MARIE THÉRÈSE

Queen of Misfortune

AMANDA BENTON

Print edition: ISBN 978-1-9162677-0-1

Ebook edition: ISBN 978-1-9162677-1-8

To David Ingram with love and thanks for your kind patience

Contents

Part I

Madame Royale

Introduction 3
1. Mousseline la Sérieuse 13
2. At the Tuileries 44
3. The Tower of the Temple 74
4. Orphan of the Temple 91
5. At the Court of Austria 110
6. Marriage and Mittau 130

Part II

The Duchesse d'Angoulême

7. Antigone and a British Exile 151
8. The First Restoration 178
9. The Hundred Days and Waterloo 205
10. The Second Restoration 230
11. The First Lady of France 259
12. Abdication and Exile 291
13. Exile and Widowhood 344

Notes 365
Bibliography 383
Acknowledgements 393

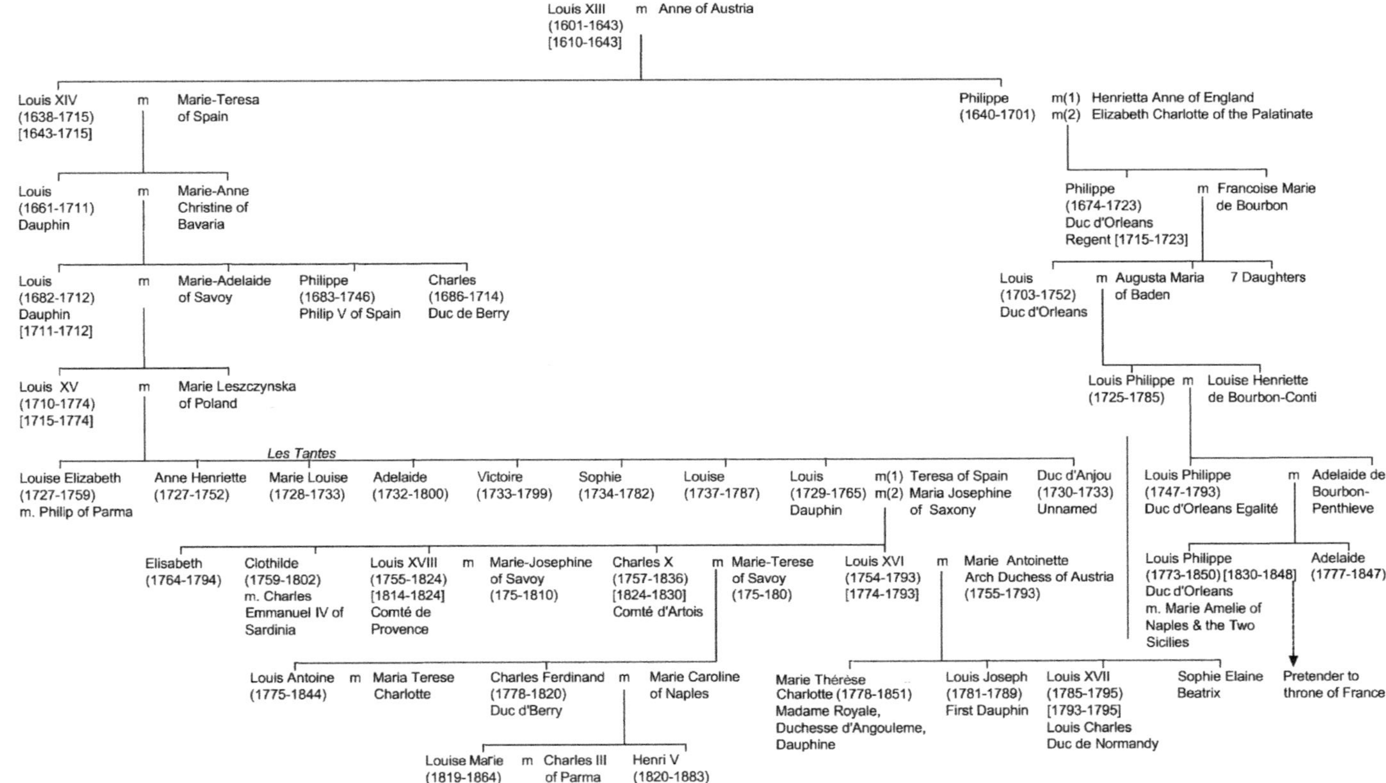

Louis XIII m Anne of Austria
(1601-1643)
[1610-1643]
Louis XIV m Marie-Teresa of Spain
(1638-1715)
[1643-1715]
Philippe m(1) Henrietta Anne of England
(1640-1701) m(2) Elizabeth Charlotte of the Palatinate
Louis m Marie-Anne Christine of Bavaria
(1661-1711)
Dauphin
Philippe m Francoise Marie de Bourbon
(1674-1723)
Duc d'Orleans
Regent [1715-1723]
Louis m Marie-Adelaide of Savoy
(1682-1712)
Dauphin
[1711-1712]
Philippe
(1683-1746)
Philip V of Spain
Charles
(1686-1714)
Duc de Berry
Louis m Augusta Maria of Baden
(1703-1752)
Duc d'Orleans
7 Daughters
Louis XV m Marie Leszczynska of Poland
(1710-1774)
[1715-1774]
Louis Philippe m Louise Henriette de Bourbon-Conti
(1725-1785)
Les Tantes
Louise Elizabeth
(1727-1759)
m. Philip of Parma
Anne Henriette
(1727-1752)
Marie Louise
(1728-1733)
Adelaide
(1732-1800)
Victoire
(1733-1799)
Sophie
(1734-1782)
Louise
(1737-1787)
Louis m(1) Teresa of Spain
(1729-1765) m(2) Maria Josephine of Saxony
Dauphin
Duc d'Anjou
(1730-1733)
Unnamed
Louis Philippe m Adelaide de Bourbon-Penthieve
(1747-1793)
Duc d'Orleans Egalité
Elisabeth
(1764-1794)
Clothilde
(1759-1802)
m. Charles Emmanuel IV of Sardinia
Louis XVIII m Marie-Josephine of Savoy
(1755-1824) (175-1810)
[1814-1824]
Comté de Provence
Charles X m Marie-Terese of Savoy
(1757-1836) (175-180)
[1824-1830]
Comté d'Artois
Louis XVI m Marie Antoinette Arch Duchess of Austria
(1754-1793) (1755-1793)
[1774-1793]
Louis Philippe
(1773-1850) [1830-1848]
Duc d'Orleans
m. Marie Amelie of Naples & the Two Sicilies
Adelaide
(1777-1847)
Louis Antoine m Maria Terese Charlotte
(1775-1844)
Charles Ferdinand m Marie Caroline of Naples
(1778-1820)
Duc d'Berry
Marie Thérèse
Charlotte (1778-1851)
Madame Royale,
Duchesse d'Angouleme,
Dauphine
Louis Joseph
(1781-1789)
First Dauphin
Louis XVII
(1785-1795)
[1793-1795]
Louis Charles
Duc de Normandy
Sophie Elaine Beatrix
Pretender to throne of France
Louise Marie m Charles III of Parma
(1819-1864)
Mademoiselle
Henri V
(1820-1883)
Duc de Bordeaux

PART I

Madame Royale

Introduction

A ROYAL ALLIANCE AND THE BIRTH OF THE PRINCESS

Royal Family of France in the prison of the Temple, 1851

The *Daily News* of 27 October 1851 reported that the Royal Academy in London had that year exhibited a picture by E. M. Ward depicting 'Royal Family of France in the prison of the Temple. At the feet of Marie Antoinette, who is mending the King's coat, and while he slumbers uneasily on the prison couch, there is seated a girl, whose fair ringlets look as yet unsullied with powder.'

The *Daily News* reported that 'The Destiny of that young captive princess has just been completed. She died the other day at Frohsdorf.'

She is Marie Thérèse Charlotte, eldest child of Louis XVI and Marie Antoinette, and this is her story.

Her parents, Louis XVI and his Queen, Marie Antoinette, had waited more than seven years for a child so they were delighted by her birth in December 1778. Theirs was not a love match, but a dynastic union. In the middle of the eighteenth century, France and Austria were competing European powers and, it seemed, entrenched enemies. Maria Theresa of Austria was fighting hard to establish and maintain her power and needed friends and allies. She offered her youngest daughter, Marie Antoinette, as a bride for the French King Louis XV's grandson and heir to the French throne, Louis Auguste, known as the Dauphin. The two countries also signed the Treaty of Versailles of 1756, which formalised an alliance of mutual protection that had been brokered by the Duc de Choiseul, ably assisted by the King's mistress, the Marquise de Pompadour.[1] The alliance with Austria was not universally welcomed in France, to say the least. Even the King's close family was strongly opposed to it.

The marriage of the young couple took place by proxy in Vienna on 19 April 1770, with the bride's brother, Archduke Ferdinand, taking the place of Louis Auguste. Two days after the proxy wedding, the new Dauphine of France, not yet fifteen years old, left Vienna accompanied by her attendants and a huge procession of fifty-seven carriages. It must have been terrifying for a young and inexperienced girl who must become a French woman in every aspect of her life and personal appearance.

Marie Antoinette met her new husband for the first time in the forest at Compiègne on 14 May 1770. She and Louis Auguste were married again, in person, on 16 May 1770. At Versailles, grand celebrations were held – including a ball in the beautiful ornate Galerie des Glaces and a wedding banquet in the theatre of the palace. In Paris, wine flowed in the fountains. There were magnificent fireworks for the enjoyment of the populace. However, other omens were not so good: a number of people were killed in stampedes at celebrations for the wedding. The young couple, stunned by the tragedy, donated a year's income to the families of the victims.

Marie Antoinette and Louis Auguste had a number of key functions as heirs to the throne: one of which was to grace the Court and please the King. Prime among the requirements was to perpetuate the royal line. The young Dauphine had the additional burden of pleasing her formidable mother by promoting the interests of her native country, while appearing a totally French princess. The wedding night was a disaster for Marie Antoinette – her husband recorded only the word 'nothing' in his diary. There is a cartoon sketch at Waddesdon Manor, Buckinghamshire, portraying the wedding night, showing poor Marie Antoinette embracing a log, so unresponsive was her husband.

Struck down with smallpox, Louis XV died after more than forty years on the throne, having long outlived his early popularity, and Louis Auguste inherited the throne from his grandfather and became King on 10 May 1774.

Louis XVI in his Coronation Robes, 1777, Joseph-Siffred Duplessis

There was a noisy stampede of courtiers as they rushed from the deathbed of Louis XV to pay their respects to the new King. The new King and Queen were young; the new King was twenty, his Queen nineteen and they were shocked to have inherited the throne of France, both bursting into tears on learning of Louis XV's death, as they knew themselves to be politically inexperienced. They were conscious of the heavy burden they were inheriting and very aware how ill-prepared they both were to fulfil the requirements of their respective roles; despite having been married for more than four years, they had still not fulfilled their duty to produce heirs. However, in the early years of their reign, they gave the people cause for hope and were a welcome change from the previous monarch. The new King and Queen were popular.

Outside the privileged confines of Versailles and the Royal châteaux of the Île de France, theirs was a troubled country. It was practically bankrupt from the cost of funding wars,[2] and full of political dissent. Lucie de la Tour du Pin, who served as an apprentice lady-in-waiting to Marie Antoinette, wrote,

> It was the height of style to complain of the duties at Court, profiting from them nevertheless and sometimes indeed often abusing the privileges they carried. All the ties were being loosened and it was, alas, the upper classes who led the way. Unnoticed, the spirit of revolt was rampant in all classes of society.[3]

She went on to write that bishops often did not live in their dioceses and colonels only spent the minimum time with their regiments. Madame de Genlis writes in her memoirs, 'You went to pay your respects at Versailles, moaning and groaning all the way. You said over and over that nothing was as boring as Versailles and the Court.'[4] It would need decisive Royal action to turn things around, and Louis XVI was not an incisive young man.

Marie Antoinette, 1767, Martin van Meytens

Co-Emperors Joseph II of Austria and his mother, Maria Theresa, feared that Marie Antoinette alone would be blamed for the couple's failure to produce a child. In Vienna, her family was very concerned that Marie Antoinette might be divorced and returned ignominiously to Austria, and that the Treaty of Versailles of 1756 might be broken. Not surprisingly, Louis Auguste's failure to consummate his marriage induced enormous frustration in his wife. Marie Antoinette fully recognised that her husband's lack of sexual competence and drive meant that she could not fulfil her own chief purpose for being in France. As a reaction to this neglect and failure, and as a product of her own fun-loving nature, she was propelled into a life of pleasure-seeking and extravagance, which tainted her reputation for sexual fidelity and damaged the monarchy.

Something urgent needed to be done, so Emperor Joseph travelled to Versailles incognito to try to save the marriage of his youngest sister and the French King. The Austrian Emperor enquired in minute and excoriating detail of his sister and brother-in-law the precise nature of their sexual problems. It became clear to Joseph that the King was easily able to achieve and maintain an erection. He would enter his wife briefly and then withdraw from her without having ejaculated. Joseph suggested that the King needed to 'be beaten like a donkey'[5] to make him perform sexually. He also rebuked his sister for her flighty ways. He exhorted her to take a more serious approach to her roles both as the Queen of France and as a wife. He did not approve of her female companions – including Mesdames de Lamballe[6] and de Polignac – and felt them to be essentially trivial women who were unworthy of the friendship of the Queen of France. Joseph instructed Marie Antoinette to pay more attention to her husband and her wifely duties. She must devote less time to gossip, gambling and spending money on redecorating her houses. Despite Joseph's criticisms of her conduct, it was wonderful for Marie Antoinette to see her brother. Joseph was convinced that rumours of her sexual exploits with members of either sex outside marriage were untrue. Her secluded life in the Trianon palace, away from Court, had persuaded many people outside her immediate circle of intimate friends that she was leading a life of financial and sexual dissipation.[7] The cartoonists and writers of the *libelle* scandal sheets were happy to exploit this to their own ends.[8] It was good business. The defamatory, and often pornographic, materials depicting Marie Antoinette and her circle in various explicit and shocking poses sold like hot cakes. They also proved to be very effective anti-monarchist propaganda.

Whatever he said, the Imperial marriage guidance counsellor seems to have solved the Royal couple's sexual problems, and on 18 August 1777 Louis XVI made love to his wife, fully and successfully. On 30 August 1777, Marie Antoinette reported in a letter to her mother that she and her husband had finally consummated their union and that they had subsequently made love again. Marie Antoinette expressed her great joy and happiness. She also shared this joyful news with Madame

Campan, who wrote in *The Private Life of Marie Antoinette: A Confidante's Account*:

About the later end of 1777 the Queen being alone in her closet sent for my father in law and myself, and, giving us her hand to kiss, told us that, looking upon us both as persons deeply interested in her happiness, she wishes to receive our congratulations … that at length she was Queen of France and that she hoped soon to have children.

Madame Campan wrote of this time, 'Dating from this happy but long-delayed moment the King's attachment to the Queen assumed every characteristic of love.'[9] The King and Queen started a new routine of spending two hours a day alone together away from other distractions in order to allow matters to take their course. Louis XVI wrote to his brother-in-law, Joseph II, 'we owe this happiness to you for since your trip, it has become steadily better and better until it has reached a perfect conclusion'.[10] By the spring of 1778, after the Emperor Joseph had returned home to Vienna, a delighted Marie Antoinette was corresponding with her Imperial mother about her pregnancy. The King and Queen were united in their happiness and delight at the prospect (they hoped) of a Dauphin. On 4 August 1778, Marie Antoinette's pregnancy was announced formally to the nation. All over France, thanksgiving *Te Deums* were sung in parish churches and city cathedrals to celebrate the impending birth.[11] Bets were taken on the gender of the child as the French people hoped and prayed for the birth of a son.

Marie Antoinette had altered her lifestyle on finding that she was pregnant. The Queen's once elaborate clothes and dramatic hairstyles were simplified. Gone were the towering coiffures several feet high and decorated with model boats and other paraphernalia. Simple white shift dresses tied at the waist with a coloured sash replaced the elaborate confections of her youth and early days at Versailles. Now she curtailed her gambling, which had been so costly to the Privy Purse and so damaging to her reputation. She was eagerly looking forward to her forthcoming motherhood, believing passionately that it would bring her fulfilment and happiness. During her pregnancy Marie Antoinette largely retired from public life to spend her days listening to music and chatting with her ladies in her apartments or at the Trianon. She took only short walks in the gardens of Versailles and avoided jolting carriage drives into Paris. It was noted that by June 1778, a few months into her pregnancy, the Queen had put on four and half inches around her waist. On 31 July Marie Antoinette felt her baby move in her womb for the first time. The summer of 1778 was very hot and Marie Antoinette slept badly, her discomfort exacerbated by her increasing size. Rather than toss and turn in her bed, bored and wakeful, she stayed up through the night with her ladies, including her sisters-in-law. Even these innocent activities caused gossip among her many detractors, who felt that her conduct was unbecoming in the mother of a possible future King.

Marie Antoinette, 1778, Élisabeth Vigée Le Brun

At the beginning of December 1778, Doctor Jean-Marie Lassonne, the Queen's Chief Physician, moved into rooms very near to her apartments accompanied by another doctor, de Vermond, the brother of the Queen's former tutor, who would also attend at the delivery of her baby.

Like almost everyone else, de Vermond hoped for a Dauphin. His reward for a safely delivered prince was 40,000 livres, but only 10,000 livres for a baby princess. Exquisite lace and other finery were prepared and the layette, the baby's first wardrobe, cost 235,965 livres. On 18 December the Queen went to bed at eleven at night in her usual way. She felt her pains start about an hour and a half later. At 1.30 in the morning of 19 December, the King was notified that the Queen was going into labour. Madame de Lamballe, as Superintendent of the Queen's Household, also communicated the news to other members of the Royal Family who were residing at Versailles. She sent letters to those of the family who were in Paris or at their châteaux informing them of the impending delivery. The King went to the Queen's apartments to be with his wife, who spent her time walking or lying on the large state bed trying to get comfortable. Marie Antoinette later moved to a small bed which had been prepared in readiness for the delivery. It was in this simple bed that the Queen would deliver her baby. As soon as the Royal Family had been informed of what was happening, the news was spread throughout Versailles that the Queen was about to give birth.

The date of 19 December 1778 became a day of (almost) universal celebration in Versailles and throughout France. Like her predecessors, the Queen was required to undertake the ordeal of giving birth in public. This was to ensure that there could be no suggestion that the child was not hers. This was, of course, an enormous ordeal for any woman. A crowd was present to observe the spectacle of royal childbirth; and Versailles was teeming with people. Two hundred nobles who usually lived in Paris had taken up residence in the château in order to participate in the events surrounding the Royal birth. The Queen's antechamber and King's council room were crowded with visitors. The doors to the Queen's bedroom were opened and there was a stampede of people determined to gain a good viewing position for the proceedings. People climbed on furniture in order to get a better view of the Royal lying-in, wrote Madame Campan in her memoirs. Members of the immediate Royal Family hastened to the Queen's apartments to take their places for the Royal birth as etiquette and custom demanded. Those not entitled to attend the birth, and who refused to leave the Queen's lying-in room when asked, were dragged out by the *valets de chambre*. Marie Antoinette made no objection to the public nature of her delivery: she had been brought up to understand that this was the way things had to be for Royal mothers-to-be.

Contemporary drawing of the birth of Marie Thérèse Charlotte at Versailles 1778

The baby girl was delivered safely and there was applause from the watching and waiting crowds. The child was then taken to another room in order to be washed, dressed and made presentable. On being informed that the baby was not the longed-for Dauphin but a baby princess, Marie Antoinette wept from exhaustion and in disappointment. The King, however, was delighted to have a healthy baby daughter. Shortly after the delivery of her daughter the Queen collapsed back on her bed in a dead faint. The boarded-up windows of her apartment had to be ripped open in order to give her fresh air. Some reports suggested that the King had himself torn down the boarding with his own hands. Medical practice dictated that the Queen be bled from her toe, in order to revive her. Marie Antoinette recovered, and was finally able to rest. While recovering from the birth, the Queen was looked after by her doctors and personal attendants.

The Queen's confidants: Princesse de Lamballe and the Duchesse de Polignac

The King spent many hours sitting by his wife's bedside chatting companionably. The Royal couple relished their sense of happiness and achievement. Couriers were sent to Paris to give the city the joyful news of the Princess's arrival, and the King wrote to the Viennese Court to announce the birth of his daughter. The baby princess was named Marie Thérèse, in honour of her grandmother.

1

Mousseline la Sérieuse

1778-1789

Marie Thérèse's early childhood was happy and secure, but under Salic Law, introduced into France in the fourteenth century, she could never succeed to the throne of France as Queen. There could be no French Queen Elizabeth I or Queen Victoria. The birth of Marie Thérèse Charlotte, given the rather clumsy, if factual, title of Madame la Fille du Roi (Madame the King's Daughter), did however mean that her parents had proved that they could produce a child and do their dynastic duty after their long failure to consummate their marriage. The next child to be born to the Royal couple might be the longed-for Dauphin. However, female *Enfants de France* were always useful in the European Royal marriage exchange. They were capable of forging links with other sovereigns and sealing treaties, acting as representatives of their native country at the very seat, and indeed the bed, of power.

As was the custom with Queens of France, Marie Antoinette did not attend the christening of her newly born daughter, which took place on 19 December, the day of the birth. Marie Antoinette was, in any event, completely exhausted following her long, strenuous and very public labour. Normally Royal children were christened after they had survived beyond the age of five or six years: a reflection of the fact that even Royal children suffered high levels of infant mortality at this time.[1] Marie Antoinette was, however, anxious that her first child should be christened immediately and her wishes in this matter were respected. The baby was handed to her newly appointed governess, the Princesse de Guéméné, who carried her new charge to the King's chapel at Versailles. The Princesse de Guéméné was from the high aristocracy and a friend of Marie Antoinette with whom, Madame Campan reports, the Queen often socialised.[2] The

Princesse de Guéméné felt her elevated status strongly and had a fascination with the occult. Madame de Boigne, the diarist, described Madame de Guéméné as 'a remarkable woman exceedingly clever, but [she] debased her intelligence by devoting herself to the follies of spiritualism'.[3]

The Grand Almoner of France, Cardinal Rohan, christened the child Marie Thérèse Charlotte in honour of her powerful maternal grandmother and godmother, the Empress of Austria and Queen regnant of Hungary, Maria Theresa, and Charlotte after her godfather Charles IV of Spain, a 'Borbon' cousin.[4] The Empress required that the first daughter born to each of her own children should be named Maria Theresa, or an appropriate local variant, in tribute to her. The child's aunt, 'Madame' (as Marie Joséphine of Savoy, Comtesse of Provence, was known), stood as representative at the christening of the baby Princess's grandmother and godmother. Her husband, 'Monsieur' the Comte de Provence, acted as proxy godfather for King Charles IV of Spain at the christening of his niece. The Comte de Provence, clever, ambitious and jealous of the status of his elder brother, Louis XVI, was in a provocative mood at the ceremony, pointing out that the officiating Cardinal Rohan had failed to ask the names and status of the child's parents, as was required by convention. It was suggested by some observers and commentators that he was trying, by pointing out this omission in the required formalities, to cast doubt on the baby Princess's paternity and legitimacy.

Marie Antoinette, Louis XVI and Marie Thérèse

The Comte de Provence had long had a difficult relationship with Marie Antoinette, as had his wife. He was happy to question her role as a wife and now mother. He wrote to his friend the King of Sweden Gustav III (1746-92), whose own Queen had very recently produced a son, that he was glad that Marie Thérèse was not a boy. He was, however, reconciled to the fact that his brother the King and Marie Antoinette would, in due course, produce a son who would oust Provence from his place in the French succession. The birth of Madame la Fille du Roi did not change Provence's place as heir presumptive. Nor did it alter their places in the order of succession to the throne of Louis XVI's younger brother, the Comte d'Artois, and his sons the Duc d'Angoulême and Duc de Berry, in the event of Louis XVI's death. It did, however, show that matters might change and that the question of the Royal succession was by no means settled.

The Royal couple rejoiced in the safe delivery of their first-born child. The King had a communicating door built between his apartments and those of Marie Thérèse so that he could visit the nursery easily and without any tedious ceremonial. It was noted by the courtiers that he saw his daughter, Madame la Fille du Roi, every day in her nursery.[5] It is strange to our modern notions that this conduct should have been worthy of comment, but it was clearly not the usual way of Royal fathers. It was also remarked upon that the King, usually so unprepossessing and lacking in confidence in his public life, was relaxed and comfortable in the role of a father. He evidently enjoyed spending time with his daughter in playing and romping, obviously far more at ease in the nursery than in carrying out official functions. Marie Antoinette, usually so upright and dignified in her posture, relished sitting on the floor of the nursery apartments.

Comte de Provence, c.1778, Joseph-Siffred Duplessis

Comtesse de Provence, c.1780, Rosalie Filleul

Comtesse d'Artois, c.1780, Jean-Baptiste André Gautier-Dagoty

The Comte d'Artois, Joseph-Siffred Duplessis

Marie Antoinette was, by contemporary eighteenth-century royal and aristocratic standards, unusually involved in her daughter's upbringing, even breastfeeding the baby Marie Thérèse for a number of months. A *nourrice*, or wet nurse, named Madame Laurent was engaged for Marie Thérèse for those times when the Queen preferred not to feed her baby daughter herself or was separated from her. The Queen shared this approach to child-rearing with her English friend Georgiana, Duchess of Devonshire. Our modern view would be to regard this as entirely natural and appropriate maternal behaviour and to admire it in a woman who was also a Queen. Marie Antoinette's contemporaries, on the other hand, thought her conduct in this respect strange to the point of being distasteful, and certainly not a practice to be encouraged among aristocratic ladies. It would have been much more fitting for the task of feeding the infant Princess to be given over entirely by the Queen to Madame Laurent. It was felt by some courtiers that the Queen's active involvement in her daughter's upbringing kept Marie Antoinette from the real business of being a Queen, namely presiding over the ceremonial rites of the Court, being actively involved in public life and producing male offspring. Marie Antoinette's approach was in part a product of the influence of the Enlightenment movement and its encouragement of a love for the bucolic and natural, which had greatly influenced the Queen's thinking. It also reflected the more relaxed family life of the Austrian Court where she had grown up. The Marquis de Bombelles, whose wife was a lady-in-waiting to Marie Thérèse's aunt, Madame Élisabeth, reported that the Queen was very involved in caring for her baby daughter when she fell ill with fever in

1780. Marie Antoinette, he reported, stayed up all night with her daughter to oversee her nursing. He praised the Queen for her maternal ways.[6]

The King and Queen, in a spirit of simplicity, did not formally present their baby daughter to the Court soon after her birth. It was normal practice for politicians, ambassadors and courtiers to be presented to newly born princes and princesses. Louis XVI and Marie Antoinette preferred to wait to do so. Marie Antoinette's conversations with Madame Campan rejoiced at having produced a daughter, who would be hers at least until her daughter's marriage; whereas a son would belong to the state and would be taken from the Queen to be educated by male tutors in his own separate household. Marie Antoinette nevertheless fully recognised the necessity of producing a son to secure the succession for their branch of the family. Even at this early stage of Marie Thérèse's life, Marie Antoinette was thinking of her daughter's future marriage, hoping that she could marry a Frenchman and therefore stay in her native land – not the usual fate of princesses. Marie Antoinette, of all people, understood the pain of being obliged by political needs to leave one's homeland and family to make a foreign dynastic marriage. As early as this, Marie Antoinette and Louis XVI considered an alliance with Madame la Fille du Roi's cousin, the four-year-old Duc d'Angoulême, elder son of the Comte d'Artois, as a serious matrimonial possibility for their daughter. The young prince combined, in their eyes, the significant advantage of being in the direct line of succession to the throne of France, thus able to make his cousin a Queen, and the further enormous benefit of enabling their daughter to stay in France with her own family even after her marriage.

On 3 January 1779, reclining on a day bed, Marie Antoinette held a reception at Versailles for all the ladies of the Court to receive their congratulations on the safe delivery of her daughter. Afterwards, as a celebration of the birth of the Princess, there was a comedy performance in a makeshift theatre set up in the Gaming Salon of the palace for the entertainment of the Court. As well as enjoying professional theatrical performances, the Queen and the young royal set were very keen on performing in amateur dramatic productions. As long as the performers and audience were confined to members of the Royal Family and close members of their households, there was no particular comment or gossip about their amusing themselves in this way. As the audiences were extended more widely away from this intimate grouping, however, there was competition among the courtiers at Versailles for the privilege of attending performances, and resentment on the part of those excluded. This exclusivity, which was not based on the usual rules of etiquette, caused great trouble within the palace. Those not admitted to performances were greatly offended. This damaged the Queen's reputation and alienated many members of the nobility who were not included in her exclusive clique of friends and companions.

Madame Royale on the knee of her governess the Princesse de Guéméné: Jean-Pierre-Julien Dupin (le Jeune), from an engraving held at the Château of Versailles

Contrary to popular belief, the Queen did not pretend to be a shepherdess in the gardens of the Trianon. She did, however, take the part of a shepherdess in the amateur theatricals performed by herself and other members of the Court. The theatre at the Trianon in which Marie Antoinette performed is exquisite. Simple on the outside, the interior is richly decorated with carved and painted wood and rich hangings. There is seating for only about fifty people on padded benches. Marie Antoinette loved dressing up in theatrical costumes that were very carefully made for her by her dressmaker, Rose Bertin, as Madame Campan recalls in her memoirs. The other amateur royal players included Marie Antoinette's handsome brother-in-law, the Comte d'Artois, as well as the Comte de Provence, her two sisters-in-law, and the youngest of the King's siblings,

Madame Élisabeth. The King himself did not take part; he preferred practical pursuits like carpentry and metalworking, producing intricate locks for cupboards. Louis XVI was, however, happy to be a member of the select audience and to enjoy watching his wife and other members of the Royal Family dress up and play act. He found nothing in their activities of which to disapprove.

The baby Princess was initially given the title of Madame la Fille du Roi by her father, but after the age of five she was known by the more elegant title of Madame Royale. Marie Thérèse's new title came as a relief to her uncle, the Comte de Provence. He was stung by the birth of a child to the brother for whom he felt contempt and jealousy; he was fearful that his wife, 'Madame', would lose her studiedly simple title and would be seen to be demoted in the Royal hierarchy. In this rarefied world of Versailles etiquette, the view was that the simpler the title, the greater the prestige of the bearer. Within the Royal Family itself, formality was the norm and even in private the more formal French *vous* rather than the *tu* form of the pronoun 'you' was used. The King was always addressed in the third person. No individual, whatever his rank, could address the King before the King himself spoke to the person. Furthermore, strict rules governed who might sit in the presence of the King or Queen and any other member of the Royal Family. Ladies who were Princesses of the Blood or duchesses were able to sit in the Royal presence on foldaway stools known as *tabourets*. This privilege was regarded as a great status symbol, as well as being considerably more comfortable than standing for hours in high, red-heeled court shoes during long Court ceremonies. It was this very formal but loving world, governed by strict protocol and etiquette, which provided the backdrop to the childhood of Marie Thérèse and influenced her thinking and approach to life as she grew up. She was treated with deference by many of those with whom she had regular contact. She seems to have come to expect this as her due. It was an aspect of her daughter's character that caused Marie Antoinette concern.

There were public ceremonies to mark the birth of Marie Thérèse befitting her status as an *Enfant de France*. Services of thanksgiving were held on 8 February 1779, six weeks after her birth, at the Church of Notre Dame and Sainte Genevieve in Paris to celebrate the safe delivery of the Princess. Marie Antoinette was well received at her 'Churching' ceremony, which signalled to the world that she had recovered from the ordeal of childbirth and was now spiritually clean and able to go back into society. The Queen showed her great happiness at the birth of her daughter and her charitable disposition by providing for one hundred young Parisian women to be married in a mass ceremony. Marie Antoinette funded the brides' dowries of 500 francs each and supplied their wedding outfits. Other charitable gifts were also made by the Queen to mark and give thanks for the arrival of her long-hoped-for child: in Paris, gifts of money were distributed to the needy on behalf of the King and Queen as a mark of their delight. Once again, Parisians enjoyed a fountain running with free wine, set up to celebrate Marie Thérèse's birth.

The baby Princess's royal cousin, the Duc d'Orléans, put on a display of fireworks in Paris to mark the birth of Marie Thérèse; however, they were regarded by the populace of Paris as being somewhat paltry and disappointing by royal standards. This may have been because the newest member of the Royal Family was 'after all only a girl'; but equally it may have been an indication of the troubled relationship between the senior branch of the House of Bourbon and its junior Orléans members, who were descended from Louis XVI's younger brother, Philippe Duc d'Orléans. Their relationship had deteriorated after there had been accusations of cowardice and misconduct against the Duc d'Orléans, who felt that his cousin the King had not defended him sufficiently against his detractors. He felt slighted and tended to stay away from Court at Versailles, hardly ever using his apartments there, preferring to spend his time in Paris at the Palais-Royal, building up his own power base. His wealth, generosity and approachability made him very popular with the Parisians, among whom he had many supporters. The Orléans family looked to the possibility of a future marriage between Louis Philippe, the Duc's son, and his cousin Marie Thérèse. Marie Antoinette rejected this possibility, partly because of her enmity towards the family and partly because of their lower status of only 'Serene Highnesses'. A proposed marriage between Mademoiselle Adélaïde, the daughter of the Duc d'Orléans, and her cousin the young Duc d'Angoulême was abandoned – much to the chagrin of her family – when he was earmarked as a possible future husband for Marie Thérèse. The princesses and cousins Adélaïde of Orléans and Marie Thérèse were near contemporaries, Adélaïde being only a year older.

Much of Marie Thérèse's childhood was spent at Versailles, the magnificent palace just outside Paris. Louis XIV,[7] the great-great-grandfather of Louis XVI, had experienced the indignities of being a powerless boy King during the Fronde series of religious civil wars in the 1630s and grew to loathe Paris. He also wanted to be able to indulge the Bourbon passion for hunting with ease, and so extended and remodelled what had been a modest royal hunting lodge at Versailles used by his father, Louis XIII, into one of the grandest royal palaces in Europe. Its grounds were enormous. The beautiful gardens and small palaces added by his successors provided a huge playground for the Royal Family, their children, courtiers and servants.

The Trianon and Petit Trianon and their lovely gardens had been created by Louis XV and his mistress *en titre* and later platonic friend, the Marquise de Pompadour. They were private retreats for Louis XV,[8] an intensely shy and private man, and her close friends and family; a refuge from the stifling protocol and crowds of the main Palace of Versailles. She adored building, renovating and embellishing properties, designing and creating wonderful gardens for the enjoyment of the King and his companions. The Marquise de Pompadour may have been a bourgeois Parisian and in the eyes of many of the French people a spendthrift whore, but she had wonderful taste and an exquisitely refined eye for the decorative arts, building and garden design.

Louis XVI gave his wife the Trianon Palace including the Petit Trianon and its beautiful gardens as her private domain. Marie Antoinette relished a life away from the main palace, enjoying the charms of the Trianon with her own clique of friends, her children and close family members, thus escaping the stultifying etiquette of Versailles. Marie Antoinette's desire for privacy and to escape etiquette was understandable, as was her desire to spend time with the friends and family she loved, rather than those individuals who had the right to her time and attention bestowed by etiquette alone. However, the Queen's use of the Petit Trianon was damaging to her image and reputation because it created jealousies and alienated those members of the Court who were not included in her close group of intimates. At a time of worsening economic conditions and failing harvests, the expenditure caused deep resentment within France. Madame Campan commented in her memoirs on the intimate gatherings favoured by Marie Antoinette and the resentment they caused in the Court and country: 'people ... never forgive any fêtes but those they share in'. She had also lost the love of many of the ordinary people of France who expected to be able to see and even speak to the Royal Family. Any member of the public, as long as they were respectably dressed,[9] could visit Versailles (and many did) to rub shoulders with or at least see the Royal Family, watching them at their formal meals or just moving around the palace following their daily routine as prescribed by the prevailing etiquette. The most senior Princesse or Duchesse would not be admitted to Marie Antoinette's Château de Trianon unless she were a member of the Queen's favoured group and the recipient of an invitation to join the Queen. Marie Antoinette's selection of companions, not based on the understood principles of rank but her own personal likes and dislikes, caused enormous resentment among all sections of society. The monarchy thereby lost support of its natural constituency among the nobility, or at least those not in Royal favour. The Orléans family, for example, certainly did not bother going regularly to the Court at Versailles where they feared that they would be snubbed by their cousins. They preferred to stay in Paris and build up their power base, frequently fraternising with those who would, in due course, make a Revolution.[10] The focus of French life, both social and political, gradually began to move away from Versailles and back to Paris as the reign of Louis XVI progressed. There was no point in being in Versailles if you, as a nobleman or woman, could not obtain easy access to the Royal Family. By the late

1780s Versailles often seemed almost deserted of company and very quiet at times.

A charmingly elegant dairy provided fresh milk, which was drunk by the Queen and her companions from specially designed Sèvres porcelain. This was the living embodiment of bucolic simplicity and harmony with nature as advocated by Jean-Jacques Rousseau. The carefully contrived decay of the village and farm exteriors belied interiors formed of light, airy, classically proportioned rooms where the finest fresh fruit was served to the Queen and her guests and music performed for their entertainment. Marie Antoinette lived informally at the Trianon and Madame Campan reported that etiquette was relaxed to such an extent that 'She entered the sitting room without driving the ladies from their piano forte or embroidery.'[11] Normally they would have been required to stand up immediately and curtsey each time the Queen entered a room and to have remained standing in her presence, except for those ladies entitled to use a *tabouret.*

Marie Antoinette's guests also had the opportunity to wander freely in the grounds of the Hermitage, a small, specially constructed mock village, and to enjoy musical performances. Madame d'Oberkirch wrote of the le Petit Trianon, 'What a delicious walk, through groves perfumed with lilac and filled with the charming songs of a thousand nightingales … how delightful this charming retreat must be to the queen, who spends the greater part of every summer there.'[12] The Queen found the time spent at the Trianon was relaxing and reminded her of the happy and informal family life she had enjoyed as a child with the Imperial family at the Palace of Laxenberg near Vienna. As Madame Campan wrote, the Queen would sometimes spend a month at the Trianon with her friends, the children being brought by their governesses from their apartments in the main palace to visit her and spend time with their mother. The Princess and her aunt, Madame Élisabeth, had their own small rooms in the attics at the Petit Trianon. The *London Chronicle* of 5 August 1784 reported that the Queen and her daughter were at the Petit Trianon and likely to stay there for an extended visit of three weeks.

Madame Élisabeth stayed overnight with the Queen at the Trianon, but there was not sufficient room for most of the other ladies of the Court to be accommodated. They had to return to the main palace and their apartments there. The King and princes visited regularly to have supper, but always by invitation from the Queen. They too did not stay overnight, returning to the palace to sleep. Many were offended by the independence which the 'Austrian' Queen asserted in making these arrangements, even requiring that the King have an invitation to enter her territory rather than being entitled by right to visit as and when he wished. Even the furniture was stamped 'Château de Trianon' on the underside with her own mark.[13]

Madame Élisabeth by Louise Élisabeth Vigée Le Brun

Royal lives were meant to be lived out in public. No wonder the people of France thought the Queen was up to no good, and they were not slow in saying and writing so. Increasingly it was remembered that she was not even really French, but *L'Autrichienne*, 'the Austrian', and by extension '*la chienne*', or 'bitch'. In 1789, even her sisters-in-law (themselves foreign Savoyard princesses), jealous of her role and perhaps her charm, disloyally referred to her in these disparaging and personal terms. Her perceived and real extravagances, the accusations of sexual impropriety with both sexes, the thought that she dominated an ineffectual King and her seclusion had brought Marie Antoinette the contempt, even hatred, of many of her people. The King had no mistress; usually, the incumbent of this role was the woman at whom such public venom for excessive indulgence and spending was principally directed. This had been the role assigned to La Marquise de la Pompadour and later Madame du Barry in the previous reign. Louis XVI's interests lay in the smithy rather than the bedroom, and he was sexually faithful to his wife. The blame for royal decadence and the opprobrium that followed fell squarely on the foreign-born Queen. She was the convenient scapegoat for the King and his government's mistakes, as well as her own follies. In a slightly grudging defence of Marie Antoinette, the Marquis de Bombelles[14] wrote that Marie Antoinette was not as extravagant as Louis XV's last mistress Madame du Barry, who herself had been so loathed by the Austrian princess on her arrival at Versailles in 1770. It was to damn with faint praise.

Whatever the political problems surrounding her family, Marie Thérèse was growing up to be a healthy, pretty, happy child with ruddy cheeks and bright blue eyes. We see her rude good health illustrated by the portraits by Madame Vigée Le Brun, her mother's favourite portrait painter, whose diary also charts the lives of her Royal patrons. The Princess enjoyed the best of everything: a world of beautiful châteaux, glorious parks and the simple elegant beauty of her apartments surrounded by a Household dedicated to serving her needs. Furthermore, she enjoyed the status of an *Enfant de France*, the devoted care of two loving parents and the love of her extended family. The children were closely supervised as one might expect; for the first five years of her life Marie Thérèse was watched over every night by a fully-awake, uniformed night nurse. The Bourbons feared cot deaths for their children, just as we do.

Marie Antoinette was determined to be an active and involved mother. Her own childhood experience had been one of benign neglect by her mother, the Empress Maria Theresa, who was too preoccupied with the business of ruling her country to be actively involved in her upbringing and education. Marie Antoinette adored the Empress, as we see from the very dutiful and affectionate letters she wrote from France to her mother, but she felt keenly Maria Theresa's lack of input. Perhaps recognising that this neglect and her own laziness in pursuing her studies had left her ill-equipped to fulfil her role, Marie Antoinette was determined that this omission would not be repeated in the upbringing of her own daughter. While very loving, Marie Antoinette felt it very important that Marie Thérèse be brought up strictly as befitted her station in life, and also be prepared adequately for difficulties that she might meet later in life. It is sometimes said that Marie Thérèse preferred her father to her mother. The little girl felt that Marie Antoinette was too strict, did not listen to her or take her own wishes and preferences sufficiently into account. The child for example complained that while she and the Queen were on a visit to her Carmelite great-aunt Louise, the Queen strode ahead of her daughter ignoring her; whereas her father's approach was to hold Marie Thérèse's hand and to explain things to his daughter as they walked along together.

As well as her *gouvernante*, the Princesse de Guéméné, Marie Thérèse had a considerable Household. To assist Madame de Guéméné in her duties, there were four under-governesses. All ladies of the aristocracy, they were the Baronne de Mackau, who had previously been governess to Madame Élisabeth; the two Mesdames de Soucy; and Madame de Demaulet. In addition the baby Princess's Household comprised twenty clerics, among them almoners and assistant almoners,[15] and in time, as the Princess's education started, masters for pianoforte, viola, clavichord, dancing, writing, mathematics, as well as grooms and hunt masters.

The cultured and well educated Madame Henriette Huë[16] acted as the young Princess's reader. In addition, there were staff to look after the fruit room, manage the storage of furs, laundresses to keep all the many household and personal linens washed and pressed, cellarers, librarians, nursery nurses, plus the usual cooks and other domestics. The servants required servants of their own, and all these people needed to be fed, provided with clean clothes and accommodation. It was a significant undertaking. The medical needs of the Household were looked after by nine doctors. At the time of her birth and in her early childhood, the Princess's Household consisted of approximately 85 individuals. Huge and overblown as this Household must seem to us, it was fairly modest compared with that maintained by her aunts: Madame, the Comtesse de Provence's Household consisted of 496 individuals; and the Comtesse d'Artois had 296 staff to serve her. Even the young, modest and religious Madame Élisabeth felt the need for an establishment of 78 people. In the mid-1780s, Marie Antoinette reduced the size of her daughter's Household, both as an economy measure – France was in deep economic trouble and the Royal expenditure had to be reined in – and to encourage simplicity and humility in her daughter.

The Princess's apartments were under the Hall of Mirrors and very near to those of the King and Queen, linked with connecting doors. While the state apartments at Versailles were enormous and of gilded elaborateness, the private apartments behind the scenes, where the Royal Family went to escape life in the public eye, were of livable dimensions and decorated with delicate, simple, beautiful furniture and florally inspired colour schemes. The Queen created a small private garden for her daughter to play in by having a fence put up to screen off part of the park that was used by members of the public visiting the palace grounds. It was here that Marie Thérèse learned to walk at the age of eight months. Marie Antoinette was proud of her daughter accomplishing this feat at such a young age. The Queen was delighted to be able to write to her mother to let the Empress know of her granddaughter and namesake's progress. Every development of the baby was noted, for example Marie Antoinette wrote to her mother in November 1779 happily announcing that her eleven-month-old granddaughter had four teeth.[17] In October 1780, Marie Antoinette informed her mother that the toddler Princess was again teething and bearing the discomfort of her sore gums with great fortitude.[18]

Father and daughter were devoted to each other and it is appropriate that the first word spoken by the Princess was 'Papa' as Marie Antoinette reported in a letter[19] to the Empress. In March 1780,[20] Marie Thérèse at the age of fifteen months was asked to point out her mother and immediately stretched out her arms to the Queen wanting to be picked up and taken in her mother's arms. Not surprisingly, Marie Antoinette was delighted by this affectionate display by her baby daughter and wrote to tell the Empress Maria Theresa in Vienna what had happened and her pleasure in it. It was the first time that the little Princess had so obviously recognised and identified her mother. Marie Antoinette felt that she loved her daughter even better than before following this happy incident. Marie Antoinette also commented on how well grown her daughter was, almost like a two-year-old. She was also in robust health, though she did not speak much. There was sad news for the family on 29 November 1780, when Marie Thérèse's august godmother and grandmother died. The King could not bear to give his wife the news of her mother's death. He sent the Abbé de Vermond, her former French language tutor from her last days in Vienna, to tell her of the demise of the Empress. Marie Antoinette was devastated by the loss of her powerful mother. She felt keenly the absence of the maternal love, advice and support through her letters, even from the distance of the Court of Vienna.

Marie Thérèse Charlotte of France by Adolf Ulrich Wertmuller

There was cause for rejoicing within the Royal Family when on 22 October 1781 a long-desired Dauphin was born. This time the King had spared the Queen the indignity of a public birth. Immediately following the delivery of her second child, the Queen did not know whether she had given birth to another Princess or to a Dauphin. The King, apparently in a state of almost euphoric happiness, informed his weary wife of the delivery of a son in these mock formal terms: 'Madame, Monsieur the Dauphin begs to be presented to you.'

Madame Campan wrote, 'The birth of the Dauphin appeared to give joy to all classes.'[21] Marie Antoinette was overjoyed to have provided her husband and her adopted country with an heir. The King and Queen's first son was named Louis as was customary with the Bourbons and Joseph in honour of his Austrian Imperial uncle, Joseph II, who had been so instrumental in bringing about the conception of their first child.[22] Marie Thérèse was two-and-three-quarters when her brother arrived. No doubt as an intelligent and alert girl she was fully aware of the birth of this important child who, as a boy, was the heir to the throne of France.

The Queen was utterly delighted. Her duty to her family (both French and Austrian) had been done. It must have saddened her greatly that her mother was not alive to see her triumph. The King was profoundly moved by the arrival of his son and referred to him often in conversation with members of the Court, clearly relishing the arrival of 'Monsieur le Dauphin'. There were elaborate celebrations from all classes of society in honour of the birth of a Dauphin. Lucie de la Tour du Pin, whose mother La Comtesse Dillon was one of Marie Antoinette's twelve ladies-in-waiting, first stayed as a young girl at Versailles just after the birth of the Dauphin. She wrote in her journal of Marie Antoinette at a ball held to celebrate the birth of her son, that 'wearing a blue dress strewn with sapphires and diamonds, she opened the ball with an unknown young guardsman. She was young beautiful and adored by all. She had just given France a Dauphin and it was inconceivable to her that the brilliant career on which she was launched could ever suffer a reverse.'

It is reported that following the birth of the Dauphin the six-year-old Duc d'Angoulême commented to his father, the Comte d'Artois, how small the new baby boy was. To this remark the Comte d'Artois replied that the Dauphin would soon be great enough. The Comte was fully conscious of the fact that he and his sons had moved down the Royal order of succession. The intense attention and affection that the King had given to Marie Thérèse in her first few years was in some measure transferred to her younger brother. Louis XVI remained, however, a loving and devoted father to Marie Thérèse and his affection was fully returned by his daughter.

On the baby Dauphin's arrival in 1781, Madame de Guéméné was appointed governess to him. At the time, the care of Royal infants was in the charge of female aristocrats. Princesses remained with them, whereas boys were passed over to male tutors and governors from the age of seven. Marie Antoinette assured the Princesse de Guéméné, who feared the heavy workload involved in rearing two Royal children, that she herself would be more involved in the upbringing of her daughter in order to free Madame de Guéméné to care for the Dauphin. In 1783, the four-year-old Princess was at the château of La Muette with her mother for her inoculations against smallpox, which Pauline de Béarn says she approached with great fortitude, and then for recuperation. At that time her *gouvernante*, the Princesse de Guéméné, was forced to resign from her prestigious post because of financial scandals, which had engulfed her family. Once rich and influential, the Prince de Guéméné had run his financial affairs so badly that his many creditors had forced him into an ignominious and humiliating bankruptcy. This necessitated the sale of a number of the de Guéméné properties, including one near Versailles which the King bought as a present for his sister, Madame Élisabeth. It was also a gesture of support and practical aid to the now impoverished family. The Guéméné family was forced into retirement from Versailles and Court life, a terrible blow for ambitious courtiers with senior appointments that they could no longer keep. The King felt in the circumstances that he had no choice but to accept the resignation of his children's governess. The King and Queen regretted the Princesse de Guéméné's departure from their service, although some of the Court had felt that the princess's family pride had become excessive, and the King was criticised for the financial aid he gave the Guéméné family when the state finances were in such a dire state.

The departure of Madame de Guéméné meant that a high-status post at the centre of the Court was available to be granted by the King and Queen to another lady. The individual chosen to be the next Royal Gouvernante to the Enfants de France was Yolande, Duchesse de Polignac.[23] Marie Thérèse came to know Madame de Polignac throughout her childhood as one of her mother's closest friends and a member of the Queen's intimate social circle. In any event, she also had the involvement and continuity of her loving parents and Madame de Mackau and the other assistant governesses. Her mother was happy to have as governess to her daughter someone who would welcome her active participation in the upbringing of Marie Thérèse, as the Queen explained to Madame Campan. She felt that Madame de Guéméné had, in carrying out her duties, tried to exclude her from her daughter's nursery and to limit her involvement in her upbringing. Marie Antoinette discussed the new appointment with Madame Campan, who reported that the Queen saw it as an opportunity for superintending the education of her children, without running any risk of hurting the pride of the governess; and that it would bring together the objects of her warmest affections: her children and her friend. The Queen hoped that Madame Campan would make her thinking clear to those who did not approve or were jealous of the Duchesse de Polignac's appointment to such a prestigious Court post.

The Polignacs were widely disliked at Court and beyond in France for their pride and their greed for money, lands and political influence. This was a plum role, providing contact with the King and Queen on a regular basis and influence over the next generation of Royals. Although the Duchesse herself was regarded as largely unambitious and not particularly self-seeking, it was felt that her rather laid-back and lazy ways might not suit the demands of her new role as Gouvernante to the children of France. Madame d'Oberkirch described Madame de Polignac as being greatly loved by the Queen. She reported that Marie Antoinette said of her friend, 'whilst I am with her, I am no longer a queen; I feel that I am myself'.[24] Lucie de la Tour du Pin, the daughter of one of the Queen's ladies-in-waiting known for her memoir of the period, wrote of Yolande de Polignac that she was 'very pretty but not very clever'. Yolande de Polignac may not herself have been ambitious or greedy for offices and financial rewards, but the same could not be said for the rest of the Polignac family. Madame de Polignac's relationship with the Queen was engineered by her sister-in-law Diane who, with the rest of the family, was keen to milk the friendship with the affectionate and generous, if rather naïve, Queen for all the advancement and financial advantage they could get. In the process the Polignac clan became widely loathed both at Court in Versailles and in the rest of France – a byword for greed and ambition.

Marie Thérèse was nicknamed 'Mousseline la Sérieuse' by Marie Antoinette,[25] indicating not only the deep affection the Queen had for her daughter but also her recognition that, even from an early age, her daughter was a rather serious introverted person. In 1783, when she was four, the Princess was installed in the Petits Appartements at Versailles close to her mother. Here she lived with her Household a life of ease, surrounded by the clean muslin dresses of her mother, a woman ahead of her time for the custom of taking a daily bath, and the fresh linens of her attendants and governesses. Marie Thérèse had a number of visitors to her apartments apart from her parents. Her paternal aunt, Madame Élisabeth, fourteen years the Princess's senior and a model of piety, kindness and simplicity – qualities not often abundant at Versailles – was a regular visitor to the Royal nursery. She too had been brought up by Madame Mackau, who had to be very strict with the infant Élisabeth in order to mould her into the religious woman she became, since as a small child she had been demanding and spoilt. Élisabeth embraced her religion and it influenced all aspects of her life. She found it a source of joy and comfort. She had been well-educated and enjoyed music and played the harp; she also acted with Marie Antoinette and her troupe of Royal actors. She was generous, making many charitable grants to the poor and needy. She would be very influential in the life of Marie Thérèse.

Her great aunts Mesdames Adélaïde, Victoire and Sophie also spent time with Marie Thérèse as she grew up, despite the fact that their intriguing had made Marie Antoinette's life so difficult when she had arrived at Versailles. Others among Marie Thérèse's visitors were her paternal uncles and aunts, Monsieur and Madame and the Comte and Comtesse d'Artois. One must also assume that she was visited by her cousin Louis Antoine, Duc d'Angoulême, three and a half years her senior, and his younger brother Charles Ferdinand, Duc de Berry, who was nearly a year older than Marie Thérèse. Marie Thérèse also spent time with her mother's friends and their children. The Queen's circle included Madame de Noailles, Madame de Polignac, Madame de Lamballe and later Madame de Tourzel, whose daughter Pauline (later Madame de Béarn) was a childhood friend and companion of Marie Thérèse. She also played with the children of members of her mother's Household.

Marie Thérèse and, in due course, her younger brothers were able to enjoy roaming and romping in the Royal playground. Marie Antoinette took the property which she had been given by the King and incorporated her great love of flowers into the decorative schemes of the walls and draperies. She also created a naturalistic or 'English' garden for herself and her circle of friends and family in the grounds. The Queen achieved the kind of elegant, seemingly artless, simplicity and effortless naturalism that can only be produced by the expenditure of enormous sums of money and great effort. For Marie Thérèse, her siblings and playmates there was a small farm inhabited by well-scrubbed and groomed animals with which they could play. The pets were led about the farmyard on coloured ribbons by cheerful and deferential farm workers.

The summer of 1783, when Marie Thérèse was four years old, was a glorious one. The Royal Family enjoyed spending leisurely days fishing in the lakes around the Château of Versailles hoping to catch carp and tench on a line. Marie Thérèse was very proud of having caught a fish and ran to show her parents her catch. The ladies relaxed in the beautiful gardens wearing brightly coloured dresses that made them look like flowers. No doubt four-year-old Marie Thérèse looked on with interest when in September 1783 the Royal Family viewed the first ever launching of a hot air balloon which had been developed by the Montgolfier brothers. Before the ascent, the King, who was always very interested and intrigued by scientific and technological matters, inspected the basket of the balloon. The Royal Family continued to be intrigued by ballooning. The Duc d'Angoulême with his father and brother travelled by balloon to the small but very attractive Château at Bagatelle, which had been built by the Comte d'Artois as a country retreat from Versailles, and also to the horse races at Longchamps.[26]

The winter of 1783/84 was by contrast extremely cold. One Court lady resorted to wearing a bear's skin as a coat in an attempt to keep warm. Marie Antoinette encouraged her daughter to be charitable to the poor, and at Christmas Marie Antoinette displayed the gifts which were to have been given to her daughter on a table; she appealed to Marie Thérèse's conscience, asking the little girl to make a sacrifice of her toys so that the money saved could go to buy food and fuel for the poor and needy. Marie Thérèse clearly understood what her mother was asking of her and readily agreed to give up her Christmas presents. In addition Marie Thérèse's almoner made donations of more than 8,000 francs from the monies allocated to the Princess's Household to aid the poor. Madame Campan reported that the King himself gave 3 million livres for the 'relief of the indigent'.

By way of compensation for the loss of her Christmas presents, and no doubt also as a reward for her good behaviour, Marie Antoinette took her daughter to see a performance at the theatre in Paris. The Parisians received the Queen coldly, aggrieved by their own sufferings during the freezing winter and her perceived extravagance and isolation. Marie Antoinette's reputation was increasingly being vilified and damaged by the defamatory *libelles*. Many of them were deeply obscene. They poured into the country from publishers in Holland, England and Germany, attacking the Queen for her perceived extravagances and baseless accusations of sexual immorality. The booklets were written by journalists such as Jacques René Hébert, who will feature again in the life of Marie Thérèse: Hébert wanted to combine making a good living with promoting social and political change through the *libelles*. Clearly there was discontent even at Court as copies of the offensive materials appeared on the Queen's bed, deeply distressing her according to Madame Campan. The Austrian-born Queen refused to dignify the attacks by responding to them, and was thus an easy target.

The relationship between mother and daughter was not without its strains while Marie Thérèse grew from babyhood. Marie Antoinette was a doting mother who spent a lot of time with her children, but not one who was blind to their faults or unwilling to attempt to take steps to remedy these as she felt necessary. In Marie Thérèse she felt that she saw pride, even arrogance – perhaps not surprising in a child brought up in such an atmosphere of deference. Marie Thérèse was only too aware of her status as a Princess of France and a descendant of both the Royal houses of the Habsburg Empress Maria Theresa of Austria and Bourbon Louis XIV of France; a lineage in which she took great pleasure and pride.

It was in order to counter her fear that her daughter might be proud that in 1784 the Queen introduced Marie Philippine Lambriquet to the Household of her daughter, now aged five so formally titled Madame Royale. Marie Philippine was known within the Royal Household as 'Ernestine' after the heroine of one of the Queen's favourite novels, written by Madame Riccoboni. Ernestine was, according to some commentators, the daughter of Madame Élisabeth's *valet de chambre*. Other reports suggest that she was the daughter of a bailiff and a chambermaid. Ernestine was more or less the same age as Marie Thérèse, having been born in July 1778. It was intended that Ernestine should share the young Princess's daily routine and activities. When she first joined the Household, Ernestine spent all day with the Princess but returned to her own family and home to sleep at night, rejoining the Court the following day. Marie Thérèse was required by her mother to look after Ernestine and to put her companion's needs before her own; for example, serving Ernestine her food first and treating her always as an honoured guest in the nursery and schoolroom.

The girls were dressed in identical outfits and received the same lessons from their tutors in music, mathematics, dancing, languages and horse riding. Like both her parents, Marie Thérèse loved to ride (her father was a particularly keen huntsman who rode out from the palace hunting most days) and she learned to ride well and with pleasure and confidence, as befitted a Bourbon princess. She was an accomplished horsewoman who came to know the bridleways of the Île de France like the back of her hand. Marie Thérèse's education, both academic and in terms of the social accomplishments thought necessary for a princess, was taken very seriously by her parents. She was regarded as being of above average intelligence and with an aptitude and desire for learning. She was equipped with the usual ladylike accomplishments of her generation: the playing of musical instruments, drawing, and the creation of elaborate needlework. Marie Thérèse had a marked liking for reading and other academic pursuits and worked hard at her studies. There are examples in the National Archives of France of her handwriting, showing that she was required to copy out lines of improving texts. The Princess learned German, her mother's native language, as well as French and Italian. Marie Antoinette would often attend lessons to test her daughter's understanding of her studies and to provide additional teaching. The King, who loved maps, taught her geography by cutting up maps like jigsaws. He enjoyed sitting with her while she put them back together.

From an early stage, Madame Royale was interested in, and serious about, her Roman Catholic faith and practised acts of charity – very much a Habsburg characteristic – showing kindness in making gifts of food to the poor. She was taught religion and spirituality by her aunt, Madame Élisabeth. Marie Thérèse also enjoyed visiting her great aunt, the former Madame Louise (1737-87), who had become a nun, and was later Abbess at the Convent of the Carmelites of St Denis, near to Versailles. Marie Antoinette prepared her daughter for her first visit to the convent by having a doll made which was dressed as a nun, to accustom her daughter to a nun's unusual outfit and appearance so she would not be frightened or discomforted when visiting the convent. In fact, Marie Thérèse loved the convent atmosphere and asked the sisters to pray for her, which charmed and impressed them. The memoirs of Pauline de Béarn[27] recount how the nuns thought that Madame Royale might well make a good nun herself, so struck were they by her religious spirit and self-discipline. Her saint's day, St Theresa, was celebrated on 15 October each year.

In the gardens of the Petit Trianon, Marie Thérèse and Ernestine each tended the flowerbeds that had been allocated to them with specially made miniature garden implements. The girls also shared a herd of sheep and goats, given to them as pets. It was hoped from this relationship and in caring for her companion that Madame Royale would learn humility and service to others. The Queen found the time at the Trianon relaxing, reminding her of the happy and informal family life she had enjoyed as a child at the Palace of Laxenberg near Vienna. The Queen would sometimes spend a month at the Trianon with her friends, the children being brought from their apartments in the main palace to spend time with their mother. Madame Royale and her aunt Madame Élisabeth had their own small rooms in the attics at the Petit Trianon. The *London Chronicle* of 5 August 1784 reported that the Queen and her daughter were at the Petit Trianon and likely to stay there for an extended visit of three weeks.

Ernestine's mother died in 1788, when the girls were ten, and from that time Marie Antoinette took the young girl completely into her care, to live permanently with the Royal Family. The English Royals at the time of George III made similar arrangements for the upbringing of the princesses and princes by introducing a poor child to be brought up with them as a companion, as did the Orléans family.[28] It is also said that Marie Antoinette, as part of her plan to train Marie Thérèse to be humble and think of others, would drop her fan on occasion, so that her daughter would have to pick it up for her mother herself, rather than leaving the task to one of the many servants.

In due course, Marie Thérèse was presented with further siblings. On 7 March 1785, Marie Antoinette gave birth to her second son, Louis Charles, who was known during his early years as the Duc de Normandie; and then on July 9 1786 a second daughter, Sophie Hélène Beatrix, who sadly died ten months later. There is a well-known portrait from this period by Madame Vigée Le Brun of Marie Antoinette and her three surviving children looking at the empty cradle of the dead baby princess, who has been painted out of the picture.

In the wonderful grounds of the Royal residences, Marie Thérèse was able to enjoy a range of leisure pursuits. The English newspapers reported that a large party led by the Comte d'Artois spent time sledging during March 1786. The sledging party included the seven-year-old Marie Thérèse. The Queen also arranged for children of members of the Court to perform plays for the amusement of the Princess and the Dauphin. Madame de Gontaut, one of the child actresses, recalls in her memoirs a performance in which she took part as a seven-year-old of Euripides' *Iphigenia at Aulis*. After the play the children, both performers and audience, were served supper by members of the Royal Family.

In 1787, when Marie Thérèse was nearly nine years old and the Dauphin, Louis Joseph, was six years old, the Queen started a series of Sunday evening children's dances at the Trianon to which all children, whatever their social backgrounds, were welcome as long as they had clean clothes and looked respectable. The Queen served cake to the guests as a treat. She was able to do this as she was within the confines of her own private château. The Dauphin and his sister were encouraged to dance with other children, whatever their rank in society. The Queen's intention was to teach her children to be socially at ease and to encourage in them humility and approachability to all classes, as well as to perfect the important skill of elegant and accomplished dancing. Contemporary observers of the royal children at the Sunday evening dances reported that Marie Thérèse was cold, stiff and clearly did not seem to be enjoying herself. This said, she may have been frozen with shyness or filled with resentment at having to dance with strangers; or she may have felt this to be a heavy-handed lesson in morality, which she resented.

Whatever the truth of her feelings about the dances, Marie Thérèse's relationship with her father was easier than that with her mother, and she more clearly favoured the Bourbon side of the family. There is a story of Marie Thérèse's reaction in early childhood when the Abbé de Vermond told her that her mother had taken a fall from her horse and could have died from her injuries (Marie Antoinette had nearly fractured her skull). Marie Thérèse apparently expressed no concern. Even when challenged by the shocked Abbé de Vermond at her lack of emotion at the news of this dreadful accident, she said that she did not care about what had happened to her mother. The Abbé further pressed her by asking if she understood what it meant that a person was dead. She replied that she did and said, 'You do not see dead people any more. I would not see the Queen any more and I would be very glad about it, because I would be able to do what I wanted.' Marie Thérèse may have simply been frightened by the news or resentful, as children are, of being pushed to show appropriate emotions to order. It would be dangerous to read too much about the relationship between mother and daughter into this report. It is, nevertheless, an interesting early insight. Her reference to her mother as 'the Queen' also illustrates the formality in which the Royal Family referred to each other.

Madame Royale's under-governess Madame de Mackau was a close friend of Madame d'Oberkirch,[29] who had been introduced to Marie Antoinette at Strasbourg when the newly married Dauphine was travelling through France to join her new family. Madame d'Oberkirch was able to observe Marie Thérèse at very close quarters as she was growing up and recounts a number of stories that give us an insight to the young Princess and her childhood in the years before the Revolution swept away the world of the *ancien régime*. She recalls in her Memoirs a visit to the Royal nursery in the mid-1780s, writing that:

> Madame de Mackau had the goodness to take me to the apartments of the Royal children. The Princess Royal is a miracle of beauty, intelligence and precocious dignity, and very like her august mother. She looked at me attentively and asked my name; when she was told, she said:
>
> 'You are German, Madame.'
>
> 'No Madame, I am French and from Alsace.'
>
> 'I am glad of that for I could not love foreigners.'[30]

Madame d'Oberkirch, who was a great admirer of royalty and was always inclined to regard them and their actions in a tolerant light, remarked how charming this was in so young a child. Marie Thérèse was to display her less charming side to Madame d'Oberkirch on another occasion, when the Princess was about seven and half years old. Madame d'Oberkirch was visiting the nursery at the invitation of Madame de Mackau, and on meeting Marie Thérèse again after some time commented on how well the Princess was looking and how much she had grown since they last met. The little Princess was taken aback that this lady should presume to comment on her appearance even in such complimentary terms, and said so frankly. No sooner had she done so than Madame de Mackau made it clear by a stern glance at her charge that such a riposte was not seemly in a princess, even if etiquette had been breached by Madame d'Oberkirch in commenting so freely on the Princess's appearance. Madame d'Oberkirch noted that the Princess quickly recognised that she had behaved arrogantly and apologised as well as curtseying to the older lady and graciously holding out her small hand to be kissed. Madame de Mackau had had more than enough experience in taming uppity princesses during her time spent with the once unruly, but now very gentle and self-controlled, Madame Élisabeth. Marie Thérèse, while somewhat proud of her position and ancestry, was not vain about her appearance despite being regarded as an attractive child. Her upbringing under the supervision of her mother and governesses was strict and required application to her work and neatness in her dress and appearance.

During 1785, Marie Thérèse was a witness to one of the key scenes of the 'Affair of the Queen's Necklace',[31] an episode which illustrated how low Marie Antoinette's stock had fallen in France, and which was to damage further her reputation. The unpopularity of the Queen and the mistrust felt by many in France towards her had been very obviously demonstrated. Her good name was in the dust. Her reputation for extravagant self-indulgence had brought the monarchy to a very low ebb. This atmosphere of contempt for the monarchs would help to fuel dissent and revolt.

It seems that, at this time of her life, Marie Thérèse much preferred the ceremonial life offered at Court to the public and rather egalitarian children's dances organised by her mother. She enjoyed participating in the 1788 visit of three exotic envoys of the Indian Potentate under Tippoo Sahib, Sultan of Mysore.[32] He had come to ask for the help of the French in their war with Britain as he was attempting to 'create an alliance to drive the British … out of India'. Lucie de la Tour du Pin, who was at Court during the visit, wrote in her Journal, 'They had come to ask the support of France against the English.' She goes on to say that they received only kind words and encouragement in their struggle, but no practical aid. France was in no position to get involved in another war against the old enemy. French involvement in the American War of Independence had had terrible consequences for the public finances. The envoys stayed for several months in Paris at the expense of the King, travelling in a carriage with six horses and attending the opera where a fine box was reserved for them. Madame Royale and other high-ranking ladies of the Court observed the colourful proceedings from a canopied dais when the exotic envoys were presented at Court.

The King and Queen themselves did not enjoy this distraction, concerned as they were by the political and economic situation in France and preoccupied by the failing health of the seven-year-old Dauphin who had became very ill with rickets 'which within a few months curved his spine, and rendered his legs so weak that he could not walk without being supported like a feeble old man'.[33] The Dauphin was in great distress and pain. He had been sent to the Château of Meudon, approximately five miles from the centre of Paris and in an elevated position. Here the ailing boy was able enjoy peace and quiet and fresh country air. The King had lived there at times and remembered it with fondness. The Dauphin's fragile health and sufferings naturally worried his parents and his governess, Madame de Polignac. Yolande de Polignac noted that whenever the Dauphin received a treat or gift from his parents or others, he generously wanted Marie Thérèse to be treated similarly.

Royal childhoods were short. By 1787, at the age of ten years, possible future marriage alliances for Marie Thérèse were being openly discussed and speculated about at Court. Potential suitors for her hand included her maternal cousin, the hereditary Prince of Naples, the son of Marie Antoinette's favourite sister Maria Carolina, Queen of Naples and the Two Sicilies. A possible marriage between the Dauphin and his cousin Princess Marie-Amélie of Naples was also discussed and seriously considered by Marie Antoinette. The young Princess came to think of herself as a future Queen of France. In the summer of 1787 the Queen of Naples sent her envoy, the Chevalier de Bressac, to see the Queen about this possible alliance.

For Madame Royale the Duc d'Angoulême, Louis Antoine, was another possibility, with the advantage that marriage to him would mean that she would not need to leave her native land and family. Marie Antoinette said to Madame Campan that in marrying the Duc d'Angoulême, Marie Thérèse would not 'lose her rank as the daughter of the Queen' and that her situation would be 'preferable to that of the Queen of any other country'. Since the birth of Madame Royale, Marie Antoinette had regarded the Duc d'Angoulême as the favoured candidate for her daughter's hand in marriage. The Duc's father, Comte d'Artois, was also in favour of gaining the hand of this Princess for his son. In addition, so long as Madame Royale had no brothers, the young Duc d'Angoulême was the heir to the throne. The birth of Marie Thérèse's two younger brothers would change this, but he was still regarded as a serious possibility. Marie Antoinette always behaved generously to Louis Antoine, giving him gifts and seemingly regarding him not only as a nephew but also as a possible future son-in-law.

The Duc de Chartres, Louis Philippe, heir to the rich Orléans dukedom and five years older than the Princess, was also considered as a possible husband. Marie Antoinette did not like this option as she felt that it would be an overly favourable union for the younger branch of the Bourbon dynasty to marry the daughter of the King. The King and his Orléans cousin had never got on well and the early friendship between the Duc d'Orléans and Marie Antoinette had ended in a quarrel. Madame de la Tour du Pin wrote, 'The Queen hated the Duc d'Orléans who had spoken ill of her in public, for example, during the Affair of the Diamond Necklace. He had wanted his son, the Duc de Chartres, to marry Madame Royale. The Duc d'Orléans took this preference as a mortal affront. His visits to Versailles were rare.' The Swedish Crown Prince, the son of Gustav III, the Bourbon family friend and ally, was another option as a possible husband for Madame Royale.[34] He was a near contemporary of Marie Thérèse. The rumours and reports in the English newspapers that the Princess might marry the Prince of Wales (later Prince Regent and King George IV) were highly unlikely, given the Bourbons' attachment to their Roman Catholic faith and the prohibition in the Act of Settlement against the British sovereign marrying a Roman Catholic.

As the Princess grew to adolescence, her life in Versailles and the other châteaux of the Île de France was pleasant and ordered. She was surrounded by loving parents, siblings, an affectionate extended family and an attentive Household. However, the political scene was much less happy. France was practically bankrupt. Costly foreign wars, extravagant monarchs and an inequitable and ineffective tax system had all contributed to this situation. The tax burden fell most heavily on the poorest sections of society, while the generally richer nobility and clergy had legal exemption from taxation. Louis XV during his long reign had shied away from problems and pursued his pleasures with vigour. All these factors were exacerbated by recent cold winters and failed harvests. The winter of 1788/89 was terrible. Many people in France were hungry and there was agitation against an absolute monarchy that seemed to them increasingly remote, ineffectual and extravagant. Lucie de la Tour du Pin wrote that while the Duc d'Orléans was making generous gifts to the poor in Paris, 'In contrast, whether rightly or wrongly there was no mention of any charitable gifts from the Royal princes or from the King and Queen.' Whatever the realities, the propaganda battle was being lost by Louis XVI and his Queen. Decisive action was needed and Louis XVI, with all his many good points, was not a decisive man. The Queen no longer went regularly into Paris to attend the theatre. Lucie de la Tour du Pin wrote, 'The people never saw her or her children. Nor did the King ever show himself. Hidden away at Versailles or hunting in the nearby forests, he suspected nothing, foresaw nothing and believed nothing he was told.'[35]

In late 1788, the King felt compelled to take action by the dire condition of the public finances. He summoned the Estates General, the general assembly that represented the three Estates into which the French realm was divided: the First Estate was made up of the clergy, the Second Estate consisted of the nobility, and the Third Estate was that of commoners. The Estates General was instructed to assemble, and the following year they gathered at Versailles to try to involve all sections of society in finding a solution to the country's many problems. The ten-year-old Marie Thérèse observed the elaborate ceremony that accompanied the political activities. The meeting of the Estates General was preceded by a grand procession from the Château at Versailles to the parish church of Notre Dame. The British newspapers of June 1789 reported:

> All the state coaches belonging to the King, his brothers, sister and aunts, preceded, and made as brilliant a show as ever was seen in this kingdom; for the sun darting his rays on the gold, silver and glasses of the magnificent carriages, and the rich trimmings and caparisons,[36] their manes adorned with variegated plumage, spread a refulgent splendor [37] on the eyes of every beholder. Next, with almost as splendid cortege, came the Queen, majestically seated, facing Madame,[38] and accompanied by the Princess de Lamballe and Madame Élisabeth.

The nobility and clergy were richly attired and were followed by the soberly dressed Third Estate, among whom lawyers were numerous. The Duc d'Orléans chose not to join the other Princes of the Blood, but to accompany his colleagues among the Third Estate. He had been elected as a Deputy (representative) for the town of Orléans. This gesture of solidarity with the populace caused the crowd watching the procession to cheer loudly. The King was still popular with his people, if the cheers of the crowds were a reflection of this; the Queen and clergy less so. The day was filled with six hours of ceremony, including a Mass at which the Duc d'Angoulême participated with his father, holding the strings of the canopy under which the Holy Sacrament was carried by the Archbishop of Paris. The Dauphin attended as an observer, despite his poor health. The real business would begin the next day when the King went to the Estates General and gave a short speech. He then handed over proceedings to Monsieur Necker, the Minister of Finance, who made a speech to the assembled representatives about the dire financial troubles facing France.

The condition of Marie Thérèse's brother, the Dauphin, worsened and on 4 June 1789 he died, aged eight, greatly mourned by his family. His younger four-year-old brother, Louis Charles formerly Duc de Normandie, a healthy and amenable child, was now the Dauphin and heir to the throne of France.

On 20 June 1789, in an atmosphere of national tragedy, the Third Estate section of the Estates General vowed that it would not disband until it had introduced a constitution in France. This was known as the Tennis Court Oath. From this time onwards the assemblage was known as the National Assembly. The initiative had moved away from the King to the legislators.

The political situation was growing more troubled, and Madame Campan writes that although the people still spoke of the King with affection and felt that he was genuinely in favour of reform, they believed that he was badly advised and under the influence of the Queen and the Comte d'Artois, who were attempting to persuade him to retain the status quo and resist political reform. The King's younger brother, the Comte d'Artois, was particularly loathed for opposing the creation of the three estates, nobility, clergy and commons, within the Estates General. He wanted only two, combining clergy and commons, thus diluting their voting powers. In Paris there were uprisings and disorder on the nights of 11 and 12 July, and on the afternoon of 14 July the Bastille, the notorious state prison, was stormed and fell to the Parisian mob – a major attack on a symbol of Royal authority, even if it in fact held fewer than ten prisoners.

The Queen was bitterly upset. On 15 July, the King went to the Estates General accompanied by his brothers and declared to the assembled representative: 'I trust myself to you; I only wish to be at one with my nation, and, counting on the affection and fidelity of my subjects, I have given orders to the troops to remove from Paris and Versailles.' The army was disbanded and its members returned to their homes. The King responded to requests for his presence in Paris by going to the Hôtel de Ville on 17 July. Nesta Webster's account of the French Revolution noted that the King was in Paris:

> Meanwhile the Queen, holding the Dauphin in her arms and little Madame Royale by the hand came onto the balcony... The children of the Comte d'Artois came to kiss his hand; the Queen stooped to embrace them, holding the Dauphin towards them. The little boys pressed him to their hearts, and Madame Royale, slipping her head under mother's arm, joined in the caresses. The King arrived at this moment and appeared on the balcony amidst the cheers and benedictions of his people.

Tensions built during the summer of 1789, but as Lucie de la Tour du Pin wrote, there had been food riots before and they had not signalled a full-scale revolution. 'It must also be admitted that encroachments on the Royal authority were so novel that neither the King nor Queen realised there was any real danger.' The Comte d'Artois left Versailles with his wife and two sons, Angoulême and Berry. The Comte d'Artois went on first, ostensibly on a visit to his father-in-law, Victor Amadeus III, King of Sardinia, in his capital Turin, followed shortly afterwards by the rest of the Artois family. He was a fierce opponent of reform and upholder of autocracy. It was no longer safe for him to remain in France. Madame de Gontaut in her memoirs illustrates this:

> In order to give you some idea of the exasperation of the people at this time, I will mention that a chasseur wearing the livery of the Comte d'Artois, and bringing a note for my mother, was attacked, beaten, and had nearly all his clothes torn off in the Place Louis XV;[39] he was able to bring only a fragment of the letter with which he was charged.[40]

Accompanying the Comte d'Artois out of France were the Prince de Condé and his children. In 1791, the Prince de Condé would establish an émigré army known as the Condé Army, or Princes' Army, comprising many young aristocrats and other émigrés who were committed to fighting against Revolutionary France. It was funded at different times by foreign powers and fought over a number of years in alliance with Russia, Austria and Great Britain. They were initially based in Coblenz,[41] a great centre for the French émigré community. Also leaving France were Louis Charles' former governess, who had resigned her duties to go into exile; Marie Antoinette's dear friend, Madame de Polignac; her husband and daughter, the Duchesse de Guiche;[42] Madame de Gramont; Comtesse Diane de Polignac, sister of the Duc de Polignac; Madame de Polastron; and the Abbé de Balivière. The Queen was devastated by the loss of so many friends and close members of the family.

Closely watched by her enemies as she was, the Queen could not express her full emotions as she said goodbye to her beloved companions on their departures from Versailles and France. Wild rumours of an Austrian invasion spread through France. These inflamed the people against the Queen whom they believed was plotting with her Austrian family to reimpose royal autocracy and counter the gains made by those who wanted political change.

On 5 October, a mob of Parisian market women and fishwives marched from Paris to Versailles in what has become known as the Women's March. Many of the participants were in fact men dressed as women, in the expectation that the King, who was well known for his kindness, would not order his troops to fire on women. The previous day the 'women' had marched to Versailles from Paris to demand bread. They had called on the Queen to show herself on the balcony and had howled obscene abuse at her when, bravely, she went out to face them. She presented the second Dauphin, Louis Charles, and Madame Royale to the crowd in order to gain their sympathy, but they screamed at her, 'No children!' The visibly upset Dauphin and Madame Royale retreated back into the palace, being handed over by the Queen to their new governess Madame de Tourzel, who had taken up her post in early August.[43]

Marie Antoinette bore all this abuse with great courage and dignity, impressing the crowd with her bearing, according to reports. At last a few cries of '*Vive la reine*' were heard from the crowd. Marie Thérèse later wrote, 'The courtyard of the Château presented a terrible sight. A crowd of women almost naked, and men with pikes threatened our windows with dreadful cries.' Madame de Boigne described 'the streets of Versailles being filled up with a flood of horrible looking people, uttering wild cries while gunshots could be heard in the distance'.[44] Marie Thérèse later referred in her memoirs to these autumn days as being the 'beginning of the outrages and cruelties'.

Madame Royale had been at her lessons on the morning of 5 October 1789 when the palace was invaded; she heard the terrible cries and noise of the mob. The Royal Family gathered in the King's apartments. The Queen had previously been forced to flee from a mob threatening to kill her, escaping through a concealed door moments before the mob arrived in her apartments. She had been saved from the mob's anger by the courage of one of the guards who delayed the attackers long enough to allow her to get away. He was badly injured but not killed.[45]

The family had spent a sleepless and frightened night awaiting developments. Following the attack on Versailles by the market women and their male supporters, the cry of 'To Paris!' went up. The Royal Family was forced into a coach to make the journey to Paris. Seated in the coach, according to Madame Campan's account of events, were the King, the Queen, Marie Thérèse, the Dauphin, Madame and Monsieur,[46] Madame Élisabeth and Madame de Tourzel. When Marie Antoinette had gone up to Paris for balls or to the opera from Versailles, the journey would take about an hour; on this occasion, it took more than six long, stressful, frightening hours. All the occupants of the coach were in a state of barely concealed terror. Louis Charles and Marie Thérèse suffered especially. The Royal coach was accompanied by a huge crowd shouting horrible abuse at the family, particularly regarding Marie Thérèse's mother. Some of the marchers carried with them the heads of murdered Royal guards, mounted on pikes. The crowd of some 30,000 people included the women and the men who had invaded the Palace of Versailles, as well as the National Guard, which led the procession. The Marquis de Lafayette had been appointed the head of the newly created National Guard. He was known as a moderate reformer and hero of the American War of Independence, but was unable to prevent the family from being forced to leave Versailles. He could only hope to maintain sufficient control of his men, many of whom were sympathetic to the demands of the mob, to enforce some order and protect the Royal Family from the worst threats of violence. Marie Antoinette – who disliked the Marquis anyway – never forgave him for what she saw as his failure to protect Royal authority.

Following the procession into Paris were members of the National Assembly, which had been in session at Versailles. The mob rejoiced at their humbling of the once-autocratic monarchy, and sang lustily of bringing the 'Baker' (a reference to the stores of grain held by the Royal Family), his wife and son back to Paris with them. As the King left Versailles, he turned to Monsieur de la Tour du Pin who had been left to guard the château and said, 'You are in complete charge here. Try to save my poor Versailles for me.' His wife Lucie went on to write, 'The only sound that could be heard in the Château was the fastening of doors and shutters which had not been closed since the time of Louis XIV.' At Passy, on the family's route into Paris, according to the memoirs of Madame de Tourzel the Duc d'Orléans had hired a house; from its balcony he could observe the humiliation of his cousins as they were forced by the mob to leave the security and tranquillity of Versailles for Paris.

2

At the Tuileries

OCTOBER 1789–AUGUST 1792

Marie Thérèse was nearly eleven years old when the Royal Family made their journey from Versailles via the Hôtel de Ville to the Tuileries Palace in the centre of Paris. They were ceremoniously greeted and welcomed by the Mayor of Paris, Monsieur Bailly. But when the exhausted and shocked family finally arrived at the Tuileries Palace on the evening of 6 October, nothing was prepared for them. Events had moved with such speed and in such an unexpected and shocking manner that no one had had an opportunity to make any arrangements. There were insufficient beds and linens to accommodate the family and their attendants in anything like the style and comfort to which they were accustomed. Madame Royale and particularly her younger brother Louis Charles, a cosseted and sensitive four-year-old, Marie Antoinette's beloved *chou d'amour* or darling cabbage, were disturbed and frightened by the violent events. Their parents tried to comfort them and provide some stability in the chaos.

At least the children had the comforting presence of their newly appointed governess, Madame de Tourzel, who had a reputation for being a woman of the highest morals and strong religious principles. She was a widow whose husband had been killed in an accident while hunting with the King at Fontainebleau. She had apparently brought up her own five children (four daughters and a son) in an exemplary way. The King and Queen were happy to put her in charge of the upbringing of the *Enfants de France*. Marie Antoinette said to Madame de Tourzel that previous governesses had been appointed because of their rank (as with Madame de Guéméné) or their close personal relationship with the Queen (Madame de Polignac), but that she had been given the prestigious post because of her many virtues and her sense of duty. Madame de Tourzel's daughter

Pauline writes of her mother's devotion to her obligations. According to her daughter,[1] Madame de Tourzel slept in the same room as the Dauphin and was on duty constantly, very conscious of her obligations to the family and her young charges.

Louis Charles of France

The Tuileries Palace had been built in the sixteenth century by Catherine de' Medici, the Italian-born wife of Henry II, Regent of France, during the reigns of her sons Francis II,[2] Charles IX and Henri III. It was a vast, imposing building situated in the heart of Paris near the Louvre. The Tuileries Gardens are now the only surviving remnant of the palace that Marie Thérèse knew; the palace was very badly damaged in 1871 during the Franco-Prussian War and the remains were finally pulled down in the 1880s. Louis XIV had finished the construction of the building and furnished the Tuileries before deciding, in 1682, to move the seat of Royal government, and his main residence, from Paris to Versailles. The Tuileries was occupied by Louis XVI's grandfather, the boy King Louis XV, between 1715 and 1722 before he too moved to the comforts of Versailles. The Tuileries Palace had not been well looked after in the absence of Royal occupants over the previous century. However, it did have some happy memories for the King and Queen, as it had been the venue for the Paris celebrations of the birth of the recently deceased first Dauphin, Louis Joseph. The palace comprised three sections: the Pavillon de Flore at the southern end, the Pavillon de Marsan in the centre, and to the north the Pavillon de l'Horloge. The palace's 386 rooms[3] were divided into a number of apartments occupied by retired Royal servants, courtiers and artists. There were also tradespeople and artisans accommodated in the palace, operating their businesses from it. The occupants were speedily evicted to make way for the Royal Family and their attendants, leaving behind them furniture and other equipment which were purchased by the Royal Household to provide for their immediate needs. Over the next few days a steady stream of carts travelled between the abandoned château at Versailles and the Tuileries Palace, bringing supplies of furniture, clothes, linens, bedding, silver plate, glass, books, toys for the children, musical instruments and the other personal necessities required to conduct Royal life in the capital.

On 8 October 1789, Marie Antoinette and Louis XVI toured the numerous rooms of the Tuileries Palace to decide how the available apartments should be allocated to different members of the Royal Family and their Households. The King, Queen, Madame Royale and the Dauphin were housed more closely together than they had been at Versailles. The King had rooms on the ground floor with views over the gardens. His study and bedroom were on the second floor. The Queen was next to her husband, with Marie Thérèse and Louis Charles immediately above their mother. The rest of the accommodation chosen for the Royal Family comprised a drawing room, billiard room and several antechambers. Madame Élisabeth and Madame de Lamballe occupied the Pavilion de Flore overlooking the River Seine. The Comte and Comtesse de Provence did not join the King and the Queen and their immediate family at the palace, but retired to their own Paris home, the magnificent Luxembourg Palace. They came daily to the Tuileries to eat with the rest of the Royal Family. Naturally, the courtiers themselves were accompanied by a retinue of their own domestic servants and cooks. Marie Thérèse had with her Ernestine Lambriquet as her playmate and companion.

The King's aunts, frightened after their unsettling experiences at Versailles, were allowed to retire to their château at Meudon. They did not actually come into Paris but went straight there from Versailles; nevertheless they were forced to travel some distance surrounded by a screaming mob and forced to wear the tricolour insignia of the Revolution. The diarist Madame de Boigne speaks of how her mother, the Comtesse d'Osmond, found that Mesdames Victoire and Adélaïde, completely terrified by the invasion of Versailles, had locked themselves in their apartments on the morning of the departure for Paris. Their apartment doors and windows were firmly closed and there was only one candle to light the gloomy room. The windows of the princesses' rooms had been fired at by the mob and not 'a single pane of glass remained unbroken'. One can only imagine how these events traumatised these middle-aged women, whose whole lives had been spent within the privileged and secluded confines of convent and Court.

After the initial chaos of the unexpected forced removal of the King and his family from Versailles, in some ways the Royal routine continued much as it always had for Marie Thérèse and her family. There were the usual King's *Levée* and *Coucher* and the Royal Family's daily attendance at Mass in the Chapel of the Tuileries Palace. The Queen held courts on Tuesdays, Thursdays and Sundays, and otherwise spent her days supervising Madame Royale's studies, doing needlework, and writing letters to the courts of Europe to try and drum up support for her cause. Of this time in Marie Thérèse's girlhood, Madame Campan writes that 'When the King and the Queen were suitably established at the Tuileries, as well as Madame Élisabeth and the Princesse de Lamballe, the Queen resumed her usual habits; she employed her mornings in superintending the education of Madame, who received all her lessons in her presence.' The Queen and her sister-in-law worked during this period on weaving a large carpet.[4] Marie Thérèse, always a keen reader and hardworking student, threw herself into her studies with even greater diligence, seeking perhaps a distraction from the horrors she had seen around her and trying to cling on to whatever normality and order she could find. Madame Campan writes that 'their Majesties found some consolation in their private life; from Madame's gentle manners and filial affection, from the accomplishments and vivacity of the little Dauphin, and the attention and tenderness of the pious Princess Élisabeth, they still derived moments of happiness'. The Dauphin continued his lessons with his tutor the Abbé Davaux, while Marie Thérèse was a dutiful and supportive daughter to her parents at this difficult time.

Despite the familiar ceremony and grand surroundings, the Royal Family felt themselves to be prisoners of the mob. They took no pleasure at being in Paris. They were resentful of their position and it showed. When questioned about this, the Queen remarked that she had been much disturbed by the way they entered Paris, preceded by people holding pikes on which were the heads of their decapitated guards. The Queen gave up her boxes at the *Opéra*, *Comédie Française* and *Comédie Italienne* (known as the *Opéra Comique*), which had given her and Marie Thérèse so much pleasure on their visits to Paris in the past. Despite being in the centre of Paris, the Queen rarely went out. There were no royal balls, fêtes, plays or concerts – the staples of the life of a pleasure-loving Court. By behaving as virtual prisoners and not carrying on normal Court life, the King and Queen fed the perception of being captives. Lucie de la Tour du Pin writes that this was a tactless approach by the Queen that damaged her husband's cause and was 'very natural, but most unfortunate for it made the people of Paris more hostile than ever towards her'.

The Parisians, curious to see their humbled monarchs, were admitted to the Tuileries Gardens as had been the custom at Versailles. This was a far cry from the secluded privacy of Marie Antoinette's Trianon and its gardens, where not even the King might enter without her permission and the children could play and relax unobserved. Madame de Tourzel writes that on one occasion a mob of women invaded the apartments of Madame Élisabeth, who was so traumatised that she begged the King to change her accommodation. The Tuileries Palace was guarded by the National Guard, and the King and Queen encouraged the children to be friendly with them. The Dauphin was happy to oblige and charmed the soldiers. One suspects that the older and more reserved Marie Thérèse would have found this enforced camaraderie with the soldiers more difficult to cope with than her affable sibling. She would also have been much more aware of the events happening around her than her young brother. Marie Thérèse must have noted the changes she and her parents were experiencing, including a marked lack of the previous deference from some of those with whom the Royal Family had daily contact.[5]

An aviary was installed in the Tuileries Gardens, on the orders of the Queen, to divert and amuse Marie Thérèse, Ernestine and Louis Charles. The King also attended his daughter's classes and heard the children reciting their lessons. The Dauphin was particularly good at learning verses and then reciting them to his family and attendants in a charming way. He had a precocious intelligence and wit, which he would sometimes use to tease his elder sister.

Marie Antoinette wrote to her confidante Madame de Polignac, who was in exile in London, of Marie Thérèse and her younger brother at this time, saying 'they are always with me and are my consolation'. Marie Thérèse and her mother liked to walk for exercise and fresh air in the gardens of the Tuileries, but they missed the open expanses of the gardens of the Trianon. As they walked in the grounds of the Tuileries Palace, they were often exposed to insulting and sexually abusive remarks from Parisians also enjoying the gardens. The Queen's reputation had been damaged by the sexually explicit *libelles*. The normal constraints were broken and she was reviled by many of the people. It must have been particularly unpleasant and shocking for Marie Thérèse. The Queen could hardly approach an open window without being subjected to insults and abuse in the most violent and explicit sexual terms. Following a particularly unpleasant encounter, Madame Royale and the Queen no longer went out to take exercise. The family's lives were becoming increasingly circumscribed and restricted.

In October 1789, the National Assembly followed the Royal Family back to Paris and established itself in the indoor riding school that was part of the Tuileries Palace. The National Assembly was determined to diminish the powers of the once absolute monarchy. It was populated by a large number of lawyers (making up approximately half of the Third Estate) who were undertaking the task of writing a new Constitution for France. Louis XVI's speech of 4 February 1790 to the National Assembly in the Salle du Ménage at the Tuileries was an act of studied self-preservation. He energetically committed himself and the Queen to support for the newly drafted Constitution and appealed for all counter-revolutionaries based in Coblenz and elsewhere, including his brother the Comte d'Artois, to work together to restore France to its former glory. His speech was well received. The Deputies then escorted him to meet Marie Antoinette, who in turn presented the Dauphin to the parliamentarians. The Queen spoke briefly and received a gracious response. It was all part of the charade they felt obliged to perform. Following the speech, the King and Queen went out and about more, even attending the theatre again. The King reviewed the troops. The Queen made visits to the Paris Orphanage, the Foundling Hospital and a glass manufactory in Faubourg St Antoine. The French Royal Family had since the time of Louis XIV and Louis XV been keen patrons of the manufacturers of luxury goods of France. Marie Thérèse and her brother were also part of the campaign of re-establishing normality. Marie Antoinette often took them out for drives around Paris. It is also recorded in the writings of Madame Campan that Marie Antoinette received a deputation of mothers from the Charité Maternelle, which had been founded in 1788 with the Queen as patroness to help improve the circumstances of impoverished mothers and their infants.[6] The magnificence of the Queen's apartments was noted by the visiting women. It was also observed that the ladies of Court were seated in the Queen's presence: already a relaxation of the etiquette of Versailles and more akin to the way Marie Antoinette had liked to live when she was at the Trianon.

We gain another rather different insight into the character of Marie Thérèse from the writings of Madame de Tourzel, who followed the young girl as she was growing up during the late 1780s and 1790s. Madame de Tourzel expresses the view in her memoirs that Marie Thérèse was far from proud and haughty, and that the Queen had been given the wrong impression by reports from servants and courtiers. On the contrary, she wrote:

> the young Princess was good, affable, timid, and ever in need of being inspired with confidence. It would have been far more useful for her to have seen more people than to be forever alone with her women and the young person[7] who was permitted by the Queen to share her studies and amusements. Deprived when so young of all support, left to herself in cruel captivity, she alone finished her own education; unhappiness was her tutor, and, fortunately, it did not alter those great qualities which

> circumstances developed to their greatest extent during the whole of her life.

Madame de Tourzel denies the suggestion that Marie Thérèse did not seek and enjoy the company of girls of her own age as playmates and friends.

On 8 April 1790, Easter Day, at the age of eleven and a half, Marie Thérèse took her First Communion. This was a significant spiritual event in the life of a serious and religious girl. Madame de Tourzel says in her memoirs that 'her piety seemed to be born with her, rendered this ceremony very moving'. While not particularly religious herself, Marie Antoinette required that her children be brought up with the strictest religious principles. The Queen attended her daughter's First Communion incognita and the service was short and simple. The ceremony was marked by her parents giving alms to the poor of the parishes of Paris, as was usual on such occasions. The family's changed circumstances were illustrated by the absence of the traditional gift of a diamond necklace. Her parents explained to Madame Royale that this would not be appropriate in their current position. Marie Thérèse entirely understood their reasoning and accepted their decision without question. In any event, clothes and jewellery were not important to her.

On the day of her First Communion Madame Royale was dressed all in white, as was customary for all girls taking the rite. Marie Antoinette led Marie Thérèse into her father's rooms, where Madame Royale knelt before the King and asked for his blessing. The King replied to his daughter that she:

> might not stay in this kingdom. But into whatever place the hand of God may lead you, remember that you are called upon to edify by your example, to do good whenever an opportunity occurs and, above all, to succour the unfortunate to the uttermost extent of your power. You are young and you have already beheld your father heavily afflicted more than once.[8]

He understood how difficult it must have been for her to bear the humiliations and pain she had observed her beloved father experiencing. She was powerless to do anything to prevent the causes of his sadness. Louis XVI, who regarded himself as having been anointed by God at his coronation at Rheims on 11 June 1775, likened his own sufferings to those of Christ when speaking with Marie Thérèse. His words made an indelible impression on her. The King's reference to a possible foreign marriage for his daughter suggests that at this stage the King still envisaged, despite the problems they were experiencing, a 'normal' Royal life for his daughter. It also shows that it was not absolutely certain at this point that she would marry the Duc d'Angoulême, who had left France with the rest of his immediate family.

With the loyal and devoted exception of the King of Sweden, Gustav III, help was not forthcoming from other European monarchs. Marie Antoinette's position was not improved by the fact that Joseph II, the brother to whom she had been close, had died in February 1790. He had been succeeded as Emperor by their younger brother, Leopold II, whom Marie Antoinette hardly knew. They had both been in their teens when she left Vienna. The Emperor Leopold, safe in Austria, encouraged Marie Antoinette to take a softly, softly approach to her changed position, exhorting her to bide her time and go along with the views of the majority of the National Assembly. The Borbons of Spain were no more helpful and were even evasive in their responses to requests for fraternal support. In June 1790, all noble titles and aristocratic dues were abolished. At the same time, the National Assembly made grants of money to maintain the Royal Family. Under the emerging Constitution, the King had control of foreign policy but his decisions had to be ratified in advance by the Assembly. He had the right to withhold his consent from certain laws for set lengths of time, but not from laws concerning matters of finance or impeachments. The Assembly could also reject the royal veto. It was a far cry from the absolute power previously enjoyed by the monarchy.

The King and Queen persisted in their attempts to get foreign help against the Revolution. Marie Antoinette and Louis XVI's views and those within their family did not always coincide. The Queen advocated a less compromising approach to the demands of the politicians in the National Assembly. The Comte d'Artois, from the safety of exile on the borders of France, having been granted refuge by the Elector of Treves in Coblenz at the Palace of Stolzenfels, advocated taking a hard-line approach to the Revolution in order to restore Royal authority. He plotted an invasion with the aid of foreign powers. Marie Antoinette was angered by his interference. Madame de Gontaut wrote that the atmosphere in Coblenz among the dispossessed aristocrats who had taken up residence there was jolly and optimistically confident that they would soon be able to return home having defeated the 'rebels'. The King's orders were ignored in Coblenz, the refuge of the émigré princes, as well as in Paris. Madame Élisabeth, for all her modesty and piety, echoed the political views of the Comte d'Artois, in wanting their elder brother to take firm, decisive counter-revolutionary action. Even such a clever politician as Catherine II, Empress of Russia, seemed unable to comprehend the dire position of the imprisoned monarchs. She wrote to Louis XVI and Marie Antoinette that 'Kings ought to proceed in their career undisturbed by the cries of the people, even as the moon pursues her course unimpeded by the baying of dogs.' What a far cry from the reality of their circumstances. Some individuals, such as the poet Wordsworth who had travelled in France, welcomed the dawning of a more egalitarian new order.[9] The King and Queen and their children were trapped between revolutionary enemies and counter-revolutionary 'friends'.

The romantic love of Marie Antoinette's life was Axel von Fersen, an enormously wealthy and handsome Swedish nobleman. The same age as Marie Antoinette, he made his first appearance at Versailles in 1774 and met and fell into conversation at a masque ball with an unidentified woman who was, unbeknownst to him, the Dauphine, Marie Antoinette. Over the years the Swede spent time at the French Court and became a close member of the Queen's coterie, often dining in company with her. He was a man of action, taking part in the American War of Independence and spending several years there, returning to France in 1783. Over the years they corresponded and became closer. Relations between von Fersen and Louis XVI were perfectly amicable. We can only imagine what, if anything, Marie Thérèse thought of the relationship between her mother and Axel von Fersen. Did Marie Thérèse sense the closeness of the relationship? Did she speculate as to whether it was purely emotional or also a physical one? Or did she simply not yet think in those terms of the relations between men and women? She may have observed the cordial relationship between her father and Axel von Fersen and have felt that everything was as it should be, and not a cause for concern. Indeed, we may never know the precise nature of the relationship between Marie Antoinette and Axel von Fersen – letters between them that might have revealed it were destroyed by von Fersen's family in the nineteenth century. We can be confident, however, that they were devoted to each other and much in love. Certainly, large groups of the National Assembly and the French people were happy to believe that he was her lover.

The highly influential Marquis de Lafayette used rumours of her affair with the Swede against the Queen. He threatened her with the possibility of being forcibly divorced from Louis XVI and banished from France, separated from her beloved children and subjected to international public disgrace; no wonder Marie Antoinette loathed him. Lucie de la Tour du Pin writes in her memoirs that Marie Thérèse shared her mother's views on the Marquis de Lafayette, noting that 'Madame la Dauphine inherited the Queen's hatred of him. She listened to all the absurd tales told about him.' Whatever the nature of the romantic and sexual relationship with Marie Antoinette, Axel von Fersen was regarded by both the King and Queen as the trusted representative of the friendly King of Sweden. Equally importantly, the Count von Fersen was known to be a man who kept his promises and was both personally courageous and capable of decisive action. Others did not agree. Lucie de la Tour du Pin, for example, did not share the high opinion of von Fersen, regarding him as stupid and incapable of proper organisation, as she writes in her memoirs.

To avoid the summer heat of Paris, the Royal Family left the Tuileries in early July 1790[10] and spent more than four months at St Cloud[11] – a country retreat away from the restrictions of life at the Tuileries and an escape from the palace itself, which Madame Campan describes as being a 'very disagreeable residence during the summer'. The nearby Seine was used as a drain by Paris, which did not make a fragrant neighbour for the Royal Family. They were followed to St Cloud by the National Guard of Paris, who remained with them at the palace. They were able to go out into the countryside without guards, accompanied only by an *aide-de-camp* of the Marquis de Lafayette. They did, however, return regularly to Paris as their public duties required. During this time, the family dined in public so that they might be seen by the populace. The Royal Family (the King and Queen, Marie Thérèse, her brother, Madame Élisabeth and the Comte and Comtesse de Provence) returned briefly to central Paris on 14 July 1790 to participate in the 'celebrations' to mark the first anniversary of the fall of the Bastille, known as the *Fête de la Fédération*. The intention of the revolutionary government was to create a feeling of national unity and common purpose. It is hardly likely that the Royal Family shared this interpretation of events. The fête was held on the Champ de Mars (situated between where the Eiffel Tower now stands and the École Militaire), and the Royal Family, including the children, were seated on a stand under a huge tent, which was fortunate as it poured with rain. On their arrival at 8 p.m., there was enthusiastic applause despite the rain, and cheers when the Queen held up her five-year-old son so that the crowd could see their future King. To shelter Louis Charles from getting wet, Marie Antoinette wrapped him in her shawl, drawing a sympathetic reaction from the people who appreciated this gesture of simple maternal care by a Queen – particularly one with such a dreadful reputation for dissipation. Following this ceremony, Marie Thérèse and the rest of the family returned to St Cloud and stayed there until early November 1790, when they resumed residence at the noisy and very public Tuileries.

Even in these changed times and at St Cloud, much of the exacting etiquette of the Versailles Court still applied. Madame de Béarn writes of etiquette as '*la loi*' or 'the law'. Before Pauline de Tourzel, as daughter of the Dauphin's *gouvernante*, was permitted to dine with the King, there was prolonged discussion among the Royal Family, including the aunts Victoire and Adélaïde, as to whether this was appropriate. Eventually, after much debate, it was agreed by the family that Pauline could join them. It was during this time that Pauline and Marie Thérèse made friends and Pauline came to appreciate 'her excellent heart and precious qualities'.[12] Pauline was also charmed by a poem sent to her as a surprise through the post by the King. On Sundays the public were admitted to watch the Royal Family dining and were able to circulate among their tables and speak to them.

The King and Queen felt increasingly uncomfortable with the political developments within the National Assembly, which was becoming more radical. Once absolute royal power started to fade, Louis XVI felt strongly the compromise of the concept of absolute rule with which he had been brought up, and about which he had written as Dauphin, and the requirements of the new Constitution. This was brought to a head when he was required, on 26 December 1790, to sign the National Assembly's decree, 'The Civil Constitution of the Clergy'. The National Assembly, increasingly under the influence of the radicalised and violent Parisian mob, felt that the majority of the clergy were still committed to the *ancien régime* and operated outside their control. The decree would give the National Assembly control of the clergy. They would become, in effect, civil servants paid for by the state and therefore subject to it. The signing of the clergy decree that the Constitution required of the King would cause an inevitable schism with Papal authority once priests were required to swear loyalty to the Constitution. As a faithful son of the Roman Catholic Church, Louis XVI agonised about signing this decree. It was threatened that if he did not give his consent, there would be civil discord. Louis hated violence; he passionately did not want to be the cause of it. He felt himself to be the father of his people, and yet was humiliated. He was devastated by having to make this choice; but in the end he felt he had no option but to sign.

Following the implementation of the clergy decree, Lucie de la Tour du Pin reports that the Royal routine changed and the King and Queen and the Court no longer attended daily Mass. They could not bring themselves to attend services or take the sacrament presided over by a 'state-controlled' priest. For Marie Thérèse, after recently taking her First Communion, this break with tradition and the normal Royal routine of religious observance must have highlighted to her the ignominious position of her family. It must have been both alarming and bewildering. The Queen at this time was even more engaged in a massive correspondence – sometimes clandestine and in code – with the European powers to try and rally support for her cause. As the indecisive Louis XVI drifted into inactivity and depression, more of the burden of this work fell to the Queen, and she took it up with an energy belying her reputation for indolence and frivolity. But Marie Antoinette felt emotionally and physically exhausted by the considerable strain of trying to orchestrate a clandestine foreign policy on behalf of her depressed and passive husband. She felt drained by being obliged to live so closely monitored, as a hated foreigner and the architect, as they saw it, of the people's woes. She wanted to escape.

In February 1791, Mesdames Les Tantes, Adélaïde and Victoire, left the Château of Bellevue at Meudon, where they had settled following the departure from Versailles. But they were delayed on their way out of France by local officials who initially refused to allow them to leave. Eventually they were permitted to proceed and made their way to Italy. Les Tantes spent time at the court of Marie Antoinette's elder sister, Maria

Carolina, the Queen of Naples. They were kindly received and lived happily for a number of years, housed at the beautiful summer palazzo at Caserta, fourteen miles from Naples and one of the largest palaces in Europe.

The King had encouraged his ageing aunts to leave France. He wanted them safely out of France before he and his own family made their own plans to flee to the borders of France. The princesses very much hoped that their niece, Madame Élisabeth, would go with them into exile. Madame Campan writes, 'Mesdames were desirous of taking Madame Élisabeth to Rome. The free exercise of religion, the happiness of taking refuge with the head of the Church, and the prospect of living in safety with her aunts, whom she tenderly loved, were sacrificed by the virtuous Princess to her attachment to the King.' Mesdames Adélaïde and Victoire hoped that their exile would be of short duration and that they would soon be able to return to their homeland. These religious ladies were uncomfortable living in a country where their nephew had been forced to bring the French church under the control of the state, abandoning the traditions of their Roman Catholic faith and turning priests into civil servants. The departure of the sisters was presented as being for religious grounds. Following the aunts' departure, the National Assembly and its aides monitored the rest of the Royal Family and their intentions even more closely than usual, knowing that it could be a signal that the rest of the family would attempt to follow their example.

Madame Royale was growing up in an atmosphere of tension and fear. She must have been fully aware of the pressures on her family. Her life was still taken up with lessons, her religion and family, but was circumscribed by the continual presence of the National Guard's taunts and insults. Now the once reluctant King would think seriously about leaving France, with the idea of returning to restore the monarchy to govern in the old way. This was what the Queen wanted and was trying to achieve. Marie Antoinette desired a foreign military invasion of France followed by a full restoration of the powers of the monarchy. To bring this about it was first necessary for the Royal Family to escape from France and the control of the National Assembly. Discussions and plans of escape now began in earnest. The main protagonists were the King and Queen, Axel von Fersen, and François Claude, Marquis de Bouillé, a Royalist general, and his eldest son.

The resolve of the family to leave France was further strengthened by the events of 18 April 1791. They had planned to spend the Easter holiday in St Cloud to enjoy fresh air and privacy away from the confines of the Tuileries, as they had done the previous year. Madame Campan reports that the rest of the Household had gone ahead to St Cloud and that the King's dinner awaited him there. The carriages taking the Royal Family attempted to leave the palace courtyard at about noon. Before they had even gone a little way, they were halted by the National Guard, brandishing their weapons and supported by a mob including a number of fishwives, a group well known for their previous encounters at Versailles with the Royals. The mob feared an escape attempt by the family, which they were determined to prevent. The Guards at the palace shut the gates and would not let the family pass. The Royal party was subjected to insults and their servants were beaten up. Not even the intervention of the Marquis de la Lafayette could persuade the mob to release the family and allow them to continue their journey. This went on for two hours before the family gave up the attempt.

The Comte de Provence later wrote of his niece at this time:

> It was on this occasion that I first saw my niece in her true colours. All the strength the King and Queen and my sister had hitherto drawn from their natural firmness, courage, and piety now seemed exhausted. We stared at each other in melancholy silence. My niece, who was then twelve years old, stood alone in the centre of this miserable circle. Her expression, as she flitted from her father's side to her mother or her aunt, showed she was well aware of her position, but rose above it: tears were in her eyes but her lips were smiling. Her innocent caresses, her tender thoughts for us all, and her comforting words were balm upon all our wounds. When she came to me I clasped her in my arms and said: 'Oh, my child, may Heaven shower upon her all the happiness, that is denied to your unhappy family.'

Frustrated and frightened, Madame Royale and her family were forced to abandon their trip to St Cloud and return to their apartments in the Tuileries Palace.

It was agreed that the escape party would comprise the King and Queen, Madame Élisabeth (who was not part of the planning of the escape), the Dauphin, Madame Royale and their governess Madame de Tourzel. The plan was that the family would head for Montmédy, a fortified town under the command of General de Bouillé, situated in eastern France near the border with modern Luxembourg. This town could readily be reinforced or give easy access to refuge in Austrian territory if the Royal Family and their supporters came under attack. Their advisers wanted the family and their attendants to travel in two parties in light fast carriages, but Marie Antoinette was adamant that the family must stay together. Axel von Fersen was determined to provide transport fit for a Queen and the woman he loved. The King and Queen also wanted the services of Madame de Tourzel to look after Madame Royale and the Dauphin as they travelled. Despite the recommendation of the General and others that the Royal Family should have with them a military man who would be capable of resolute action if this was required, the Royal couple preferred the services of the governess.

Even at this crucial stage, Louis and Marie Antoinette were unable to break away from the trappings of royalty, which were such an engrained part of their daily lives. Madame de Tourzel rejected strongly the suggestion that it was she who insisted on going with the family, thereby taking the place of a soldier.[13] The Comte de Provence and his wife would make their own separate arrangements, but attempt their escape at the same time as the rest of the Royal Family. The Comte had planned an earlier escape, but had been persuaded by the King and Queen to abandon the idea because if he made good an escape, it would focus attention even more closely on the rest of the Royal Family and make the possibility of their flight even more difficult.

The plan was that the Royal Family would travel the first 90 miles as far as Châlons-sur-Marne alone and unaccompanied by any soldiers, other than their bodyguards. At Châlons they would meet a detachment of troops who would then provide an escort for them to Montmédy. Von Fersen set about making the practical arrangements. The escape was scheduled for June 1791. In deference to the Queen's wish that the family travel together in one carriage, von Fersen had had specially made a magnificent Berline coach. It was elaborately appointed but, more to the point, cumbersome and slow, and to some minds very conspicuous. Madame de Tourzel states in her memoirs that while comfortable, the coach was not in any way extraordinary or particularly conspicuous, contrary to the statements of others.

Passports were applied for in the names of a Russian noblewoman, the Baronne de Korff, with whom Marie Antoinette had become friends, the Baronne's children and servants. The party comprised Madame de Tourzel, who would pose as Madame de Korff accompanied by her *valet de chambre*, Durand (the King); the children's governess, Madame Rucher (the Queen); and two 'daughters' Amélie and Agläe (the Dauphin dressed as a girl and Marie Thérèse). Madame Élisabeth was to play the part of a lady's companion. Travelling in a cabriolet, their waiting women would go ahead of the Royal party out of Paris and meet up with them later in the journey. They were also to be accompanied by three bodyguards who were also given pseudonyms: Saintjean (M. de Maldon), Melchior (M. Daumoutier) and François (M. de Valory), each of which was in fact part of their respective Christian names. This was a complicated escape attempt involving a large number of people.

The finances for the journey were put in place. The real Madame de Korff had helped to fund the escape with substantial loans on which the Queen was already paying interest. Axel von Fersen also used significant sums of his own money to facilitate the Royal Family's escape. In preparation for the departure from Paris, Marie Antoinette was determined to ensure as far as possible the financial future and independence of the family. To this end she set about packing up and sending out of the country her impressive collection of diamonds and other jewels. Madame Campan describes how Marie Antoinette 'shut herself up with me in a closet in the entresol,[14] looking into the garden of the Tuileries, and we packed up all the diamonds, rubies, and pearls she possessed in a small chest'. Madame Campan continues, 'The box was handed over to Léonard, her Majesty's hairdresser, who left the country with the Duc de Choiseul.' Madame de Gontaut reports in her memoirs that the potential escape attempt was an open secret among the émigré community in Coblenz, and that escape was talked of 'openly and imprudently'. A number of families loyal to the monarchy, including her own, were asked to provide funds to aid the Royal Family's escape, and did so. The Duc de Castries suggests that Lafayette and a number of others were aware of the planned escape and its proposed route.

Madame de Campan reports that Marie Antoinette wished to appear as a Queen, elegant and beautifully adorned when she reached freedom, not a destitute refugee. She set about making the necessary arrangements. The Queen was planning to order new outfits for herself, Madame Royale and the Dauphin. Despite Madame Campan's advice that this activity might alert their captors to the fact that they were planning an escape, the Queen was determined on this point. Madame Campan shopped for the Queen, the Dauphin and Madame Royale using her own son and niece as models to ensure that the outfits for the Royal children were the right size. Marie Antoinette, using Madame Campan as her go-between, also arranged for the production of a magnificent travelling case under the pretext that it was being made as a gift for her sister, the Archduchess Christina, who was based in the Netherlands as its Governor. In the end, the elaborate trunk took too long to manufacture and Marie Antoinette sent her own travelling case out of the country, ostensibly as a present to the Archduchess, to await her arrival. So long surrounded by hordes of servants and bound by etiquette, the Royal Family could not conceive of making an escape without the Royal infrastructure that was normal and natural to them.

The plan was that the specially made Berline coach would await the Royal Family some miles from the Tuileries. They would travel to it in a simple vehicle that should not arouse suspicion as it waited in the vicinity of the Tuileries Palace. The escape was originally planned for the night of 19 June 1791. The troops who were to provide an escort were operating on this basis. Among the staff assembled at the Tuileries to serve the Royal Family, there were many who shared to a greater or lesser degree the views and aspirations of the revolutionaries; some wanting to abolish the monarchy altogether and others who wished to curb its powers within a constitutional framework like the English model. The King and Queen feared that there were spies among their staff, particularly the wardrobe woman who was believed to be having an affair with a revolutionary. They felt it prudent to wait for her to be off duty before making their escape attempt. Eventually, they decided that the escape attempt should be made on 20 June. This, however, meant that new orders had to be communicated in secret to their escort reflecting the altered date, with all the possibility for muddled communication that flowed from the changed plans.

Marie Thérèse reports of the escape in her very clear and dispassionate memoir, noticing that 'During the whole of the 20 June my father and mother appeared to me to be extremely agitated and much occupied, without my being aware of any reason for their being so.' She was a sensitive and observant child. Madame Élisabeth, who had not as yet been privy to the escape plan, was now informed by the King and Queen. They locked themselves up with her to inform her of their intention to quit Paris. Beloved as Élisabeth was by her brother and sister-in-law, they were not always in political sympathy. Madame Élisabeth shared her brother the Comte d'Artois' reactionary political views, and Marie Antoinette was distressed by how much time she spent with Madame Mackau, the Princess's former governess, who shared her opinions.

At 5 p.m. on the afternoon of 20 June, Marie Thérèse, her brother and their governesses went for a walk in the gardens with the Queen. It was here that her mother told Marie Thérèse of what was going to happen later that night. Madame Royale wrote of being given this information: 'My comprehension was so dull that I could not make out what she meant.' Marie Antoinette told her not to be afraid if anything unusual happened that evening. To present a picture of normality to those watching, Marie Thérèse retired to her room as normal at about 7 p.m. and had only one servant with her, Madame Brunyer. This lady was not included in the escape party but had shown her loyalty by saying that she was willing to leave her own family to go with the King and Queen, if so required. She was married to Pierre-Edouard Brunyer[15] who was the personal physician to the Royal children, an illustration of how closely knit relationships were within the Royal Households. Marie Antoinette was touched by Madame Brunyer's courage and devotion. Just before the escape was put into action, Marie Antoinette sent Ernestine, who had been Madame Royale's companion for the last seven years, away to safety.[16] She was not to be included in the escape party.

The Comte and Comtesse de Provence joined the King, Queen and Madame Élisabeth for supper that evening. All were aware of the significance of the farewells they made except for the Comtesse de Provence, who had not been included in the plan. They did not trust her discretion. The King and Queen played billiards as they usually did every evening and then retired to bed. Madame de Tourzel, with the Queen, woke the children and took them into the Queen's apartments where they were dressed to play their parts. The Dauphin, when asked why he thought he was wearing girl's clothes, said he thought they must be taking part in a play. Then, accompanied by one of the bodyguards, M. de Maldon, Marie Antoinette took the children and Madame de Tourzel to the carriage to wait for the rest of the party. It was 10.30 p.m. Madame Élisabeth arrived about an hour later and accidentally trod on the Dauphin who was sleeping on the floor of the carriage. He had the presence of mind not to cry out. She was able to assure the children and their governess that all was quiet in the palace. Axel von Fersen, who was disguised as the coachman, then drove the carriage around Paris so that it would not draw suspicion while waiting for the arrival of Louis and Marie Antoinette. The King, meanwhile, was having his customary evening meeting with the Marquis de Lafayette.

The King and Queen eventually arrived separately at the coach. The Queen had been delayed. The servant who was supposed to escort her to the carriage had got lost in the maze of small streets around the Tuileries and had had to ask for directions. Marie Antoinette and her guide had also encountered the Marquis de Lafayette who knew the Queen so well. Fortunately, he did not recognise the heavily veiled woman as being Marie Antoinette. The King, when he arrived at the meeting point, was concerned by the Queen's non-appearance and had gone off to find her. At last all the party were assembled. Eventually the coach set off and, after delays, Axel von Fersen was able to locate the Berline coach in which they were to travel to Montmédy and freedom. The Royal Family and their companions were on their way. They were already more than an hour behind the planned schedule. As it was mid-June the hours of darkness were at their shortest; time was slipping away. Axel von Fersen was driving the coach and the party had a jolly feel, enjoying being away from the confines of the Tuileries and their guards. Von Fersen drove the coach as far as Bondy, approximately seven miles east of Paris. Here he parted company with his beloved Marie Antoinette and her family. They hoped to meet up again soon.

The coach was equipped with picnic gear and the family, especially the Dauphin, relished the opportunity to play in the fields when the carriage stopped – the Prince even running away from his father. Madame Campan later reported that the Queen had told her that she got out and walked beside the coach up an incline. This, and some small necessary repairs, further delayed their progress. Making haste should have been the top priority, but it was not and nearly three hours were lost. The Bourbon facial features and gait were distinctive and well known. The obviously smart coach and its aristocratic occupants aroused suspicion as they travelled east. Marie Thérèse in her memoirs reports that they feared that they were spotted at Etoges, about 75 miles from Paris. It did not take a genius to recognise them for who they were. There were numerous images of the King and Queen in circulation.

By Châlons-sur-Marne the travellers were sure that they had been recognised. Marie Thérèse recounts that 'many persons thanked God that they had seen the King and addressed prayers for his safety and escape'. Being behind schedule by several hours and confused orders meant that their escort had dispersed by the time the Royal Family arrived in Châlons-sur-Marne. The family waited there until 8 p.m. on 21 June, hoping that the promised 'escort of cavalry' would appear to accompany them to Montmédy. They then moved on to Clermont where there were troops loyal to the Bourbons, but the people would not allow the soldiers to mount up. As night closed in, despite 'agitation and anxiety'[17] according to Madame Royale's memoir, the exhausted family fell asleep as the coach moved on towards the border.

By Varennes the postilions were exhausted and the horses could go no further without rest. The coach drivers could not find any fresh horses for hire or purchase. By this time, the Royal Family's coach was surrounded by angry townspeople, apparently only too aware of the Royal Family's purpose and destination. Marie Thérèse describes them in her writings as an armed mob. The identities of the travelling party had been spotted by Jean-Baptiste Drouet, the local postmaster. He had seen the coach leave Clermont and had ridden cross-country to Varennes. Here he roused the people and blocked the Royal Family's passage with an overturned cart. He had recognised the King when Louis put his head out of the coach to look for their mounted escort. It was 11.30 p.m. The family was jolted awake. The King attempted to deny who he was but could not sustain the fiction. The postilions wanted to fight off the mob and make good their escape. The King, as always, ordered them not to use force. As so often, his compassion and love for his people worked against his own interests. At first, dozy with sleep and frightened, the family refused to get out of the coach; but when threatened with death, at last they did so. The local Procureur Syndic[18] of the commune of Varennes was a grocer by the name of Monsieur Sauce. The exhausted Marie Thérèse and the rest of the Royal Family were taken to his home. Lucie de la Tour du Pin recounts in her memoirs that 'The entire flight organised by M. Von Fersen, who was a fool, was a succession of blunders and imprudences.'

The King appealed for assistance, stating 'I am not going to destroy, but to shelter and guarantee the Constitution', but neither the grocer nor his wife, when appealed to by the Queen, were prepared to risk the wrath of the government in Paris to help them. Madame Royale and her family were entertained kindly with food by the local people, but all momentum had gone and their escort – when it did arrive – was not allowed by the King to fight to aid the family's escape. The King and Queen tried to play for time, hoping that an overwhelming military force would arrive to rescue them. This did not happen. One of the children's woman-servants pretended to be so unwell as to be unable to travel and thus delay their departure for Paris, hoping that rescue might come. The National Guard had been called out to prevent a rescue attempt. By now the Revolutionary government in Paris was fully aware of the escape attempt and had sent three commissioners, Messieurs Barnave, Pétion[19] and Latour-Maubourg, to bring the Royal Family back to Paris. The commissioners had met the Royal Family at Épernay on the return leg of their journey and travelled back with them to Paris.

Marie Thérèse and Louis Charles

The return journey to the Tuileries was a terrible ordeal for Madame Royale and her family. The family spent three days in their coach travelling slowly in the intense June heat, through a mob of angry people shouting insults and abuse and demanding that their prisoners be displayed to them at will. The coach was uncomfortably crowded with eight occupants (the King, the Queen, the Dauphin, Madame Royale, Madame Élisabeth, Madame de Tourzel, Barnave and Pétion). Antoine Barnave and Jérôme Pétion were members of the National Assembly, where Barnave was admired for his oratory. He was a young lawyer and impressed by the Queen, and realising this Marie Antoinette set out to charm him, hoping that he might be of use to her in the future. She would later follow up with a clandestine correspondence with him intended to win friends among the more moderate members of the Assembly. Jérôme Pétion suggested, later, that Madame Élisabeth developed a '*tendresse*' or romantic liking for him during the journey in the confined space of the coach.

The family could not get any fresh air. Marie Thérèse and Louis

Charles were covered in dust from the dry roads and drenched with sweat. They were filthy and uncomfortable. A loyal gentleman, Monsieur Dampierre, attempted to approach the coach to present his respects to the King and Queen but was hacked to pieces by the angry mob. Madame Royale was so stunned and shocked by the sight of blood and violence that she fainted dead away. A cordon of between three and four thousand troops from the National Guard surrounded the carriages. The government had put about the face-saving fiction that the King and his family had been kidnapped from the Tuileries Palace by counter-revolutionary forces. It was said that they had been taken towards the border against their will, rather than that they had attempted an escape. At times shouts were heard of 'God Save the King'. There were also long tirades against the King's betrayal of his people in allowing himself to be taken from them. Insults and accusations were hurled at the Queen. The family, especially the Dauphin, was traumatised. They were all terrified, wondering what their fate would be on their return to Paris.

As the journey progressed, it was clear that the National Assembly members were controlling its pace. The commissioners, not the Royal Family, decided when to stop for food or rest. The commissioners were impressed by the closeness of the Royal Family and their obvious love for one another. These were not the monsters of popular imaginings, nor cold heartless despots as presented in the *libelles*. Madame de Tourzel had very nearly been accosted by a mob at one of their stops, so was particularly overwhelmed by events and near to collapse. The Queen, whilst maintaining her dignity, was greatly affected by the journey and her already thinning hair turned white overnight. She was only thirty-five years old. This brought home to Marie Thérèse the great sufferings of her parents and allegedly contributed to her deepening seriousness in character, despite her youth. The family stopped to eat at Sainte-Ménehould. In Châlons, they stayed in the Hôtel d'Intendance where Marie Antoinette had rested when she had arrived in France so many years earlier. They continued to Épernay and then Dormans, where Madame de Tourzel reports that the Royal Family were threatened with the possibility of a priest being killed before their very eyes. The family slept at Dormans. The young Dauphin was tormented by horrible nightmares in which he was in a forest being attacked by wolves.[20] As the family neared Paris, the crowds became thicker and more threatening. The family arrived at Ferté-sous-Jouarre where they dined. They were prevented from pulling down the blinds and so were continually in public view. They slept at Meaux. So crowded was the coach that there was no seat for Marie Thérèse; she sometimes sat on the knee of Madame de Tourzel and sometimes the lap of Madame Élisabeth. They were sunburnt and very uncomfortable, in a sorry state.

On 25 June 1791, the dejected procession at last reached the capital.

Orders had gone out from the Revolutionary government to the citizens of Paris that no abuse should be directed at the Royal Family, but equally that no royal honours should be shown to them. The crowds stood watching them pass in insolent silence, their hats firmly on their heads. No arms were presented by the soldiers as the Royal carriage passed by. The return to Paris was presented to the people as a successful rescue attempt by the forces of the Revolution. The King's flight exposed the fallacy that the political changes taking place in France were sanctioned by him. The revolutionaries were conscious that the desire for political change was by no means embedded in French life, and that there were serious threats from counter-revolutionaries supported by foreign powers.

For Marie Thérèse, the failed escape was yet another humiliation for her family, in particular her beloved father. It was also a terrifying experience prolonged over a number of days. The crowd abused Marie Antoinette, shouting out that her son was not the King's child. Marie Thérèse realised that her parents' concern was focused on the Dauphin. Her own Bourbon features made evident her own ancestry. The Bourbon relatives outside France had initially received news that Marie Thérèse and her family had made good their escape, only to be disappointed by the later reports that the family were in fact back in Paris and under arrest. Their celebrations turned to despair and fear.

The family returned to the Tuileries, completely exhausted and depressed. The children were nearly collapsing; Madame Royale and her brother had to be carried into the palace by members of the National Guard. Marie Antoinette relished the relaxation of a warm bath after the family's ordeal. But the conditions of imprisonment of Madame Royale and her family were to become harsher. The King and Queen's attempt to escape had demonstrated their real view of the Revolution, and they had lost their bid. The King, Queen and Dauphin were now put under guard, but not Marie Thérèse or her aunt. Madame Campan reports that on returning to the Tuileries, 'The Queen's attendants found the greatest difficulty in making their way to her apartments; everything had been arranged so that the wardrobe woman, who had acted as spy, should have the service;[21] and she was to be assisted in it only by her sister and her sister's daughter.' Not only were the family prevented from having with them their usual servants, but they were allowed very little privacy. Madame Campan notes that 'the measures for guarding the King were vigorous' and the family was ordered to keep open the door of the Queen's bedchamber 'in order that they might have their eyes upon the Royal Family'. How profoundly unpleasant this close and intrusive supervision must have been for Marie Thérèse and her family. The family members were not able to communicate freely among themselves. The atmosphere was full of tension, and Marie Thérèse being an intelligent and sensitive girl must have been only too aware of this and deeply affected by it.

The Comte de Provence and his wife had been more fortunate (and pragmatic) in their escape attempt. On the night of 20 June, after supper with the King, Queen and Madame Élisabeth, they returned to the Luxembourg Palace to retire to bed. The Comte de Provence then got up again, dressed simply as an Englishman (in an era when fashion varied significantly from country to country) and travelled out of Paris with his *maître de la garde-robe*, Monsieur d'Avaray.[22] In order to complete his disguise, the Comte de Provence also spoke French with a marked English accent. Meanwhile the Comtesse de Provence was woken by her reader and companion, Jeanne-Marguerite de Gourbillon (1737-1817), who explained that she had been commissioned by the Comte de Provence to take Marie Joséphine from Paris and to safety 'out of the Kingdom'. Monsieur and Madame met in a post town en route to the border, but pretended not to know each other. They eventually met up in Brussels. The Comtesse de Provence then travelled on to her father's court in Turin, where she was able to take refuge. Two of the King's brothers were now established outside France, trying to influence internal French politics from beyond the borders. They were free to set up their own diplomatic networks and to pursue policies at variance with those of the King and Queen in the Tuileries. Marie Antoinette's brother, the Emperor Leopold, also got involved in French politics. Madame de Tourzel writes that the Emperor issued a manifesto supporting the Constitution.

The King fell into despair and was only roused by pleas from the Queen and his children. In an attempt to create an atmosphere of normality and routine on their return to Paris, Madame Royale resumed her lessons with Madame Mackau. Ernestine returned to join Madame Royale and to share her life once again at the Tuileries. Their lessons were often interrupted by the frightening cries of the mob. Marie Antoinette, as usual, sat in on and supervised Marie Thérèse's classes herself. The Queen once more spent her time reading late and writing numerous letters, often in cipher, to her family and other sovereigns trying to summon their support. She often found it difficult to sleep. For fear of attack, she had her bed moved from the ground floor to the first floor of the palace. Late in June 1791, Madame Élisabeth was once more offered the opportunity to leave France and join the other exiled members of her family. The offer was made by the Marquis de Lafayette who had been appointed by the National Assembly as Governor of the Tuileries and Keeper of the King and the Royal Family. Madame Élisabeth refused this second offer. She had promised to stay with her brother and his family in their hour of need, and she would do so whatever the consequences for her own well-being.

Opportunities for fresh air and exercise were restricted. This was very harsh for a family who loved to be outside, hunting, riding, fishing and walking. Madame de Tourzel reports that Marie Thérèse and her family were occasionally able to visit St Cloud, where the children could play in the grounds. So fearful were they of assassination that the King wore a padded jacket to deflect a possible knife attack. There were also rumours of poisoning by supporters of the Revolution employed as chefs in the Royal Household. The family took the precaution of ordering only simple roasted meats without easily contaminated sauces, and eating only pastry smuggled in from loyal suppliers. As time passed, the harshest restrictions eased and Madame Campan reports that by August 1791 'the doors were not kept open; greater respect was shown to the sovereign; it was known that the constitution soon to be completed would be accepted, and a better order of things was hoped for'.

The Revolution was, however, gaining a head of steam. By July 1791, there were many factions operating within French politics with different views of the role, if any, that the monarchy should have. Madame Campan describes the struggle between the Jacobins (the more extreme revolutionaries) and the constitutionals on 17 July 1791, noting that cannon were fired on individuals who called for the King to be put on trial. The newly drafted Constitution was presented to the King on 3 September. Those who supported it felt, and advised the King, that it should be accepted wholesale and without derogation or amendment. Louis XVI was inclined to follow this approach. It was felt that this would give him most protection from the extremists who would seize on any debate to try to persuade others of the impossibility of a constitutional monarchy, the need for its complete abolition and the creation of a republic.

In September 1791, the King accepted the new Constitution. Louis XVI's role had changed from being King of France by the Grace of God to King of the French People by the Grace of God and the Constitutional Law of the State. Now the King, too, was subject to the law. The King and particularly the Queen played along with these changes. They tried to remain, at least outwardly, calm and sanguine while at the same time corresponding with other sovereigns trying to gain support. Monsieur de Breteuil coordinated this clandestine diplomacy and was in frequent contact with Louis XVI and Marie Antoinette. The strain of maintaining the appearance of outward calm in such difficult circumstances must have been enormous. They did not know who they could trust; even the loyalty of their own staff could not be relied on. Marie Thérèse must have noticed and felt their stress as she went about her lessons and daily routine.

In September 1791, Marie Thérèse was present when the Deputies went to the Tuileries to express their pleasure that the King had accepted the Constitution. As they were admitted to see the King, he made a speech to them, noting, 'you see there my wife and children, who participate in my sentiments'. Marie Antoinette, very much against her real views and instincts, indicated her pleasure. It must have been upsetting for the twelve-year-old Princess to be confronted with the need for her parents to dissemble their true feelings, and indeed to observe the difference in her parents' views on such crucial matters. These early experiences influenced her own political views as she grew to adulthood. Despite some reported praise for the King's signing of the Constitutional act, he was humiliated when the Assembly received him with a marked lack of deference. This was made worse for the King by the fact that Marie Antoinette was there to witness the scene. Celebrations followed the acceptance of the Constitution, and the King and Queen made a trip to the opera. On another occasion Marie Thérèse went out to the theatre with her mother and Aunt Élisabeth, and received a warm welcome from a selected audience.

The spring of 1792 brought more bad news for the beleaguered family. Madame de Tourzel records in her memoirs that 'The Emperor Leopold, brother of the Queen, was attacked by so severe an illness that it carried him off in three days.' The news of his illness and his death arrived simultaneously on 1 March 1792. Madame de Tourzel notes that:

> The Jacobins, who thought themselves well rid of an enemy, rejoiced over his death, without reflecting that, as the Cabinet of Vienna would remain the same and would not change its principles, no alteration would take place in the existing state of things. The Queen was of this opinion. She persuaded herself that … Francis II … would infuse greater energy into a war which the arrogance of France in regard to foreign powers made her look upon as inevitable. She was mistaken in this expectation, and the same dilatoriness continued to be conspicuous in the preparations of the Court of Vienna.

From Stockholm, in April, came the dreadful news that their ally Gustav III had been assassinated. Madame de Tourzel writes, 'The King and Queen were thrown into consternation by the news.' Marie Antoinette expressed the fear that the same fate might befall her family. According to Madame de Tourzel, the family then discussed the age of the Prince Royal of Sweden, Gustav Adolf:

> 'I know it well,' said the King. 'I heard of his birth[23] just as the Queen was about to be confined and I said to her, 'You may expect a daughter, for two kings have not two sons in the same month, and a few days afterwards [he looked at Madame] Mademoiselle came into this world.' 'Will your Majesty permit to ask if you regret her birth?' 'Certainly not,' said the King, folding her in his arms; and looking at her with tears in his eyes he kissed her with an amount of emotion that completely unnerved the Queen and Madame Élisabeth, and produced the most distressing effect. The young princess burst into tears.

One of the last thoughts of the King of Sweden before his death was for the sufferings of the French Royal Family, and that his death would mean that he could not be of assistance to them. Once again the Jacobins rejoiced in the death of someone who might have been able to help Madame Royale and her family. On 20 April 1792, France declared war on Austria. 'The position of the Royal Family became worse and worse every day,' wrote Madame de Tourzel. There was a suggestion that Marie Antoinette, already loathed by huge sections of the populace and now, since the declaration of war against her homeland, 'an enemy alien', should be sent away from the family. Assisted by Madame Campan, the Queen began to burn her papers. Interest in the Affair of the Queen's Necklace was revived by the arrival from England of the *Mémoires de Madame de la Motte*. Madame de Tourzel writes, 'The King … fearing justly the eagerness with which the lies they contained would be received, thought it prudent to prevent their circulation, and bought up the edition himself.' The whole edition was then incinerated in the ovens of the porcelain factory at Sèvres. The Royal Family's position was made more difficult by the King's refusal to sanction a decree that all priests who refused to take the oath of loyalty to the state were liable to banishment.

Paris was in a state of turmoil. At this time there were a large number of people living there who had come from other regions of France, in particular the very radical city of Marseilles, and their presence affected the popular mood. There were accusations against the Royal Guards of disloyalty to the Revolution, and an attempt to have them disbanded was approved, although the King continued to pay them and many remained loyal to the King and Royal Family. The decree to disband the Royal Guard reduced the level of protection given to the family. There had already been an attempt by a mob to invade the Tuileries Palace, which was foiled. As Madame de Tourzel reports:

> It was passed at night, and sent at once to his Majesty. Nobody in the Castle had gone to bed; everybody was in a state of consternation… But the Ministers, who, independently of their agreement with the Assembly, dreaded for themselves the withholding of the sanction, so strongly represented to the King the danger he would bring on his family, those who were attached to him … they tormented him so with the idea of the excesses to which the populace would give way, that they drew from him this fatal sanction, which filled the King with bitterness, and was one more weapon in the hands of the rebels.[24]

Marie Thérèse was present at the departure of the Royal Guards. Madame de Tourzel writes, 'The departure of the Guard … was a very touching sight. Everybody, with tearful eyes and a sad heart, was at the windows to do a last homage to this brave and faithful Guard. The King, the Royal Family… were plunged in the most profound grief.' The celebrations for the third anniversary of the storming of the Bastille were approaching, and a decree was passed to set up a camp of 20,000 men elected from different regions of France. In the Assembly there were accusations of a pro-Austrian plot to restore the monarchy to its former power. In the streets there were cries against Monsieur and Madame Veto, the nicknames applied to the King and Queen as a reference to their attempts to slow down revolutionary change. Ministers resigned. The King attempted to form a new government despite the difficulty of finding suitable people to serve as ministers – so fearful were the potential candidates of the consequences of joining the government. Madame de Tourzel wrote:

> The King informed the Assembly of the change of Ministry. It was so assured of the speedy destruction of Royalty that it appeared insensible to the dismissal of men who had every right to its gratitude... It became more and more bitter against the King, and received with every honour the most inflammatory, insulting, and menacing petitions against the Royal authority, even against the person of his Majesty.

The date of 20 June 1792 was a terrifying day for Marie Thérèse. She and her family were confined to the Tuileries Palace while it was surrounded by a mob 'armed with pikes, hooks of various kinds, clubs, pitchforks, hatchets, stakes and scythes. The crowds had gathered from ten o'clock in the morning to hear speeches. They marched, sang, made the most infamous remarks about the King and the Royal Family.'[25] The mob made its way to the National Assembly, to mark the anniversary of the Tennis Court Oath. Several Deputies tried to prevent their admission in case an armed band might try to 'influence its decisions',[26] but this was rejected by the Jacobin element of the Assembly. Anti-monarchist speeches were made in the Assembly by members of the *sans-culottes* groups, then there was a march-past. On hearing what was happening in the Assembly and streets of Paris, the Royal Family had taken refuge in the King's apartments. They were guarded only by the National Guard who 'filled the Castle but refused to defend it'.[27] They even drove from the palace those who might have defended the monarchy, according to Madame de Tourzel. At about three o'clock in the afternoon, a gate was opened which allowed the crowd to enter the palace gardens. The soldiers took no action against the trespassers. Emboldened by this lethargy, the crowd then surged into the palace itself. Madame Royale and the rest of the family were gathered in the King's small bedroom; with them were a small group of loyal servants. The crowd was approaching the room and the King, fearing that the door might be forced, proposed to go and meet them. He first asked that the Queen and the children be taken away to a safer part of the palace. This done, the King went out from his bedchamber to meet the mob. Madame Élisabeth, seeing the danger to her brother, elected to stay with him rather than go with her sister-in-law and the children. Together they were confined to an embrasure of a window.

The mob mistook Madame Élisabeth for the Queen, the hated 'Autrichienne'. Madame de Tourzel writes that the Princess, despite the horrible threats of the crowd to kill her, 'spoke these sublime words to those around her: 'Do not undeceive them; if they take me for the Queen, there will be time to save her.' The crowd was full of threats and insults against the King. He was forced to wear a tricolour cap and to sit on the window seat so that the crowd could see him. The room was stiflingly hot and the King was parched. A soldier gave him a water bottle from which to drink. Hundreds of people marched past the King and Madame Élisabeth, who was also forced to wear a cap in revolutionary colours. Meanwhile, the Queen and the children tried to find a safe hiding place: first in Madame Royale's rooms and later in those occupied by the Dauphin. The Queen was distraught at the thought of abandoning her husband and could only be persuaded with great difficulty not to go back and join him. Madame Élisabeth got word to Marie Antoinette that Louis was behaving with great courage and that her presence would only inflame the situation. It was better that she stayed away.

Marie Thérèse, her mother and her brother were forced to retreat back to the King's bedroom by the advance of the mob, which was breaking down doors in an attempt to find them. The three were in the King's bedroom when news came that the mob was closing in on the family. Madame de Tourzel wrote:

> It was resolved that the Queen should go into the Council Chamber, through which Santerre was leading his men in order to make them leave the Castle. She presented herself to these rebels in the midst of her children… Her Majesty sat down behind a table having Mgr the Dauphin on her right and Madame on her left, surrounded by the Filles Saint Thomas battalion, who constantly opposed an impenetrable wall to the bellowing crowd, which abused it without ceasing.

Eventually the King was able to return to his bedchamber and Marie Thérèse and the rest of the family were able to join him there. Madame de Tourzel continued, 'The Queen, in tears, threw herself at his feet with her children; he held them all for some time in a close embrace, and this touching scene affected all those who witnessed the happiness they felt at meeting each other once more safe and sound.' The King and Queen were immensely grateful to Madame Élisabeth for her selfless courage. Madame Royale's room, as well as her brother's, had been ransacked during the invasion of the palace. Doors had been smashed, locks and bolts stolen and panelling damaged.

The King issued a proclamation denouncing the use of violence. He acknowledged that he had refused to ratify certain decrees. He stated that violence would never force him to give consent to legislation that he felt was not in the interests of the French people. In the Assembly, there was a proposal that the need for Royal consent should be disregarded in the case of certain special decrees. Shortly after the invasion of the palace, Pétion was made mayor of Paris and was received by the King and the Royal Family; he excused the conduct of the mob, saying that their intentions were peaceful and that the King could not be harmed. Angrily, the King dismissed him from his presence, citing the events of the day as evidence of the lack of respect with which he had been treated. In the following days, members of the National Assembly spoke against the monarchy, blaming the King for errors made by the army. Some even accused him of treason, referring to the activities of the émigré princes in Coblenz as evidence. The National Assembly and the country were increasingly incensed by the threat of invasion by foreign powers that had formed a coalition against revolutionary France. A few days after the incident with the crowd, Marie Thérèse was present when her father received a deputation from the National Assembly swearing to uphold the Constitution and the monarchy. Louis was touched and gratified by this act of loyalty. Meanwhile, others were working against the monarchy with equal fervor, accusing the King of treachery and demanding that he be put on trial. The Jacobin clubs demanded the establishment of a republic.

The third Fête de la Fédération celebrating the fall of the Bastille, on 14 July 1792, was attended by Marie Thérèse and the rest of the Royal Family, accompanied by Madame de Lamballe. They travelled by carriage to the Champ de Mars, escorted by their ministers and Court. When they arrived, they were greeted by anti-monarchist shouts. In the following days, feeling that the sentiments were getting out of hand, some of those loyal to the King pleaded with him to flee Paris for a safer place. The King decided against these proposals. He could not face the idea of a second Varennes. In the days that followed, the National Assembly cleared Paris of regiments that they felt were still loyal to the King. There were further petitions calling for the King to be put on trial. The fear of invasion was mounting. Paris was tense: awash with rumours that aristocrats had assassinated supporters of the Revolution and that huge caches of arms were stored at the Tuileries. All this was designed to stoke the fears of the people. According to Madame de Tourzel, 'The position of the Royal Family became worse and worse every day. Shut up in the Tuileries, whence not even Mgr the Dauphin was allowed to emerge lest he fall in with a crowd of rebels, they were deprived of fresh air and any distraction.' On one evening they did venture out only to be subjected to insults from the crowd who had been allowed access to the Tuileries Gardens from the Feuillants Terrace. Tensions grew between the dissidents from Marseilles and members of the National Guard and there was violence.

The Queen's apartment was felt not to be safe from invasion by the mob, so she slept in the Dauphin's room, determined to be close to her son.

Counter-revolutionary coalition forces were massing on the borders of France. The Duke of Brunswick, who was in command, issued a declaration requiring the French people to put an end to the anarchy persisting in France, to end the attacks on the King and the Royal Family and to restore Louis XVI to his authority. The Duke offered to protect those who submitted to Royal authority. The National Assembly was incensed by the declaration. The King was forced to issue a declaration requiring that the foreign armies should not invade France. Paris was in ferment. By the beginning of August, the King feared for his safety and that of his family. The National Guard could no longer be relied on. More and more of its members were sympathetic to the Revolutionary cause. The King could only rely on his force of Swiss mercenaries, the Swiss Guard. The family spent a restless night on 9 August, and by 7 a.m. on the morning of 10 August 1792 the mob was advancing towards the Tuileries. There were orders from the National Assembly to defend the King, but there was widespread mutiny against the order. The King and Queen were persuaded to leave the Tuileries and to make their way to the Assembly. The Queen had initially resisted this suggestion, as Madame de Tourzel reports:

> The Queen, who was standing by the King, remarked that it was impossible to abandon all the brave men who had come to the Castle solely to defend the King. 'If you oppose this step,' said Roederer to her in a severe tone of voice, 'you will be responsible, Madame, for the lives of the King and your children.'

The distressed Queen did not trust the advice, but felt she had no alternative but to comply. Madame de Tourzel continues, 'There was general consternation when the King was seen leaving for the Assembly; the Queen accompanied him holding her two children[28] by the hand. By their side were Madame Élisabeth and the Princess de Lamballe.' When the family reached the Assembly, they were initially seated on the ministerial bench with the King by the side of the President of the Assembly. It was then decided that they should be relocated to the reporters' gallery behind the presidential chair. Meanwhile, there was rioting at the Tuileries, which had been set on fire. Reports came through to the family that in the fighting many of the Swiss Guard, who had been ordered not to fire on the crowd, had been killed. The family were devastated by the news of the deaths of men they had known and relied on for protection.

The National Assembly now moved to diminish the power of the crown. It was proposed that the Prince Royal, as the Dauphin was now called, should be handed over to a governor. The income of the family was to be severely curtailed and they would be required to live within the environs of the National Assembly until they could relocate to the Luxembourg Palace. Marie Antoinette was able to persuade some of the sympathetic members of the Assembly that she should not be separated from her son. Many were indifferent anyway as to whom should be his governor. The upbringing of a prince was of little matter in a republic. The family spent twelve hours in the stuffy gallery subjected to insults and abuse, while the Tuileries was looted of jewellery, wine and documents.

That night the family slept in hastily prepared rooms in the Feuillants, a nearby former monastery. Marie Thérèse shared a room with her mother. Madame de Tourzel writes, 'As may well be imagined we spent a wretched night, and could distinctly hear the uproar and applause in the Assembly; and with the exception of Mgr the Dauphin and Madame,[29] who, worn out with fatigue, fell asleep directly, not one of us could close our eyes throughout the night.' The King's servants were sent away. The family spent three nights here overhearing the jubilation of the Assembly as it swept away Royal authority. The Commune of Paris, which was in charge of the family, decided not to house them in the Luxembourg but the Temple. The events of 10 August 1792 marked the end of power for the French monarchy. Marie Thérèse had been a witness to the final collapse of her father's authority. She and her family were now in the hands of the revolutionaries.

3

The Tower of the Temple

AUGUST 1792–MAY 1794

On 13 August 1792, the family was taken to close captivity in the Temple. As the Royal Family travelled to the Temple they passed by the now prone statue of Louis XIV, which had been toppled by the mob. They were treated with scant respect by those who escorted them to prison on the two-and-a-half-hour journey, which was deliberately slow in order to expose the family to the insults and scorn of the mob. However, at those times when the party was brought to a complete standstill, even their guards became nervous for their safety, fearing violence.

The Temple had belonged to the Comte d'Artois, given to him by Louis XVI in 1787 as his Paris residence before the Revolution. The Temple, situated in central Paris, had been designed as a fortress completely encircled by a crenellated wall more than 12 metres high, with a large gate onto the Rue du Temple and a gatehouse manned by a gate-keeper. Within the walls was a spacious courtyard with lime trees, and what had been the Palace of the Grand Prior of the Order of the Knights Templar, where was situated the gloomy-looking Tower which Marie Antoinette had always hated and dreaded when she observed it on her visits to Paris. She had apparently often asked the Comte d'Artois to have it demolished, so depressing did she find it. Within the confines of the Temple there were the luxurious apartments that had been used by the Comte d'Artois on his visits to Paris. The family was soon disabused of the idea that their imprisonment would be in these comfortable surroundings.

Strict security measures were in place, designed to incarcerate the family and prevent escape or rescue. They included a force of 190 soldiers led by a commandant-general, an adjutant, major and ensign plus fourteen gunners. Two canons were mounted in the courtyard. At the Tower itself there were two manned gates. To access the Tower and its prisoners it was necessary to use two keys simultaneously: one from the outside and one from the inside. The Revolutionary authorities would not countenance a repeat of the escape from the Tuileries. In due course the family were taken to the Tower of the Temple. This was a prison worthy of the name, not the palace-arrest of previous times.

The former Royal Family, now referred to as Citizens Louis and Louis-Charles Capet and Citizenesses Antoinette, Élisabeth, Charlotte,[1] were confined with their remaining attendants[2] in a few ill-furnished rooms on two floors. Nothing had been prepared for the arrival of the family, and the rooms were devoid of any of the comforts to which they were accustomed. There were not enough proper beds, so Marie Thérèse slept on a camp bed. Madame Élisabeth and Marie Antoinette's dear friend la Princesse de Lamballe,[3] who had returned from exile and safety in England to be with her friend and Queen in her times of trouble, slept in the kitchen. The King had his own bedchamber while the women and children shared sleeping accommodation. From 26 August onwards the family was cared for by the King's former valet, Jean-Baptiste Cléry. The princesses were delighted to see him. They had not been able to dress their hair properly for several days and his arrival solved this problem. He had heard what was happening to the family and had managed to present himself to the authorities as a loyal Revolutionary in order to be able to resume his role in caring for the King and the rest of the family. He had to be careful to conceal his true loyalties. Baron Huë,[4] Louis XVI's *valet de chambre*, was with the family until his arrest in late September 1792.

The former Royal Family was at first accompanied in their imprisonment by Madame de Tourzel, who wrote:

> The Queen who never ceased thinking of everything that could mitigate the trouble of those around her, being anxious to give me the consolation of having my daughter Pauline with me, with the greatest kindness offered to ask Pétion to allow her to come. I was petrified by this proposition, as I foresaw only too clearly that we should be left for a long time in the Temple; I shuddered at the idea of exposing my daughter, young and pretty, to the mercy of the fanatics; I was too well acquainted with the firmness of her character, and the happiness she would experience from being able to ameliorate the cruel position of the Royal Family by her care, respect and attachment, to allow myself to calculate the danger she would incur elsewhere. Mgr the Dauphin and Madame[5] seeing me give way to momentary hesitation, threw their arms round my neck, begging me to give them their dear Pauline; Madame added with inexpressible grace, 'Do not refuse us; she will be our consolation, and I will treat her as my sister.'

Madame de Tourzel could not refuse the Royal children their request. Pauline came to live with them. Madame de Tourzel reports that all the Royal Family treated Pauline with the greatest kindness and affection during the time she spent with them during their confinement. In a letter to her sister, Pauline says of the time when she arrived at the Temple prison to join her mother and the Royal Family that 'Mgr the Dauphin and Madame kissed me, displaying the most touching friendship for me, and telling me that we should never part any more.'[6] The girls shared a fondness for dogs.

Marie Antoinette and Louis XVI were no longer in a position to influence their fate by negotiating with those in power at home or to intrigue abroad. Perhaps the Royals were able to reconcile themselves to their circumstances knowing that there was nothing more they could do to affect the outcome of events. They settled down to a quiet domestic life. The family routine was simple: they took breakfast together and then the King spent time teaching Louis Charles his lessons in Latin and geography. After a walk in the courtyard, they would dine at 2 p.m., then nap for an hour or so. Between 6 and 9 p.m., the ladies would sit together and embroider while the King worked at lessons with his son or played with him. Cléry writes of this time that the Dauphin would play football or skittles with his father. Then a light supper was eaten by the family, following which the King would read until retiring at midnight. It would seem that they were well fed. The kitchen was managed by M. Meunier, who had previously belonged to the commissariat of the King. Louis, as was his way, ate well; too well, exposing himself to the derision of their captors who called him 'a fat pig'. It is interesting to note that the kitchen feeding the family and their companions consisted of two chefs and eleven under-cooks. There was an extensive library in the Tower to provide the King with reading materials, which gave him much pleasure. The Queen and children also borrowed books from the library. The Queen had a harpsichord in the Tower of the Temple and she played for the Dauphin and Marie Thérèse in an effort to distract them from their troubles. Marie Antoinette and the family took great comfort from this diversion. The Queen had loved music from the time of her childhood in Vienna. Often these songs were light romantic airs such as 'Boston de Rose', composed by the Princesse de Lamballe, a close confidante of the Queen, in 1791 while resident at the Tuileries, as well as lullabies with lyrics by the poet Bruin. Friends and servants smuggled sheet music into the Temple.

The family surprised their guards by settling into an affectionate and routine family life. This was not the debauchery and decadence the guards had been led to believe of 'Messalina'[7] Antoinette and her family. The King spent his days reading and teaching his children, coaching the Dauphin to recite passages from the writings of Corneille and Racine, something at which the young Prince excelled, as Cléry[8] reports. Marie

Antoinette and her sister-in-law worked at knitting, sewing and supervising the lessons of Marie Thérèse and the Dauphin. Madame Élisabeth taught the children religious subjects and mathematics.

The family were guarded round the clock and given very little privacy. A commissioner sat with them at all times. They were forbidden to correspond with the outside world. Abbé Edgeworth records that he was able to communicate with Madame Élisabeth by the use of letters written in invisible ink (lemon juice) and sent to and from the outside world concealed in balls of sewing thread. Their guards would even cut into fruit intended for the family, suspecting that messages might be concealed within. Nevertheless, the family managed to develop a series of signals in order to obtain news from the outside world from Cléry and even pass notes among themselves.[9]

Life was full of humiliations and irritations for the family. Their guards took pleasure in insulting them and subjecting the women, in particular, to crude and embarrassing comments and jibes. Those supervising the family relished smoking in the presence of the King and Queen without asking for or receiving permission, and then blowing smoke in the King's face or in the direction of the Princesses. The family tried not to give the guards the satisfaction of reacting to their treatment and to remain aloof, but it was a continual trial for the nerves and morale of the prisoners. The Royal Family were always formal in their mode of address, using the formal *vous* – which had been abolished as elitist and counter-revolutionary – even among themselves, both when speaking and in writing. They were offended to be spoken to in the familiar *tu* form by their guards, with its implication of familiarity or close relationship. The use of this informal form of address was a continual irritation and one of the things mentioned in Marie Thérèse's account of this period of her life. When the family was allowed out of their quarters for exercise, Marie Antoinette encouraged the Dauphin to behave charmingly towards their guards. Even this opportunity for fresh air and exercise was made unpleasant by continual insults directed at the family.

Outside the confines of the Temple, the atmosphere in Paris, and France, was by no means so peaceful. A Prussian army had invaded France on 19 August in support of the Royal captives; panic and fear were rife. A special tribunal had been set up to try those involved in defending the Tuileries Palace and firing on the people of Paris. Paris was in uproar, terrified by the invasion of the Austro-Prussian forces and the possibility that they might attack Paris itself. Gangs roamed the streets accosting anyone they feared might be in league with the enemy or sympathetic to the Royalist cause. More than 3,000 people were imprisoned and 1,400 murdered by the mob, including twenty-four priests who adhered to pre-Revolutionary religious doctrines. The Royal Family could hear the sounds of turmoil and sense the tension within the city, even from the confinement of the Tower of the Temple. They heard the chimes of the *tocsin*, the alarm indicating the curfew, and the sounds of the rampaging mob in the distance. Officials informed the King, 'Sir, you do not know what is happening in Paris? The people are infuriated and demand vengeance … it is you who have unleashed against us a ferocious enemy determined to massacre us.'[10] They blamed Louis for abandoning his duties as King and father of his people by attempting to flee France, and thus bringing on France the trauma of invasion and occupation by foreign forces, with all the attendant horrors. The guards' treatment of the family worsened as the political atmosphere grew darker in the country.

The Revolutionary government took upon themselves draconian powers: houses were searched and counter-revolutionary suspects dragged off into custody. On the night of 19/20 August 1792, Princesse de Lamballe, Madame de Tourzel and her daughter were taken from the Tower of the Temple, interrogated and then imprisoned in the notorious prison of La Force. It was formerly the home of an aristocratic family and had been purchased by the government to provide additional prison places at this time of national crisis. Marie Thérèse was speechless with distress at being parted from her friend. A guillotine had been installed on 21 August in the Place du Carrousel in front of the Tuileries Palace. This was the period of the Revolution known as The Terror, when violence reigned and the guillotine was in regular use.

On 10 September, the former Royal Family were at dinner when they heard a tremendous noise from below the windows of their prison. Outside the Temple a screaming mob were calling for the King, and more especially the Queen, to come and see the decapitated head of Madame de Lamballe which had been stuck on the end of a pike. The Princess had been taken from her prison to be tried by the Revolutionary Court and subjected to swift and rough justice. The outcome was never in doubt, and she was condemned to death. Once the sentence had been pronounced, the mob seized the Princess. Some commentators suggest that she was raped, others that this was an exaggeration of the horrors to which she was subjected in order to gain sympathy for the Royalist cause and to revile the French people. She was horribly hacked to death and her body was then dismembered. In a gruesome twist, the mob had her hair – long, blonde and of great beauty – dressed by a hairdresser before they marched to the Tower, with the intention of displaying her head to the imprisoned Royal Family. Forced to go to the windows by officials who threatened that, if she did not, the mob would be allowed into their apartments, the Queen fainted dead away shocked by the sight of the sad remains of her beloved and loyal friend.

Following these terrifying events, the tension and stress in the Royal apartments can readily be imagined. Harder to evaluate is the emotional effect on a young girl of thirteen of being subjected to continual fear and threat of violence, seeing the norms and certainties of her childhood world collapsing around her, and the daily humiliations of those she loved most. Her calm objective memoirs suggest that she reacted with great courage and fortitude under these daily strains and was a source of comfort to her parents and the rest of the family. Forty years later, she told the Marquis de Villeneuve that '*Mes parents m'avaient fait en Temple de ne pleurer jamais, et ce devoir que j'observai est devenue une habitude.*'[11] Not showing emotion was a form of self-protection for her and became a key element of her personality.

On 20 September 1792, the army of Brunswick that had invaded France with the objective of rescuing the Royal Family and restoring the *ancien régime* was defeated by French Republican forces at the Battle of Valmy near Châlons-sur-Marne in eastern France. The invading army, overconfident and dismissive of the Revolutionary rabble – as they viewed the French soldiers – virtually melted away when faced with the superior French numbers and artillery. Marie Antoinette had long plotted and wished for this attack on France and the rescue she hoped for from counter-revolutionary forces, but in vain. The following day, 21 September, the French monarchy was abolished; gone were the throne of St Louis and the glories of the Sun King. This was announced to the prisoners in the Temple by a procession of Parisians shouting the news to their captives. France was now a Republic. The victory at Valmy had given the government the confidence to move against Louis XVI and the monarchy as it wished, knowing that there was no immediate foreign military threat to the Republic and the Revolution.

The former King was informed on 11 December 1792 that he would be put on trial, charged with conspiring with the European powers against the state and the Revolution of France. During a period of some six weeks, he was not permitted to see or speak to his family except under the closest supervision by their guards and at prescribed times of day. The former King was offered the invidious option of being able to see his family more freely, but only if then the Dauphin would be removed from the care of Marie Antoinette. Louis Auguste, always the kind husband and loving father, could not voluntarily impose this suffering on his wife and son. Instead, he opted for isolation from his family during the period of his trial. He was provided with legal counsel, M. de Malesherbes and M. de Sèze, and was able to offer a defence to the charges made against him. On 19 December 1792, he noted to his servant Cléry with sadness that it was the fourteenth birthday of his daughter and he was not able to be with his beloved Marie Thérèse on this special day. Cléry reported this conversation to the orphaned Princess later, when they were both in exile in Mittau. It was bittersweet news to her. Louis Auguste spent Christmas Day of 1792 apart from his family and his trial resumed the next day. This was a time of frantic anxiety for Marie Thérèse, so devoted to her beloved father. She must have missed him terribly during this enforced separation.

The court trying the former King came to the unsurprising conclusion that Louis was guilty of the charges against him. The court then voted as to how he should be sentenced. Some voted for exile and others for life imprisonment. By a majority of one, the court voted for a death sentence to be carried out by guillotine. Those voting for the death sentence included the ex-King's own Bourbon cousin, the Duc d'Orléans, Philippe Ėgalité. The schism in the Bourbon family had reached its apogee, with one cousin voting for the death of another. The duke was later traumatised by the decision he had made to vote for the death sentence. But it is ironic that not even this act of revolutionary fervour would save the Duc d'Orléans. He too was guillotined during the Terror on 6 November 1793. His family went into exile, wandering Europe in search of refuge, alienated from many of their family and class.

On 20 January 1793, Louis was able at last to see his family, albeit briefly, to tell them of the outcome of the trial and his fate. He was to be executed the next day. The eve of his execution was agonising for Marie Antoinette, Madame Élisabeth, Marie Thérèse and Louis Charles. They spent the little time they had together talking and praying. Even this meeting took place under the close supervision of their guards, who watched the family through a glass screen. Marie Thérèse and her family were stunned by the severity of the sentence and the speed with which it was to be carried out. They were in a state of deep shock. When it came time for him to leave them, Louis Auguste promised that he would see them all one final time the following morning. Marie Thérèse, who had always maintained a great restraint over her emotions and attempted to be a steadfast companion to her family in their troubles, fell down in a dead faint at her father's feet. Her father was able to help to revive her before being taken away from the family and back to his own room. Marie Thérèse had always been so close to her father and devoted to him. The relationship between father and daughter had always been easier than that with her mother, and the thought of his death was unbearably painful. In her memoirs of this time, she wrote of her father:

> He showed me so much affection that I should have been very ungrateful not to love the best father that ever lived. His death was an irreparable loss for me, and as long as I live I shall not cease to mourn for him ... such was the life of my father during the severe imprisonment. Pity, magnanimity, firmness, gentleness, courage, kindness, patient endurance of the most horrible calumnies, wholehearted forgiveness of his assassins, and the most profound love for God, his family and his people – these and only these were the qualities he showed until he breathed his last and went to his reward for them in the bosom of an almighty and pitiful God.[12]

The King's will begged his son not to try to take revenge on the people who had executed him and to think only of doing good to the people of France. Marie Thérèse tried to be guided in her life by this approach, but it was one that required great personal sacrifice and effort.

The Abbé Edgeworth, the King's Irish confessor, was ordered on 20 January 1793 to go to the prison in the Tower of the Temple. His presence there had been requested by the individual now known to the political establishment of Paris as Louis Capet, the deposed and condemned former King of France. Edgeworth, who knew the Royal Family well and was well regarded by them, had an interesting and unusual history of his own. His family had made significant sacrifices for their Roman Catholic faith. Edgeworth's ancestors were Protestants living in County Longford, Ireland, having moved there from England during the reign of Elizabeth I.[13] Abbé Edgeworth's father was the Protestant rector of the eponymous Edgeworthstown, and the family was connected by marriage and schooling to many in the Irish Protestant elite.[14] The Abbé's father, the Reverend Robert Edgeworth, resigned his living and converted to Catholicism with his entire family: a bold and unusual move in an era before Catholic emancipation in Britain.[15] To avoid the possible social, religious and legal stigma of his conversion to Roman Catholicism, the Abbé's father moved his family, including the young Henry Essex Edgeworth, to France. The boy grew up in Toulouse where he studied theology, later moving on to the University of Paris.

He was later ordained as a priest and came into contact with the Royal Family when Madame Élisabeth requested a recommendation for a replacement confessor for her Household. Henry Edgeworth's name was put forward and approved by the Archbishop of Paris and he was introduced at Court. In 1792, the Archbishop was forced to leave Paris as his life was at risk from the revolutionaries, and he appointed the Abbé Edgeworth as his Grand Vicaire. The appointment gave the Abbé full delegated powers, leaving the affairs of the Archdiocese of Paris completely in his hands. Despite the dangers and the pleas of his friends, Edgeworth refused to seek sanctuary in England or Ireland. He wrote to a fellow priest in London, a Monsieur Maffey, saying:

> Almighty God has baffled my measures, and ties me to the land of horrors by chains I have not the liberty to shake off. The case is this wretched master[16] charges me not to quit this country, as I am the priest he intends to prepare him for death. And should the iniquity of the nation commit this last of cruelty, I must also prepare myself for death, as I am convinced the popular rage will not allow me to survive an hour after the tragic scene; but I am resigned. Could my life save his I would willingly lay it down and I should not die in vain.

As was his usual custom, the former King ate a hearty meal and, amazingly, slept well the night before his execution. The Abbé spent the night of 20/21 January at the Tower of the Temple and in the morning said Mass in the King's apartments. He heard Louis' last confession and they talked on religious subjects. Louis had been deeply distressed by his distraught family's understandable reaction to his dreadful news the previous evening. Louis decided that he would not see them again on the morning of 21 January, preferring to spare them the pain of another farewell. The Abbé supported his view. What agonies Marie Thérèse and her family must have suffered as they awaited his visit and a last chance to say goodbye and then, as time passed, finally realised that they would not see him again. Accompanied by the Abbé, Louis travelled to the Place de la Révolution[17] in a closed carriage. The journey from the Temple to the place of execution took about an hour. The streets of Paris were lined with 30,000 troops and members of the National Guard to keep the peace and deter any rescue attempt by Royalist supporters, and to control the thousands of bystanders. Rescue attempts were planned by Royalists led by the Baron de Batz, but were foiled. Munro Price's book *The Fall of the French Monarchy* suggests that it is highly unlikely that the former King knew that any rescue attempt had been made. There was to be no escape for him. When Louis reached the scaffold, he was required to have his hair cut. At first he tried to resist this further indignity, but the Abbé reminded him of the sufferings of Christ, so Louis agreed to allow the executioner, Sanson, to cut his hair in preparation for the guillotine. His hands were tied.

An estimated crowd of 20,000 gathered to see the execution of the former King. At the guillotine, Louis Auguste attempted to make a speech of forgiveness and reconciliation. The speech was largely drowned out by the noise of the beating of fifteen drums. As Louis was about to be executed, Abbé Edgeworth apparently, by way of comfort, said the words 'Son of St Louis, ascend to Heaven', and then Louis Auguste was executed. Whether this is an accurate account of the event is a matter of conjecture, but those words came to be part of the Royalist mythology surrounding the death of Louis XVI.[18] Later in his life, the Abbé was often asked to confirm whether he had indeed said the words. He refused to confirm or deny having said them, stating that he simply did not remember the events of the moment when the King was executed as he was too moved and agitated to do so. His memoirs, detailed in many other ways, are silent on this point. Whatever the reality, the words were a powerful and moving motif.

Accounts differ of the exact events of the execution. Some reports say that the first descent of the blade of the guillotine could not cut through Louis' sturdy neck. According to some reports, he cried out in pain but then was silent as the second blow killed him. Other accounts of his execution speak of his being killed by the first and only blow of the guillotine. As his bloody severed head was held up to the crowd by one of the guards, a cry went up which was audible to his imprisoned family in the Tower of the Temple. It was in this way that Marie Thérèse knew that her father was dead. Some of the spectators dipped their handkerchiefs in the blood of the former King to obtain mementoes, or relics, depending on their viewpoint.[19] The Abbé Edgeworth, contrary to his fears and expectations, was able to leave the Place de la Révolution without being accosted by the assembled mob.[20]

The Dauphin, Louis Charles, was now, in Royal theory, if not reality, Louis XVII. The 'Widow Capet', as Marie Antoinette was called, and her family struggled on in their prison: spending their days in reading, sewing, prayer, teaching and playing games with the boy they now regarded as being the rightful King of France. The Queen, Madame Élisabeth and Madame Royale treated Louis Charles as a monarch as well as a little boy. There was little contact from the outside world to intrude on their grief. The boy's uncle, the Comte de Provence, declared himself Regent from his exile in Ham in Westphalia. The Declaration of Regency from the St James Chronicle stated:

> Whereas the most criminal of men have by the perpetuation of the most atrocious of crimes, completed the weight of their iniquities… We declare that the Dauphin, Louis Charles, born the 27th day of March, the year of our lord 1785, is King of France and Navarre, under the name of Louis XVII. We furthermore declare, in virtue of our birth-right, and the fundamental laws of France, that we are and will act as Regent of France during the minority of the King, our nephew.

Joined in the declaration were 'our dearest brother Charles Philippe of France, Count of Artois to whom are united our dear nephews, grandsons of France, their Royal Highnesses Louis Anthony, Duke of Angoulême, and Charles Ferdinand, Duke of Berry'. The other princes of the blood, Prince Condé, the Duke of Bourbon and Duke of Enghien, also signed this declaration. The new Regent took the opportunity to create the Comte d'Artois 'Lieutenant-General of the Kingdom' and to exhort all subjects to 'show obedience to the orders that may and will be issued by our dearest brother'.

The declaration further stated that, aided by the allied sovereigns, the Bourbon princes in exile – i.e. the Comte de Provence, Comte d'Artois and his sons, Prince de Condé and his family – would:

> do our utmost endeavours to recover the liberty of our Royal nephew King Louis XVII; of her Majesty, his august mother and guardian; of the Princess Royal, Maria Theresa, his sister and our niece; and of her Royal Highness the Princess Élisabeth his Aunt and our dearest sister; all held in the severest captivity by the chiefs of a faction.

In the Tower of the Temple, the agony deepened for Marie Antoinette and the other Royal women. The conditions of their imprisonment deteriorated. Madame de Tourzel reports in her memoirs that Marie Thérèse had problems with her leg and, worn down by anxiety and grief at the death of her father, she was badly affected by it. The children's doctor, M. Brunyer, was summoned to attend the Princess and provided fresh linens to bind her leg.[21] Madame de Tourzel was able to obtain news of Marie Thérèse, and the doctor spoke to them of the Princess's 'gentleness amid her profound grief, and the patience with which she bore her sufferings'. The family was offered the opportunity to walk in the garden. They could not bring themselves to walk through the gate through which the former King had gone to his execution, so passed up the chance for fresh air and exercise that they so craved. On 3 July 1793, a decree of the Convention[22] ordered that the boy King should be separated from the rest of his family and put under the supervision of the Commissioner Antoine Simon and his wife. Simon had been appointed as a Commissioner in the Temple in October of the previous year. A former cobbler and bankrupt, he had a well-deserved reputation for vulgarity and cruelty. Marie Thérèse wrote, 'My mother's anguish was at its height when she learned that Simon, the shoemaker, whom she had seen as a municipal was entrusted to the care of the unfortunate child.' Madame de Tourzel agreed with this view of Simon, calling him 'an atrocious man'.

The guards came at ten o'clock at night to take away the little boy from his mother and family. Marie Antoinette fought and argued for an hour, pleading hysterically with the guards to be allowed to keep her son with her, but to no avail. Marie Thérèse wrote later in her memoirs – which were written in detached third-person terms recounting her experiences and observations – that Louis Charles threw himself into his mother's arms, emitting loud cries and begging not to be separated from her:

> The unfortunate Queen … did not want to give up her son, and against the municipal authorities, she defended his bed where she had placed it. But they menaced her with the use of violence… The Queen responded that they had only to kill her rather than to snatch her son from her. Finally, they threatened so positively to kill the child if she did not deliver him to them that her maternal tenderness forced her to this sacrifice.[23]

Marie Thérèse wrote further, 'We rose, my aunt and I, for my poor mother no longer had any strength. After we had dressed him, she took him and gave him in to the hands of the municipals herself, bathing him with her tears and overwhelmed with a sense of foreboding that she would never see him again.' The young King kissed his sister, aunt and mother and went away with the guards. He was taken to the room that had previously been his father's. He was terrified by the room and the memories of his father that it evoked.

His mother, aunt Élisabeth and Marie Thérèse spent hours trying to spot him at play, looking out from various vantage points. They were ill-rewarded for their efforts: the unfortunate eight-year-old, who had been so cared for and loved by his family, was ill-kempt and often forced to drink alcohol to get him drunk. The women of the family were to be traumatised by the crying of the frightened child. He was found by his guards to be masturbating – this habit was encouraged by those supervising him, as they felt this was a way of demeaning him and weakening his spirit. Madame de Tourzel, who had loved and cared for the young Dauphin, wrote, 'One cannot help regretting that Heaven did not ordain that he should die for he would have been spared the ill-treatment he experienced, and the frightful captivity he endured from the time that the Royal Family were separated – a piece of barbarity that brought him to the grave.'[24]

The story of his confinement is one of cruelty and inhumanity. The Royal ladies heard the boy singing revolutionary songs, as he had been trained to do by his jailers, and shouting sexual explicit insults about his mother, sister and aunt – 'the whores' as he had learnt to call them. The women's despair must have been great. Years before, Marie Antoinette had written to Louis Charles's governess that he was easily influenced; not surprisingly, given his youth and vulnerability, this had proved to be only too true. In the outside world, concern was expressed about his condition. The Austrian Archduchess Marie-Anne, sister of Francis II and a cousin to the Royal children, wrote of the captive family, 'the one I pity the most is the poor little King, who, unless God have the mercy to take him from this world, will become a little monster'.[25]

On 2 August 1793, in the middle of the night, just a month after the removal of her brother, Madame Royale's mother was taken away from the Tower of the Temple. Following a further decree of the Convention, Marie Antoinette had been sentenced to even closer confinement in the Conciergerie in preparation for her trial. Marie Thérèse was so agonised by the shock and pain of the departure of her mother, not knowing where she was going, that she was not able to say farewell properly. She writes movingly of the departure, 'At last my mother left us, after kissing me again and again, and bidding me be brave and careful of my health. I did not answer my mother at all, being convinced that this was the last time I should see her.'[26] The former Queen's new prison was a room shared with a maid, screened only by a curtain from her two male guards. She was suffering from untreated heavy menstrual bleeding, which further added to her woes. For a fee, members of the public were able to observe their former Queen in her prison cell. A young maidservant, Rosalie Lamorlière, showed Marie Antoinette many small kindnesses as she waited on her during her ordeal, serving her meals and helping her to dress, and even providing her with a small, shoddy mirror.

The Queen and Madame Royale were very different characters, and although there had been clashes and difficulties, they were still devoted to each other. Close confinement in the Tower had built love and closeness to one another in a way that a life of greater etiquette and physical distance at Versailles or even the Tuileries Palace could not. Madame Royale and Madame Élisabeth spent the night of 2 August in tears. The next day, the Princesses begged their jailers to be permitted to join the Queen, wherever she might be. This was not allowed and they received no news of the Queen's fate. At this point, their only servant was also dismissed. Madame Élisabeth and Madame Royale would have to look after themselves. These ladies who, in their old world, had had whole Households of tens of people devoted to their welfare were now required to do their own cleaning, laundry and bed-making. No doubt it relieved the boredom to have something to occupy their time and hands.

The prison regime is described in the memoirs of Madame Royale, or 'Charlotte Capet' as the Princess was now known by her revolutionary guards. Having been separated from her mother, father and brother, fortunately she still had the company of her beloved aunt Élisabeth. Unbeknownst to Marie Thérèse and her aunt, a petition for the trial of Madame Élisabeth had been addressed to the National Assembly just a few days after the execution of her brother the King in January 1793, but had not as yet been acted upon. Marie Thérèse had always admired and loved her aunt for her piety, her commitment to her brother, her resignation in the face of their troubles and courage in refusing offers of escape from France. It is not an exaggeration to say that Madame Élisabeth had a profound impact on her niece's moral, religious and political thinking. They had been close from Madame Royale's earliest childhood. Although they were aunt and niece, there were only fourteen years separating them in age, and Madame Élisabeth was more like a much-admired and loved elder sister to Marie Thérèse. The Princesses were subjected to daily deprivations and humiliations, and kept without news of family and friends. They were able to bear this as at least they were together and able to pray and talk of happier times, family and friends.

In early October 1793, Marie Thérèse was separated from her aunt and taken from their shared quarters by members of the National Guard, despite requests from Madame Élisabeth that she be allowed to accompany the child. On reaching an interrogation room, Marie Thérèse was confronted by a panel of men including Jacques René Hébert,[27] the lawyer and editor of *Le Père Duchesne*, a radical revolutionary newspaper, who had been appointed by the government as the Prosecutor. He was responsible for the trial of Marie Antoinette. With him was Pierre-Gaspard Chaumette, a fierce anti-monarchist who had voted for the execution of the King and was Procureur of the Commune; not that Marie Thérèse knew of the particular roles of either of these individuals. The men were there to gather evidence against the Queen for the trial that was planned. Their intention was to blacken Marie Antoinette's deeply damaged reputation beyond any hope of repair. Hébert intended to use the Royal children's testimony against their mother and then against Madame Élisabeth. Louis Charles, a vulnerable and easily influenced eight-year-old, had already been coerced or persuaded by his captors into making allegations that his mother and aunt had sexually abused and committed incest with him.

At first the questioning focused on the communications and contacts that Marie Antoinette had maintained with foreign courts while the family were living at the Tuileries. Marie Thérèse apparently answered with cool courage, giving away nothing. Her composed responses seem to have disconcerted her interrogators. She was also confronted by her younger brother, whom she had not seen since July, and who repeated to her face his accusations of sexual misconduct by their mother and aunt. Marie Thérèse went to embrace the traumatised child. She was separated from her brother by the guards. He was taken into another room for questioning.[28] Marie Thérèse was torn between disgust at what her little brother was saying and outrage that he had been so abused by his captors that he had been persuaded to make these terrible accusations. He had signed a statement confirming the terrible charges against his family. At first, she was so stunned by the whole implausibility of the crimes alleged that she could hardly believe her ears. She vehemently denied the charges against her mother and aunt. The persistent questioning of this lone young girl lasted three hours. It was the stuff of nightmares. In her memoirs, Marie Thérèse describes how, in this distressing incident:

> they proceeded to question me on a host of dreadful things of which my mother and aunt were accused. I was overwhelmed by the horror of it and so indignant that, in spite of the terror I was in, I could not help saying that it was an infamous thing to do. In spite of my tears, they pressed me hard for an answer. They said things I did not understand; but those I did understand were so horrible that I wept with indignation.

Marie Thérèse confirmed none of their accusations, but she did concede that she was not always present when her mother and aunt were with Louis Charles. She was then returned to her cell. Madame Élisabeth was subjected to similar questioning and denied all the accusations made against her and her sister-in-law. Madame Élisabeth was outraged by their allegations. They had seen only too vividly how appallingly the isolated boy King was being treated. His captors had succeeded in their objective of degrading the little boy and turning him against his family for their own ends.

The captives in the Tower were unaware that on 14 October the former Queen was put on trial. The trial lasted many hours. Marie Antoinette put up a spirited and intelligent defence, albeit an untruthful one, denying conspiracy against the Revolution and collusion with foreign invaders. The personal loathing of her felt by many of the French people was much greater than that felt for her late husband. The accusations of sexual misconduct with her dearly beloved son were put to her and provoked a reaction in her of abhorrence and denial. At one point she appealed to the mothers in the court who responded favourably to her. It was clear that Hébert's efforts to attack her mothering had backfired and were in danger of creating sympathy for Marie Antoinette. Those accusations against the former Queen and her sister-in-law were quietly dropped.

The outcome of the Queen's trial was, in any event, a foregone conclusion. As Anthony Trollope wrote in his 1850 novel *La Vendée*, 'Her fate was already fixed, and had only to be pronounced.' Marie Antoinette was taken to the guillotine on the Place de la Révolution[29] on 16 October and executed at approximately midday. For her there was to be no closed carriage or the ministrations of a kind confessor, as there had been for the King nine months earlier, but an open cart and a specially extended route through a baying and vitriolic crowd from the Conciergerie to the place of her execution. She was not able to wear her black mourning clothes, but was obliged to change into a fresh white dress and an ugly cap. Ironically, for many years previously it was white rather than black that had been the traditional colour of mourning for Queens of France. Her hands were bound behind her back. The once elegant and glamorous princess was now gaunt and grey-haired. She bore all the humiliations and fear with enormous dignity and the upright queenly posture that had been noted in better times. Even the small sketch by the revolutionary sympathiser, David, of her on the way to execution – drawn from life as she passed on the tumbrel along the Rue St Honoré – illustrates this proud bearing. The revolutionary newspapers, however, preferred to characterise it as anger and contempt for the people.

Marie Antoinette on her way to execution, sketched by Jacques-Louis David

In her courage and dignity, Marie Antoinette proved herself a true daughter of her mother, the Empress. The people of Vienna responded by rioting in the streets, so shocked were they at the way their Archduchess Maria Antonia had been treated by her adopted country.

The Princesses in the Tower did not know what had happened to the former Queen. The moving letter of farewell that the Queen wrote to her sister-in-law in the hours before she was taken to be executed, begging for forgiveness for the accusations made by Louis Charles about his aunt and commending her children to Élisabeth's care, was never received by Élisabeth. Of this letter, how it was eventually received by Marie Thérèse and its contents, more later. At the Conciergerie, Marie Antoinette had been able to do some knitting to pass the time and to keep her hands occupied. After her death, her handiwork was passed to François Huë by the keeper of the Conciergerie prison, Bault, and thence eventually to Marie Thérèse, who kept her mother's knitting with her until the end of her life.

By this time, the physical conditions in the Tower of the Temple were deteriorating for the prisoners. Madame Royale and Madame Élisabeth had no candles and therefore no choice but to go to bed when the light in their room faded. Sugar and soap were in short supply. In addition to the confinement, lack of fresh air and exercise exacerbated the discomfort of their living conditions. The Princesses' quarters were subject to inspections up to three times a day, with each search lasting up to four and a half hours. Cupboards and drawers were ransacked. The ladies wondered if the guards had nothing else to do with their time but to carry out these protracted and unpleasant searches. Their sheets were taken away and replaced with ones so coarse that it would be impossible to twist them into a rope to aid escape. As a child, Marie Thérèse normally enjoyed robust good health, but in November 1793 her imprisonment caused her a bout of whooping cough. The cramped conditions, lack of exercise and stress had taken their toll.

There were physical deprivations, but most difficult to cope with were the anxiety for her mother and the sounds of her brother's suffering and distress, which she heard (or thought she did) but about which she was powerless to do anything. The guards were aggressive and insulting. It seems highly likely that, however suppressed, there was some element of sexual threat with two young women being imprisoned so closely by male guards. This would have been unnerving to any woman, but particularly so to ones who had led such protected lives prior to the departure from Versailles. Things were to get worse still for the Princesses and Louis Charles.

4

Orphan of the Temple

MAY 1794-DECEMBER 1795

In May 1794, the fifteen-year-old Marie Thérèse was left in solitary confinement in her prison room. She must have long feared that she and Madame Élisabeth might be separated. On the night of 8/9 May 1794, this dreaded event happened. Roughly dragged from her niece and their quarters, Madame Élisabeth was reprimanded by their guards for trying to reassure and comfort Marie Thérèse by saying that she would soon return to their shared room. The Princesses embraced and kissed each other tenderly.

From the Tower of the Temple, Madame Élisabeth was taken to the forbidding Conciergerie. From there she was taken to be tried at the Council Hall of the Revolutionary Tribunal – at ten o'clock at night. The Princess was taken to the Assize Court where she was prominently displayed to the assembled crowd on the upper bench of the courtroom. She was described in the court paperwork as 'Marie Élisabeth Capet,[1] sister of Louis Capet, the last tyrant of the French, aged 30 and born at Versailles'. As early as November 1793, the municipality of Paris had addressed to the National Assembly a petition requesting that 'you will send the infamous Élisabeth before the Revolutionary tribunal at the earliest moment'. The indictment against her claimed that she had been 'involved in all those crimes; she has co-operated in the plots, the conspiracies formed by her infamous brothers and by the wicked and impure Antoinette'. The Princess was also accused by the prosecutors of engaging in counter-revolutionary activity and 'promoting the re-establishment of tyranny by lavishing with Antoinette, on the son of Capet, homage to Royalty, and the pretended honours of a King'.

When Madame Élisabeth was asked by her accusers about the allegations of sexual misconduct with her nephew, she vehemently denied the repulsive and untrue charges. She was offered neither legal counsel to defend herself nor a priest. She did not ask for either comfort, knowing it was hopeless to do so. A brave lawyer, Monsieur Chauveau, heard of Madame Élisabeth's distressing situation and went to the courtroom where she was on trial to offer the Princess legal advice and to offer to speak on her behalf. He was not allowed to see or speak to her and was turned away from the revolutionary tribunal. However, a speech was made in Madame Élisabeth's defence saying that the court that was trying her had not followed the due process of law in conducting her trial; this did not help her. Despite her protestations of innocence, the sentence of the court was death. There could be no other. Madame Élisabeth was to be executed the next day, 10 May, at the Place de la Révolution, by guillotine.

After the trial, the Princess was taken back to the Conciergerie and held overnight in a cell with twenty-four other prisoners who, like Madame Élisabeth, had been tried, found guilty and were awaiting execution the next day. The reports are that she acted with calm dignity and courage, giving what comfort she could to the others who were to die with her. It was only now that Madame Élisabeth learned from her fellow prisoners of the trial and execution of the Queen in October of the previous year. The next day she was taken to the guillotine in an open cart, subject to abuse from the bystanders. In a further twist of cruelty, she was forced by her executioners to sit on a bench and watch her twenty-four companions die in front of her eyes. It is said that the women who were about to die kissed the Princess before going to the guillotine and the men bowed before her. Other reports indicate that even the stoic and devout Élisabeth could not bear such suffering, and that she fainted away at the sight of such horrors. Her decapitated body was buried in a common grave.[2] The day of her execution, 10 May 1794, was effectively the twentieth anniversary of the accession of her brother, Louis XVI, to the throne of France. Her family in exile was stunned by the news of her death, except for Marie Thérèse, who was not told of the fate of her beloved aunt.

Outside the Tower of the Temple, the violence of the Terror was rampant. Paris was still in a state of turmoil. On 10 May 1794, the day following the departure of her aunt, Marie Thérèse was visited by a person she later found out to be Maximilien Robespierre.[3] The Head of the Committee of Public Safety inspected with interest the small collection of books that Marie Thérèse had in her room. They had provided Marie Thérèse and Madame Élisabeth with intellectual stimulation and spiritual sustenance and helped to sustain their morale. Madame Royale was not aware of Robespierre's identity at the time of this visit, but later recorded in her memoirs[4] that the man was treated with great respect and deference by the men guarding her. Marie Thérèse bravely took the opportunity to ask his permission to tend to her brother, who was very unwell and without proper nursing care. Marie Thérèse notes in her memoirs that she told her visitor 'my brother is ill. I have written[5] to the Convention for permission to nurse him. The Convention has not yet answered. I now repeat my request.'[6] It is reported that Marie Thérèse also handed Robespierre a letter setting out her request to go to the assistance of Louis Charles. Her efforts on his behalf are a testament to her love for her younger brother. She had been upset and repulsed by his horrible accusations about their mother and aunt, but he was, after all, only a very young and frightened child in the hands of cruel and manipulative revolutionaries wishing to turn him against his family and use his evidence against them. Sadly Marie Thérèse's request to be allowed to look after her brother was ignored, and she was neither able to see nor to care for the unfortunate boy. It was agonising for her to know of his sufferings; to be so physically close to him and yet unable to do anything to aid him in his troubles.

In the Tower the routine continued much the same for Marie Thérèse, but without the companionship and support of her aunt. There were still the three daily inspections of her room by the commissioners. Marie Thérèse had developed a series of rituals and activities that helped her to survive the torments of anxiety for herself and the pain of not knowing what had happened to her family. The Princess spent her days cleaning her room and making her bed. She took particular pains to keep herself and her clothes, worn and mended as they were, neat and clean. She washed her own linen by hand and pressed it under the mattress. Madame Royale mended her stockings and even tried to repair her shoes, which were worn out with use. This was important to her sense of order and in maintaining her spirits. This was in sharp contrast to the filthy conditions in which her poor brother was confined. He made no effort to keep himself or his surroundings clean and tidy but allowed himself to sink into degradation and filth. Marie Thérèse's room was kept shuttered and was rather dark. She could hear little from the world outside: only the occasional peals of bells, an especially loud drum roll or the muffled cries of a news vendor. Deprived of news from the outside world, she quickly lost track of the days; and in any event, France was following the new Revolutionary calendar.[7] Kindly, the Temple cooks[8] who prepared her meals, aware of her strict religious principles, ensured that she had fish rather than meat on Fridays, in the old way. This served to act as a crude calendar; at least once a week she knew with some certainty which day of the week it was. She did not have enough firewood to keep warm, so in the cold weather Madame Royale's hands were covered with painful chilblains. Later in life, she empathised with anyone who was suffering with this uncomfortable condition.

In the world outside the Tower of the Temple, there were rumours suggesting that the ascetic bachelor Robespierre, the 'sea-green incorruptible', was intent on marrying Marie Thérèse in an attempt to bolster his political position. Paul Barras, who succeeded to power as one of the Directors, wrote in his memoirs[9] of the time that a number of people asserted:

> that Robespierre had conceived the idea of entering into a matrimonial alliance with the daughter of Louis XVI, then a prisoner in the Temple. I did not believe a word of these allegations, yet they absorbed the minds of the people; although there was perhaps very little probability about the reports, it did no harm to let them circulate among the masses, who could not persuade themselves that he was a tyrant except by associating him with the ideas of ancient Royalty.

By the end of July 1794, Robespierre had himself been overthrown from power in a *coup d'état* and was guillotined on 27 July 1794. The death of Robespierre heralded a change of regime in the world outside the Tower of the Temple, as the crazed state violence and excesses of the Terror ceased. Marie Thérèse later wrote in her memoirs that the physical conditions of her imprisonment improved after the death of Robespierre.

Later in May 1794, Marie Thérèse asked for permission to send fresh linen to her aunt. This permission was refused. She was not told that her aunt had been executed several weeks before, nor given any information about her health or whereabouts. Marie Thérèse hoped that she had been sent into exile to join Les Tantes in Italy. As well as cleaning and exercising, Marie Thérèse filled the lonely days with practical pursuits and reading. As a child at Versailles she had learned to make clothes for poor children; and while imprisoned she knitted, which she loathed, but which helped to pass the time, finishing off some stockings that had been started by Madame Élisabeth. She also continued work on a tapestry that had been previously worked on by Marie Antoinette but which the Queen had been forced to leave behind when she was taken away to the Conciergerie in August 1793.

Before Madame Royale's aunt departed, she had told her niece if she were ever to be left alone to request a female companion from her guards. Madame Royale did this in obedience to her aunt's wishes. Later she told Madame de Tourzel that she really preferred to be alone than have as a companion anyone whom her jailers might consider suitable. Her request for a companion was anyway ignored. She was left very much alone with no human contact except with her jailers, who were terse and unpleasant in their dealings. Marie Thérèse, a frightened young girl, had months of broken and disturbed nights, sleeping in a chair for fear of being found undressed and in her bed by her guards. In order to have some exercise and to pass the tedious hours of her captivity, Marie Thérèse walked backwards and forwards across her room, which was 15 feet square, for an hour each day, looking at her watch as she did so to 'prevent any stagnation of the blood'.[10] Her self-discipline and determination to survive this terrible time were great. She channelled all her pride and courage into withstanding her fears and the harsh physical conditions in which she was confined. She later reported to Madame de Tourzel that:

> My aunt, who foresaw only too clearly the unhappiness for which I was destined, had accustomed me to wait upon myself and to do without assistance. She mapped out my life so that every hour had its occupation; the care of my room, prayer, reading, work, all was laid down. She, moreover, neglected nothing that could conduce to my health. She made me scatter water about to freshen the air in my room.

To keep her mind occupied and to try to distract herself from her gloomy surroundings, Madame Royale applied herself to the mental discipline of learning by heart *La Journée d'un Chrétien sanctifée par la Prière et la Meditation*, one of the religious books that Madame Élisabeth had left behind. Inspired by the training of her aunt, Marie Thérèse seems to have displayed amazingly good practical sense in adapting to imprisonment, in particular her solitary confinement: understanding how vital it is for a prisoner's morale to keep the body as clean and healthy as circumstances permit and not allow oneself to drift into inactivity, depression and physical degradation. She recognised the need to stimulate the mind as much as possible, despite the searing boredom of solitary confinement. Madame Royale also wrote later in her memoirs that there were times during her captivity when she thought that she would be kept in solitary confinement for the rest of her life. She was left alone with her thoughts and fears. She did not know what was happening in the outside world, nor did she know the fate of her family; she did not know what would become of her. She was also mourning the death of her beloved father whom she knew, for certain, was dead.

Madame Royale kept herself as separate from the guards as possible, rarely speaking to them unless it was absolutely necessary. The lonely Princess was thrown back on her own internal resources. Her strict upbringing and early training helped to sustain her in this terrible period of her life. Marie Thérèse's few requests for material necessities and, in particular, for news of the rest of her family were rejected harshly. She had been demonised along with her brother as the children of the hated Marie Antoinette. Marie Thérèse later wrote of this time of her life as 'the door was shut and the bolts were drawn and no one answered me'. The guards or 'commissioners' guarding the former King's children were drawn from the three hundred members of the Commune of Paris. They were characteristically men from the lower middle class of Paris, clerks and tradesmen. Four of them were chosen each day to be on duty in the Tower of the Temple; they were on guard for a twenty-four-hour shift. The guards were often drunk and therefore even less predictable than usual. The prospect of any contact, let alone the prolonged daily inspections, must have been nerve-racking to a young, lone girl. This was exacerbated by additional surprise inspections when the guards were particularly jumpy. Any kindness shown by a guard to their prisoners would bring on him the suspicion of being a Royalist sympathiser and counter-revolutionary by his comrades. Few dared to show any humanity towards the captive Royal offspring. She hardly heard a word that was not harsh or cruel from her guards. At times the children were referred to as 'the little wolves' by their captors.

Her religious faith was a great consolation to Marie Thérèse. She later told Madame de Tourzel, when asked how she had survived so many misfortunes, 'Without religion it would have been impossible; it was my only resource, and procured for me the only consolation of which my heart was susceptible; I had kept the devotional books belonging to my Aunt Élisabeth; I read them, I fixed their counsel in my mind. I sought never to stray from it, but to observe it faithfully.' Her loneliness was terrible, and Madame de Tourzel later wrote:

> In spite of all her courage she confessed to us that she was so weary of her profound solicitude that she said to herself, 'If they end by placing me with anybody who is not a monster, I feel that I shall not be able to prevent myself loving her… My dreams were haunted. One night I awoke to the echo of my own screams, and lay awake weeping until the first cold light crept through the shuttered windows. That morning only my fear that the guards would force their way in if I didn't answer the door made me get up and drag on my clothes. I picked up a knitting needle and not really knowing why I did it, scratched a message on the plaster wall of the chamber: "Marie Thérèse is the unhappiest person in the world". Live, my good mother, whom I love so much but of whom I can hear no tidings. O my father watches over me from heaven!"[11]

Responding to rumours that the closely guarded child prisoners had somehow managed to escape from the well-guarded Tower of the Temple, in July 1794 Director Paul Barras[12] went to the Temple to see for himself. By his account, he ordered that the Royal children should be reunited and that the appalling conditions in which Louis Charles was imprisoned, surrounded by his own filth and plagued by fleas and rodents, should be improved. He also apparently gave instructions that the children should be allowed out of their cells for a twice-daily walk in the prison yard. According to Barras' account of events, he ordered that the young boy's cell should be cleaned and two women be appointed to care for him. Inspection of the boy showed that he was traumatised by his cruel treatment, hardly able to stand and obviously in pain. His clothes were far too small for him and had to be cut open, revealing his limbs to be very swollen and an unhealthy colour. But according to Barras' account the boy was still able to speak, despite some suggestions that he had become mute. This account of the visit reported that the boy should be provided with medical attention. 'Consequent upon the report I made to the Committee of Public Safety, I obtained leave for medical men to examine the youthful sufferer.' The doctors reported back that the boy's illness was 'a most serious one'. Mistreatment and fear had also made Louis Charles retreat into himself. He tried to placate his guards for fear of later retaliation, so when asked about his treatment he replied, 'I have no complaints to make against those who have charge of me.' He was obviously terrified to make a complaint and then be left to the attentions of those about whom he spoke out once Barras had left. Barras' memoirs recount that his orders for improvements to be made in the conditions in which Louis Charles was imprisoned were ignored, and the boy continued to live in isolation and degradation.

Paul Barras also went to see Madame Royale on this visit. Marie Thérèse noted in her own memoirs that she recognised him from the old days. He was an aristocrat by birth and must presumably have attended the Court, either at Versailles or during the time spent by the Royal Family at the Tuileries before their imprisonment. Barras wrote in his memoirs, 'I then went to see Madame. Her room was a little less indecently kept. Madame had dressed herself at an early hour.' Marie Thérèse recollected Barras asking if she objected to being kept in the Temple, to which she replied that the accommodation was satisfactory but informed her visitor that she was sad at not having news of her mother despite asking for information about her.[13] Barras and his companions said nothing about what had happened to Marie Antoinette. Marie Thérèse reports in her memoirs of feeling fearful of her mother's fate. By way of comfort, she was told by her visitors to be patient and to trust in the goodness of the French people. The lack of information left her mind to wander amongst terrible imaginings and speculations, and this was the aspect of her imprisonment she found most difficult to bear; much worse than her physical deprivations. Barras was mindful of the need to be seen to guard the children closely, so ordered that the number of guards at the Tower be doubled. He was taking no chances regarding security or his own political position.

Paul Barras' visit to the Royal children was eventually to have some positive results for them, as on 29 July 1794 Christophe Laurent[14] was appointed as *Gardien des Enfants du Tyran*, apparently on the orders of Barras. Conditions for both the children improved significantly during the period of his guardianship. Louis Charles had been in solitary confinement since January 1794, and Laurent was disgusted by what he found on first visiting the boy in his cell; the stench was horrendous. Laurent set up a formal enquiry to establish why the boy had been treated in this way and who was accountable for the abuse. He made a full report setting out the condition of the child prisoner. Laurent was humane in his approach; but equally, as a canny public servant, he had no intention of being held accountable for any mistreatment that had happened before his appointment. Other commissioners inspected the cell and the child and confirmed Laurent's assessment of the situation, including the insanitary conditions in which Louis Charles was being kept and how this had affected the health and morale of the Prince.

It was only after considerable efforts that Laurent was able to ensure, at the beginning of September 1794, that the cell was cleaned and the boy had the first glimpse of daylight for more than six months. At last he was washed, his hair, finger and toe nails cut, and his injuries dressed by a doctor. From then on the abuse ended and his captors politely called him Monsieur Charles. Security, however, was still incredibly tight. The Revolutionary authorities – ever fearful of Royalist plots or foreign agents attempting to rescue the children – deployed more than 500 guards over the boy King and Madame Royale. In October 1794, Laurent was provided with an assistant in his task of caring for the sick boy and his sister. The Committee of General Safety appointed Jean-Baptiste Gomin.[15] Marie Thérèse writes that Gomin showed great kindness and 'took extreme care of my brother. For a long time my brother had been without lights; he was dying of fear.' Gomin ensured that he had light in his cell. This information must have been passed to Marie Thérèse by Gomin as, even with improved conditions and despite her pleas to be able to visit Louis Charles, brother and sister were kept apart. Laurent was able to give her comfort that her brother's conditions and health were improved, but he was forbidden to allow the children even to see each for a moment or communicate in any way. Louis Charles and Marie Thérèse were at least now allowed some exercise outdoors, albeit separately. All her life Marie Thérèse felt that outdoor exercise was essential to her feeling of health and well-being. The outside world knew little of the fate and condition of the children.

Better conditions, a clean cell, medical treatment, company and improved food could not save Louis Charles. He died on 8 June 1795, almost certainly from tuberculosis made worse by the period of neglect and cruelty that he had suffered. He was ten years and nearly three months old. Marie Thérèse was not informed of her brother's death nor allowed to attend his funeral. She later wrote of this time of her life, 'My brother died in the room below me; even, of this, I was left in ignorance.'[16] She wrote, 'He was not poisoned, as some have believed. The only poison that shortened his days was filth, made more fatal by horrible treatment, by harshness and cruelty, of which there is no example.' Despite being his closest relative, she was not allowed to see him, nor was asked to identify the body of the dead boy as that of her brother. Before leaving the Tower, in deference to the feelings of the boy's sister, the funeral director did not nail down the coffin lid until the coffin was out of the area where she might hear the hammering and guess what had happened to her brother.

Speculation about the death (or otherwise) of the young King was to set up one of the great Royal mysteries and would cloud Marie Thérèse's later life. She was plagued by 'Dauphins' claiming to be her dead brother and thus the rightful King of France in place of her uncles, Louis XVIII and the future Charles X. The body of Louis Charles was buried at last on 10 June, after delays to obtain the necessary permissions, in a communal grave at Sainte Marguerite. No prayers were said and no member of his family was present. Unbeknownst to those burying the child's body, it was incomplete. At the autopsy, Dr Philippe-Jean Pelletan had stolen the heart of the dead boy. He concealed it in a handkerchief and removed it from the Tower of the Temple; he took it home with him to keep in a jar filled with alcohol to preserve it. Madame de Tourzel was stunned by the news of the death of her charge. 'I heard of this appalling event when I was out walking and was utterly unprepared for I fell at once into a state of extreme despondency; everything became a matter of indifference to me…'

Laurent and his assistant, Gomin, ended the intrusive and protracted three-times daily inspections of Madame Royale's room. Now inspections happened just once a day at noon and were conducted by only one of the commissioners, rather than mob-handed as before. Marie Thérèse had been given Coco,[17] a dog, as a companion. Three times a day either Laurent or his deputy would check on Marie Thérèse to ensure that the fire in her room was lit, that she was warm enough and that her room had been cleaned satisfactorily by the servants. She no longer did her own housework, not that she had minded this task. The laundry, which she had previously done herself, was now sent out for washing and pressing. Laurent and Gomin also checked that her meals had been properly delivered to her rooms. She was given a bell to summon assistance, more books, and drawing materials. The *tutoyer* practice – addressing her with the familiar *tu* rather than *vous* – that had so offended her and other members of the Royal Family now ceased. Her new jailers sympathised with her plight and sufferings and eased the physical conditions of her incarceration. The very relaxation of the regime freed her mind from the needs of immediate physical survival to a desperate need for information about what had happened to her family. News was a commodity in very short supply during her sojourn in the Tower of the Temple. Marie Thérèse still thought she could hear her brother moving about in the cell beneath hers, even after he was in fact dead.

In November 1794, new linen, stockings and shoes were provided for Madame Royale to replace articles that had long worn out. In the spring of 1795, it was noticed that Marie Thérèse was looking very pale and in need of fresh air; she had been largely confined indoors in an ill-lit room for many months. She was allowed by Laurent to go up on the roof of the Temple to take some exercise in the open air and the light. Outside the Temple, the Terror was quietening and people began to think once more of Madame Royale and to wonder how she had fared. She was dubbed the *Orpheline du Temple*, the Orphan of the Temple. There were petitions requesting that Marie Thérèse be set free from the Tower, including one from the city of Orléans in June 1795. The death of Louis Charles and the application of Salic Law meant that her political significance had faded.[18] Laurent left his post in March 1795;[19] he had done much to improve the conditions of the child prisoners and was 'the first person to improve her lot in prison'.[20] She became very attached to him.

In June 1795, Marie Thérèse was at last allowed what she had long requested, a female companion. On 11 June, the Committee decreed that the Commissioner of Police should, within two hours, draw up a list of three women who could be recommended for their Republican virtues and morals and would act as a companion to the '*fille de Capet*' as Madame Royale was styled. Madame de Tourzel and her daughter were released from imprisonment in October 1794, and she recalls in her memoir, 'As soon as we were out of prison, and had a little more liberty, we tried to obtain news of them;[21] but such complete silence was observed in regard to their situation that we could only indulge in conjectures, which were frequently contradicted by events.' Madame de Tourzel attempted to get herself appointed as the Princess's companion but her pleas were rejected by the Committee of Public Safety, as were those of Madame Huë.

Madeleine de Chanterenne,[22] who was thirty years old and married to a policeman, was selected from the shortlist of respectable Republican matrons.[23] Sometimes known affectionately as Renete, she was the daughter of a ship-owner who had lost his money before the Revolution. She had been brought up in good provincial society and was regarded as being refined and sensitive. A woman of some education and culture, she spoke Italian, a language that Madame Royale had previously studied. She had a reputation for being kind, cherishing and compassionate. She was also a highly skilled embroiderer, something she had in common with Marie Thérèse. On first being introduced to Madame Royale, Madame de Chanterenne knelt before her and wept a little as she tried to explain why she had come to be with her. Madame de Chanterenne observed her new charge and reported that the young woman of sixteen and a half standing before her had reddened hands, no doubt from the chilly conditions of her imprisonment, the scanty fires and the work of washing her own clothes and bed linen. She was wearing a worn grey dress, which she had long outgrown, and two kerchiefs, one around her neck and one on her head.

It was only now, more than a year and half after the trial and execution of her mother and more than a year after the execution of Madame Élisabeth, that Madame Royale was finally given the news of what had become of them. Madame Royale recounts in her diary that she asked Madame de Chanterenne:

> 'What of my mother?'
> 'You have no mother.'
> 'And my aunt?'
> 'She is dead.'
> 'And my brother?'
> 'He, too, died a week ago.'[24]

She wrote of her fears for the rest of her family, 'I suspected the fate of my unfortunate relatives only too shrewdly; but since the sorrowful like to flatter themselves, there were moments when I still had hope.'[25]

Madame de Tourzel wrote that the Princess felt it particularly difficult to reconcile herself to the loss of her aunt:

> She had never been able to believe that the fury of the mob could be carried to such an extent as to attack the life of a Princess who had no concern whatever with the government, and whose virtue was so much respected that profound silence reigned as she was taken from the Conciergerie to the Monceaux barrier.

Marie Thérèse spent some of the time she had available following her release from domestic duties in writing the first version of her memoirs, covering the period of her life from the time in the Tuileries, the abortive escape attempt and recapture at Varennes and the time spent in the Tower. In a further relaxation of the regime, from 21 June the Committee of Public Safety ordered that the remaining inspection of her rooms be abandoned. Now that she knew that her immediate family was gone, Marie Thérèse began to think of her wider family. She records in her memoirs that she thought of those of her relatives who were still alive: her uncles, Provence and Artois, and their wives; her great-aunts; the Orléans, the Condés; Madame Clotilde; the Borbons of Spain, and the Bourbons of Naples and Parma. She did not know her Austrian relatives. She assumed that she would be put into the care of her uncle, the Comte de Provence, and probably go to live with her great-aunts in Italy.

In the outside world there was a resurgence of interest in Marie Thérèse. The Princess was touched to note that whenever she walked out, windows looking onto the Temple garden were always full of onlookers. Bands played and she heard familiar Royalist songs. François Huë, her father's former *valet de chambre*, had returned to the area and rented an apartment on the fourth floor of a building from which it was possible to view the Princess through a telescope as she walked on the roof of the Tower for exercise. According to Madame de Tourzel, he spent time trying to find out about the fate of the Royal children. Madame de La Briche, an aristocrat who survived the Terror, wrote in her journal that she had watched the Princess in her prison:

> I saw Madame come out of the Tower. A little dog[26] preceded her and turned back to caress her. Madame de Chanterenne followed behind at a distance. Madame was dressed in white; a fichu tied around her head and descending very low on her forehead prevented one from seeing her hair. She carried her head high like her unfortunate mother, which made her appear taller than she is.

After the death of Louis Charles, Francis II of Austria approached the French Directory government and asked for Marie Thérèse to be given into his safekeeping in exchange for General de Beuronville, formerly Minister of War, who was in the custody of the Austrians.[27] The other captives for whom she was to be exchanged were Drouet, the man who spotted her family's escape attempt, Marat, Semonville, Cannes, Lamarque, Bancal and Quinette. All of them had voted for the execution of the King. At this point the Revolutionary government was feeling more established and confident of its position in discussions with the Imperial government of Austria. The French government recognised that Madame Royale, as the cousin of the Emperor of Austria, could be useful as an exchange pawn in negotiations. At the Court of Vienna, her dead mother's Habsburg relatives were discussing the possibility of Marie Thérèse marrying a Habsburg Grand Duke, namely her cousin the Archduke Charles. The Viennese Court was considering the notion that, while Salic Law debarred Madame Royale from claiming the majority of France, it could be argued that there were certain regions that were not affected and which could pass to Madame Royale and then to her husband and the Habsburgs. Alsace, Lorraine, Brittany and possibly Franche-Comté were regarded as being divisible from the rest of France, and therefore capable of being inherited by a woman. This was an attractive idea for the Austrians.

Following the arrival of Madame de Chanterenne, it was also possible for the Princess's former governess Madame de Tourzel and her daughter Pauline to visit Marie Thérèse. The ladies had been trying to see her for some time and were at last successful in persuading the authorities to allow them to do so.

Madame de Tourzel describes their first meeting in her memoirs:

> When we reached the Temple I handed my permit to the guardians of Madame, and I asked to be allowed to see Madame de Chanterenne in private. She told me Madame was fully acquainted with all her misfortunes, that she expected us, and that we could go. I begged her to

> tell Madame that we had come. I was afraid of the impression that might be made on the Princess by the sight of the two persons who, when she went to the Temple, were in attendance on those she held dearest in the world, and whose loss she was reduced to deplore; but fortunately the emotion she experienced had no disastrous result. She came to meet us, embraced us tenderly, and took us to her room, where we mingled our tears over the objects of our regret.

After being so long isolated and unable to speak with anyone, let alone sympathetic old friends, the Princess spoke 'incessantly' of her family and 'gave a most touching and distressing account of the moment of her separation from the King, her father whom she loved so tenderly, and to whom she was so attached'.

The presence of these old friends was an enormous source of joy, as well as being a sad reminder of the terrible losses that Marie Thérèse had suffered. The Princess enquired after many of those who had been known to her and the family before their imprisonment in the Temple. Madame de Tourzel, who was in regular contact with the Comte de Provence, reported to him that Marie Thérèse had grown and was in good health, full of dignity and fine feeling. Madame de Tourzel was struck by her likeness to both her parents and Madame Élisabeth; she wrote, 'Heaven, which destined her to be a model of that courage which, without diminishing the softer parts of the character, renders it capable of great action, did not allow her to succumb under the weight of so many misfortunes.'

There was some tension between the middle-class ship-owner's daughter and Madame Tourzel and her daughter, former aristocrats who were used to the ways of Versailles. Madame de Chanterenne felt patronised and undermined by these noblewomen who had known Madame Royale in the days before the Revolution. By their own account, they were polite to her but by no means friendly or intimate. The aristocratic ladies felt that the bourgeois Madame de Chanterenne had become puffed up with pride and arrogant as a result of being the companion of the former King's daughter, whom, they felt, she did not treat with sufficient deference. Madame de Tourzel noted that Marie Thérèse did not seem to be aware of the over-familiarity. At first Madame de Chanterenne left the Princess alone with the ladies, but sat in on later visits. She was, after all, the appointee of the Revolutionary government. It would seem she was careful not to leave Madame de Tourzel and her daughter alone with Marie Thérèse. There was undoubted mutual affection between the Princess and Madame de Chanterenne to whom Marie Thérèse referred as 'my dear Renete' in her writings. Marie Thérèse was also very attached to Madame de Tourzel and Pauline. As she had said previously, after months of isolation she was happy to give her affection to anyone who was not a monster.

On receiving the news of the boy King's death, the Comte de Provence had declared himself to be the King of France, taking the title of Louis XVIII. He used Madame de Tourzel and her daughter as conduits for correspondence with his niece. Madame de Tourzel wrote to the King the day after her first visit to Marie Thérèse. Louis XVIII was very keen to ensure that Madame Royale supported and recognised his claims to the throne – her acquiescence was vital to him. In correspondence with Madame de Tourzel, he was keen to promote the marriage of the Princess with her cousin the Duke of Angoulême. Madame de Tourzel writes that 'He desired me to tell Madame of his wish to see her wife of the Duke of Angoulême. This marriage was so thoroughly in accord with her attachment to his august family, and also to France, which had so ill-treated her that she was spontaneously inclined to it.' Madame de Tourzel also notes that during their lifetime, Louis XVI and Marie Antoinette had made it very clear to her that their intention was that Marie Thérèse should marry the Duc d'Angoulême. Apparently, they had not discussed their thoughts for her future with Marie Thérèse for fear of distracting her from her studies. While they were at liberty, she had been too young for such conversations; and once they were captives, there were other more pressing matters to deal with, quite apart from the fact that they were not free to broker any marriage. The young Princess asked many questions about her husband-to-be. Madame de Tourzel was not able to be very informative as she had little knowledge of events outside France. She, too, had not seen the Duc d'Angoulême since he left France in 1789.

Madame de Tourzel and François Huë received a letter dated 8 July 1795 from Louis XVIII, who was in Verona. The letter, which had been written in cipher, was decoded by Huë and then passed to Marie Thérèse by Madame de Tourzel on one of her visits to the Princess. Louis XVIII wrote warmly to his niece:

> I am writing this letter on the chance of its reaching you, my dear niece, although I do not know if it will ever do so; but my affection for you refuses to be silenced at so heartrending a moment. Nothing can repair the dreadful losses we have suffered; but I trust you will let me temper their bitterness. Regard me, I implore you, as if I were your father, and be very sure that I love you and shall always love you as tenderly as if you were my own daughter.

He exhorts her to reply only if it is safe for her to do so, and signs off, 'Farewell my dear niece, I love you and embrace you with all my heart'. Huë was also allowed to visit the Princess and she was delighted to see her father's former *valet de chambre*. Huë wrote to Louis XVIII of his visit to the Princess: 'Your Majesty's good and sensitive heart can guess, far better than I can describe, the touching nature of this delightful meeting. I can only say that Madame Royale, who has been told of all her losses, bears them with a degree of courage and strength worthy of her august descent.'

Madame de Tourzel reported that the Princess was determined to reply to her uncle's letter, despite being closely watched by her jailers. Louis XVIII received a reply to his letter on 18 September in Verona, where he was based. It was addressed to 'her dear Uncle'. However, Marie Thérèse resisted the invitation of her uncle to regard him as a replacement father. To her way of thinking there could be no substitute for her dear father and the very close relationship they had shared. She may have quite logically read into Louis's apparently kind gesture an assertion of paternal authority over her and preferred to keep her independence for the time being, whilst simultaneously expressing her affection and respect for him. Her reply read:

> No one could be more touched than I am by the kindness you so graciously show towards a poor Orphan, in wishing to adopt her as a daughter. The first happy moment that I have known for three years was when I received your assurance of good will.[28] I love you as much as ever, and long for the day when I shall be able to tell you myself of my gratitude and affection.

On 5 September 1795, Madame de Mackau, who had been with the Royal Family through so many of their tribulations, and had herself been imprisoned in La Force, was at last able to visit Madame Royale. She was by now ageing and sick, but Marie Thérèse was delighted to see her former sub-governess.

Even from within the Temple, Marie Thérèse could sense the tension in Paris. There was factional rioting in early October. From her prison, Marie Thérèse hoped that it might be a Royalist uprising, but she was to be disappointed. Napoleon Bonaparte was called on by the Convention to suppress the rioting, which he did using much force. He took the opportunity to stage a military coup known as the 13th Vendémiaire, establishing a new Directory government with himself, Paul Barras and three others as the dominant players in French politics.[29]

Despite the dangers of crossing Paris, Madame de Tourzel and her daughter continued their visits to Marie Thérèse. Madame de Tourzel writes that they:

> returned to the Temple the following day, and Madame welcomed our arrival with great pleasure. She was uneasy in regard to what was happening in the city, and was anxious for our return… In spite of the commotion in Paris, we continued our visits to the Temple in peace, and without experiencing the slightest inconvenience we walked there alone and unattended, and we did not return until night, so as to spend as much

time as possible with Madame. We walked with her in the garden when the weather permitted, and we then played at tennis with her. We brought her some tapestry work, and did all we could do to procure a little distraction for her.

On one visit to the Tower, Marie Thérèse took Madame de Tourzel and Pauline to see the room where her brother had been incarcerated and died. In her memoirs Madame de Tourzel writes:

> She entered, followed by Pauline with saint-like respect. The loss of the young King was still so recent that I felt I had not the courage to look at the place where he had suffered so much, and I begged Madame to allow me to stay behind. I went into the rooms of the little Tower, and I was very glad not to have shown the same weakness about them... Madame took us to the library and we spent the afternoon there. She began to chat with Pauline, and said to me, 'If you are curious enough to look into the register that is on that table, you will find the diary of the Commissioners from the date of our coming to the Temple.' I needed no second request, and I set to work at once to examine this register. In it I saw the daily account rendered to the Convention in regard to its august prisoners. They confirmed me but too surely in my opinion that not even the slightest hope could be held that the young King was still alive.

The Register detailed in chilling terms the progress of the boy King's decline, death and burial despite the best efforts of Gomin who had, as Madame de Tourzel put it, 'neglected nothing in order to procure for the young Prince the assistance which was so constantly refused him'.

The Directory government learned that letters from King Louis XVIII in exile were being smuggled into the Tower of the Temple to Marie Thérèse by Madame de Tourzel. In early November 1795, Madame de Tourzel was briefly imprisoned in the Collège des Quatre-Nations[30] and forbidden to visit Madame Royale again. She was saved from perhaps a harsher fate by her sharp-witted daughter. Pauline had got rid of incriminating evidence of the correspondence her mother was conducting with Louis XVIII, and she managed to get up-to-date messages to her mother of what was happening. Marie Thérèse was questioned by government representatives about the correspondence between her and her uncle. She gave nothing away. Long experience had taught her discretion. Madame de Tourzel reports that she was allowed no more visits to the Princess. She was forbidden to write to the Princess and could only convey messages to Marie Thérèse via Monsieur Gomin.

Despite the fact that France and Austria were still formally at war, talks about the fate of Madame Royale were taking place in the city of Basle between the head of the local government, who was representing the

Emperor of Austria, and Monsieur Bacher, who represented the French government. As an indicator of the changed mood of Paris, in October 1795 Marie Thérèse's portrait was displayed in the window of a building near the Temple. Among some French people, and especially Royalists, Madame Royale had achieved almost mythical status as the romantic young prisoner and the tragic *Orpheline du Temple*. By early November, there were rumours circulating within Paris of the negotiations between France and Austria which would provide for the freedom of the *Orpheline du Temple* in exchange for French prisoners held by Austria. The gossips confidently asserted that there was a suite of ladies from the Imperial Court in Vienna waiting to receive Marie Thérèse at the Swiss border. By 27 November 1795, news was out of the agreement between the two countries to exchange Marie Thérèse for a number of Revolutionary leaders who had been captured by the Austrians during the wars between Austria and the armies of Revolutionary France. On 28 November, the Directory government ratified the treaty with Austria, agreeing to the trading of Madame Royale for the French Revolutionary captives.

The news of her impending release and her exile to Austria under the care of her Austrian cousin, the Emperor, was announced to Madame Royale by Pierre Bénézech, the French Minister of the Interior. Bénézech also informed Marie Thérèse that the Austrian Imperial Court had made it clear to him that they were not prepared to accept any of the ladies who had been with her in the Temple. This edict prevented Madame de Chanterenne from being a possible companion for Marie Thérèse in Vienna. Madame Royale was devastated at the prospect of being parted from 'her dear Renete' whom she had quickly come to love as a friend and kind companion. In her place, the Princess debated between the merits of Madame de Tourzel and Madame de Soucy, the daughter of her former sub-governess, Madame de Mackau. Madame Mackau herself was felt to be too old and frail to accompany Marie Thérèse to Vienna. However, the incident of the smuggled letters had put out of the question the possibility of Madame de Tourzel accompanying Marie Thérèse. She was not acceptable to the French government. Marie Thérèse wisely recognised that she needed mature guidance and support in exile, following her imprisonment and her isolation from political events, and she wrote, 'In the position I am in, in my loneliness and absolute ignorance of the manners of the world, I need someone who can give me good advice.' In the event, she was accompanied on her journey into exile by Madame de Soucy. She also asked for Cléry, her father's last servant in the Tower of the Temple. She requested that, if she were to be accompanied into exile in Austria by one of her warders, it should be Monsieur Gomin, for whom she had a great deal of respect and affection. He had been so thoughtful and kind to her and her brother during their imprisonment.

Louis XVIII's fears about Austria and their intentions towards

Madame Royale were great. Before Marie Thérèse's departure from Paris, he wrote to Madame de Tourzel describing 'How very difficult it is to believe in the disinterestedness of the Court of Vienna, and I cannot help suspecting that its apparent generosity hides ulterior views, and a definite plan to make me buy my niece's freedom very dearly.' His desire was that Marie Thérèse's exile, until the hoped-for and planned marriage to the Duc d'Angoulême, should be spent in quiet retirement with her great-aunts who were living in Italy. This arrangement would combine appropriate chaperonage of a young unmarried princess with a respect for family feelings and affections. At the same time it would keep Marie Thérèse well away from the influence of the Austrian Court and the possibility of a marriage not to the liking of her uncle. In response to hearing Louis' concerns, the Princess wrote:

> Sire, I am impatiently awaiting any orders my King and Uncle may be good enough to give me regarding my future conduct. I am longing to be with you and to be able to tell you how much I love you and feel my affection for you will never change. I am going to Vienna, where I shall show the Emperor all the gratitude I owe him for the service he has done me in giving me my liberty. But I assure you my uncle that I shall never dispose of my future without your knowledge and consent; and you can count upon your niece, who like her father, will always love the French and her family.

This was what Louis wanted: an acceptance of his authority, albeit that of an uncle rather than the father figure he wanted to be to her. Also reassuringly for Louis, she reiterated her love for her country of birth and her family. The last thing he needed, politically, was a Bourbon Princess and martyr figure who hated her country and countrymen. Understandable as that might have been, given her very real sufferings, it would not help his cause. Louis XVIII certainly felt the need to keep Madame Royale's support for his cause and goodwill. Her youth, prettiness and dignity in her troubles and the impact of her tragic story were valuable commodities in securing help from other monarchs and the nobility of Europe. Madame Royale begged her uncle and King to forgive the French 'who have gone astray' and said that she brought with her from France 'the prayers and homage of every good Frenchman'. In her correspondence with Louis XVIII and her other relatives scattered in exile all over Europe, the theme of her love for France and its people recurs. Madame de Tourzel speaks in her memoirs of the attachment and affection that Marie Thérèse retained for her native country despite all her sufferings.

On the evening of the 18 December 1795, Bénézech came to fetch the Princess from the Tower of Temple. An extensive trousseau of new clothes had been quickly prepared for Marie Thérèse on the orders of the French government, so that she might appear every inch the well-dressed French Princess on her journey through France and not be embarrassed by any deficiencies of her wardrobe on her arrival at the Court of her cousin. Madame Royale said her farewells to Madame de Chanterenne in the gardens of the Temple, returning several times to kiss her friend again. It was at this time that Marie Thérèse slipped into her dear companion's hand the first draft manuscript of her memoirs. They covered the period of her and her family's imprisonment from August 1792 to the death of her brother in June 1795.[31] At the request of her uncle, Louis XVIII, Madame Royale later wrote a more detailed version of the account of her experiences and those of her family during her imprisonment. They were published much against her wishes – Madame Royale had intended her writings to be a private document. To Louis XVIII, however, they were useful Royalist propaganda. In due course, she requested her original draft back from Madame de Chanterenne so that she could work on it further. A copy was returned to Madame de Chanterenne to replace the one borrowed by the Princess.

Madame Royale walked out of the Temple on the arm of Monsieur Bénézech. She had spent three of her formative years imprisoned in the Tower of the Temple, including many months when she was held in solitary confinement, fearing that she would never see the outside world again. She left on the eve of her seventeenth birthday, having lost all her immediate family, to go into exile with her Austrian cousins. It was a devastating experience and an enormously influential period of her life, affecting her entire personality. The experience informed her approach to politics, personal relationships, her own role as an *Enfant de France* and her perception of herself as a Frenchwoman. On leaving her prison, she had inscribed on the wall of her prison room the words 'My God, forgive those who have put my kinsfolk to death.'

5

At the Court of Austria

DECEMBER 1795–JUNE 1799

Awaiting Marie Thérèse outside the walls of the Temple prison was the carriage that would take her from France to her cousin's Court in Vienna. Already seated in the coach were Madame de Soucy and Monsieur Méchin, the Captain of the Gendarmerie who was to accompany Marie Thérèse to Basle in Switzerland as the representative of the government of France. Here the formal exchange of the Princess for the French prisoners of war was scheduled to take place. In a second carriage were Madame de Soucy's son, plus François Huë, three domestic servants and Coco. Marie Thérèse also had with her a number of mementoes of her brother, including his backgammon board.

The passports for the journey from France to Switzerland and on to Austria had been issued to Monsieur Méchin and were ostensibly for him, his 'wife' (Madame de Soucy), 'daughter' Sophie (Marie Thérèse) and 'servant' François Huë. Méchin was keen to maintain this fiction about the identity of the travellers and make the departure from Paris as uneventful as possible. No doubt the Directory, as the government of France was known, wanted to keep to a minimum the publicity attached to the departure of the daughter of the former King for enemy Austrian territory. The news did, however, appear in the newspapers, which was how Madame de Tourzel found out about the Princess's departure. It was refreshing for Marie Thérèse once again to be treated as a princess. However, she was not best pleased that while Madame de Soucy had a maid with her, Marie Thérèse herself had no personal servant.

Marie Thérèse was no doubt the object of great curiosity for the people whom she met as she travelled towards Vienna. She was dressed in the deepest mourning clothes, a symbol of her many sufferings. On

Christmas Eve, the Princess's party reached Huningue on the French left bank of the Rhine, and stayed overnight at the Corbeau Hotel.[1] A regular correspondent, now that she was free to write as often as she wished, Marie Thérèse wrote two letters from here on 27 December, one to Madame de Chanterenne:

> I was recognised the very first day at Provins.[2] Ah, my dear Renete, it hurt me very cruelly and did my heart good at the same time. You cannot imagine how the people came running to see me. Some of them called me their good Lady, others their good Princess. Some of them shed tears of joy and I very nearly did so myself. My poor heart was greatly agitated, and more than ever regretted leaving the land that it still loves so dearly.

She also wrote to Renete of the rumours that were circulating that she was to marry her cousin Archduke Charles of Austria. Some newspapers even reported that she had already married him. The exchange of the Princess for French Revolutionary prisoners took place on 28 December 1795, although some sources suggest the exchange took place two days earlier on 26 December in a merchant's house near the town gates of Basle.[3] Present at the handover ceremony were the Prince de Gavre and Baron Dégelmann, representing the Austrian Emperor, as well as a suite of six carriages full of observers. The Princess was being given to the Austrians in exchange for French prisoners, including Drouet of Varennes fame.[4] In due course, he had been captured by the Austrians during the fighting between the two countries. In a rather undignified piece of bureaucracy, the French officials demanded a receipt for Madame Royale's person and safe delivery. They wanted no comeback from her cousin, the Emperor. The receipt was signed by Baron Dégelmann, the Imperial Austrian government representative, and read, 'I, the undersigned in virtue of the orders of his Majesty the Emperor, declare that I have received from M Bacher, the French Ambassador charged with this duty, Madame la Princesse Marie-Thérèse-Charlotte, daughter of his Majesty, King Louis XVI.'

The formalities done, Marie Thérèse and her party then travelled on to Vienna. She was closely guarded as she travelled. Louis XVIII had been plotting with the Prince de Condé, Commander of the counter-revolutionary Royalist army, to intercept the Princess as she journeyed towards the Austrian capital and secure her 'freedom'. Aware of this possibility and determined to foil any such attempt by the French in exile, the Princess was given a large escort of Austrian Imperial soldiers. This was a mark of honour and respect, as well as a way of ensuring her safe delivery to her cousin's Court. Her uncle's plan to intercept her failed because of delays in communication between the Bourbons, but it illustrated the deep suspicion with which Louis regarded Marie Thérèse's Austrian family and their intentions towards his niece. On 30 December 1795, the Princess's party arrived at Fussen in Bavaria. Here a party of émigré French enthusiasts were waiting to greet Madame Royale and to pay their respects to her. However, they were prevented from meeting the Princess and having an audience with her by her Austrian escort. Similar scenes occurred at Innsbruck. Her supporters were disappointed at being deprived of the opportunity to pay their respects to the Princess.

En route to Vienna, however, Madame Royale was able to meet her great uncle, the Elector of Treves, and his sister Princess Cunegunde. Marie Thérèse took advantage of Princess Cunegunde's offer to ensure that a letter would be safely and securely delivered to her uncle Louis XVIII in Verona. She wrote to him that she had been treated 'with the greatest friendliness' during her journey out of France and into Austria. In an age of telephones, email and texts it is almost impossible to appreciate fully the frustration and delay in communication and the propensity for confusion, misunderstandings and working at cross-purposes. On 2 January 1796, Marie Thérèse met the Archduchess Abbess Marie Elizabeth, an elder sister of Marie Antoinette, with whom Madame Royale later spent time in Prague.

Madame Royale was received by the twenty-eight-year-old Emperor Francis II in Vienna on 5 January 1796. In many ways this was a sort of homecoming for her. Vienna was, after all, the former home of her powerful namesake and grandmother, and the birthplace and childhood home of her dead mother. She must have heard stories throughout her childhood about the Viennese Court. Marie Thérèse had always taken great pride in her Habsburg ancestry. At the Court of Vienna, Madame Royale was housed in the magnificent and richly furnished apartments in the Hofburg Palace, which had been occupied previously by her uncle, the late Emperor Leopold I. The Emperor provided her with the same scale of Household as his sisters and daughters, her cousins the Austrian archduchesses. She made friends with some of these ladies and was especially close with the Archduchess Anne Marie. The Prince de Gavre was appointed Grand Master of her Household.

The Emperor Francis's wife – another Marie Thérèse named in honour of their mutual grandmother – was, as a daughter of Queen Maria Carolina of Naples, Marie Antoinette's sister, also a cousin. The Empress was very taken up with her daughter, the baby Archduchess Marie Louise,[5] and was not particularly kind or welcoming to her exiled cousin. It was suggested that the young Empress was jealous of Madame Royale, her attractiveness and her celebrity. It is thought that she feared that her husband, the Emperor, was attracted to the other Marie Thérèse.[6] Madame Royale had learned German as a child. It was reported that two months after her arrival at the Imperial Court, she was conversing easily in her mother's native language. On her departure from France, Marie

Thérèse had been provided with a trousseau by the French government. She did not feel comfortable keeping the clothes that had been provided by her jailers, so they were returned to France with the hope that they would understand her reluctance to accept the gift.

Awaiting Marie Thérèse in Vienna was a reminder of her mother and her preparations for the family's unsuccessful escape attempt. In the hope of gaining her freedom, Marie Antoinette had sent a casket of her jewellery to Brussels. This was Marie Antoinette's practical response to the needs of her family. Madame Campan reports in *The Private Life of Marie Antoinette* that 'The box remained a long time in Brussels, and at length got into the hands of Marie Thérèse, being delivered to her by the Emperor on her arrival in Vienna.' The jewels must have represented for her a symbol of previous times and a vivid physical reminder of her mother. They also offered the possibility of some financial independence from her Austrian cousins.

Louis XVIII had long had difficulties with the Viennese Court. The Emperor Francis II was keen to keep revolutionary principles out of his territory, but had been less than supportive to Marie Antoinette and her French family in their troubles. He was not above trying to exploit internal French strife to gain territory or other advantages for Austria. At times, the Emperor even refused to correspond with Louis XVIII, simply not replying to his letters.[7]

At the time of Marie Thérèse's arrival in Vienna, Louis was pushing hard to secure her consent to marriage with the Duc d'Angoulême. He wrote to plead the cause of his nephew and begged that she write or send word of 'something that I can show him to prove that you will have no repugnance in accepting the husband whom your father and mother chose for you … and whom they would choose for you again today if we were happy enough to have them in my position'. The King was prepared to use any emotional pressure to achieve the marriage of his nephew and niece. He made reference to her parents and was happy to cite their wishes in support of his case. There was an element of truth in what he wrote. Before the arrival of her younger brothers, Louis Joseph and Louis Charles, when the Duc d'Angoulême was the heir apparent to the French throne, he was indeed an attractive match for Marie Thérèse. This was very much Marie Antoinette's wish. Louis XVIII even provided a script for her should an alternative bridegroom be put forward. If challenged on the matter, he wrote, she should reply that 'I was pledged to my cousin the Duc d'Angoulême by my own desire and in accordance with the wishes of the King, my uncle, and in whose hands I have deposited my promise.'

Madame de Soucy reported to the King that the Princess had a great deal of courage and high principle with which she combined a quick intelligence and a sensitive heart. At the same time, Madame de Soucy noted that during the years after her uncles, the Comte de Provence and Comte d'Artois, had left France to go into exile, Madame Royale had received a bad impression of them and their apparent lack of loyalty to their elder brother in his time of trouble. There had been an inevitable conflict between Marie Antoinette and Louis XVI, who were imprisoned and trying to manage an enormously difficult and complex political situation, literally fighting for their lives, and the position of the émigré princes who, from the safety of exile, felt it appropriate to pursue a more hard-line approach to the unfolding Revolution. Furthermore, the refusal of the Comte de Provence and Comte d'Artois to return to France, despite their brother the King's order for them to do so, did not endear them to the beleaguered family.

Highly unwelcome to Louis XVIII was a suggestion from Madame de Soucy that the Princess was happy about the idea of marrying the Archduke Charles. This view was not supported by other observers, who indicated that although the twenty-four-year-old Archduke was a brave and competent soldier[8] who undoubtedly admired his French cousin, his feelings were not reciprocated by Madame Royale. Madame de Soucy herself had seen to that by intimating to Madame Royale that Charles's moral conduct was not all it should be; she knew that these allegations of licentious behaviour would not endear him to the upright and pious Marie Thérèse or help to promote a match between them. Charles also suffered from epilepsy, a condition that was not in his favour as a potential husband for Madame Royale. Moreover he was not French, nor heir to the throne of her beloved France. Marriage to him did not offer the possibility of being Queen of France.

To be subjected to this degree of emotional pressure from both her French and Austrian families seems cruel in the extreme. Louis XVIII was content to use her to his own political ends. At one point Madame Royale reports that she 'was sent for to the Emperor's cabinet' in an attempt to persuade her to change her mind and contemplate an Austrian marriage. At the Austrian Court, she was also called briefly Madame de Bretagne, as part of the attempt to make claim to those parts of France that might be inherited by a female. There were suggestions that Madame Royale had been subject to physical pressure and even abuse by her Austrian cousins in an attempt to persuade her to support them in pushing her claims to French territories that could then, they hoped, be transferred to the control of an Austrian husband. There were rumours that Francis II's Empress had even boxed Marie Thérèse's ears in an attempt to cajole her into going along with their plans for her future. In Vienna, after the initial welcome and under the formality and etiquette where she might have hoped for compassion, she found, with a few notable exceptions, a tendency to use her to further her cousins' political agenda. It seems to have been a hardening and embittering experience for her. She was only seventeen years old and had been imprisoned in chillingly severe isolation for more than a year; prior to that she had suffered a cruel imprisonment with her family. In addition, she had lost parents, her aunt and brother. One gets no real sense that anyone in a position of power or influence was protecting her interests or giving her the chance to recover from her ordeals.

By late January 1796, Madame de Soucy had been ejected from Vienna for her indiscretion in informing the Emperor of Madame Royale's negative feelings about his plans for her marriage to his brother. Marie Thérèse was delighted by the prospect of the departure of the trouble-making Madame de Soucy and wrote to her, 'Madame, I am writing to beg you very earnestly to go away from here without any further delays. If you cannot go today let it be at all events tomorrow after hearing mass. It is time this matter should end. I wish you a pleasant journey.' Madame de Soucy did indeed leave the next day, having received a farewell grant from the Imperial Treasury and her travelling expenses. Marie Thérèse was relieved to learn that she had left and could no longer embarrass her Royal mistress.

During this period of her life, there is almost an element of desperation in Louis XVIII's letters to Marie Thérèse in his wish to keep her on his side and malleable to his wishes. It is difficult to say how much he really felt for her. The cynicism and coldness of the early years of her life, when he felt little warmth for her mother and contempt for his brother, her father, may have been changed by the adversity experienced by the family. The twenty-three-year-old Duc d'Angoulême was not in love with his cousin. How could he be? He had not seen her since she was ten years old and he fourteen. He had his own problems to distract him from her concerns and had had no contact with her since 1789. Boys of fourteen are rarely enamoured of their ten-year-old cousins. Even if they are, it is unlikely that this affectionate feeling would survive many years of separation and relative hardship. Despite this, Louis XVIII was extremely keen to ensure that the alliance would go ahead and determined to counter the possibility of a marriage with the Archduke Charles. The King felt that it would be useful to foster a relationship between the cousins by encouraging the fiction that the Duc d'Angoulême had the most passionate and affectionate feelings for his cousin. Meanwhile, the young man's father, the Comte d' Artois, with whom Louis Antoine was staying in Edinburgh, was exhorted to encourage his son in his supposed passion for Marie Thérèse. Louis XVIII apparently wrote that his nephew had long felt the tenderest sympathy for his cousin in her horrible imprisonment. This may well have been the case, but it was not indicative of romantic feelings. Apparently, the Duc d'Angoulême had said that there could 'be neither happiness nor peace for him until his dear Thérèse was out of France'; this wording feels more like the uncle putting words into the mouth of his nephew.

In mid-January 1796, Marie Thérèse had a meeting with her father's former servant, Jean-Baptiste Cléry.[9] He reported back to Louis XVIII that

Madame Royale was determined to make the 'French match'. She wrote to her uncle in the same terms, saying, 'I can positively assure my uncle that I shall always remain faithfully attached to him, and also to the wishes of my mother and father with regard to my marriage, and that I shall reject all the Emperor's proposals for his brother. I will have nothing to do with them.' This cannot have been an easy position to take, while living under the Emperor's roof and being financially dependent on him. Emotionally, she must have wanted, and in some way needed, to please her rescuer and to live within a united and loving family. Her devotion to France and her French family was, nevertheless, unwavering. She articulated her difficult position to Louis XVIII:

> My Uncle, you have known me for a long time; but I hope you will never doubt me. My position is very difficult and delicate; but I have confidence in the God who has already helped me, and brought me out of so many dangers. He will never let me be false to the illustrious blood that flows in my veins. I would rather share the misfortunes of my relations, as long as misfortune is theirs, than be at the Court of a prince who is hostile to my family and my country. I have been well received in his dominions; but all this does not dazzle me. There are well-disposed people with me, but there are also some who are ill-disposed.

Despite all her sufferings since 1789, she wrote commending the French people to her uncle, saying, 'your heart is so kind: forgive them [the French people] and put an end to the war. Alas if my good father were alive I am sure he would do so.' She strongly advocated a peaceful approach to the restoration of the family to the throne, as had her father during his lifetime at Varennes, the Tuileries Palace and later in his Will. She felt that public opinion in Paris was beginning to turn against the Revolutionary government and its excesses, prompted by starvation and the bloodshed caused by the Terror. Louis XVIII received her remarks about France and the political situation with great pleasure and interest. He was impressed by her clear written expression of her feelings and the strength of her views. She noted that even members of the French Revolutionary elite were quite happy to hedge their political bets. Monsieur Bénézech, after negotiating the treaty for her release, had asked her to 'convey his homage' to Louis XVIII. Shrewdly, the Princess wrote, 'This is really true; the man is ambitious but he is an aristocrat at heart.'

Her religious faith had always been a great source of comfort to Marie Thérèse. After a gap of four years, she was able to take communion at an early morning Mass for the Dead on 21 January 1796. This was the third anniversary of her father's execution. At last, she was able to mourn publicly her dead family.

Madame Royale was delighted to be reacquainted (albeit only by the exchange of correspondence) with her uncle, but equally determined to behave as she felt right. The Abbé Edgeworth had been with her beloved father at the guillotine and Madame Royale wrote to him warmly once she was settled in Vienna. Louis XVIII had suggested to her that her letter, which was clearly intended for publication and propaganda purposes by the King-in-exile, would have more impact if she dated it immediately upon her release from the Tower of the Temple. Marie Thérèse would have no truck with this sort of deception. Despite her affection and respect for her King, she dated her letter accurately. She wrote to Louis XVIII explaining her action and her disobedience to his wishes. 'I will not hide from you that it would distress me to antedate my letter… But it is more suitable to my age and character to be as simple and accurate as truth itself. I hope my very dear uncle, that you will forgive this little act of resistance, in consideration of the reasons that prompt it.' She was also keen that her letter was not published, as she did not want a public display of her deepest feelings. This was very different from Louis' own approach: he was happy to have his letter about his feelings exposed to public scrutiny and comment, and to take any possible propaganda advantages that it might bring.

In Vienna, the physical circumstances of the Princess were comfortable but she was still kept apart from the French men and women who wanted to meet her. She must have felt keenly that she was living in a country at war with her native land, and the consequent conflicting loyalties. Even her uncle Louis XVIII's envoy in Vienna, Monseigneur de la Fare,[10] an émigré of longstanding, was not permitted to see her. He wrote, 'Madame is invisible to everyone, except for a few members of the family.' He went on, 'There is a fixed determination to keep our interesting Princess sequestered in this way until further orders.' Louis XVIII was very concerned that she was being kept deliberately isolated by her Austrian family to keep her away from French influence. She later wrote to her uncle denying that she had in any sense been kept prisoner at her cousin's Court; on the contrary, she asserted that it was she 'who begged that I might be alone. It was not suitable for me in my deep mourning and in my present position, to see people.' Her French Household comprised only Cléry and Huë, who were allowed to stay with the Princess and were provided with pensions from imperial funds.

At the time of her release from the Temple, the Princess's French family were scattered all over Europe and Marie Thérèse now went about trying to re-establish contact with them. Louis XVIII was in Verona and the Comte d'Artois was in Scotland, as was the Duc d'Angoulême. The Duc de Berry was with the Royalist army on the Rhine along with Condé and his son, the Duc d'Enghien. Madame Clotilde[11] and Marie Thérèse's surviving great aunts, Madame Adélaïde and Madame Victoire, were established in genteel poverty in Rome. The princesses were doing their own housework, including changing beds. The family of the disgraced regicide, the Duc d'Orléans, were wandering Europe and the United States of America in search of a comfortable refuge. Louis XVIII's Queen, Marie Joséphine, and her sister, the Comtesse d'Artois, were in Turin in northern Italy at the Court of their father, Victor Amadeus III, King of Sardinia.[12] She wrote that the greatest pleasure she had experienced in Vienna was hearing the qualities of her aunt universally acknowledged and praised. The two women had never met, but they had one vital link in common: Madame Élisabeth.

On the arrival of Madame de Chanterenne in the Tower of the Temple and during their early conversations, Madame Royale had listed her surviving relations and noted to Renete that she looked forward to establishing a warm correspondence with them, in due course being able to spend time with them. A few months after her arrival in Vienna, as we have seen, a very frequent, frank and warm correspondence had been established with her uncle, Louis XVIII. She was also regularly in touch with her great aunts in Italy and Louis XVIII's Queen, Marie Joséphine, who was settled by this time in Budweiss[13] in Bohemia. She and the Duc d'Angoulême wrote often to each other. Marie Thérèse felt aggrieved and hurt that other relatives, such as the Spanish Borbons, had been so much less forthcoming and regular in their correspondence. Deprived of her beloved close family, she was very keen to re-form and strengthen other family connections. The Comte and Comtesse d'Artois (her aunt and uncle and parents-in-law to be) were noticeably bad correspondents. More than six months after leaving prison, she had received only one letter from the Edinburgh-based Comte d'Artois, and nothing at all from his wife in Turin.

On 16 October 1796, the Comtesse d'Artois' father died,[14] and Marie Thérèse wrote to express her condolences but received no response. However, while the Duc d'Angoulême's mother was living in Turin, she suffered from terrible depression so perhaps her lack of letter writing may be excused by her own sufferings. The Comtesse d'Artois would spend the days locked up in her darkened bedroom, and even seriously contemplated giving up the world and going into a convent. Helped by her sister-in-law, Madame Clotilde, she eventually managed to overcome her depression. Despite not being a good correspondent, the Comtesse d'Artois was prepared to bestir herself in an effort to go and see her niece and prospective daughter-in-law. However, she was refused permission to travel to Vienna by the Imperial Court. The ladies were no doubt disappointed, and Louis XVIII was outraged that the visit of such a close relation was forbidden. The refusal may have compounded fears that his marriage plans for his niece were somehow under attack. Madame Royale's cousin and prospective brother-in-law, the Duc de Berry, had also written to her very affectionately, if not frequently. She was delighted to hear of his exploits with the Condé Army, noting that he was brave almost to the point of recklessness. Her maternal aunt, Maria Carolina, Queen of Naples, was a very infrequent and tardy correspondent. To her great aunts, Madame Adélaïde and Madame Victoire, Madame Royale wrote that 'my respect and affection for you have never changed, that I often think of you'. She went on to say, 'We must not think of the past, it is too dreadful. It would give me great pleasure, *mes tantes*, to be with you in Rome; but I am quiet here, which pleases me much.' Not even with her closest family was she able, or willing, to discuss the traumatising events she had experienced during her years of imprisonment. It is difficult to believe that such a suppression of her experiences was beneficial to her.

Marie Thérèse by Heinrich Füger, 1796

Marie Thérèse sent to Louis XVIII a portrait of herself which had been painted in Vienna early in 1796. She had grown up and changed considerably since the last time he had seen her at the Tuileries Palace in June 1791. Monseigneur de la Fare was finally allowed access to see the

Princess by the Austrian authorities, on 6 March 1796. Following the visit he reported back to Louis XVIII that he had been received kindly by Marie Thérèse. He wrote, 'I was greatly touched by the kindness Madame Royale showed me, and I took careful note of every expression of her profound interest in the Royal cause and in the émigrés of every class.' She was particularly interested in discussing the well-being of her relatives who were exiled throughout Europe.

Marie Thérèse was chaperoned at this meeting by Madame de Chanclos, a middle-aged lady of French descent who had married an Austrian nobleman and was Grand Mistress or governess to the Emperor's daughter, Marie Louise.[15] She was loved at the Austrian Court for the diligent way she carried out her duties. Madame Royale described her as 'an excellent person'. Marie Thérèse was fully aware of Madame de Chanclos' devotion to the Emperor and his family, but equally confident of the lady's loyalty to her. It was comforting to Marie Thérèse that Madame de Chanclos had known her mother during her childhood in Vienna, and was good, just and upright. She had living with her two nieces who were pretty and charming girls of eighteen and twenty, whose lively and youthful company Marie Thérèse very much enjoyed. A long-standing and close relationship was established with one of Madame Chanclos' nieces, Marie Françoise de Roisin, later the Comtesse d'Esterhazy,[16] who married into the prominent and enormously wealthy Hungarian art-collecting family. They had been well liked by Marie Antoinette, no doubt a recommendation to her daughter. Madame Royale was also introduced to Anne Charlotte Henriette de Choisy,[17] a Frenchwoman and émigré, by Monseigneur de la Fare. She showed warmth and kindness to the lonely Princess. Despite the difference in their ages, Mademoiselle de Choisy being eighteen years older than the Princess, they became friends and Mademoiselle de Choisy joined Marie Thérèse's Household. According to Madame du Montet, the niece of M. de la Fare, this friendship provoked jealousy among other émigrés who wished for their womenfolk to hold posts close to the Princess, and Mademoiselle de Choisy's family had not even been in service at Versailles!

We have a description of Madame Royale's appearance at this time from the memoirs of a niece of Cardinal de la Fare who was living as a boarder at the Convent of the Visitation next door to the Princesses' residence at the Belvedere, and she visited often during her stay in Vienna. She described Marie Thérèse as having inherited her mother's oval face, blue eyes and small mouth; otherwise she looked like her father. In terms of figure, she was short-waisted. Her voice was harsh like the voices of many of the women of the Bourbon family (Madame Campan noted this in Madame Adélaïde);[18] Marie Thérèse's words might be kind, but they did not always sound that way. This was often off-putting to those meeting her. She seems to have totally lacked her mother's passion for clothes and fashion, not even interested in the symbolic importance of costume for royalty. During her sojourn in Vienna she was dressed in deep mourning. She walked energetically and purposefully. She enjoyed taking part in the Convent girls' games and they tried to get hold of a strand of her hair as a souvenir of the Princess.

Early in 1796, Marie Thérèse was presented at a special Court in Vienna with the sisters of the Emperor. This was her first public appearance since her arrival in her cousin's capital city. She had had to be schooled in the etiquette and manners of the Austrian Court on her arrival in Vienna. 'Everyone who could possibly attend, whether Austrian or foreign, was eager to appear on the occasion. Madame won all the success that she deserves on so many grounds, and her praises were on every tongue. The Neapolitan Ambassador presented various Frenchmen and women to Madame Royale. She showed marked pleasure on seeing the Frenchmen who were present,' wrote Monsieur de la Fare. The Princess took satisfaction from the attentions she received and was very clearly moved by the kind reception given to her. She had become a fashionable celebrity in Vienna and a figure of romance and curiosity. Gouverneur Morris, the American diplomat who saw her at this time, comments on her resemblance to her father and that she was looking well. The evening after her presentation, members of the Imperial family accompanied her to the theatre. This was a return to the Court formalities she had known in her pre-Revolutionary childhood, and she relished it. Later in the week, she received ambassadors and foreign ministers, and the next day their wives. Monseigneur de la Fare noted that the Princess was amiable and charming to her visitors during these presentations. It seemed to him that she had not been embittered by her experiences and sufferings during her imprisonment: 'Madame's strength of mind enables her to repress her grief,' he wrote. Other commentators were equally complimentary about her, praising her intelligence, her circumspection, her willingness to learn and her passionate commitment to France. She had learned the art of keeping her thoughts to herself during her captivity, and she was able to utilise these lessons in tact and discretion during her time at her cousin's Court.

Marie Thérèse was sometimes aggrieved at not being adequately informed by her family of the doings of other members of the Bourbon family. The Habsburg Court was happy to play on this deficiency and exploit the divisions within the Bourbons. This feeling of being let down by her Bourbon family was exacerbated by the failings of the postal system. On 22 August, the Duc d'Angoulême fell from his horse and broke his collarbone. Madame Royale was embarrassed and hurt to be informed of this accident by her Austrian cousins rather than hearing it directly from the patient, or their uncle. In fact, shortly after the incident, the injured Duc d'Angoulême, had dictated a letter to Louis XVIII informing Marie Thérèse of what had happened, since he was unable to write himself. The letter was reassuring about his well-being and expressed his deep affection for her. Unfortunately, the letter did not arrive in Vienna until 2 September, long after the news had been given to her by the rather gleeful Austrians. Madame Royale was soon mollified on hearing of the efforts made by her cousin to keep her informed of his health; however, this incident highlights that even the most diligent correspondent could be frustrated by postal delays, leading to otherwise unnecessary misunderstandings and annoyances.

In April 1796, the exiled King suffered two mishaps: being ejected from his temporary home in Verona, and being the object of an assassination attempt from which he received minor wounds – although some suggested that the assassination was faked to try to gain sympathy from the various courts of Europe. His forced departure was the result of Bonaparte having conquered Venice and the government of the defeated Republic of Venice being ordered to ensure that Louis XVIII leave Verona. He had hoped to be able to join the Condé Army, led by Louis Joseph Bourbon, Prince of Condé, but was prevented from doing so. Louis XVIII was subsequently offered refuge by the King of Prussia, Frederick William II, at Blankenburg in the territory of Brunswick. He was joined there by the Duc d'Angoulême and the Abbé Edgeworth.

Marie Thérèse meanwhile spent the summer of 1796 at the Schönbrunn Palace with the Austrian Emperor and his family, enjoying country pleasures. The younger archduchesses became like sisters to her. She visited her maternal aunt Marie Elizabeth,[19] who was the Abbess at the Imperial and Royal Convent for Noble Ladies in Prague.

By November of that year, however, the King of Prussia had died and the unwillingness of his successor Frederick William III[20] to give Louis XVIII and the Duc d'Angoulême sanctuary meant that they were on the move again in search of asylum. The Bourbon princes appealed to the goodwill of the Russian Emperor Paul I, who had dazzled the court of Versailles with his intellectual brilliance and sophistication in happier days, and was acquainted with the Bourbons. Louis XVIII wrote of the Russian Emperor: 'One must admit that, of all the Sovereigns, he is the only one who has preserved any sense of honour. He has pride and, he is a man of feeling.' He had succeeded to the throne on the death of his mother Catherine the Great[21] in November 1796. On the occasion of the Empress's death, Marie Thérèse had written that she hoped that the Emperor Paul would prove as good a friend to the Bourbons as had his mother, who had been so kind in trying to help them. He did. In January 1797, Louis received the offer of the use of the Castle of Mittau in the Duchy of Courland in Russian territory. Mittau is now known as Jelgava in Latvia and is approximately 40 miles from Riga and the Baltic coast, and 450 miles from St Petersburg. It had been the capital of Courland until 1795. Madame de Gontaut wrote in her memoirs:

> The King, Louis XVIII, was then at Grodno[22] but he had a great desire to come to England. To this end he sent Monsieur thither to obtain permission for him to seek shelter in this kingdom. But the Emperor Paul having proposed that he should settle at Mittau, with the other members of the Royal Family, he felt that he could not refuse, although it was the desire of his heart to be as near to France as possible. Monsieur departed for London and the King for Russia, both hoping to meet again soon.

As the months passed, Marie Thérèse's novelty value to Viennese society, as the romantic and tragic *Orpheline du Temple*, began to fade. As she wrote in a letter to her aunt, the Archduchess Abbess, she was able to lead a quiet, even retired, life at the Belvedere Palace with a small Household of attendants. She resumed her interrupted education and studied with masters. This reduced scale of Household also helped her financial situation. However, it was a narrow and restricted life for a young woman who had suffered so much and needed warmth and affection to help her recover from her terrible experiences. Despite this, Marie Thérèse wrote to her uncle that she was 'happy' in Vienna, which unsettled Louis XVIII; was she being 'Austrianised', he asked himself? Louis had written around this time, 'It seems to me that her resolution[23] is not as firm as it was, and I am told that the French who are permitted to pay Court to her do not receive the welcome they have a right to expect from her.' Later, he would instruct one of his émigré courtiers to visit Marie Thérèse to assess her views and feelings and to gain comfort that she was not being influenced by the Austrian Court against her French family. Rather reluctantly, the Marquis de Bonnay called on Madame Royale in order to establish her real views. The issue of the apparently chilly welcome received from her by her co-patriots was broached. It would appear that the French were not popular in Vienna, often being seen as arrogant spongers. While Madame Royale had received with all appropriate warmth the French men and women of whom she approved, the less virtuous and worthy had not been so warmly welcomed by the Princess.

Regarding the Angoulême marriage, Monsieur de Bonnay was able to give his royal master complete reassurance about Marie Thérèse's intentions. He reported back that during her early days in Vienna her cousin the Emperor had indeed tried to put pressure on her to marry his brother Charles, but she had made it entirely clear to Francis II that she was committed to betrothal to her French cousin. Madame Royale's resolute approach had secured from Francis II his 'solemn promise' that he would 'not do anything to prevent her marriage to the Duc d'Angoulême'. As Monsieur de Bonnay wrote, the only thing that would override these sensible practical considerations was 'passion'. Madame Royale was not a passionate person, but one of practical common sense and 'essentially reasonable'.[24] Having dealt decisively with the question of her marriage,

Marie Thérèse had secured her position and therefore did not feel it necessary to restate it forcefully; it was an established fact in her own mind that she would in due course marry the Duc d'Angoulême. She was, however, in no immediate hurry to marry her cousin. She would do so when she felt it was an appropriate time and all the necessary practical and financial arrangements had been made. She also hoped that her family would be settled in a more permanent home before her wedding.

One of the problems that beset Marie Thérèse during her exile in Vienna was lack of money. She was well provided for by the Emperor for her own immediate needs. She was also included in the ceremonial at Court; for example, she accompanied the Archduchess Amalia to a magnificent party given by the Emperor at his villa in Luxembourg in October 1798, at which the other guests included Prince Augustus of England.[25] Her financial resources were, however, greatly stretched by the requests for financial aid from the numerous émigrés who appealed to her for help. She was distressed by the calls on her finances and her inability to respond positively to all the requests. Trained by the years of austerity in the Temple, she lived as economically as possible in order to be able to help those who asked for her assistance. In an attempt to manage and respond to the flow of numerous letters asking for aid, she appointed Monseigneur de la Fare to become her *premier aumônier* in 1815. He had the authority to decide who was deserving of charitable grants and who was just chancing their luck.

One of the most interesting appeals came from Count Axel von Fersen, on behalf of Madame de Korff. In order to facilitate the French Royal Family's escape attempt in 1791, Madame de Korff had lent significant sums (over 250,000 francs) to Louis XVI and Marie Antoinette. The Royal couple had signed loan bills promising to pay interest from 1 June 1791. Marie Antoinette had honoured the interest payments as long as possible, but as her captivity became more confined and closely supervised, and her resources reduced, she was unable to keep up payments. Madame de Korff, now herself in exile with her mother and in severely straitened financial circumstances, appealed to Marie Thérèse for repayment of the loan made to Marie Antoinette. The honourable Princess was determined to repay the Baroness de Korff. Axel von Fersen, who was himself owed 600,000 francs spent trying to rescue the Royal Family, had hoped that the Emperor would repay the loan made to his aunt and uncle at a time of great need. Marie Thérèse was distressed by the privations of Madame de Korff and her mother, and also by her own inability to help them, so appealed to the Emperor and was able to secure the sum of 1,000 Austrian ducats. During the remainder of her time with the Austrian Court, by virtue of being economical, Marie Thérèse was able to repay some of the money owed by her parents to various other creditors. She was able to send Madame de Korff 3,000 ducats on the eve of her departure for

Mittau, in the spring of 1799. This did not finally settle the matter of the repayment of debts, which was still going on in 1815, but Marie Thérèse shrewdly wrote that she was not in a position to quantify the total debts of her parents, and therefore not able to decide fairly to whom the available funds should be allocated. Nevertheless she was anxious to give assistance, wherever possible, to the cases that she and her adviser felt to be the most deserving of her help.

A British sponsored invasion of France at the Quiberon peninsula in Brittany took place in June 1795. Encouraged by exaggerated reports of support for counter-revolution, 3,000 men landed there, equipped with supplies for twenty times that number. They were joined by only 10,000 supporters. Though well equipped, they were lacking discipline and clear lines of command so the Republican General Hoch was able to defeat them easily; the peninsula was retaken and the 6,000 prisoners captured were treated very harshly. Of the émigré prisoners captured, more than 600, some estimates say 750, were executed, along with 108 local Royalist and counter-revolutionary supporters. The Republican government was anxious to suppress this guerrilla-like uprising and to ensure there were no copycat revolts. Resentment of the severe treatment of the rebels by the government festered long afterwards, and this and subsequent uprisings were difficult to suppress. Marie Thérèse very much wished to support the victims of the failed Quiberon invasion of 1795, but she was not in a financial position to do so. Indeed, Monseigneur de la Fare wrote to Louis XVIII that he sometimes found Marie Thérèse in low spirits and pessimistic about the future.

Marie Thérèse was profoundly saddened by the sufferings of the émigrés. In his biography *The Youth of the Duchesse d'Angoulême*, Imbert de Saint Amand wrote of the suffering of Marie Thérèse at her inability to aid her compatriots:

> Noble and generous herself, she was inconsolable at being unable to relieve such miseries; and the decay, the poverty, the humiliations and anguish of these unhappy nobles whom she had seen so brilliant and so haughty at Versailles in her childhood, incessantly caused her painful reflections. At every instant her heart bled. One day she heard of the Quiberon disaster and the odious massacre of prisoners; on another, of the catastrophes in Vendée and the execution of François Athanase de Charette.[26] Again it was the proscriptions of which the royalists were victims after the 18th Fructidor,[27] the fusillades in the plain of Grenelle, the deportations in iron cages, the exiles to Cayenne,[28] which was called the dull guillotine. All the families in which the daughter of Louis XVI felt any interest were attainted. The wind of misfortune blew from all the cardinal points at once, and the French aristocrats, tossed from one tempest to another, were hounded by an implacable fatality from every

> shore. All that was occurring overwhelmed with grief a patriotic Princess, for whom, as a poet has said, it was an inexpressible vexation to ascend and descend the staircase of another. She was astonished at the levity of the émigrés when she saw them amuse themselves and smile. She sympathized less with them than with the loyal and heroic peasants of Vendée, who had waged what Napoleon called a war of giants, and to whom the Restoration showed itself so ungrateful later on.[29]

One of the main concerns expressed by de la Fare was the spiritual development of 'Madame de France', as he referred to Madame Royale, during her time in Austria. He wrote to the Archduchess Marie Anne, who had become something of a mother figure to Marie Thérèse, saying that he believed that 'she was the best person to guide' Marie Thérèse. He suggested that Madame Royale should 'saturate her mind' with the spiritual writings of Bossuet, Fénelon, Massillon and many others. He was keen that she should not only read widely, but meditate on Monsieur Bossuet's *L'Histoire Universelle*, *Politique sacréee tirée des livres saints*, and his principal work *Craisons funèbres*. He also suggested Massillon's *Petit Careme* and *Telemarque*; *Les Entretiens de Phocion*; *Les Dialogues des morts*; *La Vie de Theodose*; and all works by Monsieur de Fénelon. The Archduchess described the difficultly of obtaining quality French books at a time of war between Austria and France, but she noted that some of the books mentioned were already in the Princess's possession.[30] Marie Thérèse had always taken her religious and spiritual life seriously. The time spent so intimately with Madame Élisabeth in the Tower of the Temple had developed and strengthened her religious faith. We learn at this time, June 1797, that she had herself written prayers for the times when the words of prayer did not come easily to her. In them she thanked God that she felt no hatred for the 'authors of her misfortunes'. Her eager forgiveness is a great credit to her and her developed, though youthful, spirituality.

The motivation of de la Fare in recommending this reading matter was 'the desire to see Madame de France as perfect as possible'. He noted that she would always be an object of public interest. His anticipation and hope was, no doubt, that she would one day be Queen of France and it was to be hoped the mother of '*enfants de France*'. He also recommended wide-ranging secular reading to Madame Royale to continue her education, which had been so circumscribed during her years of captivity with her family, and even more so during her period of solitary confinement.

Napoleon Bonaparte figured large in the life of Madame Royale. She detested him with a passion and regarded him as the agent of all her troubles and those of her family and her beloved France. In 1797, his victories throughout Europe sent the Imperial children and Marie Thérèse fleeing from Vienna to seek safety in exile in Prague. The peace settlement, articulated in the Treaty of Campo Formio on 17 October 1797 between France and Austria, meant that they were able to return to Vienna. However, Louis XVIII felt it better that Marie Thérèse stay in Prague rather than return to join the rest of the Imperial family in Vienna. Madame Royale had apparently settled comfortably with her aunt, the Archduchess Marie Élisabeth, and could safely remain with her. His niece did not agree with his recommendation. Louis XVIII was always keen to detach Marie Thérèse from Austrian influence, and he felt that her absence from Vienna could be beneficial to his cause. He also expressed concern that if she returned to Vienna she would be brought into contact with negotiators from the French Revolutionary government, which would cause her distress.

Unbeknownst to Madame Royale, Louis was also planning for the Duc d'Angoulême to visit his fiancée during her stay in Prague. Whilst determined to push forward with the match, Louis felt it important that the young people should get to know each other better before their marriage. He was very conscious from his correspondence with his niece that she was brighter than her intended husband. He wanted to be sure that Madame Royale understood the position and was content to go ahead with the union, knowing the character of her husband to be.

Marie Thérèse was more than capable of resisting her uncle and doing what she felt was right. She returned to Vienna, against her uncle's advice and wishes, travelling with her cousin, the Archduchess Amalia, and Madame de Chanclos. She later justified her decision to return to her uncle by explaining that the Archduchess Marie Élisabeth was suffering from a chest disease. It was therefore not suitable for Madame Royale to spend time with the Archduchess for two reasons: firstly, the potential strain on the Archduchess's own health, and secondly, the Bourbon family's history of susceptibility to lung diseases – Marie Thérèse did not want to expose herself to this health risk. Louis had not been aware of the Archduchess's ill health and the words 'chest disease' had a particular resonance and dread for him; his father the Dauphin Louis Ferdinand, his mother the Dauphine Marie Josèphe, and his eldest brother the Duc de Bourgogne had all died prematurely from chest complaints, almost certainly tuberculosis. He concurred with his niece's decision in this matter and was content to be guided by her judgement.

Foiled in his attempt to arrange a meeting between Marie Thérèse and her cousin Louis Antoine in Prague, Louis XVIII hoped that the young people might be able to meet and get to know each other in Vienna, so set about organising this. The Comte d'Artois was also keen that the young people should have an opportunity to meet before their marriage. Louis XVIII's intention was that the visit of the Duc d'Angoulême to his cousin should be incognito and therefore not require the usual formalities of a royal visit of a prince to a princess. However, the bride-to-be did not favour the idea of an unofficial visit by the Duc d'Angoulême, writing to her uncle that it was 'not possible for Angoulême to be incognito – all is known by the Court. Everyone who comes to see me is known.' Marie Thérèse felt that if the Emperor did not receive the Duc d'Angoulême 'as he ought', the Bourbon Prince would be offended. Alternatively, if the Prince did not meet the Emperor Francis II, the incognito visit and any perceived discourtesy to her host would be blamed on her and would undermine her position at the Viennese Court. No doubt she was also more than aware that her Austrian cousin was negotiating with the new French government and that an unannounced visit by a scion of the former ruling family of France had the potential to be embarrassing to the Emperor. Her view was, further, that an incognito visit would only be appropriate if the date of their marriage was imminent. It was not, and therefore it would be better to wait patiently for a visit. Marie Thérèse had learned patience in the hard school of the Tower of the Temple. In this case, Louis XVIII's eagerness to secure the marriage seems to have outrun his normally highly honed political sense. Marie Thérèse wrote to him, 'I ask your pardon, my very dear uncle, for all these observations; but my affection for you and my whole family makes me speak frankly when their interests are at stake.' A subsequent conversation between Madame de Chanclos and Francis II confirmed that Marie Thérèse's view of the political situation was accurate; the Emperor would have found an incognito visit by the Duc d'Angoulême 'impossible' as it might well have alienated the French Directory government at a time of delicate negotiations.

Marie Thérèse was fully aware of the financial practicalities of life, the expense of maintaining a Royal Household and the need to secure her financial independence. General Jean-Baptiste Bernadotte,[31] the future King of Norway and Sweden, who had been sent to Vienna as an envoy of the all-conquering French republican Directory government was present in Vienna during 1797 and in talks with the Austrian government. Marie Thérèse was hopeful that her cousin Francis would include an income for her in the terms of any treaty with the French. She wrote to her uncle during this period:

> I confess I should like the Emperor to do something for me so that I might live independently of the Republic, especially, but also of all other Powers. I do not like being a burden, and I think that at this moment there is not a single ally to be depended upon. I even think that you need not congratulate yourself on the Spanish ones this is why I feel since we can count on no one that it would be best to live independently. These are the reasons that make me wish the Emperor[32] did something for me, in his Treaty with France.[33] But from the Republic I look for nothing in the world; I detest it quite as much as I should.

In addition, there was the suggestion that Marie Thérèse should receive those legacies from her grandmother, the Empress Maria Theresa, which had been left to Marie Antoinette and apparently never paid over to her by the executors of the Empress's Will. There was even debate as to whether Marie Antoinette's dowry on her marriage to the Dauphin in 1770 had ever been paid to her new family.

During Marie Thérèse's time in Vienna and Prague, she became close friends with Francis II's youngest sister, the Archduchess Amalia; but she died tragically in 1798. As often in Marie Thérèse's life, those she loved died prematurely. Marie Thérèse was devastated by her death and wrote to her uncle in heart-rending terms of her sense of loss. She was increasingly anxious to leave Vienna and go to join her French family. By late March 1798, Louis XVIII and her fiancé the Duc d'Angoulême had arrived at Mittau. An entourage of a hundred émigré courtiers had followed the Bourbons east. Now at last one of her paternal relations was in a position to provide a stable home for Marie Thérèse.

In May 1799, as an assured Princess and with an understanding of her social obligations, she held a Court to say farewell to the émigré community in Vienna. There was nothing now to stop her from leaving Vienna and travelling to meet the remnants of her French family. Nevertheless, Louis XVIII feared that the Emperor would attempt to prevent her departure. His fears were unfounded. The Emperor had clearly given up any hope of a marriage between his brother Charles and the Princess. Marie Thérèse set off from Vienna for her new home in Russia on 4 May 1799 accompanied by Baron Huë and his wife. She travelled 700 miles over a month. The Emperor Francis II ensured that she travelled with all due ceremony, as was fitting to a young woman who was a French Princess, his cousin and about to marry an heir to the throne of France. The Emperor of Russia treated her with equal respect as she travelled through his lands to meet her fiancé. She was greeted at the border by the Duc de Villequier, Louis XVIII's premier *gentilhomme*. Her life as a married woman was about to begin.

6

Marriage and Mittau

JUNE 1799–JANUARY 1801

What of Marie Thérèse's husband-to-be? His experiences had been very different from hers in the ten years since they had last met. He had endured exile from France, but not a nightmarish imprisonment nor the death of mother, father and brother – experiences which had been the lot of his bride to be.

Louis Antoine, Duc d'Angoulême, was born at Versailles on 8 August 1775. He was the son of Charles, Comte d'Artois, the second younger brother of Louis XVI and Princess Marie Thérèse de Savoie,[1] to whom the Comte d'Artois had been married as a sixteen-year-old. The Comte d'Artois was very much part of Marie Antoinette's select Trianon set. Handsome, rather suave, he was a keen participant in the amateur dramatics so loved by the young royals. Lucie de la Tour du Pin's description was that 'the Comte d'Artois was young with the charming good looks which he never lost'. Enjoying life's pleasures to the full, a passionate lover of horse racing, decadent and not particularly intelligent, he was reactionary and hard-line in his political views. He believed that reforms of the French system of government were unnecessary and to be resisted.

The birth of Louis Antoine was greeted with joy not only within the family and Court, but throughout France. Coming after his Uncle Louis Stanislas the Comte de Provence and his father in the succession, he was third in line to the throne until such time as the King and Queen produced a son of their own. Madame Campan's memoirs[2] described Marie Antoinette's reaction to the birth of Louis Antoine:

> custom required that the Royal Family and the whole court should be present at the *accouchement* of the Princesses; the Queen was, therefore,

> obliged to stay a whole day in her sister-in-law's chamber. The moment the Comtesse d'Artois was informed a Prince was born, she put her hand to her forehead and exclaimed with energy, 'My god, how happy I am!' The Queen felt very differently at this involuntary and natural exclamation. Nevertheless her behaviour was perfect. She bestowed all possible marks of tenderness upon the young mother, and would not leave her until she was again back in bed.

On her way back to her apartments following the birth of Louis Antoine, the outwardly calm Marie Antoinette was confronted by the fishwives of Paris urging her in the crudest language to produce a son of her own. In the privacy of her rooms alone with Madame Campan, the Queen wept with disappointment and frustration at her lack of a child.

Louis Antoine was brought up at the Château Beauregard in St Cloud, about three miles from Versailles, with his younger brother Charles Ferdinand, Duc de Berry, who was born in 1778. Marie Antoinette treated the little Duc d'Angoulême with marked favour, for example presenting him with a very fine diamond clasp for his epaulettes. The plan for his upbringing was that he would be trained to be a soldier. In 1785 he was given his own regiment, which had previously been known as the Régiment de Savoie Carignan. He was short in stature. Books and study did not appeal to him and he showed a marked lack of intellectual curiosity. As a child, the young Duc d'Angoulême was regarded as a rather apathetic, listless boy lacking in initiative and rather cold in nature. Lucie de la Tour du Pin's memoirs record that she was not impressed by the education given to the young Prince and his brother by their tutor, the Duc de Sérent. She compared it unfavourably with the rigorous intellectual training given to the Orléans children by their tutor, Madame de Genlis. Madame de la Tour du Pin wrote that the Duc d'Angoulême and the Duc de Berry 'were never seen and knew as little of France as if they had been heirs to the throne of China'. The Duc d'Angoulême was also appointed Grand Prior of France.

As a Prince of the blood and a grandson of France, he was included in the elaborate Royal ceremonial surrounding the calling of the Estates General and the beginning of its proceedings in May 1789. The *General Evening Post* of London of 6 May reported that two days previously 'at ten o'clock his Majesty, accompanied by Monsieur, the Comte d'Artois and the Duke of Angoulême mounted his coronation coach, and proceeded to the parish church of Notre-Dame at Versailles'. There are reports of the magnificent carriages and splendid horses, their manes decorated with variegated plumage.

The Duc d'Angoulême was forced to quit France with his family when he was almost fourteen years old for '*crainte de fureur populaire*' (fear of the rage of the people). His father was one of the most loathed people in

France for his reactionary views. He was one of the first émigrés to leave France in July 1789. The Comte d'Artois travelled at a leisurely pace through France and Italy and arrived in the court of his father-in-law at Turin in September 1789. He was followed into exile shortly afterwards by his wife and their two young sons. Even after Louis Antoine's departure, the newly constituted National Assembly was discussing the level of annual allowance to be made to the young Prince and the rest of his family.

The Royal Family in exile was joined in Turin by the two surviving Tantes, Mesdames Adélaïde and Victoire, in early 1791. They had left France in February, fearful for their safety following the events of 1789 and loathing the increasing momentum of change in France. During 1791, the Bourbon family in exile was with reason greatly concerned for the safety of the King, Queen, their children and Madame Élisabeth. They watched with impotent concern as the position of the Royal Family became more and more difficult. The Comte d'Artois was, however, still clear in his own mind that the only way to stop the Revolution was by hard-line methods. He advocated the invasion of France by foreign forces friendly to the Royalist cause. In June 1791, the Bourbons based in Turin were initially told that the 'Varennes escape' attempt from Paris had been successful. Later reports instead reported that the King and his family had been forced to return to Paris in the most ignominious of circumstances. There was, however, some good news. The Duc d'Angoulême's mother eventually received a letter from her sister confirming that both she and her husband, the Comte de Provence, had made good their escape from France and had reached Bruxelles safely. The Comtesse de Provence arrived in January 1792. From the safety of his place of exile, the Comte d'Artois did not support Louis XVI's acceptance of the new Constitution in September 1792. This confirmed his deep lack of understanding of the predicament in which his brother found himself and how far Royal power had ebbed away even in the relatively short time he had been absent from France.

The Duc d'Angoulême and his brother grew to maturity in exile and relative poverty. They were, however, surrounded by their family and accompanied in their wanderings by a large contingent of loyal émigré courtiers. There was a measure of continuity and security. While the Bourbon family was based in Turin, the refugee French men and women made no effort to endear themselves to the local population. Lucie de la Tour du Pin wrote of her experiences of the émigré community: 'They all brought the airs and insolence of Paris society. They mocked at everything and were everlastingly amazed that there should exist in the world anything besides themselves and their ways.' The French émigrés seemingly took pleasure in ridiculing the customs and dress of their hosts. While the nobility of Turin sympathised with the plight of the Royal Family, the general populace was supportive of the Revolutionary changes happening in France. There were physical attacks on the émigrés. Madame Clotilde as a French Princess and the wife of the heir to the throne of Savoy felt torn between her conflicting loyalties. The King Victor Amadeus III, her father-in-law, was keen to be helpful to her family and her countrymen and loathed the tide of Revolutionary change spreading from France. But he was conscious of being the near neighbour of the larger and much more militarily powerful France. As Bonaparte proved himself to be a highly successful general and an aggressive conqueror of neighbouring territories, this fear and tension became more and more of an issue for the Royal Family of Savoy and their French guests.

During the time they spent together, Louis XVIII's observation of the Duc d'Angoulême's lack of intellectual curiosity troubled him; he himself was fond of learning, finding reading, study and intellectual conversation a comfort during the long days of exile in foreign lands. When he saw the quality of Madame Royale's thought and expression in her letters to him, Louis XVIII felt that she was very much her betrothed's intellectual superior. This was an aspect of the proposed marriage between Louis Antoine and Marie Thérèse that worried Louis XVIII; he feared that this might prove to be an area of incompatibility between the young couple. The Duc d'Angoulême wrote to his fiancée with great affection, although maybe not all his letters were his own work. Those who knew Louis Antoine well spoke of his kind-hearted, generous nature, but it was felt that he lacked easy charm and animation. He may possibly have inherited some of his mother's depressive tendencies. He longed for activity and occupation. Louis Antoine's younger brother, the Duc de Berry, possessed a *joie de vivre* and easy manner in public, which made him well liked among the army and the émigrés, or at least among those who did not disapprove of his libertine ways. His elder brother does not seem to have shared his taste for feminine company.

Like so many French émigrés, the Comte d'Artois sought a settled home outside France. Having wandered around Europe for five years since quitting France, he sought refuge in England. Here he found support for his cause. War raged with Napoleonic France, but the Channel and the British navy gave protection. The Comte d'Artois had moved to live in the British Isles in 1794, and with the exception of occasional sojourns outside the country, for example to meet his brother in Sweden 1804, was settled in the United Kingdom until 1814. A blue plaque at 72 South Audley Street in Mayfair marks his residence in London. His mistress, Louise de Polastron,[3] a sister-in-law of Gabrielle de Polignac, Marie Thérèse's governess, was settled in a small house in Thayer Street, just off Marylebone High Street. The whole area around Baker Street and Marylebone was occupied by so many French aristocratic émigrés that it was dubbed 'Versailles in Baker Street'. A French chapel was operating in King Street[4] just off Portman Square from 1793 onwards, providing Roman Catholic religious rites and the companionship of their countrymen and co-religionists for the French émigré community. The Comte d'Artois with his princely charm and good looks made himself agreeable to English aristocratic society. He was invited everywhere, attending the elegant parties of the time in London and visiting the country homes of his aristocratic English friends. He was well received by a government that was at war with Republican and Napoleonic France for most of this period. William Pitt the Younger,[5] the Prime Minister, was a keen supporter of the exiles and keen to offer them moral and financial succour, wherever possible. London offered many pleasures and distractions. Both Louis Antoine and his father sat for miniaturists, and the likenesses of the exiled Princes were advertised for sale in the exhibition catalogue of the Royal Academy in Piccadilly.[6]

In 1795 and 1796 the Duc d'Angoulême spent time in Edinburgh with his father, who had been driven away from London by the pressing demands of his many creditors. His passion for horse racing cannot have helped. According to Madame de Gontaut, there was a claim against him for debts incurred by suppliers to the Condé Army. In 1789, as the King's brother, merchants and others were happy to give him credit; but after his flight from France and the collapse of the Bourbon monarchy, creditors were less understanding. Holyroodhouse as a Royal palace, dilapidated as it was, gave the Comte d'Artois refuge from those pursuing him for money as long as he did not stray too far from its environs. The local nobility rushed to visit their Royal visitors and pay their respects. Of the time he spent in Scotland, the Duc d'Angoulême writes: 'My father and I are treated as well as possible here by the Scots, neither the country nor the climate is very fine, but the kindness of the people is very nearly perfect in every respect, and much more than compensates for these two defects.' There were entertainments and diversions to distract from the bad weather and poorly maintained accommodation. A colony of émigrés grew up in Edinburgh. *Lloyd's Evening Post* of Wednesday 13 April 1796 reported, 'The Stage Box of the Edinburgh Theatre has been fitted up in an elegant style for the reception of the Duke of Angoulême, son to the Count of Artois. His Royal Highness was attended to the play on Tuesday evening with much pomp and parade.'

The Duc d'Angoulême received visitors on Mondays and Thursdays at noon in his father's apartments at Holyroodhouse. The Princes also took part in military parades accompanied by the local aristocracy and gentry, including a number of ladies. The newspapers of 7 March reported that the Royal Edinburgh Volunteers paraded in St Andrew Square in the New Town and marched to Bruntsfield Links an area of open parkland. The exercises were watched by the Lord Lieutenant of the county, the Duke of Buccleugh, joined by the Earl of Dalkeith, the Earl of Ancrum and Major General Hamilton, accompanied by the Duc d'Angoulême. Louis Antoine is described as wearing a dark green coat, faced with pink, and a pair of silver epaulettes (perhaps the ones given to him by Marie Antoinette) plus his Orders the Star of the Order of St Esprit and the Cross of St Louis and the white cockades of the Bourbons. He was accompanied by two French gentlemen, it is reported. It had been snowing and conditions under foot were very hazardous. The Duc d'Angoulême slipped over and fell on one knee but was not hurt badly. Thoughtful and kind, Louis Antoine travelled back to London in May 1796 to comfort his former tutor, the Duc de Sérent, whose two sons had recently been killed on the same day fighting in the Vendée. The Duc d'Angoulême was only in London for a couple of days before heading north accompanied by the bereaved father, whom he had persuaded to return with him to Edinburgh, hoping that company and a change of scene would help to ease his paternal grief. Eventually, the army suppliers withdrew their claims against the Comte d'Artois; he was given protection from his creditors by the Aliens Act of 1798, which prevented arrest for debts contracted outside the UK. He and his attendants headed back south to London full of gratitude for the kindness shown by the people of Scotland. He lived in London for the next fifteen or so years.

The Comte d'Artois was eager to return to France and help restore his family to the throne. He intended using the British Isles as a base from which to lead an expedition to invade France. He hoped that large numbers of their compatriots would be inspired to join the Bourbon cause. There were Royalist uprisings, including the risings in the Vendée and the invasion at Quiberon in Brittany during the years 1795-6, but they were brutally suppressed. The Duc d'Angoulême was keen to assist his father in this enterprise, but also hoped to relocate somewhere nearer to Marie Thérèse. The Duc d'Angoulême writes of the frustration caused to him and his bride-to-be by the length of time his letters took to reach Marie Thérèse in Vienna and the responses from Marie Thérèse to reach Scotland. He asks of Marie Thérèse that she 'do me the kindness, my very dear cousin, to accept the homage of all the ardent and tender feelings that fill the heart of your most affectionate cousin'. In return, Marie Thérèse expressed her pleasure that her fiancé was so diligent in writing to her, missing no opportunity to correspond.

Suggestions were reported in the British newspapers during the late 1790s that if the Bourbons were to be restored to the throne, then the older generation (Louis XVIII and the Comte d'Artois) should be passed over and the throne go to Marie Thérèse and Louis Antoine. The young couple would provide the Bourbon cause with the attractiveness of youth untainted by *ancien régime* politics. At this point they also held out the prospect of securing the dynasty with a number of healthy children. As a young, innocent and attractive girl, Marie Thérèse always garnered sympathy for her own and her family's many sufferings during the Revolution. Marie Thérèse was shocked and appalled at such a disloyal suggestion and wrote to Louis XVIII, 'what an insult and what an extravagant idea. I shall always be much attached and faithful to you, *mon oncle*. But attempts are being made to create mischief between us. I hope they will never be successful.' Her belief in the legitimate succession was absolute and uncompromising.

Louis Antoine was a committed soldier and reported that he found a life denuded of action to be 'useless' and 'unbearable'. He expressed his wish to join Condé's Army. 'Glory and my dear cousin are the only influences capable of enlivening my existence', he wrote at this time. During the late 1790s, Louis Antoine did spend time training and fighting with the Condé Army and was in command of the cavalry from the Berri region of France. He proved himself to be a brave soldier and enjoyed the sense of purpose that army life brought him.

At the same time as Marie Thérèse left Vienna for Mittau in May 1799, Louis XVIII's wife Marie Joséphine set off from Budweiss, her base in Bohemia. She had been summoned by the King to be present for the wedding of Marie Thérèse and Louis Antoine. The King and Queen had not seen each other for more than five years. They had lived separately since Louis had left Marie Joséphine's father's Court in Turin to travel widely in search of a settled establishment. But they had corresponded in a friendly, even humorous manner over the intervening years. Their relationship conducted by letter, with the benefit of absence, proved to be more amiable than their face-to-face contact. Louis XVIII had no particular desire to see his wife again or to live with her, but the wedding of their niece and nephew, as heirs to the throne of France, could not, in all dignity, go ahead in the absence of the putative queen of France. The Queen was accompanied to Mittau by Madame de Gourbillon, who had helped Marie Joséphine to flee from Paris in June 1791. They had been living together in some intimacy ever since.

Marie Joséphine was completely devoted to Madame de Gourbillon, who was loathed by the King for her foul temper, greed and aggression and the bad influence that he felt she exerted over the Queen. There were rumours of a lesbian relationship. Marie Joséphine and Madame de Gourbillon arrived at Mittau only the day before Madame Royale, just in time to do the courtesies. The King would not allow his wife's companion to enter the castle compound at Mittau. When she tried to do so against his express orders, she was swiftly ejected. Marie Joséphine was completely incensed at the harsh treatment meted out to her friend. Devastated at being separated from her companion, she became hysterical. There were terrible arguments between the King and Queen; she spent her days writing to Madame de Gourbillon and being a morose presence around the Palace at Mittau – hardly an auspicious start to Marie Thérèse's new life. Abbé de Tressan, who was present at the events, commented that the Queen seemed happy being among loyal Frenchmen and women. He wrote, as quoted by Madame de Tourzel in her memoirs, that 'she sees every consideration satisfied by her presence; and the wishes she hears expressed for her happiness prove to her the devotion and love for their masters entertained by the French who surround her'. The good Abbé may have allowed loyalty to overcome his good judgement in taking an overly optimistic view of the situation.

Madame Royale had received a letter from her uncle during her time at the Court in Vienna describing her aunt as amiable and easy to live with – surely stretching the truth to breaking point. Marie Joséphine had envied and detested Marie Antoinette, jealous of her glamour, charm and her position as Queen, while at the same time being contemptuous of her apparent lack of intellect. Marie Thérèse may well have been fully aware of this enmity between her mother and aunt. The tense atmosphere and family discord can hardly have been a pleasant welcome for the bride-to-be, who had so looked forward to being reunited with her French family after her long separation from them. However, the Bourbons had a great knack for putting aside family differences in public to accord with their vision of themselves as a united family. Madame Royale approached Mittau after her long journey on 4 June 1799. Madame de Tourzel received a description of the proceedings at Mittau from the Abbé de Tressan, who was present with his friend Lord Folkestone. The Abbé wrote, 'We could not resist the desire to witness that arrival of Madame at Mittau. By the kindness of the King, we received permission to remain there until the marriage of the Princess with the Duc d'Angoulême.' The Abbé went on to say how earnestly the King had wished for the marriage between his nephew and niece.

The King and Queen accompanied the Duc d'Angoulême out from Mittau to meet the Princess bride just outside the town. Louis XVIII was so delighted to see his niece and to have achieved his dynastic objective that he called out to the Household, 'She is here. She has come!' On seeing the Royal party arriving to greet her, Marie Thérèse got out of her carriage and knelt before the King, who tried to raise her from the ground. Abbé de Tressan recalls, 'The long and tedious journey had not impaired her strength.' The Queen kissed her and handed Marie Thérèse to her fiancé.[7] The Abbé continued that Marie Thérèse exclaimed on meeting the King, 'at last I see you and am happy; I am your child; watch over me and be my father'. The King wept. Louis Antoine, shy and awkward in Marie Thérèse's presence, stammered a few words and kissed her hand, weeping as he did so. As she entered the castle there were welcoming cheers from its inhabitants, to whom she was presented. Louis XVIII said, according to the Abbé de Tressan, 'At last she is ours; we will never leave her; and we are no longer strangers to happiness.' All were moved.

Madame Royale then retired to her own room, as described by the Abbé de Tressan:

> [to] acquit herself of a duty as dear as it was just – that of expressing her gratitude to H.M. the Emperor of Russia. From the moment she set foot in his Empire, she had received the noblest warmest proofs of his interest, and the heart of Madame felt all that she owed to the august and generous heart to whom Heaven had entrusted the power, and confided the will, to succour unhappy kings.

Marie Thérèse wrote to the Emperor thanking him for his hospitality in welcoming her to his country, then asked to see the Abbé Edgeworth. It was from the Abbé Edgeworth (through Louis XVIII's letters to her during the years she had spent with her Austrian family) that Madame Royale had learned the details of the last hours of the life of her much loved father and his execution. At last the Princess and the priest were able to meet and talk freely in person. She then received the Royal Guards, many of whom she remembered from her time at Versailles and the Tuileries.

The Abbé Edgeworth, following the deaths of Madame Élisabeth and that of his own mother, feeling that he had fulfilled his promises and duty to both these ladies, was free to leave France. He escaped Revolutionary France and travelled to London where he spent three months feted as a hero by London society and the émigrés for his role at the King's side at the execution of Louis XVI. William Pitt, the British Prime Minister, offered him a lifetime annuity, which the Abbé felt unable to accept. He was just about to leave London to travel to Ireland to visit his family when he was asked to take confidential letters to Louis XVIII, based with his Court in exile in Blankenburg. Edgeworth arrived there in December 1796, and Louis XVIII asked the Abbé to remain with the Court as his chaplain. He did so, living and travelling with the Royal Family in their exile.

Alone with the man who had been with her father at his execution, Marie Thérèse broke down weeping, nearly fainting from the emotion of the moment. They wept together and she took comfort from this. At last there was an opportunity to show her emotions with someone who could understand her sufferings. This description of the encounter is from the account of the meeting given to Abbé de Tressan by Abbé Edgeworth. He was struck by how much she reminded him in appearance and manner of Louis XVI, Marie Antoinette and Madame Élisabeth. The Abbé was able to give Marie Thérèse further insights into her father's generous forgiveness of the wrongs done him by his accusers and his willingness to pardon his countrymen – which was so influential on her own thinking on this matter. She, and others, very much hoped and prayed that Louis XVI would be created a saint by the Roman Catholic Church.

The Duc d'Angoulême and Marie Thérèse were first cousins, and therefore required a Papal dispensation to allow them to marry. Louis XVIII was keen to do all he could to promote the marriage and to bring it about quickly, so applied for the dispensation using the Spanish Borbons and their diplomats as conduits to the Pope. Once Pius VI received the petition, he was happy to give his consent. Madame Royale and Louis Antoine were married on 10 June 1799 in the chapel of the castle at Mittau.

The Emperor Paul I sent the bride a wedding gift of a diamond necklace and a letter praising her courage in her misfortunes and condemning the actions of the Revolutionaries:

> Your misfortunes, your virtues, and your heroic courage have won for you the lasting respect and sympathy of every well-disposed and good-hearted human being. May you be happy in the midst of your loving family, and never leave my dominions till you return to France, to find there a repentant nation, weeping for the crimes of the monsters it has had the misfortune to produce.[8]

The marriage contract between the young people, drafted by the Comte de Sainte-Priest who had served Louis XVI as his *Ministre du Maison du Roi*, was read the evening before the wedding and signed by the King and Queen and a number of members of the Household.[9] It was then sent to the Emperor, who had kindly agreed to sign it and have it deposited in the Russian Imperial Archives.[10] Given that their financial situation was not clear, the disposal of the couple's property was not covered in detail. When her parents' names were read out by the Comte de Sainte-Priest, the bride-to-be sobbed.

The marriage service was conducted by the Abbé Edgeworth and Cardinal Montmorency, the Grand Aumonier de France. It was attended by many of the émigré community, officials from Russia including Lutheran and Orthodox priests, and the aristocracy of Courland. From that time onwards Marie Thérèse was known as Her Royal Highness the Duchesse d'Angoulême. In marrying her cousin she must have felt that she was doing her duty both as a Bourbon princess and as a daughter. After all, this was the match that her dearly loved parents had wanted for her when she was a young girl. Louis XVIII had written to his niece describing her bridegroom-to-be when she was living in Vienna with her Habsburg cousins. He told his niece,

> It will be easier for you to be happy with him for his heart has been given to none but you and his principles will ensure that this first sentiment will also be the last. I count very much on your influence with him, for you will, I think, not be satisfied that he should be only an affectionate husband; you would wish him to be worthy of the high position which we cannot doubt he is destined one day to occupy. Born with excellent capacities, a life of forced inaction has discouraged him. When he learns

> from you yourself that the best way to please you is to make himself worthy of you, this is all that will be needed to excite him to study and France will one day owe its happiness to you.

This was a clever appeal to a Princess who loved her country. It was also a realistic and even frank assessment of her husband.

The Vicomte de Châteaubriand, himself an émigré who had fought with the Condé Army and travelled widely in Europe and the United States, years later wrote a romantic description of the marriage between the Bourbon cousins in *Bonaparte et les Bourbons*:

> this young Princess whom we have persecuted, whom we have made an orphan, longs every day in foreign palaces for the prisons of France. She might have received the hand of a powerful and glorious Prince, but she preferred to unite her destiny with that of her cousin, a poor exile, proscribed because he was French, being unwilling to separate herself from the love of her family. All the world admires her virtues; people from all parts of Europe follow her whenever she appears in public, and crown her with blessings; we alone can forget her when she left the country where she was so unhappy, she turned back to look and wept.

Though flowery in expression, it had a strong element of truth.

The new Duc and Duchesse d'Angoulême settled down in Mittau to married life. The young couple gave every appearance of happiness. The Comte de St-Priest wrote to M. de la Fare on 27 June 1799, 'The young family continues to get along marvellously well; we need only hope soon to see the fruits of it.' Some happiness at last for the Princess who had suffered so much bereavement and sorrow. Louis commented to his brother the Comte d'Artois, Marie Thérèse's uncle and now father-in-law, in Mayfair, that now he had time to observe the new Duchesse d'Angoulême in person, she appeared to him to be 'like both her father and mother'.[11] He continued, 'Her natural gaiety has not been destroyed; when her thoughts can be turned from the terrible past, she laughs heartily. She is sweet, kind, loving, but in public, her demeanour is that of a Princess accustomed to hold her Court. She has the mind of a person of mature age but she is an innocent, and pure as the day she was born.'

Marie Thérèse was second only to the Queen in seniority among the women at the miniature Court, and as the daughter of a King she still took precedence over her husband in Court etiquette. The Queen had hated being separated from Madame de Gourbillon, but nevertheless did not return to Budweiss after the wedding, remaining with her husband and the newlyweds in Mittau.

Mittau was very remote from France, located 1,000 miles from Paris. It was made to feel even more isolated to the Bourbon family and their attendants by the restrictions applying to the hospitality given by the Russian Emperor, Paul I. As a condition of the family's residence in his lands, the Emperor required that the Bourbons and their attendants did not visit his capital city, St Petersburg. In any event, it was an uncomfortable and expensive two-day journey by carriage. Equally, he would allow none of the Russian nobility living in St Petersburg to visit Mittau to pay court to the Bourbons. But Mittau was fortunately on the European courrier routes, which helped facilitate Louis XVIII's correspondence with his agents and representatives. Paul felt that providing the exiled King of France and his Court with a refuge reflected well on him, both as a man of honour and as a monarch. It was also a way of repaying the magnificent hospitality he had received when visiting Louis XVI and Marie Antoinette at Versailles with his wife Maria Feodorovna[12] during their tour of Europe in 1782. The Russian visitors had enjoyed a number of balls, dinners and theatrical performances. They had been charmed by the hospitality and warmth of Marie Thérèse's mother, who went out of her way to ensure that everything was done to please and entertain their Imperial guests – including a supper at the Trianon.[13] This was despite the anxiety that the young Royal couple felt on being required to entertain fellow royalty by whom they were a little intimidated.[14] Ironically, when Madame Royale was a rather precocious four-year-old, she had told the then Grandduke Paul that she'd like to visit his country herself one day. Little can the Duchess d'Angoulême have expected that she would eventually have occasion to do so as his pensioner, while in exile from her own beloved France.

In a thoughtful gesture, prior to Madame Royale's arrival, Louis XVIII had ordered a fine pianoforte for his niece from London. He hoped and expected that she would enjoy playing the piano to pass the long hours, especially during the Russian winter, when outdoor activities would be very restricted. The pianoforte took a long time to arrive. When it did finally reach her, Marie Thérèse was not inclined to play the instrument. Perhaps the idea of music reminded her too forcibly of happier days, or even too strongly of Marie Antoinette playing in the Tower of the Temple when her mother had attempted to lighten the atmosphere of their imprisonment with music. On the King's instructions large supplies of sewing materials had also been stockpiled in Mittau in order to provide the Duchesse d'Angoulême with a congenial occupation. She spent many hours working on her tapestry and embroidery.

The Bourbons lived in magnificent apartments in the beautiful baroque palace at Mittau, which had previously belonged to the Dukes of Courland. The exiled Court in fact only occupied one wing of the vast chilly palace; the rest of the building was used to house a barracks and a hospital. Funded by the Russian and English governments, the Bourbons maintained much of the heavy etiquette of Versailles and Court life there, despite the relative modesty of their financial circumstances. A royal bodyguard lined the corridors of the palace. Arms were presented as the Royal Family made their daily trip to the palace chapel for Mass. The usual duty rotations of courtiers that were required to attend on the King still applied. Courtiers would often travel a considerable and expensive distance to fulfil their obligations to wait on the King for a few months. The Bourbons regarded personal service from their courtiers as being essential and of utmost importance. Failure to deliver this level of service for whatever reason would greatly damage the career prospects of any émigré courtier. There was an example of a courtier with a Protestant wife who was not made to feel welcome at the very Catholic Court. He did not travel to Mittau, preferring to arrange for a friend to undertake his duties. This did not go down well with the Royal Family and he was permanently banished from Court life. The Duc de Richelieu also suffered from the view that he was not appropriately attentive during the years the Bourbons spent in exile.

The King was an utter stickler for punctuality. Timekeeping was one of the few things he could control. Louis XVIII coined the phrase 'punctuality is the politeness of princes'. Strict adherence to the requirements of good timekeeping governed the routine of the Royal Household. The King retained the rituals relating to his dining: the King traditionally ate alone observed by his courtiers and other visitors. Behind the apparent opulence of their accommodation and Royal ceremonial, there was a severe shortage of basic household items such as plates and crockery for the family and their attendants. Supplies of bedding and table linen were insufficient for the needs of the more than a hundred exiles living in Mittau. There was no library in the castle to provide entertainment and diversion, although Louis XVIII had brought his own collection of books with him.

Court life at Mittau was uninspiring and tedious for Marie Thérèse, to say the least. By April 1800, her husband had left Mittau again to spend time with the Condé Army under the command of their cousin. Fond as he was of his new wife, Louis Antoine was desperate to return to an active military life. At the time of his wedding he had written to the Emperor Paul begging for an opportunity to serve in the Russian army:[15]

> the happier I am, the more I desire to show myself worthy of my happiness. Every man who is not deaf to the voice of honour is making all the haste he can upon the road that Paul I has opened to him. I have seen Your Imperial Majesty's soldiers speeding upon the path to glory: Europe is ringing with the exploits of Marshal Souvarof[16] and the Archduke Charles; and meanwhile the husband of a Princess whose courage, quite as much as her sorrows and virtues, has attracted the eyes and thoughts of all Europe, is condemned to inaction! Ah, sire, at such a cost there can be no happiness for me! Will Your Imperial Majesty deign to consider my

> position, and crown your many kindnesses by permitting me to fight under your flag? To serve as a volunteer in the cause of my God and my King, to fight in the front ranks of Your Imperial Majesty's army, to show the world that I am not unworthy of my ancestors, that is all that I wish and all that I ask. Being assured of the safety of the wife who is dearer to me than life itself, since I shall be leaving her in the dominions and under the protection of Your Imperial Majesty, I shall summon my honour to stifle the regrets I might otherwise feel, and shall devote all my efforts to justifying the choice of our parents and the kindness of our august benefactor.

The Emperor did not agree to his request.

Marie Thérèse took long walks around the castle itself and its grounds. She had always found exercise important to her morale and sense of well-being. Perhaps her dead brother's dog, Coco, accompanied her on her walks. Some accounts of this time of her life indicate that the Duchesse d'Angoulême spent a lot of time reading; others lead one to believe that, like her husband, she was not a great book lover. Books and the learning of extended passages of text had certainly been a great comfort to her during her time of solitary confinement in the Tower of the Temple. It is more convincing that she carried on enjoying the pleasures of reading and the escape and relief from boredom they provided while she was in exile. She had within her Household Madame Huë as her reader, which would suggest that she enjoyed this as a relaxation and as a backdrop to accompany her handiwork. Newspapers, particularly long-awaited French publications, were also important to her and the family, who read them out loud to each other. Letters from friends and family were also a great source of news and pleasure to the exiles. It has been suggested in memoirs written by her husband and quoted by Joseph Turquan in his biography that despite Madame Huë's loyalty in following Marie Thérèse into exile in Vienna and Mittau, the Princess could be a difficult and moody mistress at times and not always kind or grateful to her attendants. It is reported that she was restless and unable to settle to any particular task, feeling the need to pace. These could well be signs of low spirits, not surprising after all she had suffered in her youth. The Bourbons, in general, had very high expectations of the service that was due to them. Gratitude did not figure strongly among their characteristics.

Louis Antoine eventually got his wish for active military service. The British newspapers of 1800 reported that the Duc d'Angoulême was involved in active combat. They noted that, 'An artilleryman was wounded by the side of the Duke d'Angoulême. No other officers are known as yet to have been wounded except M. de Vasse, Adjutant to the Duke.'[17] Marie Thérèse experienced the loneliness and constant nagging anxiety of any wife whose soldier husband is away from home on active service. The newly wed Duchesse d'Angoulême at twenty years old was left alone with her aunt and uncle and members of the Court, many of whom were middle-aged or elderly. Court life at Mittau was uninspiring and tedious for Marie Thérèse. She dined every evening in the Royal Family's quarters in Mittau, sitting next to Cardinal Montmorency, a man of advanced years who was badly afflicted with deafness – though he had never been a great conversationalist. Her world narrowed and her life was without stimulus or interesting company. Furthermore, her husband's military ambitions deprived her of his companionship. The Court of Vienna, with her Austrian archduchess cousins and other friends for company and amusement, had surely been a more congenial way of life for her despite its restrictions. Vienna had had its problems for Marie Thérèse, but it was a large Imperial city with many opportunities for distractions and pleasures at the centre of European political and royal life. Mittau must have made her feel marooned in the middle of nowhere. Louis XVIII himself was only forty-two years old, but obesity and the debilitating effects of gout meant that he lived the restricted life of an invalid more usual for a much older man. Louis XVIII spent many hours in his library, sometimes alone and sometimes accompanied by his favourite d'Avaray, writing numerous letters, running his network of spies in France, corresponding with his supporters and studying European politics. He read several newspapers a day, including those from Paris. He was enormously well informed about politics in France and wider Europe. He was able to be in indirect and non-attributable contact with Napoleon through the good offices of Madame Huë, who was a close friend of Joséphine, Napoleon's wife, with whom she was in regular correspondence. This was a useful conduit for contact and negotiations between the exiled Bourbons and the new regime in France.

While the Royal Family was settled in Mittau, the Duchesse d'Angoulême's Household consisted of a *Dame d'Honneur*, the Duchesse de Sérent; her daughter, the Duchesse de Damas, acted as her *Dame pour Accompagner*; the Duc de Damas was her *Chevalier d' Honneur*; and Mademoiselle de Choisy was also with her. In addition there were the usual domestic servants and religious advisers. The Abbé Marie was Marie Thérèse's Chaplain and Father Confessor. She also had the company of the Abbé Edgeworth, her father's Irish confessor. He was a loved and respected part of the Royal Household. The Comte d'Artois wanted his daughter-in-law to have a Household of Versailles-like proportions, but Louis XVIII felt that it would be inappropriate. His view was that it should be small as befitted their current reduced financial circumstances and populated by only the most respectable people. Politely but firmly, he declined to include in the Household members of the Polignac family. He regarded them not as loyal subjects, but rather their extravagance and greed for offices signified part of the cause of the fall of the Bourbons. It took much effort to ensure that these matters relating to the Duchesse d'Angoulême's Household were in good order. The Comte d'Artois and the King had not initially been able to agree on the personnel for the new Duchesse d'Angoulême's Household. The Comte d'Artois was keen to appoint his friends and supporters irrespective of their reputations for marital fidelity and piety (essential for the maintenance of the dignity of the Household) and their suitability for the positions in question.

The years of the early 1800s were a difficult time for Marie Thérèse and her family. Napoleon was dominant on the battlefields of Europe; he carried all before him in Italy, including the once proud and independent Republic of Venice,[18] the Low Countries and Spain.[19] His enemies, the Imperial and Royalist governments of Europe, had no choice but to deal with him as the ruler of France and conqueror of huge tracts of Europe. The spring of 1800 brought to Mittau the news of the death of the last surviving Tantes, Madame Adélaïde,[20] who had died in Trieste (some sources suggest Rome), sending the Russian Court in St Petersburg into mourning for two weeks. The final blow for her had been the harsh weather when fleeing Bonaparte's army as he pursued his Italian campaign. Her sister Madame Victoire[21] had died in June of the previous year in Trieste, just before the marriage of her great nephew and niece. Although Marie Thérèse had not seen her aunts since 1791 when they left France for exile in Italy, their deaths marked the end of an era for her; one more break with the world of her happy and secure early childhood at the magnificent Versailles.

In May 1800, Napoleon Bonaparte offered to buy off Louis XVIII and his claims to the French throne. In exchange for his claims, Louis would receive a considerable annual income and possession of the Duchy of Massa and Carrara plus the Republic of Lucca – all situated in Tuscany, Italy. In order to gain these territories and the income on offer, Louis would have to give up his rights to any property held by him in France and his claim (and that of the rest of his family) to the French throne. Napoleon advised Louis XVIII, without any apparent sense of irony, 'Think no more of returning to France. You would have to trample on a hundred thousand corpses. Sacrifice your interest for the peace and happiness of France. History will thank you for it.' Louis was impoverished and in exile far from France with no prospect of restoration, so was at first prepared to enter into negotiations, with Abbé Edgeworth as his intermediary. In the end, however, after protracted negotiations, Louis refused the offer, preferring poverty and the lack of a settled home to a dishonourable surrender to the usurper of his and his family's destiny and birth right. In truth it was never a serious possibility that Louis XVIII, who from boyhood had longed to be King and was fully aware of the enormous benefits attaching to the role, would give up the prospect, however small, of being King of France. Louis XVIII felt that he was the heir of St Louis and was conscious of his descent from the great Bourbon Kings of France, Henry IV and Louis XIV. He felt an almost mythical attachment to his throne and his '*patrie*'. Napoleon was angered by what he felt to be Louis' intransigence. He was confused by the exiled Louis's refusal to accept the realpolitik that the rule of the Bourbons in France was finished, and that a new dynasty was establishing itself. Napoleon perceived Louis' clinging to his claims to be ridiculous. The Comte d'Artois, ever the hardliner, and in relatively comfortable exile as the leader of many fellow émigrés in London, was outraged that his more pragmatic brother should even think of entering into negotiations with Bonaparte about such matters.

The marriage of Madame Royale to the Duc d'Angoulême was a dynastic match intended to secure the succession and to bolster the attractiveness of the Bourbons to the French people. It was never about romantic love. The cousins were not passionately in love with each other but had much in common, not least a shared deep and active religious faith. They were comfortable together and understood each other's backgrounds and family life. Marie Thérèse noted and respected her husband's good qualities, his sexual faithfulness (so rare in a Bourbon prince and so very different from his father, the Comte d'Artois, and his brother, the Duc de Berry), his honesty and deep sense of personal integrity. She was, perhaps, the stronger character of the two, her personality having been forged and tested in the most extreme of circumstances. She was, as their uncle observed, the more intellectually able of the couple; but despite the differences, they seemed genuinely fond of each other. The Duc d'Angoulême referred to his wife as 'his Joy'. She in turn was proud of the respect that he achieved as a soldier. There is very little surviving correspondence between them to supply a fuller picture of their relationship. Marie Thérèse may have remembered her mother's burning of possibly incriminating or embarrassing letters from the Tuileries on 20 June 1792, when the mob was invading the palace and there was the danger of letters being seized. She seems to have taken a similarly cautious approach herself in burning her own correspondence and that of her husband.[22]

For all the good things about their marriage, there was one glaring deficiency which would become apparent as time passed: the lack of children. This was both a personal and a dynastic issue for the Duc and Duchesse d'Angoulême. In a previous generation, Marie Antoinette's inability to produce children drove her to the follies of frivolity. In Marie Thérèse's case her disappointments made her introspective, hardened her character and made her rather bitter and intolerant. It may well be that the marriage was consummated, but that either or both parties suffered from infertility. Jo Burr Margadant, in her survey of attitudes to Royal motherhood during this period, suggests that the Duc d'Angoulême was impotent. The years of imprisonment and severe stress in Marie Thérèse's formative years may also have rendered her incapable of bearing children. She so desperately needed love and understanding to help her achieve some equilibrium after the terrible years in the Temple. The lack of passion in her marriage and the lack of children quashed her spirit in a way that the terrible times in the Temple and even the stresses of Vienna had not done. Then she had been able to sustain herself with high hopes of life with her French family; the reality proved rather different.

The Bourbon Court in exile was reasonably comfortably settled in Mittau when, according to some accounts, the jealous rage of the Queen's favourite, Madame de Gourbillon, indirectly led to the family's expulsion from Russia. She was piqued at being kept apart from the Queen and at having been ejected so unceremoniously and insultingly from the castle on their arrival for the Angoulême wedding. As an act of revenge or stupidity, she showed one of the Russian Imperial government ministers some letters that were written by the King's favourite, d'Avaray, to another Bourbon courtier. They were less than flattering, even mocking, about the Emperor. They were in turn passed on to the Emperor Paul. Other accounts suggest that it was a female spy working for Paul I who was shown the letter by her lover, the Duc d'Havre, and who revealed the insulting contents to the Emperor. This was the last straw for the Emperor who had been so generous towards the refugees. Whatever the provenance of the letter, Paul was greatly displeased and insulted. He wrote to Louis XVIII pointing out to him that hospitality was a virtue not an obligation. The French émigrés were not easy guests and had made themselves very unpopular. In a deeply devout country like Russia, they were seen by the people as being irreligious, having to be literally dragged to church. The émigrés were thought to be frivolous, hell-raising and arrogant. Many of them had not adjusted to the change in their fortunes after being forced to leave France and their estates, and still played the swaggering aristocrats; this was almost guaranteed to make them resented and unpopular in their host countries. The content of the correspondence would have very uncomfortable consequences for Marie Thérèse and her family.

PART II

The Duchesse d'Angoulême

7

Antigone and a British Exile

JANUARY 1801-APRIL 1814

Paul I was often unstable and paranoid, despite his great intellectual gifts. On 20 January 1801, he ordered Marie Thérèse's family to leave their refuge in Mittau; Marie Thérèse herself was not included in the order to leave, but it was unthinkable to her to abandon the rest of the family. In practical terms she could hardly remain in Russia separated from her husband, uncle and the rest of the Court in exile. It was the middle of a viciously long and cold Russian winter. The Royal Family and their entourage had only two days to pack up all the possessions they could gather together and leave the palace which had been their home for the last couple of years. Louis XVIII's letters to the Emperor Paul I asking him to reconsider his decision were ignored by the Emperor and returned to the King unopened. In an age of slow communications, exacerbated by the winter conditions, this gave Louis XVIII, the family and their Households no time to make proper arrangements as to where they might next go to find refuge.

As a final blow to his prestige, the passport issued by the Emperor to Louis XVIII for his journey was in the name of the Comte de Lille, his *nom de guerre*, rather than in the name of the King of France. The Russian Court had been one of the first foreign governments to recognise Louis XVIII's claims to the throne on the death of the little Louis XVII in the Tower of the Temple in June 1795. It was very dispiriting for Louis XVIII and Marie Thérèse to find that not even the Russian Court was now willing to recognise Louis XVIII as the legitimate King of France. Furthermore, the pensions from the Russian Court, which had helped to sustain the Bourbons and their supporters, were also stopped by the Emperor.

The Royal Family left Mittau on 22 January 1801, having sold, at knock-down prices, many articles of furniture and household equipment that they were not able to take with them. The curious citizens of Mittau, who had cheered the family's arrival not so long previously, watched the departure. The weather and road conditions were appalling. The days were short and the weather achingly cold. The roads, which were never very good, were covered in deep snow. The coachmen were freezing as they were not properly clothed for the journey. Their horses struggled to make progress in such conditions. Four of the horses were drowned as they tried to cross a river. On the second day of their journey, as they left Dobele where they been housed overnight by the Baron Koyt, the carriages belonging to the French refugees were overturned due to the harsh conditions. On occasion, the obese gouty Louis supported by his young niece had to get out of his carriage and try to walk through the deep snow. At times the King and the Duchesse d'Angoulême could hardly make any headway in the awful conditions. The snow was up to their knees. Marie Thérèse gave her arm to Abbé Edgeworth. Coco did his best to follow his mistress, jumping through the snow. It was here that the legend of Marie Thérèse as the loyal and devoted 'Antigone' was born. Louis XVIII likened his niece to the eponymous heroine of the Sophocles play, in which the heroine prefers death to abandoning her principles. At other times, in less complimentary terms, he compared her with Regan and Goneril.

It was possible to present this journey in a heroic light, but it was an uncomfortable experience for the Royal party. Accommodation was hard to come by and often of very inferior quality. The stench of bodies was so bad at one inn that Marie Thérèse preferred to sleep in a cold bakehouse. On another occasion, an ungentlemanly Russian officer refused to give up his room for Marie Thérèse, who therefore had to share with three other women a room overheated by a malfunctioning stove. In the morning, the ladies emerged looking as red as lobsters from their stifling room.

At last they crossed the border into Prussian territory. Marie Thérèse hid the Royal archives under her skirts to keep them away from the prying eyes of the local customs officers. On their departure from Mittau, the King had wanted to go to Italy and settle in Naples, where he was familiar with the Italian language and liked the climate. This was not to be and they were offered asylum in Warsaw, the Duchy of Warsaw being under Prussian rule at this time. The soldiers presented arms as they crossed to the Prussian side of the border and the party spent their first night on Prussian soil in Niemmusats. They travelled on from there to Memel – modern-day Klaipeda in Lithuania – where they arrived exhausted in the middle of the night of 27 January. Marie Thérèse had never previously seen the sea, so wandered down to the port and boarded an English ship to experience the joys of sailing.

While they were at Memel, desperation drove the Duchesse d'Angoulême to write to Queen Louise of Prussia, wife of Frederick William III. Louise was a woman renowned for her beauty and her courage in defying Napoleon. The Duchesse wrote to her as one Princess to another, pleading with the Queen to give her and her family succour in their time of trouble. They waited in Memel, in a miserable and uncomfortable inn, to hear whether they were welcome in Prussia or not. Before their eventual answer, the Prussian Royal Family kept the Bourbons waiting for three long weeks. According to the memoirs of Vicomte Anne-Henri Dampmartin, a soldier and émigré,[1] Queen Louise finally replied to Marie Thérèse that she was honoured to be able to provide the Bourbons with accommodation in Warsaw. The Queen also sent the Princess a number of small gifts that she hoped would make the Princess more comfortable.

During the delay, the Prussians consulted Napoleon as to whether he had any objection to the Bourbons being given refuge in Warsaw. The First Consul of France, supremely confident of his own position, did not object to the Bourbons being given sanctuary in Warsaw. A messenger was sent to Warsaw to have apartments made ready for the arrival of Louis XVIII and the Duchesse d'Angoulême, who was travelling incognita as the Marquise de la Meilleraye. The permission to take up residence in Warsaw was presented as very much a personal favour to Marie Thérèse. The sufferings of the Duchesse d'Angoulême and the romance of her story gained her sympathy and inclined other royals to provide her, and those accompanying her, with help; she also still had the advantage of being a young and attractive woman of twenty-three, who was able to appeal to the chivalrous and compassionate instincts of her potential hosts and benefactors. Her uncle was fully aware of Marie Thérèse's value as the daughter of the martyred King Louis XVI and Marie Antoinette. The family received much practical help from the ruling classes (ambassadors, nobility, churchmen and other monarchs) of the countries in which they resided. These useful and influential people felt sympathy for their plight and respect for their status as exiled royals. They were prepared to give the Bourbons assistance by finding or giving them use of often elegant housing and providing contacts and entrée to local society, which helped to make their daily lives more palatable.

The expulsion from Mittau not only deprived the exiled Royal Family of accommodation, but also of the pension previously paid to them by the Emperor. Paul applied great speed and efficiency to cancelling the payments to the Bourbons following their expulsion from Russia. They were desperate for money for the basics of life for themselves and their accompanying Court. The Duchesse d'Angoulême used the moneys raised by the sale, or pawning, of her jewellery to pay off the family's bills for the living expenses and the other personal debts incurred during their travels since leaving Mittau. It was an expensive business keeping a Court functioning, particularly one without a settled base. The Duchesse d'Angoulême, ever practical and not wishing to create further debts, also sent money to her attendants who were travelling independently of her to meet their needs and pay off any charges they had already paid on their travels. Madame de Sérent was able to make a little money to support herself and help the Household finances by selling her needlework to the Emperor of Russia; even after their departure, he was prepared to help the Bourbons and their attendants in this way. Money was also borrowed by the Royal Family from members of the court – for example, Monsieur de Damas – who were often richer than the royals they served. Madame de Sérent was sent on a mission to the Danish ambassador to sell the diamond necklace given to Marie Thérèse by the Emperor on the occasion of her marriage; he did not purchase it, but loaned money to the family.

The Duchesse d'Angoulême and her party travelled on to Konigsberg (modern-day Kalingrad, part of the territory of the Russian Federation). The planned departure of the family from Memel to Konigsberg on 9 February was delayed by news of the suicide of the Abbé Marie, Father Confessor and Almoner of Marie Thérèse and Louis Antoine, sometimes referred to as Abbé Maria. Some commentators suggest that he took his own life because he could no longer bear the pain and shame of an inappropriate love affair with one of the other courtiers; otherwise there was no apparent reason for his suicide. He burnt his paperwork, made his will and then killed himself by stabbing himself through the heart, according to newspaper reports of the time. It was a sad end for a man of God who had served the family so loyally. Louis XVIII had been particularly attached to him: the Abbé Marie was a very able and renowned mathematician and Louis XVIII enjoyed spending time discussing history, mathematics and literature with him.[2] No doubt the event cast its pall of sadness and gloom over the life of the Court.

Abbé Edgeworth took over the dead man's role as the Confessor to the Duchesse d'Angoulême and her husband. In the end, the family did not leave Memel until 23 February, arriving in Konigsberg the following day. The English newspapers reported events in these terms:

> A private letter received by the Hamburg mail of yesterday from Konigsberg of the 14th March 1801 states as follows: 'The greater number of persons who composed the suite of Louis XVIII have separated themselves. It is known that the pension he received from Russia is now entirely discontinued. The Duchess of Angoulême was compelled by want to pawn her diamonds at Memel for 2,500 ducats. The two illustrious persons arrived at Warsaw after suffering the severest hardships during their journey thither from Konigsberg.'

The King, Queen and Duchesse d'Angoulême arrived in Warsaw early in March 1801 with a Court of about forty people and expecting to stay in the city for only a few weeks. In fact they were to live there for more than three years. The Duc d'Angoulême joined the family in Warsaw in the spring of 1801 after the disbanding of the Condé Army. The King and the Duc and Duchesse d'Angoulême had strong Polish family connections. Louis XV's wife, Louis XVIII's grandmother, Marie Leszczynska, had been a Polish princess; and Louis XVIII was named Stanislas in honour of her father, Stanislaw Leszczynski,[3] who had been King of Poland. The Bourbons were also, through their grandmother or great-grandmother in the case of Marie Thérèse, related to many of the local nobility, who were proud to be able to be of help to their French 'cousins'. The family and their attendants lived quietly and in some (relative) poverty in the aristocratic quarter of Warsaw. At first they rented the Hotel Waliszewski, and later moved to the Palais Kazanowski. As a summer residence, their cousin Prince Poniatowski provided them with the annex to the beautiful lakeside Palace of Lazienki, which enabled the family to escape the heat and smell of Warsaw during the hot summer months. On 25 August (Fête de Saint Louis) of each year, the people of Warsaw came to the Bourbon residence to pay their respects to the King and the rest of the family on his name day. Less congenially, the family was surrounded by spies planted by Bonaparte and the other powers to monitor their movements and intentions. They were also under constant police surveillance by the local authorities.

Louis XVIII applied to the British government for assistance, and was sent a one-off grant of £5,000 with a promise that a further £6,000 would be forthcoming as an annual income for the Duchesse d'Angoulême. It is interesting to put this sum of money in context in terms of its purchasing power. It will be recalled from the writings of the ever practical and money-conscious Jane Austen that the fictional Mr Darcy's[4] Derbyshire estate of Pemberley produced an income of £10,000 a year. He was regarded as a most advantageous match, having only himself, his sister and eventually the former Miss Elizabeth Bennett to maintain. Such monies did not go far though, when one was trying to run a mini Court in exile and keep more than a hundred courtiers in the necessities of life. The British pensions were intended by the British government to continue to be payable until such time as Louis XVIII was restored to the throne of France and thereby achieved financial independence. Members of the *Garde du Corps*, who had been with the Duchesse d'Angoulême and her parents on their failed escape attempt from Paris in June 1791, were also provided with small pensions. The British government led by William Pitt was sympathetic to the Bourbons and very much opposed to the Revolutionary government in France. The payment of the long-delayed Austrian dowry of Marie Antoinette, which Louis XVIII and the Duchesse d'Angoulême had been trying to obtain when the then Madame Royale was attempting to settle her financial affairs prior to leaving Vienna for Mittau in 1799, had still not materialised. Louis XVIII continued to press the

Austrian government for its payment. The Bourbons were so desperate for money that any possibility of additional resources, however remote, had to be pursued to the utmost. *The Times* of 4 December 1801 did admit that the Bourbon household were good payers: 'All the expenses of their Household are defrayed with the strictest punctuality.' This sounds like Marie Thérèse's good influence.

The Bourbons in exile had always believed that they could count on the support of what was left of the Roman Catholic Church in France after the Revolution, as well as that of the Pope in Rome and the vast majority of the aristocratic class. As the years of exile continued and Napoleon, initially as first Consul and later as Emperor, tightened his grip on the government of France and established a new status quo, these certainties started to crumble for Louis XVIII and his adherents. In July 1801, Pope Pius VII[5] and Napoleon settled a Concordat or treaty between them: the Roman Catholic Church, which had been so diminished in its role, wealth and influence in France by the Revolution and had traditionally been loyal to the Royalist cause, would accept Bonaparte's rule in return for state recognition of it as the main religion in France.

Following the signing of the agreement, 30,000 émigré priests returned from exile to France, their parishes and other roles. Many other émigrés, homesick for France and living in straitened circumstances abroad, were tempted home by the amnesty of 1802. By the end of that year, an estimated 40 per cent of the émigré community had returned to live in France. In doing so, they sacrificed their foreign pensions. Many of the returning nobility joined the army. The memoirs of the Comte Regis de Trobriand report on his relative Joseph de Trobriand:[6]

> that once loyal émigré soldiers had to choose between fighting against the forces of the Revolution and of the victorious Empire and permanent exile, can we wonder that many French nobles would shrink from accepting the latter alternative, should an opportunity to become Frenchmen again present itself? This happened when Napoleon, at peace[7] temporarily with all the world, abolished the sentence of death against the émigrés and encouraged the men serving in foreign armies to take commissions in the French Army.

As de Trobriand said, 'Bonaparte', the previous scourge of European *ancien régime* monarchies, had now become 'Napoleon' and was crowned Emperor of the French in the presence of Pope Pius VII at Notre Dame on 2 December 1804. His regime was looking very established and settled. Many younger French people could not even remember the Bourbons as rulers. This was a significant blow to the Bourbons. Restoration to the throne seemed a distant, even hopeless prospect. They were losing core support from those upon whom they utterly relied for loyalty.

Both duty to her kind benefactor and her own inclination to lead a quiet life meant that the Duchesse d'Angoulême ventured out very little into society during the years she spent in Warsaw. She had given her word to Queen Louise of Prussia that she would lead a retired life away from aristocratic society in Warsaw. She resisted the invitations of the aristocratic ladies there who saw her as a romantic and tragic figure. Abbé Edgeworth[8] described the family's daily life at this time, which he knew intimately:

> The King and the Duc and Duchesse d'Angoulême lead a most solitary life and though in a town of dissipation and pleasures far beyond any other I have seen in my life, they partake of none. A few visits are received (for they do not pay any) and these are very short; a jaunt in their carriage when the weather is fine; or a solitary walk on foot, is the only distractions they allow to their melancholy thoughts. The greater part of the day, the King especially spends in his closet, where he dispatches his own business; and certainly does in a morning what most men would do in a week.

The Times of 4 December 1801 described the daily routine of Marie Thérèse and her family, noting that they were rarely seen out except 'at the foot of the altar or in the most unfrequented walks'. What a depressing life for a woman still in her twenties who loved to ride and walk. She must surely have needed distraction and entertainment to try to come to terms with her losses and to provide relief from the narrow circle of family and courtiers among whom she lived.

Her beloved and long-term companion Coco fell to its death from a balcony at the Lazienki summer palace. Abbé Edgeworth wrote that the Duchesse d'Angoulême, usually so self-contained and apparently unemotional, was devastated and spent days in tears and mourning for the dead animal. The Abbé Edgeworth felt the strength of her emotions on Coco's death to be something of an over-reaction on her part. Perhaps it can be explained by understanding that Coco must have been a reminder to Marie Thérèse of both happier family days but also a symbol of the trials of her imprisonment and the terrible losses she had suffered. Louis XVIII arranged for the poet Jacques Delille to write an elegy for a plaque on the animal's tomb, paying tribute to the companionship and comfort he had given his mistress during her incarceration.

In March 1801, Emperor Paul's fears of plots and assassination proved to be a self-fulfilling prophecy. His many eccentricities had alarmed sufficient of his courtiers to encourage them to form a clique against him and he was murdered. On the accession of the new Emperor, Alexander I, the Bourbons had their pension restored. Their stay in Warsaw was proving much longer than the few weeks' sojourn they had originally anticipated. The Peace of Amiens, signed in March 1802, signalled another low point for the Bourbons as their friends made peace with their enemy. The Treaty led to a cessation of hostilities between France and her many foes. The British government recognised the French government. The British travelling classes rushed to enjoy the delights of the continent so long denied them by war. The sad news of the death of her aunt Madame Clotilde, in March 1802, also came while the family was living in Warsaw. Marie Thérèse had never met her aunt, but had corresponded with her. This was yet another break in the connection to her family.

The peace was brief and by May 1803 a state of war again existed between Britain, her allies and Napoleon. By 1804, the Prussians were finding it too politically difficult to carry on providing the Bourbon pretenders to the French throne with sanctuary, as they were coming under intense pressure from Napoleon. The Prussian government tried to persuade Louis XVIII to renounce his rights to the throne of France and accept whatever financial provision Bonaparte might be prepared to make for him. Louis XVIII steadfastly continued to refuse to do so. In taking this stance, the King was fully supported by his brother and heir, the Comte d'Artois, and Artois' two sons and, no doubt, Marie Thérèse. The rest of the members of the Bourbon family (including the Orléans branch) were also united on this point. They had no wish to give up their claims to the throne of France and their French properties, any more than did the King himself. Despite the apparent hopelessness of his cause, Louis XVIII refused to give up his claims. Bonaparte became increasingly angry at what he perceived to be the obstinate and unrealistic stance taken by the Bourbons in continuing to press their claims to the throne. The Bourbons had a passionate belief in their legitimacy as the rulers of France. Depending on your viewpoint, they were either stubborn or steadfast in maintaining this position whatever the circumstances. They believed in their God-given role as rulers of France and nothing or no one was going to change this. As Louis XVIII said to a delegation from the Chamber of Deputies in 1821, 'in exile and during persecution I upheld my rights, the honour of my family and that of the French name'. Marie Thérèse agreed this position with equal passion and commitment. She never wavered in her desire to return to France or her belief that her family was its lawful and legitimate ruler.

In March 1804, Bonaparte said, without any apparent irony, 'Make no mistake about it; there will be neither peace nor rest in the land until the last of the Bourbons is exterminated.' There was an attempt to kill Louis XVIII by poisoning in the summer of 1804. Some commentators suggest that this was, in fact, a Bourbon fabrication to gain sympathy and to justify Bourbon plots against Napoleon. The previous year, Napoleon had said to his court that Louis was suffering from a fatal disease, a pretty unsubtle incitement to the assassination of the King, whom he regarded as a troublesome nuisance. In 1804, there was a plot to assassinate Napoleon by gentlemen from the court who belonged to the supporters of the Comte d'Artois. As an act of revenge, one of the Bourbon cousins, the Duc d'Enghien,[9] grandson of the Prince de Condé, was executed by Bonaparte on spurious grounds of being one of the conspirators. The Duc d'Enghien was kidnapped from his residence in Ettenheim in Baden and taken across the river Rhine to Strasbourg, then executed at the Château of Vincennes. The judicial murder of the Duc d'Enghien on the orders of Napoleon damaged the Emperor's reputation and shocked the Courts of Europe and many people in France. In a side note, the exiled King of Sweden, Gustav IV Adolph, who was a keen supporter of the Bourbon claims, adopted the Duc d'Enghien's dog and put around its neck a collar acknowledging that it was the Duke's dog.

In 1804 the Duchesse d'Angoulême, her family and their 150 attendants were asked to leave Warsaw. Once again they were forced to try to find another country that was willing and able to give them refuge. In July 1804, shortly after the May proclamation of Bonaparte as Emperor, when Bourbon fortunes seemed to be at their lowest ebb, Louis XVIII and the Duc d' Angoulême set off from Warsaw to travel to Sweden. Louis was so low on funds that he was reduced to begging for books from supporters in London. The King hoped to gather all the Bourbon princes including the Duc d'Orléans for a *conseil de famille* (family conference). The Comte d'Artois had been given permission by the British to travel to meet his brother and elder son for the conference in Sweden. The Duc d'Orléans was not able to obtain permission to travel from the British, and had to make do with writing to his cousins with his comments on the situation in France. His analysis of the political situation there was that the Empire was just one more stage in the Revolutionary process. The Duc d'Orléans, resident in Richmond near London, and a keen Anglophile, busied himself in trying to obtain permission from the British government for his cousin Louis XVIII to join him and the Comte d'Artois in their exile in Great Britain. He used the contacts he had made with the government and the Prince of Wales to work on behalf of the King, Queen and the Duc and Duchesse d'Angoulême.

Relations between the two branches of the House of Bourbon were at least sufficiently warm for them to be able to work together on this vital project of obtaining a more comfortable, accessible and permanent place of exile. The Duc d'Orléans advised his cousin Louis XVIII that he should not wait for formal permission to land in Great Britain but present the British government with a *fait accompli* and simply arrive at a British port. He would be able to manage the situation as best he could from there. Marie Thérèse accompanied by Queen Marie Joséphine and most of their suite remained settled in Warsaw following their usual quiet routine. The Comte d'Artois and Louis XVIII had not seen each other for many years and Orléans had been isolated from the rest of the Bourbon family for much of his time in exile. The Bourbon family had had to rely on uncertain, and often slow, postal services to keep in touch, except for those times when they or their supporters travelled between the different countries in which the family were in exile and messages could be carried in person without the threat of loss or interception of the post. Such trips were expensive and time-consuming. The Duc d'Angoulême, having spent time with his father in Great Britain as well as with his uncle and Marie Thérèse in Mittau and Warsaw, was in better contact than his wife with the other members of the family.

The Duc d' Angoulême and Louis XVIII decided that they could not return to Warsaw. In September 1804, the King of Prussia was aggrieved by a newspaper article by the King's favourite, the Duc d'Avaray, and the disruptive, arrogant and unmannerly conduct of the French émigrés. They were often found to be contemptuous of local people and their ways. The King of Prussia decided that he, too, had had enough of the Bourbons and their followers. He would no longer give them asylum; even his generosity and patience were exhausted.

Louis XVIII appealed to the Emperor Alexander I for permission for the French Royal Family to return to Mittau. Initially, the family was informed that this was not possible. Another option was, however, available: they were told that they could go to live in Kiev in the Ukraine, if they so wished. This was not an attractive prospect to the family, either personally or politically. Kiev would be even further than Mittau from the hub of Europe and would have even more difficult lines of communication. The Emperor Alexander I relented and offered Louis XVIII and Marie Thérèse and their party the use of the palace in Mittau again. Louis XVIII referred to this period of their exile in Russia as Mittau II. This was, however, a much-reduced and diminished version of life in Mittau compared with their first period of exile. This time there was no Guard of Honour for them in the corridors of their apartments. Money was very limited. The Russian Emperor did not want to provoke Napoleon too much by treating the Bourbons as a government in exile. The isolation, long winters and short days and tedium of Mittau were, however, the same for Marie Thérèse and her family. Queen Marie Joséphine and the Duchesse d'Angoulême returned to Mittau from Warsaw in late autumn 1804, and found, no doubt to their great distress and annoyance, that many of the items of furniture and other household equipment that they had been forced to leave behind when they fled in 1801 had been stolen or sold off by the local people.

We are able to gain an outsider's view of the Bourbon Court during the Mittau II years from the accounts written by Princess Dorothea,[10] daughter of the Duke and Duchess of Courland, whose ancestral home was the palace at Mittau now occupied by the Bourbons. Fleeing Berlin following the defeat of Prussia by Napoleon at the Battle of Jena on 14

October 1806, Dorothea and her governess Mademoiselle Hoffmann travelled to Courland to find refuge from the French armies. The young Dorothea was so used to the sophistications of Berlin society that she was not impressed by her native land, finding it largely devoid of culture and economically poor. Even the nobility, to whom she was related, she described as only interested in feasting and drinking away the long winter nights and short days. During the time she spent in Mittau, Dorothea often visited the Bourbons and their Court. Mademoiselle Hoffmann was a close friend and confidante of the Duc d'Avaray, the current favourite of the King. The fourteen-year-old Dorothea spent time with the King, sitting on his knee and discussing her academic work with him. She was given the nickname of 'his little Italian' by the King – a reference to her dark, lively eyes.

She was moved by the plight of Marie Thérèse and her family. She observed them trying to maintain some Royal dignity and style in the shabby castle despite poverty and exile and little hope of a return to their homeland. Already anti-Bonapartist in her views, her dislike of Napoleon was further bolstered by her sympathy for the sufferings and privations of the exiled princes. As a wealthy young heiress of high birth, her governess and the Duc d'Avaray discussed a possible match with Duc de Berry. It was not to be. Her memoirs were sympathetic towards the exiled Bourbons in tone and respectful, particularly to the sufferings and plight of Marie Thérèse as the *Orpheline du Temple*, which appealed to the romantic young girl.

It is said that during Marie Joséphine's second stay at Mittau, she was often dressed in clothes that were practically rags and spent her days wandering around the grounds of the palace. No wonder she turned to the bottle and Madame de Gourbillon for comfort. In 1805, Marie Joséphine received the sad news of the death of her sister, the Comtesse d'Artois. Marie Thérèse had not seen the Comtesse d'Artois since she was ten years old, before the Comtesse left Versailles in the first wave of the émigrés. They had not been able to meet throughout their long years of exile.

Matters did not improve for Marie Thérèse and her family. There were arson attacks on the Bourbons. Then the extremely loyal and much loved Abbé Edgeworth died on 22 May 1807 aged 62 from a virulent fever, probably typhus caught from sick French prisoners of war to whom he was ministering in the hospital established by the Duchesse d'Angoulême in the palace. Marie Thérèse nursed devotedly and selflessly the man who had been with her father during the last moments of his life. Ignoring the risks, she nursed him day and night. Marie Thérèse remembered the many services the Abbé had rendered not only her but also other members of her family in their troubles in France and later in exile. She wrote of the Abbé that he was 'her most beloved and revered invalid, her more than friend, who had left kindred and country for her family'. Perhaps in looking after the person who had ministered to her father, it felt that she was caring vicariously for her beloved father. The Duchesse d'Angoulême was twenty-nine at the time of the Abbé's death. Abbé Edgeworth was buried in the Roman Catholic cemetery in Mittau, and the King himself drafted the Abbé's epitaph: 'I weep for a friend, a comforter, a benefactor, who guided the King, my brother, on his way to Heaven.'

Maria Edgeworth, the novelist and a relation of the Abbé, visited Paris in 1820 and was told by Madame de Rohan that the Abbé was held in great veneration and respect by the French Court. On 4 June 1820, Maria wrote, 'Some weeks ago we saw a picture of the death of the Abbé Edgeworth – pale and almost extinct supported by a venerable priest on one side –and on the other is the Duchesse d'Angoulême preparing some medicine – bending over him in all her youth and beauty.'[11]

Emperor Alexander I of Russia visited Mittau in March 1807, and was introduced to the Duchesse d'Angoulême. He spent an hour and a half with Louis XVIII, who was deeply depressed by the conditions of his exile and crippled by gout. The Emperor noted that Louis XVIII could hardly get out of his chair to greet his visitor and benefactor, so afflicted was he by his gout and perhaps a more general lethargy. The King was not yet fifty years of age. Contact with the family did not impress Alexander with the virtues and strengths of the Bourbons, whom he regarded as being arrogant, ungracious and without a talent for government. The Duchesse d'Angoulême appeared to the Emperor to be increasingly embittered. During the time she spent in Mittau and Eastern Europe in exile, Marie Thérèse's personality, which Louis XVIII had described as being so pleasing in the early days of her marriage, seemed to harden. The endless tedium of their exile had sapped the *joie de vivre* that she had previously shown, despite her many sufferings. As time passed and the possibility of children faded, Marie Thérèse became increasingly sad, often replaying the traumas of her girlhood experiences and spending many hours at prayer. As a young woman living in Vienna, she had expressed doubts about the wisdom of bringing children into a world where there was so much suffering and pain. She wrote at that time, 'But the losses I have suffered are enough to make me unhappy always, especially if I were to incur the just reproaches as time went on, of bringing others into the world to be unhappy too.' Royalist supporters were disappointed. There was no direct line of succession after the Duc de Berry.

On 7 July 1807, the Peace of Tilsit was signed between Alexander I and Napoleon on an island in the middle of the river Neman. In the light of the new alliance between Alexander and Napoleon, it was hinted to the Bourbons by the Russians that it would be better if they sought refuge elsewhere. The Bourbon family fortunately had the comfort of an invitation from the King of Sweden. Louis XVIII and the Duc d'Angoulême went to Stockholm to inspect the accommodation on offer, but meantime the

French army and Napoleon were threatening Sweden and forcing the Swedish army to retreat. Sweden was no longer in a position to be able to provide a suitable place of safety for the Bourbons. Gustav IV Adolph urged Louis XVIII and the rest of the family to seek refuge and a new home in England, which was less threatened by Napoleon than the rest of Europe by virtue of its island geography and the strength of the Royal Navy. Money worries were also troubling Louis XVIII and he wanted access to English funding; he felt he would be more likely to get the help he needed if he were on the spot. With few other options available to him, Louis sailed for England; but the voyage was horrendous and they were nearly shipwrecked at Kalmar[12] on the east coast of Sweden and in danger of being washed up on the shores of Pomerania, which was under Napoleon's control. Louis XVIII wanted refuge and to be near to France and his network of spies and informers; also close to his friend the Prince Regent[13] and the British government, if at all possible. In order to try to achieve this arrangement, he chose to stay in his boat for five whole uncomfortable days on the choppy seas of the North Sea off the coast at Yarmouth, awaiting permission to come ashore as an acknowledged King. Many of his companions were feeling less than well, to say the least. Eventually, the British government representatives allowed Louis XVIII to take up an offer from the Marquis of Buckingham of a home for him and his suite. The King disembarked to a warm welcome from the local people at Yarmouth on 2 November 1807. He was required to stay at a distance from London. The Bourbons' new home was to be Gosfield Hall, near Braintree in Essex, one of the estates belonging to the Marquis. Louis XVIII retired there under the *nom de guerre* of the Comte de Lille. He was not formally recognised as King in exile. He was, however, provided with a pension by the government.

In January 1808, Louis spent time staying with the Marquis of Buckingham, his kind and generous protector, at Stowe, his beautiful house with its fabulous gardens filled with temples and monuments. The King was accompanied by the French Princes of the Blood who were also living in exile in England – the Comte d'Artois, Duc d'Angoulême, Duc de Berry, Duc d'Orléans, Comte de Beaujolais,[14] the Prince de Condé and Duc de Bourbon and their attendants. The French Princes may well have been reminded of Versailles, so magnificent were the surroundings. A stone circular building in the grounds was renamed the Bourbon Tower in honour of their visit.[15] There were even suggestions that the King's younger nephew, the Duc de Berry, might marry Lady Mary Grenville, the Marquis of Buckingham's daughter. This idea did not come to fruition for a number of reasons: Lady Mary might be a Marquis's daughter, but Bourbons (even in exile) were more accustomed to the idea of marrying princesses from the Royal houses of Europe. There were also differences of religion. Lady Mary was a Protestant and Berry the scion of a very

Roman Catholic family. From the point of view of Lady Mary's family, the Duc de Berry was an impoverished exile with no immediate prospect of returning to France, and had a reputation for enjoying the company of English women of less virtue than Lady Mary. Other Royal families were not keen to marry into the Bourbon dynasty at this time. In 1805, the King of Sardinia forbade his daughter to marry the Duc de Berry on the grounds that it would condemn her to a life of poverty, hunger and wandering like a gypsy without a settled home. The comments about poverty and hunger were an exaggeration, but he was right about the lack of a settled home – as Marie Thérèse had experienced since her own marriage in 1799.

At Stowe there were toasts at dinner to 'The Illustrious House of Bourbon' and the absent Royal ladies, Marie Thérèse and her aunt who were still in Mittau, 'The Ladies at Mittau'. The Marquis also entertained his guests with dancing and music. The *Morning Chronicle* of 26 January 1808 reported a visit by the Comte de Lille, as the newspaper dubbed Louis XVIII, and the Duc d'Angoulême to the University of Oxford. Louis XVIII visited the Bodleian Library and browsed the rare and interesting books to be found there.

The assistance given to the Bourbons by the Marquis of Buckingham cost his family dear. The Preface to the memoirs of his son Richard Duke of Buckingham and Chandos, published in 1862, stated:

> His father had lived with princely magnificence; his expenditure in the luxuries of art and literature was enormous; and the munificent spirit with which he maintained the Royal Family of France and its numerous followers,[16] during their residence on one of his estates,[17] not only drained his exchequer, but burdened him with debt. Neither Louis XVIII nor Charles X took the slightest notice of the obligation that had incurred – apparently regarding such imprudent generosity as the natural acknowledgement of their exceeding merit. But with their benefactor the evil of pecuniary embarrassments increased year after year, till it became imperative that his expensive establishments should be reduced, and that he should go abroad till his large estates could be nursed, so as to meet the heaviest and most pressing demands.

These words give us further evidence that the Bourbons were demanding and not particularly grateful guests. They regarded such assistance as their right and due. Certainly they do not seem to have taken the opportunity in later more prosperous times to assist their former benefactor.

It seemed preferable to Marie Thérèse and Marie Joséphine to remain in Mittau rather than attempt a long and difficult journey across Europe by coach during the winter weather, topped off by a crossing of the North

Sea, to join their menfolk. It is a measure of the affection between the Duc and Duchesse d'Angoulême that by 1808 Louis Antoine was missing his wife so much that he travelled back to Mittau to escort this wife and aunt to England. Louis Antoine could not bear to be away from his dear 'joy' for too long, as he was missing the comfort of her familiar presence and support. The *Caledonian Mercury* of 16 June 1808 reported that the Duc d'Angoulême had left Stockholm and was travelling on to Karlscrona, a Swedish Baltic port, on his way to Mittau.

The arrival in Harwich on 1 September of the Duchesse d'Angoulême and the Queen of France, accompanied by the Comte and Comtesse de Damas and other members of their entourage, was reported by the *Aberdeen Journal* of 7 September 1808 in these terms:

> The *Euryalus* frigate is arrived with the Queen of France and the Duchesse d'Angoulême. On passing Yarmouth the frigate made a signal to the *Majestic*. Admiral Russel immediately hoisted the Royal Standard at the main, and the Union[18] at the mizzen, and fired a royal salute, which was repeated by Admiral (William) Douglas's flagship, the *Roebuck*.

The Duchesse d'Angoulême was thus treated with Royal honours as the romantic figure of the *Orpheline du Temple* on her journey to Great Britain. They were cheered loudly by the inhabitants.

The Queen and Duchesse d'Angoulême arrived at Gosfield Hall in the autumn of 1808. They resided there until April 1809. The Duchesse d'Angoulême apparently liked Gosfield, as it reminded her of France. Here the Royal Family lived a quiet, rather isolated life, not that different from the kind of routine they had followed in Mittau and Warsaw. They were devout Roman Catholics in an almost entirely Protestant country. Louis XVIII spoke very good English. It was reported that by the time he was resident in England in 1809, Louis was able to read the English papers and translate and read their contents out in French. The Duc d'Angoulême spoke some English from the time spent with his father, the Comte d'Artois, in Britain; but the Queen and Duchesse d'Angoulême and many of the family's attendants did not speak the language of their new home. The local gentry in Essex were intimidated by their Royal rank and felt inhibited from visiting the Bourbons. They were also reluctant to attempt social visits during which they might be expected to speak French.

The Comte d' Artois had spent most of his life since 1789 in exile in London and Edinburgh. He was regarded by many of the longer established émigrés based in Britain as their leader and the legitimate representative of Royal authority. As Fanny Burney[19] reported, 'French titles had become as plentiful as blackberries in several parts of England.' However, many of the French émigré community in England felt little inclination to spend time and money travelling to remote Essex (and later Buckinghamshire) to pay their respects.

In April 1809, the Bourbons left Essex and moved to live at Hartwell House, two miles outside Aylesbury, Buckinghamshire. The French Royal Family had leased the house from Sir Henry Lee for an annual rent of £600. Hartwell was a Jacobean house built by the Hampden family in the early 1600s. The Lees later intermarried with the Hampden family, hence their possession of Hartwell House and its estate by the 1800s. The house had been extended in the mid-eighteenth century in the Georgian style. The grounds were designed in the style of Capability Brown with lakes, rivers and ornamental buildings, and the surrounding countryside was very attractive. The King enjoyed walking in the grounds very much when his health permitted exercise. On the entrance porch there was (and still is) a carved stone fleur-de-lys. It is said that when the King first arrived at Hartwell and noticed the symbol of France, he said, 'This is a happy omen; it means I shall return to assume my throne.'

Hartwell House

There was intense pressure on space at Hartwell. The large airy rooms in the house were divided into smaller units to provide extra accommodation for the large retinue of attendants and servants who accompanied the Royal Family during their exile in the English countryside. Estimates vary as to exactly how many they were; a letter from Charles Francis Greville[20] to the Seward family following a visit to Hartwell speaks of 150 people being housed there. The *Victoria County History of Buckinghamshire* of the period refers to 140 occupants of the house and its stables and other outbuildings. Whatever the precise number of attendants and family, and no doubt it fluctuated from time to time, it was a large number of people to accommodate, feed and clothe. It is a testament to the regard in which the family were held by their staff that even when restoration to the throne seemed least likely, and the new Imperial regime was most firmly established, this number of people were still prepared to follow them around

Europe and Great Britain, and not always in the most comfortable of circumstances.

The fabric of Hartwell House took something of a battering in an attempt to modify it to accommodate so many people. The parapets on the roof were demolished so that even those occupying rooms in the attics could have external views from their garrets. Vegetables were grown in a roof garden to provide cheap food for the occupants. Chickens were also kept on the roofs for eggs and meat. Members of the Court opened shops in the stables of the house to provide the residents with essentials, and also to supplement their incomes. This was something that had also been done at Versailles. Every inch of space was used to try to make money or to make life more comfortable for the occupants of Hartwell. As Roman Catholics the French Royal Family were not able to use the chapel at Hartwell House or to attend the local village church. As daily attendants at Mass it was essential that the family, their courtiers and servants had access to an appropriate chapel, and so one was created for their use in a wood-panelled room on the ground floor of the house.[21]

Hartwell House boasts a fine Jacobean staircase, the handrails of which are decorated with a number of wooden statuettes of mythical beasts and knights. Terrified by the shadows cast by these wooden carvings (and perhaps they were a little the worse for wear), Marie Joséphine insisted that the statuettes be chopped of at their bases and removed from her sight; so much did she loathe them. The statuettes were indeed taken away. Unfortunately, no record was kept of the order in which they should be replaced when the Bourbons left. To this day no one can be sure whether the restoration of the staircase has put the severed statuettes back in their original places.

Philip Mansel writes in his excellent biography of Louis XVIII of the handicap the King felt from not having children of his own[22] who could be heirs to the throne he claimed. Louis XVIII might be King of France in name, but he was only too conscious of the reality of the situation that he was the pensioner of foreign governments and merely a figurehead. Even among his own family his authority was diminished by the fact that the first loyalty of his heirs – the Duc d'Angoulême and the Duc de Berry – was not to him but to his brother and successor and their father, the Comte d' Artois. Louis XVIII had none of the levers of control that he would have had if he had been on the throne of France; for example, the control of the huge income and lands which he could bestow as he wished. He also desperately needed to maintain unity among his family to secure the aid of other governments. Louis XVIII felt pulled between his own more liberal and compromising political approach and the hard-line approach taken by his brother and the Duchesse d'Angoulême. In 1801, Louis XVIII had wanted to visit Naples – instead of heading for Warsaw when the family were thrown out of Mittau by the Emperor Paul I – and to be accompanied to Italy by the Duc and Duchesse d'Angoulême. Louis XVIII liked to have them with him as he felt they presented the most appealing and sympathetic side of the Bourbon dynasty, particularly Marie Thérèse, the *Orphan of the Temple*. But the Comte d'Artois forbade the Duc and Duchesse d'Angoulême from travelling with the King to Naples, and Louis Antoine and Marie Thérèse obeyed the Comte d'Artois rather than the King. The Comte had taken this position because he had learned that his brother was secretly negotiating with Napoleon, and this was something he could not countenance. In any event, it was not possible for the Bourbons to travel to Italy as they were prevented by Napoleon's victories. Louis XVIII wrote of his brother, the Comte d'Artois, '*Il connaît bien tous les droits d'un père*' (He knows well all the rights of a father).

The Duc de Berry energetically set about creating his own family life with an Englishwoman, Amy Brown, with or without the formalities of marriage. Madame de Gontaut's memoirs report that while they were resident in England, 'Having very simple tastes, Duc de Berry led a quiet life in London, dining every day with Monsieur, frequently spending his evenings with him at the house of the Duchesse de Coigny.' He did, however, enjoy the opera very much and was able to enjoy invitations including those from the Duke of Portland. Madame de Gontaut's memoirs continue:

> From the box of the Duke of Portland ... we enjoyed his pleasure; but not far from us we noticed a very distinguished person whom everyone was looking at, but whom no one knew. She was very beautiful, but extremely pale, and well, though simply, dressed. We were greatly amused at the curiosity she seemed to inspire in our compatriots, all the more so as she seemed to be perfectly indifferent to it. A young man named La Chastre one day offered her a programme, which she refused. M. de Clermont, with more audacity, offered her a bouquet, whereupon she froze him with a glance of magnificent disdain. On this occasion we observed that Monseigneur looked grave and cold, apparently thinking it bad taste to annoy the young woman. M. de Clermont, who persisted in his attentions and his curiosity, told us at length that he had succeeded in finding out her history. 'Where she lives they call her Mrs. Brown,' he said. 'She lives near the Park, where she walks out every day with her child, a little boy about six or seven, upon whom she lavishes maternal cares. They say she is good, charitable, and kindly, but very reserved.' We could not learn anything more from M. de Clermont, who seemed to grow mysterious all at once, and we forgot the whole matter. This happened about the time of the wars with Russia and Spain. Several years afterwards, I learned that Madame de Montsoreau and Vicomte d'Agoult had become sponsors for a little girl, to whom they gave the name of Charlotte. Two years later, the Duchesse de Coigny became godmother to another little girl named Louise. The

> Duc de Berry, they said, seemed to be interested in these children. The two godmothers were discreet, and the curious public could draw but one conclusion. Society became accustomed, and so did my daughters and I, to seeing them sometimes at the houses of the Duchesse de Coigny and Madame de Montsoreau. They were taken good care of, they had a governess who taught them French, and they spoke English with their mother.[23]

The daily routine for Marie Thérèse and her husband when he was in residence at Hartwell revolved around the King and his daily pursuits and habits. Here the King rose at 8 a.m., as was his habit, and worked on his correspondence and papers until 11 a.m. Then, accompanied by the Duchesse d'Angoulême, and whoever else of the rest of the Royal Family was at Hartwell and the members of the Court who were in attendance, he would go to Mass. The family then ate a large dinner together followed by taking some fresh air, perhaps a walk in the gardens of Hartwell House or a carriage ride in the surrounding Buckinghamshire countryside. Marie Thérèse loved to ride and acquired a new saddle and riding gloves during her time at Hartwell. The Bourbon men took every opportunity to hunt. There would then be a formal reception followed by a light supper. Marie Thérèse spent some time in the gardens and particularly enjoyed grafting plants, especially roses. The family played whist. The Duchesse d'Angoulême would often watch the game while working with her ladies at her needlework.

The Royal Family was surrounded by servants and courtiers as in the days of Versailles. These attendants argued among themselves and jockeyed for position and preferment just as they had in grander circumstances. A number of English guests were invited to have dinner with the family and to stay overnight. Included among their visitors were the Grenvilles, Lady Mary Grenville and her mother, Lady Buckingham. The time spent at Hartwell was not without pleasures and distractions for the Royal Family. They may not have been in London but it was only 50 miles away and there were no restrictions on their receiving visitors. Louis XVIII travelled widely in England as a tourist, enjoying the sights of Oxford, Cambridge, the magnificent Warwick Castle and the curative waters of Bath Spa. He visited with interest the up and coming town of Birmingham, then an expanding and very interesting industrial centre renowned for its innovations in technology and engineering. Marie Thérèse preferred to stay at Hartwell out of the public view. She did, however, spend some time with the King in Bath, for example in 1813. The city had become home to many of the French émigré community. The King relished the attention and courtesies paid to him and was in good health. Occasionally the Duchesse d'Angoulême would venture up to London to have lunch with the Duc de Berry, attend Mass at King Street and dine with her cousin, Condé. She was closely observed by many 'interested in her melancholy charms'.[24] She did not enjoy the attention attracted by her celebrity and tragic history.

At least during the English exile, money worries were not so much of a problem as they had been during the earlier years of the family's exile. The British government provided for them handsomely.[25] The Duc d'Orléans, who was also living in exile in England at Twickenham with his family, visited Hartwell House. While Marie Thérèse, as a Christian woman and in deference to her father's wishes, was prepared to forgive the Duc d'Orléans' family for their part in her father's downfall and death, she felt the pain in doing so. His family's betrayal of her family was great. The Duc d'Orléans' own views had changed significantly over the years. As a young man he had been a keen adherent of Revolutionary principles and thinking. He had fought bravely for the Revolutionary cause against the foreign counter-revolutionary forces invading France in November 1792 at the Battle of Jemappes. His courage had been mentioned in despatches. Despite being a Prince, hardly a recommendation during Revolutionary times, he was rated as a brave and competent soldier. He too had come to see the violence of the Revolution with the execution of his own father in 1794, and had spent long years in exile during which he and his family had suffered hardship. He had sought and gained reconciliation with Louis XVIII through the good offices of the Comte d'Artois.

It was important for all the Bourbons to present a united front against the claims of Bonaparte, if they were to have any hope of regaining the throne of France and maintaining the support of foreign governments. When the Duchesse d'Angoulême first saw Louis Philippe, who had arrived at Hartwell before Mass was finished, she fainted away. She refused his offer of help to get up. Marie Thérèse went up to her room, a large handsome apartment overlooking the gardens of Hartwell, to recover from the distress she felt at seeing the Duc d'Orléans and the dreadful memories and associations evoked by him. Later in the day she was sufficiently recovered to be able to join the rest of the party for luncheon. She was able to converse with the Duc d'Orléans on the subject of her health, a frequent and safe topic of conversation at the Bourbon Court in exile.

During Marie Thérèse's period of exile in Britain, Napoleon ordered that the Temple, including the Tower in which she had been imprisoned, be razed to the ground. The Emperor feared that the Temple and all the memories it evoked was becoming an attraction for Royalist supporters in search of martyrs to their cause. He was conscious that it might become a place of pilgrimage or even a shrine to the dead Bourbons and that its continuing existence might encourage sedition and pro-Royalist sentiment among the French people. When the Duchesse d'Angoulême heard of the destruction of the Tower, she was saddened. It was a place which held memories of her great sufferings and those of her family during their captivity. It was equally the last place she had seen, spoken to and embraced her father, mother, aunt and younger brother, so provided a tangible link with them. One day she must have hoped to return to visit and pray there for her family. Like the deaths of the Abbé Edgeworth, those of her aunts and Coco, it was another break in the connection with her girlhood, family life and happier times.

In April 1810, the eighteen-year-old Archduchess Marie Louise of Austria[26] was married to Napoleon. It was part of the settlement following the Battle of Wagram in July 1809 at which Napoleon had defeated the army of the Austrian Empire commanded by the Archduke Charles. The Archduchess became Empress of France. Napoleon had divorced the Empress Joséphine because of her inability to bear him a child. The young Empress was Marie Thérèse's second cousin. The Duchesse d'Angoulême had known Marie Louise as a little girl, during her days at the Viennese Court. Marie Louise for her part remembered with fondness her French cousin. The Duchesse d'Angoulême felt herself to be shamed that a Habsburg Princess, and her cousin,[27] had been offered in marriage to the usurper Bonaparte by the Emperor Francis of Austria. Marie Thérèse had always been proud of her Habsburg family, and this marriage felt like a further humiliation. It gave the Napoleonic regime respectability, particularly in the eyes of the French nobility and ruling classes, as well as in the eyes of other European rulers. The marriage was also an indication of the permanence of the French Imperial regime, which was difficult for Marie Thérèse and her family to accept. It was, after all, only sixteen years since a former Austrian archduchess had been transported through the streets of Paris on an open cart through jeering crowds, her hands tied, to be executed at the guillotine; now here was another Austrian archduchess arriving in France to be its Empress.

Following Napoleon's second marriage, the English newspapers of the period, for example the *Leeds Mercury*, noted the close family connection by marriage between the exiled French Royal Family and Napoleon the usurper. By 1810, the Bourbons had been out of power and away from France for more than fifteen years. Indeed, at times when the prospect of the Bourbon return was at its dimmest, Louis XVIII had even encouraged his own courtiers to return to France and make their peace with the Imperial regime. He never gave up hope of regaining his throne, but did not wish to bear the responsibility or cost of keeping from France those who wished to return to their homes. The feeling among many of the aristocracy was that if Napoleon Bonaparte was good enough to marry into the Imperial Habsburg dynasty, he was good enough for them. His regime provided order after the Revolutionary years. Sometimes in conversation, Napoleon would refer to the executed Louis XVI as 'my poor uncle'.

Queen Marie Joséphine died aged 57 from hydropsy[28] on 13 November 1810 at Hartwell House. After a service at the French chapel in

Marylebone, she was given the honour of a state funeral in Westminster Abbey, which was the first Catholic service in the Abbey since the Reformation. The service lasted five hours. There was a large gathering of the French émigré community at her funeral, with reports of a total of 300 attending the ceremony. The funeral cortège was followed by the carriages of six princes of the British Royal Family. The Queen was buried in Westminster Abbey, but later her body was disinterred and reburied in Cagliari Cathedral on the island of Sardinia. The Duchesse d'Angoulême had nursed the dying Queen tenderly in her last illness. The two royal ladies had grown close over the years they had spent together in exile and had come to love each other dearly. As Marie Joséphine was dying, she implored the Duchesse d'Angoulême not to love her too much or to grieve too deeply for her death.

As was the usual custom with French Royal women, protocol meant that Marie Thérèse was not present at the funeral of her aunt. The Court in exile at Hartwell, never the most jolly of environments, was plunged into deep mourning by the Queen's death. Louis XVIII wrote[29] to the Comte d'Avaray on the death of Marie Joséphine, saying, 'I confess I did not realise how much I loved the Queen. I miss her a hundred times a day. I say to myself, mechanically, I must tell her this or that, and then I remember that I have no one to confide in.' The death of the Queen meant that Marie Thérèse was now the senior lady at the Court of her uncle, and would be required to play her part as his hostess. Another significant death had occurred during the year, namely the murder of Axel von Fersen during a riot in Stockholm at the funeral of King Charles Augustus. The news of his death must have given rise to a number of emotions in Marie Thérèse. She must have thought again of the abortive escape attempt of 1791, which he had been so instrumental in organising, with its hope and despair. She may have recalled the rumours and speculation about the nature of his relationship with her mother, which must have given her pain. His memory must have also brought back to her the uncomfortable time during her sojourn at the Court in Vienna when he had asked her for money. This was yet another farewell to part of her childhood and youth to trouble the Duchesse d'Angoulême.

We gain a picture of life at Hartwell after the death of the Queen from the April 1814 account of a visit two years earlier by the young diarist Charles Greville, who visited Hartwell House and his father. He wrote of the visit, 'About two years ago my father and I went to Hartwell by invitation of the King. The house is large but in a dreary, disagreeable situation.'[30] The visiting Englishmen were received graciously by the King, who shook hands with them. They were shown into the private apartments which were 'very small, hardly bigger than a closet, and I remarked pictures of the late King, Queen, Madame Élisabeth and the Dauphin (Louis XVII) hanging on the walls'. He continued:

> After the audience we were taken to the salon, a large room with a billiard table[31] at one end. Here the party assembled before dinner, to all of whom we were presented – The Duchesse d'Angoulême, Monsieur the Duc d'Angoulême, the Duc de Berry, Prince and Princess de Condé (ci-devant[32] Madame de Monaco) and a vast number of Ducs etc., Madame la Duchesse de Serron[33] (a little old dame d'Honneur to Madame d'Angoulême) Duc de Lorges, Duc d'Avaray, Archevêque de Rheims (an infirm old prelate tortured with tic-douloureux[34]) and many others whose names I cannot remember. A little after 6 o'clock dinner was announced, when we went into the next room, the King walking out first. The dinner was extremely plain, consisting of very few dishes and no wines except port and sherry. His Majesty did the honours himself, and was very civil and agreeable. We were a very short time at table and the ladies and gentlemen all got up together.[35] Each of the ladies folded up her napkin and tied it round with a bit of ribbon, and carried it away.[36]

The youthful Greville noted the extreme deference shown by Marie Thérèse to her uncle, reporting, 'Whenever the King came in or went out of the room, Madame d'Angoulême made him a low curtsey, which he returned by bowing and kissing her hand.' Time was spent after dinner drinking coffee and tea and chatting. The majority of the dinner guests reassembled in Madame d'Angoulême's apartments upstairs for a quarter of an hour before going back down to the drawing room where several card tables were laid out. The King played at whist with the Prince and Princess de Condé while the rest of the party played at billiards and ombre.[37] Greville and his father spent the night at Hartwell at the invitation of the King, but the young man was not impressed by the comfort of the accommodation provided for him. The party took breakfast at 10 a.m. and the King and family went to Mass at 11 a.m. as was his usual custom. The presence of so many elderly and infirm courtiers can hardly have made for a lively and stimulating environment for Marie Thérèse. In assessing Greville's view of life at Hartwell, one must remember his youth: he probably found even the Duchesse d'Angoulême, who was then in her mid-thirties, to be elderly.

Among the visitors to Hartwell was the exiled King Gustav IV Adolph of Sweden, who spent three months staying with the family at Hartwell. The Prince Regent did not often visit the family, but when he did come to Buckinghamshire he was always scrupulously polite to Louis XVIII. One of the most influential members of the Bourbon Court in exile, and someone with whom Marie Thérèse would have had daily contact during the years of exile, was the King's favourite, the Duc d'Avaray. He had acted as the King's confidant, adviser, favourite and secretary. When he died on 4 June 1811, his place was taken by the Comte de Blacas,[38] an aristocrat originally from Provence. The Comte had a classic émigré background: he had fought with the Condé Army and spent time in Warsaw with the family, thence following the Bourbons to England. In 1809 he was appointed to the office of *Grand Maître de la Garde-Robe du Roi.*

From 1811 onwards, the once invincible Napoleon began to look more vulnerable. His armies were humbled in Spain and Portugal by Wellington. Now Louis XVIII and the Duc and Duchesse d'Angoulême were routinely invited to London to attend the Prince Regent's Birthday Drawing Rooms held at his beautiful London home, Carlton House.[39] The Bourbons were honoured guests among the 3,000 at the magnificent celebrations in honour of the Prince of Wales becoming Prince Regent in June 1811. One newspaper of the time described:

> The illustrious family of the house of Bourbon entered through the gardens at about ten, when they were ushered into the Privy Council Chamber, where the Prince Regent was sitting under a crimson canopy of state, surrounded by the Officers of State of his Household, who, on their approach immediately rose to receive them.

Like the Emperor of Russia, the Prince Regent felt it proper and dignified for him as a brother prince to assist the Bourbons and give them succour and help in their exile. The Bourbons were treated by the Prince and the other attendants according to their Royal rank at these events. England was at war with France; it no longer mattered if Napoleon was offended by the actions of the Prince Regent in honouring the dispossessed Bourbons. Even so, at the June 1811 celebrations Louis XVIII was introduced as the Comte de Lille rather than as King of France. Marie Thérèse did not find these visits to London as congenial as did her uncle: she tired of the pomp and ceremonial of which she was so often the centre of attention, as a result of her 'romantic' and tragic history. For example, the descriptions of her attendance at the Carlton House celebrations of June 1811 report that 'The amiable daughter of Louis XVI naturally attracted the chief attention, the exhilarating effect of which was clearly visible on her interesting countenance.' Marie Thérèse was blushing, embarrassed by all the attention addressed to her. The adult Marie Thérèse had come to dislike, and find rather overwhelming and embarrassing, the elaborate ceremonial which she had so enjoyed as a child at her father's Court.[40] She was perhaps also uncomfortable with the unfamiliar manners and language of the English Court. She was certainly conscious of their ambiguous social position, royal yet not ruling, and living as the dependent pensioners of a country at war with their own beloved homeland.

At the reception of June 1811, she met once again the Duke of Sussex whom she had previously encountered in Vienna in the late 1790s during her stay with her Imperial cousins. Several years later in a conversation with Madame d'Arblay, the Princess commented on the Carlton House reception, the Prince Regent's hospitality and the noble style in which he had treated her and all her family at the Carlton House fête. In the midst of their misfortunes, 'and while so much doubt hung against every chance of those misfortunes being ever reversed, did so much honour to his heart, and proved so solacing to their woes and humiliation that she could never revert to the public testimony of his good will without the most glowing gratitude!' She declared the Prince Regent to be perfect.

Fashionable society with its frivolous occupations and preoccupations with clothes and gossip was not her thing. She seems to have preferred the pleasures of solitude and the opportunity to pray and meditate rather than the distractions of balls, parties and meeting the '*haut ton*'[41] of Regency society. Amusing to note, given Marie Thérèse's indifference to fashion, the *Morning Chronicle of* 2 December 1811 described in detail the new fashion for Mechlin lace tippets[42] 'à la Duchesse d'Angoulême' to cover the bosom at a cost of 20 guineas. More invitations to events in London followed. In early August 1812, the English newspapers reported that the Prince Regent had travelled to Wimbledon to have dinner with the Bourbon family including Marie Thérèse, who was also invited to dine at Carlton House and meet Queen Charlotte.[43] In August 1812, the Duc d'Angoulême at last received permission from the British government to join the British Army on the Iberian Peninsula. Marie Thérèse and her family were once again moving back into the centre stage of European social and political life. The Duchesse d'Angoulême spent many hours on her knees praying for the restoration of her family to the throne.

She also spent time travelling in England. The *Morning Post* of 7 August 1813 reported that the Duchesse d'Angoulême was staying in Charlton Park in Cheltenham, 'trying the efficacy of its salubrious water'. She noted in a letter to the Comte de Damas that she was suntanned from spending time in the garden provided at her lodgings, where she spent her days walking and reading. She felt the benefit of taking the waters and enjoyed a warm welcome from the local inhabitants; and for company she had with her Madame de Sérent. The Duchesse d'Angoulême and her husband had visited Cheltenham previously in 1811. Louis XVIII came from Hartwell to visit her during her stay in the spa town, and took the time to visit the site of the Battle of Tewkesbury[44] and Gloucester.

Louis XVIII and his activists tried to stir up sedition against the Bonapartist regime in France. The Comte de Blacas wrote to the holders of the great offices of state in France reassuring them that their positions would be secure under a restored Bourbon monarchy. Louis XVIII and his close advisers hoped that the power of self-interest and the reassurance of the continuation of positions they had achieved would help to facilitate the return of the Bourbons. In February 1813, Louis issued the Declaration of Hartwell from the Library at Hartwell, which set out his policies and the approach his government would take on his Restoration as King. It was a document intended to reassure the people of France that the Bourbons had indeed learned much from their exile. The Declaration aimed to show that they also understood the changes that had taken place in France during the more than twenty years since Louis XVIII had gone into exile. Louis made it clear in the Declaration of Hartwell that he was committed to peace and honour and the maintenance of existing Napoleonic administrative and legal structures in France. He promised that there would be no revenge for past acts and that there would be no future military conscription, which had come to be so loathed under the Napoleonic regime. The Declaration appealed to the Senate, the French parliament, to use their talents in support of the Restoration. The Declaration was a model of moderation, designed to appeal to a very wide constituency in France and to enrol the support of European governments. It promised the maintenance of order that Napoleon had established so firmly. It was not bloodthirsty or full of hatred for what had happened in France during and since the Revolution. It promised the possibility of national unity and peace after the long years of the Napoleonic Wars, so expensive in manpower and resources. The Bourbons also committed themselves to lay claim only to those French territorial boundaries which had existed before Napoleon. This was a reassuring position for other European rulers. The Declaration of Hartwell also signalled the end of the Bourbon view of themselves as Kings by divine right. The politically astute Louis XVIII may have been happy to promulgate this view of monarchy, but years of exile had taught him the necessity of political pragmatism. His brother and heir, the Comte d'Artois, felt very differently. Years of exile in England had not warmed him to the English way of government and constitutional monarchy. He is said to have remarked that he would rather chop wood than be the King of England.[45]

Reassuring those members of the middle and upper classes who had bought 'émigré' property during the period, the King asked that the purchasers of 'nationalised' property or '*biens nationaux*' try to come to a negotiated settlement with those whose land and other goods had been seized and then sold on to its current owner or their successor. The British government supported and encouraged the moderation of his approach and helped to promulgate the Declaration widely in France by using agents to distribute leaflets. This moderate approach might appeal to the wider France. Ironically, it was most unattractive to those who had been most loyal to Louis XVIII and his family in exile. The hard-core émigré community, who had given up so much to follow the family into exile with its attendant hardships, including the forfeiture of their property, were dismayed by its liberality and lack of recognition of their sacrifices. There was no commitment to restoration of property or compensation for their losses. The Declaration gave no opportunity for revenge on those who had destroyed the *ancien régime* and with it their privileges and property rights.

Many of the émigrés felt that the hard-line uncompromising Comte d' Artois was much more to their taste. He was, they felt, their natural leader and advocate. They barely tolerated the would-be King Louis XVIII and his 'liberal' Declaration of Hartwell and looked forward to the time when the Comte d'Artois would be their King; surely not far off given the chronic ill-health of Louis XVIII. Marie Thérèse inclined towards the political views of her father-in-law. She longed to return to France.

In 1812 Napoleon was defeated in Russia by the weather and the determination of the Russians. Napoleon lost the Battle of Leipzig in October 1813. His military star was fading. Perhaps the Princess's dream of home could come true. She prayed so.

Louis XVIII

8

The First Restoration

1814-1815

On 1 March 1814, Austria, Great Britain, Russia, Prussia, Spain, Portugal and Sweden came to an agreement known as the Sixth Coalition or Alliance.[1] The purpose of the Alliance was to crush Napoleon once and for all. Each of the signatory nations agreed to maintain a standing army of 150,000 until the war against Bonaparte was concluded. During March 1814, Napoleon was fighting and defeating the invading Russian and Prussian armies in a number of small-scale battles[2] in the eastern part of France around the area of Rheims, where the Kings of France were by tradition crowned. Napoleon was also, through his wife Marie Louise, trying to negotiate an honourable peace with the allies that would preserve his throne for his son. He was hoping to use the influence of his wife's father, the extremely vacillating and self-seeking Emperor of Austria, Francis I,[3] to save the French Imperial crown for his daughter and her son. Francis had very clearly, however, thrown in his lot with the Sixth Alliance. He now simply wanted to achieve a swift and reasonably dignified exit from France for his daughter and grandson that would not compromise his own position.

In the spring of 1814, France was occupied by foreign armies from the alliance of European powers. The question was then who would rule France in place of Bonaparte. The prospect of a possible return to France had lightened the lives of the exiles settled at Hartwell and brought Marie Thérèse and her family hope. From 1812 onwards, they read reports of Napoleon's disastrous invasion of Russia and the terrible retreat across the frozen wastes of Russia from the burning and abandoned ancient capital of Moscow, which cost thousands of French lives. In January 1814, the Comte d'Artois, Duc d'Angoulême and the King had made the very difficult decision, for loyal Frenchmen who loved their country even if they loathed and despised the upstart Bonaparte and all his doings, to support an attack on Napoleonic France by allied troops. Madame de Boigne[4] described in her memoirs the exiled Duc de Berry living in London and rejoicing in the victories of the French Navy against the British Navy in the Indian Ocean. A month later, the Comte d'Artois left Britain and went to join the Russian troops based in Holland and then travelled westwards awaiting the invasion of France by allied troops. Marie Thérèse watched developments in France and Europe with enormous interest from Hartwell. She read out loud reports of events to her uncle from the French newspapers, the delivery of which was eagerly awaited by the Household. In many ways, the Bourbons had no choice. The attack on Bonapartist France would take place with or without their support and endorsement, and it offered the only possibility of their Restoration. They would have been foolish indeed not to support the allies against Napoleon and hope themselves to benefit in the wake of any military gains. It was noted that the Duchesse d'Angoulême prayed for the sufferings of French soldiers, irrespective of whether they fought for the hated Bonaparte or were loyal to the Royalist side.

Charles Talleyrand, always the wily and shrewd politician, had been in touch with the Bourbons at Hartwell from 1813 onwards – long before the collapse of Napoleon's regime, in which he held the post of Foreign Minister. There were revolts and small uprisings throughout France in favour of the return of the Royal Family. The zeitgeist was moving away from the Empire and back towards the Bourbon monarchy. The people no longer wanted to pay the price in men and money required by the military ambition of Napoleon, particularly now that he was no longer the all-conquering hero of old. The Bordeaux area of south-west France was especially strong in its support for the Bourbons. It was in this part of France that the Duc d'Angoulême concentrated his energies to stir up support for the restoration of the Bourbon dynasty. Marie Thérèse was proud of her husband and his efforts on behalf of their family. The *Morning Post* of 25 January 1814 was full of Restoration rumours.

The *Lancaster Gazette* of 5 February 1814 reported that the Bourbon princes had left Great Britain the previous week. Marie Thérèse's husband was trusted by the King as a fellow political moderate and a safe pair of hands, in contrast to his father the Comte d'Artois. The Duc d'Angoulême headed towards Wellington's headquarters in the south-west of France, arriving there in early February. The King did not want the Comte d'Artois to be involved in this crucial area of the country where the Royalists had such strong support. He did not trust his younger brother's political judgement or his discretion. The Duc d'Angoulême based in this part of France was not, however, a free agent but was under the command of Wellington, the Commander of the British forces in France. He had to be content with being told by Wellington where he could travel within France and having his efforts to raise Royalist support and morale criticised by Wellington. The Duc d'Angoulême's younger brother, the Duc de Berry, landed in Normandy in February 1814 and apparently received a very low-key welcome from the local population. He largely disappeared from view, spending some time in Jersey until reappearing in Paris four months later.

Napoleon was by this time convinced that his former friend and admirer the Emperor Alexander of Russia had no desire to come to an amicable agreement and leave French territory, but wanted to ride at the head of his triumphant occupying troops though the streets of Paris. The allied armies had succeeded in tricking the Emperor Napoleon with a diversionary tactic, leaving a small detachment purporting to be the main army while in fact the majority of the allied forces were heading for Paris. Napoleon, usually such a brilliant tactician himself, was utterly amazed by their cunning and surprised to have been so deceived. He spent hours planning how he could move to protect his capital. Marie Louise panicked and left Paris on 29 March, initially for Rambouillet and thence to Troyes. Her flight was much against the advice of ex-Queen Hortense[5] of Holland who feared that the departure of the Empress and the little King of Rome would signal to the world the end of the Imperial regime. Napoleon himself had written on 16 March 1814 to his elder brother Joseph, the former King of Spain, who was in Paris and advising the Empress; he ordered him, one suspects not entirely seriously, 'Whatever happens you must not allow the Empress and the King of Rome to fall into the hands of the enemy… Stay with my son and do not forget that I would sooner see him drowned in the Seine than captured by the enemies of France.' In Paris there was intrigue against Napoleon orchestrated by Talleyrand, whom Napoleon referred to as 'the evil genius' in a letter to his brother Joseph. Talleyrand set about forming a provisional government to fill the power vacuum left by the absence of Napoleon, as he was by this time convinced that Napoleon should be overthrown for the good of France.

In late March 1814, a messenger arrived at Hartwell from Lord Cochrane to announce to Louis XVIII and Marie Thérèse and their courtiers that the allied sovereigns[6] were indicating that they wished to call upon Louis XVIII to return to France as King. This was not as yet, however, a formal or confirmed invitation, though Royalist fervour was mounting in Paris. Individuals read out copies of the declarations made by Louis XVIII during his years of exile committing him to guarantee various freedoms and civil liberties for the French people. Even the former servants of the Bonaparte family went over to the Royalist side, for example Bausset the Imperial *Préfet du Palais* reverted to his former title of Marquis and ceased to be a *Baron d'Empire*. Just as in October 1789, when Marie Antoinette found the Palace of Versailles practically deserted by courtiers and servants when the Parisian mob approached, so now the rats were leaving the Bonapartist ship. Even those closely and personally connected with the former Emperor changed sides; for example Claude de Beauharnais, one of Marie Louise's *Chevaliers d'Honneur* and a relation of the Empress Joséphine, resigned from his post in the second Empress's Household. In correspondence with his wife, Marie Louise, Napoleon railed against the betrayers.

One of the Comte d'Artois' agents, the Comte de Semalle, took over a newspaper office in Paris; having installed Royalist editors, he set about printing and distributing pro-Bourbon material. The historian Viscount Châteaubriand wrote that the most enthusiastic Royalists were often former Republicans or former supporters of the Emperor Napoleon, desperately attempting to cover their political tracks and hoping to ingratiate themselves and their families with the new Royalist regime. The mood in Paris had changed and where once there been cowed sycophancy to the Emperor, there was now abuse and bitterness. Few – except his old soldiers and his de Beauharnais stepchildren, Hortense and Eugène – among the many who had benefited so much from his rise to power remained loyal or had a good word to say for him. Many of the political establishment and senior military figures were running for cover.

The Duchesse d'Angoulême and her uncle were at Mass on Maundy Thursday, 24 March 1814, when from the chapel at Hartwell House they saw the arrival of a number of carriages and soldiers on horseback wearing large white cockades. The rest of the Household dashed outside to hear the news and find out what was happening. Louis XVIII and Marie Thérèse, trained by long experience to be patient and anxious to maintain royal dignity, waited inside the makeshift chapel to find out who had arrived to pay their respects. It proved to be a delegation of two deputies, Baron de la Barthe and Monsieur de Tausia from the city of Bordeaux, arriving to announce to Louis XVIII that the city had formally recognised him as the King of France. Louis was in tears of joy. Marie Thérèse was delighted to learn that it was her husband, the Duc d'Angoulême, accompanying the English army into Bordeaux, who had organised and encouraged the local Royalists to declare for the King. Bordeaux had surrendered to the English army without any resistance. The party sent to Hartwell by the citizens of Bordeaux was a response to the Duc d'Angoulême's efforts, as well as a reflection of the strong Royalist sentiments that existed in the area.

The Duc d'Angoulême had made a number of commitments to the people of Bordeaux of 'no more oppressive taxes, no more wars and no more conscription'[7] which had done much to persuade the population of Bordeaux that their city should support the Bourbons and their Restoration to the throne. Marie Thérèse's husband had received a triumphant welcome, including the reading of loyal addresses from the vast majority of the townspeople on his entering the city of Bordeaux. *The Times* of Saturday 26 March 1814 reported that the British army was greeted by the local population as liberators. *The Times* of 13 March reported:

> the Duke of Angoulême approached the city. He was met at two leagues[8] distant by a troop of two hundred young men of the first families in the neighbourhood, mounted on horseback and adorned with white cockades and sashes. As he approached the city gates the crowds increased and pressed around him, until he was literally carried by them to the Cathedral where *Te Deum* was sung.

In the evening the Duc d'Angoulême attended the theatre, which was completely full with an audience of those who wished to see him. The start of the play was delayed by poems and speeches in his honour and 'long and incessant peals of applause interrupted the performance'. There was even an *Ode sur une heureuse arrivée a Bordeaux*, which bemoaned the iron fist of Napoleon and welcomed a hero who would change the destiny of France!

Events moved apace. On Easter Saturday, the Royal Household at Hartwell learned that the French Senate had voted for the demise of General Bonaparte, as the former Emperor Napoleon was now known. Confirmation of this fact was received from London at midnight in a message from the Prince Regent. The allied armies of Great Britain, Russia, Prussia and Austria entered Paris on 31 March. The Duc de Raguse,[9] formerly Bonaparte's Maréchal Marmont, had on 31 March 1814, along with Mortier, negotiated the surrender of Paris to the Emperor Alexander I of Russia. He had then withdrawn the French troops under his command to Normandy, thus opening the way to the Restoration of the Bourbons.

The surrender document was signed by Maréchals Mortier and Marmont. Throughout France towns and cities were declaring for the King. Madame de Boigne reported in her memoirs[10] that the Emperor Alexander I of Russia, in conversation with that consummate survivor and politician Prince Talleyrand, remarked, 'Well, here we are at last in famous Paris. It is you who brought us, Monsieur Talleyrand, and now there are three things that we can do: we can deal with the Emperor Napoleon, we can establish a Regency,[11] or recall the Bourbons.' Talleyrand replied that the only option was to recall the Bourbons, stating, 'As your Imperial Majesty knows full well that the finest armies melt away before the anger of a nation.' Briefly, Maréchal Bernadotte and the Duc d'Orléans were considered as possible candidates, but Talleyrand was determined that the principle of legitimacy should determine the outcome of the debates about the succession. Alexander was persuaded that this was right despite his own lack of personal liking and respect for the elder branch of the Bourbons. So it was to be the Bourbons. The conqueror Alexander and the power broker Talleyrand had settled the fate of France and that of Marie Thérèse and her exiled family.

Napoleon wrote a letter dated 26 February 1814 from Troye to the Empress Marie Louise scoffing at the idea of the Restoration of the Bourbons, saying, 'So the Congress the allies intended to hold in my country is now under my control... The Russians tried to put forward the Bourbons. They were laughed at everywhere, and no one would second them. On this point the Austrians did not second them, nor would they hear of the Bourbons.' He was proved wrong. There was sufficient support for a Bourbon Restoration.

On 4 April 1814, Napoleon signed the Act of Abdication at Fontainebleau abandoning his throne in the hope that it could be saved for the infant King of Rome. He was persuaded to do so by many of his former loyalists, including Maréchal Ney who told the Emperor frankly and brutally that there was no chance of saving his throne for himself but that there was the possibility that something might be salvaged for his son. The Act of Abdication declared, 'The Allied Powers have proclaimed the Emperor Napoleon was the sole obstacle to the restoration of order in Europe; the Emperor Napoleon, faithful to his oath, declares himself prepared to descend from the throne, to leave France, nay to give up his very life for the country's good.' This wording was not acceptable to the alliance and two days later Napoleon abdicated once and for all. A few days later, the Treaty of Fontainebleau provided the deposed Emperor with a new domain – namely the Island of Elba. It made generous financial provision for him and his family, which in the event was not properly paid. He would be able to keep with him a small bodyguard.

The Senate had also nominated Talleyrand as the President of the provisional government and on 6 April 1814 declared that the 'French people freely call to the throne Louis – Stanislas – Xavier brother of the last King.' The existence and short, sad reign of Marie Thérèse's younger brother, the sad boy King Louis XVII who had been imprisoned and died alone in the Tower of the Temple in 1795, were conveniently overlooked. Thus Louis XVIII recognised the legality of the Revolutionary and Imperial governments of the intervening period. The offer of Restoration was ratified by the Legislative Assembly on 9 April 1814. It was made on condition that the King accept the Senate's new Constitution, which he did. The prize was simply too tempting to refuse, even if it made a nonsense of his claim to have been for nineteen years 'His most Christian Majesty the King of France and Navarre'. He could always change his mind on this point and assert his rights if the political weather changed.

Louis was going back to France as King, but as King of the French rather than as a divinely appointed sovereign and King of France. It was a profound shift in the role of the monarch and how he was seen, but the combination of the liberal Declaration of Hartwell and the military might of the Sixth Alliance had facilitated the return of a Bourbon monarch, even though he would be regarded in a very different way from his ancestors Louis XIV and Louis XV.

The Duchesse d'Angoulême was woken from her sleep and went downstairs to share in the rejoicings of the Household at Hartwell and read the illuminated address that had been sent to them by the Prince Regent. Once Hartwell and the Court in exile had been off the main political map of Europe; now all roads leading to it were crammed with traffic and travellers. Everyone wanted to congratulate the new King or send him some communication about the state of his kingdom and to jockey for position within the new regime. They were heady days for Marie Thérèse and her family. The Easter Day Mass was one of great celebration and rejoicing.

In Paris too there were celebrations. The Duchesse de Gontaut's memoirs quote a letter from a resident of Paris at this time:

> Try to imagine if you can how Paris looks at this moment, as I write in this beautiful spring sunshine, in the midst of a dense crowd — the allied armies dazzling in their gold and silver, Russians, Prussians, and Austrians, two hundred and fifty thousand men, thirty abreast, marching in through one of the magnificent gates of Louis XIV. On the Boulevards, with drums, music, flags; Cossacks calmly parading in the midst of this elegant throng, who receive them, not as conquerors, but as liberators; the streets, balconies, and windows crowded with people. As each sovereign passes, the women throw themselves at their feet, clasping their hands and crying: 'Long live our liberators! Down with the tyrant! Long live the Bourbons!' The women at the windows respond to these cries and demonstrations with similar ones. The white cockade appears everywhere as if by magic, handkerchiefs and dresses even being torn up to serve as flags. Just now everything is white, emblematic of peace, of hope — of glory, in short. Tell this to our friend; it will make her happy, and she will make it known in the proper quarter.

Artois was jubilantly received and charmed with his *bon hommerie* and good looks when he entered Paris on 12 April. Lord Byron's poem 'The Age of Bronze', written in 1823, posed the question to Louis XVIII:

> *Good classic Louis! Is it, canst thou say,*
> *Desirable to be the Desiré?*
> *Why wouldst thou leave calm Hartwell's green abode ...*
> *To rule a people who will not be ruled,*
> *And love much rather to be scourged than school'd?*

Whatever Byron might have thought, the would-be King longed for his throne and his country. However, disabling and painful 'martyring'[12]gout, to quote Byron,[13] delayed Louis XVIII's departure from Hartwell until 20 April, but he was now truly returning to his country as King. Aylesbury had been decorated with white lilies. As they travelled towards London, there were celebrations by crowds of British well-wishers lining the King and Duchesse d'Angoulême's route. Aylesbury has to this day a Bourbon Street, with a Blue Plaque commemorating the events of 1814. Things were now very different from the cold isolation of Mittau or the seclusion of Warsaw. At Stanmore in the north-western outskirts of London, the crowds unhorsed the King and Marie Thérèse's carriage. The people pulled the Bourbons' carriage to a nearby inn where the King and his niece were able to rest and refresh themselves. The Prince Regent travelled with them from Stanmore through Kilburn, down Edgware Road, Park Lane and thence into Piccadilly. London was awash with white Bourbon insignia. Outside their very smart Grillons Hotel in Albemarle Street,[14] famous for accommodating visiting royalty and the aristocracy, one hundred British soldiers wearing white Bourbon insignia provided the King and Duchesse d'Angoulême with a guard of honour, as befitted their restored Royal status. The King of France and Prince Regent of Great Britain exchanged decorative orders. The French King was invested with the ancient Order of the Garter and the Prince Regent received the Grand Cordon of the Saint-Esprit, the highest French order of chivalry.

The Russian Grand Duchess Catherine, favourite sister of Alexander I, was visiting London at the time of Marie Thérèse's arrival with her uncle. The Royal ladies exchanged visits. It was noted in the collection of letters between the Russian siblings, *Scenes from Russian Court Life*, that the Grand Duchess invited Queen Charlotte to join her to see the procession:

> [the Prince Regent] was in a gilt coach and eight, with the French King and the Duchess d'Angoulême. They came, escorted by some thousands of horsemen, great noblemen or small gentry came from London, and all the neighbouring counties' best, riding the finest horses in England, and all with the white cockade in their hats. All London was there, shouting and applauding. You might have thought it was the restoration of an English King. One cannot exaggerate the magnificence and splendour of the sight or the effect of these acclamations. The King got down at the Grillon Mansion in Albemarle Street. There the body of Ambassadors and the English Cabinet were gathered. It was in their presence that the King and the Prince exchanged Orders, and that Louis uttered to the Regent the memorable words that History has endorsed: 'Under God it is to your Highness that I owe my crown.'

That same day the King dined at Carlton House. After dinner there was a reception, where the Duchess (Grand Duchess Catherine) made his acquaintance; the ladies were presented to him by the Regent.

I saw him again afterwards under his own roof: he received me just at his bedside, for he suffered much from his legs, and never remained standing. He kept me half an hour. His talk was clever, but had something studied about it which to my mind took away all the agreeableness of it. Our Duchess and she of Angoulême exchanged visits next day, and met in the evening at the Queen's card-party.[15]

The county of Buckinghamshire had provided refuge for the Duchesse d'Angoulême and her family, and so sent a delegation to London to participate in the celebrations:

> An address, in that language (English), was read to His Majesty, which was presented by the Noblemen and Gentlemen of the County of Buckingham, congratulatory upon his happy restoration, and filled with cordial thanks for the graciousness of his manners, and the benignity of his conduct, during his long residence among them; warmly proclaiming their participation in his joy, and their admiration of his virtues. The reader was Colonel Nugest, a near relation of the present Duke of Buckingham.

Fanny Burney, Madame d'Arblay, was presented to Louis XVIII in London, and described his poor physical state, 'An avenue had been cleared from the door to the chair, and the King moved along it, slowly, slowly, slowly, rather dragging his large and weak limbs than walking, but his face was truly engaging!' She was invited by the King to visit Marie Thérèse at South Audley Street. This visit did not in fact take place, but the ladies did meet later in Paris. Miss Frances Williams Wynn, a relation of the Grenvilles and the Marquis of Buckingham, did attend one of Marie Thérèse's receptions and was not impressed, saying in her rather waspish *Diaries of a Lady of Quality*:

> [I] went one evening to the Duchesse d'Angoulême's, in Monsieur's dark two-roomed house in South Audley Street. It was literally hardly possible to see across the room, and the whole thing was, if one could have entertained such a feeling, a burlesque upon royalty. The sour, ill-tempered, vulgar countenance of the bleary eyed Duchess was a great damp to the interest one was prepared to feel in one whose fate had been more melancholy than that of any heroine of romance.

Madame de Sérent was described as 'little and crumpled' and Marie Thérèse was observed to be wearing a 'dingy brown dress'.

The Prince Regent, whose government had not allowed Louis XVIII to live in London when he had arrived in England as an asylum seeker from Mittau, was now happy to fete and honour his Royal guests. Louis XVIII certainly seems to have very much enjoyed the celebrations in London; the Duchesse d'Angoulême less so. A grand party was held at the Prince Regent's London home of Carlton House in honour of the Duchesse d'Angoulême. It was attended by all the London society glitterati. Marie Thérèse, it was noted by observers, was quiet and unprepossessing though dignified in her bearing during the celebrations. Her manner was reported by some commentators as being somewhat cold and formal. Kinder members of society recalled the Duchesse d'Angoulême's own imprisonment. Her dowdy appearance was noted by fashionable London society. The Duchesse d'Angoulême, it would appear, was not comfortable with what she felt to be the ambiguity of their position as the celebrated guests and pensioners of the conquerors of their beloved native land. Unlike her menfolk, she was never able to rejoice in the defeats of France, even one led by their arch-enemy Napoleon.

Madame de Gontaut's rather gushing memoirs describe the scene in these touching terms:

> Carlton House was dazzling with lights and gilding. The Prince Regent,[16] who had very good taste and was always gracious, kindly, and affable, tried to show his respectful affection for the King of France, and his pleasure in seeing him in his own house, by delicate attentions, which made this sight a delight to us all. The Prince had invited not only the princes and princesses of England, but had taken particular care to collect about the King the faithful émigrés those illustrious names of France, who had afforded a distinguished example of self-devotion. I had never seen the Prince so amiable; the King was very happy, and I must confess I was enchanted. It was in the midst of this that an interesting incident occurred. The Duchesse d'Angoulême met the Duc d'Orléans again for the first time.[17] They were in the embrasure of a window, and everyone was looking at them. An expression of sadness and sweetness was engraved on the interesting features of the Princess, where might be read pardon and oblivion. Everyone was affected.

Their departure from England was accompanied by ceremonial. The *Gentleman's Magazine* reported that the French King was escorted by members of the nobility and greeted as he travelled into Kent by the Lord Lieutenant of the county and a number of mounted soldiers. They were seen off on their journey to France by the Prince Regent himself, bringing with him parting gifts of travelling coaches and horses for the King and the Duchesse d'Angoulême: six horses for the King and four for the Duchesse d'Angoulême and her husband.

Marie Thérèse arrived back in France on 24 April 1814 after an exile from her beloved homeland of nearly nineteen years. At thirty-six years of age she was a very different person from that optimistic and forgiving young Princess who had left France for Vienna in December 1795. Exile and many disappointments, including her lack of children, seem to have hardened her nature, sapping some of her compassion for the sufferings of others, but deepening her piety and resignation to the will of God. She landed in Calais from an English warship, appropriately named *The Royal Sovereign*, escorted by six Royal Navy vessels. She gave her arm to support her gouty and obese uncle to help him walk ashore in France, just as she had once supported him in walking through the snowy wastes of Russia. The crossing of the English Channel (La Manche) was accomplished in lovely early summer weather and took only two and half-hours. The Admiral commanding the fleet was the Prince Regent's younger brother, the Duke of Clarence; [18] a sailor prince. The Duchesse d'Angoulême herself had never previously visited the northern part of France[19] around the Pas de Calais and could scarcely believe that she was back home in her beloved native land after so long away. Madame de Gontaut reports that 'The Duchesse d'Angoulême was greatly agitated, and could not restrain her tears. She inspired profound respect.'[20]

The arrival of Marie Thérèse and her uncle in France was greeted by a welcome of peels of church bells and, perhaps rather alarmingly, by artillery fire. Marie Thérèse was the first lady of the kingdom. The King and Duchesse d'Angoulême were accompanied on their return by their elderly cousin the Prince de Condé and his son the Duc de Bourbon, both of whom had been in exile in England with them. The Prince de Condé had been living in some style as he had managed to get some of his fortune out of France before the Revolution prevented it. In a speech to the people of Calais, the King said of the occasion 'after more than twenty years of absence, Heaven gives my children back to me, Heaven gives me back to my children; come, let us thank God in his Temple'. Sixteen burghers of Calais came forward to pull the Royal coach themselves.

The procession to the church was led by the clergy, including a Curé who had remained loyal to the *ancien régime* and had not sworn the Constitutional Oath of November 1790. The route to the church was lined with soldiers from the National Guard and the troops of the line, who had so recently been loyal to Bonaparte (who was by now on his way to exile in Elba). Napoleon had expressed a desire to live in England as a retired country gentleman following his abdication and surrender to the British, much as Louis XVIII had lived at Hartwell. He had been well received by cheering British crowds when the ship carrying him, *The Bellerophon*, was sighted off the coast of Britain. Meanwhile in Calais, the white flags of the Bourbons were displayed everywhere and the buildings were bedecked in white drapings. The King walked into the choir of the church under a canopy and was seated in its middle. The Duchesse d'Angoulême, as was her wont, was dressed very simply and in an English style. Her hat was small, too small for French taste, and without decoration. The King kept repeating over and over again. 'How happy I am to be in the midst of the good French people.'

A *Te Deum* was sung and the Duchesse d'Angoulême joined in the singing, weeping as she did so with joy at being back in her beloved homeland. The Royal party received the civil and military élite. The people of Calais placed a bronze plaque where the family had landed; their intention was that it contain an imprint of the Royal foot to mark where the Bourbons returned to their inheritance;[21] they were welcomed almost as Roman gods. The sight of the Duchesse d'Angoulême who had suffered so much moved many of the people. The surviving servants from her days as a young girl at Versailles were lined up to meet her (or if the servant had already died, he was represented by a son). Furthermore, forty ladies who had known the young Madame Royale before the Revolutionary times were presented to the Duchesse d'Angoulême. Many of the ladies were, not surprisingly, barely recognisable to Marie Thérèse. The returning Princess had not seen them since her family's forced departure from Versailles in October 1789, nearly 25 years before, when she was only a child of ten. It was an enormous strain on her nerves and memory to struggle to recognise the individuals and to respond fittingly to their eager greetings. It must have felt to Marie Thérèse as though she was moving in a world of dreams and shadows from a different age.

The plan was now for the Royal Family to travel at a dignified pace towards Paris: a speed calculated to build up anticipation for their return and interest in a family almost entirely forgotten by the people – and certainly one not greatly missed by the majority of the French. Marie Thérèse with her romantic and tragic story was the one who was both most attractive and most memorable. The Empress Joséphine's daughter, Hortense, the ex-Queen of Holland, while hardly an impartial witness, nevertheless reflected the view of many people in writing of the Bourbon family: 'like the majority of the French people I did not know of how many persons it was composed. The only one known to us was the Duchesse d'Angoulême.' Former Queen Hortense was daughter of the beautifully groomed and gracious Joséphine, and was herself an elegant and accomplished woman. She had been partly educated at the school in St Germain en Laye[22] for young ladies. It had been founded by Marie Antoinette's former First Woman of the Bedchamber, Madame Campan, following the collapse of the monarchy and the end of the Queen's Household. Madame Campan had needed a means of supporting herself and her school came to be very well regarded. Hortense reports that during her school days she had often heard from Madame Campan[23] of the sufferings of the Bourbons 'whose misfortunes had made so deep an impression when Madame Campan used to tell me of them'. Hortense wrote that 'Paris salons spoke of Marie Thérèse as an angel,[24] whose return would bring happiness. Everyone was touched by the thought of the suffering she had been through, and the memory of her mother was mingled with the romantic attachment she inspired.' This view was echoed by English people whom she had met during her time in exile and later visited her in Paris. Thomas Whalley wrote in his journals, 'The Duchesse d'Angoulême is adored, and with reason, for she is an angel.'

Louis XVIII travelled slowly towards his capital at a rate consistent with his poor state of health and passion for comfort. He was also able to savour the pleasures of the return after so many years of exile. The Comte d'Artois was already established in Paris, as Lieutenant General of the Kingdom and the representative of his brother. The Comte d' Artois had been the first of the Royal Family to quit France at the beginning of the Revolution in July 1789, and he was the first of the family to return to France for the Restoration. Madame de Boigne[25] reports that 'Monsieur', as the Comte d'Artois was now known following his brother's Restoration, was 'gracious, courtly, debonair, anxious to please and good-natured, but at the same time dignified'.[26] He looked every inch the prince, slim[27] and graceful unlike both his elder brothers who tended to obesity[28] and the distinctive Bourbon waddling gait. The Comte d'Artois had the bearing expected of a prince and the easy conversation and facile charm associated with the Court. What he did not understand or choose to recognise was the complex political position of the Bourbons in a France very different from the one he had left in July 1789. The need to compromise the interests and requirements of the returning émigré community and those individuals who had prospered under the Revolution and Napoleon was outside his comprehension. Even at this early stage of the Bourbon Restoration, the Comte d'Artois was building around him a reactionary party in opposition to the studied compromises of his brother, Louis XVIII. Marie Thérèse understood and sympathised with the Comte d'Artois' views and approach to politics. She wanted to return France to the way it had been in her childhood. She felt that in the interim the people had been misled by aberrant rulers. The former Queen Hortense wrote in her memoirs of these days that, 'The Comte d'Artois was already in Paris and everyone crowded around him. Madame de Rémusat, who so shortly before had been lady-in-waiting to the Empress Joséphine, came to Malmaison one morning and gave her to understand that it was advisable for her (my mother) to pay some mark of respect to the family who were about to ascend the French throne.' Joséphine, however, declined to sign the sycophantic letter addressed to the Bourbons drafted for her by Talleyrand.

Amongst the returning Royal Family, Marie Thérèse's position and experiences were singular. Her father-in-law, husband and brother-in-law had fled Versailles in the summer of 1789 and had not experienced the October 1789 attack on Versailles and the terrible six-hour trek into Paris or house arrest in the Tuileries. Louis XVIII himself, though remaining longer in France and seeing more of the Revolution, had made good his escape from Paris in June 1791. Marie Thérèse alone had experienced the horrible journey from Varennes to Paris; captivity; the bloody and vicious murder of the Swiss Guards at the Tuileries on 20 August 1791; the dreadful interview about the sexual mores of her mother and aunt; heart-rending partings from her father, brother, mother and aunt; solitary confinement in the cold Tower of the Temple without information about her family; and finally the knowledge that all her immediate family were dead. She had six years of appalling memories from when she left Versailles on 6 October 1789 until 18 December 1795 when she was released from the Tower of the Temple. So many places and so many people revived excruciatingly painful memories for Marie Thérèse, even after so many years.

On 26 April the Royal party left Calais, having spent two nights there, and travelled the 25 miles to Boulogne-sur-Mer where they spent the night and were greeted with similar outpourings of emotion from the local population. Marie Thérèse was accompanied by her ladies-in-waiting who included Mademoiselle de Montboisier, the Comtesse de Simiane and the Duchesse de Duras. Still in her simple travelling clothes, Marie Thérèse and the King held a Court reception at Boulogne, at which some reporters suggested that Talleyrand was present.[29] Whatever the location, Marie Thérèse had no desire to meet him. Despite all her self-discipline and Royal training, Marie Thérèse could not bring herself to meet or to receive him. Her essential honesty would not allow her to dissemble and hide her feelings so as to enable her to meet the politician with equanimity. Even among Royalist supporters, the Duchesse d'Angoulême was criticised for her lack of display of what they felt to be appropriate emotion. The absence of effusiveness and warmth, even towards her family's most loyal supporters, was noted. It would seem that she felt too much. Marie Thérèse was not about to play to order the tragic role of the Orphan of the Temple just to suit others. Her sufferings and losses were a personal tragedy, not a useful political tool. That said, it was acknowledged that she held Court with dignity as befitted her rank, as she had done previously as a young woman in Vienna. Much of the Court etiquette of former times was reinstated. Marie Thérèse had six ladies-in-waiting, two of whom were on duty in rotation at any one time. Each lady was in attendance on the Duchesse d'Angoulême for a week and then had two weeks off.

Marie Thérèse was delighted to be reunited with Pauline de Tourzel,[30] the daughter of her former governess, the Marquise de Tourzel.[31] Companions of happier times, the girls had played together at the Tuileries and St Cloud. Pauline also understood some of Marie Thérèse's sufferings as someone who had known her during the days of her imprisonment in the Tower. Pauline had been one of her first visitors, with

Madame de Tourzel, when the prison regime had softened in mid-1795 prior to Madame Royale's release and departure to Austria. Pauline herself had also suffered imprisonment in the notorious La Force prison. The old friends embraced and conversed at length and with great warmth and affection, recollecting all that had happened since they last met. With close old friends such as Pauline, Marie Thérèse was able to relax and show her true feelings in a way not possible for her in public or with those with whom she was not intimate. Pauline's husband had interestingly been one of Napoleon's Chamberlains – an example of a marriage across the political divide. Louis XVIII was also delighted to meet up again with Pauline and welcomed her warmly, with his customary polished politeness, saying how happy he was to see her again.

Louis XVIII and Marie Thérèse reached Abbeville on 27 April. The next day at Amiens cries of 'Long Live the King' were heard from the assembled crowd. Preceded by twelve young ladies of the town dressed in white and led by Cécile de la Tour du Pin (Lucie's daughter), the King and Marie Thérèse were drawn in procession in their carriage into the town by twelve members of the Millers' Company. It was that guild's ancient privilege to do so. The millers wore suits and wide white felt hats in honour of the Bourbons, newly purchased at their own expense. The carriage was taken first to the cathedral where the Bishop sang a *Te Deum*. According to Lucie de la Tour du Pin, who was at this time living in Amiens where her husband was the *Préfet*, the cathedral was packed with people wanting to participate in the celebrations for the return of the King. She reports that 'Madame, who was in tears, prostrated herself at the foot of the altar and I share with all my heart the feelings she was experiencing.' Their carriage was then drawn by the millers to the Préfecture where Lucie de la Tour du Pin[32] wrote that the King 'received the municipality and the entire city, both men and women with the courtesy and ready interest, as well as wit and charm with which he had been so generously blessed'. Madame de la Tour du Pin had arranged a banquet at the Préfecture in Amiens at which the young girls of the town dressed in white costumes to sing Glück's chorus. This was the same chorus, written by one of her favourite composers, that had been sung for Marie Antoinette when she had arrived in France as the young Dauphine in 1770. The King was apparently very impressed by the food and in particular the selection and quality of the wines provided. The King and Duchesse d'Angoulême stayed overnight, and this gave Lucie de la Tour du Pin an opportunity to observe Marie Thérèse at close quarters.

Two examples of the returning Duchesse d'Angoulême's conduct disappointed Lucie de la Tour du Pin, suggesting the Princess's intransigence and her lack of tact and charm. Once again the question of clothes arose. Edward Jerningham and his wife were members of the English Roman Catholic gentry and cousins of Lucie de la Tour du Pin. They had been stalwart supporters of the Bourbon cause during their exile, writing supportive articles in the British press. They had crossed the Channel with the King and Marie Thérèse and were travelling on with the Royal entourage to Paris. Lucie writes:

> Both Edward and his wife feared that Madame's wholly English style of dress would displease the members of Napoleon's Court who had gathered at Compiègne to await their new sovereign. They both realised it was essential that the first impression should not arouse antagonism. At their urging I spoke of this to Mademoiselle de Choisy, lady-in-waiting to Madame, and also to Monsieur de Blacas who mentioned it to the King. But the obstinacy of the Princess was not to be moved.

Lucie de la Tour du Pin was equally unimpressed by Marie Thérèse's reception of a woman who had shown Marie Antoinette great kindness during her imprisonment in the Conciergerie, despite much risk to herself. Lucie writes of the Duchesse d'Angoulême, 'On the morning of her departure, she received several ladies whom I presented to her. One was Madame de Maussion, wife of the Rector of Amiens University, a woman of noble virtue and conduct, worthy of the greatest respect.' Mademoiselle de Choisy was described by Fanny Burney as being 'becomingly dressed, wearing a smile over a sensible face', and one of the Duchesse's ladies had been told about her history, so that she could notify Marie Thérèse that

> Madame de Maussion was a prisoner in the Conciergerie at the same time as the Queen. She (Madame de Maussion) was given an opportunity to escape and found means to suggest to that unfortunate Princess that they should exchange clothes, and that she should lie in the Queen's bed while the Queen left the prison. Madame de Maussion was only 18 at the time and such devotion on the part of such a very young woman surely merited at least a courteous acknowledgement. This was not given; Madame did not even speak to her.

It is important to contrast this cold reception of a lady who had suffered with Marie Antoinette with the kindness shown by the Duchesse d'Angoulême to Rosalie, the young woman who had served and helped to relieve the sufferings and humiliations of the Queen with many small kindnesses in her last weeks while imprisoned in the Conciergerie. Marie Thérèse may well have been completely overwhelmed by the stories she was told and unable to respond as was expected. She was rarely able to show the required emotion that would have given easy satisfaction to those who supported her and her family. Nevertheless, it does seem churlish on her part.

By 29 April, the Royal party reached Compiègne,[33] about 40 miles from Paris. Here they rested and received visits from, among others, the former Maréchal Bernadotte[34] who had been elected as Crown Prince of Sweden in 1810 and was now one of the allies who had been fighting against Napoleonic France. Years before, Bernadotte had been sent to Vienna as an envoy of the French republican Directory government in 1799 when the Duchesse d'Angoulême, as Madame Royale, was living there at the Court of her cousin. Louis XVIII had, at that time, feared that meeting Bernadotte or any of the other Revolutionaries would have been very distressing to his niece and worked to ensure that they should not meet. Now, in order to fulfil her role as the first lady of France, she would have no option but to engage with those who had once been the enemies of her family. Wherever she went, the greatly moved but rather inarticulate Duchesse d'Angoulême repeated the phrase, 'How happy I am to be in the midst of the good French people!'

The French people encountering the Duchesse d'Angoulême almost certainly sympathised with her many sufferings, but even the most committed Royalist supporters were shocked by her lack of style. During the years of conflict between France and England, the isolation meant that English fashions had diverged greatly from those in the rest of Europe. English people, normally great travellers and keen enjoyers of continental pleasures, had not been able to visit Europe for most of the previous twenty years. When at last they were able to travel and visit European cities again, the women's outfits caused amazement among their continental hosts: they were shocked by their (relatively) short skirts and the smallness of their hats. Marie Thérèse was very like her father, of whom Lucie de la Tour du Pin wrote, 'He took no interest in his clothes, putting on without a glance whatever was handed to him.'[35] Exile and the passing of the years had not been kind to the once attractive young Princess. It was felt even by her most devoted adherents that the Duchesse d'Angoulême had aged badly and looked significantly older than her 36 years. On a visit to the Vendée in 1823, a little six-year-old scallywag (in Emperor's new clothes fashion) commented that she was not beautiful. The Duchesse d'Angoulême agreed with him, saying that she might be ugly but she was good. The boy received a coin for his honesty and courage. Her once beautiful complexion, so redolent of her mother's excellent skin, had coarsened and reddened. Her pretty fair curling hair, noted by the convent girls of Vienna in 1799, had faded to a dull brown. Her formerly slim figure had gone the way of so many gourmand Bourbons to stoutness. Marie Thérèse resembled all too closely her beloved father with an ungainly gait and large rather unfeminine features – especially her nose. What remained was her general air of dignity and solid, if rather unexciting, worthiness. But her shyness and reserve did not help her to respond to the people as they wanted and felt was their due. As a grown woman, Marie Thérèse had not changed essentially from the shy child who did not enjoy dancing with strangers at her mother's children's Sunday balls at the Trianon. The people felt her sadness and grief, and acknowledged her many sufferings as a living reproach.

Emperor Alexander of Russia, who had been instrumental in restoring the Bourbon family to the throne, came to Compiègne to visit the King and Marie Thérèse on 1 May. Not greatly impressed by the accommodation provided in the château for him, Madame de Boigne reports that he said of Marie Thérèse, 'Madame la Duchesse d'Angoulême looked sufficiently like a housekeeper to have been able to take the matter in hand.'[36] He had apparently been put in very inferior rooms while the splendid apartments allocated to the absent Bourbon princes, the Duc d'Angoulême and Duc de Berry, were not even being occupied. It was noted that Louis XVIII sat in a very comfortable armchair while Alexander I, who was provided with an uncomfortable straight-backed chair, preferred to stand. Louis did not even do Alexander the courtesy of rising when the Emperor entered the room. Louis XVIII was served first at dinner and in all matters of protocol was treated as the senior monarch, as he obviously felt himself to be. These discourtesies did nothing to recommend the Bourbons to Alexander. The Russian Emperor noted their rudeness and arrogance and was not favourably impressed.

At Compiègne a celebratory dinner was attended by the Royal Family, Court and officers. The King toasted the French army in the presence of the gathered Maréchals, and was gracious to all who attended, making polite conversation and complimenting his hosts. The Maréchals were pleased and flattered by the reception they received from the returning monarch. They were particularly impressed that they were allowed to be seated in the presence of the hereditary monarch, Louis XVIII. Napoleon, the self-made monarch, had not allowed his Maréchals such liberties. There may have been regime change, but the same Maréchal Berthier Prince of Wagram and Neufchatel who had arranged the ceremonial for the marriage of Napoleon and Marie Louise in 1810 also orchestrated the arrangements for the ceremonies to mark the return of the Bourbon family and the Restoration of their dynasty. Maréchal Ney[37] and Maréchal Marmont went to greet Louis XVIII and the Duchesse d'Angoulême. Maréchal Ney's wife, Agläe, had been a childhood playmate of Marie Thérèse at Versailles, where her mother had been one of the Household of Marie Antoinette. Other Maréchals were also present, namely Macdonald, Moncey, Serurier, Mortier, Brune, Lefebvre, Oudinot and Kellerman. The assembled Maréchals announced to the King, 'Sire, let your Majesty consider us the pillars of the throne. We will be its firmest supporters.' They were delighted to welcome the Bourbon King back to France. No doubt they were fully conscious that they had achieved much under Napoleon and wanted to ensure that their gains would be secured under the Bourbons. As Hortense shrewdly wrote in her memoirs, 'those who had taken part in the Revolution feared the return of the family it had driven from the throne. They were now in office, and a change would threaten their position.' Throughout the ceremonies Louis XVIII was badly affected by painful gout.

At the request of the King, the Emperor Alexander took the Duchesse d'Angoulême into dinner. Madame de Boigne reports, 'Madame did not have sufficient distinction of mind to realise that in these circumstances a warm welcome would have been the most dignified reception.' Equally, one needs to recall that Madame de Boigne was herself a passionate admirer and supporter of the Orléans family, which must have affected her views on the returning Bourbons. The Bourbons always had a very grand idea of their Royal status, and Marie Thérèse seems not to have been an exception to this. Apparently neither the Duchesse d'Angoulême nor her uncle the King expressed thanks to Alexander for the generous assistance they had received from him and his family over the many years of their exile, including the years spent in Mittau as his pensioners. The Emperor Alexander noted the length of the meal and the evident pleasure taken by the Bourbons in their food. The handsome Emperor with blond rather thinning hair, a well-built 37-year-old, was not a great fan of the Bourbons. He had brought with him as a gift to the family the marriage contract of the Duc and Duchesse d'Angoulême. He pointed out to Napoleon's sister-in-law that 'what a change in the inhabitants of the Tuileries; it was a great man who lived there not so very long ago whereas today…' tactfully not finishing the sentence. For relaxation during his stay in Paris, the Emperor Alexander preferred to spend time chatting with Napoleon's warm, charming and sophisticated ex-Empress Joséphine and her de Beauharnais children, Eugène[38] and ex-Queen Hortense, at her country house of Malmaison outside Paris, playing with her grandchildren (Hortense's sons by Louis Bonaparte), rather than with (as he saw them) the rather stuffy, cold and boring Bourbons.

Alexander I apparently remarked to Eugène de Beauharnais, 'I do not know but that I shall repent having re-seated the Bourbons on the throne; we have had them in Russia, and I know how to conduct myself as far as they are concerned.' It does not sound a ringing endorsement, but then he was speaking to Napoleon's stepson. Alexander I apparently spoke to Hortense with whom he was friendly (some suggested a more intimate relationship existed between them) about his relationship with Marie Thérèse's family. Hortense recalls in her memoirs that the Emperor said to her of his stay at Compiègne with the Bourbons, 'I have just returned from Compiègne. And I am sad. I love France. I wish her prosperity, and I fear that this Bourbon family will not know how to ensure it.' He was surprised that Louis XVIII went so far and was so politically naïve as to date his proclamation as being in the nineteenth year of his reign. This was very much against the advice of the Emperor who felt it was foolhardy to ignore the events of the years of the Revolutionary and Bonapartist years in France. He felt that such an attitude flew in the face of reality and common sense. Nevertheless, this was what the newly restored King chose to do. Alexander had apparently wanted to extract guarantees from the Bourbons as to how they would govern the country. His cautionary advice was ignored: 'in the first moment of enthusiasm it did not seem as though the Comte d'Artois could get to Paris fast enough to please people. It is not my fault if they are mistaken in their expectations.' Despite his close relationship with the previous regime, Eugène de Beauharnais was well received at the Court of the returning Bourbons, using his *ancien régime* title of Marquis de Beauharnais.[39] He wrote to his wife of this time, 'Everybody is fighting for their share of the cake.'

The day after the dinner at Compiègne, the Royal party continued on their journey towards Paris, staying overnight on 3 May at Saint-Ouën. Echoing the Montgolfier hot air balloon ascent of 1783 that Marie Thérèse had witnessed as a child, Madame Blanchard went up in a balloon holding a white Bourbon flag in each hand, in celebration of the return of the Bourbons. Meanwhile Napoleon was sailing towards his new domain of Elba, arriving there on the same day as the restored King Louis XVIII reached his capital. The Senate came to Saint-Ouën, situated very close to Paris,[40] to meet the King and the Court, led by Talleyrand. The King had expected that the Senate would be difficult to handle, but soon found that it was inclined to be biddable and accommodating to the royal will. In his Declaration of Saint-Ouën, Louis XVIII set out his plans for government. He sketched out his ideas in writing, but the detailed work of drafting the Declaration was done by his advisers, namely Messieurs de Blacas, de Vitrolles and de la Maisonfort. The final draft of the Declaration was not in fact seen or formally approved by the King. He had fallen asleep while it was being finalised. It had to be issued immediately in order to achieve its deadline for publication in the *Moniteur* newspaper. The courtiers, scared of waking the sleeping King, preferred to take the risk of his possible displeasure at their wording of the Declaration, rather than wake him from his siesta. The liberally worded Declaration was duly published the next day and was well received by the readers of the *Moniteur* and others. The *Moniteur* had been one of the French newspapers read avidly by Louis during his many years of exile from France in order to keep him up to date with developments in French politics and society.

The former Queen Hortense, who was interested in Marie Thérèse and her sufferings, enquired after her. She was anxious to hear what Alexander felt about the Duchesse. Jaundiced, perhaps, by the treatment he had received at Compiègne and a sense that his efforts on their behalf had not been sufficiently appreciated or recognised by the proud Bourbons, Alexander commented, 'She may have virtues but if you saw her you would change your opinion of her. Even her voice is harsh[41] and she has nothing of a woman's gentleness about her.' On 14 May 1814 a Mass was held at Notre Dame for the souls of Marie Thérèse's parents, Louis XVI and Marie Antoinette. Marie Thérèse did not attend but spent the day in prayer and reflection in her apartments in the Tuileries. Conspicuous by his absence from the service was Alexander, who preferred to spend the day picnicking at Hortense's estate of St Leu with the former Empress Joséphine and other members of the Beauharnais family. He commented on this to his companions, saying blithely, 'I ought to have been in Paris today with the other Kings.'[42] His choice was regarded as disrespectful and did nothing to endear him to the Bourbons or to warm relations between the families. Alexander's preference for and his intimacy with the family of the deposed Emperor did not go down well in the Tuileries with Marie Thérèse and the rest of the Bourbons.

Hortense wrote, 'Everyone laughed at certain old-fashioned customs that they attempted to revive.' When Hortense presented herself to the King, he found her to be charming; but despite his invitation to return to Court, she declined any further contact with the Bourbons. She wrote about the suggestion that she should visit Marie Thérèse: 'She is doubtless a respectable and interesting personage, but I have no reason for waiting upon her.' She wrote of how little, she felt, the Bourbons understood the country to which they had returned. Queen Hortense reports that there was a feeling of hatred from the émigrés towards their compatriots and that those returning mocked what they saw as the pretensions of those who had made good under the previous regimes. She writes, 'The laughter and jests in the salon of the Duchesse d'Angoulême had been unending; it was doubtless considered most absurd that *parvenus* should have dared to assume arms.'[43] But she felt of such open derision: 'It is not only in bad taste, but it proves that they have not studied the new institutions of the country, and fancy that they find it as they left it; but they must grow accustomed to the emancipation of France, if they wish to govern it.'

Louis XVIII also courted the ex-Empress Joséphine. During the long days of exile in Mittau, Louis had used the Empress and her large network of friends drawn from both the *ancien régime* worlds and the new Revolutionary and then Imperial regimes as a conduit for messages and information to pass to Napoleon. Louis XVIII admired Joséphine as a sophisticated and worldly woman and as someone who understood and was comfortable in the pre Revolutionary world as well as supremely well connected with the powers that replaced it. She was warm and kindly and Louis XVIII was prepared to overlook her lapse in marrying Bonaparte and thereby connecting herself to the upstart. The Duc de Polignac was sent to visit Joséphine at Malmaison, her country home outside Paris where she lived following her divorce in 1809 from the Emperor. During the years of their marriage, Joséphine had used her feminine influence plus her apparent ability to cry at will to persuade her husband to be merciful to his enemies. She understood the power of compassion and how charitable acts could be used to bind the people to their rulers. The Empress Joséphine, in conversation with her confidante Mademoiselle Cochelet which that lady recorded, said of the Bourbons that she 'did not believe for one minute that they would ever return to France but I was pleased to help their friends; they were French people who had suffered, many of them were old friends or acquaintances of mine, and the position of princes I had known when they were young moved me.... It was because of my supplications that he [Napoleon] allowed them a pension that was paid to them abroad.' Very few of the people she had helped made the effort to come to Malmaison to thank Joséphine for the efforts she had had made on their behalf during the Napoleonic era – which must have disappointed and saddened her.

As Philip Mansel writes, 'The Charte of Louis XVIII, proclaimed in June 1814, one month after his entry into Paris, which left ample powers to the monarch, became the principal model for other constitutions.'[44] Philip Mansel says that the King approved the Constitution because the people wanted one and it was better to grant it graciously than be forced to do so reluctantly. The Charte gave freedom of the press and provided for a bicameral legislative body,[45] the retention of titles, honours and appointments and senatorial control over taxation. It gave protection against arbitrary arrest, and all classes of society were subject to tax which provided for equality for all. Artois and his party hated its provisions and its liberality. The King retained the power to appoint ministers and officials and to declare war and peace.

The Bourbon Court was a strange mixture of the returning émigré courtiers of the *ancien régime* world and the self-made men and their wives of the Revolutionary and Imperial times. It was not always a comfortable mix. The Duchesse d'Angoulême herself was not convinced by the rapid, self-serving and undignified conversion of the once fervent supporters of Napoleon who now wooed the Bourbons with their pretty speeches. Louis XVIII referred to those who had been ennobled during the time of the Empire as '*les valets de Bonaparte*'.[46] The King remarked that he was taken aback by finding 'a New France, new habits, manners and costumes, and underneath an outward show of deference, much self-esteem and a profound conviction of individual worth. What greatly surprised me was the avidity for titles, rank, crosses of honour, etc. I said to myself, where be the true Republicans, those who were so contemptuous of Kings, nobles and privileges?'

The observer could not help but be struck by the difference in demeanour between the bulky, slow monarch and the restless energy of the former Emperor. Sycophantically, Maréchal Ney said to the new King that while Napoleon had been raised to Imperial power by the efforts of others, including those of his Maréchals, Louis XVIII's Royal Majesty came from long established precedent. It was suggested to Louis XVIII by Talleyrand that Princess Dorothea of Courland, now the Comtesse Edmond de Périgord, would be a suitable lady-in-waiting for Márie Thérèse. Despite the affectionate relationship she had had with Louis XVIII in 1807 during her stay at Mittau, her candidature for the post of lady-in-waiting was rejected. She was just too closely associated by marriage with Talleyrand (the defrocked priest turncoat, as the Duchesse d'Angoulême regarded him) and had also been a previous lady-in-waiting to the former Empress Marie Louise. The King would not ask his niece to have a person so connected to be a part of her Household, even to oblige Talleyrand.

The King attended Mass in the chapel at the Château of Compiègne accompanied by the Duchesse d'Angoulême dressed in a white silk robe, her head covered by a lace veil and a wreath of flowers. The Royal Family and the Court left Compiègne on the morning of 2 May and spent that night at Saint-Ouen, then a village on the River Seine situated between St Denis[47] and Paris. The family was lodged in a small château overnight. The crowd of courtiers accompanying the King was growing as the party moved towards Paris. The King as always behaved with quiet dignity. The Baron de Vitrolles described the Duchesse d'Angoulême in the following terms: 'Madame stood up hardly distinguishable, if one may say so, from the persons in waiting on the King.'

The Royal party set out from Saint-Ouen at 10 a.m. on 3 May to travel towards their final destination: Paris. It was a beautiful clear May Day and the sky was a bright blue. The King and Duchesse d'Angoulême rode in a large green open calèche which had belonged to the Emperor, so his coat of arms had been painted over. It was drawn by eight white horses, which had been lent to them for the procession from the stables of the Emperor Alexander of Russia. The Comte d'Artois rode on horseback beside their carriage. They were preceded along the processional route by a detachment of mounted troops of the National Guard and another detachment of Cavalry of the Line. There was an artillery salute to celebrate the arrival of the carriages and their royal occupants. The Bourbons had clearly only been restored with the help of foreign military forces. Paris was a city under military occupation by the Russians, Prussians and British, but this was not apparent on the day of the restored King's entry into his capital. In a tactful gesture, no foreign troops were present on the route; they had made themselves scarce to save the blushes of the restored King and his government. Political allegiances could be changed more easily than uniforms, and it was noted that the rather sulky and reluctant soldiers, still loyal to their former Emperor, were all wearing their Napoleonic military uniforms. There had not been time or money to prepare new uniforms for the military. This group of the population in particular, not surprisingly, maintained their loyalty to the former Emperor now imprisoned in his tiny kingdom of the Island of Elba. But along the route followed by the procession there were white standards and white flags to be seen everywhere in honour of the returning Bourbons.

The King's favourite and adviser, Louis Duc de Blacas, had presciently arranged for between 40,000 and 50,000 silver coins to be minted with the King's image on them, which were to be distributed to the crowds of Parisians who lined the streets to watch the ceremonial processions. The coins were scattered in front of the King's carriage and eagerly collected by the watchers. The coins were engraved with the words '*Ludovicus reduce, Henricus redivicus*', a reference to Henry of Navarre, the beloved founder of the Bourbon dynasty who reigned as Henry IV of France. This popularist gesture met with Marie Thérèse's approval. The Duc de Blacas wrote that 'the Duchesse d'Angoulême approached and took out of my hand some of the medals which I could have wished to present in a more respectful manner and she was so gracious as to seize this occasion to say some words expressive of that favour and kindness of which I have experienced affecting evidence'. The Duchesse d'Angoulême was not always cold and remote; she could be gracious and full of charm when she chose.

In their carriage, the Duchesse d'Angoulême sat on the left of the King wearing (after persuasion from her French fashion advisers) a high-necked French-style white dress embroidered with silver leaves and with a ruff. Her hat was a torque topped with a feather. She carried a delicate umbrella, but wore no jewellery. It will be recalled that much of her collection of jewellery had been sold to fund life in exile. Despite the best efforts of her ladies, the outfit was still criticised by members of the watching crowd as looking too English. She had insisted on altering the dress provided for her by shortening it, so to some observers she looked like a walking bell. The distribution of coins had not greatly lifted the mood of the crowds; they were numerous and curious to see the spectacle, but were largely unenthusiastic for the monarchy, despite their largesse. It was felt that the Duchesse d'Angoulême looked dour and was not particularly forthcoming in acknowledging the crowds and responding to their greetings. Where there was any cheering or applause from the crowds, Louis XVIII pointed to his niece as if to direct their acclamations to her. She was unable to play up to this – too honest to conceal her real feelings and no doubt recalling all too vividly other carriage rides through Paris in less agreeable circumstances.

Louis was aware that his age and bulk did not endear him to the populace. He wanted to use Marie Thérèse and her sufferings to appeal to the people. When the market women of Paris greeted them, Marie Thérèse must have remembered them as the screaming mob baying for the blood of her mother at the balcony at Versailles and that horrible journey to Paris on 6 October 1789 when she and her family were forced to leave their home. The Vicomte de Châteaubriand, that most flowery of Royalist writers, noticed that it was not always the Royalists who were keenest to celebrate the return of the monarchy, for example by putting out flags or banners. Ironically it was often the former Republicans and supporters of Napoleon who tried harder to prove their monarchist credentials, thereby forcing genuine Royalists to display monarchist flags and decorate their houses with white Bourbon hangings.

At Notre Dame there was a *Te Deum* attended by even the regicide members of the government like Joseph Fouché. From there, the Royal Family and their approximately 50 attendants processed to the Tuileries Palace, passing the Conciergerie Prison (from which Marie Antoinette had gone to her execution in October 1793) on their way. Travelling very slowly they reached the Tuileries at 6 p.m. Here the Duchesse d'Angoulême was greeted by ladies from the different *arrondissements* of Paris waiting to be presented to her, each carrying garlands of flowers with which they wished to adorn her. Marie Thérèse was by this time completely emotionally and physically exhausted by the ceremonies and experiences of the day. She could not respond to the ladies and their thoughtful gesture. But instead of seeing this as reserve or exhaustion, it was unfairly interpreted by some observers as the coldness and sulkiness of a haughty princess. She had last been at the Tuileries on 10 August 1792, leaving to seek shelter with her family in the National Assembly. They were not pleasant memories for her, to say the least. Eventually after joining a presentation to the crowd on the balcony, the Duchesse d'Angoulême was able to retire to her quarters and weep in the privacy of her apartments; she could rest alone with her thoughts of her dead family and the sad recollections of former times.

The next day, 4 May 1814, a conqueror's review was held in Paris to celebrate the role of the allies in restoring the Bourbons to the throne of France. During the Emperor Alexander's 'stay' in Paris, he did everything to endear himself to the Parisians. He spoke excellent French. He went to the Opera where he was well received and applauded loudly by the audience; here he observed the Parisian ladies with the white flowers symbolic of the Bourbons decorating their hair. Florists were apparently under intense pressure to keep up with the demand for white flowers. At the Opera House the young Royalists covered the Napoleonic eagle decorating the former Imperial Box with a white flag in deference to the Bourbons. Later the eagle emblem was destroyed, presumably by supporters of the Bourbons and their Restoration. At the end of the month, the former Empress Joséphine died. She had caught cold while entertaining the Emperor Alexander in her rose garden at Malmaison, and with terrifying speed died of pneumonia at the age of 50. Alexander purchased part of the Malmaison collection from her heirs, and today it is in the Hermitage in St Petersburg.

On 30 May, by the Treaty of Paris, the new French government under Talleyrand signed away all the territories won for France by Napoleon's military prowess. The Duchesse d'Angoulême neither liked nor approved of Talleyrand. He was the consummate politician turncoat and survivor, serving the Revolution, Napoleon and the restored Bourbons. She must have remembered how it was he who had preached at the *Fête de la Fédération* Mass marking the first anniversary of the Storming of the Bastille, 14 July 1790. The Royal Family had been dragged back from their summer trip to St Cloud, the Château given to Marie Antoinette by her husband as a present in 1785, where they were enjoying a break from the heat and confines of the Tuileries Palace to attend the celebrations on the Champ de Mars.[48] Talleyrand, the *déclassé* aristocrat, had preached a sermon on that occasion that was very derogatory of the King and the monarchy. His lack of principles and previous conduct did not endear him to the Duchesse d'Angoulême, even if he had enabled the Restoration of the Bourbons to the throne of France. Louis XVIII, that stickler for punctuality, treated him politely enough during their meetings; but one suspects that he enjoyed keeping Talleyrand waiting in an anteroom for several hours before receiving him at audiences.

The Bourbons were not obliged to endure his presence for too long. In late September 1814, he and his niece by marriage arrived in Austria to attend the Congress of Vienna, which would decide the post-Napoleonic political map of Europe. He was there to represent French interests and she to be his hostess for the dazzling social round required of the representative of the French government. Adam Zamoyski writes in his introduction to *The Rites of Peace, The Fall of Napoleon and the Congress of Vienna*:

> The reconstruction of Europe at the Congress of Vienna is probably the most seminal episode in modern history. Not only did the congress redraw the map entirely. It determined which nations were to have political existence over the next hundred years and which were not. Not only was it a key political event but a social whirlwind characterised by wonderful dances and dinners. Given that France was a defeated and occupied nation merely losing the territories gained by Napoleon this really was not a bad deal. The conquering powers could have sought to exploit their advantage much more powerfully had they so desired.

Madame de Gontaut reported that 'Among the festivities which took place to celebrate the King's return to Paris, that of the opera was the first, the finest and most brilliant, each box being brilliantly lighted; the king's box was perfectly dazzling.' The opera being performed was *Oedipus*: 'A very affecting part was the well-known air where Oedipus addresses Antigone beginning with these words: "She has lavished upon me her affection and her care." The King put out his hand to the Duchesse d'Angoulême, who kissed it; and everyone shouted "*Vive le Roi! Vive la Duchesse d'Angoulême*!" with an enthusiasm difficult to describe.'[49] It was at this performance that the Duc de Berry, after time spent in Jersey, was reunited with Amy Brown, whom he had invited to attend the Opera. Madame de Gontaut states rather surprisingly, given that they had had two daughters together, 'Mrs Brown, having led a very retired life, was entirely ignorant of Monseigneur's exalted rank, and on learning it so suddenly, its brilliancy, far from dazzling her, only made her understand the immense gulf between herself and him, which it would be impossible for her ever to cross.'[50]

On 1 June, the King and the Duchesse d'Angoulême bade farewell to the Emperors of Austria and Russia at the Tuileries Palace; they now returned to their own countries to observe events in France as they developed. A contingent of Austrian and Russian troops remained and would do so for another few months 'to settle in' the new regime. Court life continued and *The Times* of 12 September 1814 reported that on 6 September ambassadors and foreign ministers paid court to 'The King, the Princes of the Family and the Duchesse d'Angoulême'. The next day the King and the Duchesse d'Angoulême appeared on the balcony at the Tuileries Palace to greet the large crowds down in the gardens. The King called the Duchesse d'Angoulême forward and the Royal pair were visibly moved by the warmth of the reception they received. The King took a walk that afternoon and later attended a ceremony to honour officers who had taken part in the disastrous attempt to invade France at Quiberon in Brittany in 1795. The Comte d'Artois gave a dinner for a number of English ladies accompanied by his son the Duc de Berry, who was well known for his liking for English ladies. The Duc d'Angoulême visited the Polytechnic School in Paris and hunted with the Duke of Wellington on 12 October 1814 at Rambouillet.

Portraits of Marie Thérèse were put on display in Paris. Royal life for Marie Thérèse and the rest of the family was settling back into its normal routines. On 29 August Dr Whalley described 'a most splendid fête at the Hôtel de Ville, for the king and the Royal Family, at which between three and four thousand persons were present' to mark the traditional Bourbon celebration of the Fête de St Louis. The Comte de Lally Tollendal, a friend of Fanny Burney, wrote that he was going to see Louis XVI's daughter who was now being honoured in her ancestral palace after having once been incarcerated in a prison. Marie Thérèse must have found the return full of the same combination of the very familiar and the vastly changed. What was clear was that it would be very difficult (even if desirable) to turn back the clock to the ways and manners she had known as a child during the years before the Revolution.

9

The Hundred Days and Waterloo

1814-1815

The Duchesse d'Angoulême was not able to escape her tragic and sad past on her return to France. In what they thought was a gesture of kindness and respect, people would place portraits of her parents in all the places she frequented. Everyone wanted to speak to the Duchesse d'Angoulême of his or her experiences of the Revolution or share with her their recollections of her dead family. Wherever Marie Thérèse went, local government officials would greet her arrival with songs and poems reminding her of the virtues of her dead parents and her terrible sufferings during the years of the Revolution and exile. Even a theatre visit was not without emotion for Marie Thérèse; at Lyons, for example, she was greeted at the theatre by an address recounting her many sufferings and lauding her courage during her imprisonment during the Revolution before the curtain at last lifted and the performance started.

The French monarch and his family lived together in the Tuileries Palace and spent time together most days. Following the Restoration, the Duchesse d'Angoulême and her husband lived in the Pavilion of Flora at the Tuileries Palace, which had been occupied by Madame Élisabeth and the Princesse de Lamballe during the Royal Family's house arrest. Perhaps Marie Thérèse recalled the severed blonde head of her mother's beloved friend the Princesse de Lamballe on the end of the pike and her mother's dead faint from shock and grief at seeing it from her place of confinement in the Tower of the Temple. Writers of the time, including the diarist Charles Greville, commented on how comfortable and grand the palace was, even if it was not always clean. Marie Thérèse's own sitting room at the Tuileries Palace was decorated with the white velvet hangings embroidered with fleurs-de-lys, which was the last piece of work done by Marie

Antoinette and Madame Élisabeth. Marie Thérèse also had in her apartments the magnificent jewellery cabinet which had belonged to her mother and which was refurbished for her. Louis XVIII and the Duchesse d'Angoulême would often breakfast together as they had done during the long years of exile. Later, she would be joined by Louis Antoine while the King was working on his papers and correspondence. Together the family would attend daily Mass. Marie Thérèse was always punctilious (in exile and in power) in treating her uncle with the deference she felt was due to a reigning monarch.

Early among those to visit the Duchesse d'Angoulême in 1814 was her mother's former Woman of the Bedchamber, Madame Campan. She was not well received. The Duchesse d'Angoulême was clearly aware of the strong connections that Madame Campan had had with the Imperial regime. Napoleon's sister Caroline and stepdaughter Hortense de Beauharnais had been educated at her school in St Germain. Later, she had been appointed by Napoleon to run a school at St Écouen founded to educate the daughters and sisters of members of the *Légion d'Honneur*. The school was closed down in 1814 on the Restoration of the Bourbons. Marie Thérèse asked a clearly emotional Madame Campan what she had done during the reign of Napoleon. When informed that Madame Campan had run her schools in order to earn a living, Marie Thérèse cut her off abruptly and said that she would have been better off staying at home. There was no talk of their shared past or the troubles experienced by Madame Campan and her family. Marie Thérèse was uncompromising in her expectations regarding the loyalty of former and current Royal servants.

Marie Thérèse gathered about her memorabilia of her dead family: her father's black silk waistcoat and cravat which he had worn at his execution; her own *prie-dieu* (prayer stool) made from a stool on which her mother had sat during the family's imprisonment in the Tower of the Temple; a cap worn by Marie Antoinette during the sad times of the family's imprisonment; and part of the fichu[1] reputedly worn by Madame Élisabeth at her execution by guillotine in May 1794. The memoirs of the Comte d'Osmond[2] under the title *Reliques et Souvenirs* noted that Marie Thérèse kept the blood-stained shirt supposedly worn by her father at his execution on 21 January 1793. The Comte d'Osmond reports that nearly twenty years later, at the time of the Restoration in 1814, the shirt was faded by the passage of time. The Comte d'Osmond reports that Marie Thérèse kept it almost as the relic or the icon of a saint, surrounding it with candles. The Princess certainly regarded her father as a saintly figure. There were moves to have the executed former King canonised by the Roman Catholic Church for his sufferings at the hands of the Revolutionaries and his religious spirit. The Comte and Comtesse d'Osmond were greatly moved by a remark of Marie Thérèse that she had cried too much and could cry no longer. It was touching to them in its simplicity. It was perhaps a plea to be allowed to move on from the harrowing recollections of her youth and family and form a new life.

At the Pavilion de Flore and elsewhere in the Tuileries, clever and speedy needlework was required to turn the Napoleonic NN into the more appropriate Bourbon LL embroidery decorations on the curtains and soft furnishings filling the palace. As time passed, the Duchesse d'Angoulême became vigilant in hunting down and replacing the insignia of the previous regime. The Empire-style furnishings remained nevertheless. The restored Royal Family rather liked this simpler style of decoration and did not attempt to return to the highly ornate rococo decorations of Versailles from the days of Louis XVI and Marie Antoinette. In any event, all those furnishings of former times had been sold off shortly after the Revolution. The Bourbons were impressed by how well Bonaparte had maintained their palaces. They liked his taste in furniture and decoration, if nothing else.

Once she had obtained consent from the King, the Duchesse d'Angoulême often went to the site of the Madeleine, where it was believed that her parents were buried, to kneel and pray, accompanied by Pauline. In getting to the Madeleine from her apartments at the Pavilion de Flore at the Tuileries Palace, the Duchesse d'Angoulême's carriage had to drive across the Place de la Concorde[3] where Louis XVI and Marie Antoinette as well as Madame Élisabeth had been guillotined. Unable to bear the sad thoughts and memories that the Place de la Concorde brought back of her dead family, she ordered that her coachman should never again drive her that way. The route reminded her too strongly and painfully of the dreadful hot, dusty and distressing drive through Paris on 25 June 1791 following the Royal Family's abortive escape attempt from Paris.

Some of the old customs and etiquette were restored by the returning Court, but it was a different world. The Bourbons had been absent from France for 25 years, and in the meantime a new elite had established itself firstly during the Revolutionary years and latterly under Napoleon and his Empire. Louis XVIII and the Duchesse d'Angoulême as the first lady of the land held Courts regularly to receive and entertain the ruling class. It was noted with pleasure by observers that the King kissed his niece's hand with respectful affection on meeting her each day. He was always fully conscious of her propaganda value as the tragic 'Orphan of the Temple'. Her lack of interest in fashion did not stop her introducing new Court dress. Marie Thérèse wore the newly modified ladies' Court dress for the first time at a Whitsun Court in 1815. It comprised a high-waisted white silk dress cut narrowly at the skirt with a long train and a mantilla or long veil of lace hanging from a coronet. Madame de Boigne wrote that 'Madame made a very serious business of this. Such strict attention given at such a time to the length of lappets and the size of mantillas appeared to me to be a triviality unworthy of the situation… Madame would have liked to return to hoops, as at Versailles, but the rebellion against this was so general that she gave way.'[4] Men, including the King, wore plain frock-coats, the '*frac*', or their uniforms. The King in a very *ancien régime* way continued to have his hair powdered, even though this fashion was beginning to die out before 1789. Ironically, it was Robespierre who continued the custom during the Revolution, even after it was fading. The King, despite never having been a soldier, always sported a sword. Those attending Court were first received by the King, over a few moments of polite conversation; they then passed on along the Long Gallery of Diane to be presented to the Duchesse d'Angoulême. This was not an environment that suited Marie Thérèse or played to her strengths. Her harsh voice, grating and unpleasant even when saying the kindest things, gave an embittered, grumpy impression that may have often disguised her true intent.

The extent to which France and Court life had changed during her long exile also surprised her. She found the women ennobled by their connections with the Imperial regime difficult to accept, referring to them rather uncharitably as 'Napoleon's cooks';[5] she refused to refer to them by their Napoleonic titles. For example, she referred to the Duchesse d'Abrantès,[6] wife of one of Bonaparte's Maréchals, as Madame Junot rather than giving her proper title. She addressed the Princess of Moskowa as Madame Ney, maybe because she was already acquainted with Agläe Ney as they had played together as young girls at the Palace of Versailles before the Revolution of 1789. Agläe Ney's mother had been a member of Marie Antoinette's Household and the sister of Madame Campan. Madame Ney was subsequently befriended by the Empress Joséphine, who had been responsible for arranging her marriage to Ney. Following the divorce of Joséphine and Napoleon and the arrival of the Empress Marie Louise, Madame Ney had joined the young Empress's Household. Madame de Boigne describes the offence caused to Madame Ney by the Duchesse d'Angoulême:

> On the same day ... when Maréchal Ney's wife came to pay her court Madame called her Agläe. She was very much horrified at this. She saw in it the reminiscence of the time when she was admitted to Madame's presence, as her mother was chambermaid to Queen Marie Antoinette. I am convinced that Madame meant, on the contrary to show her great politeness, just as she did to me when she referred to me by the name of Adèle. Her tone, though, was so unpleasant, her speech so curt, her gestures so brusque, and her expression so cold, that it did not ever seem as though her words could be kindly meant. People have told me, that when one knew her intimately, these surly ways disappeared, but I never had the honour of being admitted into her intimacy.[7]

From a woman like the Duchesse d'Angoulême, who was so punctilious in observing the proper forms of etiquette even within her own family, this could have been either a calculated and insulting gesture, or else a note of warmth and intimacy in the conversation. Her conduct did not endear her to the new elite, who may well have felt intimidated by her. In his book *In Flight with the Eagle*, Raymond Horricks recounts that Maréchal Ney was so incensed by this treatment of his wife that, still in his muddy riding boots, he stormed into the Duchesse d'Angoulême's rooms, brushing past her ladies to remonstrate with her in a loud voice. In the most crude of terms he informed Marie Thérèse exactly what he thought of her and her family, even insulting their appearance. Every attempt was made to keep this encounter private, and certainly it appears in few of the accounts of the period. Marie Thérèse who had suffered so much was not able to make easy compromises and cover her true feelings to flatter others or to ingratiate herself with the French elite, unlike her uncle. The Duchesse d'Abrantès herself was struck by the kindness of Marie Thérèse, writing, 'I was touched by the kindness and fascination of the Dauphiness.'[8] She had enquired after Madame d'Abrantès' young son and 'She fixed on me that kind look which secured her the love of all by whom she was surrounded. It seemed evident that Madame d'Angoulême, rigid and severe to the world, had been particularly kind to me.'[9]

A solemn Mass lasting more than an hour and half and attended by a heavily veiled Marie Thérèse was held for Marie Antoinette, Louis XVI and Madame Élisabeth but not, interestingly enough, for the Dauphin, Louis Charles, so briefly and sadly Louis XVII. The reason for this is not entirely clear. The Duchesse d'Angoulême believed that Louis Charles had died and an investigation into the events of June 1795 in the Tower of the Temple by Madame de Tourzel, his former governess and a trusted confidante of the Duchesse d'Angoulême, supported this view. Marie Thérèse did not, however, have any direct personal evidence of what had happened to her brother, despite their proximity during his last days in the Tower of the Temple prison. In recent years, Deborah Cadbury's excellent book *The Lost King of France* has demonstrated by the means of modern DNA testing that the little boy who died in the Temple was, indeed, Marie Antoinette's son and the Duchesse d'Angoulême's younger brother.

In the early years of the nineteenth century his sister did not have these scientific advantages or certainties in deciding what had become of him. Marie Thérèse spent much time in fruitless, inconclusive and painful interviews with a number of young men who claimed to be her brother, and more to the point to be the rightful King in place of Louis XVIII. Among the claimants were Messrs Hervegault, Mathurin, Bruneau and perhaps most famously and most long drawn out Karl Wilhelm Naundorff, whose family persisted in the claim long into the nineteenth century. There were lawsuits in Paris in an attempt to prove the veracity of claimants' assertions. The Duchesse d'Angoulême even made a point of meeting with Madame Simon, the wife of her dead brother's cruel tutor, in the hope of gaining more information about Louis Charles's last days and his fate. While seemingly largely convinced that her brother had died, she could not be sure and must have been tortured by doubt and anxiety as to what had happened to him. She certainly supported her uncles as the rightful Kings of France – which would indicate that she had no doubts about their right to rule and the bogus claims of the Pretenders. It is almost inconceivable that women of principle such as the Duchesse d'Angoulême (a loving sister) and Madame de Tourzel (appointed to her post for her integrity), both devoted to the young Dauphin, would collude with any plot to conceal the truth of what happened to him. Nevertheless, numerous plays, books and more recently film and TV programmes have been based on the idea that the young Prince survived imprisonment and came back to claim his throne. Marie Thérèse visited the site of the destroyed Tower of the Temple where she planted a weeping willow in memory of her dead family.

The Duc d'Angoulême arrived in Paris from the south of France, where he had been touring since his return to France in late May 1814, to a triumphal welcome. He displayed a great deal of tactlessness by wearing English military uniform.[10] This was hardly likely to endear him and his restored family to the French people. He also hunted in the Forest of Rambouillet with the newly appointed English ambassador, the Duke of Wellington, who had spent so many years fighting against the French. Marie Thérèse and Louis Antoine resumed their life together at the Tuileries, occupying the Pavilion de Flore. Their gentlemen attendants were well-born and well-bred, including among them the Duc de Montmorency. They were in general older than the Royal couple and perhaps did not provide the liveliest or the most stimulating of company for them. This was, however, very much the atmosphere in which they had lived for their whole married life. Their physical circumstances were significantly more comfortable than their first married home in Mittau. Their Household consisted of about 150 people. After years of financial stringency during their long exile, the Duc and Duchesse d'Angoulême were allocated a generous Civil List independently and separately from the provision for the King, the Comte d'Artois and the Duc de Berry.

Despite being well provided for financially, the Duc and Duchesse d'Angoulême entertained little and lived simply, apart from keeping very smart horses and elegantly appointed carriages under the management of the Duc de Guiche. It was noted with disappointment that the Duchesse's household 'was less impressive than the Empress's'.[11] Greville noted how well the restored King lived in contrast to the austere years when he had visited him in Buckinghamshire and there had been no wine at dinner and few courses. Greville's Diary described the food and accommodation now enjoyed by Louis XVIII as being 'sumptuous'. The Duc and Duchesse d'Angoulême had hereby achieved the financial independence the Duchesse d'Angoulême had always wanted, indeed longed for since her days at the Viennese Court when she had scrimped and saved to pay off creditors and try to satisfy the requests of petitioners for her assistance. The Duc and Duchesse d'Angoulême saw less of the Comte d'Artois, but were regularly in attendance on Louis XVIII. The Comte d'Artois, or Monsieur as he was now known,[12] was distrusted by the King who feared the unhelpful influence of his reactionary views and preferred not to see much of him. The Duchesse d'Angoulême spent time engaged in charitable work, particularly supporting religious charities. She assisted a number of nunneries which were attempting to re-establish themselves in and around Paris following the Restoration of the Catholic Bourbons after the anti-religious and very anti-clerical Revolutionary and Empire periods. The French newspapers reported with interest her programme of activities. She also gave generously to individuals in need. The writer René de Chazet suggested that she compensated for her lack of children by her charitable activities.

Always keen to take exercise, Marie Thérèse liked to walk without ceremony or fuss along the River Seine in the Left Bank area of Paris attended by a single lady-in-waiting. She found it difficult to respond in a relaxed and warm way to the attention of the Parisians when they recognised her. She would also ride out on horseback. Both of the Angoulêmes were rather reserved and uncomfortable in public and therefore could easily appear to be stiff and disdainful when in fact they were merely shy and ill at ease with public attention. The Parisians were certainly not taking to the Duc d'Angoulême, regarding him as rather ineffectual and faintly ridiculous.

As the years of their marriage passed, it was clear that the Duc and Duchesse d'Angoulême were fond of each other. While he admired and respected her many virtues, there would appear to have been no sexual passion between them. As a King's daughter she took precedence in ceremonials and he readily acknowledged this and abided by it with grace. Some observers felt that she was the dominant partner within the marriage, but she was publicly a scrupulously obedient wife to the Duc d'Angoulême in deference to her upbringing and her religious principles. The Duc d'Angoulême had been appointed a member of the King's Council and worked hard at administrative duties. His politics inclined towards the pragmatic moderation of his uncle the King, rather than the more aggressively right-wing reactionary views of his father and wife. Despite her own political leanings, the Duchesse d'Angoulême largely left her husband to his own devices politically, except to try and influence him when it came to new appointments within the Church, which were in the gift of the King and his government.

During the summer of 1814, the Duchesse d'Angoulême spent time travelling around France getting an impression of the country for which she had longed for so many years but of which she had only childhood memories. She gave some time to recreation, spending July visiting the well-known spa town of Vichy,[13] two hundred or so miles to the south of Paris, for a rest cure and to take the waters (it had an established Royal following). Marie Thérèse then made a short tour through central France, returning to Paris for the celebrations of the Feast of the Assumption at Notre Dame in August 1814. Wherever she went she was greeted warmly, and everywhere was decorated in white in her honour.

August was an emotional month for her, when she revisited for the first time since October 1789 the splendid Château of Versailles and the Trianons and their once beautiful gardens so beloved of her mother. It was her childhood home, which she and her doomed family had left nearly 25 years earlier. In an attempt to recapture more happy memories and also in a return to the old ways, Marie Thérèse's very strong preference was for the Royal Family to return to live full-time at the Château of Versailles, which she remembered with affection. By contrast, Louis XVIII felt it essential that while the dynasty re-established itself in the minds of the people of France, the monarchy should be based in Paris. This would enable the Bourbons to be in touch with the public mood and be accessible and visible to the people of the capital. Isolation in Versailles had helped contribute to the Revolutionary fervour which had toppled his brother, Louis XVI. Louis XVIII did not intend repeating the mistakes of Louis XV or Louis XVI by keeping himself and his family secluded in Versailles away from the capital and its politically influential and volatile populace. To keep himself in the minds of the people and in touch with their views the King regularly went out driving in his carriage around Paris, often accompanied by his niece in order to judge the mood of his people and to show himself to them. Occasional recreational trips to St Cloud would, the King felt, be sufficient to give the Royal Family a respite from the noise and crowds of Paris and allow them to enjoy country pursuits such as riding and walking in the countryside, which Marie Thérèse so enjoyed. Royal life at Versailles was not to be resumed.

Marie Thérèse must have been saddened that the beautiful contents of Versailles, many of which had been lovingly collected by her parents, had long before been auctioned off during the Revolution. The Château was largely denuded of furniture, hangings, carpets, mirrors, wonderful Sèvres porcelain and the other luxurious household items, which had made it such a comfortable home for the Royal Family and such a showcase of French craftsmanship and luxury. Guided public tours of the abandoned Château had started in 1790, but the wonderful contents had been purchased by private collectors, both French and foreign. The sales of furnishing and artefacts were large (more than 20,000 lots) and well publicised all over Europe. Some of the very best pieces were preserved for national collections. Many of them later joined the magnificent French paintings, artefacts and furniture at Waddesdon Manor[14] in Buckinghamshire and the Wallace Collection at Hertford House, Manchester Square, London. Versailles and its gardens were in a very different state from how she must have recalled it. The buildings themselves had not been well maintained during the absence of the Royal Family, as Napoleon used the Trianon as a residence during his rule, but not the main palace.

Marie Thérèse was pleased during 1814 to have the opportunity to become close friends with another Royal lady, her cousin the Duchesse d'Orléans, previously Princess Marie Amélie of Naples and the Two Sicilies,[15] one of the extended Bourbon clan. Marie Amélie too was a granddaughter of the late Empress Maria Theresa of Austria, daughter of Maria Carolina, Queen of Naples, and a sister of the late Queen, Marie Antoinette. She was therefore a first cousin of Marie Thérèse, both of them combining Bourbon and Habsburg heritages and only a few years apart in age, Marie Amélie having been born in 1782. She arrived in Paris in the summer of 1814 with her husband and family. The cousins shared not only a web of family connections but also the same deep religious faith and solid worthy virtues. They were also both keen horsewomen. Marie Amélie's mother-in-law, the dowager Duchesse d'Orléans, who had suffered greatly during the Revolution and her long exile from France in Spain as well as fleeing before the forces of Napoleon, was also included in the friendship of the Bourbon Princesses. The theme of strong female friendships is one that runs strongly through Marie Thérèse's life. Like her mother she seems to have had the great gift of forming and maintaining strong bonds with other women. The Duchesse d'Angoulême said of her cousin Marie Amélie, 'She is so good, so excellent, so closely related to us.'

The younger Duchesse d'Orléans had been forceful in insisting on marrying her husband. Her family had not liked the proposed match, considering it beneath Marie Amélie as a princess of a ruling house and a granddaughter of the Empress Maria Theresa. While she was a Royal Highness in her own right, her husband was only a Serene Highness. Moreover, in the eyes of many, his father had betrayed his family and his class and was a regicide. The young Duc d'Orléans was keenly conscious that this was a good match for him, connecting him to the elder branch of the family. Marie Amélie fell in love with the Prince and was determined to marry him despite opposition from her family. Marie Amélie had threatened that she would retire to a convent and take vows to become a nun unless she was allowed to marry the man with whom she had fallen in love. The 27-year-old Princess was aware of the potential difficulties of her marriage, but was very much devoted to her husband-to-be. In due course, her family relented and the young couple were married and settled down to produce children. (From them is descended. The current claimant to the throne of France, Henri d'Orléans,[16] the would-be Henri VII.) The Duc d'Orléans' mother was insistent that the consent of Louis XVIII should be obtained for the marriage before she would give her own agreement. The King's agreement was given and the marriage contract was duly signed by Louis XVIII at Hartwell on 15 November 1809. The Duc d'Orléans was delighted that this marriage joined him to the prestigious House of Habsburg and the elder branch of the Bourbon family.

Relations between the senior and junior branches of the Bourbon family had been uncomfortable for many years. Marie Thérèse found it very difficult to meet comfortably with the young Duc d'Orléans, as the son of a regicide, but with his wife relations were more relaxed. Ostensibly the Comte d'Artois and the Duc d'Orléans had healed the rift during the years they had both spent in England in exile. In February 1800, the Comte d'Artois had officially received the Duc d'Orléans at the time when Marie Thérèse and the King were resident in Mittau. Despite the apparent warming of relations, in reality the differences between the two branches of the family festered for many years and there was mutual suspicion. In particular Adélaïde d'Orléans, sister and close confidante of the Duc d'Orléans, was never on good terms with Marie Thérèse.

During 1814 and early 1815, the Orléans family was subjected to a number of perceived snubs and insults by Louis XVIII, which made it clear that they were very much the junior branch of the Bourbon family and would be treated as such. The newly restored King did, however, generously restore to the family all their possessions and properties which had not been sold off during the Revolution, including the Palais-Royal in Paris as part of the more general settlement applying to the possessions of the émigrés. The Duc d'Orléans and his sister Adélaïde had both spent many years in poverty and exile. These holdings of lands and the income derived from them made the Orléans family enormously wealthy and influential. The Duc d'Orléans was restored to the rank of Lieutenant General of the Kingdom, which he had held previously. This was the same high rank as that held by the Comte d'Artois. Louis XVIII received the Orléans family at the Tuileries Palace and their arrival was greeted with Royal honours. The Royal Guard presented arms and drum rolls sounded as they descended from their carriages. Louis XVIII was delighted to meet Marie Amélie, who impressed him with her Bourbon features. She had manners that he felt very appropriate to her status as a member of his family and dynasty.

Observers of the meeting noted that Marie Thérèse greeted her cousin Marie Amélie with great warmth and friendliness, but was distinctly cool towards the rest of the Orléans clan. She still found it hard to forgive, let alone forget, their transgressions against her beloved father. Louis XVIII wrote of the Duc d'Orléans and his wife and his niece's reaction to them in his memoirs:

> he possesses exquisite tact and knows exactly the right thing to do; it would be impossible to have more dignity and grace of manner than he has. He surpassed himself on this occasion, even Madame Royale had to acknowledge it, though she had great repugnance to meeting him, for she could not forget Ègalité.[17] However, eventually by degrees she got used to the presence of the Duc d'Orléans and received him almost graciously.[18]

Louis XVIII was clearly charmed by Marie Amélie, a Bourbon Princess like her cousin Marie Thérèse, but perhaps as a mother and the wife of a man whom she loved a more fulfilled and happier version and one easier to be around.

It was freezing cold on 21 January 1815, twenty-two years to the day after the execution of Marie Thérèse's beloved father; on this day what were believed to be the remains of her parents were transferred from their original resting place near the Madeleine to the royal vaults at St Denis, the traditional burial place of the Kings of France, which had suffered badly from vandalism during the Revolutionary years.[19] Among the more than a thousand occupants were the King and Queen and even the Duchesse d'Angoulême's persecutor and interrogator from the days of her imprisonment in the Tower of the Temple, Jacques Hébert,[20] and Philippe Ègalité, the cousin who had voted for the execution of the King and had also been buried in the Madeleine. Throughout France, in every town and village, Louis XVI's Will was read out proclaiming the dead King's message of Christian forgiveness for the sufferings he and his family had suffered at the hands of the Revolutionaries. His devoted daughter spent the day in prayer and contemplation in her own rooms at the Pavilion de Flore in the Tuileries Palace, as it was not then the custom for Royal ladies to attend funerals or similar occasions. There was magnificent ceremonial to accompany the removal and reburial of the remains, but the dignity of the occasion was not universally observed by those watching. There were cries of 'to the Guillotine' from some anti-Royalist members of the gathered crowd.

The burial ground is situated approximately half a mile to the north-west of the now Place de la Concorde, in Ville l'Évêque. During the peak periods of the executions the corpses would be dumped here and might stay unburied for several days until there was a gravedigger available. Apparently this was the undignified fate of Marie Antoinette's body. The King's body by contrast was buried speedily and with some ceremony, attended by priests who also made records of the place of interment. Living in the Rue d'Anjou near the Madeleine in 1793, at that time a largely rural area, was a Royalist gentleman by the name of M. de Desclozeaux who noted the places where the bodies of the executed King and Queen were buried. In due course, he purchased the land in which the bodies lay. Over the graves of Louis XVI and Marie Antoinette, M. de

Desclozeaux planted weeping willows. He kept the location to himself during the years of Revolutionary and Imperial governments. With the Restoration in 1814, he was able to reveal to the restored Royal Family where Marie Thérèse's parents were buried. Louis XVIII ordered that the burial site be excavated with great care over the night of 18/19 January 1815. They uncovered not only the bodies of Louis XVI and Marie Antoinette, but also remnants of clothing including the garters which Marie Antoinette was said to have worn at her execution. The remains of Marie Thérèse's parents were placed in lead-lined coffins and taken to St Denis, the ancient burial ground of the Kings of France.[21]

It was decided by Louis XVIII that a Chapelle Expiatoire should be built to mark the spot where the bodies of Louis XVI and Marie Antoinette had lain after their executions. The Chapelle is in the Place Louis XVI[22] in the eighth *arrondissement* of Paris, a tranquil place despite being very close to the grand department stores of the busy Avenue Haussmann. Louis XVIII commissioned his architect Pierre François Léonard Fontaine, who had previously worked for Napoleon, to build the Chapelle in neoclassical style. The first stone was laid on 21 January 1815. Marie Thérèse contributed more than 2 million francs of her own money towards its construction, which was completed in 1826. She often visited it. The Chapelle Expiatoire consists of an entrance pavilion on which there is an inscription describing Louis XVIII's wish to honour his brother and sister-in-law's burial place. Through the entrance there is a courtyard whose inner walls are decorated with the monograms of Marie Thérèse's parents. Within the courtyard is the Campo Santo or cemetery, created from material in the former graveyard. On each side are gravestones to commemorate the Swiss Guards who died defending the Tuileries and the Royal Family on 10 August 1792. The chapel itself is on two levels and domed, and on the walls are portrayed in bas-relief [23] religious themes including the Passion of Christ and the Tablets of the Law. On the upper floor are idealised white marble statues of Louis XVI[24] and Marie Antoinette.[25] On the pedestal of the King's statue on a black marble plaque is engraved the Will of the King; and on the statue of the Queen is engraved the words of her last letter[26] written to Madame Élisabeth on the morning of her execution. These were donated to the Chapelle in 1834-5 by the Duchesse d'Angoulême.[27]

Following the ceremony of reburial, the King was keen that the Duchesse d'Angoulême put aside her mourning and, as a Frenchwoman and his first lady, pay more attention to her appearance and endeavour to dress more stylishly. He wanted his niece to play the part of his 'Queen' at the new Court with style and elegance (dare one say, like Joséphine de Beauharnais, Napoleon's charming and socially assured first Empress who was greatly admired by Louis XVIII as exemplar of the fine manners of a grande dame of the *ancien régime*). It was not to be. By temperament and habit, Marie Thérèse was deeply attached to her rituals of commemoration for her dead family and could not cast off these long-established habits of mourning and sadness. She was perhaps suffering from a deep depression from which she found it almost impossible to rouse herself. The Duchesse d'Angoulême had long ago in Mittau lost the early spark and optimism which she had displayed so bravely after her release from the cruel captivity in the Tower of the Temple in December 1795; on her arrival at the Court in Vienna, her depression was exacerbated by the lack of children from her marriage and the joys and hope for her dynasty that they might have brought her.

We gain an impression of Marie Thérèse at this time from the reports of the courtier Madame d'Arblay, the well-known novelist writing under her maiden name of Fanny Burney and author of *Evelina*, who was presented to her at the end of February 1815. This meeting was sponsored by Queen Charlotte and had been scheduled to take place in London in April 1814. Madame d'Arblay set out to prepare herself for the meeting by taking her husband, himself a French émigré, to 'the salon of the exhibitions of pictures to view a portrait of Madame d'Angoulême that I might make some acquaintance with her face before the audience. The portrait was deeply interesting but deeply melancholy.' Madame d'Arblay was also informed that the Duchesse d'Angoulême was reading her novel *Evelina* with great pleasure, in a French translation. Madame d'Arblay understood that the Princess read English well, so obtained permission via the Vicomte d'Agoult (her equerry) from the Duchesse to send her a copy in the original language, which the Princess said she would happily read. Mathieu de Montmorency, one of the Duchesse d'Angoulême's Household, promised to be on hand on the day of Madame d'Arblay's visit to make sure that all went smoothly at the presentation.

Monsieur and Madame d'Arblay went at the appointed time to the Tuileries Palace and were taken to the apartment of the Duchesse d'Angoulême's lady-in-waiting Madame de Sérent, to be instructed in the etiquette they should follow on meeting the Princess. Then escorted by a page they were taken into a very large apartment. On her way, Madame d'Arblay asked that their friend Mathieu de Montmorency be informed of their arrival. Poor Fanny, despite all her preparations, was rather overwhelmed by events. She failed to recognise another member of the Household, the dowager Duchesse de Duras, whom she had met previously. Without her husband she was taken through to the next room. She writes that Duchesse de Duras had assured her 'that her Altesse Royale was expecting me, and that I should meet with a most gracious reception'. This was not least because Queen Charlotte had 'particularly recommended' Fanny to the Princess's notice. On through another enormous apartment, this time escorted by Mademoiselle de Choisy who was full of compliments; still no Mathieu de Montmorency!

At the end of the room, Fanny saw a lady to whom she curtsied. Fanny did not move or speak. Eventually the second lady, to whom Fanny nodded but assumed to be yet another lady-in-waiting, spoke 'enquiring politely after my health', expressing good-natured concern about her recent ill-health and saying that she was pleased to see her. Fanny was still waiting for the arrival of Montmorency and was somewhat distracted. Her account of the visit continues:

> I thanked her, with some obligation to her civility, but almost without looking at her, from perturbation lest some mistake had intervened to prevent my introduction, as I still saw nothing of M. de Montmorency. She then asked me if I would not sit down, taking a seat at the same time herself. I readily complied; but was too much occupied with the ceremony I was awaiting to discourse, though she immediately began what was meant for a conversation. I hardly heard, or answered, so exclusively was my attention engaged in watching the door through which I was expecting a summons still. At length, the following words rather surprised me,[28] 'I am quite sorry to have read your last charming work in French'. My eyes now changed their direction from the door to her face, to which I hastily turned my eyes, as she added '*Puis-je le garder, le livre que vous m'avez envoyé?*'[29]

A mortified Fanny now understood her mistake: despite her research, she had not recognised that she was already talking to the Duchesse d'Angoulême. She was shocked by her own lack of formality in the way she had behaved towards the Princess. She had sat close to her and not addressed her as 'Your Royal Highness'. She wanted to rush out of the room in her embarrassment, but thought it best to remain and hope that the Duchesse d'Angoulême would ascribe her behaviour to 'English awkwardness and *mauvaise honte*'.[30] Fanny explains her behaviour by noting, as had others, that 'nothing in her demeanour had announced her rank, and such a discovery might lead to increased distance and reserve in her future conduct upon other extra audiences, that could not but be prejudicial to her popularity, which already was injured by an opinion extremely unjust, but very widely spread of her haughtiness'.

Fanny sufficiently recovered her composure to continue the conversation, which was now full of deference and references to 'Your Royal Highness'. She hoped that the Princess would not notice the change of tone. In an attempt to cover her earlier lack of attention to the Princess, Fanny seems to have committed the *faux pas*, in dealing with royalty, of speaking without being first addressed by the Princess. Fanny seems to have chattered on without taking her lead from the Princess. The Princess at times fell silent, but Fanny continued regardless. As she wrote, 'This gave me an opportunity of mentioning many things that had happened in Paris during my long ten years' uninterrupted residence[31] which were evidently very interesting to her.' She noted that the Duchesse d'Angoulême's face was 'lighted up with the most encouraging approval'. Fanny was keen to make clear to Marie Thérèse that she and her family had not willingly lived under the 'usurpation', as she put it, pointing out that her husband had turned down three advantageous military appointments offered to him by the Imperial regime. The Princess praised M d'Arblay's loyalty. Fanny noted that the Duchesse d'Angoulême 'could not forbear smiling and her smile, which is rare, is so peculiarly becoming, that it brightens her countenance into a look of youth and beauty'.

There was then a debate between the ladies as to how well the Duchesse d'Angoulême spoke English. From what we know from Fanny's account, the Duchesse seems to have understood English well but preferred to speak French. Apart from saying in English that her English was bad, she spoke French to her guest. Fanny felt that she had been very graciously received by the Princess. She was pleased to hear Marie Thérèse's complimentary comments about 'the Royal Family of England and it was inexpressibly gratifying to hear her just appreciation of the virtues, the intellectual endowments, the sweetness of manner, and the striking grace of everyone'. The Prince Regent, however, was evidently her favourite. The meeting between the ladies, scheduled to last only a few minutes, in fact lasted 45 minutes, ending only when Marie Thérèse was summoned to join the King at dinner. This was their first and last meeting. Fanny d'Arblay was clearly pleasantly surprised and impressed, writing of 'this exemplary princess whose worth, courage, fortitude and piety are universally acknowledged but whose powers of pleasing seem little known'.

Setting off from Paris on 27 February 1815, the Duc and Duchesse d'Angoulême went on a joint Royal progress travelling through Central France visiting Châteauroux, Limoges and Périgueux, not far from the area which gave them their titles. The purpose of their visit was to bolster and cement support for the new regime and to establish its reality and permanence in the minds of the people. The reports of the visit are that the Duchesse d'Angoulême found it hard to behave in the relaxed, gracious manner expected of a Royal personage on a tour of her country. It would appear that she seemed to expect that it was for the people of France to please her, rather than vice versa. Seemingly she retained the *ancien régime* view of the role of the Royal Family and the unquestioning deference due to it. Once again, as with the negative reports of her behaviour on her return to Paris in May 1814, it may have been that her shyness and reserve did not allow her to play to the crowds in the way they wished.

The city of Bordeaux, an important trading port on the south-west coast of France where the navigable River Garonne enters the Atlantic Ocean, was a bastion of Royalist support and the Duc and Duchesse d'Angoulême arrived to a rapturous reception from the townspeople. The Duc d'Angoulême entered the city dressed in military uniform and riding on horseback surrounded by a mounted escort of officers loyal to the Bourbons, much as her husband had been in March 1814. Marie Thérèse's own open carriage was drawn through the streets of the city by a team of young girls dressed in outfits all of Bourbon white.

Everywhere in the city of Bordeaux the streets and houses were festooned with white flowers and white Bourbon drapery to celebrate the Royal arrivals. The couple were welcomed to the area by General Tureau, a former supporter of Napoleon and holder of the *Légion d'Honneur* who had been appointed a Baron of the Empire under the former regime. In his Revolutionary days he had apparently executed numerous people, including women and children, and had threatened to burn down the Royalist city of Nantes. Louis XVIII was presumably ignorant of his history but possibly just cynically keen to secure his loyalty to the new regime when giving him the Order of St Louis. It pained many loyal Royalists when Marie Thérèse held out her hand for it to be kissed by this individual; like so many of the elite in France in 1815, his loyalties were questionable. In view of the very frosty approach she took with Talleyrand and Fouché, whom she regarded with deep suspicion, it would seem highly unlikely that Marie Thérèse was aware of the allegations against him or she would hardly have allowed him such favours.

The Duc and Duchesse d'Angoulême were attending a ball held in their honour in the Hôtel de Ville in Bordeaux when it was announced to them that Napoleon Bonaparte had escaped from his island kingdom of Elba. He had landed on French soil at the Golfe Juan on the coast of the south of France on 1 March 1815. The deposed Emperor was reportedly gathering forces and was on the rampage heading north towards Paris in an attempt to restore himself to his throne. Persuaded by his wife of the seriousness of the situation, the Duc d'Angoulême left Bordeaux immediately to join up with the Royalist army, which was moving to block Napoleon's advance up the valleys of the Rhône and Sôane rivers. The Duc d'Angoulême was in nominal charge of the expedition. Maréchal Macdonald, one of Napoleon's former Maréchals who had gone over to the Royalist cause on the Restoration, was assigned to guide the Duc d'Angoulême and to give him practical military advice. His role was in part to act as liaison with the troops, many of whom had not given up their emotional loyalty to Bonaparte even though they were in theory fighting on the Royalist side.

On her husband's departure, the Duchesse d'Angoulême was left in charge of affairs in the city of Bordeaux and the neighbouring areas. She acquitted herself with great aplomb, showing courage, initiative and decisiveness in carrying out her duties. These were qualities that she had previously had little opportunity to display during her years of secluded exile, which she had filled with embroidery, writing letters and praying. Her routine during these days was to get up very early (as was her usual custom), hear Mass and then go to the various barracks in the locality to spend the day reviewing the soldiers, often on horseback, and making speeches of encouragement to the troops in an attempt to bolster their fervour and their support for the Royalist cause. Her strident voice here served her well in making speeches to the assembled soldiers. She arranged for reinforcements of troops to be sent to join and supplement her husband and Macdonald's forces. Her commitment to the Bourbon cause inspired those around her. With the Duchesse d'Angoulême in this work was Monsieur Sosthanes de la Rochefoucauld, a devoted Royalist supporter. Queen Hortense commented that the Duchesse d'Angoulême displayed strength of character worthy of her rank in her conduct during the time of the 'Hundred Days' at Bordeaux. Marie Thérèse, always loath to see the shedding of French blood, prayed that a Royalist victory might be achieved without too much violence. She regularly reviewed the list of those volunteering to be soldiers in the Royalist cause and exhorted the local authorities in the Bordeaux area to make even greater efforts to recruit soldiers.

In early March 1815, Louis XVIII addressed the international diplomatic corps based in Paris, saying, 'Messieurs, you see me in a suffering state, but it is from gout not from anxiety as to the result of Bonaparte's landing, for my cause is the cause of Europe. If Bonaparte succeeds, war will break out everywhere.' Joseph Fouché convinced Louis XVIII that the army was loyal to Bonaparte and that it was essential that he should leave Paris and wait for events to play out to his advantage. The Duc de Berry, like his sister in-law, was dismayed that his family should give up their crown so easily and without fighting for their cause and honour. He remonstrated with his uncle, saying, 'Do not let us leave without firing a shot, if only to show that we are not afraid of powder.'

Meanwhile in Bordeaux, the old soldiers who had known the glory days of French victories under Napoleon were his natural supporters; few responded to the Duchesse d'Angoulême's cry of '*Vive le Roi*'. Indeed, some of the assembled soldiers shouted for the Emperor and removed the Bourbon fleur-de-lys insignia from their uniform caps in defiance of the ruling regime. Marie Thérèse wrote to her father-in-law of her hopes of the courage and military skills of Maréchal Ney, whom she believed was the only person capable of defeating Napoleon. She wrote urging the Comte d'Artois to leave Paris and its comforts and to join the army. She believed that his presence was really needed to stiffen the resolve of the troops for the Royalist cause. Marie Thérèse was sorely disappointed by what she perceived to be the inactivity and lack of courage in a time of crisis displayed by her father-in-law. She wrote to him, 'In God's name, leave Paris, the King does not need you. Your duty is the army, not at Council where they talk nothing but inanities!' Marie Thérèse was nothing if not frank, even in dealing with the princes of her house. Her status as the Orphan of the Temple and her own evident personal resolve gave her this compulsion. Her influence within the family was great. When she went out into the city of Bordeaux, she was often greeted by groups of young girls clad in white outfits in honour of the Bourbons curtseying low before her. Marie Thérèse was greatly loved in Bordeaux and admired for her courage and fortitude at this very difficult time.

The Duchesse d'Angoulême, usually so religious, resorted to the ruthless tactic of sending a man to assassinate Napoleon as he and his growing army progressed towards Paris. Unfortunately, from her point of view, the would-be assassin failed in his mission and was captured and imprisoned by troops who supported the returning Emperor Napoleon. It is nevertheless a measure of her desperation and determination to defeat the enemy of her family that she apparently ordered such a violent act and one so seemingly contrary to her religious beliefs. Napoleon was perhaps so demonised in her eyes as to be less than human, but he was the husband (albeit estranged) of her young cousin Marie Louise. It will be recalled that Napoleon had himself ordered assassins to attack the then Comte de Provence during the early days of his exile and had ordered the judicial murder of the young Bourbon Prince, the Duc d'Enghien; so Marie Thérèse may have felt that her tactics were justified by his previous conduct. Nevertheless, her stance was a brutal one.

Meanwhile, Napoleon was travelling at great speed through France. When the former Emperor arrived back at Fontainebleau (the scene of his abdication in April 1814) he noted with pleasure and perhaps some amusement that the Bourbons during their time living there had changed nothing of the decor in his former apartments. By 12 March 1815, the situation in Paris was becoming very tense and fearful. The Duc d'Orléans had informed the King that he was about to send his family back to their former refuge in Richmond in England. The King was by no means confident of the loyalty of this Prince of the Blood, whom he felt eyed his throne with envy and might well feel inclined to take his chance to establish himself as monarch. Trust in the newly restored monarchy was ebbing away among the people of France. While there was strong passive support in the country for the monarchy and its liberal declarations, few were prepared to fight for the preservation of the regime. Those who were willing to take to arms – i.e. the standing army – were strongly Bonapartist in their sympathies and would not fight against their former commander. They were much more inclined to defect to his forces. It was said that of the 80,000 strong National Guard, only 500 were loyal to the restored Bourbon monarchy. The soldiers might raise their hats and shout '*Vive le Roi*' but continued under their breath with '*de Rome*'.[32] Even loyal Royalist troops were not prepared to provoke civil war, particularly not one against such a conspicuously successful commander as Napoleon. The King sent out an order of '*courrir sus*',[33] demanding that Napoleon be hunted down and captured. By whom was not clear.

Crippled once again by gout, the King, never a soldier himself, was not best placed to take decisive action to save his throne. His brother was clearly not capable of filling the void.

On 16 March 1815, Louis XVIII spoke to the Chamber of Deputies about the Charte in an attempt to rally the nation and steady the situation. Despite a vote by the Deputies giving support to the restored monarchy, events were already moving away from his control. Three days later the King and his brother Monsieur left Paris for Lille followed by 500 of the King's Maison Militaire. The King and the Comte d'Artois wisely took with them 8 million francs and the Crown Jewels.[34] If there were to be more time in exile for the Bourbons, at least on this occasion it would be more comfortable and less cash-strapped than previously. The Duc de Berry was devastated at having to leave Paris and his mistress, the dancer Eugénie-Virginie Oreille, who had just given birth to their child, a son. Berry told his mistress that he feared that the Bourbons would never return to France and that his family had lost everything. The retreat of the Royals from Paris on 20 March was somewhat precipitate; the King announced his intention to depart from the Tuileries Palace at 9 p.m. and was gone by midnight that night leaving behind him many private papers. According to the *Journal de Paris* and reported in *The Times*, these included some of his correspondence with the Duchesse d'Angoulême and other ladies, and medals that had previously belonged to Louis XVI. The wags suggested that the King travelled in his slippers, having forgotten to take his shoes with him; more likely he could not fit his swollen gouty feet comfortably into his shoes. The intention had been for the Royal Family to travel to Lille, eastern France, and take up residence there. This would enable the Court to flee the dangers of the advance of Napoleon while staying within French territory, thus avoiding the accusation of another flight from France. Based in Lille they would be able to play a waiting and watching game. They were invited by the King of the Netherlands to join him in Brussels. In the end, however, the Royal party left French soil and decided to settle in Ghent – now in Belgium.[35] This did not give a confident message to the people of France, and certainly caused distress to the Duchesse d'Angoulême, working as she was for the Royal cause around Bordeaux.

Maréchal Ney, who had so recently eulogised Louis XVIII and the virtues and dignities of his Royal House and his Majesty, was sent by the King to capture Napoleon Bonaparte. Ney had made extravagant vows of loyalty to the Bourbons, promising to hunt down the invading Napoleon and bring the former Emperor back to Paris as a captive in a cage. In fact, when Ney encountered Napoleon he deserted to him taking all his troops with him and made a declaration that the Emperor was the true sovereign of France. Old affections and loyalties were too strong for Ney to resist the glamour and military prowess of Bonaparte. The patina of loyalty to the Bourbons was just too thin and recent. Of the twenty Maréchals created by Napoleon, three of them – Berthier, Marmont and Victor – went into exile with Louis XVIII and four – Perignon, Macdonald, Oudinot and Grunion Saint-Cyr – stayed away from the action on their country estates.[36] The rest reneged on their oath to the Bourbons and returned to fight with the former Emperor.

The Duchesse d'Angoulême, many miles away in Bordeaux, was angered by the news coming from Paris. She was stunned that her uncles had given up control of the capital so easily, without even putting up serious resistance, and that they had once again fled into a humiliating exile outside France. Marie Thérèse had already ignored orders from the King to return to the Tuileries and continued to remain at what she regarded to be her post. The news of the departure of the King and Comte d'Artois from Paris not surprisingly damaged morale and confidence among the Royalist troops, even in the loyal south-west. If the King and his heir would not defend his throne, why should their soldiers? Marie Thérèse was fighting a losing battle, but nevertheless she struggled on. Soon she was the only Bourbon holding out against Bonaparte. The *Morning Post* of London[37] noted:

> [The] Duchess of Angoulême, a name synonymous for everything that is amiable and gentle – unhappily too for everything that is deep, though silent, in grief – has risen with the necessity of the crisis into a heroine, animating everyone by her presence and her speeches. She, like the great Queen from whom she is descended, calls upon all Frenchmen to arm for their Sovereign... She reviews the troops – she issues vigorous proclamations – orders measures of say – sends off dispatches to different towns, and is herself a host.

De Vere wrote a chivalrous Ode to the Duchess, ruing the return of Napoleon and the cowardliness of so many supporters of the Bourbons.

Across France, in Nîmes, the Duc d'Angoulême and his troops fought bravely against the Emperor's soldiers, despite suffering a number of desertions, but they were defeated. Louis Antoine's own life was threatened by Napoleon for conduct that Bonaparte labelled as actively 'defying' him. The French newspapers, for example *Le Moniteur* of April 1815, once again loyal to Bonaparte, revelled in the humiliation of the Bourbon Prince. The Duc d'Angoulême felt he had no choice but to leave the field of battle and to flee into exile, escorted by troops loyal to Bonaparte. He sailed from France to Cadiz in southern Spain, which had itself recently been liberated from the Corsican usurper who had appointed his brother Joseph as its King. Their throne had recently been restored to the Spanish Borbons after the successful Iberian campaigns of the Duke of Wellington. The Spanish Royal Family had been imprisoned by Bonaparte in France for a number of years. *The Times*' reports of the French newspapers of 19 April 1815 noted, 'The Duke of Angoulême has contracted an engagement not to re-enter France; never to approach within 60 leagues of the frontiers, to enter into no machinations against France, and to obtain from the Count de Lille the restitution of the Crown Jewels.' What a humiliating experience for him to be forced to give such an undertaking.

To the Duchesse d'Angoulême, Napoleon paid the somewhat doubtful compliment of calling her the 'only man in her family'. The memoirs of former Queen Hortense reported that during the time that Napoleon spent in Paris before heading for Belgium and the Battle of Waterloo, a letter from the Duchesse d'Angoulême to Louis XVIII was intercepted and read by the Emperor. The Duchesse d'Angoulême clearly thought that the King was still in Paris fighting for his throne, as she 'made a number of suggestions and described what she was doing to hold Bordeaux for him'. Ironically, Archduke Charles (brother of Emperor Francis II), who had taken a shine to Marie Thérèse and wanted to marry her during her stay in Vienna in late 1790, was in fact regarded as being the only man in the Habsburg family by Bonaparte. The Emperor admired Charles's courage and military skills, but felt only contempt for the character of the Emperor Francis I, his vacillating father-in-law. Given Bonaparte's rather low opinion of women in general, perhaps this was more fulsome praise for Marie Thérèse than might at first appear. Queen Hortense reported Napoleon's comments on the Duchesse d'Angoulême: he was surprised that a woman 'whose misfortunes made so strong an appeal to the sympathies, had not succeeded in winning the hearts of the French'. It had apparently been suggested to him that her lack of popular appeal could be attributed to the fact that she had a 'vindictive' nature when confronted by those who did not share her views and attitudes.

One Royal lady, however brave and determined, could not hold out against the reputation and charisma of the victor of Marengo and Austerlitz. Over the days, her troops leached away. Troops sent by Marie Thérèse to arrest the Bonapartist General Clausel, who had been ordered by Bonaparte to take Bordeaux for the Napoleonic cause, far from detaining him went over to the Emperor's cause and swelled the ranks of his forces. Royalist prisoners were sent by Clausel to try to persuade the Duchesse d'Angoulême to surrender. She replied '*C'est une gasconnade*' (a trick, or ruse) and refused to receive them. Her supporters (without her knowledge) sent an intermediary to treat with Clausel. It was made very clear to them that the Emperor had won the struggle for power in France and that Clausel himself was graciously giving the Duchesse d'Angoulême time to get away from France safely and with her dignity intact. She, however, was determined to stay at her post despite ignominious flight from Paris by her uncles. Marie Thérèse regularly undertook reviews of her troops but did not receive an encouraging response to her cries of '*Vive le Roi*', even from the officers. They preferred to shout '*Vive Madame*'. Despite the compliment to her, this response was disappointing for the Duchesse d'Angoulême. Such personal loyalty did not help her in her mission of preserving her family's hold on France. These times were challenging for Marie Thérèse, but they allowed her to show her mettle and courage in the face of considerable adversity and danger.

Undecided as to whether she too should leave France, Marie Thérèse resolved to test the feelings of the troops herself. In one final attempt to rescue the situation, she visited the barracks of St Raphael in Bordeaux on 26 March 1815. She arrived at the barracks at 2 p.m. in a carriage and surrounded by a large escort. In silence Marie Thérèse inspected the assembled ranks of troops, walking between the lines of soldiers who stood at respectful attention. Once the inspection was over, a group of officers gathered around her in the centre of the parade ground and she spoke to them. Acknowledging the events in the wider France which were going against her cause, she stated that '*Un étranger vient de s'emparer du trône de votre roi légitime.*'[38] She asked if the troops would support the National Guard in defending the city of Bordeaux and said that she had come to assess herself the mood and intentions of the troops and their officers. When asked directly whether they would support the National Guard in their efforts to fight against Bonaparte, the officers remained silent. Despite her despair and trying not to allow her emotions to show, she exhorted those soldiers who were loyal to the Royalist cause to make themselves known to her. A very few swords were raised. Marie Thérèse declared to the assembled group that at least she now knew on whom she might count for support. More individuals cried out that they would protect the Princess. She replied that the important issue was whether they would serve their King, not protect her safety. The soldiers made it clear to her that they did not want civil war and would not fight against their brother soldiers. Defeated but still fighting for her beloved Bordeaux, she asked the officers to ensure that order was maintained in the city until the Bonapartist troops arrived to take over. She requested that the members of the National Guard who had been loyal to her family did not suffer the fate of the Swiss Guards at the Tuileries Palace in August 1792. She observed that most of the soldiers had removed the Royalist insignia of three fleurs-de-lys from their uniform caps. The garrison at Blaye, north of Bordeaux and situated on the estuary of the Garonne River, would not admit pro Bourbon troops despite being ordered to do so by the Duchesse d' Angoulême herself. She could feel the throne slipping away from her family once more.

Marie Thérèse made a second visit, to the barracks at Château-Trompette; this was where her own Angoulême regiment was based, which the Duc d'Angoulême had so favoured during his time in Bordeaux. Here the atmosphere was very different from that at the previous barracks; at Château-Trompette, Marie Thérèse found to her distress a spirit of revolt and mutiny. Her escort of officers was refused entry and the commander of the regiment formally refused to obey her commands. This was the Revolutionary spirit of old. 'God,' she cried, 'it is hard after twenty years of exile to have to leave my country yet again. Yet I have never ceased to pray for France. For I am French. You are not Frenchmen; you may withdraw.' A drum beat as the Duchesse d'Angoulême left the parade ground. A guard of honour was formed along the quai side of the Garonne River by the loyal sections of the regiments. The Duchesse d'Angoulême, resilient to the end, stood on the seat of her carriage to call out, 'I ask of you a new sacrifice and a new oath. Will you swear to obey me in everything, at least?' They replied that they would and she went on to say, 'Well then, I command you to think no more of fighting. From what I have seen, any conflict would be useless. Keep a few faithful subjects for the King until happier days.' She again requested that the troops keep law and order in Bordeaux and protect the local inhabitants and their property. The soldiers cheered their Princess with enormous enthusiasm; many were in tears. Marie Thérèse presented the men with the decorations from her hat, which she handed to them as souvenirs of the occasion. She then returned to the Palace in Bordeaux to make preparations for her departure for Spain.

The Duchesse d'Angoulême dictated a proclamation to the people of Bordeaux saying that she understood and appreciated their loyalty but was leaving for fear that if she stayed longer in their city, the retributions visited on its citizens would be worse. '*Je n'ai pas le courage de voir des Français malheureux et d'être la cause de leur Malheur*.'[39] She went on to say that she was aware of their feelings for her family and would convey them to the King. She sent her and her husband's good wishes to them and said that her husband fought on in Lyon.[40] She hoped to see them again. On 3 April,[41] the Duchesse d'Angoulême drove in pouring rain to Pauillac on the west shore of the Garonne estuary where an English ship, the ironically named *Wanderer*, was waiting for her. She distributed small tokens to the crowd before embarking. They sailed first to Bilbao in Spain, and then back into exile in England once more. Marie Thérèse arrived at Plymouth on 19 April, where she was greeted by a large crowd and a 21-gun salute; they then travelled via Exeter and Salisbury to London. *The Times* of 6 April had reported that there was civil war in France and 'there were insurgents'; by 20 April *The Times* was reporting that Bonaparte was receiving 'loud acclamations' when he unexpectedly appeared in his box at the theatre in Paris.

The Duchesse d'Angoulême did not return to Hartwell, as the lease had been given up by the King and his family in more optimistic times; instead they lived quietly with Monsieur de la Châtre at the then French

Embassy, Home House in Portman Square in Marylebone, London. She visited the Prince Regent to pay her respects to him, but otherwise did not venture out in to London society, only going early in the morning to attend the first Mass of the day at the chapel in King Street. The French ambassador wrote that the Princess was visited by most of the English ministers and their wives and also by members of the diplomatic corps. Later she moved to Battersea, preferring its quiet location. Here she was visited by the Prince Regent. *The Times* reported that the Duchesse d'Angoulême was scheduled to arrive at Ghent on 27 May 1815. The Duc d'Orléans was also in London and Marie Thérèse was keen to monitor his movements and ensure that she was in a position to counter any plotting on his part. She and her uncle must have suspected that he was angling for English support to place himself on the throne. She rejoined Louis XVIII, the Comte d'Artois and Duc de Berry in Ghent, where Royalist supporters had gathered from London, accompanied by the Duc and Duchesse de Lévis and two gentlemen of the Household. She settled quietly[42] in a house described as being an elegant property outside Ghent, which had been lent to the Royal Family by the Comte d'Heune de Steenhuyse,[43] preferring privacy and seclusion at such a compromised time. She does not seem to have enjoyed Ghent. The tedium was broken by a visit from the Duke of Wellington, who on 1 June paraded 600 cavalrymen and 500 infantrymen before the Princess. There was plotting among the exiled Royalists to regain power, including trying to persuade the British government to sponsor another uprising in Brittany or the Vendée.

In an effort to gain more support from the British government for the fight against Napoleon, the Duchesse d'Angoulême once again returned to London on 4 June 1815 as the King's representative, accompanied by Hyde de Neuville, for secret negotiations with the British government. She was requesting arms for Bourbon supporters in the Bordeaux area of south-west France and also trying to gain reassurance that the allied armies would not occupy Paris as they had done during the first Restoration, once Napoleon was defeated. Once again Marie Thérèse lived very quietly at the French Embassy in London, and was only seen in public when she attended Mass in the King Street chapel.

The allied victory at Waterloo on 18 June 1815 made a Second Restoration to the throne of the Bourbon family possible. Once more Napoleon was forced to abdicate; he failed to make good an escape to the United States of America, so surrendered to the forces of the Prince Regent. In due course, he was sent to the island of St Helena in the South Atlantic, too far away from Europe to allow another attempt to re-establish his dynasty. Marie Thérèse read the news of the second return of Louis XVIII to Paris and the cheering crowds which greeted him. She did not hurry back to Paris to join her uncle. She also heard that Louis XVIII had been persuaded by the allied governments to appoint Joseph Fouché as his

Minister of the Interior. Marie Thérèse was clear in her determination that she would not receive Fouché. During the early summer of June 1815 she remained in London, staying quietly at the French Embassy. She only returned to Paris in late July, more than a month after the Second Restoration. Could she really leave politics to her menfolk? Her recent experiences had challenged her views on such matters.

10

The Second Restoration

1815-1824

The Second Restoration, especially its early years, was another painful time for Marie Thérèse. She had pleaded with the British government that the allied troops (Prussia, Russia, Austria and Britain) should not be allowed to occupy Paris. To her deep chagrin, even in mid-January 1816 more than six months after the victory at Waterloo, there were still troops in the capital. Scots and Russian[1] soldiers were everywhere, even camping in the Place de la Concorde. The Prussians were settled in the Tuileries Gardens, their washing hanging on the fencing of the Carrousel of the Louvre. English soldiers were camped in front of Notre Dame. There were reports that the Prussian and Russian armies, whose countries had experienced harsh occupation when invaded by Napoleon's troops, had been involved in incidents of rape, looting and wanton destruction of property in France. The Russians, who had sacrificed their own city of Moscow in order to prevent its resources falling into enemy hands, had scant respect for French people and property. Wellington, a fierce disciplinarian, imposed heavy penalties on any of his soldiers who indulged in this sort of behaviour. He also insisted, as he had during the Iberian campaign, that all supplies be properly paid for, rather than forcibly requisitioned from the French people. Marie Thérèse was also conscious that many of the courtiers who swarmed back to the Tuileries to attend her receptions had only recently paid their humble respects to the returned Emperor before his defeat at Waterloo. As a woman of deep personal integrity and fixed views, she found their hypocrisy and self-serving disloyalty difficult to tolerate. The political cartoons of the time showed courtiers literally turning their coats (again) from the colours of the Bonaparte family to those of the returning Bourbons. What had been tolerated during the first Restoration was no longer acceptable, and those courtiers and servants who had shown too much devotion to the Emperor were dismissed.

Louis XVIII re-entered his capital on 8 July, delighted to be back in Paris and happy to enjoy once more the pleasures and luxuries of being a ruling monarch. The statue of Napoleon in the Place Vendôme was pulled down, just as during the Revolution the statue of Louis XIV had been toppled. The figure of Napoleon was replaced by a flagpole flying the white standard of the Bourbons. The King usually liked to have the Duchesse d'Angoulême with him on his Royal 'walkabouts' and carriage rides around Paris, capitalising on her fame as the 'Orpheline du Temple'. But even without her, he went out to meet and greet his people in the streets outside the Tuileries Palace, relishing the attention and deference. He appointed Talleyrand as the President of his Council, much as he loathed doing so. There did not seem to be a viable alternative. The Duchesse d'Angoulême eventually arrived back in Paris on 27 July 1815, but refused to accept the usual ceremonials due to the senior Royal lady returning to her Court, which her status as the first lady of France usually demanded.

Marie Thérèse could not bear to re-run the triumphal entries, speeches and celebrations from the First Restoration in the previous spring of 1814. She could not comfortably receive these honours in a capital city still occupied by the 'enemies' of the country she loved, even though it was the armies of these countries which had fought for the Bourbon cause and whose efforts had restored her family (once again) to its throne. Perhaps she was also embarrassed and shamed by the unseemly haste and lack of courage shown by the male members of the Bourbon family, with the honourable, if unsuccessful, exception of her husband. Their behaviour was in contrast to her own gutsy performance in Bordeaux. Now they were established back at the Tuileries as if nothing had happened. It did not say much for the calibre of the *ancien régime* dynasty.

The period after the Second Restoration is sometimes known as the White Terror, a reference to the white emblems of the Bourbon supporters. The treacheries and counter-treacheries of 1814 and 1815 had hardened the resolve of the returning émigrés to extract revenge for their perceived sufferings. The accommodation which had existed at least pro tem between rival factions of French political life during the First Restoration had broken down. Compensation would not be given to those who had lost property. The Bourbons had been restored to their throne, but for their most loyal adherents the situation was that 'what is sold is sold, what is confiscated remains such'.[2] The King would not imperil his own position by requiring that money be repaid or property returned.

André Castelot describes Marie Thérèse as being the emotional heart of the Ultra reactionary movement and the White Terror. The occupying forces of the allies had achieved a great victory at Waterloo and the French people now felt that they were truly under occupation. In general the British army under Wellington was highly disciplined, but on occasion fights would break out between French and British officers at the theatre or at balls. The raucous celebrations of many Royalist sympathisers after the defeat of the Emperor's army at Waterloo, particularly the residents of the *ancien régime* enclave in the Faubourg-Saint-Germain, were a visible demonstration of the divisions in French society. There was violence between rival groups. Queen Hortense wrote that she was shocked at the celebrations of Royalist ladies who were happy to rejoice in the defeat of their countrymen. There were a number of assassination attempts on the life of Wellington during his second period of residence in Paris. It is suggested that some were undertaken by ultra extreme Royalists led by the Comte d'Artois, keen as they were to rid their country of the influence of Britain and the other occupying forces and get on with the business of ruling themselves. The Parisians were devastated by the repatriation of artworks previously looted by Napoleon from Italy and the many other European countries he had defeated in battle. The collections were on display in the Louvre and much visited and loved by the French people. Deep resentment turned to violence as crowds tried to stop the exhibits being shipped back to their previous homes. They appeared more disturbed by the loss of the artworks than by the change of rulers.

French royal life during the Second Restoration was more centred on Paris than on Versailles. This was perhaps one lesson the Bourbons had learned, even though they were said to forget nothing and learn nothing. The Duchesse d'Angoulême would have preferred to spend time at the family's country palaces of Rambouillet, Versailles and St Cloud, where she could ride and walk in the parks untroubled by the public, which she much enjoyed. The Duc d'Angoulême was content living at the Tuileries, even if it was somewhat grubby. Louis XVIII insisted that the family reside for the majority of the time in Paris. His personal taste, obesity and poor health – he could hardly walk – meant that country pursuits were of little interest to him. The family only quit Paris when it was necessary for the Tuileries Palace to be cleansed. As Madame de Boigne described:

> It was inhabited by eight hundred people who were by no means invariably clean in their habits. There were kitchens on every floor, and an absolute lack of cellars or sinks; consequently all kinds of filth collected and made such a smell that one was almost suffocated when going up the staircase of the Pavilion de Flore and crossing the corridor on the second floor. These appalling odours eventually reached the King's rooms.

Only then would the King agree to move out, and then for the briefest possible time.

Politicians fought to keep their power and influence. One particular example was Joseph Fouché: he had the Napoleonic title of Duc d'Otrante, having been Bonaparte's Minister of Police, but was now included in the new Royalist government as Minister of the Interior. Despite his Revolutionary and violent history, he had the support of the British cabinet and was regarded by the occupying forces as being a pragmatic and effective politician. The King was at first appalled at the idea of Fouché being included in his government, but Wellington made it clear that Louis XVIII's cooperation with Talleyrand and Fouché was a condition of the Second Restoration. Louis XVIII must have wondered how the Duchesse d'Angoulême would react to the appointment as a minister of one of the men who had voted for the death of her father. Her response was pragmatic, as she told the King: 'I will not permit anything to be personal; I will forget, if need be, that I am a daughter, but do not forget that you are a King.' She would not, however, receive Fouché.[3] She was even careful to avoid being in the same room as him.

The memoirs of the Marquise de Custine, Delphine de Sabran, noted that the Minister of Police had an 'implacable enemy' in the Duchesse d'Angoulême. Madame de Custine wrote of the Duc d'Otrante that 'he did his utmost to maintain himself in power; he had speedily forgotten his conduct during the Terror and he imagined his admirers no less forgetful of it'. The King ensured that he was not seen to speak to the regicide in public. The immediate problem of proximity and frequent contact was solved when in September 1816 Fouché was sent to Dresden as French ambassador to the Court of the King of Prussia, Frederick William III, who with his Queen Louise had helped the Bourbons during their exile. Fouché then moved on to Prague where he died on Christmas Day 1820.

Maréchal Ney was singled out as a particularly notorious turncoat. During the First Restoration in 1814 he had abandoned Napoleon, insisting that he abdicate, and had defected to the Bourbons by whom he was honoured. When Napoleon escaped from his island prison of Elba and invaded France, Ney was sent out from Paris by Louis XVIII to intercept the returning Emperor. But rather than capturing him, Ney had joined him. After the French defeat at Waterloo, in which Ney fought with great personal courage, he was captured by troops loyal to the Bourbons. Ney was then put on trial, found guilty by the Chamber of Peers and condemned to death for his treason. Ney's distraught relatives tried all possible ways to save him from the death sentence. But Louis XVIII was determined that Ney should die for his offences and refused all pleas for clemency. This was a betrayal too far for the King and the rest of the Royal Family. Ney was executed by firing squad on 7 December 1815.

The execution took place despite the pleas of Ney's wife Agläe,[4] who had known the Duchesse d'Angoulême since childhood. Back in 1795, one of the first letters from the then Madame Royale to Louis XVIII had pleaded with her uncle to show mercy and forgiveness to the French people, whatever their transgressions against the Bourbon family might have been. She had also shown her forgiveness and love for her native country when she had set up and helped at a hospital established at Mittau to care for French soldiers, even though they were fighting for Napoleon. The Duchesse d'Angoulême was the one person who might perhaps have changed the King's mind about the fate of Ney, so Louis XVIII said, and yet she refused point blank to plead the Maréchal's cause with the King. She would not respond to their pleas to ask the King for mercy. Instead she urged Louis XVIII to order the army to carry out the death sentence on him and advocated a policy of '*parti vigoreux*'.[5]

How does one square Marie Thérèse's response to Ney with her profound Christian religious principles, which surely required love and compassion towards others? This uncompromising and unmerciful stance actually echoes her actions in sending an agent to attempt to assassinate Napoleon in 1814 during the Hundred Days, when she was fighting so hard for the Bourbon cause in Bordeaux. But many people expected that because she had herself suffered so grievously that she would be more sympathetic to the pain of others and would try to save Ney from execution. Madame de Boigne wrote of the political atmosphere in Paris at this time,[6] 'it must be admitted that those who demanded an example to deter future traitors were the honourable members of the party, the Princes, the Bishops, the Chambers, and the court in addition to the foreigners. Europe told us we had no right to be generous or indulgent at the expense of European blood and treasure.' Marie Thérèse could not countenance a betrayal as clear and obvious as that of Ney; he had escorted the Comte d'Artois into Paris in April 1814 and attended the reburial of her beloved parents in January 1815 at St Denis. This was a very personal treachery for her. Loyalty to the old ways and to her religion and family were at the core of Marie Thérèse's character and approach to life. She could not and would not tolerate disloyalty in those close to her. Whatever compassion she may have felt for Ney and his wife and family on a personal level was far outweighed by the need to punish disloyalty and to be seen to do so.

Madame de Boigne reported that the King had said that if Marie Thérèse had asked for mercy for another of the traitors, M. de la Villette, he would apparently have granted it. This was a heavy burden of responsibility to put on her. She refused to make the appeals to the King. She feared that if clemency were shown to traitors, it would encourage sedition. She was also concerned that it would be viewed with dismay by those who had always been loyal to her family, and who had suffered for that loyalty under the previous regimes. When the Duchesse d'Angoulême was approached on her way back to her apartments from Mass by Madame de la Villette, she refused to get into conversation with the woman and snatched away her skirts to which Madame de la Villette was clinging.

The city of Bordeaux was always a magnet for Marie Thérèse and Louis Antoine. *The Times* reported from the French newspapers:

> Yesterday their Royal Highnesses the Duke and Duchess of Angoulême, and Mons. the Duke of Berry heard vespers at Notre Dame, and then attended the procession of the Vow of Louis XIII.[7] This religious ceremony was most solemn and impressive. All the streets through which the procession passed were hung with tapestry, as at the processions of the *Fête-Dieu*. An immense concourse joined the procession, and all were pervaded by the pious devotion, excited by the affecting example of the august daughter of our Kings.

That evening the Duc and Duchesse d'Angoulême set off on their journey to the south-west of France and visited Bordeaux where they were as usual well received by the local population. A column celebrating the Duchesse's visit to the town of Angoulême on 18 August was erected the following year, which still exists. But the journey was not without incident, as *The Times* reported that a 'private letter from Paris of the 23 instant is said to contain the subjoined account of an apparent attempt to assassinate the Duke and Duchess of Angoulême at Poitiers'. The Paris papers, however, in mentioning their arrival there, and their subsequent departure for Bordeaux, gave no indication of such an attempt. *The Times* continued:

> It appears that the Duke and Duchess arrived at Poitiers on the 18 instant, on their road to Bordeaux, and were received by the inhabitants with the greatest enthusiasm. The air resounded with the incessant cries of '*Vivent le Duc et la Duchesse d'Angoulême! – Vive à jamais la famille Bourbon!*'[8] About an hour after the arrival of these illustrious personages at the hotel prepared for their reception, a number of soldiers were seen collecting in the street, with several officers at their head, making use of very coarse and violent language towards the Duchess. After vociferating '*à bas les Bourbons*',[9] they attempted to force the doors of the hotel, when the Duke and Duchess were advised to make their escape by a pair of back stairs, and were carried off in safety by the citizens of the town and the peasants of the surrounding villages.

Despite this attack, the Duc d'Angoulême then went on to deal with the Royalist Spanish army, which was still occupying areas of the south-west of France and seemed loathe to leave French territory and return home to Spain. The Duchesse d'Angoulême spent the rest of August in Bordeaux. She then moved on to Toulouse where she was less well received, and so displayed less charm and warmth than she had done in Bordeaux. She then travelled back to Paris where she spent the winter of 1815/1816 at the Tuileries Palace in her apartments at the Pavilion de

Flore. On 21 January 1816, the 23rd anniversary of her father's death, the by now annual memorial service for her family could this year be held at Notre Dame. After the Mass, Louis XVI's Will was once again read aloud in all the churches in France calling for the forgiveness of crimes against him and peace and reconciliation in France. To most French people Louis XVI and his Will must have felt a distant and largely irrelevant memory. Marie Thérèse spent the day of the anniversary at prayer, secluded in her apartments. Her recollections and sadness were sharp and vivid.

During this period, Marie Thérèse was presented with a moving document. It had been concealed by Edme-Bonaventure Courtois, a former member of the Convention and Committee of Public Safety, and was now produced by him in an apparent attempt to ingratiate himself with the new regime. Marie Thérèse received the document presented to her by her uncle the King with great formality. She was stunned to see it so long after it had been written by her dear mother, when she'd known nothing about it. On seeing the handwriting of her long dead mother she fainted away, as she so often did at times of high emotion. It was the last letter of Marie Thérèse's mother written on the morning of 16 October 1793 from the Queen's cell in the Conciergerie, shortly before her execution. The letter was addressed to Marie Antoinette's beloved sister-in-law Madame Élisabeth, but never received by her. The letter written in such dire circumstances had remained concealed and known to only a few people since 1793. On the execution of the Queen, it was passed by her jailers to the public prosecutor, Fouquier-Tinville, and from him to Robespierre. He had apparently kept it under the mattress of his bed in the rue Saint-Honoré, at the home of his landlords and friends the Duplay family, until his own execution in July 1794. It then passed to M.Courtois, who was deputed to look after his papers. By this time Madame Élisabeth, the intended recipient, had herself been guillotined.

This last letter helped to give further insight to Marie Antoinette's thoughts and feelings very shortly before her death. It is a testament to her love for her children and her thoughtfulness as a mother. We also see demonstrated her spirituality and devotion to her Roman Catholic faith. We are able to see the thinking of a mature woman who has suffered greatly and lost all those she cared for most; a far cry from the dizzy teenager of her years as Dauphine and the early years of her time as Queen of France. Marie Antoinette from her cell wrote:

> October 16th, at half past four in the morning. It is to you, Sister, that I am writing for the last time. I have just been sentenced to death, but not to a shameful one, since this death is shameful only to criminals, whereas I am going to rejoin your brother. Innocent like him, I hope to show the firmness he showed during his last moments. I am calm, as one may be when one's conscience is clear, though deeply grieved at having to forsake

> my poor children. You know that I existed only for them and for you, my good affectionate sister. You who, in the kindness of your heart, had sacrificed everything to be with us – in what a terrible position do I leave you! It was only during the trial that I learned my daughter[10] had been separated from you. Alas, poor child, I do not dare write to her, for she would not receive my letter; I do not even know if this one will reach you. However, through you I send them both my blessing, in the hope that someday, when they are older, they will both be with you once more and will be able to enjoy your tender care. If only they will both continue to think the thoughts with which I have never ceased to inspire them, namely that sound principles and the exact performance of duties are the prime foundation of life, and that mutual love and confidence will give them happiness... In our misfortunes, how much consolation we have derived from our mutual affection! Again, in happy times one's enjoyment is doubled when one can share it with a friend – where can one find a more affectionate, a more intimate friend than in one's own family? I hope my son will never forget his father's last words[11] which I will here purposely repeat for him; let him never try to avenge our death!

The letter commended the care of her children to their aunt and begged Élisabeth to understand and forgive the horrible and false accusations of incest made by the young Dauphin about his aunt. She said, 'I know how much my little boy must have made you suffer. Forgive him, my dear sister, remember how young he is, and how easy it is to make a child say whatever one wants, to put words he does not understand in his mouth. I hope a day will come when he will grasp the full value of the kindnesses and affection you have shown both my children.'

Poor Louis Charles was never able to see his aunt again and was by the time of his mother's letter already descending into the degradations and sufferings which would eventually kill him. The Queen prayed for peace and forgiveness. She made no reference to the interrogation to which Marie Thérèse had been subjected as part of the process of gathering evidence against her mother. Perhaps Marie Antoinette had not been informed of her daughter's three-hour ordeal[12] at the hands of Hébert and Chaumette. Marie Antoinette's wish was certainly satisfied by her daughter who loved, respected and admired her aunt. Marie Thérèse was also conscious of the contribution made by Madame Élisabeth in helping her survive the period of her imprisonment, including solitary confinement, by the example of practical common sense and piety she provided. Madame Élisabeth was one of the most profound influences on Marie Thérèse's character and approach to life.

With what mixture of emotions Marie Thérèse must have read the declaration of love for her children written by a woman who knew she was to die that day. Marie Antoinette went on, 'I send you my heartfelt love, and also to my poor, dear children. How heart-breaking it is to leave them for ever and their distress is among my greatest regrets in dying. Let them know, at least, that down to the last they were in my mind.' What joy at knowing how loved Marie Thérèse was by her long dead mother, what pain at knowing all she had lost! The Queen confirmed her Christian faith but did not even hope to have the ministrations of a priest at her execution. Marie Antoinette would not accept, in any event, the help of a priest loyal to the principles of the Revolution. The Revolutionary government would never let a priest who had not sworn loyalty to the new regime attend her and hear her confession. She forgave all and begged to be remembered to her family both in France and Austria, no doubt fully conscious of how little help in her hour of need she had received from many of her family. The Austrian part of the family had abandoned her to her fate with little effort to save her. They were prepared to sacrifice her life, hoping to take political advantage caused by the outrage at her death. Marie Antoinette's brothers-in-law, the Comte de Provence and Comte d'Artois, from the safety of exile far away from the horrors of the Revolutionary years, had been self-serving, disobedient and at times positively hostile to their sister-in-law. It must have been a source of comfort to Marie Thérèse that her mother made no reference to these family divisions in her last letter. She sought only reconciliation within the family. Any other position or overt criticism of the now King and Monsieur would have been very difficult for Marie Thérèse; she had after all married the son of one of them and had lived most of her adult life with the other, acting as his hostess and close companion. Loyalty and family solidarity were essential to the Bourbons' vision of themselves as the only legitimate rulers of France.

The summer of 1816 brought happier family news. There was to be a wedding. Louis XVIII had no son, and there was no prospect of one, even though he was teased by the Comte d'Artois with the suggestion that Louis XVIII should contemplate remarrying and producing a son. As the succession currently stood, the throne of France would pass to his brother on Louis XVIII's death, and thence from the Comte d'Artois to his elder son, the Duc d'Angoulême and Marie Thérèse. There was again talk at this time that the succession to the throne should bypass the fundamentalist Comte d'Artois on the death of Louis XVIII and pass direct to the Duc d'Angoulême. Neither Marie Thérèse nor her husband would entertain such an idea. Their deep sense of family loyalty and love for the Comte d'Artois and the demands of the proper order of things made such a thought impossible to Marie Thérèse and her husband. In any event, Marie Thérèse shared with her father-in-law many of his political views and inclinations towards conservatism, tending more to his political stance than that of the more compromising one of Louis XVIII. She was not going to be complicit in attacking Artois politically. The Duc d'Angoulême was more in sympathy with the pragmatic and flexible approach of the King and was in return trusted by his uncle, but passionately loyal to his father. Sadly from both personal and political points of view the Duc and Duchesse d'Angoulême were childless, and now in their late thirties they were likely to remain so.

The hopes of some that a return to her native land might cause 'the lily' – as they called Marie Thérèse – to become fertile and produce a child were disappointed. The actress Mademoiselle Mars had a performance at the Comédie Française in May 1814 at which Marie Thérèse was present; the actress expressed the hope that the return to her native land might produce an heir. The audience applauded and the Princess stood to acknowledge the acclamation. All were to be disappointed. So it would appear that the Duc de Berry would be King on the death of his brother. The Duc had already proved his fecundity with his English mistress/wife Amy Brown, so it was now his duty to secure the line of succession for the senior branch of the Bourbon family.

Various possible princesses had been suggested as brides for the Duc de Berry during the long exile. With the Restoration, as the heir to the throne of France, he was now a much more attractive proposition as a royal bridegroom. Madame de Boigne recalls in her diaries that the Emperor of Russia, Alexander I, their benefactor, had proposed his sister as a possible bride. This suggestion was, however, rejected by the French Royal Family, causing some offence to the Russian Imperial family; the grounds given were that their dynasty was not regarded as sufficiently ancient to provide a mother for the '*enfants de France*'. Bourbon arrogance and tactlessness must have outraged Alexander I, whose family had been so generous and gracious during the émigré period; good enough to pay the bills at Mittau, but not to marry into the proud Bourbon dynasty. A more charitable interpretation of events may have been that the very Roman Catholic Bourbons were not happy with the idea of a Russian Archduchess from the Russian Orthodox Church[13] who might find the idea of a religious conversion to the Roman Catholic faith too difficult.

Madame de Boigne[14] recounts that the Duchesse d'Angoulême shared the views of the King and Comte d'Artois on this matter and did not want to see as the Duchesse de Berry a princess 'whose political connections would have given her complete independence, and who would therefore have been a personage of importance. She was also afraid of a princess whose personal accomplishments might have gathered around her people distinguished for their intellectual powers, for which Madame always felt an instinctive repugnance.' One should of course always remember Madame de Boigne's bias against 'Madame', as she refers to Marie Thérèse; but she did have excellent connections at the Bourbon Court which give her writing a great deal of interest and usefulness in reviewing events.

Other princesses considered for the role included Marie-Louise of the Duchy of Lucca and Louise de Condé, but matters did not go any further in pursuing those marriages. The possibility of the long widowed (and celibate, since the death of his beloved mistress) Monsieur[15] remarrying was also discussed; he was still youthful in appearance and might yet father further children. This idea was rejected by the family. Apparently the Duchesse d'Angoulême objected to the possibility of such an alliance because the Comte d'Artois' new wife as the spouse of the heir to the throne would outrank her at Court. This was a prospect that Marie Thérèse could not bear to contemplate after so long[16] as the senior Royal lady at the Court of her uncle and his official hostess. 'Monsieur who loved her (Marie Thérèse) tenderly, apart from other motives would not have wished to cause her this vexation,' wrote Madame de Boigne. The Comte and Comtesse d'Artois had not lived together as husband and wife since their flight from France in July 1789, living separately during the years of exile: the Comte d'Artois in Britain and the Comtesse in various towns in Europe, spending much time in Italy. Following the deaths of his wife and mistress ten years previously, the Comte d'Artois had settled into a chaste and single way of life,[17] which was comfortable to him, and he had no great desire to change it by taking a new young wife. So the possibility of the Comte d'Artois' marrying again was quietly dropped.

The web of Royal intermarriages at this time, which almost created a supranational Royal caste, meant that Marie Thérèse was closely related to the Princess chosen to be the Duc de Berry's bride. Eventually the choice of bride had fallen on Maria Carolina of Bourbon Sicilies, a granddaughter of the King of Naples, Ferdinand IV of Bourbon Sicilie and his Habsburg wife, the former Archduchess Maria Carolina, the elder and closest sister of Marie Antoinette. Her father was Francis I of the Two Sicilies and his wife Maria Clementina, herself a Habsburg Archduchess. The Duchesse d'Angoulême and Maria Carolina were second cousins. The Princesses were both related to the Empress Maria Theresa of Austria. She was grandmother to the Duchesse d'Angoulême and the great-grandmother of Maria Carolina.

Maria Carolina was a Bourbon, and the choice of this Princess was pleasing to the rest of the family. Ironically, she had first been suggested as a possible match for the Duc de Berry by the loathed Talleyrand. He could not bear the idea of a Russian Grand Duchess becoming the Duc de Berry's wife and was keen to put forward other possible candidates. It was felt appropriate by the King that the family which had suffered in all its different branches during the Revolution and the 'reign' of Napoleon should maintain its prestige and strengthen itself by marrying within itself.[18]

Maria Carolina was born on 5 November 1798 at the beautiful Palace of Caserta. She was therefore twenty years younger than her proposed husband.[19] Maria Carolina was brought up on her father's estates in the countryside around Palermo on the island of Sicily, to which her family had fled from Naples to avoid Bonaparte and his invading armies. The Neapolitan Royal Family had to be rescued by Nelson and transported to live in Sicily. So difficult was the journey that one of Maria Carolina's young uncles died as a result of the traumas he experienced. The family then settled in Palermo. It was a quiet retired upbringing. Her mother died when Maria Carolina was only three years old, but her father's second wife, the Spanish Princess Maria Isabella, was a kind and caring stepmother to the little girl. Maria Carolina learned to speak French (albeit with a strong Italian accent and rather wayward grammar) from her childhood, but the outdoors life suited her tastes better than study. In particular she loved to climb the mountains close to her home. After the defeat of Napoleon and the expulsion of his sister and her husband Murat, who had been created King and Queen of Naples, Maria Carolina's family was restored to its throne in 1815. She was 16 years old when the family returned to their capital city of Naples.

The French Royal Family proposed the match and King Ferdinand was delighted to accept the marriage proposal on behalf of his granddaughter. The prospect of being Queen of France was a great prize for any princess. They conveniently forgot the fate of Marie Antoinette. In the letter Maria Carolina wrote to her husband-to-be accepting the proposal of marriage, she wrote that she hoped to be capable of 'imitating the virtues of their Royal Highnesses the Duc and Duchesse d'Angoulême'. The couple were married by proxy in Naples in April 1816.

Maria Carolina's husband-to-be, Charles Ferdinand, Duc de Berry, was regarded as being the more worldly and more physically attractive of the Comte d'Artois' two sons. He was considered to be more charming than his elder brother the Duc d'Angoulême, but equally it seemed he lacked the solid worthiness and deep-seated religious principles of his brother. Charles's temper was quick and hot, and he was well known to be a libertine. According to some reports, though, he had been a popular soldier during his time with the army. Despite their differences, the brothers were close and loving.

The Duc de Berry had always been publicly complimentary about his sister-in-law, Marie Thérèse; although one cannot help feeling she must have disapproved of his way of life and to have found him dissolute in his lack of sexual morality. Madame de Boigne suggests that 'while doing justice to the virtues of his sister-in-law, he cared nothing for her'.[20] In appearance, the Duc de Berry was swarthy with dark curly hair, slightly bulging eyes, a high complexion and the full sideburns which were fashionable at that time. He was not tall but well-built, even sturdy, in appearance. He held great charm for women and, fortunately for the success of their marriage, Maria Carolina was susceptible to his sexual allure. The Duc de

Berry was an open and generous person and probably the most personally popular of the Bourbons. In particular, it is reported that he was greatly loved by his servants, whom he treated with kindness and generosity.

The marriage was celebrated with much of the old ceremonial that had been used for the arrival in France of previous royal brides, including the Habsburg Archduchesses Maria Antonia (later Marie Antoinette) and Maria Louisa (later the Empress Marie Louise, second Empress consort to Bonaparte). Madame de Boigne reports that many families who had not attended Court for many years during the years of the Empire were delighted to be able to participate in the wedding celebrations. On 14 June 1816, the Royal Family, the King, the Comte d'Artois, the Duc and Duchesse d'Angoulême and the bridegroom met the new bride at an elaborate marquee in the Forest of Fontainebleau; she was now renamed Marie Caroline, according to French style. The groom's English family and possible English marriage were conveniently overlooked. Carpets and mats were laid on the ground for the Royal party to walk on. Just a few days after meeting in the forest, Charles and Marie Caroline were married at Notre Dame in Paris on 17 June 1816. The ceremonial was designed to appeal to the populace by being open to their gaze, as opposed to previous Royal marriages that had been celebrated in the chapels of palaces away from public scrutiny. Louis XVIII understood the need to bind his restored dynasty to the people in a way that had not been customary prior to the Revolution of 1789.

For the wedding, the Duchesse d'Angoulême wore a white silk outfit and a headdress made of diamonds; but she was a middle-aged woman, by the standards of her time, with a rather stout figure, so all eyes were focused on the alluring nineteen-year-old bride. The new Duchesse de Berry was not a beauty, but she was attractive (despite one blue eye being smaller than the other), full of vivacity and the desire to enjoy life to the full. Her character was lively and natural and this endeared her to the people with whom she came into contact. She was noted for being appreciative of the attention given to her by the people, and also grateful for any services rendered and honours given to her. She thanked her servants and courtiers for their attentions to her. This was unlike other members of the Royal Family, who treated members of their Households as being almost invisible appendages, there only to carry out their wishes and serve their needs. Her new husband expressed himself pleased with his bride, saying 'she is prettier than her portraits'. One of Marie Caroline's first royal duties as the Duchesse de Berry was to present flags to the newly created Garde Royale. The arrival of the younger Princess and the hope of heirs shifted the focus of attention away from Marie Thérèse and her husband. They were no longer the future of the dynasty.

Members of the Court must have hoped that the arrival of a young and vivacious Princess would enliven the rather serious and turgid Court life under the leadership of the staid and pious Duchesse d'Angoulême. Madame de Boigne remarked of the relationships within the ruling family and of the new Duchesse de Berry, 'Her husband seemed greatly attached to her as also were the Comte d'Artois and Duchesse d'Angoulême.'[21] The Duchesse d'Angoulême herself was dismayed to find that, in her view, her cousin was badly educated. She was hardly able to read and write French, as a Bourbon princess, speaking their language with a noticeable Italian lilt. Marie Caroline's spelling in particular was appalling. She was provided with tutors to try to remedy the deficiencies of her education, and passed her mornings in acquiring the accomplishments required of a princess. Marie Caroline said of herself that she was as educated as a carp.

Marie Thérèse was critical of her young sister-in-law, disappointed by Marie Caroline's seeming indifference to the need for appropriate etiquette and her general flightiness and frivolity. Marie Thérèse must have been aware of the comparison between her and the new young Princess, and it would have hurt and offended her sensibilities and pride in a number of ways. The Comte d'Artois, her father-in-law, after further exposure to her ways also came to think of Marie Caroline as being lightweight and juvenile. This is certainly how she must have appeared, in contrast to her devout and rather stolid elder sister-in-law. In particular, Marie Caroline adored '*montagnes russes*'[22] as the big-dipper fairground rides were named by the Parisians. Perhaps they reminded her of the thrills of hill walking she had so enjoyed in the countryside near her girlhood home in Sicily. Madame de Boigne noted, 'Madame d'Angoulême was the only person who tried to guide her, and this she did with the acerbity of a governess.' This mode of behaviour was hardly designed to create warmth and ease between the Royal sisters-in-law. Marie Caroline herself was aware of being just as much a princess as her sister-in-law, and seems to have had no sense of deference towards her elder cousin. She wanted to have fun and enjoy life in France.

The newly-wed couple settled into their new home at the Elysée Palace, where Marie Caroline held informal dances despite her new family's disapproval. Louis XVIII was normally a stickler for good timekeeping and yet he forgave his niece-in-law her tardy ways, although he did impose a small fine by way of punishment for her waywardness and bad timekeeping. Marie Caroline was enormously generous (too generous for her resources) to a large number of charitable causes. Despite the substantial Civil List income allocated to the newlyweds and the fact that Marie Caroline brought with her a large dowry, the Duc and Duchesse de Berry were almost constantly in debt. Poor financial management was another character trait of which the punctilious and financially organised Marie Thérèse could not have approved. Other sources do, however, suggest that the Duchesse de Berry was disciplined regarding the management of her Household and that tradespeople were paid promptly and efficiently. Ironically, despite the Duc de Berry's own rather casual financial habits, he is credited with introducing the concept of a savings bank within his Household, thus enabling members of his staff to accumulate nest eggs. As a mark of honour for the city which had been first to raise the white Bourbon flag at the First Restoration, Louis XVIII promised its citizens that the first son and heir to the throne born to the Duchesse de Berry would be given the title of Duc de Bordeaux.

The Duc de Berry felt that following the Restorations fashionable society sponsored by the Royal Family should be more open and less exclusive. In order to achieve this, following his marriage, he and the Duchesse de Berry gave large parties at their home, the Elysée Palace, in order to broaden the invitation list. The Royal couple shared a more relaxed and informal and less '*ancien régime*' approach. This was in sharp contrast to Marie Thérèse, who found it difficult to accept the '*nouveaux*' who attended her receptions. Even the Duc de Berry apparently found her parties to be tedious, and suggested that she did not wish people to enjoy themselves when she was hostess. He wanted the family to entertain more often and in a more jolly way. The Comtesse de Boigne commented that the Duc de Berry had said that this changed approach was

> Not as easy as you seem to think. My father would like it and would even be ready to turn it to advantage, for he likes society notwithstanding all his religious scruples; but I do not think that it would suit the King, and I am sure that it would displease my brother and my sister-in-law still more. She does not like people to be entertained except in her way 'very sadly'.

Parties at the Tuileries required that the sexes were separated, an old-fashioned and in many ways un-French way of carrying on. Theirs was not a tradition of the ladies retiring after dinner leaving the gentlemen to their port, but one of salons where women were pre-eminent as leaders of fashionable society. It was also noted that the Duchesse d'Angoulême always left parties early, no doubt keen for an early night so that she could be up with the lark to attend to her religious duties.

'The Duc de Berry considered that court society was far too exclusive,' wrote the Comtesse de Boigne. She noted that the Duc de Berry 'sought to rectify this situation by holding a great ball at the Elysée Palace' and that

> Invitations were numerous and distributed with great liberality. The Duc de Berry had previously given dinners to which he invited peers and deputies who were famous in the political world, and he proposed to extend further the circle of his guests. He himself would have everything to gain, for he was sufficiently intellectual to benefit from the conversation and to attempt to stimulate it.[23]

The Duc and Duchesse de Berry in contrast to the Duc and Duchesse d'Angoulême entertained magnificently and with some verve. The Prince did the honours of it with full courtesy and condescension, according to Madame de Boigne.[24]

Despite his marriage, the Duc de Berry still kept in regular contact with Amy Brown[25] and their two daughters: Charlotte Marie Augustine de Bourbon,[26] Comtesse d'Issoudan ; and Louise Marie Charlotte de Bourbon,[27] Comtesse de Vierzon. There were rumours that Mrs Brown and the Duc de Berry had been married. Amy's grandson, writing many years later, said that the probable marriage of his grandparents was something not spoken of in Royal circles. There was apparently no documentary proof of the marriage and the children of the Duc de Berry and Mrs Brown always behaved as courtiers rather than relations around members of the Royal Family, especially the Duchesse de Berry and her son. To do otherwise would question the legitimacy of her marriage and his birth and claims to the throne.

It is clear that the girls were included within the family circle and that Marie Thérèse was acquainted with them. They were living in Paris and Berry visited them and their mother every day. In addition he had a number of other mistresses and casual affairs. Inevitably his wife, who was passionate in her love for him, found out about his philandering and was angry and jealous. She was only able to come to terms with his unfaithfulness when she was informed by the Prince Castelcicala[28] that she had no option but to accept the reality: with the exception of the Duc d'Angoulême, all the men in her circle had mistresses. It was normal and accepted conduct in Frenchmen, even by the very happily married Duc d'Orléans, husband of her cousin Marie Amélie. The Duchesse d'Orléans had wisely learned to turn a blind eye to her husband's unfaithfulness. Prince Castelcicala pointed out to her niece that as an intelligent wife, the Duchesse d'Orléans did not question or even acknowledge her husband's conduct but just got on with things, accepting that this way of life was the norm among Frenchmen of her husband's class and background. Marie Caroline had no real choice in the matter, but found it difficult to accept her husband's unfaithfulness. She had a passionate and possessive nature. Her husband had no desire to hurt her, but he was not prepared to give up the family life with his English mistress and their two daughters or his pleasures with attractive actresses and opera dancers; this had been his way of life long before Marie Caroline arrived in France to marry him.

Whatever the possible deficiencies of Marie Caroline in her '*métier de Princesse*', she was soon set to fulfil the most important role of a princess and produce *enfants de France*. She was unfortunate in her early efforts. In July 1817 she gave birth to a daughter, Louise Isabelle, who died the next day; in September 1818 a baby boy was born, but died shortly afterwards as yet unnamed. Madame de Berry finally produced a healthy baby daughter in 1819, Louise Marie Thérèse, known as Mademoiselle or Mademoiselle d'Artois.[29] Louise was the first Royal baby born in the immediate Royal Family since Marie Antoinette's youngest daughter, Sophie Hélène in 1786.

The two Duchesses, d'Angoulême and de Berry, so very different in character, far apart in age and experience, had not immediately become friends on Marie Caroline's arrival in France. The Duchesse d'Angoulême appeared to her young cousin to be a rather austere woman whose good points were not necessarily immediately apparent. The cousins did, however, become closer when Marie Thérèse showed great care and concern for her sister-in-law following the loss of her babies, which had left Marie Caroline feeling physically drained, depressed and sad. Madame de Gontaut, who had been appointed governess to the baby Princess, wrote, 'Monseigneur told me to call the Duchesse d'Angoulême: she came, and was absolutely perfect, caring for Madame as if she had been her own daughter.'[30]

The birth of a daughter rather than the hoped for prince was disappointing, but the Duchesse de Berry and the rest of the family were optimistic that the next baby could be an heir. Her husband was assiduous in his duties as a husband, in this respect at least. By 13 February 1820, Marie Caroline was pleased to be able to inform her husband that she was again pregnant.

The Orléans family had quit Paris and travelled to England in 1815 to escape Napoleon's advance. While Louis XVIII admired the many qualities of the Duc d'Orléans, he did not fully trust Louis Philippe and his sister Madame Adélaïde, remembering only too well the Revolutionary atmosphere in which they had been brought up by their father Philippe Égalité and his mistress/the children's governess Madame de Genlis. Madame de Genlis had herself gone into exile during the emigration years. Madame de Boigne wrote of Louis' attitude:

> As long as the emigration had lasted he had defended the Duc d'Orléans against the hatred of the Royalist party, but after his return to France he had himself adopted the exaggerations of the party. In particular after the events at Lille in 1815 he persecuted the Prince with untiring animosity. The Orléans family had been excluded from the Royal pew in the chapel of the palace, from the Royal box at the theatre, and in short from every mark of oyal distinction… Only a Prince can appreciate how these little insults may wound the feelings of others.[31]

Louis XVIII refused the Orléans family the right to return to France after the Second Restoration. It was only following pleadings to the King on their behalf by Monsieur, who was keen to establish Bourbon family unity, and the Duchesse d'Angoulême, who was very fond of the Duchesse d'Orléans and godmother to Marie Amélie and Louis Philippe's second son the Duc de Nemours,[32] that the Orléans family were able to return home to France.

The family had spent two years in England, living at first at the Star and Garter Hotel in Richmond and then at Orléans House, their home in Twickenham. Here they were visited by the Prince Regent's daughter and heiress to the throne of England, Princess Charlotte, and the Duke of Kent. The Orléans family was not able to be present at the celebrations of the marriage of Marie Amélie's niece, Caroline of Naples, to the Duc de Berry in 1816 and were only allowed to return to Paris in April 1817 long after the rest of the Royal Family. When they did, they received a rather frosty reception from Louis XVIII, despite the good offices of Marie Thérèse. The relations between the Duc and Duchesse d'Angoulême and at least some of their Orléans cousins were cordial. Following their return to Paris, the Duc and Duchesse d'Orléans held regular Wednesday evening receptions once a month at the Palais-Royal. On occasion a bell would ring indicating that the Duchesse d'Angoulême and her sister-in-law, the Duchesse de Berry, had arrived for the evening. The Duchesse d'Orléans would hurry to the top of the stairs to receive them and escort them into the salon where the party was in progress. Countess Granville, a daughter of the Duchess of Devonshire with whom Marie Antoinette had been such close friends, wrote of the Duchesse d'Angoulême at this time, 'She is very gracious, and is much gayer than she used to be.'

By 1817, Marie Thérèse's memoirs of the years of her childhood imprisonment was published. The first draft had been finished many years before and one copy left with Renete de Chanterenne on Marie Thérèse's departure for Austria. The memoirs were not published under the name of the Duchesse, but there was no doubt as to their authenticity. They created an upsurge of sympathy for the Princess and interest in the events of nearly thirty years previously. An English edition was published in 1817 and a revised edition in 1823. The *Morning Chronicle* of 12 April 1817 commented, 'The detail of the barbarous usage endured by that young innocent, the Dauphin, really requires more than common nerves to peruse', and felt that the writing had a 'touching simplicity and could not be read with a dry eye'. Various slightly different versions were produced over the years, and Louis XVIII at times edited and amended his niece's writings. In general, though, Marie Thérèse was happy that the memoirs be published as they were written. The notes to the 1823 English edition refer to the reluctance to edit the memoirs, which may be seen as yet another example of the Duchesse d'Angoulême's integrity and desire not to 'rewrite' her own version of history to suit anyone else's desires. She had shown the same approach as a young girl in Vienna, refusing to amend and redate her letter to the Abbé Edgeworth. Her unwillingness to be used as a propaganda tool does her credit. She rarely took the easy option in life. This approach may not always have made her comfortable to be around, nor have endeared her to people, but it is a testament to her solid virtue.

As the notes to the English edition put it:

> It will be observed that several passages are obscure, and one or two contradictory: there are frequent repetitions, and a general want of arrangement. All these, which would be defects in a regular history, increase the value of this Journal: they attest its authenticity, and forcibly impress on our minds the cruel circumstances of perplexity and anxiety under which it was written; and the negligence and disorder, if I may use the expression, in which the Princess appears before us, become her misery better than a more careful and ornamented attire. It is a great proof of her good taste, as well as of her conscientious veracity, that she has not permitted any polishing hand to smooth down the colloquial simplicity of her style, and the irregular, but forcible, touches of her expression. This narrative was first published in 1817; it has been lately republished with some slight variations, and a greater appearance of authority. In the first edition, the Princess was made to speak in the third person, and one or two omissions were made. The translation (which originally appeared in 1817) has been revised and accommodated to the new edition, and the variations are mentioned in the notes. There are some little differences on minor points between Her Royal Highness's account and those of M. Huë and Cléry. These might have been easily corrected or omitted: but, again, we think the Duchess has acted with perfect good taste and judgment, in leaving these passages as they were originally written. Those who will take the trouble to compare hers with the other two accounts will see that these trifling variances (and they are very trifling) instead of invalidating, support the credit of all the narrators, and prove that they all faithfully report the impressions or the information which they severally received.

At this time, the Duc and Duchesse d'Angoulême were often separated as they both travelled extensively in France hoping to build support for their family. Louis XVIII trusted his nephew as a fellow advocate of moderate middle-way politics designed to reconcile all sections of French society to a moderate Royalist government; a constitutional monarchy that could heal the divisions of the past. Madame de Boigne wrote of the Duc d'Angoulême and his politics that 'he was dominated by the idea of unlimited obedience to the King. The nearer he was to the throne, the more, in his opinion, was he bound to set an example in this respect.' Other members of his family were not regarded by the King as being so politically sound. The Comte d'Artois had not moved from his reactionary politics of the years of exile, and the King also regarded Marie Thérèse in the same way. He thought her more intelligent but as right-wing and reactionary in her political and religious views as her father-in-law. Madame de Boigne wrote that the Duc d'Angoulême was made unpopular by his moderation in politics, as it offended so many different factions of society and pleased very few. Other sources suggest that many individuals were happy to associate themselves with the Duc d'Angoulême and his more liberal policies. During 1819 the Duchesse d'Angoulême was even forbidden by the King to visit the south-west of France and Bordeaux (which she loved for its loyalty to the Bourbons and where she was loved by the people) for fear that she would be seen not to be supporting the King's compromise policy and that this would stir up trouble.

From 1819 onwards, the Duc de Berry started to receive letters threatening his life; they continued into the following year. He was rightly regarded as the person who was capable of securing Bourbon rule by fathering a son and heir to the throne. He was, therefore, dangerous to those who opposed the regime. At first he did not take the threats seriously, but as the letters continued to arrive he became more anxious about his safety. Marie Caroline was frightened and cross when he started to joke about her being left a widow. On 13 February, the Sunday before the beginning of Lent and the very day she told her husband of her pregnancy, the Duc and Duchesse de Berry went to the opera. The Duchesse de Berry's aunt and uncle, the Duc and Duchesse d'Orléans, were also present at the Opera House and the Royal couples chatted during one of the intervals in the performance. The pregnant Caroline was not feeling too well and decided to return home to the Elysée Palace before the end of the opera. She was escorted to the Opera House exit and helped into her carriage by her husband. Waiting nearby for his chance to attack the Duc de Berry was Louis Pierre Louvel,[33] a passionate supporter of Napoleon. Born at Versailles, he worked in the Royal Household as a saddler, but had been dismissed on the Second Restoration for his Bonapartist views. He loathed the Bourbons. As the Duc de Berry turned to go back into the Opera, the man leapt on him and plunged a knife into the Duc de Berry's left chest just below his lung. The Duc de Berry did not die at once, but he was very badly wounded.

Marie Caroline heard her husband cry out and pushed past her lady-in-waiting, Madame de Béthisy, to get down from her carriage and go to her injured husband, taking him in her arms. The wounded man, who was clearly aware of how badly he was hurt and that death might be imminent, called for a priest to be brought to him and asked of Marie Caroline that he might die in her arms. First aid was given by two doctors who lived nearby. Dr Charles Bougon[34] was quickly on the scene. The Prince told the doctor, whom he recognised from his sojourn in Ghent, that he was mortally wounded. The assembled doctors consulted as to what treatment they should administer. The surgeon, Guillaume Dupuytren, examined the patient's injury closely, trying to determine whether the heart and lungs were damaged. They decided the best course of action was to operate there and then. The Comte d'Artois gave his consent to the operation, trusting his son to the skill of the surgeon who promised to act with zeal. He was assisted in the operation[35] by Bougon.

Marie Thérèse arrived at the scene at about midnight, her face concealed by a large hat. She was, as so often in dire circumstances, outwardly calm and composed. The Duc de Berry had been carried back into the Small Green Salon of the theatre. The Royal Family could still hear the music and applause coming from the auditorium, even as the operation was underway. Actresses still dressed in their Spanish costumes acted as nurses. The surgeon had underestimated the depth of the wound and was unable to the stem the bleeding. Marie Caroline had used her belt as a tourniquet to try to stop the flow of blood from her husband's wounds. Also present at the scene were the Duc and Duchesse d'Orléans and Mademoiselle Adélaïde d'Orléans. They were completely overwhelmed by the events, as reported by Madame de Boigne. Aware of the seriousness of his injuries and the likelihood that he would not live, the Duc de Berry asked to see Mademoiselle Louise and his two other daughters from his relationship with Amy Brown. He kissed all three of his daughters tenderly and asked that his wife care for his half-English daughters. Marie Caroline, ever generous, embraced the girls and said that she now had three children. Marie Thérèse warmly approved of this gesture of forgiveness. She had apparently been less impressed by the earlier histrionics of her cousin.[36] Charles commended the care of his son by his mistress Virginie Oreille, the opera dancer, to the charge of the Duc d'Angoulême.[37] She was present at the scene, apparently wearing a pink tutu. The King arrived early in the morning of 14 February, and the Duc de Berry implored him to show mercy to his assassin; the King agreed that he would. The Duc de Berry was drifting in and out of consciousness and finally died at 6.30[38] a.m. He died with dignity and courage, and the Duchesse de Maillé suggested he died better than he lived. His young pregnant widow embraced her dead husband's body. The Duc de Berry's body was taken to the Louvre at 7.30 a.m. On returning to the Elysée Palace, she hacked off her pretty blonde hair as a gesture of her deep despair at the loss of her husband. The Duc de Berry lay in state and was then buried in the chapel at St Denis with his ancestors.[39] The theatres were closed for nine days as a mark of respect. Louvel, the assassin, was not spared as the Duc de Berry had pleaded that he should be, and was tried and guillotined for his offence on 7 June 1820.

The assassination of the Duc de Berry led to the collapse of the government. Marie Thérèse was instrumental in persuading the King against his own desires that the ministry of Duc Élie Decazes was by its liberal policies responsible for the death of the heir to the throne and that he must go as President of the Council.[40] For Marie Thérèse the assassination was yet another sad and violent death of a member of her close family. Marie Thérèse blamed Élie Decazes[41] for the assassination. Unable to resist the pleas of Marie Thérèse and others, the King felt he had no choice but to let him resign. Decazes tendered his resignation. Madame de Boigne wrote, 'The touching details which accompanied this dreadful catastrophe, beyond dispute because of the number of witnesses, did much to restore the credit of the Royal Family in the eyes of France, and the death of the Duc de Berry was more useful to his family than his life.'[42] Much of France mourned the loss of the Duc and felt the tragedy of the young family, including the pregnant widow he had left behind. Madame de Gontaut reported that there was also an attempt on the life of the pregnant widow – which mistakenly caused an explosion in Marie Thérèse's bathroom. Little damage was caused and neither Princess hurt.

The hope of the dynasty lay with Marie Caroline's unborn child. The Duchesse de Berry went into labour prematurely at 2 a.m. on the morning of 29 September 1820, and matters moved very quickly indeed. Detailed plans for the delivery of her child had been made, but had to be abandoned as events moved too fast. The Princess called for Madame de Gontaut, who was to be the child's governess. Madame de Gontaut herself (as Mademoiselle de Montault- Navailles[43]) had been educated in part with the Orléans children. She had also known Madame Royale as a child at Versailles where she was a frequent visitor, being related to Marie Antoinette's favourite Madame de Polignac. Influenced by her education, she was liberal in her political leanings and had been a particular favourite of the Duc de Berry. Fortunately, the Duchesse de Gontaut was sleeping nearby as she was designated to be one of the official witnesses to the birth of Marie Caroline's baby.

The Duchesse de Berry's doctor arrived an hour later in rather a state. Like the Duchesse de Berry herself, he was very concerned that those hostile to the Bourbon dynasty would question the speed of the delivery and therefore the legitimacy of the child's birth. The Bourbons certainly did not want a repeat of the doubts that had arisen at the birth of the son of James II of England, with all its disastrous consequences for the Stuart dynasty. That episode had undoubtedly made Marie Caroline only too aware of the problems of verification if she did not ensure beyond doubt the legitimacy of her son and his right to the throne. The great political virtue of the elder branch of the Bourbon family was its incontestable right to the throne: its legitimacy. Following the baby's delivery and while he was still connected by the umbilical cord to his naked mother, a rather stunned member of the National Guard was brought into the room by Madame de Gontaut so that he would be able to vouch for the parentage of the child. Three other guardsmen, including Charles d'Hardivillier, were recruited as further witnesses. Nothing was left to doubt or dignity in ensuring the child's right to the throne of France. Dr Bougon who had attended the dying Duc de Berry assisted at the birth. Madame de Boigne was disgusted by the detailed and prurient way in which the news of the baby's delivery was reported in the French newspapers.[44]

It was with great joy that the birth of Henri-Charles-Ferdinand-Marie-Dieudonné d'Artois was announced to the Royal Family and the people of France. As promised by the delighted King, in honour of the city's loyalty to the Bourbons, the miracle child was given the title of Duc de Bordeaux. Marie Caroline had done her duty and produced an heir. She was pleased and proud and settled down to receive the plaudits of her family and France. The baby was presented to the people of Paris and there were wild celebrations both inside and outside the Palace. A line of 15,000 people filed by the baby as he lay in the arms of his grandfather, the Comte d'Artois.

By the time of the birth of the Duc de Bordeaux, the allied occupying forces had at last left France in 1818, under persuasion from the Duc de Richelieu at the Congress of Aix la Chapelle. Madame de Boigne said of this period of French history, 'The wounds were beginning to heal … [and people] felt enormous relief when they no longer saw foreign uniforms strutting on our streets as though they were their own.' A later entry in Queen Victoria's journal, written in August 1855 on a visit to the Emperor Napoleon III and Empress Eugénie in St Cloud, reported that she saw the elaborately decorated cradle made of rare woods, ivory and mother of pearl which had been used first by the young King of Rome and then by the Duc de Bordeaux as babies. From the cradle the Royal infants received visitors.

Marie Thérèse was delighted by her nephew and spent hours by his cot or holding him tenderly in her arms. Chancelier Pasquier's Mémoires[45] recorded, 'It is difficult to imagine the pathos of that hard, cold countenance illuminated at last by pure, natural, womanly joy after the trials she had been called upon to endure. She seemed to regard the child as a sign from god that the times of trouble were over and that she might now look forward to a happier future.' She relished the renewed vigour of the family and the possibility of the continuance of the line. Her own disappointed and thwarted maternal instincts found an expression in the affection she was able to lavish on him.

Not all welcomed the birth of the baby Prince, feeling that the perpetuation of the elder branch of the House of Bourbon was not necessarily a good thing. Madame de Boigne reported the following occurrence on the day of the birth of the Prince, 29 September 1820:

> I remember well an incident which struck me at the time and which we have often recalled since. I was walking in my drawing room with Pozzo,[46] and had been expressing my enthusiasm at this birth for an hour when he

> suddenly stopped, put a hand on my arm, and said, 'You seem very pleased, very happy and very delighted. You hear those bells ringing? Well they are tolling the death-knell of the House of Bourbon, and do not forget what I have said.'

In Madame de Boigne's opinion, the predictions proved only too real:

> The posthumous child, who received the title of Duc de Bordeaux, induced his family to begin attempts for the re-establishment of the absolute monarchy, and also deprived the people of their hopes that the older line, with which they were not in sympathy, would become extinct. Thus it is that the prophecies of weak mortals are often overthrown by the decrees of Providence and our cries of joy turn to lamentations. I must do Pozzo the justice to recognise that he was one of the few people who predicted this fact at that time. The Duke of Wellington expressed himself in almost similar terms upon the marriage of the Duc de Berry. Someone had said that the Duchesse seemed too feeble to have much hope of children, and he replied, 'It would be very fortunate for the Restoration. The best chance for the Restoration to establish itself is to leave some hope that the reigning branch may become extinct.'

Marie Thérèse was certainly not noted for her gracious treatment of the Duke of Wellington, and he was less than enamoured of the Bourbons in general and certainly not impressed by their capabilities as rulers. Wellington was presumably hopeful that the fecund and anglophile Orléans branch would supersede their cousins on the throne and marry together the twin strands of Revolution and monarchical government.

The baby Prince was christened on 1 May 1821 at Notre Dame. The Duchesse d'Angoulême stood as proxy for his godmother, the hereditary Princess of Naples; and the Comte d'Artois represented his godfather, the King of Naples. Madame de Gontaut placed the baby on the altar of the cathedral. Henri was being initiated into his role as a Prince of the very Catholic Bourbon dynasty. During his early months there were a number of attempts on his life by assassins keen to put a quick end to the possibility of the elder branch of the Bourbon family perpetuating itself. There were rivals for the throne: in Vienna being educated at his grandfather's Imperial Court was the former King of Rome, now the Duke of Reichstadt, who was regarded by the Bonapartists as the proper heir to the throne of France. Former Queen Hortense and Louis Bonaparte had also produced sons who had a claim to the Napoleonic political legacy. To celebrate the baby Prince's christening, there were great firework displays and a fête in Paris. Sweets were distributed to the populace. A public subscription raised sufficient funds by 5 March 1821 to purchase for the baby Prince his own magnificent Château of Chambord[47] in the Loire valley.

The Duchesse d'Angoulême was not always consistent in deciding whom she would or would not receive at Court. She was quite prepared to accept Louis XVIII's mistress and to receive her. This lady was born Zoé Talon in 1785, and was the daughter of an aristocratic family who had remained loyal to the Bourbons. Madame de Boigne suggests that her father was one of Louis XVIII's network of spies. She was educated by Madame Campan and following her marriage she became Comtesse du Cayla. Zoé[48] became Louis XVIII's favourite during the last years of his life. She was increasingly influential after the departure of Duc Decazes in 1820, following his fall from office. The Duchesse d'Angoulême supported the rise of Madame du Cayla as a favourite in place of Decazes. The former favourite was sent as ambassador to London by way of compensation for loss of office. She preferred this lady, for all her avarice and ambition, to the King's previous favourite. The relationship between Louis XVIII and Madame du Cayla would seem to have been platonic, though there were suggestions that he liked to take snuff from her bosom or shoulder, according to Queen Hortense's memoirs. She accumulated a huge fortune, benefiting from Royal generosity. The diarist Charles Greville when visiting the restored King in Paris observed that Louis XVIII wanted a confidante 'to whom he could tell everything, consult with on all occasions, and with whom he could bandy literary trifles'. Madame du Cayla became the conduit to the King through whom his ministers would communicate.

Lord Byron, that keen supporter of Napoleon, described Louis XVIII in his 1823 poem 'The Age of Bronze':

A mild Epicurean, form'd, at best,
To be a kind host and as a good a guest,
To talk of letters, and to know by heart
One half *the poet's,* all *the gourmand's art:*
A scholar always, now and then a wit,
And gentle when digestion may permit; …
But not to govern lands enslaved or free;
The gout was martyrdom enough for thee.

Byron certainly did not feel that Louis XVIII was cut out to rule the volatile and divided land that was post-Revolutionary France. The Court was reformed in the 1820s. Anachronistic and superfluous posts were abolished and the number of servants reduced. Uniforms were introduced which added splendour to the King's Court.

Momentous news arrived in Paris from the British island of St Helena. It was announced that the former Emperor Napoleon or General Bonaparte had died of cancer on 5 May 1821. Most of Marie Thérèse's life had been dominated and overshadowed by his presence and his success as a soldier. After leaving France in 1795, she spent the next ten years or so of her life being forced to flee from his forces: residing with the Imperial children in Prague in the late 1790s, or taking refuge in countries which were often subservient to him. Some of the most depressing years had been when he was winning victory after victory and there seemed no possible end to his rule and the restoration of her family to its homeland. If not wholly responsible for the downfall of her family, he had certainly made sure that he was one of the major beneficiaries of it. She could not forget the humiliations of the Hundred Days when her husband was forced to leave France under threat from the resurgent Napoleon and her uncles were driven out of Paris in undignified haste. Equally, she herself had been compelled to give up the fight in Bordeaux and return to England. She may, however, have recalled the grudging respect Napoleon had given her as the 'only man of her family'. She certainly did not enjoy being connected to him by virtue of his marriage to Marie Louise of Austria.

Marie Thérèse was very proud of her husband when in 1823 he went successfully to the aid of their Spanish Borbon cousin, the reactionary and pro-Jesuit Ferdinand VII.[49] The Spanish Royal Family had suffered kidnapping and imprisonment in France at the Château of Valençay during the Napoleonic era and been replaced on the throne of Spain by Bonaparte's elder brother Joseph. Restored to the throne in 1813, thanks to the victories of the Duke of Wellington, they had returned to govern; but their conservative and religious policies (what would have been characterised as Ultra in France) led to revolt. Once again the Spanish Borbons were in peril. Louis XVIII did not like war or the expenditure it entailed, but Marie Thérèse and others persuaded him to agree to the invasion of Spain. Ferdinand was practically a prisoner of the communeros revolutionaries. Determined to help their cousins and to suppress possible anti-monarchist sedition on their southern border, the French mobilised. The Duc d'Angoulême, despite his lack of real operational military experience, was appointed Commander in Chief. His own lackings as a commander were compensated by the presence of General Guilleminot as chief of staff and the real leader of the expeditionary force. The Vicomte de Châteaubriand as the Minister for Foreign Affairs was in political control of the campaign. Marie Thérèse travelled south with her husband as far as Bayonne: just north of the Spanish border, and on the west coast of France near what is now Biarritz. She seems to have enjoyed the journey and to have been relaxed and gracious. Louis Antoine went on with a French army of 80,000, entering Spain in the spring of 1823.

Marie Thérèse returned to Paris to await her husband. Louis Antoine and his troops were greeted as liberators by huge sections of the Spanish population. Victory at the Battle of Trocadero on 31 August 1823, when French forces captured the fort guarding Cadiz, the release of Ferdinand and the capture of Madrid made for a heady cocktail of success for Louis

Antoine. In Madrid he was lauded and presented with loyal addresses expressing their gratitude and calling him 'an august prince', signed by members of the Spanish aristocracy. The Vicomte de Châteaubriand wrote in his memoirs,[50] 'on the receipt of the telegraphic despatch announcing the rescue of the King of Spain we ministers rushed to the castle. There I felt a sudden presentiment of my downfall; it was like a bucketful of cold water down my back, for the King and Monsieur took no notice of us. Madame the Duchesse d' Angoulême, delirious with joy at the success of her husband, had no eyes for anybody.' Louis Antoine returned home to a hero's welcome and a delighted and proud Marie Thérèse. Commemorative coins were struck in his honour by the Monnaie Royale des Medailles, showing his triumphal entry into Paris on one side and on the reverse his passing under the Triumphal Arch of L'Etoile on horseback 'bearing the standard of France and followed by his brave and faithful warriors'.[51] It was in part a vindication of his humiliations at the hands of Bonaparte's troops during the Hundred Days. The Royal Family processed to Notre Dame on 12 October 1823 for a service of thanksgiving.

Enjoying the relaxations of country life and finding that she could not be as private as she wished at St Cloud, the family's main summer retreat, Marie Thérèse purchased the small estate of Villeneuve-l'Étang[52] near Marnes-la-Coquette, not far from St Cloud. In a move reminiscent of her mother's to the Petit Trianon, Marie Thérèse enjoyed *'jouer à la fermière'* or pretending to be a farmer's wife.[53] She must have had happy childhood memories of spending time with her parents and siblings and their close companions at the Petit Trianon and L'Hermitage in the days before that fateful coach ride into Paris on 6 October 1789.

The property she purchased was quite isolated, and here Marie Thérèse was able to enjoy privacy and solitude spending time in the afternoons reading in the shade of the large trees in the grounds. She lavished care and money on her country home. At Villeneuve-l'Étang she was able to relax with her old friends, such as Pauline de Béarn, with whom she felt at ease. Sometimes the Dauphine would invite a group of a hundred or so children from the town of Versailles and entertain them to tea at her country house. This gave her the opportunity to enjoy the company of children and to emulate the children's parties hosted by Marie Antoinette during her own girlhood.

When at the Tuileries Palace, Marie Thérèse always had a pot of cream from her own farm on her dining table; woe betide anyone who dared suggest this was not the best cream in the world. Marie Thérèse also used her home-produced pot of cream as a way of indicating her favour or otherwise to members of the Court and government. Madame de Boigne reported[54] on the departure from political power of the Duc de Richelieu:[55]

> as the Duc de Richelieu was the Master of Hounds and First Gentleman of the Chamber, he continued to lunch at the Château but he always met with a very cold reception... The cream was placed in a little jug which stood by her side, and as a mark of favour she would share it with certain individuals. One day she made a point of offering it to guests to the right and left of the Duc de Richelieu in so marked a manner that her neglect of him became a positive insult.

The Duc de Richelieu fully recognised the ridiculous pettiness and discourtesy of this gesture, but as a courtier of the *ancien régime* he would notice such things and recognise the acerbity of the deliberate insult. He had offended the Bourbons years before, and was never forgiven for failing to give the service required of him at Mittau. When the Duc de Richelieu died in 1822, according to Madame de Boigne it was only the Duc d'Angoulême who expressed sorrow for his death. The Duc d'Angoulême apparently said to Madame de Boigne's brother, the Comte d'Osmond: 'I feel sorrow at his loss; he did not like us, but he loved France. His life was a resource, and his death will be a loss.'[56] The King, Monsieur and Marie Thérèse seemed to be relieved that he had died, so that they would not have to meet him again. Such stories of social pettiness and ungraciousness do not put Marie Thérèse and the rest of the Bourbons in a good light. Another change in the Household was when the Duchesse d'Angoulême's faithful and long-serving attendant Madame de Sérent, who had been in exile with the family, died in 1823.

The family still enjoyed excursions to the theatre. The *Morning Post* of 9 December 1823, reporting from the French newspaper *L'Etoile*, noted: 'The Princes and Princesses of the Royal Family will honour the Theâtre Français with their presence on Wednesday next.' Clearly security fears even after the assassination of the Duc de Berry did not stop them enjoying visits to the theatre. As is the way with royalty, Marie Thérèse was honoured with having all manner of things named after her. She was no doubt pleased that a hospital had been established in her name, 'the Infirmerie Marie Thérèse', by Madame de Chateaubriand as a thank you offering for the Second restoration of the Bourbons in 1815. It was opened in 1819 to provide a sanctuary and care for ill and impoverished priests and gentlewomen who had been affected by the Revolution. She was its patroness. Plaques and columns were erected to commemorate the places she visited as she travelled around France. In her 'home' town of Angoulême there is still a column in the ionic style that was erected in 1816 to commemorate her low-key visit to the town in March 1815. A more elaborate and well-prepared visit scheduled for March 1814 had been disrupted by the arrival of Napoleon in France and the necessity for Marie Thérèse to rally the troops in Bordeaux. There is also a column in St-Florent in the Vendée, which she visited in 1823. A wag noted that she had left it rather late to visit this loyal area. A pear was named after her and in 1820 a basket of the fruit was sent to the Duchesse d'Angoulême by its grower. She agreed that the bright green pear might bear her name and it is still called that to this day. There was also a richly scented 'Duchesse d'Angoulême' rose named in honour of Marie Thérèse and a ship, *The Duchesse d'Angoulême*.

French tradesmen and women were keen to associate themselves and their products with Marie Thérèse and the Duchesse de Berry. The former hairdresser to the Royal ladies announced his arrival in London and hoped for custom. The English elite was accustomed now to travel to Paris for their pleasures. Madame d'Arblay noted that 'Paris, that favoured capital, seems to be half peopled by English. The rage for Parisian excursions is almost incredible.' But the English, with their rich, conquering and often inebriated ways, were not always popular visitors to Paris when they flocked there.

The English were however always welcomed at the Court of Louis XVIII. It was said that an English accent guaranteed a good reception. Dr Whalley, a visitor to Paris, wrote that he had been kindly received by the Duchesse d'Angoulême; he commented of the Royal Family that 'Their gratitude to England is unbounded, and the name of English is a passport everywhere.'

11

The First Lady of France

1824–1830

Louis XVIII eventually died on 16 September 1824 surrounded by his family, as was the usual custom on the death of a member of the Bourbon family. Marie Thérèse was with the King to the end of his life. She had nursed her uncle, as she had previously nursed the Abbé Edgeworth and Queen Marie Joséphine, with great devotion. Madame de Boigne wrote that as it became clear that the King was dying, Louis XVIII's courtiers hinted to the dying King that he should receive the last rites of the Roman Catholic Church. He declined to do so, but replied uncharacteristically sharply to Marie Thérèse, when she made the same suggestion, that it was not yet time for him to die. The final rituals of the church could wait a little longer. Eventually the King's favourite, Madame du Cayla, managed to persuade the King to make his peace with his God. The priests were sent in to give the dying King the last rites. The Royal Family gathered around his bed, accompanied by members of the clergy, the King's doctors and courtiers. The Duchesse d'Angoulême was deeply affected by her uncle's death and her usually iron emotional restraint was breached; her face ran with tears.

Munro Price's excellent book *Perilous Crown* draws on the previously unpublished diaries of Madame Adélaïde, sister of Louis Philippe, to give us an insight to the role and reactions of the Duchesse d'Angoulême at this distressing time of her life. Madame Adélaïde reported on 11 September that Marie Thérèse was concerned that the King had refused to take the last sacraments and make peace with his God. By 13 September the King had agreed to take communion and receive the last rites. The Royal Family, accompanied by members of the Court, processed from the chapel to the King's room carrying candles and bringing with them the communion host. The King took communion and gave his family his blessing. Outside the Tuileries Palace the Paris stock exchange was closed as a sign of respect, as were the theatres. A large and very quiet crowd held vigil outside the Tuileries Palace. A few days later Adélaïde reported in her diary that the Duchesse d'Angoulême announced with some concern that Louis XVIII was still reluctant to have said the prayers for the dying, despite her repeated requests that he do so. Adélaïde wrote, 'I admit that this detail upset me. Although I had no affection or indeed any particular feelings for the King, far from it, I pitied him. Why, once he had received the sacraments, made his peace with God and set an example, go on tormenting him with these prayers?'[1]

Madame Adélaïde also described a rather macabre dinner that took place at this time. The Orléans family was invited to dine with Monsieur, Marie Thérèse and Louis Antoine in the room next to the chamber where the dying Louis XVIII lay. She wrote, 'The King's place was laid, his whole dinner service was laid out as if he was about to come and dine, except that it was covered with a veil.' Everything was done just as if the King was eating with the family while in fact he was next door dying. The King's agonies and those of his family were protracted and painful to all concerned. It seemed he was just about to die and then he would recover a little and battle on. Gangrene was eating at his body. On one foot he had only three toes. The stench in the room was apparently horrendous. At last, by the early hours of 16 September, it seemed that the King was really dying at last. His room was full of members of the Royal Family, including Marie Thérèse, her husband and father-in-law, the clergy[2] and members of the Court.[3] Madame Adélaïde reports that as the old King died at 4 a.m. the Duc d'Angoulême said several times to Monsieur, 'Father, it's over.'[4] The new King, Charles X, then knelt by the bed and kissed the hand of his dead brother, as did Marie Thérèse and her husband and the other members of the Royal Family who had been present at his deathbed, namely Madame de Berry, the Duc and Duchesse d'Orléans and M. le Duc de Bourbon. Madame Adélaïde herself reports that she pretended to do so, but could not bring herself to kiss the dead man's hand.

On the death of Louis XVIII and the accession to the throne of her father-in-law, Charles X, Marie Thérèse became Madame la Dauphine. This was the title that had last been held by her mother, Marie Antoinette, between her marriage in 1770 to Louis Auguste and 1774 when she became Queen. Marie Thérèse was, however, not a flighty young girl naïve in the ways of the French Court, as had been her mother on becoming Dauphine, but a solidly built matron in her mid-forties. For the previous 25 years of their marriage, Marie Thérèse, as the daughter of a King, had outranked her husband in terms of Royal protocol. For example, Marie Thérèse had always preceded her husband when they were both leaving a room. All changed now with the accession of the Duc d'Angoulême's father to the throne of France. Marie Thérèse dutifully and very publicly deferred to her husband's new rank as Monsieur le Dauphin. As Marie Thérèse and Louis Antoine left the presence of the now dead Louis XVIII, both were visibly deeply moved by his death and the horrible protracted manner of it. Both were weeping. Nevertheless, as the Duchesse d'Angoulême reached the door of the chamber, aware of the change in their relative seniority, she stopped and managed to utter, despite all that she was feeling, 'Take precedence, Monsieur le Dauphin.' She stood aside so that her husband might pass first through the door ahead of her, as was required by the Court etiquette instilled in her as a child.

Madame de Boigne reported this incident in her diaries from contemporary information given to her by her brother, the Comte d'Osmond, who was present at the deathbed of Louis XVIII:

> The Princes of the House of Bourbon have been warmly criticised for their sacrifices to the laws of etiquette, but it is obvious that this is a tendency inherent in their character. Certainly the Dauphin's wife [i.e. Marie Thérèse] was deeply affected by her uncle's death, even if she had not been attached to him, the terrible scene at which she had been present would have been enough to move her deeply. Only a few seconds had elapsed, and the dying man's last groan was still ringing in her ears; yet nothing could distract her from a matter of pure etiquette under circumstances when no one would have noted any breach of it. [5]

Always considerate of his wife's feelings, the new Dauphin on this occasion accepted her deference to his new rank without 'any display of astonishment or impatience'.[6] This echoes the extreme deference that Greville noted Marie Thérèse showing to her uncle Louis XVIII during the diarist's visit to Hartwell in 1812. The tradition was that the new King could not stay in the same place as the body of the late King, so the Royal Family immediately quit the Tuileries Palace. The body of the late King was left there to lie in state, while the Royal Family retired to the Château of St Cloud. The public was admitted, by ticket, to view the late Louis XVIII's body lying in state for several days in his former apartments. The rooms were decorated with black draperies, suitable to a chapel of mourning. Masses were said for the dead man's soul, and Louis XVIII was buried at St Denis with his ancestors. Marie Thérèse watched the funeral service from the gallery in the sanctuary from which 'she was accustomed to go with her pious grief', as the *Morning Post* of 30 October reported.

Marie Thérèse had been 'first lady' of the Court since the death of Louis XVIII's Queen, Marie Joséphine in 1810. With her title now changed to La Dauphine, it meant the simpler the title, the greater was the prestige within the Royal Family. The Duchesse de Berry was now keen to assume the title of Madame, but the new King and Marie Thérèse were united in denying Marie Caroline this honour. When courtiers in the first few days after the accession of Charles X spoke of Marie Caroline as 'Madame' to Marie Thérèse, she responded to them 'you mean the Duchesse de Berry'. When Marie Caroline spoke to her father-in-law about the matter, Madame de Boigne relays that he supported Marie Thérèse's position, saying, 'By what right? I am alive and you are a widow. The thing is impossible.' He was alluding to the fact that the title of 'Monsieur' (with the title of 'Madame ' for his wife) would only have gone to Marie Caroline's dead husband Berry on the accession to the throne of his elder brother, the Duc d'Angoulême, now the Dauphin. The title of 'Monsieur' with 'Madame' for his wife was strictly reserved for the brother of the King, not the widow of a second son.

The tale illustrates the enormous emphasis placed by the Bourbons, and Marie Thérèse in particular, on what must appear to the modern mind as small and entirely unimportant points of style and etiquette, even within their own very close family. Notwithstanding the approach on this matter of the King and Dauphine, those individuals wishing to curry favour with the Duchesse de Berry and close friends and members of her Household would refer to her simply as 'Madame'. Marie Caroline was, after all, the mother of the future King and there were those who looked to her in due course for favour and preferment. The Duchesse de Gontaut,[7] governess to the Duc de Bordeaux and his sister, Mademoiselle Louise, declined to refer to their mother as 'Madame' in deference to the views of the reigning King and the Dauphine. She clearly preferred to play the short, rather than the long-term, political game. The Prince and Princess's governess's insistence on using this form of address, as can be well imagined, led to rather strained relations within the Household of the Duchesse de Berry. They were clearly as a family far more interested in the required protocol of any ceremonial situation than in dealing with the very pressing and difficult political issues that needed their attention.

Things began to go wrong for the Bourbons almost as soon as Marie Thérèse's father-in-law Charles X became King. He was a complete fish out of water. He was not equipped to rule a country which had endured such change and was riven by divisions. Though socially charming, as Lord Melbourne commented to the young Queen Victoria,[8] he was rigid and deeply out of touch in his political views. Marie Thérèse, in contrast to her husband, was by inclination and conviction an ultra-Royalist. She was, therefore, in instinctive political sympathy with the reactionary and pro-émigré views of her father-in-law, uncle and now King. This was in contrast to the approach during the reign of his predecessor and his 'third way' of trying to hold a political position through pragmatism and compromise. Despite living in London and Edinburgh for more than twenty years and seeing the British system of government in operation at close proximity, constitutional monarchy and parliamentary democracy were anathema to Charles X and it would seem to Marie Thérèse too. She had taken no positive learning from having seen the model of the British parliamentary system and the restriction of Royal power. Charles X was once asked about the subject of the British monarchy and its role, and replied that he would rather not be a monarch than reign like a King of Great Britain. His niece and daughter-in-law agreed with him about this definition. Kings reigned and ruled in her view, or else had no purpose. Madame Élisabeth's influence on her niece was evident.

The Court retired to the Château of St Cloud, where Charles X received his ministers and the whole Royal Family, including the Orléans cousins. He appointed to the government as his first minister Jules de Polignac, one of the hated clan and a relic of pre-Revolutionary times. Polignac was religious to an extraordinary degree. He claimed to receive visions from the Virgin Mary, and this divine inspiration would guide him on how best to rule France. The French political system worked on the basis of an executive appointed by the monarch who had the right to propose legislation; and two parliamentary houses which reviewed and amended legislation. Despite being nominally a democracy, the electorate was tiny, approximately 80,000. All women were excluded, and only those males who owned significant property were entitled to vote. Pressure from the majority of the population was building for change.

Madame de Boigne reports that Charles X 'made a declaration of principle' regarding the political approach that he and his new ministers would take. It was surprisingly and, to many, pleasingly liberal in its stance. It supported the Constitutional Charter that had formed the underpinning of his brother's government. Many in France had thought, given Charles X's political stance during his brother's reign, that he would attempt to move sharply away from the middle way and towards more reactionary policies. Promulgated through the *Moniteur*, the announcement was well received in Paris and all over France. As a response to the new government's apparently moderate and constitutional stance, the new King was initially popular with his people. He received an extremely warm welcome when he entered Paris on horseback in September 1824. Despite the rain, Charles X seemed very happy 'getting wet with the best grace in the world, with the pleasing and open countenance which charmed the citizens of Paris in 1814' when he had first returned to Paris years before.[9] Despite the downpour, the crowds were large and enthusiastic. 'His popularity was at its height.'[10] Marie Thérèse relished her uncle's popularity as she followed him in her carriage in the procession into Paris. Madame de Boigne wrote with some irony that while 'Monsieur was most unpopular … on the contrary, Charles X is very popular.'[11]

The period in the run-up to the Coronation in May 1825 had its political difficulties. Louis XVIII had decided against an elaborate coronation, but his traditionalist and religious brother was determined to return to the rituals of the *ancien régime* and as far as possible to the old ways. The new King had at the beginning of his reign made liberal statements declaring his loyalty to and support for the Constitutional Charter promulgated by his late brother. The question which arose was whether he would swear during the Coronation service to uphold its principles and the rights given to the people. The Constitutional Charter gave individual citizens freedom of worship and personal conscience (whatever their religious persuasion); the French Roman Catholic establishment especially was unsurprisingly keen to exclude these rights to individual religious freedom. The King, as a devout Roman Catholic and committed son of the Roman Catholic Church, shared this view and wanted to make his approach very clear in his Coronation oath. As a man of profound faith, any such oath sworn at his Coronation would bind him firmly. It would be a very clear and unequivocal statement of his views and intentions. The traditionalist and religious party known as the Congrégation party, led by the clergy and especially the Jesuits and with the support of the papal nuncio to France, urged Charles X not to swear to uphold the Charter during his Coronation. Apparently[12] prompted by M. de Villèle, his former tutor, the new Dauphin was fully aware of the negative message that such an obvious and powerful omission would give to the country, so managed very sensibly to persuade his father, with much difficulty, to include a guarantee of 'freedom of worship'[13] in his Coronation oath. There was much drafting and redrafting of the King's oath in preparation for the ceremony in order to come up with a version that could be palatable to all sections of society. Marie Thérèse was closely identified in the public mind with the religious party, and the close connection did her image no good with large sections of the population.

Marie Thérèse's greatest popularity was with the Royalist army. As Duchesse d'Angoulême in Bordeaux in 1814, she had shown her courage and her resolve in leading the troops in the confusion of the Hundred Days. Marie Thérèse was fully aware of the importance of a loyal army in maintaining her dynasty's hold on power, so courted the officer corps. Her husband and his brother, the Duc de Berry, had always enjoyed 'playing soldiers'.[14] As Duc d'Angoulême, the Dauphin had shown courage and resolution, if not success, in confronting Napoleon and had been victorious during the Spanish campaign of 1823; but as Madame de Boigne reported:

> Next to hunting, the Dauphin liked nothing so much as playing at being a soldier. This amusement was permitted more readily as he cared very little about matters of military organisation. After he had drilled a few battalions, had severely reprimanded some clumsy execution, had pointed out a mistake in uniform or in the handling of a weapon, he imagined that he was a great General, and went home delighted with himself.[15]

Marie Thérèse, both as Duchesse d'Angoulême and later Dauphine, took what one might characterise as a feminine approach. She made a point of getting to know the officers personally. She knew all their faces and names. She was aware of their 'circumstances, their hopes and their family connections'.[16] Marie Thérèse worked hard to ensure that the army was strongly connected to the Royal Family in a real and personal way by the bonds of devotion and affection. She put effort into establishing and maintaining these contacts.

Whenever Marie Thérèse was able to gain a favour for one of the army officers, she always made sure that she gave her husband the credit for obtaining the benefit as a way of bolstering his popularity with the army and countering his far more formal and impersonal approach to the officers. One senses that with her gruff voice, rather peremptory manner and approach and lack of interest in the feminine arts of dress and appearance, the Duchesse d'Angoulême was comfortable and at ease with these military men in a way she was not with many of the ladies of the Court. She was much more relaxed with the army and, contrary to her reputation for severity and austerity, sought to provide the young officers with 'amusement as well as promotion'. On many occasions she secured the suspension of orders which interfered with 'the amusements of the Carnival, so that the soldiers could enjoy the jollities. Hence she was adored by these young men, for whom she relaxed the usual severity of her countenance.'[17] Marie Thérèse was regarded as the 'patroness'[18] of the newly established Royalist army.

Marie Thérèse was less relaxed in her approach and contact with the 'remnants of Napoleon's *Grande Armée*'.[19] She had experienced at first hand during the Hundred Days in 1815 the devotion of many of Napoleon's old soldiers to the now dead former Emperor. It had been shown in their refusal to fight against him and their willingness to lay aside their oaths of loyalty to Louis XVIII during the Hundred Days in the spring and early summer of 1815.

As Madame de Boigne recounts, Charles X would never voluntarily speak of the wars of the Revolutionary and Empire periods. Maréchal Marmont, one of Napoleon's former generals, who played whist with the King in the apartments of the Dauphine, would occasionally take pleasure in reminding Charles X of 'the anniversaries of brilliant exploits performed by the French army. But the King invariably disputed their brilliance with much vivacity, and described them as they appeared in the accounts (from the English press, no doubt) which he had read abroad.'[20] If anyone attempted to provide him with a more Francophile version of events he was not best pleased, disputing the details of the victories and taking out his displeasure on his whist partner. Marie Thérèse's own views on the Napoleonic victories no doubt echoed those of Charles X.

The coronation of Charles X at Rheims was a return to the ceremonial of the *ancien régime*, and Marie Thérèse as Dauphine participated fully in it. She rejoiced in the return to the ceremonial and forms of etiquette of her childhood and studied them in detail so as to prepare herself for the ceremony. On 27 May 1825, Charles X left Paris and headed towards Rheims, the traditional place of coronation of the French Kings some 80 miles from the capital. The cathedral had undergone repairs to restore it to magnificence after the years of neglect and dilapidation during the Revolutionary and Empire periods. Charles X was dressed for the ceremonial in a silver tunic and wore a small black velvet cap decorated with white feathers. Marie Amélie, the Duchesse d'Orléans, wrote that the Dauphine and other ladies of the Royal Family wore gowns of gold lamé brocade and sported their tiaras.[21] They were also festooned with diamonds on their arms, fingers and around their necks. The officials organising the ceremonial at least had the good sense and tact not to house the Dauphine in the same quarters as those from which her mother, Marie Antoinette, had watched the young Louis XVI arrive at his coronation. The Prince de Joinville, son of the Duc and Duchesse d'Orléans, observed the ceremonial as a six-year-old and was struck by 'the splendour displayed that interested us – the dresses, the carriages, and so on, of the princes and ambassadors who came from all parts of the world to greet the opening of the new monarch's reign'.[22]

The coronation took place on 29 May 1825. The King was anointed with holy oil through seven openings in his shirt, with Monseigneur Latil[23] officiating at the coronation. The crown itself was placed on Charles's head by Louis Philippe, Duc d'Orléans. The ceremony was accompanied by wonderful music. As the King mounted the throne there was a cry of '*Vivat Rex in aeternum*'.[24] The standards and flags were bowed before the King. Doves were released and the congregation cried out '*Vive le Roi*'. Madame de Boigne opted not to attend the ceremonial, but reported at second hand in her memoirs: 'The birds released in the cathedral as a sign of emancipation merely proved a nuisance' and no one gave the traditional cry of '*Noel! Noel!*'[25] Nevertheless, the ceremonial was well received and moving to those who attended. Marie Thérèse watched the ceremony from a gallery. Her virtues and those of other members of the Royal Family were hailed by Cardinal de la Fare in his sermon. He referred to her as 'This magnanimous Princess, the living image of celestial charity, the visible Providence of the unfortunate, the model of heroism as of virtue!'[26] It was noted by observers that the King prostrated himself before the Archbishop of Rheims, an early indication of his submission and devotion to the Roman Catholic Church which stirred fears among the anticlerical element in French society and among those Frenchmen and women who espoused other versions of Christianity or other religions.

Paris was packed with visitors from home and abroad. They had come to enjoy the city's wonderful theatre, galleries, restaurants, and elegant shopping and to see and participate in the Royal ceremonial which followed the Coronation and the King and the Royal Family's return from Rheims. The King and his party returned to a Paris *en fête*: he entertained foreign envoys and dignitaries at the Tuileries Palace, while the streets of the capital were thronged with people watching the many processions and ceremonies in honour of the Coronation. The weather was magnificent, which encouraged the enjoyment of the crowds. The entry of Charles X into the capital on his return from the Coronation at Rheims was 'superb'[27] according to Madame de Boigne, who was an eye-witness to these events; she watched the procession as it made its way from Notre Dame to the Tuileries. The Dauphine travelled in a coach accompanied by the Duchesse de Berry and the young princes of the Orléans family. Her husband accompanied the King and the Ducs of Bourbon and Orléans in another carriage.

On 7 June 1825, Charles X was invested with the English order of the Garter, presented to him by the Duke of Northumberland[28] acting on behalf of George IV. A day later the Royal Family was entertained by the municipality of Paris in the Salle d'Angoulême at the Hotel des Invalides, which had been built to commemorate the return of the Duc d'Angoulême from Spain in 1823. It was magnificent, but the room was intensely hot and uncomfortable for those attending. The Royal Family then processed to the ballroom where the Duchesse de Berry (rather than Marie Thérèse) opened the dancing with her partner.

The Dauphin and Dauphine were very involved in the upbringing of their niece and nephew, Louise and the posthumous Henri, Duc de Bordeaux. René de Chazet's *Vie Anecdotique* notes that the Duc de Bordeaux and his sister saw their aunt regularly as part of their daily routine. Marie Caroline was sidelined from the lives of her children by her father-in-law and the Dauphin and Dauphine. For example, she only saw her children for half an hour a day during the winter when the Royal Family lived at the Tuileries. When the children and their grandfather were at St Cloud in the summer and autumn, she drove out from Paris to see them but did not stay. Louise only visited her mother once at Rosny, her country retreat, and Henri never. The approach to their education and training was determined not by their mother but by the King, Louis Antoine and Marie Thérèse, with whom the children spent much of their time. Marie Thérèse spent a significant amount of time supervising the education of her nephew and niece, a role she took very seriously. The day-to-day care and education of the young prince and his elder sister was under the control of their governess, Madame de Gontaut. If there was conflict between the governess and the mother, the King always supported the governess. The Duchesse de Berry had on the death of her husband moved from the Elysée Palace where she had lived as a young married woman into the Pavilion de Marsan. Part of the Louvre complex, it was conveniently situated in the grounds of the Tuileries Palace. This brought the King's grandchildren within easy proximity for the rest of the family, including Marie Thérèse, and was sensible from the point of view of cost-saving. It had the disadvantage (for the Duchesse de Berry) of bringing Marie Caroline and her children under the day-to-day watchful eyes of other members of the Royal Family. The young Duchesse de Berry, hardly in her twenties, was unsurprisingly deeply bored by the mesmerisingly dull and deeply religious society that surrounded the older royals.

She found her pleasures in Paris, but paid the price of the disapproval of her husband's family. She held balls (some with exotic themes such as the Bal Turc) sometimes in her own name and sometimes in the name of Madame de Gontaut – which allowed for more relaxed etiquette. She even danced with the sons of Napoleon's Maréchals Mortier and Soult. Marie Thérèse, especially, found her cousin and sister-in-law to be essentially trivial and not capable of fulfilling the serious and demanding role of being a Bourbon princess and the mother of the heir to the throne. One may suspect that Marie Thérèse was jealous that such an unworthy princess, one so clearly less suited to royal motherhood than she, should have been blessed with children.

Being treated as second-class royalty by their cousins was enormously annoying and a continuing humiliation to the proud Orléans family. In an effort to heal the divisions between the senior and junior branches of the House of Bourbon, in September 1824 Charles X generously upgraded the royal rank of the Duc d'Orléans and his sister Madame Adélaïde from Serene Highness to Royal Highness. This distinction, insignificant as it may appear to our eyes, was important in the enormously rank-conscious Courts of the Bourbon Restoration. It was especially galling to the younger branch of the Bourbon family. An example of the drawbacks of being only a Serene Highness may help to illustrate the point. If the Duc d'Orléans accompanied by his wife and sister were to be visiting his cousins at the Tuileries Palace, then the protocol would be as follows. As the Duchesse d'Orléans was a princess of the Naples branch of the Bourbons and the daughter of a king, she was a Royal Highness. As she approached a room, both of the double doors of the room she was entering would be opened to admit her. She alone of the party of Orléans visitors was permitted to enter. Both the reception room doors would then be closed and the Orléans brother and sister, as Serene Highnesses, would be kept waiting outside. One door only was then reopened to admit their Serene Highnesses the Duc d'Orléans and his sister, Madame Adélaïde. Despite 'their claims to Enlightened Liberalism', as Madame de Boigne put it, this elevation of rank was received with 'much happiness'.[29] The d'Orléans family 'were and will be Princes and Bourbons, whatever may happen'.[30]

The close friendship between Marie Thérèse and her cousin, Marie Amélie, had done much to heal relations between the two branches of the

Bourbon family. Marie Thérèse had refused to receive the Duc d'Orléans when he visited the exiles in Mittau and would only receive him reluctantly at Hartwell, but now met regularly with the Orléans family. Madame de Boigne wrote that 'The sincere friendship between the Dauphine and the Duchesse d'Orléans had modified the prejudices of the daughter of Louis XVI.'[31] She was very fond of the charming Orléans children, as the Prince de Joinville[32] recounted in his memoirs. The Prince de Joinville wrote of his memory of Marie Thérèse in 1824 when he was five years old, 'I loved her dearly even then, that good kind Duchess! For she had always been so good to us, ever since we were babies, and never failed to give us the most beautiful New Year's gifts. My respectful affection deepened as I grew old enough to realise her sorrows and the nobility of her nature.'[33] The Dauphine seems to have loved children and to have been good with them. By this time of her life the possibility of a family of her own was no longer in question, but she showed great devotion and kindness to the young people of her family. This affection was reciprocated by some, if not all of them. Madame de Gontaut notes that Marie Thérèse did not make similar New Year's gifts to her nephew and niece, Louise and Henri. The King noticed this and made a point of giving his grandchildren a special gift of a mini coach and horses by way of compensation.

There was a very strong family affection between Marie Amélie, the Duchesse d'Orléans, and Marie Thérèse. By contrast relations between the new Dauphine and Madame Adélaïde were very cool indeed. Madame Adélaïde seemed to thoroughly dislike her cousin, Marie Thérèse. In theory they had much in common and had shared many sufferings during the years of Revolution and exile. Both were deeply devoted to their fathers and both had experienced the heartbreak of being deprived of paternal love and care at an early age by the execution of their respective fathers during the Revolution. Nevertheless, politically and religiously, they were poles apart. The shared sufferings that might have drawn them together in fact had the opposite effect. Madame Adélaïde had been brought up in a pro-Revolutionary household; her father had voted for the execution of his cousin the King before himself falling from Revolutionary favour and being guillotined. Their religious views were also very different: Madame Adélaïde did not share Marie Thérèse's whole-hearted devotion to the Roman Catholic Church. Most of all, Adélaïde passionately wanted to see her brother and his family on the throne of France, thus displacing Marie Thérèse and her branch of the Bourbons. Marie Amélie was able to maintain good relations with both Marie Thérèse and Adélaïde, so must have felt these family tensions strongly.

Madame Adélaïde's correspondence suggests that some of the younger generation of the Orléans family continued to feel hostility towards the senior branch of the family, particularly the Princesses who were strongly influenced in their views by their aunt. At this time, Charles X attempted to restore family and dynastic harmony by taking the opportunity of reminding the Duc d'Orléans that only the young Duc de Bordeaux stood between Orléans, his sons and the throne. He remarked:

> It is very important both for you and for us that we should be firmly united, because finally, my dear fellow, look here, you must be aware of your position, it is delicate and important; after all, between you and the throne there is only a four-year-old child … it is essential for us and even more so for you that if he should die, you or your offspring should succeed without difficulties or embarrassments.

The personal, if not the political, relationship between the two men was warm. It was better than that between the Duc d'Orléans and the previous King, with whom he had shared closer political views.

As we know, Marie Thérèse did not relish the social side of her role. An observer, the Princess Radziwill, wrote in her memoirs of these occasions that 'when someone was presented to her, the Duchesse would stand twirling her fan and making munching noises with her mouth, before she could bring forth a phrase'. Deeply conscious of her '*métier de princesse*', she was aware that there must be Royal receptions and entertainments at the Tuileries Palace even if she gained little personal pleasure or enjoyment from them. She initiated a weekly evening reception attended by the Royal Family. These required that all those who were eligible and wished to attend were in their places at the Tuileries Palace by a certain time. The doors of the palace were then closed and no one could enter or leave until the reception was finished. Those attending would then form into two lines through which the King and the Royal Family would process. Once this was done the Royal Family would sit down at tables: the Duchesse de Berry and the Duchesse d'Orléans to play cards and the Dauphine to embroider. Her husband might play a rather desultory game of chess with Madame d'Agoult or one of the other courtiers. Those attending were able to observe the Royal Family at leisure. When the Royal Family was not holding receptions, they dined and then retired to play whist, usually in the Dauphine's apartments. If Marie Thérèse was away from Paris, then the Royal Family would gather in the Duchesse de Berry's rooms to play their usual games of whist. Very few courtiers were admitted on these family evenings; often only enough people to make up a card school.

The whole atmosphere was stiff and formal. The Comtesse de Boigne's sister-in-law, the young Comtesse d'Osmond, was a favourite of the Royal Family and was often present during these evenings. We are able to gain an insider's flavour of the happenings at Court from Madame de Boigne's memoirs. Even the Dauphine's ladies had to receive a specific invitation to attend these parties; it was not theirs by right from their role as ladies-in-waiting. Madame de Boigne, wrote, 'The Dauphine was by no means pleasant to her ladies, and permitted no familiarity.'[34] We can compare this with her relaxed approach and manner when with her dear army officers. Frankly the Bourbons' evening entertainments do not sound much fun: a King set in his ways and stubborn; a taciturn Dauphin who preferred to play chess and disliked company; and Marie Thérèse, rather stern and rebuking particularly the Duchesse de Berry. The evenings at Court sound utterly tedious for all concerned. Eventually the Duchesse de Berry persuaded the King to discontinue them. One can only imagine that Marie Thérèse was more than happy to comply with his wishes in this respect.

By contrast the magnificent Palais-Royal, the central Paris home of the Orléans family, which had been wonderfully restored following the Duc d'Orléans' return to France from exile, provided sumptuous, lively and stimulating soirées. The purpose was to charm the influential in Parisian society and to position the family to achieve its ambitions as well as to provide some fun.

The Dauphine was generally very strict about whom she would and would not receive at Court. She was, for example, only after much pressure from the Orléans family, persuaded to receive Sophie Dawes,[35] an English adventuress and courtesan, and the mistress of her ageing Bourbon cousin, the Prince de Condé. Sophie had been banned from Court in 1824 when her marriage disintegrated. Marie Thérèse only consented to receive the lady in 1830 to please Marie Amélie, whose son the Duc d'Aumale, of whom the Dauphine was particularly fond, was promised the Condé fortune, including the Château of Chantilly, if Sophie were to be admitted to Court by Marie Thérèse. Marie Thérèse agreed to receive the Prince de Condé's English mistress, but would only acknowledge the woman's presence by a bow rather than the customary shake of the Royal hand.

Marie Caroline was young and sociable, unlike the rest of the family; after her initial mourning period for her dead husband, she enjoyed an active social life outside the confines of the palace. She was popular with the middle classes of Paris, as a result of her spending in the Parisian shops and mixing freely with all manner of people. During her period of mourning for her assassinated husband, Marie Caroline had created around her a coterie of courtiers who were loyal to her, but also jollier and younger than those attached to the King, Dauphin and Dauphine. Marie Caroline and her late husband had acquired the Château at Rosny-sur-Seine some 30 miles from Paris and she spent time there pursuing her own interests, collecting books and pictures, seeing friends and hunting rabbits.[36] She was largely excluded from the upbringing of her own son and daughter by their tutors and the older members of her family. As with so many royal mothers, their offspring were regarded as being too important dynastically for them to be left to the care of their own mothers. The King was a doting and involved grandfather and the Duc de Bordeaux and his sister were taken every morning to see him before his formal *levée*. The children called him affectionately '*bon papa*'.[37]

The Duchesse de Berry believed, probably rightly, that Marie Thérèse was influencing their mutual father-in-law against her. The Court could often hear the young Duchesse de Berry being upbraided for her inappropriate and less than regal conduct by her father-in-law. There were also tensions within the Duchesse de Berry's Household with the Knight of Honour, de Mesnard, and the children's governess, Madame de Gontaut, who were competing for the favour of the Duchesse de Berry. Madame de Gontaut was not above rumour-mongering and trying to catch the Princess in a compromising position.

The Duc de Bordeaux was much influenced by his governess. She was devoted to him and supervised his activities very closely. He was rarely allowed out of her sight. In 1825, Madame de Gontaut wrote to the Duc de Rivière[38] on the approach she took to her work as governess: 'my only method has been constant watchfulness; profiting by every occurrence to soften and instruct, not letting slip the occasion of a fault without encouraging reflection. I have seen everything.' It sounds a stifling regime for a young boy. Charles X was grateful to Vicomtesse de Gontaut for her care and devotion to his grandson and made her a duchess for her services to the family. He seems to have had a sweet and generous nature. The painter Madame Vigée Le Brun wrote in her memoirs of an incident involving the Duchesse de Berry and her son that she would never forget:

> While I was painting her one day, she said, 'Wait a moment.' Then, getting up, she went to her library for a book containing an article in my praise, which she was obliging enough to read aloud from beginning to end. During one of these sittings the Duc de Bordeaux brought his mother a copybook in which his master had written 'Very good.' The Duchess gave the boy two louis. The little Prince, who might have been about six, began to jump for joy, shouting, 'This will do for my poor – and for my old woman first of all!' When he was gone the Duchess told me that her son referred to a poor soul he often met when he went out and of whom he was particularly fond.

La duchesse de Berry et ses enfants,1822, François_Gérard

Madame de Boigne wrote of the upbringing of the Duc de Bordeaux and Mademoiselle d'Artois:

> the Duchesse de Berry troubled herself very little about them, and she hardly ever saw them. When the Duc de Bordeaux was suffering from a severe attack of measles, which caused some anxiety, she did not think of postponing a journey to Rosny. The King and the Dauphine were displeased in consequence, and expressed their feelings loudly. Yet they would have been the first to blame the Princess if she had asserted her rights as a mother against those which etiquette assigned to the governess.[39]

Marie Thérèse's niece, Louise d'Artois, to whom she was close, was observed by Madame de Boigne to be 'highly accomplished rather than pretty' but 'very pleasant'. Madame de Boigne noted that she dominated her brother 'with all the superiority of her age and her mind. She took an interest in public affairs when quite young, and she knew enough to show marked politeness to a politician, though she had not been specifically told to do so'. Like her aunt Marie Thérèse as a child, Mademoiselle was inclined to be haughty and had to be trained out of this type of conduct by her governess. Madame de Boigne reported, 'It was not difficult for a clever woman like Madame de Gontaut to make so clever a child understand the pettiness of such claims.'[40]

From an early age, the Duc de Bordeaux had a keen understanding of his family's history and was sensitive to the sufferings of his aunt. The Royal children had learnt by heart to recite the order of succession of various different members of their family. They were trained not only to know them in order, but also to identify each individual by their number in the order of succession. One day Marie Thérèse was in the schoolroom with them when the young Duc de Bordeaux was asked to identify numbers 13, 18, 19 and 24. He correctly listed Louis XII, Charles V and Henri IV. He then hesitated and went quiet. Once the Dauphine had left the room he explained to his tutor that number 24 was Louis XVII, the tragic boy King and her brother, and he did not wish to mention the name in front of his aunt for fear of upsetting her.

The death of Alexander I of Russia was announced in December 1825. He and his father Paul I, and grandmother Catherine the Great before him, had been great friends and benefactors to the Bourbons, especially during their years of exile. Alexander himself had been hugely instrumental in both the First and Second Bourbon Restorations to the throne of France. He had been staying by the Sea of Azov in the Ukraine and caught a fever that was endemic in that region and from which he did not recover. His last years were blighted by what seems to have been a mounting paranoia and distrust of all around him, exacerbated by deafness. It was a sad end. Madame de Boigne reported,[41] 'his death caused much sensation and grief in Paris. He had shown magnanimity in 1814, and had been very useful to France in 1815.'

It is perhaps ironic that while Alexander I was regarded as a liberal in Europe, he was far from being so in his own country. Nevertheless, he had been enormously influential in creating the new Europe that came out of the Congress of Vienna. If he had opted not to pursue Napoleon in 1812 and to remain more isolationist, then it is feasible that Napoleon would have been able to defeat or at least treat with the other European powers. It might have enabled Napoleon to retain his throne for himself and his dynasty. Alexander's willingness to intervene actively in battles that he could have avoided facilitated the defeat of Napoleon. The sheer weight of Russian fighting resource must have sapped the resolve of those

Frenchmen who had previously supported Bonaparte; for example, Marmont who surrendered Paris to the Sixth Alliance in 1814. Without Alexander it is possible to say there might have been no First Bourbon Restoration and no Second Restoration. He felt he was carrying out his religious duty in getting involved. He might not have liked or admired the Bourbons, but as a fellow ruler he recognised their essential legitimacy and lent his support to their cause.

The new Dauphin and Dauphine were drawn more closely into the political life of France with the accession of Charles X. During the previous reign, the Duc d'Angoulême had allied himself with the more liberal and less theocratic approach of Louis XVIII. Charles X's ministers recognised this and wanted to ensure that the heir to the throne did not create his own political party in opposition to his father's government. French émigrés based in London had seen this divisive and uncomfortable effect at close hand during the illnesses of George III and before the establishment of the Prince Regent in England. The difficulties created by a King and his heir being at loggerheads were only too apparent to them. They did not wish to replicate them in France. Observers of French political life credited the Dauphin's counterbalancing influence for the surprisingly moderate and liberal early utterings of the new regime. Madame de Boigne wrote:

> I have reason to believe that the prudence shown at the outset was due largely to the influence of the Dauphin. M de Villèle,[42] the Ultra who was leading the administration who knew by experience what could be effected by the heir to the Crown, realised immediately the strength which a reasonable Opposition under his leadership might gain, and attempted to neutralise any such movement. Pretending great admiration for the sound judgement of the Dauphin, he requested him to enlighten the Council with his presence.

The Dauphin was fully aware of what M. de Villèle was trying to do, but was unable to resist the invitation to join the Council and speak at its meetings. As the heir to the throne, he wielded some considerable influence. The Dauphin was, in any event, devoted to his father.

The government moved to restrict many of the freedoms that the French people had enjoyed on the Restoration of the Bourbons. Charles also acted against the institutions set up by previous regimes. Marie Thérèse was caught up in the reaction to these changes. In April 1827, she and the Duchesses d'Orléans and de Berry with Madame Adélaïde accompanied the King in a procession to the Champ de Mars to inspect the Garde Nationale. As the Royal party passed, there were cheers for the King himself but shouts against his ministers, their policies and the Jesuits. Deeply uncomfortable and very possibly frightened in the light of her previous experiences, the Dauphine sat stiffly upright in the carriage. She was red-faced and breathing deeply as she passed through the rather hostile crowd. Marie Caroline, also travelling in the coach, was annoyed by the impertinence shown to members of the Royal Family. Marie Thérèse looked askance at Madame Adélaïde. She regarded her as an ambitious conspirator on behalf of her brother Orléans, and moreover one who was seemingly enjoying the negative reaction of the crowd to her cousins and their rule. Marie Thérèse had been warned that there might be anti-government protests at the ceremony. She had tried to persuade the King to cancel or postpone the review. Now she put all her influence into convincing the King that he should disband the Garde Nationale; she succeeded in her objective and it was disbanded. According to Madame de Gontaut, Maréchal Oudinot[43] could not believe that the King would deliberately set out to humiliate and alienate this huge and loyal section of the population of Paris who had previously been loyal to the crown by treating them in this offhand way.

Marie Amélie was caught in the crossfire between the senior and junior branches of the Bourbon family, and with her loyalties divided looked uncomfortable and embarrassed as she drove through Paris. Marie Amélie's son the Duc de Chartres[44] wrote in his memoirs:

> My mother who was united to the Duchesse de Berry and Madame Royale,[45] not only by the ties of close relationship but by mutual deep affection, desired even more ardently the continuance of the sovereignty of the elder branch and had done her best to persuade me to consent to a marriage with the daughter of the Duchesse de Berry.

This was yet another attempt to unite the senior and junior branches of the family through the ties of matrimony, which in the event did not happen.

Henri d'Artois, 1826

The Dauphine continued to carry out her public engagements. She attended the horse races at the Champ de Mars in September 1826. In September 1827, she travelled through Rennes and a poem composed by M. L. C. Hoyan was placed in a house in the La Rue Dauphine; it entreated the daughter of the Bourbons to travel slowly across the fields of Brittany and stated that in this part of the country an invisible guard protected her: the love of the people.[46] She also visited the Foundlings Hospital and the Old Men's Hospital and received many loyal addresses, including references to the feeling that the presence of the daughter of their Kings brought the people happiness. At the Hotel Dieu (St Yves Hospital), *The Standard* related that 'her Royal Highness deigned to make inquiries relative to all that concerns the welfare of the numerous unfortunates who receive charitable assistance in asylum'. The nuns who ran the institution were delighted by her presence and interest and erected a plaque lauding her and calling her '*cet ange*'. She had, since childhood, been a great favourite of nuns. It was in this year that Charles X gave the Dauphine a fine porcelain statue of her nephew, the Duc de Bordeaux.

However, 1827 also had its lighter side. France had gone giraffe mad as one had been sent to Charles X as a diplomatic gift. The King was keen to go and see the exotic animal. Marie Thérèse's view was that it was for the animal to come to the King, not the other way round. Nevertheless the Royal Family, including the children, took a trip to see the unusual creature.

In 1828, the upbringing of the young Duc de Bordeaux came to the centre of the political stage. The heir to the throne needed a new governor to replace the Duc de Rivière, who had died. Madame de Boigne wrote that 'The King wished the post of the nomination of the Governor of the Duc de Bordeaux to depend solely upon his nomination. The Council wished to be consulted, while the King's claim was supported by the Ultra party. The country as a whole took the side of the Ministers.'[47] Despite the Dauphin's dislike of the Congrégation party, he supported his father's misjudged view, regarding it as a family matter for the King alone to decide, rather than one in which the state had an interest. Under pressure, the King conceded:

> 'he would make no decision without informing them. They proceeded to look for a suitable person … the King informed his Ministers individually about his decision saying that at ten o'clock in the evening the nomination of the Baron de Damas[48] would appear in the *Moniteur* the next day. This was what he called making no choice without informing them… The Cabinet entered a protest, but its influence then received a blow from which it did not recover.[49]

The nominee for the post, M. de Damas, was an extreme member of the Congrégation party, according to Madame de Boigne. He had previously been a member of the Households of both Marie Thérèse and Louis Antoine.

The Congrégation religious party won this victory, but it was an extremely unpopular appointment in the country. The Dauphin supported the Ordinances of 16 June 1828 against Jesuits and religious educational establishments, restricting their influence and limiting their size. Reluctantly, the King signed the Ordinances, fearing that not to do so would bring about a full-on attack against the religious party.

The education and training for kingship of the Duc de Bordeaux was a matter which deeply interested Marie Thérèse and the rest of the immediate Royal Family. The Baron de Damas was keen that the young Prince should be removed from all female influence, and was even forbidden to kiss his elder sister. He was taken from his family at the Pavilion de Marsan in Paris to live with his tutor at the Château of Bagatelle, which his mother had inherited from the Duc de Berry, in the Bois de Bologne.

The Dauphin's more liberal approach to politics and commitment to the Charter were further challenged by the election of General Clausel as the deputy for the town of Lille. It will be recalled that it was General Clausel who had been so instrumental in ejecting Marie Thérèse from Bordeaux in the spring of 1815. He had been sentenced to death following the Restoration, but had escaped and gone to live in the United States. He had returned to France on being granted an amnesty in 1820, but the Dauphin could not forgive Clausel his treachery. The General had been one of the first officers to return to Napoleon during the Hundred Days, despite having been honoured by Louis XVIII. His humiliating treatment of the Duchesse d'Angoulême at Bordeaux was also an open sore. Louis Antoine was outraged at this public insult to his wife. This sentiment pushed him into the arms of the Ultra party.

Marie Thérèse's apparent brusqueness caused offence to a number of influential people at the beginning of 1830. Madame de Boigne recalls that 'the King's Court of Justice, led by its president, M. Séguier, called upon the wife of the Dauphin. The president was about to address the customary congratulations, when she cut him short, saying in a most haughty tone "Pass on, gentlemen, pass on".'[50] More was to follow. The weather was particularly cold over the winter and many of the poorer members of the populace of Paris were suffering. A charity to alleviate their sufferings was set up and it was decided to hold a fund-raising ball at the Opera. First among those to contribute to the fund were 'the inhabitants of the Tuileries',[51] but on the night of the charity gala 'no one appeared in the box reserved for them. On the other hand the box reserved for the Palais-Royal was occupied by the whole of the family of the Duc d'Orléans.'[52] How little the senior branch of the family understood the need for positive action to keep the public on their side. How unnecessarily and stupidly did they cede the moral high ground to their cousins. They allowed themselves to look uncaring when, in fact, they had been generous contributors to the fund. How little they understood the France to which they had returned. Marie Thérèse and her family stayed away while the intelligent and streetwise Orléans clan courted popularity with well-considered gestures, like dancing with members of the public and moving freely among them. Marie Thérèse was being criticised in *La mode* for her formality and lack of fashion sense. This was contrasted unfavourably with the more relaxed and modern approach of her sister-in-law.

Marie Thérèse seems to have sensed that there was trouble brewing, but was unable to take action to reassert the popularity of her family. As was customary on 6 January each year, the Royal Family and their cousins gathered to share the Twelfth Night cake[53] or *galette* for the feast of the Magi. On this occasion the lucky bean fell to the lot of the Duc d'Orléans, and 'the Dauphine showed some ill temper at the fact'.[54] The Duc d'Orléans would be King for the duration of the feast. Was this an omen?

Marie Thérèse's lack of social ease was to offend members of her own family. In May 1830, there was a Royal visit by King Francis I of the Two Sicilies[55] and his Spanish Queen, Maria Isabella. They were the Duchesse de Berry's father and stepmother, and the Duchesse d'Orléans' brother and sister-in-law, as well as cousins of the Dauphine. The Italian monarchs were determined to enjoy to the full the pleasures of Paris and the Île de France. There were balls in their honour, at one of which the Duchesse de

Berry and thirty of the most beautiful young women from the Faubourg Saint-Germain danced the Neapolitan tarantella. One wit commented that they were truly dancing Neapolitan style, i.e. on a volcano. Other pleasures included theatre trips and outings to Rosny-sur-Seine. At a ball at the Palais-Royal the crowd was crushing. The Duc d'Orléans seemed to be using the visit of the Kings of the French and Naples to his home as an opportunity to court popularity with the Parisians by letting them see his Royal relations at close quarters. The crowds, under the influence of rabble rousers, became overexcited and set fire to piles of chairs. They had to be driven from the grounds of the Palais-Royal by force. Marie Thérèse seems not to have been best pleased. She sensed the game that the Duc d'Orléans was playing, but was unable or unwilling to take action to thwart him or to bolster the appeal of her own family to the people of France. Madame de Boigne wrote that, while they were both at the Duchesse de Berry's château at Rosny, the King in conversation with the Duc d'Orléans gave his assurance that he would abide by the terms of the Charter and the rights it gave the people of France. He apparently convinced his cousin that he meant what he said and would keep his promises in relation to the Charter.

The King and Queen of Naples outstayed their welcome. Madame de Boigne[56] wrote, 'The lengthy stay of the Neapolitan sovereigns, who were established in the Palace of the Elysée, began to weary the King, who wished to leave Paris for St-Cloud. The Dauphine undertook to ask them when they would start home, under pretext of setting the day when she could start to take the waters.'[57] The Neapolitan monarchs took umbrage and left Paris in high dudgeon. However, Charles X made them the gift of a porcelain jewel cabinet. Marie Thérèse was in an embarrassing position partly because she had already announced the date of her departure for the spa, with all the attendant ceremonial en route, which it was difficult to change at short notice. Furthermore, she did not wish to delay her journey as she wanted to be back in Paris before the Chambers (or parliament) met for business later in the summer. According to Madame de Boigne, she neither liked nor trusted the Polignac ministry, so beloved by her father-in-law and now supported by her once more liberal husband. The Dauphine feared that in her absence extreme measures would be implemented by the government. They were, for example, attempting to make the theft of the host (holy bread or wafers) from a church a criminal offence punishable by death. The Dauphine apparently esteemed the Duc as a private individual because of his loyalty to her family, but as a politician she found him most presumptuous.

The normally politically rigid and reactionary Marie Thérèse softened her views. Her husband's views hardened and moved towards the Ultra camp, while hers moved in the opposite direction. He actively supported the actions and views of the Polignac ministry. Usually unassuming and reserved, he now spoke often and at length in Council in support of Polignac. She now opposed any extreme action and was prepared to use her influence to ensure that a more moderate approach was taken. Later she would say to the Marquis de Villeneuve that the Dauphin had no doubt of his being correct in his view, despite what subsequently transpired. She apparently left for Vichy with the King's promise that he would let nothing politically significant be initiated by him in her absence. The King's commitment was not fulfilled. The tension in Paris in the summer of 1830 was palpable. The twelve-year-old Prince de Joinville, son of the Duc and Duchesse d'Orléans, observed and later wrote in his memoirs:

> Never having witnessed any kind of disturbance, I had not the faintest notion what a revolution might be like. I had always seen the King and the Royal Family treated with the greatest respect which indeed they never forfeited, and I was a hundred miles from the thought that they could possibly be banished. It is a fact, nevertheless, that the beginning of 1830 differed from other years and something seemed to be brewing.

There was some heartening international news for Marie Thérèse and her family during this period. The conquest of Algeria was one of the few lasting legacies of the brief reign of Charles X. The people of Paris celebrated enthusiastically with cannon fire when it was announced on 9 July 1830 that Algiers had capitulated and the Dey, the Ruler of Algeria, had given himself up to the conquering French army. Two days later the King attended a *Te Deum* service of thanksgiving at Notre Dame to mark the success of the invasion. The Parisians gave him a less than enthusiastic reception: the King was greeted with silent crowds. Had Marie Thérèse been present, this might well have reminded her of the brooding atmosphere that greeted her and her family on their return to Paris in June 1791 after the unsuccessful escape attempt to Varennes. But she was holidaying in the spa resort of Vichy, as had been scheduled and announced long in advance, some 200 miles away from Paris. It is possible that she would have used her influence with the King to persuade him not to sign the Ordinances or at least to moderate their content. Her husband, historically, was much more likely to put up opposition to the proposals. But by this time he was largely persuaded of the need to take strong action to maintain royal authority; he was also crippled politically by his personal loyalty to his father.

Marie Thérèse's return journey was uncomfortable and disturbing. Travelling back from Vichy to Paris, Marie Thérèse encountered hostility and saw for herself the deteriorating political situation in France and the weakening position of the monarchy. She was accompanied on the journey, as royal etiquette required, by the Préfet of Sâone-et-Loire, M. de Puymaigre, who had served with Condé. As he described in his memoirs,

Souvenirs sur l'Émigration, L'Empire, et la Restauration as quoted in *The Last Dauphine* by Joseph Turquan, 'We were hardly out of Autun when she hastily opened an enormous green bag, which she always carried on journeys, and pulled out a heap of newspapers, among which I saw the *Quotidienne*, the *Gazette de France*, the *Journal des Débats*, the *Temps*, the *Messager des Chambres*. She hastily ran her eye over them and remarked, "There is nothing new".' Her splendid coach was highly conspicuous, decorated as it was with her coat of arms and drawn by six white horses. She had a mixed reception in the towns and villages through which she passed. Some villages were frosty in their response to the arrival of the Dauphine. The politically liberal town of Chalon was surprisingly and reassuringly warm in its welcome. The townspeople had heard that Marie Thérèse was against the government's reactionary policies. A short walk on the plateau at Tournus, which afforded excellent views over the surrounding countryside, gave her an opportunity to have a conversation about the capture of Algeria – which cheered her a little. André Castelot suggests that she saw clearly that the people were not really concerned or interested by the victory in North Africa, even though it had been achieved without great loss of French life. The people were much more bothered about the political situation at home and the loss of their liberties.

Marie Thérèse learned from the newspapers that the Ordinances of 25 July 1830 restricted further the political freedoms of the French people and the French press. The first Ordinance[58] inflicted 'pre-publication censorship'[59] on the press. These restrictions applied to all newspapers, periodical journals and pamphlets which comprised fewer than 20 pages. The further three Ordinances changed the political landscape by dissolving the Chamber of Deputies (Ordinance Two)[60] which had just been elected, and announced that there would be elections in September to select a replacement Chamber of Deputies using the new electoral process. The Third Ordinance changed the electoral system by returning it to the system applying at the beginning of the Second Restoration. Deputies were to be elected for a term of five years, and a rolling 20% of the house would be up for election each year. The number of Deputies was reduced to 258. The right to vote was given on the basis of taxes paid: only those who paid the greatest amount of personal tax were able to vote. The Ordinances laid down that Deputies for the departments of France would be chosen by an electoral college consisting of the most highly taxed, and presumably the most conservative, electors in each area. Business taxes were not included in the eligibility criteria. This had the effect of excluding from the electorate the urban bourgeoisie, whom the Royalist and aristocratic government regarded as being the focus of opposition to their rule and political approach. Some estimates suggest that the number of those included in the franchise was reduced to 25% of the previous level. This was a massive and swingeing attack on the freedoms of the people and the press. Would the people, disenfranchised and outraged by the changes, seemingly in the face of all the advances made since 1789 accept this turning back of the clock to a system which wantonly ignored thirty years of French political life? Marie Thérèse thought not.

Charles X had not kept his promise to her. Marie Thérèse arrived in the afternoon at Mâcon, by the crossing of the river Saône, and after the official honours had been paid she heard via a message sent by semaphore that the Ordinances had been published in the *Moniteur* on 26 July. She was not yet aware of their detailed content. The Comte de Puymaigre[61] wrote: 'She seemed much upset; her quivering lips, her jerky movements, her broken words betrayed the depth of emotion this strong woman was suffering. She made a splendid attempt to recover her self-control, and presently signified her readiness to proceed with the ceremonies prescribed by her exalted station.' The situation was not helped by stiflingly hot weather. Fortunately the details of events unfolding in Paris had not yet reached the populace. Early on the morning of Thursday 29 July, after a sleepless night, Marie Thérèse summoned M. de Puymaigre to see her. Together they discussed the Ordinances and sadly agreed that they would have dire consequences for the future of the monarchy. During their discussions the Préfet of Lyon arrived and demanded an audience with the Dauphine. He had with him the wording of the Ordinances, and Marie Thérèse's worst fears as to their content were fulfilled. They also heard that there was insurrection in Paris.

The King settled for the time being at St Cloud. He was attended there by his ministers. It appeared that Charles X thought very deeply before signing the Ordinances, but in the end felt that he had no alternative. Munro Price[62] expresses the view that in his judgement Charles X was simply being faithful to the vision of royalty and Royal authority to which Louis XVI had subscribed and recommended at the meeting of the Estates General in June 1789 at Versailles, which Charles had attended as an observer.[63] As a young girl Marie Thérèse had seen her parents' travails at this time and was keen that they should not be repeated. She held strongly to the view that the maintenance of a strong Royal authority was essential to the good governance and good order of France. She also understood now, at least, the need for a degree of realism and compromise if her family were to survive as monarchs.

Marie Thérèse continued her journey back to rejoin her husband and the rest of the family, wanting to get back as quickly as possible. Her journey, in the way of all Royal travel, had long been pre-planned, but she made a change: she did not take the most direct route, but travelled via Lons-le-Saunier and Dole. The local police had been alerted so they could provide her with protection if necessary. Monsieur de Puymaigre accompanied her as far as the bridge that separated the departments of Saône-et-Loire and Ain. Fortunately for Marie Thérèse and her party, the journey passed without incident. It was noted that while villages and hamlets were bedecked with white flags in her honour, the larger towns were undecorated. She arrived at Dijon at about 5.30 p.m. Her route into the city was flanked by troops presenting arms. From the crowds behind them there were cries of '*Vive la Charte*'. The news of the promulgation Ordinances had clearly arrived from Paris. In her gutsy way, she decided to carry on with her planned programme, visiting the Museum and the Palace of the Ducs of Bourgogne. It was in Dijon that she heard of the protest being made by journalists in Paris.

Following the publication of the Ordinances[64] in *Le Moniteur*,[65] the negative reaction to them was slow at first to show itself but then built quickly, in part orchestrated by the journalist and protégé of Talleyrand, Louis-Adolphe Thiers. The anti-Ordinance action was largely funded by the banker Jacques Lafitte, a keen supporter and funder of the Orléanist cause and former governor of the Bank of France. The newspaper run by Thiers, *The National*, quickly published a special edition calling for a demonstration of anti-Ordinance action. He encouraged opposition by inviting the populace to refuse to pay taxes as a protest against the imposition of the restrictions on their freedoms. The journalists stated that the Ordinances were against the law. Some 48 journalists from eleven different newspapers signed a proclamation formulated by Thiers calling upon the French people to take general action against the government. Violence erupted at the Palais-Royal in the centre of Paris. Crowds called for the end of the Bourbons – not that either branch of the family was in the city to hear their calls. The Duc d'Orléans and his family were at Neuilly-sur-Seine, their country home some 5 miles to the north-west of Paris. They were maintaining a low profile and watching developments. The Duc d'Orléans and his sister, Madame Adélaïde, were however keeping in close touch with events in Paris. The Duc d'Orléans reportedly said of the actions taken by his cousins when he heard the terms of the Ordinances, 'they are mad they'll get themselves driven out'.[66]

Marie Thérèse arrived at the Préfecture in Dijon to stay the night, and was able to study the details of the protests which claimed that the Bourbon regime had lost its legal legitimacy. So shocked was she by the reaction to her father-in-law/uncle's actions that she let slip from her hands the paper in which they were reported. Despite raised emotions in Dijon against the monarchy and the fears of the Préfet, Marie Thérèse decided to attend the theatre as scheduled. She arrived there wearing her trademark feathered headdress to cries initially of '*Vive la charte! À bas les ministres*' and one cry even of 'Down with the queen', presumably a reference to the Dauphine. There was applause when one of the actors made anti-government remarks, and during the interval she was subjected to a barrage of cries of 'Down with the feathers', clearly a personal attack and a reference to her outfit. The Dauphine fiddled nervously with her fan, but remained in her box until the audience calmed down. She only left after the second act. Returning to the Préfecture, and once in her room, she collapsed muttering to herself that she still had hope that the troops would remain loyal. She bemoaned the idiocy of her menfolk and their advisers. She may well have been thinking that this was a replay of the stupidity and cowardice of the Hundred Days period when Louis XVIII had made a dash for the border leaving Paris to Napoleon. If only she had been in Paris in late July, she might just possibly have been able to prevent or delay the signature and publication of the Ordinances.

At 4 a.m. on Saturday 30 July, she left Dijon after only a few hours' sleep. A baying crowd watched her departure. She did have the comfort of being driven by a man wearing white ribbons as a sign of his loyalty to the Bourbon cause. At Semur the party stopped to eat. She heard further news of the disturbances, barricades and bloodshed in Paris. She also learned that the King was still at St Cloud. The task of maintaining law and order in Paris and holding it for the King and his government was left to Maréchal Marmont, Duc of Ragusa.[67] He was the duty Major-General of the Royal Guard, but some saw this as a deliberate provocation to the Parisians. It was after all he who had withdrawn from Paris so that it could be taken without resistance by the allies in 1814. The signs were not good. Marmont had not as yet received any instructions from the King, the Dauphin or government on the approach he was to take to the citizenry of Paris and any protests they might make. This was not a task he relished; his own politics were much more liberal than those of the Polignac regime. As a soldier, no doubt, he would much have preferred to be fighting in North Africa rather than acting as a glorified policeman on the streets of the capital. He had approximately 15,000 troops under his command. His strategy was to hold the main squares, believing that mass gatherings in these locations were the source of insurrection and that order could be maintained if he had control of the squares. It is extraordinary that Charles X and Polignac, both of whom had had experience of the wrath of the Paris mobs, had not anticipated that the Ordinances would provoke a strong reaction and planned for it by ensuring that Paris was well garrisoned with loyal troops, under competent leadership, and with clear orders. They did not. There were to be extreme consequences of this failure. Marie Thérèse was in despair that the fate of the Bourbon dynasty was left to Marmont. She held her head in her hands and called her husband, his father and their advisers idiots. How could they allow their interests to be commanded by a man who was a byword for disloyalty?

An hour later, after her brief stop at Semur, she was back on the road. She had a strong premonition that this time there really was no hope and all was lost for the elder branch of the Bourbons as the ruling family of France. The journey was wearyingly slow and frustrating. At Ancy-le-Franc it was confirmed by the *sous-préfet* that half of Paris was already under the control of the anti-Bourbon faction. This was a revolution, not a mere revolt. She rested briefly at the Château of Louvois, uncertain whether or not to go on into the town of Tonnerre. She just wished she could be with the King and give him the benefit of her advice. Typically courageous, she decided to enter Tonnerre, but to abandon her grand and closed Berline carriage and enter the town in an open-topped carriage. She was escorted through a silent brooding crowd by a group of Royalists. There may have been no cheers for her, but equally there was no abuse. While in the town she visited a home for the elderly. She did not forget her duty as a Princess. She was also pleased to meet her faithful secretary, Baron Charlet. He had travelled from his château at Bruyères-le-Châtel to meet her and be of assistance at this difficult time. Unfortunately the news he brought with him was terrible. The whole of Paris was now under the control of a provisional government set up at the Hôtel de Ville. The National Guard had been re-established and was under the command of the Marquis de Lafayette, who was also running the provisional government. The fate of the family was yet again in the hands of a man she despised.

Baron Charlet also informed the Dauphine that everyone knew of her travel plans. He was not sure if it was safe for her to pass through towns on the route planned for her journey to Paris. He feared that she might be taken prisoner. His plan was that they should leave immediately rather than the next morning. Also, he recommended that she should abandon her Berline and travel out of the town incognito in a less conspicuous vehicle, leaving behind many of her Household. His recommendation was immediately accepted by Marie Thérèse, who trusted him and his judgement. She was always decisive at times of difficulty.

She changed into a simple dress borrowed from one of her ladies and covered her head with a scarf so as not to be recognised. The National Guard was on duty, and to put them off the trail Charlet ordered Marie Thérèse's coach to go and wait for her at the end of the Promenade de Pâtis. Meanwhile Marie Thérèse climbed down a ladder followed by her attendants including Charlet, Madame de St Preuve and M. de Fauciny, an officer of the guard. They emerged in a courtyard, thence through a gate and into the open countryside. Their carriage was not waiting for them. The *sous-préfet* headed back into town to find out what had happened to their vehicle. They walked along a narrow street bordered by rocks. It was 10.30 at night. They waited increasingly fretfully for the carriage to arrive. Marie Thérèse must have been reliving the trauma of the flight to Varennes. Eventually a carriage arrived, not her own but a coach borrowed from an officer of the guard. The delay was explained by the fact that the *sous-préfet* had had to wake up the officer and explain the situation to him in order to procure the vehicle. Half a mile down the road they found the Berline and transferred to it, Marie Thérèse sitting in her normal place. Charlet sat up beside the driver and told him in no uncertain terms to head for Paris and not to spare the horses. It was by now 1 a.m., having gained four valuable hours' head-start on the official timetable. They were able to pass through the main centres of population without hindrance.

Travelling towards Paris, Marie Thérèse met her young cousin, the Duc de Chartres, son and heir of Louis Philippe, and his regiment. He greeted her politely and offered to escort her back to the city. When asked about his loyalty to the King, he did not however commit to support Charles X. No doubt shaken by his attitude, she refused the escort and headed for Paris. As they approached the capital, they met more and more coaches whose drivers were wearing the tricolour in their hats. The sight filled Marie Thérèse with fear and dread. These encounters unnerved the coachmen, so Charlet purchased a coachman's outfit and decided to drive the Dauphine's coach himself. He also obtained her grudging permission to use the fruity language of a coachman. The Duchesse d'Angoulême arrived at Fontainebleau on the evening of 31 July. Here she received further information about the disaster which had struck her family from the governor of the château, Melchior de Polignac. In Paris, Louis Philippe, the Duc d'Orléans, had already been proclaimed King. She stayed there that night. At dawn the following morning, 1 August, she got into a light travelling coach without armorial bearings, drawn by four horses, and headed towards Paris. The coach was driven in turn by M. de Fauciny and M. de Conflans. Her old friend Pauline de Béarn was the only lady in attendance. She was, like Marie Thérèse, simply dressed in an attempt to deflect attention. Baron Charlet had gone on into Paris to try to protect Marie Thérèse's interests. The Dauphine headed for Paris and St Cloud where Marie Thérèse thought her family still were. This was not the case. She found out at la Croix-de-Berny that the court had in fact left St Cloud and moved further away from Paris to Rambouillet. She headed there. She was distressed to note that many of the houses she passed were flying the tricolour flag, but relieved to see that the troops stationed near to Rambouillet were loyal to the Royal cause and wearing white Bourbon insignia.

The Dauphine met up with her husband, who was inspecting the troops. No doubt each of them was deeply relieved to see the other. They were both unharmed and now together. Louis Antoine joined her in her carriage, and it was here she noted that his hand was bandaged. The story of how he had been wounded was not edifying. Marmont was attending the Royal Family to obtain his orders from the King. The Duc d'Angoulême insisted that henceforth he, the Duc d'Angoulême, would take command of the troops himself, thus relieving Marmont of his command. He thought there would be '*vitres cassées*'.[68] Greville does not mention it in his account, but in other reports there are descriptions of an altercation between the men when the Dauphin demanded that Marmont surrender his sword. Louis Antoine was scratched in the tussle which followed when Marmont refused to give up his weapon and the symbol of his command. Louis Antoine was incensed by his insubordination. Despite being relieved of his command, Marmont issued further orders. The angry Dauphin pushed the man onto a sofa and called the guard. Charles X eventually managed to smooth the matter over and the two men were reconciled. By 24 August 1830, Greville was reporting in his diary the treatment received by Marmont from the Royal Family. The exiled Maréchal bemoaned what had happened during the July Revolution and felt he had been extremely unlucky. Greville recorded that Marmont disapproved of the reactionary Polignac and his measures 'and had no notion that the Ordinances were thought of'. He reported that no preparations to defend the King had been made and that no members of the army had been consulted or informed about what was planned. Marmont himself claimed to have sent numerous messages to the King requesting that he desist from further action but received no response from Charles.[69] This is another example of the Bourbon obsession with the minutiae of etiquette, rather than addressing the real issue in hand, i.e. trying to deal with a revolution.

Immediately on her arrival at Rambouillet, the Dauphine went to see her father-in-law. The despair and anger she had felt earlier fell away when she saw the old man and they embraced. She saw his suffering. They cried together. He asked for her forgiveness and she gave it, saying that at least they were all together. There was no point in recriminations. She found out what had been happening in her absence. She learned that while loyal troops were fighting for their cause and dying on the streets of Paris, the King and his heir had been playing whist. They had withdrawn the Ordinances but too late. The tricolour was already flying in Paris by the time they acted. If only she had been there. Power had leached away. News came that the Duc d'Orléans had been appointed Lieutenant-General of the Kingdom. He had been appointed as such by the Chamber of Peers. With no choice but to accept the inevitable, but trying to maintain some vestige of authority, Charles X wrote to his cousin giving the appointment his (unnecessary) approval. Louis Philippe did not reply to the notice of the appointment, but did promise to ensure the safety of the Royal Family. The King and Dauphin, secluded in Rambouillet, surrounded by loyal troops, believed that the situation could be saved. Marie Thérèse, fresh from her journey through a France flying tricolours, knew differently. The Duchesse de Berry, like Marie Thérèse at Bordeaux, was keen to take decisive action to save the Bourbon dynasty. She wanted to take her nine-year-old son, the Duc de Bordeaux, and present him to the people of Paris as their future King, and appeal to their affection and loyalty to the Bourbon dynasty. To this end, and to allow herself more freedom of movement, she dressed in male attire. Charles X refused her permission to take her son to Paris and instructed her in no uncertain terms to dress in a more respectable and appropriate manner for her rank and gender. The Duchesse de Berry found it difficult to forgive his passivity at this crucial moment. It was at this time that she discovered ambition and was politicised on behalf of the rights of her son. She also relished the idea of being Regent for him during his minority.

The authority of Louis Philippe was growing, and Charles X was woken on the morning of 2 August to be shown a copy of the *Constitutionnel* which confirmed this. Marie Thérèse had not slept all night, kept awake by her thoughts and the sound of gunshots from the soldiers who were hunting for food in the park surrounding the château. We do not know if she was called upon for her advice; but in an attempt to salvage the situation and clear the decks and also assert their legitimacy as rulers, the decision was made that Charles and Louis Antoine should abdicate their rights to the throne in favour of the nine-year-old Duc de Bordeaux. The Deed of Abdication was drafted by Baron Damas. Charles X copied it out in his own hand and signed. Louis Antoine was briefly Louis XIX and his wife Marie Thérèse Queen of France. Then unwillingly after 20 minutes of angst he too signed the Deed of Abdication. Madame de Maillé suggests that there was some noisy argument between the father and son before the Duc d'Angoulême agreed to give up his rights to the throne of France. Perhaps he was wondering what his wife would think of his decision. In denying his rights he denied her the opportunity to be Queen, a fate she had long believed would be hers in due course. Marie Thérèse was Queen of her much loved country for just a few minutes.

The young Prince, now King Henri V, working with his science tutor Joachim Barande, was stunned by events. His whole world was changing before his eyes. The family expected (reasonably or otherwise in view of their previous suspicions regarding his ambition) that the Duc d'Orléans in his capacity as Lieutenant-General of the kingdom would protect the boy King's interests and act as Regent during his minority. Charles wrote to his cousin the Duc d'Orléans in Paris asking him to proclaim the accession of the new King. This the Duc d' Orléans failed to do. Supported by his strong-minded sister, Madame Adélaïde, Thiers and Lafayette and the Chamber of Peers, Louis Philippe set about establishing himself on the throne of France. Marie Amélie, so closely connected to the elder branch of the Bourbon family, was devastated by events. She dreaded the accusations of usurpation that would follow, but as a loyal and obedient wife she accepted the decision of her husband.

Despite his lack of decisive action in trying to save the throne for himself, his son or grandson, Charles X was determined that his departure from his former kingdom should be dignified and stately. He wanted to avoid the undignified flights from the country of the spring of 1815. The Dauphin, shocked and depressed, seems to have been more interested in the fate of his dogs than the soldiers who formed their guard. The Royal

Family were informed that a mob of many thousands were making their way out of Paris. The family had no desire for French blood to be shed. This and the ever-present fear of a return to the '*Grande Révolution*' of 1789 and possible violence against them meant that they hurried to leave Rambouillet. Once again, Marie Thérèse was going into exile. She did not hold back. She made it very clear to the officers of the guard that the political mistakes that had led her to this situation were not of her making. A long, sad procession departed from the Château of Rambouillet.

12

Abdication and Exile

1830-1844

For Marie Thérèse, the departure from France was long drawn out and deeply sad; once more she was forced by the failure of her family to hold on to its throne to quit the country she loved so much. Once the decision to abdicate had been made by her father-in-law, the former Dauphine and then briefly Queen was anxious to leave France as soon as possible, much as she loved her country. Marie Thérèse was one of the first of the Royal party into the carriages, eager to be on her way to the coast and a ship to yet another exile. The Duc d'Angoulême rode beside the carriage in which she was travelling. Louis Antoine was always keen on military uniforms and the maintenance of correct standards of dress, so was wearing the ornate uniform of the '*cuirassiers*' or cavalrymen. Charles X, aged 72, was unsurprisingly sleeping badly and seemed to his attendants to have aged ten years overnight; whereas previously his youthful appearance had belied his age. He seemed a broken man.

As the family travelled slowly from Rambouillet, passing through the towns and villages of northern France towards the coast at Cherbourg and departure from France, they were greeted in a respectful manner by the citizenry. Arriving at two o'clock in the morning, they spent a night at the Château de Maintenon as the guests of the Duc de Noailles and his wife, the King sleeping in the apartments that had previously housed Madame de Maintenon.[1] Marie Thérèse occupied the apartments of the Duchesse de Noailles. So relaxed was the pace of the journey that the Royal party attended daily Mass before setting off for the day's journey. The Royal party did not leave the previous night's accommodation until 11 a.m., by which time the sun was shining and temperatures rising; the interiors of the carriages were boiling hot and deeply uncomfortable for the Royal travellers. In theory, three government commissioners[2] sent by Louis Philippe were supervising the journey of the Royal Family out of France, but the reality was that the departing Royal Family set their own pace and travelled as they chose, stopping at inns on the way for refreshment and rest as suited them. This was not another return from Varennes in 1791, when the accompanying government commissioners had controlled all aspects of the journey of the Royal Family and they had no option but to accept their dictates.

The travellers reached Dreux at last, approximately 50 miles to the west of Paris. The Commissioner Odilon Barrott went ahead of the party and spoke to the people of Dreux, who had festooned the town with Republican tricolour flags and other hangings that were offensive and insulting to the Dauphine and her family. He asked that the townspeople behave with generosity towards the dispossessed family and accord them some respect. The arrival of the Royal Family in Dreux passed off better than they might have expected; the National Guard formed a Guard of Honour and presented arms. While there was no cheering, at least the family were not subjected to any abuse or insulting cries. The horse guard left the family here. The *Observer* of 15 August 1830 reported that while the rest of the family partook of a meal of bread and butter and new-laid eggs, the Duchesse d'Angoulême was not able to eat. She spent the meal-time with a handkerchief to her face. She had clearly been crying and left the table early to pray at a nearby church. The de Trobriand family were, as a sign of respect, following the Bourbons on their journey into exile, travelling with their friend and fellow Royalist the Duc de Clermont-Tonnerre in his carriage from which the ducal arms had been erased. M. de Trobriand described the night-time scene from his vantage point on the box of the coach: 'It was night; torches carried by the attendants cast their lurid light on the arms and accoutrements of the '*gardes du corps*' and troops escorting the royal travellers. The neighing of the horses, clanking of swords, flash of steel, smoke and glare of torches, the rushing about and yelling of horse-boys and postillions.' De Trobriand observed '*les enfants de France*', whose blond heads were at the carriage window observing the scene with 'intense and amused excitement'. He had known the young Duc de Bordeaux during his time as a page at the Bourbon Court.

Once outside Dreux, the King decided to ride on horseback beside his grandson's carriage. The Duc d'Angoulême also preferred horseback. At least it provided an opportunity for some exercise and distraction from the realities of their plight. The former Dauphin was visibly deeply upset. The pace of travel was so slow that Marie Thérèse, who often preferred to walk rather than ride in the stuffy carriages, was able to outpace the entourage without even hurrying. She would occasionally speak with the remaining guards who were accompanying them on their journey. Sometimes she stopped to request a drink of water from farms on the way. After travelling for a whole day they reached Verneuil sur Arve and the Hôtel de la Piallère.

On 6 August, they chose as their staging post the village of L'Aigle, where there was (and still is) an attractive château. The travelling party consisted at this point of sixty vehicles of all types. The Royal visitors must have put an enormous strain on the food and accommodation resources of the towns and villages through which they passed and in which they stayed. The knotty problems of etiquette still presented themselves. In the village of L'Aigle it was not possible to find a dining table of sufficient size to accommodate the Royal Family and their attendants, except a round one. How could a King – even a deposed and fleeing one – sit at a round table whose very shape indicated that all the diners were of equal status? It was impossible. A solution was however found to this tricky problem: a carpenter was located to square off one end of the table at which the King could be seated and thus preside over the company.

It was suggested that the young Duc de Bordeaux should go to live with the Orléans family in order to preserve his claim to the throne. It was here that a representative from the British government arrived asking to see the Royal party. He was carrying a message from the Duc d'Orléans offering the throne of France to the young King Henri V on condition that the rest of the elder branch of the Bourbon family would leave France, even the Duchesse de Berry, his mother. Charles X and the Duchesse de Berry were united, for once, in rejecting the proposal from their cousin. Marie Caroline would not give up her young son to be brought up by other people or her rights as his mother to be Regent during his royal minority. The Duchesse de Berry's affection for her son and ambition for herself made such a proposal impossible. Marie Thérèse's influence in this decision was significant. The diarist Greville reports that Marmont said that the British ambassador to France had sent Colonel Craddock to see Charles X with the suggestion that Louis Philippe the Duc d'Orléans 'should carry on the Government as Regent[3] if Charles X sanctioned it'. Charles X consulted with the Duchesse d'Angoulême, but she absolutely rejected the idea of the Orléans family being involved in any way. She did not trust them with the future of her family. The Dauphine had not forgotten Philippe Égalité's part in her father's death and even referred back to the death of the Duc de Bourgogne (the heir to the throne) during the Regency of a previous Duc d'Orléans. In dismissing the suggestion, Marie Thérèse said of the Orléans family, '*ils sont toujours les mêmes*'.[4] Clearly nothing had really changed in their relationship over all the years, despite the Dauphine's friendship and family feeling for the Duchesse d' Orléans.

The Royal party reached Le Merlerault on 7 August at nightfall. The weather was fine, and while the Royal Family stayed at the Logis des Tourelles their attendants camped out. The young Duc de Bordeaux' room was full of fleas and he described it as being fit only for dogs. The

Dauphine was pleased to see the arrival of their baggage wagons, which at least provided her with fresh underwear, so essential in the hot weather. It was noted that the coats of arms painted on the wagons had been white-washed over, obscuring the fleur-de-lys insignia. The next day, at one o'clock, the Royal Family were greeted at Argentan in a very friendly manner by a number of young girls. The prevailing mood was one of sympathy for the misfortunes of the Royal Family and admiration for the dignity with which they were borne by the Bourbons. The Royal party settled for the night at the Hôtel de Raveton, owned by a Madame de Roncherolles. It was here that the party heard that the Duc d'Orléans had been declared 'King of the French by the Will of the People'[5] with the title of Louis Philippe I; this was the end of their hopes of a further restoration of their branch of the family. The King was dazed and deeply distressed by the betrayal not only by his cousins but also his friends who apparently had transferred their support to the new King and his family. During the day many visitors came to pay their respects to the deposed Charles X and the rest of the family.

The weather was now less favourable and it rained. The people of the town of Falaise were unwelcoming to the travellers and they preferred to move on. The former King ate his meal informally with the men who were gathering in the harvest at a farm on their route. On 11 August, Charles X and the rest of the Royal travelling party arrived at Vire. Observers noted the affection between Marie Thérèse and her father-in-law, seeing that he kissed the Dauphine's hand on their arrival at Vire. The King wanted to stay two days; the commissioners, for once asserting their authority, opposed the idea firmly. The family noted that the priest in Vire had quickly shifted his allegiance from the elder to the younger branch of the Bourbon dynasty. Notwithstanding the presence at Mass of the former Charles X and his family, prayers were said by the officiating priest for Louis Philippe and the new government. At St Lô where they spent the night of 12 August the family's bodyguards felt the need to sleep with their horses for fear that they might be stolen by the local townspeople. The river crossing at Carentan, an area of bogs and marshes, was difficult and uncomfortable for the family. There were comforts and consolations, though, on the journey north: on Friday 12 August at Torigni-sur-Vire a former bodyguard of the late Queen Marie Antoinette prepared an excellent meal for the family.

Finally on 15 August in the small town of Valognes on the Cotentin peninsula near Cherbourg, Charles X dismissed his guard. They had arrived at Valognes in torrential rain on Saturday 13 August. The King expressed the wish to spend Sunday in Valognes and the commissioners agreed to his request. The welcome was particularly effusive in Valognes, a town in Normandy which was staunchly Royalist, partly because it was disproportionately occupied by noblemen and their families. An area of the town was even known as Petit Versailles in honour of its aristocratic residents.

Petit Versailles

The Royal Family was lodged overnight at the Hôtel du Mesnildot de la Grille.[6] On Sunday morning at 8 a.m. the Royal Family attended Mass. The Dauphin was clearly distressed and had been unable to sleep; his eyes were red and his clothing very untidy. At times he expressed the wish that he had died in Paris fighting for his cause. The Dauphine maintained a dignified and rather distant manner. Their parting with the guards was emotional. The men were very distressed and filled with emotion and the King ended the proceedings with the words, 'My friends, is it necessary that I console you?' He was holding the hand of his grandson as the twelve oldest members of the guard came to make their farewells as representatives of their comrades. Behind Charles and his grandson stood the Dauphine and her husband, her sister-in-law and niece, and various attendants. Finally, when the guard had dispersed, Charles went on to the balcony of the Hôtel and tried to say farewell to his loyal supporters. Charles, usually so publicly assured and gracious but never a great public speaker, was so overcome by emotion that he was unable to speak to the crowd in the courtyard beneath. It rained throughout the day. Nevertheless, a line of well-wishers formed to make their farewells and pay their respects to the departing King and his niece, whose appearance and presence reminded people of her dead father, his sad fate and his, as they regarded it, martyrdom for the Royalist cause.

In 1930, a plaque[7] was erected by the Royalist Committee of the Manche to mark the 100th anniversary of the departure of Charles X from French soil. Engraved in gold lettering on marble and fixed to the lintel of the door of the old Hôtel de la Grille[8] the plaque states:[9] 'In this house, the ancient home of the Mesnildors, His Majesty King Charles X, after having given Algiers to France, and before leaving for exile, lived from 13 to 16 August, 1830. The Royalist Committee wished to commemorate the centenary, 1830-1930. '[10]

The plaque at the old Hotel de la Grille

Marie Thérèse and the rest of the Royal party left Valognes. The princes had changed from their military uniforms and decorations into civilian clothes. The streets of the town were thronged with well-wishers and the simply curious, eager for one last sight of the departing Royal Family. The Royal party was accompanied on its way by just four soldiers as a bodyguard, a far cry from the elaborate ceremonial of previous times. The sad group travelled towards Cherbourg. It was noted that partway to Cherbourg the Dauphine visited a cottage on the roadside at Brix. In due course they reached the Fort du Roule, and from this high vantage point above Cherbourg Marie Thérèse looked out across the Channel and the expanse of sea. Usually so reserved in public, on this occasion she could barely stop herself from weeping at her deep sense of loss and sadness. As a teenager M. de Trobriand and his family observed the Royal Family as they went into exile, and his observations are recorded:

> There was the King's oldest and childless son, the Dauphin, Monseigneur the Duc d'Angoulême, a colorless[11] and insignificant personage. Last, but not least, was the Duchesse d'Angoulême, niece and daughter-in-law of the King. This daughter of Louis XVI had in her youth, 38 years earlier, started in disguise with her father, mother, and aunt on the road that leads out of France. Was not her mind probably filled now with images of the flight to Varennes, of the horrible moment when, recognized and discovered, the hooting mob dragged them back to Paris, every rod of that road a very Calvary; did she hear again the revilings and vile epithets hurled at them by the filthy hordes; did she remember those threatening fists and scowling glances? Above all did she see again those prison walls, where for so many months she and her loved ones were to lead their martyrized existence, ending with the heartrending farewell to father, mother, and aunt as each in turn left her for the scaffold? Alas! poor woman! 'the Saint' as she was called — who will know what were her impressions?

The elder branch of the Bourbon family left France on 16 August 1830. The now former King wore a blue frockcoat without any decorations or ribbons. The Dauphine was wearing a dress made of silk and cotton in the colour 'adventurine', a pale green colour. The Duchesse de Berry was dressed in a riding habit. The King did not want to leave his country. He still hoped that there might be a future for his dynasty. At ten o'clock in the morning the Royal party set out for their last stopping place. Amongst their escort was Comte d'Estourmel the local Préfet. The Dauphine was able to see that up ahead of them a group of villagers had formed a double guard of honour, their hats in their hands as a mark of respect. They reached the town in the early afternoon. The few remaining guards presented arms one last time. In the harbour they could see the *Great Britain* and the *Charles Carroll*, the ships on which they were to sail to England. In a twist of irony the *Great Britain* was part-owned by William Patterson, an American businessman whose daughter Elizabeth had been married to Jérôme Bonaparte, Napoleon's youngest brother. The ships were well supplied with fresh food and there were cows and chickens on board to supply fresh milk and eggs. Despite being well-provisioned, the *Great Britain* was not stocked with bread so the Duchesse d'Angoulême and Duchesse de Berry bought bread and cheese from the various sellers on the quay, just like simple housewives. The men of the party, Charles X, Louis

XIX and Henri V, three Kings as the Légitimists[12] saw it, descended from their carriages. A few minutes later the Royal party boarded the ship that would take them into exile. The nine-year-old Henri was carried aboard ship by his governor, the Baron de Damas. Louis Antoine was dressed all in black, his clothes perhaps expressing his bleak feelings about events. Behind them came the Princesses, the Dauphine, the Duchesse de Berry and Mademoiselle. They were accompanied on the voyage by their doctor, Charles Bougon, and other courtiers. The Dauphine, as so often at times of great stress, fainted. Once she had recovered enough she put her hand in the fist of M. de la Rochejaquelin for him to help her board. Marie Thérèse was obviously distressed and her skin was blotchy; to observers she seemed thinner and somehow diminished in size and spirit. Charles X was the last of the party to board the boat.

At a quarter past two, the ship left port. What Marie Thérèse dreaded had happened again: exile to a foreign country with no settled home or role for her or her family. The commander of the ship taking the family to England was Jules-Sébastien-César Dumont d'Urville (1790-1842), the French explorer whose adventures had been sponsored by Charles X. He wrote in his journal, 'The King is the most spiritual, then the Duchesse d'Angoulême. Madame de Berry is light-hearted and the children good and pleasant. The Dauphin seems hopeless.' Madame de Maille, another of the party, felt differently, considering that the 'Dauphin had good judgement and good principles. He showed good sense and wisdom.' As they left the harbour, the Dauphine was looking around her trying to spot the ship *Duc de Bordeaux* named in honour of her nephew. She could not see it, as the ship had already been renamed *Friedland*. In Paris streets with names which honoured members of the old regime were hastily renamed, for example the rue d'Angoulême became rue de la Charte.

The Dauphine held her niece and nephew close to her as the coast of France retreated from their view and they headed for refuge in England. All the Royal Family, apart from the Dauphine and her father-in-law, were affected by seasickness. The family spent time on deck trying to feel better and get some fresh air. The family was forbidden to speak to the English sailors in English, for fear of conspiracy and an attempted escape or change of destination. Later there were accusations that d'Urville had behaved with scant courtesy to his Royal passengers, but he denied this. He had ensured that the family had bread rather than ship's biscuits to eat. The ship's captain slept on the bridge to give his cabin to the family so they could have some privacy. Knowing that they hated the colours of the tricolour, he desisted from wearing his uniform. The family and their 50 companions were, no doubt, all apprehensive about their future. Among those travelling with them was Maréchal Marmont. At one point during the voyage they believed that they were being taken to St Helena. Shocked and frightened, they failed to realise that the St Helens referred to was not in the South Atlantic but on the Isle of Wight.

The Bourbons' ship set anchor outside the town of Cowes on the Isle of Wight on 17 August 1830. The next day, the Princesses disembarked; their menfolk stayed on board for five more days awaiting the response of the British government to the Bourbon family's request for asylum. William IV, formerly Duke of Clarence, had recently succeeded his brother George IV to the British throne, and George had been a close friend of the Bourbon family. William IV was acquainted with the family but was not particularly sympathetic to their cause or interested in helping them. They were welcomed to the island by the Marquis of Anglesey, Governor of the Isle of Wight, accompanied by the American consul from Portsmouth. Marie Thérèse, Marie Caroline and the children settled into the Fountain Hotel. Battered and exhausted by their flight from France, they attempted to regroup and come to terms with yet another period of exile.

As their party consisted of 50 people, it took some feeding and maintaining. Accompanying Marie Thérèse were the Comte Charles O'Hegerthy, Mesdames de Saint-Maur and d'Agoult.[13] The King was keen to reduce the number of people in their Households, to save money and to make the party more manageable and manoeuvrable. The Royal Family were joined in exile by Cardinal Latil, who had fled France dressed as a woman, and Minister d'Haussez who was more fortunate than many of his ministerial colleagues in being able to seek sanctuary in England.

Many of the courtiers were unsurprisingly concerned about their own futures. It was the time of the regatta and the arrival of the Royal party caused much excitement, according to a history of the Royal Yacht Squadron, which noted that early risers on 19 August observed the two Duchesses walking with the children. The Royal ladies spent their time visiting places of interest on the Isle of Wight, including Newport and Carisbrooke Castle,[14] riding in a typically local carriage. They also attended the Royal Yacht Squadron escorted by Lord Deerhurst to watch the race for the King's Cup. It was noted that the Duchesse de Berry seemed to enjoy the occasion very much indeed. The Duc d'Angoulême, still on board the *Great Britain*, apparently missed his wife enormously and was filled with gloomy thoughts and depression at the events of July 1830. Louis Antoine came ashore to visit Marie Thérèse, despite not yet having the permission of the British government to land on English soil. This devotion to his wife gives the lie to suggestions that theirs was a marriage without affection. They were close and loving companions who missed each other during times when they were separated.

Greville wrote in his diary of 24 August 1830, 'The French King continues off Cowes, many people visiting him.' Of Madame d'Angoulême and Madame de Berri, he wrote:

> 'They came off without clothes or preparations of any kind, so much so that Lady Grantham has been obliged to furnish Mesdames de Berri and d'Angoulême with everything; it seems they have plenty of money.' Greville may have been referring here to the deposit made years before by Louis XVIII at Coutts, the royal bank. The Bourbons felt themselves to be far from affluent and lack of money was for them a problem. Gone were the generous Civil List income, fine horses and carriages enjoyed by Marie Thérèse and the rest of the family during the years of the Restoration. Marie Thérèse's nephew was greatly affected by the family's change of fortune. Used to the splendours of The Tuileries, St Cloud, Rambouillet and to being treated as the heir to the throne of France with soldiers presenting arms as the boy passed them, he was disturbed and traumatised by the family's changed circumstances. Now the security, order and deference were gone. The journey from the Paris and to the coast must have been a shocking and unsettling experience journey for the ten-year-old Henri just as the journey from Versailles to Paris had marked the end of the ordered routine and luxury of the ten-year-old Marie Thérèse's life in 1789.

The family was granted permission to stay in Britain on 20 August 1830 on the basis that they would live as ordinary citizens. The King and the rest of the family and their many baggages were eventually disembarked[15] at Weymouth on 23 August and met by a large, curious crowd, which apparently shocked the elderly King. According to Dumont d'Urville[16] Charles X thanked him warmly for his many kindnesses and courtesies to the family, shaking hands as he departed the ship. As the King left the ship he said to the captain that he did not intend staying long in Britain; he hoped to find a comfortable exile in Austrian territory, either in Venice or Verona.

The Bourbons then moved on to more permanent accommodation at the beautifully situated but remote Lulworth Castle in Dorset, some 15 miles from Poole, which was provided for them by the Weld family. Thomas Weld[17] was a member of the local gentry and a Roman Catholic who was sympathetic to their plight. The Welds had helped other French émigrés, especially the dispossessed French religious orders. On first seeing the castle, Charles X exclaimed that it was the Bastille; it was certainly reminiscent of it. From the outside Lulworth appeared to be a classic medieval castle with a central square and four round towers surrounded by woodland. The inside of the castle was less prepossessing: badly maintained and poorly furnished. It was said by Madame de Gontaut to be impossible to live in Lulworth Castle without a good umbrella, even in the summer months, so leaky was the roof.

Lulworth Castle, with thanks to George Bull

Marie Thérèse however wrote to Baron Charlet reporting that the family were in good health and not overwhelmed by their troubles. Greville commented that 'The king says he and his son have retired from public life; and as to his grandson, he must wait the progress of events; that his conscience reproaches him with nothing.' The family had left behind them in France many personal items, including the royal silverware, so they were forced to eat with steel utensils. Creditors who had still not been paid for supplies made to the Condé Army again threatened the King as he walked around the grounds. He listened patiently to their claims but dismissed them as exorbitant and said that he had no means of paying them.

They were visited at this time by Lady Arundell, who had known the family in Paris in happier days. She wrote to her sister-in-law with her observations:

> The park entered by that side is certainly fine, but it is gloom itself. I never saw a more dismal place, even to our English eyes; what then must it be to the poor French! I turned so sick and shook so much as I walked up the steps, dreading the interview so completely that I would have for a moment given anything to run away. At the door they took up our cards to the Duchesse de Gontaut, who acts Dame d'Honneur, in the absence of the real one, and ushered us into the great drawing room, but it being empty I had a moment to recover myself; then entered a valet de chambre: S. A. R. la Dauphine *va descendre elle-même, du haut l'escalier, elle m'a demandé les cartes, elle a fait un cri et elle descend*:[18] — he could hardly end, when the King

and Dauphin ran down the steps from the upper end I rushed forward and the dear Old Man, who was quite composed and cheerful, led me to the window, holding both my hands and thro' my sobs I heard nothing but, *allons Marie, quand on a la conscience bonne on ne s'afflige de rien;*[19] and I had hardly listened to that when my tears redoubled at the sight of the Dauphiness, who fell on my neck for an instant weeping bitterly, but the next moment her usual heroism returned and she was calm, but during the hour she stayed with us, to look at her was heart breaking, for I see that the iron has entered into her soul. She is haggard, pale, except a flushed spot on each cheek, and as she talked of France and of her dreadful journey, all her fortitude for a moment gave way and several times she shed tears and her voice faltered. The Dsse de Berri was gone *faire des emplettes à* [20] Wareham! and to see poor Mons. and Mme. Charette,[21] who have been obliged to take a wretched lodging there, for the misfortune of Lulworth is that not only is it much too small and they are wretchedly crowded, but there is no accommodation in the neighbourhood. They spoke in praise of Mr. Weld's civility, but tho' they did not complain, still they are evidently very uncomfortable. The King had written in answer to my offer of Wardour the kindest of answers, expressing his regret that this decision of Lulworth put it out of his power to do what he wished, but that he promised should his as yet undecided plans end in remaining in England beyond the time for which Lulworth is engaged, he would certainly accept our Château, and this promise he renewed by word of mouth as soon as I became decent and composed.

The Dauphiness and the King putting me between them on a sofa, then the Dauphin making Edward sit next to him on two chairs opposite, they all began the most unreserved conversation with us, no attendant being in the room. The King seems quite resigned and even not to regret his throne; he said I only regret the few good people that still remain in that *malheureux pays.*[22] My throne I cannot regret, for it was accompanied by endless cares and anxieties. I now have none; magnificence and luxury I do not regret. I long have thought them a bad people, a nation demoralised, that could be ruled only with a *bras de fer.*[23] Bonaparte only could govern them, so it was painful to me to govern them and it is happiness *a'en être débarrassé et de pouvoir s'occuper du ciel.— C'est là, Sire, qu'une couronne vous attend. —J'essayerai de la gagner, et en attendant, je me sens heureux d'avoir ma liberté. Sire, la dernière fois que j'eus l'honneur de voir V. M. à Paris, vous me disiez que vous portiez une couronne à épines et que vous regrettiez Londres et Hartwell. Combien j'ai pensé à ces mots depuis. C'est vrai,*[24] I often regretted England. All that I now feel is for the poor people who may suffer for the attachment they have shown me, for France is not quiet yet, and for the poor souls who have followed me here and whom I may not always be able to support. Then he talked of d'Orléans, but with so much more of pity than of anger that it was beautiful; that he suffered himself to be the tool of the Republicans, who would sacrifice him when they wanted him no longer—*pourtant il a fait bien mal, il a long temps tramé contre moi et il a saisi le premier moment pour se déclarer et se prêter à tout ce qu'on désirait.*[25]

Lady Arundell discussed with Charles X the invidious position in which Marie Amélie found herself. She continued:

> Then he pitied the Dsse d'Orléans, who was, he said, an excellent woman, and who utterly condemned this entire affair, and how she must suffer to see her sons brought up in these principles. In all this the Dauphin joined, but he spoke with bitter aigreur against the French nation. He seems resigned and cheerful but much more irritated; in fact he is a younger man than the King. He naturally looked to several years of a throne. The King has not many more years to live in the course of nature and seems to me to look upon all in this world as perfect dross. What a place he will have in our happy valley. After a long discussion the Dauphiness said, *envoyons pour nos enfants,*[26] *Marie et Lord A. aimeraient les voir,*[27] and in bounded the heir of a long race of kings, whom I had last seen in the cradle of luxury, surrounded by guards and attendants! He is much grown and improved, looks very healthy, and tho' retaining the likeness in the upper part of his face to his dear father, is getting also like the King. I think he may turn out handsome and very well made and active. He has for a child a very good manner, and his sister who came in more gravely, followed by the Duchesse de Gontaut, has a most winning manner, and in very good English said how glad she was to see me, and squeezing herself into the couch by my side talked and quite won my heart. After some time they went out to walk and we again set in for discussion on Spain and France again.

Knowing that the Royal ladies had no means of transport and that Marie Thérèse longed for exercise and liked to ride, Lady Arundell wrote, 'I am going to send my pony carriage and ponies, as the Dauphiness and children have no means of getting about the park, and if I hear of a lady's horse, I am going to send one with my side-saddle, for riding is necessary for her. If I can get two, *tant mieux,*[28] for there ought to be one for her lady-in-waiting.' Kind Lady Arundell was distressed at seeing her friends so shocked and brought so low and wrote, 'I am still quite upset by this visit.'

In late August 1830, the Dauphine received the sum of 100,000 francs forwarded to her by her secretary the Baron Charlet from Worth, her London bankers. Marie Caroline was fortunate in still having property of her own in Naples. The 200,000 francs which had been given to Charles X at Cherbourg had long gone: spent on feeding and housing his family and their still numerous attendants. Presciently, the late Louis XVIII during the First Restoration had in 1814 sent the Duc de Blacas to England with the equivalent of £200,000, which was deposited with Coutts Bank in the Duc de Blacas' name as a buffer against possible future exile and hard times. The funds came in very useful. Creditors even tried to seize the carriages which the Royal Family had brought with them from Paris. Madame de Gontaut reports that on one occasion the King was out walking when he was surrounded by a group of disgruntled creditors. An Act of the English Parliament had given Charles X immunity from his English creditors, but not from foreign ones. Now he was no longer King of France and with his credit-worthiness drastically reduced, they wanted payment and quickly. One cannot help but wonder why Charles had not dealt with his creditors during the two Restorations, when he and the rest of the family enjoyed generous Civil List incomes.

Étienne-Romain de Sèze, a French Royalist, visited the family at Lulworth in late September 1830 and wrote about his observations in his *Souvenirs de Lulworth, d'Holyrood et de Bath.* He arrived uninvited at Lulworth, not knowing if he would be able to see the King and the rest of the Royal Family. He was told by some Frenchmen whom he met that he should present himself at the castle the next day in the hope of seeing the King at on his way to Mass. He sent his card up to M. de Damas, who welcomed him warmly but made it clear that the King was seeing no visitors. Another courtier, M de Polignac, gave him more hope. M de Polignac went to see the King who was happy to receive M de Sèze in recognition of the services rendered by his father at the trial of Louis XVI when de Sèze the elder had defended the King with courage and fine oratory. He was invited to go into the room where the Royal Family gathered before Mass. So moved was he that he cried. The family welcomed him warmly and invited him to join them for dinner. At table, the King sat between his two grandchildren. M de Sèze sat next to Marie Thérèse and during their conversation she recalled the tale of her flight from Dijon when for two stressful days she had had no news of what was happening to her husband and father-in-law. She also mentioned her encounter with the Duc de Chartres and how affected she had been by his offer of assistance. She talked about the great fear that she had of being sent into exile in the United States when she had boarded an American ship at Cherbourg. She explained that on his last visit to the United States, the Marquis de la Fayette had promised the Americans that he would send the Royal Family to them. She was terrified that they were about to be transported across the Atlantic to fulfil his promise. As they spoke, Marie Thérèse recalled with fondness her neighbours at her estate at Villeneuve L'Étang. He was impressed by how well she maintained her morale and good spirits.

As Lady Arundell suspected, the family did not stay long at Lulworth. The King's pressing debts and the leaky roof and high rent at Lulworth Castle necessitated the family's removal to Scotland and Holyroodhouse. Here they would be protected from aggressive creditors. It was also at this time that the family adopted new titles more suited to their altered circumstances: Charles X becoming Comte de Ponthieu, Marie Caroline Comtesse de Rosny and Louis Antoine and Marie Thérèse, Comte and Comtesse de Marnes.[29] The would-be boy King took the title of Comte de Chambord from his beautiful Château on the Loire.

Marie Thérèse lived in Edinburgh from the autumn of 1830 for two years. Charles and the young Duc de Bordeaux set off by boat for Scotland on 17 October 1830. They spied the coast of France on their voyage north, as he told his sister with pleasure. Two days later, they were followed to Edinburgh by the rest of the Royal party who travelled the more than 450 miles from Dorset to Scotland by carriage. This was another long and no doubt tedious journey to be endured as stoically as possible. Marie Caroline spent time in London socialising and meeting the Duke of Wellington among others, which did not please the new regime in France (they wondered what she was up to), before travelling on to Scotland. Charles X, on returning to live in Scotland after many years, remarked to the Duc de Brissac, one of his attendants, 'Well, we are here once again. We must be resigned. God wills it.' Once again the French Royal Family took up residence in Edinburgh in and around the Palace of Holyroodhouse. The Palace provided protection against creditors, but it did not provide privacy and on certain days visitors were admitted to the palace and its grounds. The Bourbons felt that they were rather like exhibits in a museum or animals in a zoo.

Concerned that recent negative articles about the Bourbons in the British newspapers had stirred up the people of the city to abuse or insult the returning family, Sir Walter Scott wrote an article in an Edinburgh newspaper, *Ballantyne's*, of 20 October, exhorting the people to compassion and saying, 'it would be unworthy of us as Scotchmen, or as men, if this unfortunate family should meet with a word or a look from the meanest individual ending to aggravate feelings which must be at present must be so acute'. He made it clear that the Court would be few in number (mainly women and children), that they would as previously live unobtrusively, and that their stay was likely to be of short duration. He noted that 'Whatever may have been his errors towards his own people', Charles X should be treated with 'civility and respect'. He also reminded his Scottish readers that Charles had been a generous benefactor towards Edinburgh, sending funds to help people whose homes had been destroyed by fire. The letter seems to have had the desired effect and the family was kindly received.

There were strong historic links between Scotland and the French monarchy. The romantic heroine Mary Queen of Scots had lived in France as a child and was briefly its Queen Consort, as the wife of the young King Francis II, before returning to her homeland. The Catholic Stuart monarch James II of England and Scotland and his family, on fleeing his kingdom in 1688, had been received generously by his cousin

Louis XIV and lived on in the style of a king at St-Germain-en-Laye. The Stuart pretenders to the English throne were supported by the French monarchs when they invaded the British Isles in an attempt to regain their throne in 1715 and 1745. Of course, there was also their shared distrust of England.

M. de Sèze described Edinburgh as a place very much of two halves: the old town with its many-storeyed grubby tenement buildings, contrasting with the recently built new town of large squares and wide straight streets. At Holyroodhouse it was noted by the French exiles that the rooms which they had occupied during their previous sojourn here and to which they returned were in exactly the same condition of decoration and furnishing (no better and no worse) than they had been on their departure from Scotland more than fifteen years before. Madame de Gontaut claimed that Mademoiselle Louise's room was cold and damp and the chimney smoked terribly. Some refurbishment work, including painting, was done in the spring of 1831. The Duc and Duchesse d'Angoulême preferred to live away from the rest of the family in more secluded circumstances and with greater privacy, though they spent a lot of time at Holyroodhouse They decided to settle at 21 Regent Terrace,[30] renting a newly built and modern house (the stone still bright and clean according to M. de Sèze). P. J. Fallon visited Edinburgh in the autumn of 1831 and reported in his memoir *Voyage à Holyrood* that the Princess and her husband had moved into a very modest house consisting of only seven or eight rooms over two storeys. The house was a short walk from the palace, which it overlooked; she had had a path to it specially built for her, called 'The Queen of France's way' by the people of the area. Before the construction of the path the route was considerably longer. While more of a home for Marie Thérèse than Holyrood, Regent Terrace looked out over a cemetery: hardly a view to lift the spirits. To try to preserve family harmony, Marie Thérèse arranged for Marie Caroline to move out of Holyrood and to live in the same street near her and the Duc d'Angoulême. The sisters-in-law got on better when they did not have to spend too much time together. Marie Caroline opted to live at 11 Regent Terrace, but was forced to leave her children with her father-in-law and their tutors and governess at Holyroodhouse. But she ate all her meals except breakfast with Henri and Louise, and passed much of the day with them. She spent some time away from Edinburgh in Bath, seeking amusement and congenial company, leaving her children in the care of their second mother, the Dauphine, as de Sèze called her.

In exile in Edinburgh, the family was accompanied by a number of courtiers loyal to them: Maréchal de Bourmont, Baron d'Haussez, Comte de Montbel,[31] Duc de Blacas, Duc and Duchesse de Guiche, Duc de Polignac and the O'Hegerthys. Their doctor, Bougon, was also with them. Charles X's health was good, so his physician spent most of his time playing whist with the King. The family missed France and longed for news of it, eagerly awaiting the arrival of the French newspapers in Edinburgh. They also scoured the English newspapers for articles about France. The news from France was not cheering: many of the former Royal government ministers, including Jules de Polignac,[32] had been arrested and were imprisoned for life in the Castle of Ham in Picardy in northern France. Marie Caroline was deeply frustrated and angered by their fate and the loss of her son's throne, as well as what she regarded as the passive acceptance shown by Marie Thérèse, Louis Antoine and Charles. The Duchesse de Berry was fascinated by the story of the life and tragic end of Mary Queen of Scots[33] and adored the works of Sir Walter Scott; she spent time in Scotland reading and rereading his works.

Regent Terrace, Edinburgh

The Duchesse de Berry was keen to take positive steps to regain the throne for her son, so tried to persuade the King that a further Restoration of the elder branch of the Bourbons was possible and that prompt action was needed to achieve this objective. The King, in his mid-70s, had neither the energy nor the desire to make this happen. If the Duchesse de Berry wanted action to achieve this end, she would have to initiate it herself. She started to plot on behalf of her son. In January 1831, news of the death of Francis I of Sicily was received in Edinburgh. The loss of her beloved father was very saddening for the Duchesse de Berry in Edinburgh and also for Queen Marie Amélie in Paris, who had been close to her brother.

We have accounts from M. d'Hardivillier, an artist, royal drawing master to Henri and his sister and former member of the elite Garde du Corp, that the Duc de Bordeaux at the age of eleven and twelve years was enjoying living in Scotland and spoke English fluently. He made a number of very pleasant trips out from the confines of Holyroodhouse with his tutor and grandfather's courtiers to explore the countryside, which in its ruggedness was so very different from that of the Île de France in which he had grown up. In 1832 he visited with his sister and science tutor Joachim Barande[34] the site of the Battle of Culloden and Loch Leven Castle where their mother's heroine Mary Queen of Scots had been imprisoned. The young Duc de Bordeaux also visited Loch Awe, and on entering an inn in the village of Tyndrum near Loch Lomond he remarked on the presence of engravings of his aunt while in prison as a young girl, trying to give comfort to her mother and Madame Élisabeth; he also noticed a print of his great uncle Louis XVI on his way to his execution. The young Duc wore tartan outfits as a compliment to his hosts.

The Scots magazine observed of the deposed Charles X's time in Edinburgh: 'The Scottish gentlemen, full of respect for the grey hairs of the noble old man, entertained Charles with great kindness, sympathising with his sufferings and treating the Princes as if they were still in a position of power.' The family accepted invitations from Scottish noblemen who were sympathetic to their plight. These trips helped to fill their days and perhaps to forget, at least for a short time, their deep sense of loss and homesickness. The dispossessed King was only able to leave the confines of the palace of Holyroodhouse and its grounds on Sundays, as on this day his creditors were unable to pursue their claims against him and he could move freely around Edinburgh and the surrounding countryside. He attended the Catholic chapel in Edinburgh and was joined at Mass by members of the local nobility. He had rented three horses for a month at a time and a very modest carriage for drives. During the week his carriage was lent to friends and members of the family, as the King was unable to venture outside the immunity area of the palace.

The Duchesse d'Angoulême rode once a week with the King. She went for frequent walks to pass the time and get the exercise she craved. On her walks she was on a number of occasions followed and accosted by an old man shouting abuse at her. He was apprehended by passers-by and taken before the local magistrates who fined him. His defence was that he was not of sound mind.

P. J. Fallon met the Princess a number of times during his visit to Edinburgh. On one occasion he met her when he was out riding. She too was on horseback and accompanied by her husband and the Duc de Guiche. She recognised Fallon from their previous meetings and stopped her horse for a quarter of an hour to converse with him and his travelling companion. He was struck by her affability, and contrasted his experience of her demeanour with her reputation for coldness and disdain spread by her enemies. The King also went out for coach rides or walked in the park with his grandson. There was a small Roman Catholic chapel within Holyroodhouse and on Sundays forty or so French people attended the service. Fallon noted, in the autumn of 1831, that the King was flanked on his right by the Duc d'Angoulême and his nephew and on the other side by the Duchesses d'Angoulême and her niece.

The warm welcome of the Scottish nobility could not disguise the cold damp weather and the long dark nights of an Edinburgh winter. The damp atmosphere affected Marie Thérèse's health badly; she suffered from painful arthritis in her limbs. The family struggled to keep up their spirits in the city, which they found to be foggy, sad and mournful. M. de Sèze visited the family in May 1831 and was struck by her low spirits: she seemed sad and beaten. She could speak of nothing but France, and yet he feared discussing France with her. She recalled over and over again her flight into exile. He recalled chatting with Marie Thérèse about their mutual friends; she wanted to know all about them, and tears welled in her eyes when some names were mentioned. Despite all her sufferings, it was clear to him how much she still loved France. She seemed to relish the company of those who had recently been in France. He noted that the people of Edinburgh whom he met and conversed with were full of compassion for the plight of the exiles and admired their courage in adversity. He was filled with compassion and conscious of the aid she had given so many people in France and elsewhere.

As the government of Louis Philippe established itself in France, it became more difficult, diplomatically, for the British government to offer his dispossessed cousins refuge. The Bourbons began to look around for another place of safety and preferably warmer weather. The former King and the Duc d'Angoulême felt a deep sense of despair at the loss of the throne. Money worries beset the family, as de Sèze noted. Louis Antoine became increasingly depressed by their situation. He could barely bring himself to entertain or go out. He was unable to speak of French politics without being completely overcome. Marie Thérèse too was deeply affected by the reversal of their fortunes. Madame de Meffray[35] was from an émigré family and had been brought up with Marie Caroline. She was also one of the Duchesse de Berry's ladies-in-waiting and wrote of the Dauphine at this time:

> She is, as usual, admirable. She is not able to speak of France and the idea of never seeing it again without crying. The dignity and the loftiness of her character are always the same and do not fail her. She knows how to be at one and the same time a Christian woman and a Princess. Her only thoughts of the future are for the young Prince; I believe he will be King she says.[36]

Madame de Meffray felt that the Duchesse d'Angoulême would have been a truly great heroine if her intelligence had been equal to her other merits. For what it is worth, Madame de Boigne thought Madame de Meffray stupid.

Marie Thérèse's husband may have found it too painful or depressing to discuss developments in French politics, but she herself was enormously interested in events. She would ask detailed questions about what was happening in France of any French visitors. P. J. Fallon reported that on meeting her, the Dauphine expressed her concern for the people of France and their sufferings. He noted her eyes were red-rimmed from so much crying. She closely questioned visitors on the strength and popularity of the new regime under her cousin Louis Philippe I, trying to discern whether there was any hope for the Restoration of the elder Bourbon line.

Even the exiled minister d'Haussez could hold out only the hope of a possible Restoration of her nephew. He was convinced there was no hope for the Restoration of her husband or his father as King. Nevertheless she did not give up, and despite the very low spirits of her husband, she hoped for better things. The Dauphine was keen to hear the reality of the political situation. Disciplined and organised in order to support the possible Restoration of the Duc de Bordeaux as King, Marie Thérèse started a letter-writing campaign. She was in regular correspondence with the officers of the regiments, which had previously formed the Royal Family's bodyguard. She had always had an affinity with the military and had displayed great personal courage herself in 1815 in trying to fight against the advancing Napoleon on his return from Elba.

Marie Thérèse kept herself informed of events in France by reading the French newspapers to her husband and father-in-law. The family scrupulously avoided the anti-Louis Philippe, pro-Carlist *La Mode*. The former King would not allow any mockery of the new King, even if he was a usurper. According to the Duchesse de Dino, both the Dauphine and the former King wrote complaints to the paper's editor, M. Mennechet. He was shocked and resigned while commenting:

> Just fancy; for five years I have been leading forlorn hopes on behalf of the Prague people and I have only had two letters from them, one from King Charles X bitterly complaining of the caricatures of Louis Philippe which we had sent him and which he ordered us to stop, and the other from Madame la Dauphine who two months ago wrote me a very severe letter, sending me back my paper and saying that she would give up her subscription because we had published an article in which it was said that we had seen or received a letter containing good news about the Duc de Bordeaux.

The Duchesse de Dino felt that 'the letters are very reasonable and very creditable to the writers'. Other French newspapers were less kind to Marie Thérèse. They accused the Princess of having many lovers, including improbably the Archbishop of Paris. This episode was obviously ridiculous to anyone who knew her and her very strict principles, and evoked strong echoes of the untruthful and hurtful accusations against her mother in the *libelles* before the Revolution.

The French papers had noted in September 1830 that the Royal Family had been putting their affairs in France in order, aided by the new regime. *The Standard* of 9 September 1830 noted from the French paper the *Courrier Français* that following the departure of Charles X and his family, their agents had been active on their behalf 'preferring claims on the civil list, demanding everything that had belonged to the ex-Princes and Princesses, the Dauphin and the Dauphiness, the Duke of Bordeaux, his mother and sister'. Contrasting the position with the expulsion of the Bonaparte family, the paper went on to say:

> legitimate princes are more exacting, and the revolution more polite. Everything is returned to them with the most scrupulous fidelity-plate, libraries, linen and money. Searches have been instituted in every quarter after what might have been removed from their apartments; and those wrecks which the people had carried off as trophies have been brought back, with that integrity which so much distinguishes the population of Paris. Everything has been returned, even fragments of silver covers bearing the arms of the exiled Princes.

Horses and carriages were among the items. Inspection of the Bourbons' private property had given rise to some wry comments. The article went on to say that examination of the contents of the library of the Duc d'Angoulême and other images and autographs owned by the family had confirmed its view that the family was 'of narrow and anti-rational mind' and that it 'bears all the stamps of monkish mysticism'. It continued: 'Certain volumes and annotations have been found in the Dauphin's own handwriting; and the public will, perhaps, be astonished that several male and female saints were worshipped who had no place in the calendar; for instance, several volumes were inscribed thus "The gift of my friend Saint Edgeworth".'

Marie Thérèse passed the hours of tedium during the long winter days in Edinburgh as always with monstrous amounts of embroidery and some knitting. The products of her efforts were sold in aid of her former servants who had fallen on hard times with the change of monarch and the departure of the Bourbons from France. She was very concerned that those who had not found alternative employment should not suffer deprivations during the winter. The Dauphine also arranged for the sale of furniture, crockery and glassware from her former country retreat at Villeneuve-l'Étang and for the sale proceeds to go to her former servants, many of whom were lodged near the Tuileries Palace. It was noted in the September article in *The Standard* that 'powers have been received by their agents, at Paris, to sell the personal property of the Duchess of Berri, and of the Dauphiness, Rosny and Villeneuve L'Étang: but this requires more time than the claiming of the furniture of the Princes'. The article noted that the family had left debts in Paris and the writer hoped that they would be equally assiduous in ensuring that their debts were paid as they were in collecting together their property. The comment was made that the family had in 1816 received a huge grant of 30 million francs to repay the debts, which had accumulated during the years of exile. He hoped that they would in their turn make sure they would pay their debts to the tradesmen and other businesses that had supplied them during the Restoration.

Marie Thérèse was always punctilious in managing her financial affairs. On her departure, she had arranged to return to the Royal collection a valuable trove known as the Parure of the Duchesse d'Angoulême; it consisted of a diadem or tiara of wonderful emeralds, a necklace, a comb, a pair of earrings, a girdle, three clasps and a pair of ruby bracelets comprising 24 oval rubies and surrounded by 356 diamonds of stunning brightness, part of the Crown Jewels of France. They had been remodelled in a contemporary style for her by Paul-Nicolas Menière, to the designs of Evrard Bapst, on the instructions of Louis XVIII after the Second Restoration in 1815. They had previously been worn by the Empress Marie Louise. This is surely a testament to her integrity and her love of France. Marie Amélie and the Empress Eugénie later wore these jewels, some of which can now be seen in the Louvre.

Marie Thérèse made stringent economies, even to the extent of cancelling her subscriptions to various French magazines in order to be able to support her former Household. Her actions recall her thrift during her sojourn at the Viennese Court in the late 1790s before her marriage. Her trusted secretary, the Baron Charlet, worked hard on her behalf to place her former servants in other posts or to provide them with funds. Charlet sold what he could from her estates in France to raise funds, but crates of items which had only sentimental value were sent to Edinburgh. As the winter of 1830/31 progressed, Marie Thérèse became depressed, and her aches and pains troubled her. She was also upset by the tensions within the family, especially those between the lively and no doubt bored Duchesse de Berry, who missed her life in Paris and quarrelled with her father-in-law. The Duchesse de Berry was angered by the fact that he stood on ceremony about petty matters of etiquette, and when challenged on this he insisted that he was master in his own house. She replied challengingly but with some truth that if he had been more the master of events while they were in France, he would not have lost his throne and her son his inheritance. According to Fallon, the Duc and Duchesse d'Angoulême moved back into Holyrood in October 1831 once some repairs had been made to the apartments intended for them. He bemoaned the meanness of the government and blamed the influence of Wellington for not providing better for the family in exile; but then the Bourbons had never been favourites of the Duke.

On 2 February 1832, the eleven-year-old Duc de Bordeaux took his first communion at the Catholic chapel in Edinburgh; his aunt in particular exhorted him to pray for the good of his homeland. Marie Caroline was not present at the ceremony, as she meanwhile had more dramatic plans to restore France to 'happiness' and to place her son on the throne of France. Marie Caroline had already decided to leave Scotland and seek out a more congenial climate by returning to her native Italy. At least this was what she told the world. She had left Scotland in the summer of 1831, and

Marie Thérèse wrote to Charlet that she feared for her. Instead of settling in Naples with her family, however, the adventurous Duchesse de Berry headed for the Midi area of southern France. On her way there, Marie Caroline visited Lucca and the Duc of Modena travelling with the Duc de Blacas, Comte de Mesnard and Comte de Rosanter. She also made brief trips to Rome and Naples, but her objective was France. Throughout her time travelling she was spied on by French agents and by the agents of governments who did not want to offend Louis Philippe by being seen to support her efforts to restore her son to the French throne. Even her own family, closely related as they were to Queen Marie Amélie, did not want to provoke the government of Louis Philippe.

Her hopes of Restoration were buoyed up by a riot which took place at a Mass to mark the anniversary of the death of the Duc de Berry; it lasted three days. Within France her supporters distributed money and plotted to bring people to her cause. She was determined that the Restoration of her son should not be achieved by foreign invaders, but be a reflection of the wishes of the people of France. She had also received more than five hundred letters of support from French Royalists who looked to the young Duc de Bordeaux as their King. In order to maintain some family unity, Charles X was at last persuaded to appoint his daughter-in-law as Regent for her son on the rather unachievable condition that her attempts to restore the monarchy in France were successful. He was keen to have deniability if and when things went badly for the Duchesse de Berry.

Scotland had become an increasingly uncomfortable place of refuge for the Dauphine and her family. In November 1831 Marie Thérèse fell ill with rheumatic fever brought on by the cold house in which she was living. She also blamed her age, now she was 53 years old. She was confined to bed for a fortnight and her recuperation was slow, lengthened by a particularly harsh Scottish winter. Her spirits were further lowered by the anniversary of the July Revolution a few months earlier. The diplomatic situation had deteriorated for Marie Thérèse and her family as the new regime in France established itself as the de facto government of her country; but relations between it and the British government actually warmed. Moreover, Scotland was not safe from the cholera spreading around Europe. The *Caledonian Mercury* of 9 February 1832 noted the incidence of cholera in Scotland and the deaths occurring as a result. The newspaper also mentioned that Charles X's doctor had attended a demonstration at the Drummond Street Cholera Hospital of a special metal cholera stretcher for transporting patients comfortably and warmly to hospital.

Louise Marie Thérèse d'Artois, c.1840

It was time for the Bourbons to move on. By May 1832, the Dauphine was writing to Charlet that she planned to leave Scotland shortly and move to Austria. Once again, as in 1795, her cousin, the Austrian Emperor Francis I, came to Marie Thérèse's aid. He offered the family a refuge within his territories. It was not as yet entirely clear where the family would be able to make their home, but they hoped for somewhere warmer and nearer to other family members. Travelling in Europe was made no easier by the outbreak of cholera. The family decided that it would be sensible for Marie Thérèse and her niece, Mademoiselle, to go ahead of the main travelling party and sort out arrangements for the family's accommodation. The then Princess Victoria of Kent, later Queen, was acquainted with Louise, whom she described later in her diary[37] as being 'very agreeable & clear & easy to get on with'. The Princesses travelled through England, spending a fortnight in Cambridge and London before boarding a ship for Rotterdam in the Netherlands on 15 September 1832.

During her time in London, Marie Thérèse was visited by Queen Adelaide, the wife of William IV. Mary F. Sandars' biography of Queen Adelaide recounts:

> About this time the Duchesse d'Angoulême and Charles X passed through London on their way from Holyrood where they had been given asylum by the English Government to Austria, and the Queen paid a visit to the Duchesse d'Angoulême. The English Government was criticised for want of cordiality to the fallen Royal Family. The fact that Charles X and a party of loyal courtiers crossed in an ordinary trading boat from Newhaven[38] to Hamburg and the Dauphine travelled in a passenger boat

> to Rotterdam because the government was late in its arrangements for providing anything else, excited comment, and hurt the Duchesse d'Angoulême's feelings. She was, therefore, all the more grateful for the Queen's visit, and Queen Adelaide must indeed have felt much pity and sympathy for one whose views she shared to a great extent, and whose fate of exile in a foreign land she must have conceived as likely to be her own.[39]

The Duchesse d'Angoulême also gave receptions at the Cobourg Hotel (now The Connaught) near Grosvenor Square before travelling on to Europe. The ladies journeyed at a leisurely pace through Europe, opting to travel some of the way by barge down the Rhine rather than by carriage over uncomfortable roads. From their boat the Princesses could see the French bank of the river – an emotional experience for them both. They were delayed by the need to stay in quarantine in a village near Mayence[40] for a number of days, for fear of cholera. They reached Frankfurt on 29 September and eventually arrived in Vienna on 6 October, where they were very kindly and attentively received by the Emperor; he came every day to spend time with his cousins. Marie Thérèse and Francis had not seen each other since she had left Vienna to go to Mittau in May 1799 to marry the Duc d'Angoulême. The Empress Maria Theresa, who had been jealous of Marie Thérèse's charms during her stay in Vienna following her release from prison, had died in 1807. The Emperor was never happy unless he had a wife, so had remarried twice since; the current Empress was Caroline-Augusta, a Bavarian princess.

The Duchesse d'Angoulême found a sympathetic female friend at the Habsburg Court in the person of the young Archduchess Sophie,[41] married to the Archduke Franz Karl, second son of the Emperor Francis I of Austria. Following her marriage in 1824, the Archduchess had become great friends with the Duc de Reichstadt,[42] son of the deposed Emperor Napoleon and Marie Louise, who had been brought up despite his French origins at the Viennese Court of his grandfather, as an Austrian archduke. Sophie and the Duc de Reichstadt were even rumoured to have been lovers. The truth seems to have been that theirs was a deeply loving but platonic friendship between individuals who felt themselves isolated from those among whom they lived. They sought understanding and congenial company.

The Duc de Reichstadt had died recently and the Archduchess Sophie continued to mourn the loss. The Archduchess Sophie told the Duchesse d'Angoulême a story which moved the French Princess and flattered her husband. Apparently, shortly before his death, the Duc de Reichstadt had recounted that when his regiment was trying to honour the Duc d'Angoulême, they presented him with a pair of woollen epaulettes and the soldiers declared him to be a 'French grenadier'. The Duc de Reichstadt had apparently contrasted this French attitude with the Austrian approach, saying 'See the difference between countries; with them, when you wish to disgrace an officer you make him a soldier; with us,[43] when you wish to honour a Prince, you make him a grenadier.' The Duchesse d'Angoulême had not heard from her rather modest husband this compliment paid to him by his soldiers and was delighted to hear of the esteem in which her husband was held: she blushed with pleasure at being told this story by the Archduchess. Despite the fact that the young Duc de Reichstadt had left France when he was three years old in 1814, he had never forgotten his French origins and was fiercely proud of the achievements and military prowess of his father.

During her visit to Vienna the Duchesse d'Angoulême was able to spend time with two old friends: the Countess Zichy-Ferraris and the Countess Esterhazy. Along with the Vicomtesse d'Agoult who had travelled as lady-in-waiting with Marie Thérèse and her niece, the ladies had much to talk about and must have enjoyed being together. They had corresponded much over the years. An article in the *Journal of European Studies*[44] states that the Countess Esterhazy apparently ran a very pleasant salon in Vienna and wrote daily to the Duchesse d'Angoulême. The Duchesse also took the opportunity to try once more to sort out her financial affairs. She had not been in Vienna since 1799, and some of the financial problems that had beset her then had still not been resolved. She had money held at the bankers Heninkstein based at rue de la Carinthie; she held investments there of 512,125 florins which provided the Princess with an annual income of 25,000 florins or 64,600 francs. These monies were derived from the deposits made with the Belgian bank Nettine de Bruxelles in 1792 at the time of the flight of the Royal Family from their palace arrest in the Tuileries, which was halted at Varennes. The funds held with the failed Worth Bank in London were so meagre that Marie Thérèse instructed her secretary Charlet not to bother pursuing her claim against the bank. The main funds available to the Duchesse d'Angoulême came from France and amounted to approximately 200,000 francs per annum. While not rich by Royal standards, she possessed a handsome enough fortune and was able to maintain a respectable Household from her resources.

The Duc d'Angoulême, his father and nephew arrived in Europe from Great Britain on 20 September 1832. They were received everywhere with the honours and respect due to their rank. The King of Prussia and the Emperor of Austria both sent *aides de camp* to welcome them. The long journey had been blessed with good weather: only two days of fog (a reference to the Scottish weather). They had travelled slowly towards Austria, spending time in Spandau and Frankfurt an der Oder. The young Duc de Bordeaux seems to have enjoyed himself visiting a troop of soldiers and charming all he met, according to Damas. The Royal couple were delighted to be reunited in Vienna. Together the French and Austrian

Royal Families marked the 39th anniversary of the death of Marie Antoinette on 16 October 1832. Marie Thérèse was delighted by the warmth of the reception she received from her Austrian family, and thoroughly enjoyed her stay in Vienna. She wrote, 'I was happy (a rare thing) during my short stay with my mother's family, where they were so good, so friendly, so attentive, so full of care for me.' Their stay of ten days or so was brief by the standards of the time, when travel was difficult and expensive so visits to friends and relatives were often of long duration.

The Duchesse d'Angoulême and her niece then travelled on to Prague to take up residence in the huge Hradschin Palace,[45] the use of which the Emperor had kindly offered to his cousins in exile. When the ladies arrived from Vienna on 27 October, the Royal menfolk were already there. The palace complex was and is magnificently sited in Prague, sitting high above the city and the banks of the Danube. Its cathedral was dedicated to St Vitus, built in the sixteenth century and designed by the French architect Matthias d'Arras. Extending over some 700,000 square metres the opulent palace complex included a convent, several churches and 440 apartments and enclosed magnificent squares within its walls. The Duchesse d'Angoulême's grandmother, the Empress Maria Theresa, as Queen of Hungary had done much to renovate and improve the castle buildings during her reign. A huge portrait of her hung on a wall in the first-floor apartments, used by the Austrian Emperor on his infrequent visits to Prague. The Bourbons were pleased with the apartments provided for them on the second floor of the palace. The Comte de Damas,[46] who had gone ahead of the Royal Family to make sure everything was in order for their arrival, wrote to a friend in Edinburgh that the apartments allocated to the Bourbons had wonderful views over the city: they could see the river and the nearby mountains. Prague itself was a beautiful if not modern city (unlike the New Town of Edinburgh), full of gothic towers dirty with age and adorned with statues, though with Russian or Slavic features. Soldiers lined the corridors, and at the entrance to Charles X's apartments two grenadiers in white Bourbon colours kept guard. The Duchesse d'Angoulême found everything to her satisfaction and wrote to her secretary Charlet that 'the establishment is good'.

Prague, by Eduard Gurk, c1838

The Marquis de Villeneuve recalled his first visit to the family in June 1835, and his memoirs remarked that the Duchesse d'Angoulême took comfort from the evident status of her maternal family and wandered with evident pleasure through the reminders of Habsburg Lorraine triumphs. They seemed to help her to assuage the bitterness of exile. She also enjoyed the relative proximity of Prague to Vienna and her family there. The family was treated outwardly with respect and deference by the local officialdom, but the Marquis de Villeneuve sensed an underlying 'shadow of disdain'. His observations of her character are useful. He says that, 'her noble spirit was more suited to family affection than to political combination. Her intelligence was instinctive rather than reasoning. In some respects she lacked breadth of judgement. She gave small heed to a well-balanced summary of opinions; she would silently make her decision, and stick to it through thick and thin.' The accommodation was nevertheless certainly much more congenial than that in Scotland where the Princess had suffered so badly with rheumatic complaints. The Czech climate was drier and more pleasant. The men of the family, however, did not fare so well. Charles X suffered badly with gout in Prague, and the Duc d'Angoulême lost weight to such an extent that his clothes no longer fitted him.

Life in the Palace in Prague was highly ordered and regimented. The Marquis de Villeneuve, to whose daughter Marie Thérèse was godmother, described it as: '*Tout était réglé et ordonné comme à Paris*'.[47] The dictates of etiquette governed every aspect of daily life for the Royal Family. Many of their supporters had left them to return to their homes in France, but enough courtiers remained to satisfy the demands of protocol. Some of their attendants chose to commute between Paris and Prague, dividing their time between the two cities to enable them to savour the pleasures of Paris while still fulfilling their duties to the Bourbons. The family were accompanied in Prague by Monseigneur Latil, the Duc de Gramont, Comte de Montbel, and Comte de Saint-Chamand (the Prince's governor), Madame d'Agoult and Madame de Gontaut, the children's governess. The Marquis de Villeneuve described Madame de Gontaut (who was incidentally his aunt) as brave, devoted to her duties and very able.[48]

Also with them in Prague was Louis XVIII's former favourite the Duc de Blacas, whose speciality was the maintenance of etiquette within the court in exile. We have a description of him from the Marquis de Villeneuve. Rich and decisive, he dominated the life of the Court and, so it seems, the Bourbons themselves. He was the paymaster and gatekeeper of the Court and governed everyday life with a strict eye for the application of etiquette. To obtain an audience with the family it was necessary to write to him and then wait for a response. He was firmly of the view that Charles X was King and would in due course be succeeded by his son. A man of cultivated tastes, a lover of the arts and a collector of antiquities, he had made the choice at some personal cost to himself to serve the Bourbons rather than live in great comfort on his estates in Provence and in his town house in Paris. He was proud of the loyalty he had shown to the Bourbons over their years of exile. He created a cordon around the King and guarded access to him, thus creating a power base. A man of few words, he had a natural gravitas if a rather cold and proud manner. He was not always respectful of his Royal masters, saying to the Marquis de Villeneuve that he was forced to listen to the inane chatter of Charles X. The courtiers were disunited, grouped in factions and fought viciously among themselves for the favour and notice of their Royal masters. They can hardly have been comfortable companions for Marie Thérèse and her family, but then perhaps they knew nothing different. Simon Winder's book *Danubia* describes the Court in exile as 'being an angry and rather mad group waiting for the call to return, thronged by needy toadies and decayed snobs while real life in France continued without them'.

In exile, the Bourbons became obsessed by time and punctuality; each day was regulated by the numerous clocks in the palace and their 'deafening volley' of chimes. Louis Antoine seems to have learned this behaviour from the time he shared with Louis XVIII. The Marquis de Villeneuve wrote, 'An excess of exactitude occupied too great a place in their thoughts and actions.' The Royal Family dined together: the meal presided over by Charles X, flanked at the table by his son and daughter-in-law.[49] M. de Blacas sat opposite the Royal Family and was able to observe three generations of Bourbon monarchs. A dozen black-clad servants stood behind their chairs and served the food. The atmosphere when the Marquis de Villeneuve dined with the family was affectionate and polite, even homely within the Royal Family. He observed that Charles X himself served the *fricassée du poulet* to his fellow diners. It was a mixture of simplicity and grandeur. Dinner-table conversation was distinctly limited, focusing on the weather and the Duchesse d'Angoulême's health. They had long ago run out of more stimulating conversation. Her husband spoke little: perhaps stopping eating to discuss with Monseigneur Latil the meaning and interpretation of the gospel reading of the day. Meals lasted about an hour, then the King would lead his family and their guests into the salon where they would read the newspapers. At least the views over Prague from the salon were magnificent and provided some topics of conversation. The Marquis de Villeneuve recalls the Duchesse d'Angoulême commenting on how the river iced over in winter and pointing out the summer sun shining on the banks of the Danube. She also had conversation with him about Jules de Polignac and was less than complimentary, feeling that he had not recognised his many failings. Her husband reminded her of Polignac's loyalty and sufferings, including imprisonment in the Bourbon cause.

Etiquette required that all the men remained standing in the presence of the King. When he left, the male courtiers could rest briefly and be seated until the King returned to the room and they would have to be upstanding once again. On entering the King's presence a woman was required to wait at the doorway until her presence was noted by the King, at which point she was required to bow three times before entering the room. The King's great deafness could mean that her wait was long if he was alone in the room and there was no one to draw her presence to his attention. At eight o'clock in the evening the King would start to play cards, joined by the Duc d'Angoulême and Monseigneur Latil; a fourth player would be invited to join them. The Duchesse d'Angoulême sat in the window working on a piece of needlework or knitting, except if she were joined by her nephew and niece in which case she would play games of lotto, casino or whist for low stakes with the young people for their amusement. The Duc de Bordeaux enjoyed drawing and spent his time sketching in the corner of the room. At nine o'clock the evening's entertainment, such as it was, stopped. By this time Marie Thérèse was yawning and looking forward to her bed. The Duchesse d'Angoulême retired early so that she could be awake the next morning in time to get up at 4 a.m.[50] to attend the first Mass of the day. Mademoiselle bade her grandfather an affectionate goodnight. At the door of the room she curtseyed deeply before her grandfather and the rest of the party before retiring for the night. Charles X wished his family and courtiers a good night as they bowed before him. Another day of exile had passed in Prague.

The monument to the visit of Marie Thérèse to Carlsbad.
Picture by David Ingram, September 2014

On 20 May 1833 the Duchesse d'Angoulême accompanied by the fourteen-year-old Mademoiselle Louise travelled to Carlsbad,[51] some 80 miles west of Prague, to take the waters for her health. Carlsbad is situated in a valley surrounded by wooded hills. Torrents of hot water gush from the ground feeding many drinking fountains of different temperatures. It was a fashionable spa resort and cultural centre for the European nobility and others. Beethoven and Goethe enjoyed its delights, as did Peter the Great and other Romanovs. Founded in the mid fourteenth century by the Holy Roman Emperor Charles IV, the baths of Carlsbad had been rebuilt in 1762 by the Duchesse d'Angoulême's grandmother. The Empress Maria Theresa had also sponsored the bell-towers housing the bells that summoned her granddaughter to her prayers. According to local sources, the Princesses stayed in the 'Gottes Auge' or God's Eye lodgings on the site of the current Grand Hotel Pupp, which had been occupied by Beethoven in 1812. Marie Thérèse, travelling under the guise of La Comtesse de Marnes, was able to move freely among the other people taking the waters, which she must have found comforting. Anonymously dressed, the exiled Dauphine was just one more middle-aged woman up early in the morning trying to cure her aches and pains at the Muhlenbad baths. The Vicomte de Châteaubriand describes her as being 'dressed in a shabby robe of grey silk; round her shoulders hung a worn-out shawl and she had an old hat on her head. She looked as though she had patched her clothes together like her mother in the Conciergerie.'

Meanwhile the Duchesse de Berry had landed on French soil near Marseille on 29 April 1832 with a small group of supporters. Here Marie Caroline had declared herself 'Regent' for her son Henri V, and put herself at the centre of a plot to murder the new King and his family. On 3 May, at a Légitimist demonstration attended by only 60 people at the Hotel de Ville in Marseille, the white flag of the Bourbons was raised; but the demonstration was easily broken up by a regiment of soldiers loyal to the new Orléanist regime, and the crowd which had gathered to support the Duchesse de Berry's cause was quickly dispersed. Some of the Duchesse de Berry's adherents were arrested. Dressed in male peasant gear, Marie Caroline escaped her would-be captors and started to walk towards the Vendée, the region of western France south of Brittany traditionally loyal to the Bourbon cause and the Roman Catholic Church. She was still committed to drumming up support for her son's cause. She took refuge on 17 May with her husband's daughter by Amy Brown, the Comtesse de Charette, and her husband. The Comte de Charette was one of the very keen Vendéan supporters of the Légitimist cause. This would certainly indicate that Marie Caroline had fulfilled her promise to her dying husband that she would treat his daughters as her own and that the relationship with her step daughter was warm and trusting.

The feisty Duchesse de Berry remained at large in rural France during the summer 1832, operating under the pseudonym of 'Petit Pierre'; she was finally betrayed for money by a former supporter, Simon Deutz.[52] She was found concealed with a number of other people in a fireplace and literally smoked out from her hiding place, her dress catching on fire. The Duchesse de Berry was taken into custody, captured by government agents on 7 November 1832 after nearly six months at liberty, thereby causing embarrassment for the government and her Royal relatives in Paris, Edinburgh, Naples, Vienna and Madrid. All were outraged by her undignified and unprincess-like conduct. Her normal kindly and affectionate aunt, Louis Philippe's dignified Queen Marie Amélie, was so shocked and dismayed by her niece's conduct that she refused to correspond with her. She was taken to the castle at Nantes and from there to the Citadel at Blaye[53] near Bordeaux. Marie Caroline was treated with the deference due to her rank and connections. She was after all the niece of the King and Queen of the French and a half-sister of the Queen of Spain.[54] She was housed comfortably and provided with fresh clothes and books but allowed no visitors. Her lady-in-waiting, the Comtesse de Hautbois, was however permitted to accompany her in her imprisonment. A number of gallant gentlemen, including the Duc de Fitzjames, offered themselves as hostages in exchange for the Princess. Their offers were refused by the French government.

Marie Caroline's time since she had left Scotland had however not been entirely unproductive. It was found that she was pregnant. Something had to be done and quickly to save face. The Légitimist cause in the form of Madame du Cayla, Louis XVIII's former favourite, rallied round and brokered an arranged marriage with Hector Charles, Count Lucchesi-Palli,[55] an Italian nobleman some years the Duchesse de Berry's junior. He and Marie Caroline had become friendly while she was in Rome. He was prepared to assert that he and Marie Caroline had been married in secret during her brief sojourn in Italy and that he was her husband and the father of the child she was carrying. The Duchesse d'Angoulême wrote to Emperor Francis I of Austria to try to engage his aid in obtaining the release of her sister-in-law by his putting pressure on the French government. Marie Thérèse wrote to Marie Caroline expressing her concern about her plight and sending news of the children, Henri and Marie Louise. She prayed fervently for her and sent her loving good wishes.

Marie Thérèse was deeply perturbed by the news from France. The government of Louis Philippe made public a letter from Marie Caroline to her jailer General Bugeaud, dated 22 February 1833, in which she declared that she had been secretly married during her stay in Italy and that her pregnancy was the result of that marriage. She claimed that she had been obliged by circumstances to keep her marriage secret, but now felt it appropriate to make it public. Whatever the reality of the situation, it was deeply convenient for the Princess and her family and the letter should save something of her reputation. It is much more likely that the father of her child was in fact Achille Guibourg, the handsome young lawyer and passionate supporter of the Légitimist cause who had shared her hiding place in Nantes during the hot summer of 1832.

Marie Thérèse and her husband, in particular, were deeply shocked and mortified by the Duchesse de Berry's undignified actions. The exiled family was not even aware of the identity of her new husband. Marie Thérèse at first disowned her sister-in-law, humiliated by her conduct and no longer able to regard her as being a member of the Bourbon family. The King said that he would only receive his former daughter-in-law if he had evidence of her second marriage. At last a friendly priest was persuaded to sign a marriage certificate back dated to December 1831. The disgraced Princess gave birth to her daughter Anna Rosalia[56] on 10 May 1833 and was then deported from France to Naples to join her new husband and to retire from public life. The possibility of another Légitimist Restoration would have to wait. Marie Caroline's behaviour confirmed and strengthened Marie Thérèse's view that Marie Caroline had no understanding of her role as a Bourbon princess and that as the mother of the would-be King of France she should behave with utmost respectability and decorum. Marie Caroline's impulsive and reckless action had not helped her son's cause. From now on, with a new family, she was largely uninvolved in Henri and Louise's day-to-day lives and upbringing. In her absence the direction and supervision of their education and upbringing passed to the Dauphine, her husband and father-in-law and the tutors appointed by them. Shocked as Marie Thérèse was by her cousin's unworthy behaviour and actions, she did appeal to Charles X for his clemency, begging that he at least receive the déclassé former Duchesse de Berry and allow her occasionally to visit her two elder children. Perhaps because Marie Thérèse had herself shown courage and energy so far from the normal feminine role during the defence of Bordeaux in 1814, she had a glimmer of understanding of Marie Caroline's desire to be active and do something dynamic to restore her family to their throne, however hair-brained the scheme had turned out to be.

While in Carlsbad, Marie Thérèse had received a visit from her long-time admirer the Vicomte de Châteaubriand. He had written warmly about her at the time of the First Restoration. He brought with him letters from the imprisoned Marie Caroline, and she welcomed him warmly. He presented to the Duchesse d'Angoulême the letters which Marie Caroline had given into his safekeeping. Marie Thérèse was clearly moved by the events of the day and placed the letters on the sofa beside her. She asked the Vicomte de Châteaubriand to sit down and continued with her sewing. Marie Thérèse enquired kindly after him. He noted that she had started to cry and observed that she wiped the tears from her eyes with the back of her hand as might a child. Eventually the Duchesse d'Angoulême enquired as to the health and welfare of her imprisoned sister-in-law. She was visibly affected by her plight and obviously felt sympathy for her sufferings. The Vicomte reported that the Duchesse de Berry had put her children under the protection of Marie Thérèse during her imprisonment. She found it a great comfort that the young Duc de Bordeaux had a second mother in his 'excellent aunt' and guardian. In correspondence with the Duchesse d'Angoulême, Marie Caroline made reference to her sufferings as a prisoner and said, 'your example will teach me to suffer with patience'.[57] During this conversation, Marie Thérèse was referred to as '*Votre Majesté*', a clear reference to the minutes in late July 1830 when her husband had briefly been King of France and she its Queen. The Duchesse d'Angoulême was clearly pleased to be referred to in this way, although also slightly embarrassed by it.

The correspondence between Marie Caroline and Marie Thérèse was at this time clandestine. The Duchesse d'Angoulême must have recalled the time when she and Madame Élisabeth during their captivity in the Temple had received letters written in lemon juice and revealed their contents by exposing them to heat. The Duchesse d'Angoulême wrote in this way and Marie Caroline was also clearly privy to this technique. Marie

Thérèse held a flame to the apparently banal letter from Marie Caroline to reveal her further words. Marie Caroline begged her to care for both her children and especially placed the young prince under her supervision. Marie Thérèse promised to look after the young Duc de Bordeaux, saying how much she loved her nephew and that he was healthy and strong, although perhaps a little nervous in temperament. The Vicomte and the Duchesse d'Angoulême spent two hours together in conversation. This he felt was an unusual honour.

The Vicomte was invited to return later in the day and joined the Princess for what he describes as a poor and meagre meal eaten at three in the afternoon. They were joined by the Comtesse Esterhazy, Marie Thérèse's girlhood friend from her days at the Court of Vienna in the late 1790s; the Comtesse's daughter, Madame d'Agoult; Monsieur O'Hegerthy,[58] Marie Thérèse's riding instructor; and Monsieur de Trogoff. The meal was eaten in the sitting room as the Duchesse d'Angoulême did not have a separate dining room. He remarks that the Duchesse d'Angoulême spent her day observing from her sofa vantage point the doings of her fellow takers of the spa waters, all of whom she appeared to know and of whose daily comings and goings she was fully aware. She spent her time at her embroidery and enjoyed a number of stories told by Monsieur Trogoff. The Vicomte de Châteaubriand was amused that this Princess who had seen and participated in so many elaborate ceremonies and suffered so much should spend her days in this parochial and very ordinary way. At five o'clock the Princess went for a drive in her carriage in order to get some fresh air. In the evening, a number of those also taking the waters joined her for supper. Although the Princess addressed a few words to each, in order to ensure that she had been polite and kind, she soon reverted to her usual silence, the Vicomte de Châteaubriand reported. He noted the strong resemblance that the Princess had to her late father Louis XVI, especially in profile, which particularly reminded Châteaubriand of the portraits of Louis XVI at his execution.

The Vicomte de Châteaubriand left Carlsbad on 1 June 1833, carrying a letter from the Duchesse d'Angoulême to Marie Caroline in France. To avoid possible exposure if the letter was captured by the French authorities, Châteaubriand copied out the letter in his own handwriting on his return to France, so that it could be passed off as being from him. Marie Thérèse had had experience of her letters falling into the wrong hands. For example, Louis XVIII had left her letters to him at the Tuileries Palace on fleeing Paris in 1815, only for them to be found and given to Napoleon Bonaparte. Some of her correspondence with her husband had been captured during the Hundred Days and intimate details of her relationship with him had been published. She did not enjoy such publicity and was keen to avoid the possibility of it happening again. The Vicomte de Châteaubriand, whose own style could be florid in the extreme, felt that the letter lacked warmth; but the wording feels entirely appropriate and fitting in the circumstances. The letter was dated 31 May 1833 and marked 'Carlsbad' and signed 'M-T':

> I feel a deep contentment, my dear sister, to receive your news at first hand. You fill my thoughts. You may always rely on my constant concern for you and especially for your dear children, who are more precious to me than ever. I am not yet able to carry out your requests in respect of your family as I am forced by my ill health to come here to take the waters. I will acquit myself of them as soon as I return among them, and please believe me that we, they and I, will always share the same feelings about everything. Farewell my dear sister, I embrace kiss you tenderly.

The Vicomte de Châteaubriand noted during his conversation with Marie Thérèse that the young Duc de Bordeaux would in September 1833 celebrate his thirteenth birthday and thereby achieve his royal majority. The Vicomte already regarded him as the King, taking the view that Charles X and Louis XIX had given up their rights to the throne by virtue of their abdications in 1830.

The waters of Carlsbad apparently did little to cure Marie Thérèse and relieve the pain she felt in her side. She returned to Carlsbad for several more cures of drinking the hot waters during the period 1833-6. Her visits to the spa town were commemorated by the local authorities with the construction of a monument recounting the story of her life, which was unveiled in her presence on 21 June 1834. After her first visit in 1833, she rejoined Charles X at the spa town of Teplice or Teplitz some 50 miles from Prague, where he was treating his gout. As the summer heat intensified, the Royal Family left the city and moved out to the countryside beyond Prague and settled there for the summer on a farm. They were based near to a property that was part of the estate of the Duchy of Lucca – at this time being governed by Marie Louise, Napoleon's second wife. At other times the Bourbons enjoyed the hospitality of the émigré Rohan[59] family at their estate of Sychrov to the north-east of Prague, which they had purchased in 1820. The Rohan family had opted not to return to France at the time of the Napoleonic amnesty and '*toutes ses resources étaient mises à la disposition de la famille royale de France*'.[60] They were loyal servants of the Bourbon Légitimist cause.

There was pressure for the celebration of the Comte de Chambord's thirteenth birthday. There was a call from the Légitimists of France for the occasion of the Duc de Bordeaux's coming of age to be marked by ceremonial. This, it was felt, would help to remind the people of France that there was a very real alternative to Louis Philippe and his branch of the Bourbons. Such events would also help to bolster the spirits and commitment of the Légitimist supporters. Marie Thérèse was having none of this.

The Duchesse d'Angoulême made it very clear to her secretary Baron Charlet that there would be no public ceremonial marking the Duc de Bordeaux attaining his Royal majority. It was enough to her mind that the law and right were on the side of the exiled Bourbons. They needed no elaborate ceremonial to assert the right of her nephew to the throne of France; to her it was self-evident. The Marie Caroline affair, which had caused them so much embarrassment, must also have fed her desire to keep a low profile. Marie Thérèse had never been one for spin or public relations gestures, and was not about to change. In particular, the Royal Family did not want an influx of French people coming to Prague to disturb their peace and quiet and no doubt bring problems with them. The family may have recalled the proclivity of the French émigré community to make themselves unpopular with those who gave them refuge. They wanted to do nothing to provoke or annoy the Emperor of Austria who had provided them with a comfortable place of exile. Charles X went one better and asked the Austrian Emperor to deny passports to French men and women (or have them stopped by the guards at the borders) if their sole wish was to see the Bourbon Prince in Prague. As if the Bourbons really knew how to win friends and influence people. They might well be regarded as their own political worst enemies.

Adversity did not lead to unity in the Légitimist camp. The divisions may be characterised as Villeneuve versus Walsch.[61] The Marquis de Villeneuve believed that the abdications of Charles X and Louis Antoine (or Louis XIX as he thought) were invalid. He argued that royalty and the throne could not be given up unilaterally and that therefore nothing had changed. To his thinking they continued to be King and heir apparent respectively.[62] To support his argument, the Marquis de Villeneuve put forward the scenario that if Marie Thérèse should predecease her husband and he remarry and (unlikely given his sexual history) have a son, that that child would stand before the Duc de Bordeaux in the line of succession. Vicomte Walsch took the contrary view that the abdications had been effective and lawful and that the Duc de Bordeaux was now the King. This approach to the succession also raised the possibility of his mother the Duchesse de Berry as an influence in her son's life son as a possible Regent. This was not a prospect that caused Marie Thérèse and her family any joy. Not surprisingly, Marie Caroline was of the view that her son was King in law and that action should be taken to make him King in fact. Charles X and the Duc and Duchesse d'Angoulême preferred the Marquis' approach that the abdications were null and void. They were rather offended that the other faction of the Légitimist camp was apparently so happy to pass over the rights to the throne of France of the older Bourbon princes. These internal divisions and controversies certainly did not help the position of Marie Thérèse's family in France, which was itself divided between Republicans, Royalists of various types, and those who supported the

Bonapartist cause. In addition there were many who were indifferent to whosoever ruled but wanted to live in peace, prosperity and order.

Despite all discouragements, a few hardy Légitimist supporters made their way to Prague. Led by Vicomte Walsch they shared his view regarding the young King Henri V. Finding the family out of town for the summer, they followed them to their summer retreat. They were duly refused permission to see the Royal Family. Charles X retired to his bed claiming to have a bad fever. Marie Thérèse locked herself in her room and refused to come out until they had gone. Tired and thirsty French visitors were refused even a glass of water, let alone any food. They had to retreat to an inn nearby to toast the health of their Prince. They celebrated his coming of age in Prague with a banquet at which the young King was present, but in effigy only.[63] Despite all their protests the family did take part in a small private ceremony to commemorate the majority of Henri, designed and organised by the Duc de Blacas. The young putative Henri V wore a green suit and a white ruff in the style of his ancestor and namesake Henri IV.[64] Having listened to an address by Vicomte Walsch, he swore to make himself worthy of the great role to which his birth had called him. The young Duc de Bordeaux was also dubbed a knight. The Vicomte de Nogent presented the prince with a pair of golden spurs and M. de May gave him a sword.

The Royal Family left their summer home. The Duc d'Angoulême returned to Prague and the Hradschin Palace. He refused to have anything to do with 'that woman' whom he must have felt had betrayed and disgraced her family. He said of her '*ne me parlez point*'.[65] He did not relent even when it was pointed out to him by the Marquis de Villeneuve that she was the mother of the future King. Meanwhile his wife, father and nephew and niece travelled on to Styria in Austria to meet up with the Duchesse de Berry, now the Comtesse de Lucchese-Palli, and her new husband and baby. The rest of the family met up in the town of Leoben at the Hôtel de l'Empereur. The Duc de Bordeaux and his sister eagerly awaited the arrival of the mother he had not seen since she had left Edinburgh for her disastrous Vendée adventure.

The family reunion took place on 13 October 1833. Charles X, as an expression of his disapproval of her conduct, would not allow the disgraced Princess to kiss his hand but politely shook hands with her new husband. Marie Caroline was overwhelmed with delight at seeing her children and kissed them passionately. At first she was unable to speak. She quickly regained her voice, crying and exclaiming to such effect that the Duchesse d'Angoulême had to order the windows to be closed lest her sister-in-law allow their family quarrels and private conversations be heard on the street by the townspeople. The Duchesse de Berry attacked her sister-in-law and the adoptive mother of her children in hectoring tones; 'the proud and unfortunate Dauphine was reduced to floods of tears'.[66]

Her husband, on hearing what had happened, was deeply aggrieved on her behalf, and the old King was (yet again) shocked by the Duchesse de Berry and her unruly conduct. The Edinburgh papers were speculating as to the reception Marie Caroline would get from her family. They contrasted her waywardness with the virtue of the Duchesse d'Angoulême and suggested that she would not put up with any nonsense from her young sister-in-law. The Duchesse de Dino wrote in her diary for October 23 1833:

> Charles X himself took his grandchildren to their mother at (*sic*) Leoban[67] with the precise object of preventing the Duchesse de Berry from coming to Prague; from Leoban[68] it is said she will return to Italy. Monsieur le Dauphin and Madame la Dauphine refused to go...[69] They say that Charles X is much broken and the Dauphine is aged, and very thin and nervous, always in tears. Certainly, however, strong her character may be, her misfortunes have been such as to break the highest courage and the most masculine spirit. Beyond doubt she has been more persecuted by destiny than any character in history.

The perception of the Duchesse de Dino was that 'M de Blacas is in supreme command of the little court and is more opposed than anyone to the proposal'. The arbiter of etiquette of the Court in exile as well as its paymaster, the Duc de Blacas, did not want the distracting and often disruptive presence of the former Duchesse de Berry robbing it of whatever dignity and gravitas it had managed to maintain. He was equally ruthless in getting rid of courtiers who did not share his views or to whom he took a dislike, so la Villate, the Duc and Duchesse de Guiche and Joachim Barande were dismissed in this way. The Duc and Duchesse d'Angoulême put up no opposition to their departures. They seem to have been rather in thrall to him and were passive in the face of the dominant personality and financial might of Blacas.

The King made it clear to the widow of his younger son that he could not receive her at his Court. Some accounts suggest that the Duc and Duchesse d'Angoulême had presented him with an ultimatum saying that they would quit the court in exile if Marie Caroline was allowed to rejoin it. In any event, Charles X felt he had no choice but to reject her and her new husband. Other accounts suggest that Charles X took the initiative and would not receive Marie Caroline back into the Court in exile, whatever the views of the Dauphin and Dauphine. In any event, his former daughter-in-law threw herself on her knees before him, begging to be reconciled to him and was told firmly to shut up as his mind was made up. Marie Caroline threatened to go to the newspapers and tell them that the Royal Family wanted to separate her from her adolescent son. The noisy arguments went on for several days and were pursued from room to room.

She upbraided Marie Thérèse in the harshest terms, apparently without giving any credence to or respect for her good qualities, her devotion to the children or her own many sufferings. Recognising how influential the Dauphine was within the family, Marie Caroline deeply resented this and her own lack of political and family clout, even though she was the mother of the heir to the throne and had at least tried to promote the interests of her son. The Duchesse d'Angoulême asserted that Charles X preferred her and her husband to the mother of his grandson and heir, and that their interests would not be sacrificed to hers. By the evening of the next day things had calmed a little and Marie Caroline came to the realisation that the others no longer regarded her as a member of the Bourbon family or as a French Princess. Her failed attempt to regain the throne for her son, her embarrassing pregnancy and hasty second marriage had fundamentally altered her standing within the Bourbon family and Court.[70] Marie Caroline was usually absent from the children's lives. Their upbringing was left to Charles X, Marie Thérèse and her husband, with whom the children lived.

Marie Thérèse was very instrumental in maintaining the stance against her cousin. The Marquis de Villeneuve said of Madame de Berry that between her and her French relatives there was '*un contraste absolu en opinions, en sentiments, and et en actions*'.[71] One can perhaps blame Marie Thérèse for her rather narrow view and rigidity, but she had spent her entire life trying to maintain the dignity of her house. She had made sacrifices in doing so; she could not change now. Charles X promised that Marie Caroline would be able to visit the Court in Prague the following year, when it was to be hoped that the scandal of her hasty marriage and prison baby would have somewhat died down. Marie Caroline decided to depart for her new life in Italy. Sad to say, her baby died, apparently to its mother's great relief at this time. The three days spent in the company of Marie Caroline had badly affected Marie Thérèse's nerves. Normally the Bourbon court was noticeable for its quietness and order. Marie Caroline destroyed this. For the Dauphine and her husband, their nephew and niece, Henri and Louise, were however a source of great personal joy and pleasure as well as of dynastic hope.[72] Marie Thérèse travelled slowly back to Prague. She was happy once more to be alone and left in peace and quiet without the constraints and demands of hordes of visitors.

Marie Thérèse devoted herself to the education and Royal upbringing of her nephew. Charles X had selected two members of the Jesuit order, Pères Druilhet and Deplace, to undertake the education of his grandson. This choice was fiercely opposed by French Légitimists who threatened to throw the priests into the River Moldau.[73] They enrolled the Emperor of Austria in support of their campaign to get rid of the Jesuits. Charles X was astonished by the negative response to his plans for the heir's education. The very pro-Jesuit Baron de Damas had resigned as the Prince's governor in 1833 and returned to live in France to promote good works and write his memoirs. The Comte de Saint-Chamand was briefly the Prince's governor. In August 1834, Charles X agreed that the Jesuits should be replaced as the Prince's tutors. Their places would be taken by the aged, paralysed, but highly respected preacher, academic and government minister, Bishop of Hermopolis, Mgr Frayssinous[74] who was Marie Thérèse's father confessor. As his assistant, there was the young, lively and pleasant Abbé Trébuquet. His many virtues and talents were a real boon to the Household. It was a Bourbon characteristic to have a fierce if short-lived temper. The Prince had a quick temper and the Abbé was able to overcome it. The Abbé Trébuquet proved himself capable of educating Henri well in spiritual and moral matters, as well as the academic subjects required. The Comte d'Hautpol would be the Prince's governor. The Duc de Bordeaux did have some youthful companions, including the nephew of his one-time governor the Comte de Saint-Chamand, who joined him for his recreations. The Duchesse d'Angoulême appears to have supported the dismissal of the Jesuits. It would also seem that Marie Thérèse, usually so strict in matters of conduct, indulged and spoiled her nephew who had inherited some of the wilful and volatile temperaments of both his parents. There is a story that in an exhibition of temper, he seized his shy and retiring mathematics tutor by the collar and threw him against a door. Fully aware of the sexually passionate nature of both his parents, Marie Thérèse is said to have refused the adolescent Henri permission to visit neighbouring noble families. She feared that he would meet unsuitable young women whilst he was out and about and might form inappropriate liaisons.

General Hautpoul's time as tutor to the Légitimist heir to the throne was short-lived. He was suspected of the twin transgressions of plotting with Marie Caroline and supporting liberalism, neither of which was acceptable to his employers. He decided to return to live in France. Madame de Berry wrote with increasing sadness of her life, citing her former sister-in-law as the source of many of her woes. Marie Caroline had settled herself and her new family a short distance from Prague at the Hradschin Palace. Her proximity was a cause of continual hurt and embarrassment to the Bourbons. During the summer of 1834 she required that her two elder children were constantly with her, disturbing the peace of her family and acting as a disruptive influence on the behaviour of the young people as Marie Thérèse saw it. By November 1834, Marie Thérèse was writing to her secretary Charlet that the presence of her sister-in-law was more upsetting than ever. Marie Caroline refused to leave Prague and its environs, even though she knew her family wished her gone. Despite his age, the King being more than 70 years old, Marie Caroline continued to heap troubles on her father-in-law. The devotion of her political supporters and followers lessened over time. Her inappropriate behaviour caused them embarrassment and they became objects of ridicule to their political opponents. Despite the disruptions of their lives, there were some pleasures and compensations for Marie Thérèse and the family. On 18 November 1834, Talleyrand[75] wrote to Madame Adélaïde of the Bourbons 'with reference to Charles X and Madame la Dauphine, who often comes to Vienna and who there receives all the honours due to her rank, her misfortunes and her near relationship to the Imperial family. In Austria they are Princes almost pretenders.'

In a shock move in 1834, Madame de Gontaut was dismissed from her post as governess to the young Princess, Louise d'Artois. She had been with the Princess since she was a baby, and the infant was very attached to her. But Madame de Gontaut had become too involved in Royalist factional infighting. Like many people, she felt that the Jesuits were too influential in the education of the Duc de Bordeaux and had helped to persuade the King and the Duc and Duchesse d'Angoulême to have his Jesuit tutors dismissed. It was the word on the streets of Paris that the would-be King of France was being brought up as a monk. It was said that he was receiving a narrow religious education, which would not endear him to many of the French people or fit him to rule. As the Marquis de Villeneuve put it, the same mistakes were being made in Prague as had previously been made in Paris. By contrast, the sons of the usurper Louis Philippe were being educated at the public Collège Henri IV in Paris with the sons of his subjects. The reality was that the contact between the Princes and their classmates was very limited, but it had been a clever propaganda coup by the Orléans branch of the family.

Madame de Gontaut's more liberal views brought her into conflict with the hard-line Duc de Blacas. She passionately wanted the Duc de Bordeaux to be King and regarded him as being so following the abdications of his grandfather and uncle. She was clearly of the view that the older Bourbons (Charles X and Louis XIX) should be passed over in favour of the fresh young Henri. Her views were in sharp contrast to those of the Duc de Blacas. She was loved and respected by the young Prince, who had known her all his life. Her nephew, the Marquis de Villeneuve, understood (as did the Duchesse de Dino) that the Duchesse de Gontaut's correspondence with her daughter was intercepted. In her correspondence, she advocated marriages which would unify the senior and junior branches of the Bourbon family. In other words she wanted her charges to marry their Orléans cousins and unite the family and their claims to the French throne. Charles X showed the intercepted letter to Marie Thérèse. She, in turn, took it to Madame de Gontaut and challenged her with its contents. Madame de Gontaut was confident of her position and the affection in which she was held by the King; she suggested that, in reversal of the normal order of things, she and Marie Thérèse should go to see the King. During the discussion that followed, Madame de Gontaut, proud and eloquent, defended her position, saying with force that arrogant and incompetent ministers (yes, you, Blacas) would imperil the future of the monarchy. Such presumption could not be forgiven. Despite all her service and that of her family to the Bourbons, she was dismissed on the spot. Within days she was ejected from Hradschin Castle. She never saw Charles X again. The Bourbons were uncompromising in dealing with servants who displeased them. Thus was she brutally separated from her charges, Henri and Louise. Madame de Dino reported this in her diary:

> London, May 13, 1834. Charles X said to Madame de Gontaut on April 25: 'Louise's education is finished. I should be glad if you would go the day after to-morrow — the 27th.' Mademoiselle who is much attached to Madame de Gontaut was in despair. The Duchesse de Gontaut behaved with great courage, and spent the 26th in vain attempts to console Mademoiselle, whose new governess is said to be, provisionally, the Vicomtesse d'Agoult. This is to replace a clever woman by a Saint. All this happened before the Duchesse de Berry arrived; she did not get back till May 7.[76]

When the Marquis de Villeneuve visited Prague in 1835, it was clear that Louise was still missing her former governess. As he was leaving Prague to return to France, she gave him a lock of her hair asking him to take it to Madame de Gontaut with a message saying, '*Souvenir à la Duchesse de Gontaut*'. He was disappointed by the lack of energy and determination shown by Charles X and his son to regain their throne.

The year 1836 was a difficult one for Marie Thérèse and her family. The Bourbons were asked to move from the Hradschin Palace in Prague, where they had settled on their arrival from Scotland. The Emperor Francis I of Austria[77] had died the previous year and his son Ferdinand I[78] succeeded him as Emperor of Austria and King of Bohemia.[79] The coronation of the new King of Bohemia was to take place in Prague and he needed a lot of accommodation to house his entourage. The Hradschin Castle Palace is absolutely vast, but apparently not large enough to house both the new Austrian Emperor and his Court and the French Court in exile. Perhaps the new Emperor simply did not want his rather sad and, certainly as monarchs, very unsuccessful French cousins spoiling his coronation celebrations and drawing attention to the failures of Royal rule. Marie Thérèse and her family were back on the road once again in search of a comfortable and settled home. Marie Thérèse was also personally distressed at the death of her cousin Francis, whom she had known since the years she spent with the Habsburg family on her departure from imprisonment in the Temple. He had, on the whole, been a kind and generous benefactor over the years. It was also a break in the close connection with her mother's family at the highest political level. The new

Emperor was only a second cousin. The Bourbons and their attendants headed for the small town of Goritz, situated within the Austrian Empire on the border of modern-day Slovenia and the extreme north-eastern border of Italy, between the Adriatic and the Alps, as the Marquis de Villeneuve expressed it.

Cholera raged throughout Europe in the mid-1830s[80] and was a big factor in deciding where the Royal Family would locate themselves. Not surprisingly, they tried hard to avoid infected areas, though disease spread fast. Accurate information on which towns were affected was hard to come by. As was her usual custom, in June Marie Thérèse, accompanied by her niece Louise, travelled to Carlsbad for her visit to the spa and rest cure. From the beginning of her stay in Carlsbad, Marie Thérèse was badly affected by a painful skin infection on her head. Her husband and Doctor Bougon travelled to Carlsbad to be with her and care for her. She spent some time convalescing from the attack of cellutis[81] in Bad Ischl,[82] leaving for nearby Salzburg in mid-July. Here she heard that cholera had reached Trieste and had to change her travel plans. More distressing news followed. Marie Thérèse and her niece heard that the Duc de Bordeaux, to whom they were both devoted, had been struck down with a brain fever while staying at Budweiss. There was a horse-drawn tramway which gave easy communications between Linz and Budweiss, built during 1825-32. The Royal Family may well have used it as they travelled around the Habsburg lands. The Duchesse d'Angoulême and Mademoiselle hurried to be with Henri and nurse him.

The young Prince was settled at the Hotel des Trois Coqs in Budweiss, some 80 miles from Vienna. His grandfather was absolutely beside himself with anxiety. Doctor Bougon was again on hand to provide medical care for the boy. Fortunately, by the time the Princesses reached the hotel, Henri was well on his way to recovery. Several nasal bleedings seemed to have relieved the pressure. The Duchesse d'Angoulême wrote on 4 August to her secretary that her nephew was much better. The family decided to go and stay in the countryside near Kirchberg, about 20 miles from Vienna, until the autumn. This was partly to aid Henri's convalescence and partly to avoid the cholera epidemic, which was approaching that area of Austria. They would then travel on to Goritz when they felt it was safe to do so. The Marquis de Villeneuve's memoirs report that the young Prince had hated Budweiss and begged to leave the town as soon as possible, whereas he liked Kirchberg very much indeed. So the rich and obliging Duc de Blacas purchased the castle there, from the Comte d'Orsay,[83] for the Royal Family to occupy as a summer residence.

Baron Charlet next heard from the Princess on 5 September 1836, saying that she did not know where the family was going to spend the winter months. Six weeks later, during which time he had been very anxious about their welfare and health, Marie Thérèse wrote to Baron

Charlet from Goritz, where the Royal Family was now settled. She confirmed that she and the Duc d'Angoulême had safely arrived there a fortnight before. They had had an excellent journey enjoying the superb weather and all had passed off without any problems. The Duchesse d'Angoulême was impressed by the beauty of Goritz, which was compared favourably by travellers with Nice. M. de Villeneuve by contrast described it as a 'small and sad town'. It had provided a comfortable home to Mesdames Victoire and Adélaïde, the Duchesse d'Angoulême's great aunts, during their travels in exile from France following the Revolution. Mademoiselle Louise, her brother and grandfather did not arrive until late October. Charles X greatly feared the possibility that his grandchildren might catch cholera. So the devoted grandfather and his beloved grandchildren travelled very cautiously and slowly in an attempt to avoid infected areas. The Duc and Duchesse d'Angoulême, however, hoped that the rest of the family would arrive soon and they would spend the winter months together in Goritz. The Duchesse d'Angoulême wrote that the town had escaped cholera and the nearby area was now free of the disease.

By 21 October all was ready in Goritz to welcome Charles X. He had recently celebrated his 79th birthday at Linz on the Danube, on 7 October. Charles X had leased from the Comte de Corononi-Gronberg the castle of Grafenberg, which he occupied with his grandchildren and their attendants. The Angoulêmes lived separately from the rest of the Bourbons on the opposite side of the town, but the family saw each other often. Just as the Royal Family had settled into their new home, the old King was struck down with the disease he had so long feared. On 3 November he played whist as usual, but the next day he felt unwell. Despite the fact that 4 November was his saint's day, he did not dine with the family and only made a brief appearance. In the night he was ill, struck down with violent stomach cramps and vomiting. He called for his doctor and his priest. Bougon reckoned that the advanced age of his patient could not give the family much hope for his recovery. He also told them, after some consideration, his diagnosis that the former King had cholera.

The Duc and Duchesse d'Angoulême were heedless of the threat to their own health and sat up all the night of 5/6 November watching over the aged King. They were accompanied in their vigil by M. de Blacas, so long his faithful courtier. Louis Antoine held his dying father's hand to his lips. The King was still lucid and received the last rites from Cardinal Latil, who had been his confessor and companion for more than thirty years. At half past one in the morning the doctor announced the death of Charles X. He had died peacefully.

Marie Thérèse wrote to Charlet that she was devastated by the death of her uncle; it was the last break with family members of her parents' generation. She had been the close companion and political ally of Charles for more than thirty years. She was deeply affected by his passing.

It took her many months to start to recover from the deep grief she felt. More than a year later she discussed with the Marquis de Villeneuve the death of her uncle with, as he put it, '*une sensibilité exquise*'.[84] Ironically, according to the Marquis de Villeneuve, Charles X was the only victim of cholera in Goritz. In Paris there were questions of etiquette as to how the death should be treated at the Court of his usurping cousin, Louis Philippe. In the end the Orléans family did not wear mourning for the former King and no memorial services were held. Newspapers loyal to the former King and Légitimist cause announced his death by means of black-bordered editions. The former King's body was interred in the Franciscan convent of Castagnavizza, which overlooked and dominated the town of Goritz. His remains are still there.

Who was now the King following the death of Charles X? At a time of transition when a clear and simple statement of the position was necessary to bolster the status and claim of the elder branch of the Bourbons to the throne, as so often before, Louis Antoine prevaricated. Initially, he refused to accept the title of King and would not be referred to as Majesty. The Duc d'Angoulême regarded his nephew as being the rightful heir to Charles X.

As the Marquis de Villeneuve wrote, '*ces équivoques ne simplifiaient pas les situations des royalistes français*' (this lack of clarity did not simplify matters for French royalists). Eventually, Louis Antoine said that he and Marie Thérèse were to be addressed as the Comte and Comtesse de Marnes in a move that made it clear that he would be taking the title of King – but not using it – as long as the family was in exile. As soon as the Légitimist line was re-established in France, he would pass the crown to his nephew, the Duc de Bordeaux. Marie Thérèse was Queen once more, albeit only while the family was in exile. Henri V would be known henceforth as the Comte de Chambord (as we shall use going forward in this book). At last the French loyalists knew to whom to give their loyalty. The debates about validity or invalidity of French law on the succession to the throne produced feelings of 'pity and discouragement', according to the Marquis de Villeneuve. Certainly other European rulers were confused. They had been notified by the Comte de Marnes of his father's death. How should they reply to him? Most addressed him as his Royal Highness the Comte de Marnes. Only the Duc of Modena referred to Louis Antoine as '*Sire, Votre Majesté*' for which he and Marie Thérèse were rather perversely pleased and grateful. The winter of 1836/7 passed sadly for the family. They missed Charles X enormously and mourned his loss. The Duc d'Angoulême felt particularly downcast by the death of his beloved father and the void in their lives that his death had left.

The family spent the summer of 1837 at Frohsdorf near Kirchberg, in a castle surrounded by fir trees in the Austrian countryside. The town itself consisted of one street with manor houses and fountains.

On 21 July a group of their supporters, including Vicomte Walsch, presented themselves and were received by Marie Thérèse in a very gracious way. She was full of smiles. Marie Thérèse was very keen to have the Vicomte's confirmation that the Duc de Bordeaux was being brought up as a good Frenchman and was good-looking as well. She was besotted with her nephew and proud of his many perceived virtues. She asked Vicomte Walsch what he thought of the boy and he responded that the young man was excellent and a true Bourbon. What else could he say? Vicomte Walsch went on to blot his copybook with the family by writing untrue articles about them which were published in Paris. Marie Thérèse liked to keep herself informed of political developments in France and up to date with all the news from her beloved country. She was distressed to learn that the ground-floor apartments she had occupied as the young Madame Royale at Versailles had been converted into a museum (open to the public) as part of the very necessary restoration work undertaken at the palace by Louis Philippe.

The Marquis de Villeneuve visited the family in July 1837, and was forcefully struck by the extreme simplicity of their – rather bourgeois – lives and surroundings in contrast to the magnificence and sophistications of Prague where he had previously visited them. The Duc and Duchesse d'Angoulême passed their time peacefully enough. The Comte de Montbel describes the extreme simplicity of the accommodation used by Louis Antoine. They rose early from their shared marital bed – unusual among royal and aristocratic couples – and attended daily Mass at five o'clock in the morning in the chapel of the château. On her return from the chapel during the week, the Duchesse d'Angoulême would check on her nephew. She would then work with her staff on the Household accounts. The Duc de Bordeaux and his sister had fortunes that were held in trust for them and which needed to be managed. The Duc d'Angoulême, as their adoptive father and with his typical generosity, paid for all their personal and educational expenses. A meal was taken at eleven o'clock. Marie Thérèse ate quickly and quite lightly. As soon as she had emptied her plate it was removed by the servants. When she had finished eating she left the table immediately and retired to the salon. Etiquette demanded that she was served first, and all those eating with her were required to leave the table at the same time that she did. The result was that her guests were often left hungry, having only had time to half eat their meals, or with indigestion because of eating quickly to keep up with her. Apparently no one dared point this out to the Princess. On Sundays the family and the rest of the Court went to Mass in the town church.

Saturdays were taken up with the testing of Henri and Louise on their studies. Marie Thérèse and Louis Antoine participated in these examinations, which lasted about an hour and involved each tutor testing the Prince on his studies – which included Latin, poetry, science, history, literature, politics, maths and geometry. He was required to recite Racine, Corneille, Shakespeare and Schiller. At the session attended by the Marquis de Villeneuve, the Duc de Bordeaux rather fluffed his maths test and Louis Antoine supplied the answer, saying that he had always been good at maths in his youth. The Prince also rode or walked with his young companions and Blacas for two hours every day. The Princess was also tested on her studies –which included English, French and Italian. She was unfortunate in not having companions of her own age. If the weather was good, the party would walk on the terrace or take a trip to one of the many nearby lakes.

The summer of 1837 was especially rainy and the Royal Family and its Household entertained themselves with readings from Don Quixote (carefully edited to protect the ears of the young Princess), read aloud by the Duchesse d'Angoulême's ladies-in-waiting. The family's dinner guests arrived at about six o'clock. The Duc de Bordeaux amused himself watching from the windows of the castle as arriving guests negotiated the twin horrors of an open sewer and the muddy street. Visitors were often followed to the château by their servants carrying clean pairs of shoes. There was not sufficient space for most visitors to stay with the family. They were therefore lodged at the nearby inn or at the home of the local pharmacist, who had a large property capable of housing many visitors. Whatever Louis Antoine's other limitations, he seems to have been a generous host, for example paying for the Marquis de Villeneuve's accommodation. After dinner, according to the Marquis de Villeneuve, Louise would sing sweetly and play on the harp for their guests. Her brother spent his evening drawing in a small corner of the room and laughing as he had done in Prague. Mademoiselle Louise's governess in attendance was the '*sèche et rébarbative mais respectable et sure*'[85] Marquise de Nicolay. They had been less than frank in their dealings with Madame de Gontaut. Clearly the young Princess still had need of a governess, contrary to Charles X's words at the time of her dismissal.

When sad memories were evoked, Marie Thérèse tried to keep up the family's spirits saying that they should not dwell on the bad times. The Duc and Duchesse d'Angoulême were happiest when alone with their nephew and niece and their small Household. It was almost cell-like. The life of Marie Thérèse and her family was uneventful, even idle, but pleasant enough. Louis Antoine was content in his inactivity. When not at church or attending to correspondence, he read aloud to his wife (in French, German, Italian and English). She listened while she made items of sewing, which would be sold to relieve the sufferings of the poor. Occasionally roused from his stupor, he said that had he remained in France he would have particularly interested himself in the administration of justice, the alleviation of poverty and the supervision of the education system. Rather bizarrely, he also advocated moving the centre of administration from Paris to Tours. Unlike Louis XVIII at Hartwell, who had spent many hours at his desk writing letters, organising his spy network and generally intriguing in an attempt to regain his throne, Louis Antoine made no such efforts. He trusted to God and providence for Restoration. Their time was enlivened by the Comtesse de Montbel, who was a lively and charming woman. They also received visits from Princess Berthe de Rohan and the Comte and Comtesse de Montholon, who had been with them in exile in Edinburgh. One of the topics of conversation was the suspicious circumstances surrounding the death of the Prince de Condé.[86] Another visitor was the Comte d'Estourmel who had been the Préfet in Cherbourg in 1830 when the family went into exile and had assisted at their embarkation for England.

Châteaubriand reported that Marie Thérèse loved to gossip about trivialities and was intrigued by the lives of others, whatever their station in life. He seems to have regarded this as a rather degrading characteristic in a Princess. It seems just human. The Court was divided into factions, but Louis Antoine and Marie Thérèse lacked the energy or skills to unite their courtiers, so the bickering and jostling for position persisted. As Villeneuve pointed out, the Court was utterly dominated by the Duc de Blacas who was '*en maître absolu*'.[87] Many topics of conversation were thorny and therefore off limits. The Marquis de Villeneuve observed that these individuals, i.e. Marie Thérèse and her husband, who had been at the centre of momentous and historic events, seemed to have no desire or ability to discuss or analyse them. When the Marquis de Villeneuve, keen to promote a third Restoration of the Légitimist Bourbon monarchy, asked for a meeting with Louis Antoine to discuss plans, including a draft *Manifeste au Peuple Français* and strategies for a further Restoration, he was rebuffed. Louis Antoine followed his arguments and views with close attention and interest, but he made it clear that he had no intention of taking any action and would leave events to the will of God. Depression and disappointment at what he felt was his ungrateful treatment in France had robbed him of ambition and drive. As time passed, Marie Thérèse more and more concurred with her husband's fatalistic views. As a parting gift, Marie Thérèse gave Villeneuve a book marked with her initials and expressed the hope that they would meet again; but her husband did not receive him, expressing that they had nothing to say to each other. She was content to let matters take their course without active intervention. She would pray for regime change and hoped to see her nephew on the throne, but that was all in God's hands. In conversation with the Marquis de Villeneuve, she thanked him for his efforts but did not wish to pursue matters further. He knew it was best to let the question of Henri V and his possible Restoration rest.

The future marriage of the sixteen-year-old Duc de Bordeaux was, however, a topic in which Marie Thérèse was both very interested and about which she was prepared to converse. As the Duc de Bordeaux's adoptive mother and the 'Queen', this was an area of Royal Family policy that was, very clearly, within her domain. The Marquis de Villeneuve advocated a match with one of the Russian grand duchesses. He felt that the wealth and connections of one of these princesses would be of great benefit to the Légitimist cause. Speaking clearly and quickly, Marie Thérèse expressed her concerns about the differences in religion. She believed that this was a fundamental objection to such a marriage. Marie Thérèse did not feel that the Russians would countenance a change of their princess's religion from Russian Orthodox to Roman Catholic. The Marquis, however, suspected that this was not in fact the real reason behind Marie Thérèse's objection to such an alliance.

When the Royal Family lived in Prague, they felt that they had been snubbed by Emperor Nicholas I.[88] In 1835, at the time of the accession of Ferdinand of Austria, the family had moved out of the Hradschin Palace and were living temporarily in Buchistrad; the Emperor of Russia was meanwhile travelling through Prague on his return from Vienna, where he had been paying his respects to the new Austrian Emperor, but he did not visit Charles X despite a strong suggestion from Metternich, the Austrian Chancellor, that it would be politic to do so.

The Bourbons, always sensitive about matters of etiquette, were incensed by his lack of manners. When Charles sent his equerry O'Hegerthy to the Russian Emperor, Nicholas apparently said to the messenger, 'How is Henri V? Because I only know Henri V' – thus making it clear that he did not recognise Charles X as King. The Emperor went one step further and sent his ambassador to enquire after the health of the young 'King', rather than his grandfather. The Bourbons said that they would not receive him, but the ambassador went to visit them anyway, though this time not dressed formally. The Emperor was confused. He thought he was doing the right thing. After all, had not Charles abdicated? This was typical of the behaviour often displayed by the Bourbons, wanting it both ways and putting such emphasis on protocol. Marie Thérèse could not understand why the Russians had been unable to humour an old man and treat him as a King. She was further upset by the Russian Empress Alexandra Feodorovna[89] who had politely sent her apologies that she was not able to visit Marie Thérèse because of the brevity of her stay in Vienna. Marie Thérèse did not understand why the Empress had not invited her to go to Vienna. Apparently she would have been more than happy to travel to see the Empress, but the wound was so deep that it made impossible a marriage between the two clans.

During October the Bourbons returned to Goritz to spend the winter in its clement climate. They stayed at the Hotel Strassoldo and were accompanied by two guards of honour. The pattern of life here was very similar to that in Kirchberg. During the winter months the Duchesse d'Angoulême left for Mass before the sun was up. She was asked why she did not take a servant with her to carry a lantern to light her way or take a carriage rather than walk to church. She replied that she was happy to look after herself. She did not want to disturb her staff and the rest of the Household so early in the day when it was so cold. She was not without thought and care for others. She was often accompanied by her husband, who would carry the lantern for both of them to light their way to Mass. They mixed with the other churchgoers, unnoticed and unheralded. On their return to their residence they would light their own fire without the aid of their staff in order to warm themselves; she clearly remembered the lessons of self-sufficiency learned in the solitude of the Tower of the Temple. Exercise was essential for Marie Thérèse's good health and sense of well-being. The family would walk in the afternoon to local beauty spots, often towards the Forest of Panovitz. Here, the views extended to the Adriatic in order give her this opportunity for physical activity. In the spring they walked out into the countryside and enjoyed cutting wild asparagus, which would then be cooked for them. Sometimes the men of the household would go out shooting birds in the local countryside.

The Court in exile did undergo some changes. In 1838, the dominant Duc de Blacas and his wife left the Court and returned to live in France. He died the following year and was buried beside his late master, Charles X, at Goritz, following a funeral service in Vienna. The obituary in the *Morning Post* recognised that he had been a controversial figure, not universally loved for his views but noting his talent and loyalty to the Bourbons in exile. The paper said, 'If exiled royalty have still a tear left that it will fall on the tomb of him whose life was devoted to their service.' The Bourbons had a very practical reason to be grateful to him. As the *Morning Post* reported, the Duc de Blacas willed to the young Duc de Bordeaux 3 million francs which had been left to the Duc de Blacas by Louis XVIII, but which the Duke had always regarded as being held in trust for the young Prince. Blacas' eldest son succeeded to his titles and also to his duties as '*Premier gentilhomme de la chambre du Roi*'. Cardinal Latil who had been with the family for so many years died in January 1839. That same year[90] news came from France of the death of Renete de Chanterenne, to whom Marie Thérèse had briefly been so close. They had kept in touch over the years by letter, and a pension had been paid to Renete in recognition of her services and kindnesses. Marie Therese had also gone to visit her former companion at her home in Ablis to the east of Paris during the Restoration. Marie Thérèse instructed Charlet to send her condolences to the grieving son and continue paying the pension at half rate to him. This action illustrates her loyalty to old friends and her generosity even in her now reduced circumstances. Equally she shows by this approach her lack of effusiveness. She seemingly felt no need to write herself to the Chanterenne family. Marie Thérèse's companion and friend of nearly forty years, Henriette d'Agoult, died in March 1841 aged 84 after a short illness. For Marie Thérèse this was a further loss of one of her close and valued female friends. Old adversaries were also passing away, and on hearing of the death of Talleyrand, she apparently remarked that he had died stoically. Time had softened her views.

July 1841 brought further family worries for Marie Thérèse. The Comte de Chambord was injured in a riding accident. Dr Bougon arrived at the scene to diagnose a broken femur. The Prince spent several months in great pain, and the break was not healing. Weeks later, he was transferred to Vienna for further treatment, a painful and exhausting journey. He eventually recovered from his injuries and was able to walk and ride again, but was left with a limp. The Prince hated shaving and grew a beard. He was cursed by the Bourbon love of food (especially sugary) and became obese (weighing some 120 kg while only of medium height). The Comte de Chambord also loved to swim and set out to emulate the swimming exploits of Lord Bryon whose prowess in the water he greatly admired, by swimming the same distance as crossing the Hellespont.

As Henri grew to maturity, he needed to get away from the enclosed and restricted society of his aunt and uncle, so he travelled widely in Europe. His ambiguous status as the pretender to the throne of France and the diplomatic issues that it raised for the government of the countries he visited meant that he often travelled incognito. When he was in Vienna he did not receive the royal honours to which he was entitled, but preferred to visit his relatives there informally as a private person. He even travelled to visit Rome on a false passport. That said, Queen Louise of Belgium, his cousin and daughter of Louis Philippe and Marie Amélie, wrote that he had the patronage of the Archduchess Sophie, of the Empress, of Princess Metternich, 'and of all Society' (while her own Orléans family often felt the difficulty of their position among the royalty of Europe, reigning in France and yet being regarded as usurpers by many of their peers). The Comte de Chambord did not lack influential friends. Proximity to Vienna allowed the family to visit their relatives at the Court of Austria regularly. The *Manchester Guardian* of 12 August 1843 announced that 'the Duchess d'Angoulême with her niece Mlle de Rosni[91] sister of the Duc de Bordeaux, are at present on a visit to the Imperial family at Schoenbrunn'.

In July 1842, the Duc and Duchesse d'Angoulême went into mourning for the untimely death of the young Duc d'Orléans. The eldest son and heir of Louis Philippe was killed in a road accident. Despite the cool relations with the Orléans family, Marie Thérèse and Louis Antoine were devastated by the tragic death. He was after all the son of their beloved cousin, Marie Amélie and her husband, a young man whom they had known as a boy before their exile from France. Political differences and the betrayals of 1830 were put on one side. The Duc d'Angoulême declared full mourning[92] at the Court in exile for the young man. A letter of condolence was sent to the King and Queen at the Court of Vienna via the French ambassador, who was at this time the Comte de Flahaut.[93] Marie Thérèse added the young man to the list of those for whom she prayed. The letter from Marie Thérèse to the grieving parents said that she was 'utterly crushed by the news from Paris. We feel it as a family tragedy.' The letter was forwarded from the Embassy in Vienna to Paris. It was well received by Louis Philippe, who sent an affectionate message back via Monsieur de Flahaut, which he duly passed on to Marie Thérèse and the rest of the family at Kirchberg. The Duchesse de Dino wrote:

> The Dauphine was to go to Vienna for the birthday of the Emperor as usual, but on learning of the death of the Duc d'Orléans she wrote to excuse herself, and to say that in such circumstances she could not appear at any festivity and would stay in the country. I think she has shown excellent dignity and good taste. [Writing further on 5 August 1842.] Yesterday I went to the Sacré Cœur to say farewell to Madame de Gramont. She had just received letters from Kirchberg which told her that the day after the news of the death of the Duc d'Orléans had arrived a black Mass was said at which the Dauphin, the Dauphine and Mademoiselle had both been present and had communicated, in prayer for the soul of the deceased. I have heard of nothing more touching or more Christian.

In 1843, Marie Thérèse became the subject of a biography by Alfred Nettement, *Vie de Marie-Thérèse de France, Fille de Louis XVI*. Despite the author's protestations of respect and admiration for her virtues, she did not enjoy this invasion of her privacy. She had no wish to share the details of her life with those outside her immediate circle. She must have hated the renewed discussion of the sufferings of her family and the speculation as to the fate of her brother, Louis Charles, as the book went to a second edition in the year of its publication.

13

Exile and Widowhood

1844-1851

Marie Thérèse was widowed in June 1844, just a few days short of the couple's 45th wedding anniversary. Their marriage proved to have been a long and reasonably happy union. Theirs had been a dynastic match, not one based on romantic love or physical passion. All the indications are that the marriage was not one in which sexual passion played a significant part, and certainly it did not produce children. Nevertheless, they had had an enormous amount in common, seemed to be affectionate and respectful of each other and were sexually faithful to each other always. They had missed each other very badly when circumstances forced them to be apart. Louis Antoine's death was a further sadness for Marie Thérèse and one more narrowing of her world. Fewer and fewer people shared her life experiences. He had always been a great support and comfort to her, particularly in their later years together. In her turn she had respected him and admired his abilities as a soldier. She loved him as a devoted and affectionate husband. He was a man of honour who regarded the promise he gave to his brother to care for his children as being a binding obligation and one that he fulfilled to the full. They shared a devotion to the Roman Catholic Church and its rites.

The Duc d'Angoulême's last days were painful and difficult. He fell ill in December 1843 with what was initially diagnosed by his doctors as being an aneurism or broken blood vessel. The poor man writhed in agony on the floor of his bedchamber, so excruciating was the pain. He lost enormous amounts of weight and became as thin as a stick. Later on, a further examination in January 1844 by Doctor Bougon in collaboration with Professor Jacomini of the University of Padua concluded that he had been struck with cancer of the stomach. The Comte de Chambord was travelling in England as part of his extended Grand Tour and had to be called home in January 1844. The Duc d'Angoulême's cancer was spreading. He had spent the autumn of 1843 in London, arriving there on 23 October. The Comte de Chambord established himself and his entourage in the Belgrave Square Hotel in London's fashionable West End. His arrival put the English Royal Family in a difficult position, and Queen Victoria found it diplomatic to be away from London and in Windsor for the duration of his stay. Victoria and her family had long been friends with Louis Philippe since his exile in England during the years of Revolution and Empire. Her father, the Duke of Kent, had lent money and given other help to the Orléans family in exile. She did not want to be caught between the rival factions of the Bourbon family. Furthermore, her uncle Leopold of Belgium[1] was married to Louise,[2] one of Louis Philippe's daughters. The Comte de Chambord only just missed overlapping with a visit to London by the Duc de Nemours, second son of his cousins King Louis Philippe and Marie Amélie. Queen Victoria noted in her diary for Monday 13 November 1843:

> Nemours, who led me in & sat next to me, talked much about the different members of his family, & is so sensible about everything. He talked of the Duc de Bordeaux having, it is said, an H, with a regal crown on his carriage, which means Henri V. While all the French Princes wear the Ducal coronet, & never the foreign crown. Nemours observed that this was such a poor gratification. Uncle Leopold wrote to me at great length on the subject, adding that [*sic*] Dauphin had been against the duke's journey, while the Dauphine was for it, which Neumours [*sic*] believed to be true.

The Comte de Chambord

The presence in London of the pretender to the throne of France stirred up strong emotions. The Comte de Chambord was visited by many supporters of the Légitimist cause and there were noisy demonstrations in his favour. In France there was a surge of support for the Légitimist cause. In France five Deputies resigned from parliament and several newspaper editors[3] who reported favourably on events in London and the Comte de Chambord were fined. The pleasant and no doubt exciting trip was cut short, and on 13 January 1844 the Comte de

Chambord left London to travel back across Europe to Frohsdorf, to be with his very sick uncle and his beloved aunt in her time of trouble. Queen Victoria noted in her diary of 16 January 1844, 'The Duc de Bordeaux has suddenly left, on account of the Duc d'Angoulême's serious illness, & I must say I am glad that he is gone at last.'

To give Louis Antoine some respite from the pain, he was prescribed high doses of morphine. His body was skeletal, so much weight had he lost. Marie Thérèse nursed him tenderly as she had nursed so many others before[4] and hardly left his bedside. By 3 June it became clear that the Duc d'Angoulême was fading away and the devoted Duchesse d'Angoulême called for the priests to come to him quickly and give her husband the last rites of the Roman Catholic Church to which he had been so devoted throughout his life. Half an hour later the Duc d'Angoulême died. The *Gentleman's Magazine* of July 1844 reported:

> on the 8th June his funeral was celebrated in the cathedral of Goritz and thence proceeded to the chapel of the Franciscan convent, situated on a height to the west of the town. The Duc de Bordeaux followed the car on foot in a mourning cloak. Count de Montbel, Viscount de Champagny, and the Duke de Blacas, also in mourning cloaks, walked behind the Duke: next came the French now at Goritz, the authorities, and the inhabitants. The body was placed in the vault where the mortal remains of Charles X rest.

His death left a massive emptiness in Marie Thérèse's life, one from which she felt she would never recover. The *Gentleman's Magazine* was less than fulsome in its comments on the life of the Dauphin, noting that 'The Duc d'Angoulême seems to have been a harmless character, of no marked talent, and no decided propensities … during the exile of his house he was content with doing nothing. In private he appears to have been an amiable man.'

Following the death of Louis Antoine, the would-be Henri V of France issued a circular to the Courts of Europe setting out his position:

> Having become by the death of Monsieur the Comte de Marnes the Head of the House of Bourbon, I regard it as a duty to protest against the change which has been introduced in France in the legitimate order of the succession to the Crown and to declare that I shall never renounce the rights which in accordance with the ancient French laws I hold by my birth.

Queen Victoria wrote in her journal of 26 June 1844:

> After dinner I talked with Lord Aberdeen,[5] of a very extraordinary letter from the Duc de Bordeaux to me, the copy of which Lord Aberdeen had sent me, in which he calls me 'Soeur et Cousine' announcing the death of his uncle the Duc d'Angoulême, & then he goes on to protest against the present state of things in France, that he has not renounced his claims, & only awaits the proper moment, when he may be of use to his country. But that till then, he will only assume the title of Cte de Chambord!!! Ld Aberdeen answered the Cte de Mouttel, who had sent him the letter & the copy, — that he could not lay such a letter before me. Ld A. was quite surprised at it, but Louise had always told me, that should the Duc d'Angoulême die, Bordeaux would not remain quiet.

Queen Victoria clearly took an interest in the Bourbon family and her diary of 22 June 1847 records that she was in the process of collecting portraits of the Bourbons, including Charles X and the Duc d'Angoulême.

Schloss Frohsdorf

Everything at Goritz reminded Marie Thérèse of her dead husband. She was unable to restrain her tears, so conscious was she of her great loss. She decided that it would be better for her health and well-being if she left Goritz, despite its clement climate and pleasant environment. She decided to move to live in Frohsdorf, where they had previously spent the summers. Her plans were that this would now be her permanent home. The château and its park, which had been left to her in the will of M. de Blacas, were situated approximately 25 miles from Vienna near to Wiener Neustadt. The large park allowed the Comte de Chambord to indulge the classic Bourbon pastime of hunting and gave Marie Thérèse space for exercise and recreation. The castle was huge and divided up into individual apartments to accommodate the courtiers and guests. In addition there were communal areas providing reception rooms and dining rooms as well as a library comprising 15,000 books for the entertainment of the family and their attendants.

The château was also decorated with some of the many portraits collected by the Duchesse de Berry to educate her son in the history of his family, by training him to recognise the depictions of his ancestors. There are further examples of this at the Château of Chambord. Amusingly, as Marie Caroline pursued a full set of images of his antecedents, she was not always too fussy as to whether the picture was actually of the individual which it purported to be as long as the clothing was of the relevant period. Frohsdorf to this day contains items of embroidery produced by Marie Thérèse and furniture used by the Royal Family while they were in residence there. It also contains memorabilia collected by Marie Thérèse relating to her family. Owning the property gave Marie Thérèse security and control over her life. At last, she had the promise of a permanent home of her own during her long exile. The gardens, which were well known in Austria, were partly in the English style and partly French. There was even a fuchsia plant in a pot that had once been in the Tuileries garden of the young Prince before his long exile. The property was decorated with many portraits of the Bourbons and depictions of episodes in their lives, including the proud moment for the Dauphine when her husband returned triumphant from Spain.

Marie Thérèse lived on in Frohsdorf in seclusion from the Royal Courts of Europe, accompanied by her nephew. We have a description of her years there from the memoirs written by the Prince de Faucigny-Lucinge,[6] who visited her in 1845. She was 67 years old at this time, still upright in stance and had not put on any additional weight. She kept an air of dignity and majesty. Her hair was partly covered by a lace cap and curled at her ears. Her face retained its oval shape and her complexion was rather high in colour, her eyes a deep blue. On first meeting her, people were first struck by her rather serious manner and put off by her harsh voice. These first impressions were soon forgotten after getting to know her, although there was nothing she could do to soften the impression given by her voice. Writing in 1850, Baroness Blaze de Bury described meeting the Dauphine and noted her impressions of Marie Thérèse. The keen supporter of the Bourbon cause wrote:

> There is about this sorely-tried Princess a majesty, before which you bow down abashed as it were, by her mere aspect, at the crimes your fellow men could commit. No consecration has failed her, for no suffering has been spared. The Dauphine was rather of a decided and manly than of a gentle nature: but she has achieved gentleness, and in her presence you feel only pardon is around. So purely, truly pious is the Duchesse d'Angoulême, that, as far as outward appearances go, you can barely call her austere. All the ineffable indulgence she now so largely extends to others is compensated by severities which attain but her alone.

Not all the former spirit that had damaged her relationships during her years as La Dauphine and alienated many had been extinguished. The Baroness noted, 'Nor has this victory been cheaply bought, for there are moments still when the descendant of Louis Quatorze, and the grand-daughter of the Empress-Queen speak out, in the quick glance, the active step the rapid word; but instantly you see that is mere accident, and that nothing can ever more compromise the conquest that religion has made.' She was not a saint, then, but she was trying to be one.

She spent her last years as she had spent so many of the previous years, albeit in different circumstances and different countries: sewing, praying, corresponding with friends, family and business contacts, especially her devoted secretary, the Baron Charlet. Even in retirement and relative isolation, etiquette and correct form were important. During the day, the gentlemen attending the Dowager Queen (as they regarded her to be) wore frockcoats and top hats. In the evening, they wore formal evening dress. The ladies curtsied three times on entering Marie Thérèse's presence. It was noted by her great nephew, the Prince de Faucigny-Lucinge, that when Henri V, her beloved nephew and the king of France in her eyes, entered a room, all stood including Marie Thérèse. She always knew the honours due to a King of France, whether he be a frightened child imprisoned and abused in the Tower of the Temple or her exiled nephew. At their meals, Marie Thérèse sat in a place of honour on the right-hand side of the Comte de Chambord. Each dish was individually presented to the guests. Guests as a matter of etiquette served themselves drinks and were required by the rules of etiquette not to offer wine to their neighbour at the table. Meals were served and eaten quickly, in less than half an hour. Conversation at the table was limited by the need for courtiers to eat quickly to keep pace with the Princess or to go hungry. After dinner the Princesses retired to the grey drawing room, which was on the first floor of the building and worked at their needlework. Marie Thérèse, rather off-puttingly for her visitors, sat facing the fireplace and away from the room. Without raising her eyes from her embroidery, she would address random remarks to her guests in other parts of the room.

Even during the last years of her life, Marie Thérèse continued to travel and to receive many visitors. In 1845, for example, Marie Caroline was at Frohsdorf for her son's birthday in September. Marie Thérèse was after all not far from her Imperial cousins in Vienna, and there were convenient transport links. In winter, she might only have a Court of twenty or so people; but come the better weather, there were visits from numerous cousins. Her extended family was large: Marie Antoinette had twelve brothers and sisters; Leopold II of Austria had fourteen children and Francis II had eight children by four different wives. Furthermore, there were the half brothers and sisters to the Duc de Bordeaux and Mademoiselle produced by Marie Caroline during her second marriage to the Count of Lucchese-Palli. In addition, there were the two half-English daughters of the Duc de Berry by Amy Brown and their families.

Visitors came to Frohsdorf from France, Austro-Hungary and Italy to see Marie Thérèse and her niece and nephew. Charles II of Bourbon-Parme, whose Duchy had formed part of the settlement made on Marie Louise,[7] the former Empress of France and widow of Napoleon, visited the Bourbons in exile in 1845. His son and heir, Ferdinand Charles,[8] met and fell in love with Marie Thérèse's niece Louise and asked to be allowed to marry her. The Princess, aged 26, was married with great ceremony in Frohsdorf on 10 November 1845. Her brother escorted her to the altar followed by Marie Thérèse and the Empress Marie Anne[9] of Austria, wife of the Emperor Ferdinand.[10] The ceremony was also attended by Archduchess Sophie of Austria, another of Marie Thérèse's friends and the mother of the future Emperor Franz Joseph of Austria and the ill-fated Emperor Maximilian of Mexico.[11]

As the head of the family following the death of the Duc d'Angoulême, Henri announced his sister's marriage to the Courts of Europe. The manner of his doing so, which appeared to his cousin Louis Philippe as if he thought himself to be a reigning monarch and his sister the member of the ruling family, caused great offence to his cousins in Paris. Louis Philippe took up the matter through his rather exasperated ambassador M. de Flahaut with the Austrian Chief Minister Metternich. He was able to reassure the King that the Austrian government, who were providing the elder branch of the Bourbon family with a place of exile, did not share the family's view of their status; they continued to recognise the rule of the Orléans family. Nevertheless, Louis Philippe was irked that so many Habsburg cousins of the bride attended the wedding in Frohsdorf, thereby lending weight, he felt, to the claims of the Légitimist party.

The supporters of the Légitimist cause in France hoped that the Duc de Bordeaux would follow the good example set by his elder sister and marry. He was by now 25 years old and it was felt to be time for him to settle down to married life and produce heirs to support his claims to the throne of France. His own fancy had fallen on a Russian Grand Duchess.

The Romanovs had given the elder Bourbons great support during their years of exile and been very instrumental in the two Restorations to the throne in 1814 and 1815. Offence had been caused in the 1810s when the Duc de Bordeaux's father, the Duc de Berry, had been looking for a bride and the Russian Grand Duchess Anne had been proposed but rejected by the Bourbons on the grounds of religious differences – plus objections to the lack of antiquity and even legitimacy of the Imperial Romanov family. It was widely understood that Catherine the Great had sought a father for her children away from the Imperial marriage bed. No doubt they also recalled the insulting behaviour of Nicholas in 1835. Marie Thérèse had very different ideas on a suitable bride for her nephew: a nice Roman Catholic princess, preferably a Bourbon or Habsburg princess, was much more to her taste. Marie Thérèse, her husband and father-in-law had certainly succeeded in bringing up the Duc de Bordeaux as a devout Roman Catholic; the *Caledonian Mercury* of September 1847 reported that he was visited weekly by Redemptionist priests to be confessed and take communion.

Assisted by the Empress of Austria, Marie Thérèse persuaded her nephew that the Archduchess Marie Thérèse of Modena-Este[12] would be a much more appropriate choice as his bride. A report in the *Morning Post* of Monday 25 August 1845 noted that the Duc de Bordeaux had earlier that month driven into Vienna to visit 'members of the Archducal family of Este … then dining with the Emperor and Empress at Schoenbrunn'. By November 1845, the British papers were noting that there were rumours that the Duc de Bordeaux was to marry one of the Modena princesses.[13] The family liked the Modena family for their support of the Bourbons whom they had always regarded as the rightful Kings of France during the years of exile. The Archduchess was the daughter of Francis IV Duke of Modena and his wife Maria Beatrice of Savoy. She was closely connected to the Austrian Imperial family, which would no doubt have endeared her further to the Duchesse d'Angoulême. The women were able to convince the young man that the Princess was not only a good potential partner, but also that she was already very much in love with him. Her appearance was not particularly attractive: she had a red nose, but her figure was good. She was older than her husband, having been born in 1817; and sadly she was already going deaf.

The wedding took place in November 1846. Marie Thérèse, at least, was delighted by the marriage that seems to have rejuvenated her, observers reported. The *Daily News* of 10 December 1846 noted, 'The Comtesse de Marnes so tried by misfortune, is at the moment enjoying all the felicity which Providence has granted to the exile. She seems to find in her new daughter her whom she lately lost, when she married the Prince de Lucca.'

Another relationship seemed to have improved: Marie Thérèse had earlier that autumn visited her sister-in-law, Marie Caroline, at Brunnsee Schloss near Graz in Styria, Austria, which Marie Caroline had made her home since 1835. This allowed her easy access to the children. They had clearly drawn closer together.

Comtesse de Chambord

Concerned by deprivation in France, even though he was not living there, the Duc de Bordeaux busied himself with relief projects, setting up work schemes in the forests around Chambord and at the château itself. He advocated that such schemes be extended throughout France.[14] He also wrote to the people of Orléans to thank them for their kind congratulations wishes on the occasion of his marriage. He was happy to reassure them that his new wife's heart 'is as much French' as his own. Perhaps this was at last a Bourbon Prince of the elder branch of the family who understood the need for positive publicity and action.

The ageing court must have felt very flat following the departure of the youthful and lively Mademoiselle and the rest of the wedding guests. But Marie Thérèse was not always solemn and dignified. M. de Trobriand was living in Venice, from which he often visited the family and was able to observe their doings. When he was invited to visit the Princess in Goritz, he observed an incident when a child snatched at the headdress worn by the Dauphine and pulled from her head not only the headdress but also her wig, revealing a rather bald head. He noted wryly that the child was not invited to sit on the Royal knee a second time. Marie Thérèse had left Frohsdorf to spend the winter of 1845/6 staying with her friend the Comtesse d'Esterhazy at the Comtesse's townhouse in Vienna; but during that year Marie Thérèse's girlhood friend sadly died in 1845. While in Vienna, the Duchesse d'Angoulême also took the opportunity to spend time at the Court of her cousin, and according to the M*orning Chronicle* of 25 December 1845 attended the Opera House to see *Don Sebastian* by Donizetti, sitting in the Royal box with the Empress Mother.

In 1847 the former Empress of France, Marie Louise, then aged 56, travelled to Frohsdorf to visit her cousin, Marie Thérèse, whom she admired for her stoicism and restraint in her many sufferings. Marie Thérèse seems to have had the great gift of strong female friendships throughout her life. The cousins enjoyed conversing together, talking over old times and discussing the prospects for their families. During her visit Marie Louise reportedly commented to her cousin that she hoped she would live long enough to see the fall of Louis Philippe I of France from the throne and his replacement on the French throne by the Duc de Bordeaux, reigning as King Henri V. Her wish was not to be fulfilled as she died on 16 December 1847. The Duchy of Parma[15] reverted to the Bourbon–Parme family on the death of the former Empress, and Mademoiselle Louise's family by marriage were thereby restored to their throne. If only the ex-Empress Marie Louise had survived another year, she would have seen at least part of her wish for France and the senior branch of the Bourbon family fulfilled. In February 1848, Louis Philippe was toppled from his throne by one of the wave of revolutions sweeping Europe[16] and deposing rulers in France, Austria and Italy. He once more fled into exile in England with his family. The Emperor Ferdinand V of Austria abdicated in 1848 in favour of his nephew, the Archduke Franz Joseph (the son of Marie Thérèse's friend, Sophie) who reigned for the next 65 years.

Despite the fact that he would appear to be a possible successor to the fallen Orléans family, the Duc de Bordeaux took no steps to reclaim the throne, apart from ordering a smart new uniform to wear for his triumphal entry into Paris, and moving from Venice to be a little closer to French territory by settling in Lucerne in Switzerland. He took no decisive action to rally his support or to put his case to the French people. He preferred to leave events, as he had been brought up to do in large part by his aunt, Marie Thérèse, to God and fate; not for him the decisive, if ill-conceived actions of his mother. Into this political gap came rumour and forged letters setting out the supposed policies and approach of the would-be Henri V. Charles Didier, it was reported in the *Manchester Times* of June 1849, was travelling between Croatia and Vienna when a fellow passenger pointed out the abode of the Bourbon heir. Intrigued, he decided to visit the Duc de Bordeaux. The writer was a well-known Republican. Four months later, he gained admission to Frohsdorf and an interview with the Duc de Bordeaux, who was fully aware of his political leanings. His recollections were written up in a brochure entitled (not surprisingly) *A visit to the*

Duc de Bordeaux. It was enormously popular and rapidly went into many editions. He wrote of Henri, 'Either I am very much mistaken, deceived, or the Duc de Bordeaux is deficient in initiative, power, and probably deficient in resolution. His mind is cultivated rather than inventive, he conceives rather than creates, and takes in more than he gives out. From his education and from his nature, indolence in him prevails over the power of execution. In a word – and perhaps it is fortunate for his repose – he appears to me more suited to expectation than to action.'

According to Charles Didier, as quoted in a piece by Charles Augustine Saint-Beuve, Marie Thérèse took no pleasure in the fall of the Orléans family. She prayed for the French people as they suffered yet another period of revolution and instability. She said that she found the hand of God in all things. She apparently took comfort from noting that Charles X at least had left France a lasting legacy of his reign in the form of the French territories of Algeria. We also gain a description of Marie Thérèse and her life. Didier noted:

> She keeps in her bed-chamber, the austerity of which is almost monastic, only small objects as are calculated to revive the tragic scenes of her early youth, – the portraits of her father, her mother, and her mother's friend the Princess de Lamballe: and near her bed, which has not even a curtain, stands a prie-dieu full of objects most sacred in her eyes, – the black vest which her father wore when he ascended the scaffold, – the lace cap which her mother made with her own hands to appear in before the revolutionary tribunal. She alone has the key of those sad relics and once a year, on the 21st of January, she takes them from the reliquary in which they are enclosed, and surrounds herself with them, in order to bring herself into closer communion with the beloved dead by whom they were worn. On that day she buries her tears in complete seclusion; she sanctifies the blood-stained anniversary by solitude and prayer.

Marie Thérèse's niece, Louise, was also affected by the 1848 Year of Revolutions, which saw monarchies throughout Europe come tumbling down. On the death of the former Empress Marie Louise[17] in 1847, the Bourbon–Parme family was restored to its Duchy of Parma and Louise's father-in-law became King of Etruria. Revolutionaries forced his abdication a year later and imprisoned Louise's husband. He was eventually released and went into exile joined by his wife. Queen Victoria noted in her journal on 22 May 1848:

> we read Despatches in the train, & many private letters. I have received one from the Heredy Pss of Parma (Lucca that was), the former Mademoiselle who has been driven with her young mother-in-law, at a moment's notice from Parma, she, herself, being near her confinement this

> was done by the King of Sardinia's orders. They are both in a state of destitution, which is really shocking. The Duke also was expelled & the Prince, a prisoner at Milan. This behaviour of the King of Sardinia is most despicable.

Queen Victoria clearly had contact and friendly relations with both sides of the Bourbon family. Her late father, the Duke of Kent, had been very good friends with the Duc d'Orléans. Mademoiselle and her husband visited Victoria and Albert in October 1848. Marie Thérèse herself left Frohsdorf, fleeing in fear of approaching revolutionaries, but was able to return to the normally sleepy and peaceful Frohsdorf a month later. The Prince de Faucigny-Lucinge said in his memoirs that Marie Thérèse always kept with her a bag of diamonds in case she should be forced to flee at short notice. Once again, her life had been affected by Revolution. Even in her late sixties there was no guarantee of the quiet retired life she craved. During 1849 there were rumours in the British newspapers that the French government was looking to restore the legitimatist branch of the Bourbon family with Henri V as King. Nothing came of it.[18] Marie Thérèse spent time with the Imperial family in 1849 while the Comte and Comtesse de Chambord were staying with the Archduke Maximilian, their uncle. She travelled to Prague to sojourn with the deposed Ferdinand I and his wife, Maria Anna. She then moved on to Salzburg to see her friend the Dowager Empress who was residing there. Despite her age she made the effort to keep contact with her family and to spend time with them away from Frohsdorf. Marie Thérèse also had the pleasure of becoming a great-aunt as Louise and her husband produced four children.

Rumours and speculation about the fate of her younger brother still circulated. The British newspapers of the summer of 1849[19] reported that a claimant by the name of the Baron de Richemont was about to be acknowledged by the Duchesse d'Angoulême as her long-lost brother. The French newspaper *The Atlas* claimed that the Pope had released Marie Thérèse from the oath she had given to her uncle not to reveal the truth of her brother's being alive. According to the newspaper reports, this oath had been extorted from the Princess by the threat of making public revelation contained in correspondence from Marie Antoinette, which would call into question the legitimacy of her children. She was now free to recognise him. Nonsense, she must have felt: but irritating and distracting for the ageing Princess.

Within the wider Bourbon family, the thinking had developed that on the death of Louis Philippe the claims to the throne of the senior and junior branches of the family would revert to the senior and be united in the persons of the Duc de Bordeaux and his successors. During 1850 there was upsurge in interest and support for the Légitimist cause. The *Berlin State Gazette*[20] noted that there was a steady stream of visitors to Frohsdorf from among the aristocracy of Europe and that they were kindly received by the Duc and Duchesse de Bordeaux and their aunt. It was remarked that the young couple were given the title of 'Majesty'. This warm reception is in stark contrast to the reception given to visitors at the time of the Duc de Bordeaux attaining his majority. Marie Thérèse was clearly prepared to soften her previous approach to gain support for the Restoration of her beloved nephew. The *Daily News* of 16 April 1850 reported that 'The neighbouring village of Frohsdorf; the residence of the Duke de Bordeaux and Duchess of Angoulême was never so full of French legitimatists. There are some hundreds in the neighbourhood at this moment; they are very well received in the Palace of the Duke and are frequent visitors at his table.' They were closely watched by the local police for fear that they might be 'red republicans' in disguise. The development of the railway system made such visits much easier and cheaper than previously. Marie Thérèse was for her age a great traveler and frequently used the railway to make her journeys from Frohsdorf. Châteaubriand was struck by the notion of Marie Antoinette's daughter riding in such a modern contraption as a train.

The former King Louis Philippe died in exile in his house in Twickenham in London in August 1850. A letter of condolence was sent by the Comte de Chambord to his cousin's family. While leading a conference at Wiesbaden discussing the Restoration of the Bourbons, the Duc de Bordeaux and he attended a memorial service for the life of Louis Philippe which was also attended by many of the conference participants. Queen Victoria wrote in her journal of 26 September 1850 that Lord Aberdeen 'showed Albert a very interesting letter from Guizot, who said that Salvandy had carried a kind message of condolence from the Cte de Chambord (Duc de Bordeaux) to poor Queen Marie Amélie & the family & had taken a civil one in return; this is a good beginning'. The civilised contact between the cousins must have been a comfort to both Marie Amélie and Marie Thérèse. Salvandy reported that Marie Thérèse had asked many questions about her cousin and also enquired in detail about her children. In order to progress matters the Orléanist grouping demanded as a condition of their support for his claim to the throne that the Duc de Bordeaux accept the idea of a constitutional monarchy supported by the will of the French people and the tricolour flag as the symbol of France rather than the flag of the Bourbons.

The Duc de Bordeaux could not accept the price asked of him for the support of the Orléanist faction. To his family, and in particular to Marie Thérèse, the tricolour flag symbolised for her all the worst times of her life as the outward symbol of the success of the 1789 Revolution with all its attendant horrors for her and her family. She no doubt recalled her father and younger brother being humiliated by being forced to wear hats in its hated red, white and blue. The sacrifice of the white Bourbon flag was not one that Marie Thérèse could make. It was almost as though she was allergic to the tricolour flag. To have anything to do with it, and certainly the idea of willingly embracing it, were anathema to her. She clearly loved and respected as the symbol of her family and her house the white flag of the Bourbons. Brought up so closely and loving her as he did, her nephew shared her views and refused to compromise on this point. It is an irony as the succession of their family to the throne of France in 1589 was based on the willingness of their revered ancestor Henri IV[21] to give up his Protestant faith in order to be able to become King of Roman Catholic France.

In her seventies, Marie Thérèse continued to travel and spent the first three months of 1850 in Venice living at the Palace Cavalli[22] on the Grand Canal – which had been purchased by her nephew.[23] The huge palace was on three floors. She was not overly impressed by the beautiful city, finding it gloomy and rather sad, even if the winter climate was better for her health than that in Frohsdorf. Her daily routine whilst in Venice was much the same as in Austria. She went to Mass at the church of Saint-Vital, travelling there by gondola. She then spent the afternoons embroidering, sitting at one of the gothic arched bay windows of the 'Salon des Oiseaux' overlooking the Grand Canal. Always keen to take regular exercise, she complained that Venice did not provide sufficient space for her to take long walks. Marie Caroline, who had by now grown stout but was still flirtatious, spent time with Marie Thérèse and her son, the Duc de Bordeaux, in Venice. Marie Caroline was supposedly sewing but in fact making little progress with her work, too concerned was she with gossiping and according to one visitor scratching her behind and picking her nose. The relationship between the two Princesses, Marie Caroline and Marie Thérèse, once difficult and full of recriminations, had mellowed into a more relaxed companionableness. At the other end of the room members of the family and friends, including the Archduke Maximilian of Austria who suffered with deafness, struggled to conduct a conversation – not a particularly attractive picture of Royal Family life. As was the usual custom in Marie Thérèse's Household, meals were eaten very quickly despite consisting of more than ten different dishes. Whichever country the family was in, its members created a French atmosphere. Baroness Blaze de Bury wrote in *Germania: its Courts, Camps and People* of the Comte de Chambord, of whom she was a great admirer, that he had 'created about him an artificial atmosphere; and that atmosphere is France'. She noted that 'In the drawing room of the Comte de Chambord, wherever it may be, in Vienna, Frohsdorf, or Venice, you are in France, and everything around you is so impregnated with this perfume of the absent home.' This sounds very much a reflection of the upbringing given him by his aunt. Her love of France, her desire to return home and interest in its well-being never dimmed, however long she spent in exile. The family was well informed about events in France. They kept up with all the latest developments, including the changing and developing language, keeping themselves abreast of the latest slang and gossip.

Marie Thérèse returned to Frohsdorf and spent time talking with and comforting her niece, Louise, who had found out that her husband, Ferdinand, was having a number of affairs. The once slim Princess had put on enormous weight and now appeared to be as wide as she was tall. A large appetite and propensity to put on enormous weight was one of the curses of the Bourbon family, as illustrated by Louis XVI, Louis XVIII and their sister Madame Clotilde with her unfortunate nickname of 'Madame Grossesse or Gros'.

Having comforted her niece, Marie Thérèse travelled on to Vienna. She must have thought that she was rare among those married to Bourbon princes in not having to put up with the unfaithfulness of her spouse. Marie Thérèse's appearance started to reflect her age; she no longer had the upright bearing of a soldier. Time had softened her. She was happy with her lot, content to be a symbol of the *ancien régime* and a focus of the Légitimist cause. These days she wore black always; there were so many to mourn for – her father, her mother, her brothers and sister, Madame Élisabeth, her uncles and her husband, and his brother and so many old friends. She still prayed and hoped that her nephew would be able to return to France as King, but for herself she no longer thought she would see her beloved country again. It was now more than twenty years since she had trodden on French territory; most of her life had been spent away from her own country and in exile.[24]

Marie Thérèse was in good spirits on 12 October. She appeared to the Frenchmen who had gathered in Frohsdorf to celebrate her upcoming name day on 15 October to be in good health. She welcomed them all warmly [25] and was happy to show them around her home. As always she reiterated her love of France, bemoaning the fact that she was too old to see it again but hoping for the Restoration of her nephew. On 13 October 1851, while attending Mass as usual, Marie Thérèse felt faint and started to shake and shiver. She left the chapel so as not to cause a fuss. She was pale and clearly unwell. She did, however, join the rest of the family after Mass so as not to cause them concern. The Comte de Chambord and his wife insisted that she rest. Her new Doctor Thevenot was summoned to her. His assessment was that she had probably caught flu and recommended that she stay in bed and rest. Dr Bougon, who had been with the family in exile for twenty years, had died in March in Venice, where he was attending the Comte de Chambord. His life had been a model of loyalty and service, both personally to the Bourbons and to their cause. Her dear friend the Archduchess Sophie came to visit Marie Thérèse in Frohsdorf on 14 October to celebrate her name day the following day. The Archduchess had written very sweetly that she hoped to see her, saying, 'In the event of your being prevented from receiving me I will delay my visit, but I do not renounce it; for, my dear aunt, I shall consider it a fête for me to see you.' Marie Thérèse tried to insist on getting up from her bed to welcome the Archduchess, but was overruled by her doctor. The Archduchess Sophie came to see her in her room. The ladies had a long and affectionate chat about family matters. She seemed much better: cheered up by the presence of her dear Sophie.

On 15 October, her name day, Monseigneur Viale the Papal Nuncio came from Vienna to say the Mass for the Sick for her recovery at Frohsdorf. The Archduke Ferdinand d'Este came to see her but was not able to do so. Her doctors forbade all visitors except the Comte and Comtesse de Chambord. The name day itself passed rather sadly. The next day was the anniversary of the death of her mother. This day was invariably spent by Marie Thérèse in prayer and quiet contemplation, with many hours in chapel. This year she was not well enough to get up and follow her usual rituals on the anniversary. Her family and doctors were concerned about the strain on her of the emotions of this difficult day and that they would be too taxing for her. Marie Thérèse had a terrible night; she was clearly deteriorating, saying to Madame de Sainte-Preuve that she could hear the 'death rattle' in her chest. The Princess was delirious. Madame de Sainte-Preuve was deeply distressed by how ill she was. Marie Thérèse was praying fervently, beseeching God to protect her nephew and save France. Nevertheless, she was determined to attend the service for her mother. Her servants managed to stop her getting out of bed by saying that Monseigneur Viale would be saying Mass for her mother. She asked for her thanks to be conveyed to him for his kind offices.

On the suggestion of Abbé Trébuquet, on 16 October she received Holy Communion in her room accompanied by Madame de Chabannes. It helped to calm her. During 16 October, Marie Thérèse could hear that there were serious problems with her breathing and she started to say her prayers. Dr Sceburger, the Emperor's Chief Physician, hurried from Vienna to her bedside. Dr Thevenot and Dr Sceburger held a consultation on the 'state of the patient', and the best means of saving her. They found that her disease was inflammation of the lungs, of such a violent kind as to be almost beyond the reach of medical treatment.[26] In an age before antibiotics, there was little to be done to combat pneumonia. There was little hope that she would recover. Marie Thérèse understood the position. She was convinced that she was very close to death. She was clearly very unwell, shivering and with a strange high colour. Madame de Sainte-Preuve, her Woman of the Bed Chamber, sat up all night with her. She prayed for France and for her nephew.

She seemed to rally a little during the night of 16/17 October and her doctors started to hope that she might recover. She felt well enough to be moved from her bed to a sitting room where she reclined on a sofa. Taking the opportunity to put her affairs in order, she asked that her papers be brought to her so that she could ensure that everything was as she would wish. She was even able to tidy her own desk. Her secretary, Baron Charlet, was summoned from Paris to help to put her affairs in order. Helping with this process was the Marquis de Pastoret who acted as Administrator for the Comte de Chambord in relation to his French estates and interests. Marie Thérèse with her usual practicality and clear-sightedness worked for two hours. She ensured that all her papers and affairs were in order and that she had discharged her duty towards the charities that she supported and cared about so much. She read outstanding correspondence, arranged for replies to be sent to well-wishers including the Duchesse de Lévis, asked questions of her staff to ensure that her wishes had been carried out and gave orders to M. de Saint-Preuve.[27] With her secretary Charlet, she made arrangements for small gifts of money to be made to a number of people about whom she was concerned and for whom she wanted to make financial provision.

She then asked to see various people, including Charles de Sainte-Maure. She had been very fond of his mother, Antoinette, who had been one of her ladies. She wanted to see M. de Blacas, whose family had served hers so diligently and over so many years. She would have liked to speak to her nephew's tutor, M. de Villette, but he was deaf and she did not have the strength to raise her voice so that he would be able to hear her. She wanted to have conversation with Madame de Chabannes. She spoke with the Duc de Lévis. Her doctors tried to persuade her to rest. That night she weakened and the fever returned. She was confused but continually praying asking God for forgiveness for her sins. Her doctors spent the night close to her. Despite her confusion she seemed to recognise the Comte de Chambord's voice. Regaining some clarity, she told him that she was exhausted and said farewell. She was surrounded by her household and family.

She did not speak again.

Madame de Sainte-Preuve tried to keep her comfortable, moistening her parched lips. The Abbé was saying the prayers for the dying and Marie Thérèse was clearly weakening. Around her the Comte and Comtesse de Chambord were on their knees praying at her bed, accompanied by members of the Household. As she finally drifted away, it was noted by the Comte de Pastoret:

> A sudden and deep silence chilled every heart. Over the head of the dying Countess was a painting representing the consoling angel pointing out to Louis XVI the glory of heaven. The worthy priest raised his arms and the cross towards this painting, thus uniting the idea of the great expiation of cavalry with the painful souvenirs of the 21st January, and the present sacrifice of proscribed virtue expiring in exile. Our hearts understood his

> feelings, and repeated with his Daughter of St Louis, and of Louis XVI, ascend to heaven.[28]

This ending is another of the Bourbon set pieces, providing a narrative of faith, order, family unity and continuity.

Marie Thérèse succumbed to pneumonia at 11 a.m.[29] on 19 October 1851, two months short of her 73rd birthday. At Frohsdorf on the first floor of the building where she died there is inscribed on a marble tablet the following words: 'Here after a long life full of suffering and troubles, Marie-Thérèse-Charlotte, Dauphine of France, Duchesse d'Angoulême gave her soul to God, 19 October 1851.' Her funeral took place on Saturday 25 October and the service was celebrated in front of a crowd assembled in the chapel of the Castle of Frohsdorf. Her nephew, Henri, Comte de Chambord, was not able to restrain his tears of grief for the woman who had been a second mother to him. He said that the death of his aunt who had so influenced his life and thinking was an enormous sadness to him. On 26 October the coffin containing Marie Thérèse's body was taken to the railway station at Murzzaschlagg, from which it was transported by rail to its final resting place, the Franciscan Convent at Castagnavizza near Goritz. Here lay already the bodies of her husband, the Duc d'Angoulême, Dauphin and briefly Louis XIX, and her uncle and father-in-law, Charles X – under the chapel which was dedicated to Our Lady of Carmel. She would lie between them. All the Courts of Europe went into mourning to mark her death. In Paris high society went into black, wearing mourning clothes as a mark of respect on hearing of the death of the Orphan of the Temple.

Marie Thérèse chose for her tombstone the following inscription: '*O vos omnes qui transitis per viam, attendite et videte si est dolor similis sicut dolor meus*' or 'All who walk past, stop and look to see if there is any sorrow as great as mine'. Hers was a great tragedy. She lost to violent or degrading deaths four of the people she loved most in the world. At an age when she should have been enjoying a safe and protected childhood and adolescence, she was unjustly and cruelly imprisoned.

She loved France with passion the whole of her life. In her will she said, 'I pray God to spread his blessings on France, which I have always loved, in the midst of most bitter afflictions.' Perhaps she loved a France that did not really exist and was the product of her idealism and imagination, but the love was genuine and generous throughout her whole life.

She wanted to turn the clock back to the *ancien régime* and realised too late that it could not be done. Despite everything, she never ceased to pray for the happiness of her countryfolk, however misled they might be, in her view. In death she forgave them and thanked all those who had remained faithful to the Bourbon cause, recognising the sacrifices they had made to support her family's claims. Exile from France was her fate and one she never ceased to bemoan. She was not, however, prepared to sanction the compromises that might have helped her nephew to regain the throne. The qualities of determination, even stubbornness, and pride which had allowed her to survive her experiences in the Temple did not always help her in her later life. She was generous in giving money and her support to institutions and individuals. Despite being a woman of charitable instincts and practical generosity, her lack of understanding of others' perceptions and sensitivities, for example during the difficult years of the Restoration, did not allow her to communicate with the bulk of her compatriots or to understand them and how France had changed.

Her sufferings were great, but not all her life was bleak. There were great compensations. She was a woman of deep religious faith and trust in God. She believed she would be reunited with her murdered family. In her will she said that she 'died in the Roman Catholic and apostolic religion, in which I have lived as faithfully as it is possible for me to do, and to which I owe all the consolations of my life'. She was married for more than forty years to a husband who might have been uninspiring but was kind and faithful. Her maternal instincts were not satisfied, but she was a most loved and loving aunt and second mother to her niece and nephew. In her will she also said, 'I have always considered my nephew Henri and my niece Louise as my children, and I give them my maternal benediction.' Marie Thérèse thanked the Emperor of Austria for the years of refuge, the kindness and 'proofs of interest and friendship' he and the Imperial family had given her family during its long exile. She thanked the inhabitants of Goritz and other Imperial possessions for their kindnesses. She shared close and lasting relationships throughout her life with a number of close female friends and took great pleasure from them. Within her own circle of friends and family she was loved even venerated. She was a woman of essential, even rather simple, honesty who would not compromise her own views and principles.

When called upon to be courageous and decisive, she was. She did not enjoy the demands of a public life but was diligent, if not always gracious, in fulfilling her duties. On the morning of the day she was to be executed, Marie Antoinette wrote a letter of enormous warmth and forgiveness, demonstrating her great love for the children she was leaving to what fate she knew not. Not only did she express her love and longing for them, but articulated the standards and personal ethics to be applied to achieve contentment in life. It was said of Marie Thérèse by the Duchesse de Dino that 'Certainly, however strong her character may be, her misfortunes have been such as to break the highest courage and the most masculine spirit. Beyond doubt she has been more persecuted by destiny than any character in history.'

All her sufferings may have damaged her spirit, but they did not break it. Looking back over her life it seems fair to say that Marie Thérèse with all her failings had fulfilled her mother's last wishes for her and those expressed by her father before her first communion that she edify by her example and help the unfortunate. She had done her duty and she had lived true to her own principles and her family.

Postscript

The Comte de Chambord never did become King of France. He died in exile and childless at Frohsdorf in 1883.

Notes

Introduction

1. La Marquise de Pompadour died in 1764.
2. Wars funded included the American War of Independence against the British and the Seven Years War 1756-63.
3. *Memoirs* of Lucie de la Tour du Pin, edited and translated by Walter Geer, Jonathan Cape, 1921.
4. Madame de Genlis was an aristocrat and governess to the children of the Duc d'Orléans, younger brother of Louis XIV. *Mémoires de Madame de Genlis*, Paris, Firmin-Didot, 1878.
5. As quoted in D. E. D. Beales, *Joseph II In the shadow of Maria Theresa*, Vol 1, Cambridge, 1987, p. 374.
6. Born Marie Louise Thérèse de Carignan, the Princesse de Lamballe (1749-92) was a wealthy heiress and the virtuous widow of the Duc d'Orléans' brother. She was, therefore, sister-in-law to Philippe Égalité and aunt to the future Louis Philippe I.
7. In 1775 Louis Auguste made a gift to Marie Antoinette of the Trianon, including the Petit Trianon villa, situated in the grounds of the Château of Versailles, for her private use.
8. *Libelles* were pamphlets used for political and social satire and comment, often highly derogatory of their subject.
9. Madame Campan, *The Private Life of Marie Antoinette: A Confidante's Account*, 1500 Books, 2006.
10. Beales, *Joseph II in the Shadow of Maria Theresa*, Vol. 1.
11. A hymn beginning *Te Deum laudamus*, 'We praise Thee, O God', sung at Matins or special occasions such as thanksgiving.

1. Mousseline la Sérieuse

1. The Princess's uncle, the Comte de Provence, was without a baptismal name until he was five years old.
2. Madame Campan, *The Private Life of Marie Antoinette.*
3. Comtesse de Boigne, edited and with an Introduction by Anka Muhlstein, Afterword by Olivier Bernier, *Memoirs of the Comtesse de Boigne, Vol. I, 1781-1815*, Helen Marx Books, 2003.
4. Following the war of the Spanish Succession, Louis XIV's grandson Philip acceded to the throne of Spain in 1700 as Philip V, thus spreading the dynasty further throughout Europe. He had renounced his claim to the throne of France. Charles IV, his grandson, had succeeded to the throne of Spain in 1778. The Spanish family had deleted the 'u' from their name to conform to Spanish spelling conventions.
5. This was in contrast to his predecessor Louis XV whose numerous daughters, 'Les Tantes', were sent to a convent, the Abbaye de Tontevraud, as babies and did not return to Versailles for many years as a way of saving money on their upbringing.
6. Marquis de Bombelles, *Journal*, ed. Jean Grassion and Frans Durif, Geneva, 1977.
7. Lived 1638 to 1715, King from 1643.
8. Louis XV was born in 1710, acceded to the throne in 1715 and died in 1774.
9. Men were required to wear swords which could be hired from outside the palace – a source of income for the monarch
10. They were friends with Messieurs Barnave and Pétion, who would later play significant parts in the downfall of their cousins. It is also suggested that Madame de Genlis, the governess to the Orléans children, was instrumental in writing *libelles* against Marie Antoinette.
11. Madame Campan, *The Private Life of Marie Antoinette.*

12. Baroness d'Oberkirch, *Memoirs of Baronne d'Oberkirch*, London: Colborn & Co. Publishers, 1852.
13. As can be seen on furniture from the Queen's collection at Waddesdon Manor near Aylesbury.
14. An assistant to the Baron de Breteuil who attempted to preserve the power of the monarchy after the Revolution, was ambassador to Venice and later Almoner to the Duchesse de Berry.
15. Marie Thérèse was allocated an allowance to enable her Household to make grants and gifts to selected causes, individuals in need and institutions.
16. Née Victoire-Madeleine-Henriette Hutin.
17. *Correspondance de Marie-Antoinette 1770-1793, établie, présentée et annotée par Evelyne Lever*, Tallandier, 2005: Marie Antoinette to Maria Theresa, 16 November 1779.
18. Ibid., Marie Antoinette to Maria Theresa, Versailles, 11 October 1780.
19. Ibid., Marie Antoinette to Maria Theresa, Versailles, 16 August 1779.
20. Ibid., Marie Antoinette to Maria Theresa, Versailles, 16 March 1780.
21. Madame Campan, *The Private Life of Marie Antoinette.*
22. Born 1741, became Holy Roman Emperor in 1765 and died in 1790.
23. Lived 1749-93, and usually known as Gabrielle.
24. Baroness d'Oberkirch, *Memoirs.*
25. Some sources suggest that it was the Comte d'Artois who coined the nickname for his niece.
26. Situated in the Bois de Boulogne, and constructed in less than three months as a bet.
27. Pauline de Béarn, *Souvenirs de Quarante Ans 1789 to 1830: Récits d'une dame de Madame la Dauphine*, Paris: Jacques le Coffre et Cie, 1861.
28. The Orléans family at this time introduced into their family an English foundling by the name of Pamela, who was educated with the children of the family and later married Lord Edward Fitzgerald. One of the aims of this arrangement was to help the Orléans children with their English.
29. She was a close friend of the wife of Czar Paul I of Russia.
30. A rather strange reaction for a princess who was herself of partly Austrian descent and prided herself on her Habsburg origins.
31. For a fuller description, see Frances Mossiker, *The Queen's Necklace – Marie Antoinette and the scandal that shocked and mystified France*, Phoenix, 2004.
32. Also known as Tipu Sultan, the Tiger of Mysore (in southern India). He was born in 1750, crowned in 1782 and died in battle in 1799.
33. Madame Campan, *The Private Life of Marie Antoinette.*
34. It was to his father that the Comte de Provence had written on the birth of Marie Thérèse in December 1778.
35. Lucie de la Tour du Pin, *Memoirs.*
36. An ornamental covering spread over a horse's saddle or harness.
37. *Sic*, meaning brightly shining.
38. La Comtesse de Provence.
39. Later Place de la Révolution and now Place de la Concorde.
40. Mme de Gontaut, *Memoirs of Duchesse de Gontaut, gouvernante to the children of France during the restoration (1773-1836)*, London: Chatto and Windus, 1894.
41. Now Koblenz in Germany, south of Cologne and to the east of Belgium and Luxembourg, and situated on the Rhine.
42. The Duchesse de Guiche had been married at the age of thirteen to M. de Gramont, who was made Duc de Guiche. This advantageous marriage had attracted much enmity and jealousy at Court, according to Madame Campan.
43. Louise-Félicité de Tourzel, *Memoires de Madame la Duchesse de Tourzel, Gouvernante des Enfants de France Pendant les Années 1789, 1790, 1791, 1792, 1793, 1794, 1795*, Paris: E. Plon, 1883.
44. Comtesse de Boigne, *Memoirs, Vol. I, 1781-1815.*
45. The guardsman, M. de Miomandre de Sainte-Marie, recovered from his wounds and went into exile, returning to France in 1814.
46. Other accounts indicate that Monsieur and Madame travelled to Paris separately from the rest of the Royal Family in their own carriage. Whatever their mode of transport, the trauma of their terrible journey must have been great.

Notes

2. At the Tuileries

1. Pauline de Béarn, *Souvenirs de Quarante Ans.*
2. Briefly husband of Mary Queen of Scots before his untimely death.
3. Some suggest 366 rooms.
4. This carpet survived the Revolution, and years later it was drawn to the attention of the Empress Joséphine, who arranged for it to be preserved so that Marie Thérèse might appreciate the handiwork of her mother and aunt.
5. As noted by Madame Campan.
6. Madame Campan, *The Private Life of Marie Antoinette.*
7. Presumbably Ernestine.
8. Imbert de Saint-Amand, translated by Elizabeth Gilbert Martin., *Marie Antoinette at the Tuileries 1789-1791,* Charles Scribner's Sons, 1902.
9. William Wordsworth, 'The French Revolution as it Appeared to Enthusiasts at its Commencement'.
10. 24 May 1790, according to Madame de Tourzel.
11. The château was destroyed during the Franco-Prussian War of 1870-71. The palace was situated in what are now the leafy suburbs of Paris. The gardens are open to the public.
12. Pauline de Béarn, *Souvenirs de Quarante Ans.*
13. Madame de Tourzel, *Mémoires.*
14. Mezzanine.
15. Lived 1729-1811. In 1783 he married Antoinette Chappuis, a lady-in-waiting to Madame Royale.
16. Some writers suggest that Ernestine went to her grandparents in the countryside, others to a convent with Madame de Mackau.
17. Marie Thérèse Charlotte, Duchesse d'Angoulême, *Private Memoirs ... which complete the History of the Captivity of the Royal Family of France in the Temple,* John Murray, 1817.
18. Minor local official.
19. Jérôme Pétion was a close associate and friend of the Orléans branch of the Bourbon family. It is suggested that he was also the lover of Madame de Genlis, governess to Philippe Égalité's children, including Louis Philippe, King of the French (1830-48). He travelled with the Orléans family to Bath in 1790 and was Mayor of Paris November 1791-October 1792.
20. Madame de Tourzel, *Mémoires.*
21. I.e. be on duty.
22. Antoine Louis François de Bésiade Comte d'Avaray (1759-1811), created Duc d'Avaray by Louis XVIII in 1799.
23. Gustav IV Adolf of Sweden, 1 November 1778–7 February 1837; King 1792-1809, when he abdicated the throne.
24. Madame de Tourzel, *Mémoires.*
25. Ibid.
26. Ibid.
27. Ibid.
28. Ernestine Lambriquet was able to escape from the Tuileries and rejoin her own family. Her father was tried and guillotined. His crime seems to have been to be too closely associated with the Royal Family, and this connection included his daughter's close relationship with Marie Thérèse. His daughter survived and seems to have worked in Paris; in 1810 she married Jean Charles Germain Prempain, a widower with children. She died in December 1813 in Passy, now a suburb of Paris, shortly before the return of her childhood companion to France.
29. Marie Thérèse.

3. The Tower of the Temple

1. The Revolutionaries always referred to Marie Thérèse by her third baptismal name of Charlotte. Why is not clear; perhaps they did not like to be reminded of her Imperial antecedents by referring to her as Marie Thérèse.
2. Madame de Tourzel recounts that the King was allowed one attendant, M Cléry (1759-1809); plus Madame Thibault for the Queen; Madame Navarre for Madame Élisabeth;

and Mesdames Basire and Saint Brice for the Dauphin and Marie Thérèse. M. Huë was also permitted to attend the family.

3. Madame de Tourzel reports that she was subject to nervous attacks and that the Queen did everything she could to persuade the Princess to leave, but she insisted on remaining with the family.
4. Baron François Huë (1757-1819), *valet de chambre* and later treasurer of Marie Thérèse's Household. His wife Henriette and later son André also worked in the Royal Household. He returned to France with the family in 1814.
5. Marie Thérèse.
6. Letter to the Countess of Sainte-Aldegonde from her sister Pauline de Tourzel, dated 8 September 1792.
7. A reference to the licentious wife of the Emperor Claudius.
8. Jean Baptiste Cléry, *Journal of Cléry During the Captivity of Louis XVI at the Prison of the Temple from 10 August 1792 to 21 January 1793*, Paris: E. Terquem; New York: Brentano's, 1906.
9. Pauline de Béarn reports that she once ate a letter rather than allow it to fall into the hands of her guards.
10. François Hüe, *The Last Years of the Reign and Life of Louis XVI*, Cadell and Davies, Strand, 1806.
11. My parents forbade me ever to cry when I was in the Temple, and this duty that I practised became a way of life.
12. Duchesse d'Angoulême, *Private Memoirs.*
13. Elizabeth I, 1558-1603.
14. Including the writer Maria Edgeworth.
15. Roman Catholics did not achieve equality before the law until 1829.
16. Louis XVI aka Louis Capet.
17. Formerly the Place Louis XV and now Place de la Concorde.
18. By 1799, at the time of Marie Thérèse's arrival in Mittau, it was being treated as a fact by the émigré community according to Abbé de Tressan.
19. Marie Thérèse in later life collected many relics of her family that she kept with her almost as religious icons. She was given in 1798, for example, a miniature of her father by the painter Pierre-Noel Violet.
20. In due course, the Revolutionary clubs of Paris threatened the Abbé with execution and he was forced to leave Paris and take refuge at Bayeux in Normandy, an easy escape base for England should the need arise. He was, however, loathe to leave France and his duties to the Royal Family and his own family. He had promised Madame Élisabeth, still imprisoned with her sister-in-law and family in the Tower of the Temple, that he would remain in France and available to her as long as she needed him. Equally, Edgeworth's mother and sister were trapped in Paris and he wanted to stay as close as possible to them in case they, too, needed his help. Madame de Tourzel met up with the Abbé in 1793 and was able to take comfort from the account by the Abbé of the death of Louis XVI. Travelling in ordinary clothes rather than priestly garb and living under a number of pseudonyms, Abbé Edgeworth survived in hiding in France until 1796, by which time all the Royal Family were dead with the exception of Madame Royale. His own mother had also died. He therefore felt able in all conscience to leave France and travel to safety in England, landing at Portsmouth in the summer of 1796.
21. Madame de Tourzel reports that he wished to go with Marie Thérèse when she left France for Austria in 1795.
22. The Convention had replaced the Legislative Assembly, which had in turn replaced the National Assembly, which had superseded the Estates General summoned in 1788. It first met at Versailles in 1789. It was a single chamber assembly from 2 September 1792 to 26 October 1795 and voted for the execution of Louis XVI.
23. Duchesse d'Angoulême, *Private Memoirs.*
24. Madame de Tourzel, *Mémoires.*
25. Quoted in Ernest Daudet, translated by Mrs Rudolph Stawell, *Madame Royale, daughter of Louis XVI and Marie Antoinette – her youth and marriage*, London: William Heinemann, 1913.
26. Duchesse d'Angoulême, *Memoirs.*
27. Lived 1757-94. He was himself guillotined during the Terror.
28. This was the last time that the boy saw any members of his family.
29. Now Place de la Concorde.

4. Orphan of the Temple

1. She had previously used this name ironically in her letters to friends.
2. Her remains were never found, but she is commemorated at St Denis with a plaque.
3. Born in Arras in 1758, the petit-bourgeois Robespierre trained as a lawyer and attended the 1789 Estates General as a representative of the Third Estate. Hard-working and personally incorruptible, he rose through the revolutionary ranks to become head of the Committee of Public Safety which ruled France. He presided over the Terror – a period of state-endorsed violence against the enemies (as he saw it) of the Revolution – during which thousands died.
4. Duchesse d'Angoulême, *Private Memoirs*.
5. Other accounts suggest that she did not in fact have any writing materials at this time, but there is no reason to disbelieve her account of events.
6. Duchesse d'Angoulême, *Private Memoirs*.
7. With a ten-day week.
8. Madame de Tourzel reports that M. Meunier, formerly of the King's commissariat, stayed at the Temple until December 1795 and Marie Thérèse's departure for Austria.
9. Paul Barras, *Memoirs of Barras, Member of Directorate*, New York: Harper & Brothers, 1896.
10. Madame de Tourzel, *Mémoires*.
11. Madame de Tourzel, *Mémoires*.
12. Paul François Barras, Vicomte (1755-1829), lover of Joséphine de Beauharnais, who introduced his mistress to her husband-to-be, Napoleon Bonaparte. Barras, *Memoirs*.
13. Barras' own account of the visit makes no reference to the Princess's enquiries about her family or any other conversation.
14. Christophe Laurent was a native of Martinique (like the Empress Joséphine) and was appointed to his role by Joséphine's lover, the Director Barras.
15. Marie Thérèse refers to this man as Gomier in her *Memoirs*, but M. Huë called him Gomin, as does Madame de Tourzel. I have used their version of his name.
16. Duchesse d'Angoulême, *Private Memoirs*.
17. Called Mignon in some accounts
18. As a female she could not inherit the throne herself, nor transmit it to her children.
19. To return to Martinique to care for his mother.
20. Duchesse d'Angoulême, *Private Memoirs*.
21. I.e. Marie Thérèse and Louis Charles.
22. Sometimes spelt Chantereine.
23. According to Madame de Tourzel, her husband was very keen that she should be appointed and had been canvassing for the role for her.
24. Duchesse d'Angoulême, *Private Memoirs*.
25. Ibid.
26. Coco.
27. Beuronville and his four companions had been captured by the Austrians when in April 1793 in his capacity as Minister of War he delivered to General Demouriez an order from the Convention Government to return to Paris to answer charges that he was a counter-revolutionary trying to return to the Constitution of 1791. Fearful of his own fate, the General had betrayed the Minister of War to the enemy. The Frenchmen were arrested by 40 Austrian Hussars. Beuronville attempted to escape but was forced back into the carriage at sword point. The future Louis Philippe was present at these interviews, and therefore his own position with the Revolutionary powers was compromised. This led in part to the charges against his father that led to Philippe Égalité's death.
28. This is subtle flattery, ignoring the arrival of Madame de Chanterenne and the visits of the Tourzel ladies, Madame de Mackau and M. Huë.
29. 5 October 1795 in the new post-Revolutionary calendar.
30. Formerly one of the colleges of the University of Paris and now the Palais de l'Institut de France.
31. Madame de Tourzel's memoirs record that by November 1795 M. Huë had written the first draft of *his* memoirs, which were with her for her comments and review; memoirs of the Revolution were becoming quite an industry.

5. At the Court of Austria

1. Over the centuries the town has moved between German and French sovereignty. At the time of Marie Thérèse's departure from France in December 1795 it belonged to France, as it does now.
2. 60 miles south-east of Paris.
3. Also known as Bâle and Basel.
4. Since orchestrating the detention of the Royal Family in June 1791 on their way to the border, Drouet had used his celebrity to get elected to the National Assembly where he voted for the execution of the King.
5. Born 1791 and later to become Empress of France when she married Napoleon Bonaparte in 1810.
6. The Diaries of Queen Hedwig Elizabeth Charlotte of Sweden suggest that the Empress was pathologically jealous and possessive of her husband.
7. The Emperor Paul I of Russia, by contrast, was quick to acknowledge Louis XVIII as the rightful King of France.
8. Acknowledged for his bravery by his arch-enemy Bonaparte.
9. Cléry had been arrested in September 1793 but was released. He spent some time in London, where he gave moving readings to groups of émigrés of this account of the last meeting of Louis XVI and his family. See Lucie de la Tour du Pin, edited and translated by Walter Geer, *Memoirs*, London: Jonathan Cape, 1921.
10. Lived 1752-1829, Bishop of Nancy prior to the Revolution.
11. This aunt had left Versailles to marry the Prince of Piedmont in 1775, so was unknown to Marie Thérèse in person.
12. Lived 1726-1796, King from 1773.
13. Situated in the modern Czech Republic and now known as Ceske Budejovice.
14. Coincidentally, the third anniversary of the death of Marie Antoinette.
15. Later Empress Marie Louise of France, second wife of the Emperor Napoleon I.
16. Lived 1776 (some sources say 1778) to 1845.
17. Lived 1760-1841, becoming Vicomtesse d'Agoult after her marriage in 1815.
18. Madame Campan, *The Private Life of Marie Antoinette*.
19. Lived 1743-1808.
20. Lived 1770-1840, and King from 1797.
21. Lived 1729-1796.
22. In Belarus, close to the borders with Poland and Lithuania.
23. I.e.to marry Louis Antoine.
24. As her Uncle Louis XVIII wrote of her.
25. Son of George III, later Duke of Sussex.
26. One of the rebel leaders who was captured and executed in March 1796, aged 32.
27. The Fructidor *coup d'état* that suppressed Royalist uprisings and established further the power of Bonaparte.
28. Capital of French Guyana, to which the Royalist prisoners were sent.
29. The Duchesse d'Angoulême visited the Vendée in 1823 to thank the local people for their support of her father. Some wags suggested that she had left it rather late to come and show her appreciation for their support. But a column was built to mark her visit at St Florent, 45 miles from La Rochelle.
30. The Archduchess Marie Anne felt that such guidance would come better from the Bishop, as a man of God, rather than from her.
31. Lived 1763-1844.
32. Francis II.
33. The Treaty of Campo Formio, 17 October 1797.

6. Marriage and Mittau

1. Her elder sister Marie Joséphine married his elder brother, the Comte de Provence.
2. Madame Campan, *The Private Life of Marie Antoinette*.
3. Lived 1764-1804.
4. *The Tablet* (the Catholic newspaper) of May 1899 reported that the chapel was a modest building with a gallery which later was occupied by Louis XVIII on his visits to London, sitting in an armchair.

5. Lived 1759-1806.
6. The Duc d'Angoulême was painted by W. J. Thompson and his father by F. Ferrière.
7. In one account by the Abbé de Tressan, the Queen was waiting at the Palace and there met her niece again for the first time since 1791.
8. Quoted in Daudet, *Madame Royale.*
9. Cardinal de Montmorency, the Duc de Fleury, the Duc de Villequier, the Duc de Guiche, the Marquis de Nesle, the Comte de la Chapelle, the Comte de Brissac, the Comte d'Avaray, Abbé Edgeworth, Abbé Marie, the Comte de Saint-Priest, the Marquis de Dancourt and the Vicomte de Virieu.
10. Imbert de Saint-Amand, *The Duchess of Angoulême.*
11. It will be noted that the Comte de Provence had written in very derogatory terms about Marie Antoinette during the early days of his exile.
12. Born Princess Sophia Dorothea of Württemberg.
13. Madame Campan, *The Private Life of Marie Antoinette.*
14. Ibid.
15. As quoted in Daudet, *Madame Royale.*
16. Lived 1729-1800; a very successful Russian field marshal who is mentioned in Byron's *Don Juan.*
17. *London Gazette*, 20 December 1800.
18. Napoleon Bonaparte brought to an end the Republic of Venice.
19. Kingdom of the Spanish Borbons who were descended from Philip V, a grandson of Louis XIV, who had succeeded to the vacant throne of Spain. His descendants still occupy this throne.
20. Lived 1732-1800, buried after the Restoration at St Denis in 1817.
21. Lived 1733-1799, buried after the Restoration at St Denis in 1817.
22. One of their letters was captured by Napoleonic forces during the Hundred Days in 1815 and published, much to their embarrassment.

7. Antigone and a British Exile

1. A. H. Dampmartin, *Mémoires sur Divers Événements de la Révolution et de l'Émigration,* Paris: Chez Hubert Libraire, 1825.
2. *London Gazette*, 31 March 1801.
3. Lived 1677-1766.
4. Jane Austen, *Pride and Prejudice*, published in 1813.
5. Pope from 1800 to 1823.
6. He was an émigré who served in the Austrian army but returned to France after the amnesty. He was involved in the Russian campaign of 1812, returning from Russia to France on foot. Later, under the Restoration, he was involved in the Spanish campaign of 1823 with the Duc d'Angoulême – an interesting example of how a French aristocrat and soldier changed loyalties. In Bourbon terms, he blotted his copy book and remained in service during the Hundred Days; so in the Second Restoration he was put on half pay. But he did refuse to serve under Louis Philippe after the 1830 Revolution.
7. The Peace of Amiens.
8. As quoted in Vivienne Abbott, *An Irishman's Revolution: the Abbé Edgeworth and Louis XVI,* Dublin: Kavanagh Press, 1989.
9. Lived 1772-1804.
10. Lived 1793-1862; later Duchesse de Dino, niece and close companion of Talleyrand, the French politician and ultimate survivor who was her uncle by marriage. She lived in Paris off and on from 1809 and was lady-in-waiting to the Empress Marie Louise. She was also Talleyrand's hostess at the Congress of Vienna, at which the fate of post-Napoleonic Europe would be settled.
11. One of the few references to Marie Thérèse's attractiveness after her early youth.
12. Sometimes known as Calmar.
13. Then Prince of Wales.
14. Younger brother of the Duc d'Orléans.
15. It can still be visited.
16. It is suggested in excess of 350 people.
17. Gosfield Hall.
18. Union Jack.
19. Lived 1752-1840; author and Keeper of the Robes (1786-91) to Queen Charlotte.

20. The diarist C. F. Greville (1794-1865) confirms his father's reports to the Seward family, saying that the King 'had subdivided almost all the apartments in order to lodge a greater number of people'. The property 'resembled a small town' with the servants running shops in the out buildings.
21. Now used as the Bar of the hotel at Hartwell House, Aylesbury, Buckinghamshire, a National Trust property.
22. This lack of direct heirs of Louis XVIII was one of the arguments put forward in 1814 for the accession of Louis Philippe rather than the senior Bourbon line, as he was the father of sons.
23. Mme de Gontaut, *Memoirs of Duchesse de Gontaut.*
24. Letter from Mrs H. Piozzi quoted in Thomas Sedgewick Whalley, ed., *Whalley DD: journals and correspondence of Thomas Sedgewick Whalley DD of Mendip Lodge, Somerset*, London: Richard Bentley, 1862.
25. Philip Mansel reports that the English government provided Louis XVIII with £16,000 per annum, a similar amount to that provided for the sons of George III; in addition, Louis received a pension of approximately £4,000 per annum from the Russian government.
26. Born 12 December 1791.
27. Her mother, the Empress Marie Thérèse of Naples, was herself a Bourbon princess, a daughter of Maria Carolina of Naples.
28. Now known as Oedema OED condition, characterised by an excess of watery fluid collecting in the cavities or tissues of the body.
29. As quoted in Philip Mansel, *Louis XVIII*, Blond and Briggs Ltd, 1981.
30. This was not the King's view after the Restoration: he sent painters back to Hartwell to capture its beauties for him.
31. A favourite Bourbon recreation.
32. Previously.
33. *Sic* for Madame de Sérent.
34. Trigeminal neuralgia, literally a painful tic.
35. As opposed to the English custom which was for the ladies to leave the gentlemen at table to drink their port.
36. Evidence perhaps of the shortage of napery that they had experienced during Mittau II, and the desire perhaps not to create unnecessary and expensive laundry.
37. A trick-taking card game for three players using forty cards.
38. Pierre Louis de Blacas, 1771-1839.
39. It was situated on the southern side of Pall Mall and its gardens abutted St James's Park. The site of the Prince Regent's home has now been replaced by Carlton House Terrace.
40. For example, the visit of representatives of Indian rulers just before the Revolution, when she had sat on a small dais to receive the representatives with the other ladies of the Court.
41. The social elite of the Georgian and Regency period.
42. A ladies' long scarf or cloak; *Morning Chronicle* of 2 December 1811.
43. George III's wife and mother of the Prince Regent.
44. A success for Edward IV in the Wars of the Roses, 1471.
45. See Malcolm Pearce and Geoffrey Stewart, *British Political History 1867-2011: Democracy and Decline*, London: Routledge, 1992.

8. The First Restoration

1. Unbeknownst to Napoleon, who from his letters in early March 1814 to his wife clearly still hoped and believed that his father-in-law, Francis I of Austria, would facilitate an honourable peace between France and its enemies and thereby protect the interests of his grandson the infant King of Rome.
2. Craonne (7 March), Rheims (13 March), Arcis-sur-Aube (20 March).
3. As Holy Roman Emperor (a title he had been forced to give up by Napoleon), he was Francis II, but Francis I as Emperor of Austria.
4. Comtesse de Boigne, *Memoirs, Vol. II, 1816-1830.*
5. Hortense was unhappily married to Louis, younger brother of Napoleon. Her son Napoleon-Louis became the Emperor Napoleon III of France.

6. The King of England, Emperor of Russia, Emperor of Austria and King of Prussia, known as the Holy Alliance.
7. Conscription to fight his continental wars had made Napoleon very unpopular in France, particularly amongst women: the wives, mothers, sisters and sweethearts of the soldiers. More than 1.4 million men had died fighting during the Napoleonic Wars.
8. About 6 miles.
9. Ragusa is a town in the south of Sicily.
10. Comtesse de Boigne, *Memoirs, Vol. I, 1781-1815.*
11. For Napoleon's son, the King of Rome.
12. Lord Byron, 'The Age of Bronze', 1823.
13. Gout is a very painful and disabling affliction caused by an inflammation of the joints. It is often viewed as the curse of good living, and regarded as somewhat comical; it is nevertheless very painful for the sufferer.
14. Near the modern New Bond Street in the heart of Mayfair and ten minutes' walk from 72 South Audley Street, the home in exile of the Comte d'Artois.
15. Havelock, Henry, translator. *Alexander I and the Grandduchess Catherine. Scenes from Russian Court Life, being the Correspondence of Alexander I with his sister Catherine with an Introduction by Grand Duke Nicholas,* Jarrolds Publishers.
16. *The Court Historian*, the house journal of the Society for Court Studies, Vol. 15, 2 December 2010, reported that the Prince Regent, later George IV, collected busts of Louis XVI and Marie Antoinette. In 1817 Louis XVIII gave the then Prince Regent the magnificent Sèvres Table of the Grand Commanders, which had been designed for Napoleon but was never used by him. It is still in the Royal Collection.
17. Despite Madame de Gontaut's intimate acquaintance with the family, she would appear to be mistaken in thinking that this was the first time Marie Thérèse had met her cousin. They had met at Hartwell previously (see Chapter 8), but this may well have been the first time they had been together outside the privacy of their family circle and in a public place. Equally, other sources suggest that the Duc d'Orléans was in fact in Sicily with his wife's family at this time.
18. Later William IV (1830-1837).
19. The *ancien régime* Royal family rarely travelled outside the Île de France. Louis XVI made one trip to Le Havre during his reign.
20. Duchesse de Gontaut, *Memoirs.*
21. A column was also erected, which still exists, but was moved from its original site to protect it when work was undertaken on the port at Calais.
22. As was one of Napoleon's sisters, Caroline, wife of Murat and former Queen of Naples.
23. At the Restoration, Madame Campan came under suspicion of being less than loyal to Marie Antoinette. She was damned for her close association with the Imperial regime, as she was involved in the education of Caroline Bonaparte and Hortense de Beauharnais. Madame de Tourzel's Memoirs defend Madame Campan, saying, 'she always kept profoundly secret whatever her Majesty confided in her'.
24. This term was also used by the Duc de Berry in describing Marie Thérèse to his future wife Marie Caroline of the Two Sicilies.
25. Comtesse de Boigne, *Memoirs, Vol. II, 1816-1830.*
26. Ibid.
27. Queen Victoria reports that he was very strict about his diet.
28. Louis XVIII weighed at least 17 stone and was often confined to a wheelchair by gout.
29. Others noted that Talleyrand met the Royal party at Compiègne for the first time.
30. Now a married lady and Madame la Comtesse de Béarn.
31. She was created a Duchesse by Louis XVIII for her many services to the Bourbon family.
32. Lucie de la Tour du Pin, *Journal.*
33. Compiègne was the place where the Duchesse d'Angoulême's parents had first met following their proxy marriage and Marie Antoinette's arrival in her new country. It served a similar purpose when another Archduchess, Marie Louise, cousin to the Duchesse d'Angoulême, travelled from Vienna in 1810 to marry Napoleon.
34. There was a suggestion that he might be an alternative candidate for the role of King, rather than restoring the Bourbons.
35. Lucie de la Tour du Pin, *Journal.*
36. Comtesse de Boigne, *Memoirs, Vol. II, 1816-1830.*

37. Michel Ney, 1769-1815, also had the Napoleonic titles of Prince de la Moskwa and 1st Duc d'Elchingen.
38. Eugène de Beauharnais married Augusta, the daughter of the King of Bavaria, who had been pleased during the ascendancy of the Bonapartes to connect his family to the arriviste Napoleon. The King of Bavaria's niece Princess Elisabeth married Maréchal Berthier. The marriage between Eugène and Augusta seems to have been successful and happy. Following the fall of Napoleon in 1814, Eugène established himself in Bavaria as Duke of Leuchtenberg. His daughter Joséphine, named after her grandmother, married Oscar, the son of the Bernadotte and heir to the throne of Sweden, and is an ancestress of the present Swedish Royal Family.
39. This practice was soon abandoned, and he was received at Court using his Napoleonic title of Prince Eugène.
40. Four miles from central Paris and now part of the suburbs.
41. Hortense was noted for the musical quality of her own voice.
42. Emperor of Austria, King of Prussia and Wellington as representative of the British King.
43. I.e. heraldic coats of arms
44. Bavaria (1818), Piedmont (1848), Prussia (1850).
45. A Chamber of Peers and a Chamber of Deputies, which was elected by all males who paid more than 300 francs a year in tax. It was to meet every year. The Crown had the right to propose legislation. There would be annual elections at which 20% of the seats in the Chamber of Deputies would be contested.
46. I.e. the servants of Napoleon.
47. The location of Madame Louise's Carmelite convent, so often visited by Marie Thérèse accompanied by her parents and Madame Elisabeth, and the Royal Mausoleum.
48. Location of the *Fête de la Fédération* of 14 July 1790.
49. Duchesse de Gontaut, *Memoirs.*
50. Ibid.

9. The Hundred Days and Waterloo

1. A scarf to cover the bosom.
2. Courtier to the Bourbons and brother to the diarist Madame de Boigne, as quoted in Joseph Turquan, edited by Lady Theodora Davidson, *Madame Royale – the Last Dauphine Marie-Thérèse-Charlotte de France, Duchesse d'Angoulême*, London: T. Fisher Unwin, 1910.
3. Known as the Place de la Révolution during the Revolutionary time and previously Place Louis XV, site of many executions.
4. Comtesse de Boigne, *Memoirs, Vol. 1, 1781-1815.*
5. According to André Castelot.
6. Née Laure de Saint-Martin-Permond, 1784-1838.
7. Comtesse de Boigne, *Memoirs, Vol. 1, 1781-1815.*
8. The later title of Marie Thérèse.
9. Madame d'Abrantès, *Memoirs.*
10. Munro Price suggests that the Duc d'Angoulême was in Paris in early May and took part in the ceremonial.
11. Philip Mansel, *The Court of France 1789-1830*, Cambridge University Press, 1991.
12. Monsieur, the title by custom used by the eldest brother of the King.
13. The Orléans family often visited Marie Thérèse during her stays. This had been a favourite spa and holiday resort for her great-aunts, Mesdames les Tantes Victoire and Adélaïde, before their departure from France into exile in 1791. The Princesses' visits had helped make it a fashionable watering place. Marie Thérèse continued this trend and returned to Vichy for cures five times further in the years 1816, 1818, 1821, 1826 and 1830. It was written of Vichy in Douglas P. Mackaman's *Leisure Settings: Bourgeois Culture, Medicine and the Spa in Modern France* that 'Vichy in the 1820s represented one important model of spa development'. Owned and administered by the French government, Vichy was a spa of the French system. Majestically situated on the banks of the Allier River in a valley of striking beauty, the town of 900 inhabitants welcomed slightly fewer than 1,000 bathers every year in the 1820s; it boasted a well-founded reputation for lively society in the summer season, as well as waters which were highly regarded by continental doctors. While she was there the Duchesse d'Angoulême received petitions and deputations. The combination of Vichy's reputation and the

advantages it enjoyed as a state property placed it among the premier watering places of Europe.

14. Which was purpose-built as a home for the collections.
15. Marie Thérèse referred to Marie Amélie as her real cousin, as opposed to the rest of the Orléans clan.
16. Born 1933.
17. His father and a regicide.
18. Louis XVIII, *Memoirs of Louis the Eighteenth written by himself*, La Mothe Houdancourt, afterwards La Mothe Langon, Etienne Léon de, Baron. London: Henry Colburn and Richard Bentley, 1830.
19. They were first attacked in August 1793, and over a three-day rampage 51 royal tombs were destroyed.
20. The originator of the terrible accusations of incest against Marie Antoinette and Madame Élisabeth.
21. The tombs at St Denis had been attacked and damaged during the Revolution.
22. Very nearby is Rue Tronson du Coudray, named in honour of the advocate Guillaume-Alexandre Tronson du Coudray who made a speech in defence of Marie Antoinette at her trial. He opposed the Directory in 1797 and was deported to Guiana, where he died the following year.
23. By François-Antoine Gérard.
24. By Joseph Bosio.
25. By Jean-Pierre Cortot.
26. As she kneels before the figure of 'Religion'.
27. Following the end of the Restoration in 1830, the Chapelle was regarded by many to be an inappropriate relic of the *ancien régime*, a rebuke to the French people for rebelling against their rulers. There were attempts to have it demolished, but its survival was due to the Empress Eugenie who took a particular interest in all matters connected with Marie Antoinette and her story. Religious services were said at the Chapelle until 1883, and it was listed as a historic monument in 1914.
28. These words were spoken in French but translated into English in her diaries.
29. 'May I keep the book which you sent me?'
30. Shyness.
31. Fanny and her French husband and son returned to France in 1802 following the Peace of Amiens. The peace was short-lived and the family was trapped in France when hostilities between Napoleon and Britain resumed.
32. A reference to the young son and heir of Napoleon who had fled into exile with his mother, the Austrian born Empress Marie Louise, and was living in Vienna at the Court of his grandfather, the Emperor Francis II, being brought up as an Austrian Archduke while continuing to assert his love for his father and France.
33. A *courir sus* order means an order to harry and disrupt.
34. Some sources suggest 5 million francs.
35. Created in 1830.
36. Mansel, *Louis XVIII.*
37. Friday 7 April 1815.
38. A stranger comes to usurp the throne of your legitimate King.
39. I have not the strength to see the French people unhappy and to be the cause of that unhappiness.
40. In fact he never made it to Lyon, being intercepted 200 kilometres away by forces loyal to the returning Emperor.
41. Some sources suggest 2 April.
42. *The Times* reported that she had planned on living in a hotel which had been prepared for her, near to the palace occupied by Louis XVIII.
43. Sometimes spelt d'Hune de Steenhuye.

10. The Second Restoration

1. It was at this time that the word '*bystro*', Russian for 'quick', found its way into the French language as conquering Cossacks called for rapid refreshment.
2. Declaration of Saint-Ouen, 2 May 1814.
3. However, she later received at Court his daughter, Madame de Terme, who had a reputation of unimpeachable virtue.

4. Lived 1782-1854.
5. Resolute action and policy.
6. Comtesse de Boigne, *Memoirs, Vol. I, 1781-1815.*
7. This commemorated the dedication in 1638 by Louis XIII of France to the Virgin Mary. A picture depicting the Vow of Louis XIII was painted by Jean-Auguste-Dominique Ingres (1780-1867) and exhibited at the Paris Salon of 1824.
8. Long live the Duc and Duchesse d'Angoulême. May the Bourbon family live for ever.
9. Down with the Bourbons.
10. Marie Thérèse and her aunt had not in fact been separated at this time, but this was perhaps another example of the emotional pressure put on Marie Antoinette by her prosecutors during her imprisonment in the Conciergerie and her trial.
11. Marie Antoinette had obviously been closely informed of the events surrounding her husband's execution.
12. See Chapter 4 for more details of these episodes.
13. Even less lofty partners for Berry were proposed during the years of exile. Their English benefactor the Marquis of Buckingham had thought his own daughter Lady Mary a very suitable match for the refugee Bourbon Prince.
14. Madame de Boigne, *Memoirs, Vol. I, 1781-1815.*
15. The Duc d'Angoulême's mother, Marie Thérèse of Savoy, had died in 1805 in Turin when the Angoulêmes were based in Mittau.
16. The Queen Marie Joséphine had died at Hartwell in 1810.
17. His beloved mistress Madame de Polastron had died in London in 1804 after a long illness, and his wife in 1805. Moved by his deep faith and grief at the loss of Madame de Polastron, he did not take another mistress.
18. The Duc de Berry had once been proposed as a possible suitor for Princess Marie Amélie, who subsequently married the Duc d'Orléans and was Maria Carolina's aunt. Maria Carolina's strong-minded mother, Queen Maria Carolina of Naples, did not consider the then exiled Prince, who was also a younger son, to be a suitably grand match for her daughter
19. Lived 1778-1820..
20. Comtesse de Boigne, *Memoirs, Vol. II, 1816-1830.*
21. Comtesse de Boigne, *Memoirs, Vol. II, 1816-1830.*
22. Literally Russian mountains.
23. Comtesse de Boigne, *Memoirs, Vol. II, 1816-1830.*
24. Ibid.
25. There are suggestions that the couple were in fact married, albeit without having obtained the necessary Royal permissions, and that the marriage had to be dissolved before the Duc de Berry could marry Marie Caroline.
26. Lived 1808-1886.
27. Lived 1809-1891.
28. An adviser to the Royal Family.
29. Lived 1819-1864, also called la Petite Mademoiselle.
30. Duchesse de Gontaut, *Memoirs.*
31. Comtesse de Boigne, *Memoirs, Vol. II, 1816-1830.*
32. Louis-Charles-Philippe-Raphaël d'Orléans, Duc de Nemours; born 25 October 1814, Paris; died 26 June 1896, Versailles.
33. Lived 1783-1820.
34. Charles-Jacques-Julien Bougon (1779-1851), the last Surgeon Ordinary to the Bourbons, was a committed Royalist who had followed Louis XVIII to Ghent in 1814. He served the family for many years.
35. There was criticism later of the treatment given to the Prince and Dupuytren was called before the Chamber of Peers to explain and justify his actions. He was ennobled by Louis XVIII in recognition of his services.
36. Jo Burr Margadant, 'The Duchesse de Berry and Royalist Political Culture in Postrevolutionary France', *History Workshop Journal* no. 43, Spring 1997.
37. Madame de Boigne reported that both Marie Caroline and the Duc d'Angoulême lived up to their promises to to care for the dying man's illegitimate children. Marie Caroline helped to bring up the girls, provided them with dowries and gave them posts in her Household. They appeared at Court.
38. Some reports say that 5.30 a.m. was the time of death.
39. There had been restoration of the tombs, damaged during the Revolution.
40. A role equivalent in the English system to that of Prime Minister.

41. Lived 1780-1860.
42. Comtesse de Boigne, *Memoirs, Vol. II, 1816-1830.*
43. Born Marie Joséphine Louise de Montault-Navailles, 1773-1857. Her own father had supervised the education of a previous generation of Royal children, namely Louis XVI, Louis XVIII and Charles X.
44. Comtesse de Boigne, *Memoirs, Vol. II, 1816-1830.*
45. As quoted in Turquan, *Madame Royale.*
46. Charles-André Comte, later Duc Pozzo di Borgo, 1764-1842, was a Corsican nobleman who supported independence for Corsica and entered the service of the Emperor. He was Russian ambassador to France during the Restoration.
47. During the Revolution it had been suggested as a possible place of imprisonment for Louis XVI and his son.
48. She survived Louis XVIII by many years, dying in 1852.
49. Ferdinand VII (1784-1833) was King for a few months in 1808 and then again 1813-1823. He was married to the Duchesse de Berry's sister, Maria Christina.
50. As quoted in Turquan, *Madame Royale.*
51. *Morning Post*, 9 December 1823.
52. This estate was later used by the Emperor Napoleon III and the Empress Eugénie.
53. Monique de Huertas, *Madame Royale, L'enigmatique destinée de la fille de Louis XVI*, Feryane, 1999.
54. Comtesse de Boigne, *Memoirs, Vol. II, 1816-1830.*
55. He proved to be unpopular with the Ultras and the liberals alike.
56. Comtesse de Boigne, *Memoirs, Vol. II, 1816-1830.*

11. The First Lady of France

1. As quoted in Munro Price, *The Fall of the French Monarchy: Louis XVI, Marie Antoinette and the Baron de Breteuil*, Pan, 2003.
2. Archbishop of Paris, Grand Almoner, Bishop of Hermopolis.
3. D'Avaray, Blacas and Boisgelin and Talleyrand.
4. Diary of Madame Adélaïde.
5. Comtesse de Boigne, *Memoirs, Vol. II, 1816-1830.*
6. Ibid.
7. The Duchesse de Gontaut (1772-1857).
8. Queen Victoria's Journal of Monday 19 November 1838 reports that she was told by her beloved Lord Melbourne that the Comte d'Artois was 'a very lively, agreeable, pleasant man, very easy'.
9. Comtesse de Boigne, *Memoirs, Vol. II, 1816-1830.*
10. Ibid.
11. Ibid.
12. Ibid.
13. Ibid.
14. Ibid.
15. Ibid.
16. Ibid.
17. Ibid.
18. Ibid.
19. Ibid.
20. Ibid.
21. Memoirs of the Duchesse d'Orléans.
22. Prince de Joinville, translated from the French by Lady Mary Lloyd, *Memoirs of the Prince de Joinville: 'Vieux Souvenirs'*, New York and London: Macmillan & Co., 1893. He was the third son of Louis Philippe and Marie Amélie, born 14 August 1818 and died 16 June 1900.
23. Jean Baptiste Marie Anne Antoine (1761-1839), made Cardinal in 1829.
24. 'Long Live the King forever'.
25. Comtesse de Boigne, *Memoirs, Vol. II, 1816-1830.*
26. Saint-Amand, *The Duchesse de Berry and the Court of Charles X.*
27. Comtesse de Boigne, *Memoirs, Vol. II, 1816-1830.*
28. Hugh, 3rd Duke of Northumberland, 1785-1847.
29. Comtesse de Boigne, *Memoirs, Vol. II, 1816-1830.*

30. Ibid.
31. Ibid.
32. Prince de Joinville, *'Vieux Souvenirs'.*
33. Ibid.
34. Comtesse de Boigne, *Memoirs, Vol. II, 1816-1830.*
35. Baronne de Feuchères, 1795-1840.
36. Comtesse de Boigne, *Memoirs, Vol. II, 1815-1830.*
37. Duchesse de Gontaut, *Memoirs.*
38. Charles François de Rivière (1763-1828). He took over as the Duc de Bordeaux's governor in 1826.
39. Comtesse de Boigne, *Memoirs, Vol. II, 1816-1830.*
40. Ibid.
41. Ibid.
42. Jean Baptiste (1774-1854), Comte de Villèle.
43. Nicholas Charles Oudinot, 1767-1847, Duc de Reggio.
44. Ferdinand Philippe, 1810-1842.
45. He used Marie Thérèse Charlotte's title from before her marriage.
46. *The Standard*, 29 September 1827.
47. Comtesse de Boigne, *Memoirs, Vol. II, 1816-1830.*
48. Lived 1785-1862.
49. Comtesse de Boigne, *Memoirs, Vol. II, 1816-1830.*
50. The *Journal des Débats* reported this, and its editor M. Bertin was prosecuted. He was initially sentenced to six months' imprisonment and a fine, but this was revoked on appeal. Marie Thérèse made her displeasure at this very clear to the members of the Appeal Court.
51. I.e. the Dauphine and her family.
52. Comtesse de Boigne, *Memoirs, Vol. II, 1816-1830.*
53. In which a lucky bean was hidden: whoever found the bean in their section of the *galette* was king or queen for the evening.
54. Comtesse de Boigne, *Memoirs, Vol. II, 1816-1830.*
55. Lived 1777-1830, and King 1824-1830.
56. Comtesse de Boigne, *Memoirs, Vol. II, 1816-1830.*
57. At Vichy.
58. Drafted by the Comte de Chantelauze, the Minister of Justice.
59. Quoting Munro Price, *The Perilous Crown: France between the Revolutions*, Pan, 2007.
60. Drafted by the Comte de Peyronnet.
61. Jean François Alexandre Boudet de Puymaigre, 1778-1843.
62. Price, *The Perilious Crown.*
63. As had the Duc d'Orléans and the Duc d'Angoulême.
64. They had been delivered in great secrecy to the newspaper's offices the night before, and the Editor of *Le Moniteur*, Sauvo, was shocked by their contents.
65. Itself subject to censorship under the provisions of the Ordinances.
66. Prince de Joinville, '*Vieux Souvenirs*'.
67. Marmont was one of Napoleon's marshals and had been deputed to hold Paris for the Emperor against the invading forces of the Russian Emperor Alexander I. Far from holding out, he surrendered Paris to the Russian Imperial forces and withdrew with his troops to Normandy. His action was regarded as being one of the factors which led to the Second Restoration in 1815, following the defeat of Napoleon at Waterloo. His ducal title, from the town in Sicily, gave the French language a new verb *raguser*, to betray or go back on promises.
68. Literally 'broken windows' i.e. trouble or unrest.
69. Marmont went into exile in England after the departure of Charles X. He felt that he had been given an unrealistic task and had not been supported by the King and the rest of the Royal Family.

12. Abdication and Exile

1. Morganatic second wife of Louis XIV.
2. Odilon Barrot, Schoenen and Marshal Maison.
3. For the under-age Duc de Bordeaux.
4. Translated as 'they are always the same'.

5. Louis Philippe was not, it should be noted, King of France as had been many of his predecessors, but the much more democratic King of the French, ruling with the consent of the people, not by right.
6. There are various different spellings.
7. The writer visited in September 2010.
8. Now part of a Catholic nursery school and situated in an area of the town known as Petit Versailles.
9. *Dans cette maison, ancien Hôtel du Mesnildot, après avoir donné Algérie à la France et avant de partir pour l'exil a séjourné du 13 au 16 août 1830 sa Majesté le Roi Charles X. Le comité de la Manche a voulu commémorer le centenaire, 1830-1930.*
10. Writing in the 1930s, commentators compared the position of the then contemporary Spanish Royal Family with that of their French cousins a hundred years earlier on being forced into exile. Baron de Brix, *A French King in Holyrood.*
11. Published in the USA, hence the spelling.
12. The name given to those Royalists who supported the claim for the restoration of the elder or legitimate branch of the Bourbons.
13. Some accounts suggest that Madame d'Agoult did not arrive in England until later.
14. Where Charles I had been imprisoned.
15. It took two days of comings and goings to unload everything, including the carriages in which they had travelled to Cherbourg.
16. M. J. Dumont d'Urville, *Extrait du voyage du capitaine Dumont d'Urville en Angleterre pour y conduire Charles X et sa famille (mémoires inédits),* included in *Voyage au Pole sud de M. J. Dumont D'Urville*, Paris: Gide et Cie, 1846.
17. He was appointed as a Roman Catholic Cardinal in 1830.
18. Her Royal Highness is coming down herself, at the top of the staircase she had asked for the calling cards, uttered a cry and is coming down.
19. Mary, when one has a clear conscience, there is no suffering.
20. Gone to do errands.
21. Her husband's daughter by Amy Brown, whom she treated as her own following the Duc de Berry's death.
22. Unfortunate country.
23. An iron fist.
24. To be relieved of cares and to be able to be free to concentrate on matters pertaining to heaven. It is there i.e. in heaven, Sire, that a throne awaits you. I will try to regain it, but while I await it, I am happy to have my freedom. Sire, the last time that I had the honour of seeing your Majesty was in Paris when you said to me that you bore a crown of thorns and that you longed for London and Hartwell. How often have I since thought of those words. It is true.
25. Nevertheless he has behaved badly; for a long time he has plotted against me and he took the first opportunity to seize what he wanted.
26. It is interesting to note how Marie Thérèse refers to her nephew and niece as 'Our children'.
27. Let us send for our children, Mary and Lord Arundell would like to see them.
28. So much the better.
29. Title taken from the name of her estate.
30. Some sources suggest that they lived at 31 Regent Terrace, which was a modern house completed only four years before. It is now numbered 22 Regent Terrace.
31. Loyalty seems to have been the defining quality of the family. The Comte's brother followed Napoleon into exile on St Helena. It also illustrates how many families were split by different political ideologies.
32. He was released in 1836 and went into exile, but was allowed to return to France before his death in 1847.
33. At the Tuileries she had held a Scottish-themed fancy dress ball. The Duchesse de Berry herself came dressed as Mary Stuart. Her choice of character, according to Madame de Boigne, apparently offended and upset Marie Thérèse, who was only too familiar with the fate of another Queen who was decapitated. Madame de Gontaut states that the Dauphine was only too happy to lend her jewels to those taking part. Now the Duchesse de Berry was living in rooms in Holyroodhouse Palace opposite those previously occupied by her heroine.
34. Lived 1799-1883.
35. Suzette née de la Tour.
36. Madame de Meffray, *Memoirs.*

37. 14 October 1848.
38. A small port on the coast near Leith, now part of Edinburgh.
39. Mary F. Sandars,. *The Life and Times of Queen Adelaide*, London: Stanley Paul & Co., 1915.
40. The city of Mainz.
41. A Bavarian princess.
42. Formerly King of Rome, 1811-1832.
43. The French (!).
44. *European History Quarterly* 35 (2005), quoting William D. Godsey Jnr, *Émigrés, Aristocracy and the Court at Vienna*, referring to the Diary of Count Eugène Czernin.
45. Now a UNESCO World Heritage site.
46. *Caledonian Mercury*, 22 November 1832.
47. Everything was regulated and arranged in the same way as in Paris.
48. Marquis Pons Louis François de Villeneuve, *Charles X et Louis XIX en exil: Mémoires inédits du Marquis de Villeneuve, publiés par son arrière petit fils*. Paris: E. Plon, Norrit et Cie, 1889.
49. In the absence of Marie Thérèse, the King sat by his son and grandson.
50. During the summer months.
51. Carlsbad or Karlsbad was a popular spa town with many of the European elite, including the Duchess of Dino, niece and companion of Talleyrand. Its Czech name is Karlovy Vary.
52. See Simon Deutz, *Arrestation de Madame*, Paris: Les Libraires Associés, 1835, in which Deutz defends himself and denies any betrayal.
53. Blaye figured in the adventure of the Duchesse d'Angoulême during the Hundred Days in 1815.
54. Queen Maria Christina, fourth wife of Ferdinand VII of Spain.
55. Lived 1806-1864.
56. The child only lived for a year, but Marie Caroline had three further children – two girls and a boy – half siblings to Mademoiselle and her brother the Duc de Bordeaux.
57. Marie Caroline to Marie Thérèse, as quoted in the London *Standard* of 21 January 1833.
58. Sometimes spelt O'Heguerty or O'Hegarthy, with whose son it was suggested that Marie Thérèse rather uncharacteristically enjoyed salacious gossiping, despite (or perhaps because of) his somewhat unsavoury reputation. The Duchesse d'Angoulême sometimes had a weakness for charming if slightly raffish young men.
59. The friendship continued into the next generation and the Duc de Bordeaux is noted by the *Morning Post* of 1847 to have visited the de Rohan estates in Bohemia in that year. The de Rohan family lived here until 1945.
60. Marquis de Villeneuve, *Charles X et Louis XIX en exil*: 'All their resources were put at the disposal of the French royal family.'
61. Villeneuve clearly far more in favour with the family than Walsch.
62. The young Duc de Bordeaux would in due course come into his inheritance, but not until his grandfather and uncle were both dead.
63. Other accounts suggest that there was a portrait of the young Henri V 'present' at the feast.
64. Henri IV (1553-1610), King from 1589, First Bourbon King of France.
65. 'Don't even speak to me.'
66. Marquis de Villeneuve, *Charles X et Louis XIX en exil.*
67. Should be Leoben.
68. Leoben is in Austria on the River Mur, approximately 100 miles from Vienna.
69. Other reports suggest that while the Dauphin refused to go, the Dauphine was one of the party; and this is the view taken by the writer.
70. The powerful Duc de Blacas, for example, no longer recognised her as a Princess.
71. Marquis de Villeneuve, *Charles X et Louis XIX en exil.*
72. She had three daughters and one son with her second husband.
73. In Czech the River Vltava.
74. Denis-Antoine-Luc, Comte de Frayssinous (9 May 1765–12 December 1841).
75. As reported in Duchesse de Dino, edited with notes and Biographical Index by the Princess Radziwll, *Memoirs of the Duchesse de Dino 1831-1835*, London: William Heinemann, 1910.
76. Duchesse de Dino, *Memoirs.*
77. Also known as Holy Roman Emperor Francis II (1768-1835).

78. Lived 1793-1875, reigned 1835-48, when he abdicated. He lived the rest of his life from 1848 at the Hradschin Castle in Prague.
79. Approximately modern Hungary.
80. Cholera is an acute intestinal infection caused by ingestion of food or water contaminated with the bacterium *Vibrio cholerae*. It has a short incubation period, from less than one day to five days, and produces an enterotoxin that causes copious, painless, watery diarrhoea that can quickly lead to severe dehydration and death if treatment is not promptly given. Vomiting also occurs in most patients. This is the World Health Organization definition. The epidemic lasted over 1830-47 and killed tens of millions of people, prompting the First International Sanitary Conference held in Paris in 1851.
81. A skin infection leading to blisters and underneath the sores very inflamed skin, also known as 'St Antony's fire'; it is now treatable with antibiotics.
82. A spa town in Austria near Salzburg, later famous for its connection with the famously beautiful Empress Elisabeth, wife of the Emperor Franz Josef, son of the Archduchess Sophie, with whom Marie Thérèse made friends during her stay in Vienna in 1833.
83. Some sources suggest a different vendor of the property.
84. With great feeling and sensitivity.
85. Marquis de Villeneuve, *Charles X et Louis XIX en exil*, in which he describes Madame de Nicolay as rather dry and forbidding, but respectable and reliable.
86. He had apparently committed suicide, but foul play by his English mistress, Sophie Dawes, was suspected.
87. Meaning 'absolute master' or 'in total control'.
88. Lived 1796-1855, Emperor from 1825.
89. Formerly Princess Charlotte of Prussia, 1798-1860.
90. Some sources suggest that she died in 1836, others 1838.
91. Usually spelt Rosny.
92. Some accounts indicate the opposite, namely that mourning was not declared lest this should highlight the absence of official mourning in Paris following Charles X's death in 1836.
93. He was the illegitimate son of Talleyrand and the lover of Napoleon's step-daughter, ex Queen Hortense of Holland, with whom he fathered the Auguste du Mornay, half-brother of Napoleon III of France and one of his ministers. He had been an *aide de camp* to Napoleon, fighting with him in Russia and at the Battle of Waterloo.

13. Exile and Widowhood

1. Leopold of Belgium (1790-1865), King from 1831, her mother's brother who had been so influential in engineering her marriage to Prince Albert.
2. Louise (1812-1850).
3. Editors of *La Quotidienne*, *La Mode* and *Opinion Publique*.
4. Including Abbé Edgeworth, Marie Joséphine, Louis XVIII and Charles X.
5. Lived 1784-1860, Diplomat and later Prime Minister.
6. Grandson of the Duc de Berry: Prince de Faucingy-Lucinge, *Dans l'ombre de l'histoire: Souvenirs inédits du Petit-Fils du Duc de Berry*. Paris: Librairie Académique Perrin, 1971. The Comte was appointed as an *aide de camp* to the Duc de Bordeaux following his marriage. His uncle had assisted Marie Thérèse on her journey back to Paris from Vichy, which had proved so uncomfortable and frightening. She spoke warmly of him.
7. Marie Thérèse had known Marie Louise during her exile in Vienna, after the exchange for French prisoners held by the Austrians and exit from the Tower of the Temple in 1795.
8. Known as Charles III.
9. A princess of Savoie.
10. Emperor 1835-1848.
11. He was executed by firing squad in June 1867 in Santiago de Queretaro in Mexico.
12. Modena is in the now Emilia–Romagna region of northern Italy and 25 miles north of Bologna.
13. *Morning Post*, 25 November 1845.
14. *Rotherham and Sheffield Independent*, 21 November 1846.
15. The Duchy of Parma centring on the town of Parma is in the Emilia–Romagna region north-west of Modena.
16. Marie Thérèse's friend the Archduchess Sophie saw the abdication of her brother-in-

law the Emperor Ferdinand on 2 December 1848 and the accession of her 18-year-old son Franz Joseph to the Imperial throne of Austria.
17. Duchess of Parma.
18. *York Herald*, 10 November 1849.
19. *Freeman's Journal and Daily Commercial Advertiser*, 5 June 1849.
20. As reported in the *Morning Post*, 10 July 1850.
21. Famously quoted as having said that Paris was worth a Mass. Born 1553 and King of France from 1589 until his assassination in 1610.
22. Now the Palace Franchetti.
23. He spent the winters of the years 1846-66 there, living the rest of the time with his aunt in Frohsdorf during her lifetime.
24. 1778-1795 in France; 1814-1815 First Restoration; 1815-1830 Second Restoration, and reigns of her uncles.
25. According to reports written by the Comte de Pastoret and reported in the *Morning Chronicle* of 31 October 1851.
26. According to reports written by the Comte de Pastoret and reported in the *Morning Chronicle* of 31 October 1851.
27. Henry-Frédéric Binet de Boisgiroult, Baron de Sainte-Preuve, and his wife Louise-Marie née Dufour de Montlouis. The couple followed the family into exile in 1830 and thence all round Europe, ending in Frohsdorf.
28. According to reports written by the Comte de Pastoret and reported in the *Morning Chronicle* of 31 October 1851.
29. According to the report in the *Observer* of 26 October 1851.

Bibliography

- Abbott, Vivienne. *An Irishman's Revolution: the Abbé Edgeworth and Louis XVI*. Dublin: Kavanagh Press, 1989
- Abrantès, Madame Laure Junot d'. *Memoirs*. Richard Bentley & Son, 1883
- Acton, Harold. *The Bourbons of Naples*. Methuen, 1956
- Alexander, Robert. *Rewriting the French Revolutionary Tradition*. Cambridge University Press, 2003
- Andress, David. *The Terror: Civil War in the French Revolution*. Little Brown, 2005
- Angoulême, Marie Thérèse Charlotte, Duchesse d'. *Private Memoirs ... which complete the History of the Captivity of the Royal Family of France in the Temple*. John Murray, 1817
- Arnaud, Raoul. *Louis-Philippe and his sister: The political life and role of Adelaide of Orléans 1777-1847*. D. Nutt France, 1908
- Artemont, Louis Leopold d'. *Marie Adelaide Clothilde Xaviere, Consort of Charles Emmanuel IV King of Sardinia, A sister of Louis XVI (1759-1802)*. John Murray, 1911
- Aumule, Duc d'. *Correspondence du Duc d'Aumule et de Cuvillier 1848-1859*. Paris: Librairie Plon, 1910
- Barras, Paul. *Memoirs of Barras, Member of Directorate*. New York: Harper & Brothers, 1896
- Béarn, Catherine. *A Leader of Society at Napoleon's Court*. London: T Fisher Unwin, 1904
- Béarn, Catherine. *A Queen of Napoleon's Court: The Life Story of Desirée Bernadotte*. London: T Fisher Unwin, 1905

- Béarn, Catherine. *A Sister of Marie Antoinette: The Life Story of Marie Caroline of Naples*. London: T Fisher Unwin, 1907
- Béarn, Catherine. *Heroines of French Society in the Court, the Revolution, the Empire and the Restoration*. London: T Fisher Unwin, 1907
- Béarn, Pauline de. S*ouvenirs de Quarante Ans 1789 to 1830: Récits d'une dame de Madame la Dauphine*. Paris: Jacques le Coffre et Cie, 1861
- Bernardy, Françoise de. *Son of Talleyrand*. London: Collins, 1956
- Bernier, edited by Olivier. *Imperial Mother, Royal Daughter – The Correspondence of Marie Antoinette and Maria Theresa*. Pan Macmillan, 1986
- Best, Geoffrey. *The Permanent Revolution: The French Revolution and its Legacy 1789-1989*. Fontana, 1988
- Blanning, T. C. W. *The Origins of the French Revolutionary Wars*. Longman, 1986
- Boigne, Comtesse de, edited and with an Introduction by Anka Muhlstein, Afterword by Olivier Bernier. *Memoirs of the Comtesse de Boigne, Vol. I, 1781-1815*; *Vol. II, 1816-1830*. Helen Marx Books, 2003
- Bombelles, Marquis de, ed. Jean Grassion and Frans Durif, *Journal*. Geneva, 1977
- Bourgeois, Armand. *Etudes Historiques sur Louis XVII (1905) suivie de Marie-Thérèse-Charlotte depuis sa sortie du Temple jusqu'à Vienne et d'un post scriptum à l'arrestation de Louis XVI à Varennes*. Kessinger Publishing, 2010
- Brown Jnr, Marvin L. *The Comte de Chambord, The Third Republic's Uncompromising King*. Durham, NC: Duke University Press, 1967
- Buckingham and Chandos, Duke of. *Private Diary, Vol. 1*. London: Hurst and Blackett, 1862
- Burney, Frances. *The Diary and Letters of Madame d'Arblay (Frances Burney) with Notes by W. C. Ward and prefaced by Lord Macaulay's Essay, Vol III (1972-1840)*. London and New York: Frederick Warne and Co., 1892
- Cadbury, Deborah. *The Lost King of France*. Fourth Estate, 2002
- Campan, Madame. *The Private Life of Marie Antoinette: A Confidante's Account*, 1500 Books, 2006
- Cartron, Michel Bernard. *Louis XIX, Roi sans Couronne*. Paris: C&T, 1996
- Cartron, Michel Bernard. *Marie-Thérèse Duchesse d'Angoulême: La vertu et le malheur*. Paris: C&T, 1999
- Castelot, André, translated by Denise Folliot. *Paris: the Turbulent City 1783 to 1871*. London: Barrie and Rockliff with Valentine Mitchell, 1962

- Castelot, André. *Madame Royale*. Librairie Académique Perrin, 1962
- Castelot, André. *Charles X ou la fin d'un monde*. Librairie Académique Perrin, 1988
- Castelot, André. *La Duchesse de Berry: Revolutions and Empires 1770-1870*. Librairie Académique Perrin, 1998
- Chateaubriand, François René de. *De Buonaparte and the Bourbons, et de la nécessité de se rallier à nos Princes légitimes pour le bonheur de la France et celui de l'Europe*. Libelle, 1814
- Chazet, René de. *Vie anecdotique de Henri-Charles-Ferdinand-Marie-Dieudonné d'Artois, Duc de Bordeaux, depuis sa naissance jusqu'à ce jour. Souvenirs de Paris, de Saint-Cloud, de Bagatelle, de Cherbourg, de Lulworth et d'Holyrood*. L.-F.Hivert, 1832
- Cohen de Vinkenhoeff, Albert. *Notice biographique sur Marie-Thérèse-Charlotte de France, Duchesse D'Angoulême*. Jeanne, 1851
- Cléry, Jean Baptiste. *Journal of Cléry During the Captivity of Louis XVI at the Prison of the Temple from 10 August 1792 to 21 January 1793*. Paris: E. Terquem; New York: Brentano's, 1906
- Cole, Hubert. *The Betrayers, Joachim and Caroline Murat*. Eyre Methuen, 1972
- Creevey, Thomas. *The Creevey Papers*. Penguin, 1986
- Cronin, Vincent. *Four Women in Pursuit of an Ideal*. Collins, 1965
- Custine, Marquise de. *Memoirs of the Marquise de Custine Delphine de Sabran from the French of Gaston Maugras and Le Cte. P. de Croze-Lemercier*. William Heinemann, 1912
- Dallas, Gregor. *1815, The Road to Waterloo*. Pimlico, 2001
- Dampmartin, A. H. *Mémoires sur Divers Événements de la Révolution et de l'Émigration*. Paris: Chez Hubert Libraire, 1825
- Daudet, Ernest, translated by Mrs Rudolph Stawell. *Madame Royale, daughter of Louis XVI and Marie Antoinette – her youth and marriage*. London: William Heinemann, 1913
- Deutz, Simon. *Arrestation de Madame*. Paris: Les Libraires Associés, 1835
- Dino, Duchesse de, edited with notes and Biographical Index by the Princess Radziwll. *Memoirs of the Duchesse de Dino 1831-1835*. London: William Heinemann, 1910
- Doyle, William. *Oxford History of the French Revolution*. Oxford University Press, 1989
- Droz, Jacques. *Europe between Revolutions, 1815-1848*. Collins Fontana, 1967
- Dumont d'Urville, M. J. *Extrait du voyage du capitaine Dumont d'Urville en Angleterre pour y conduire Charles X et sa famille (mémoires inédits)*, included in *Voyage au Pole sud de M. J. Dumont D'Urville*. Paris: Gide et Cie, 1846

- Dyson, C. C. *Life of Marie-Amélie, Last Queen of the French 1782-1866*. London: John Long, 1910
- Edgeworth, Maria. *Maria Edgeworth in France and Switzerland; selection from Edgeworth family letters*. Oxford: Clarendon Press, 1979
- Elliot, John. *The Way of the Tumbrils: Paris during the Revolution and Today*. London: Max Reinhardt, 1958
- Evans, Joan. *Madame Royale*. London: Museum Press, 1959
- Fairweather, Maria. *Madame de Stael*. Constable and Robinson, 2005
- Faucigny-Lucinge, Prince de. *Dans l'ombre de l'histoire: Souvenirs inédits du Petit-Fils du Duc de Berry*. Paris: Librairie Académique Perrin, 1971
- Fife, Graeme. *The Terror: The shadow of the Guillotine: France 1792-1794*. Portrait Books, 2004
- Foreman, Amanda. *Georgiana, Duchess of Devonshire*. HarperCollins, 1998
- Fraser, Antonia. *Marie Antoinette: The Journey*. Weidenfeld and Nicolson, 2001
- Gassier, J.-M. *L'Antigone francaise, ou Mémoires historiques sur Marie-Thérèse-Charlotte de France*. Paris: l'Imprimerie d'Aubry, 1814
- Genlis, Mme. *Mémoires de Madame de Genlis*. Paris: Firmin-Didot, 1878
- Gontaut, Mme de. *Memoirs of Duchesse de Gontaut, gouvernante to the children of France during the restoration (1773-1836)*. London: Chatto and Windus, 1894
- Goodden, Angelica. *A biography of Elisabeth Louise Vigée Le Brun*. André Deutsch, 1997
- Granville, Countess Harriet, edited by her son, The Hon. F. Leveson Gower. *Letters of Harriet Countess Granville (1810-1845)*. London: Longmans, Green and Co., 1894
- Greville, Charles, edited by Philip Whitwell Wilson. *The Greville Diary (1794-1865)*. Heinemann, 1927
- Hardivillier, Charles Achille d'. *Souvenirs des Highlands: à la suite d'Henri V en 1832*. Chez Dentu, 1835
- Hart, Gwen. *A History of Cheltenham*. Alan Sutton, 1981
- Harvey, Robert. *Liberators: Latin America's Struggle for Independence*. Overlook, 2000
- Havelock, Henry, translator. *Alexander I and the Grandduchess Catherine. Scenes from Russian Court Life, being the Correspondence of Alexander I with his sister Catherine with an Introduction by Grand Duke Nicholas*. Jarrolds Publishers.
- Hibbert, Christopher. *Nelson, A Personal History*. Viking, 1994

- Hibbert, Christopher. *Wellington, A Personal History*. Perseus Books Group, 1999
- Holmes, Richard. *Wellington, the Iron Duke*. Harper Collins, 2003
- Horricks, Raymond. *In Flight with the Eagle: Napoleon's Elite.* New Jersey: Transaction Publishers, 1995
- Hortense, Queen, compiled by Sir Lascelles Wraxall and Robert Wehrhan. *Memoirs of Queen Hortense, Mother of Napoleon III.* London: Hurst and Blackett, 1864
- Howarth, T. E. B. *The Life of Louis Philippe, Citizen-King.* E&S, 1961
- Hüe, François. *The Last Years of the Reign and Life of Louis XVI.* Cadell and Davies, Strand, 1806
- Huertas, Monique de. *Madame Royale, L'enigmatique destinée de la fille de Louis XVI.* Feryane, 1999
- Johanet, Auguste. *Souvenirs du séjour de M. le comte de Chambord et des Français à Ems.*
- Johanet, Auguste. *Voyages de Henri de France en Ecosse, en Angleterre, en Allemagne et en Italie*. Kessinger Publishing, 2010
- Joinville, Prince de, translated from the French by Lady Mary Lloyd. *Memoirs of the Prince de Joinville: 'Vieux Souvenirs'.* New York and London: Macmillan & Co., 1893
- Lamballe, Princesse. *Secret Memoirs of the Royal Family of France, during the Revolution … by a Lady of Rank.* Treuttel & Würtz, 1826
- Le Notre, G. *The Daughter of Louis XVI.* London: John Lane, 1908
- Le Notre, G. *Memoires et souvenirs sur la Revolution et l'Empire Publiés avec documents inédits.*
- Lenotre, G., translated by J. Lewis May. *Marie-Thérèse- Charlotte de France Duchesse d'Angoulême*, London, 1958
- Lever, Evelyne. *Correspondance de Marie-Antoinette 1770-1793, établie, présentée et annotée par Evelyne Lever*, Tallandier, 2005
- Lever, Evelyne. *Louis XVI.* Paris: Fayard, 1985
- Lever, Evelyne. *Louis XVIII.* Paris: Fayard, 1988
- Longford, Elizabeth. *Wellington: The Years of the Sword.* Panther, 1971
- Longford, Elizabeth. *Wellington: Pillar of State*. Panther, 1975
- Loomis, Stanley. *Paris in the Terror*. London: Jonathan Cape, 1964
- Louis XVIII. *Memoirs of Louis the Eighteenth written by himself.* La Mothe Houdancourt, afterwards La Mothe Langon, Etienne Léon de, Baron. London: Henry Colburn and Richard Bentley, 1830
- Macaulay, Thomas Babington. *Napoleon and the Restoration of the Bourbons.* Columbia University Press, 1977

- MacCarthy, Fiona. *Byron, Life and Legend.* John Murray, 2002
- MacKenzie Stuart, A. J. *A Royal Debtor at Holyrood.* STAIR Society Miscellany, 1971
- MacKenzie Stuart, A. J. *A French King in Holyrood.* Edinburgh: John Donald Publishers, 1995
- Madelin, Louis. *The French Revolution: the National History of France.* Heinemann, 1916
- Maillé, Blanche-Joséphine, Duchesse de, presenté par Xavier de La Fournière. *Souvenirs des deux Restaurations; journal inédit.* Paris: Perrin, 1984
- Maillé, Blanche-Joséphine, Duchesse de, avec introduction et notes de Frédéric d'Agay. *Mémoires, 1832-1852.* Paris: Perrin, 1989
- Mansel, Philip. *Louis XVIII.* Blond and Briggs Ltd, 1981
- Mansel, Philip. *The Court of France 1789-1830.* Cambridge University Press, 1991
- Mansel, Philip. *Paris between Empires 1814-1852.* John Murray, 2001
- Montbel, Comte de. *Le comte de Marnes, Fils Ainé du Roi du France. Notice sur son exil, son caractère, sa mort et ses funerailles.* Versailles: Librairie de l'évêche, 1844
- Montet, Baronne Alexandrine du. *Souvenirs de la Baronne du Montet 1785-1866.* Paris: Librairie Plon, 1904
- Moorehead, Caroline. *Dancing to the Precipice: Lucie de la Tour du Pin and the French Revolution.* London: Chatto and Windus, 2009
- Mossiker, Frances. *The Queen's Necklace – Marie Antoinette and the scandal that shocked and mystified France.* Phoenix, 2004
- Nettement, M. Alfred. *Vie de Marie-Thérèse de France, Fille de Louis XVI.* De Signy et Dubey, 1843
- Normington, Susan. *Napoleon's Children.* Alan Sutton, 1993
- Oberkirch, Baroness d'. *Memoirs of Baronne d'Oberkirch* London: Colburn & Co. Publishers, 1852
- Orczy, Baroness. *The Turbulent Duchess.* London: Hodder and Stoughton, 1935
- Page, William. *Victoria County History of Buckinghamshire.* James Street, 1905-28
- Palmer, Alan. *Alexander I, Tsar of War and Peace.* Phoenix Giant, 1997
- Palmer, Alan. *Napoleon and Marie Louise, The Second Empress.* London: Constable, 2001
- Pearce, Malcolm and Stewart, Geoffrey. *British Political History 1867-2011: Democracy and Decline.* London: Routledge, 1992
- Pimodan, Comte de. *Les Fiancelles de Madame Royale Fille de Louis*

XVI et la Première Année de son Séjour à Vienne. Paris: Librairie Plon, 1912

- Post, Marie Caroline. *Life and Memoirs of Comte Régis de Trobriand, Major-General in the Army of the United States by his daughter*. New York: E. P. Button and Company, 1910
- Price, Munro. *The Fall of the French Monarchy: Louis XVI, Marie Antoinette and the Baron de Breteuil*. Pan, 2003
- Price, Munro. *The Perilous Crown: France between the Revolutions*. Pan, 2007
- Ravignant, Patrick. *La Comtesse des Ténèbres*. Encre Editions, 1979
- Reiset, Vicomte de. *Autour des Bourbons*. Paris: Editions Emile-Paul Frères, 1927
- Rocher, Philippe. *La Jeunesse du Dernier Bourbon, Le duc de Bordeaux (1830 to 1844)*. Paris: Librairie Ancienne Honore Champion, 1923
- Romer, Isabella F. Mrs, completed by J. Doran. *Filia Dolorosa, Memoirs of Marie Thérèse Charlotte Duchesse of Angoulême*. London: Richard Bentley & Son, 1852
- Ronciere, Charles de la. *The letters of Napoleon to Marie-Louise*. Hutchinson & Co., 1935
- Rounding, Virginia. *Catherine the Great: Love, Sex and Power*. London: Hutchinson, 2006
- Saint-Amand Imbert de, translated by Elizabeth Gilbert Martin. *The Youth of the Duchesse d'Angoulême* London: Hutchinson & Co., 1892
- Saint-Amand, Imbert de, translated by James Davies. *Duchess of Angoulême and the Two Restorations.* London: Hutchinson & Co., 1892
- Saint-Amand Imbert de. *The Duchesse de Berry and the Court of Louis XVIII*. London: Hutchinson & Co., 1892
- Saint-Amand Imbert de. *The Duchesse de Berry and the Court of Charles X*. London: Hutchinson & Co., 1892
- Saint-Amand Imbert de, translated by Elizabeth Gilbert Martin., *Marie Antoinette at the Tuileries 1789-1791*. Charles Scribner's Sons, 1902
- Sandars, Mary F. *The Life and Times of Queen Adelaide*. London: Stanley Paul & Co., 1915
- Scurr, Ruth. *Fatal Purity: Robespierre and the French Revolution*. London: Chatto and Windus, 2006
- Seward, Desmond. *The Bourbon Kings of France*. London: Constable, 1976
- Sèze, Étienne Romain Comte de. *Souvenirs de Lulworth, d'Holy-Rood, de Bath*. 1831

- Sherriff, Mary D. *The Exceptional Woman Élisabeth Vigée Lebrun and the cultural politics of art*. University of Chicago Press, 1996
- Sion, Madeleine Louise de. *Le Vrai Visage de Madame Royale*. Beauschene, 1959
- Skuy, David. *Assassination, politiques and miracle: France and the royalist reaction of 1820*. McGill Queens University Press, 2003
- Stenger, Gilbert. *The Return of Louis XVIII*. W. Heinemann, 1909
- Stoeckl, Agnes de. *King of the French: A Portrait of Louis Philippe, 1773-1850*. John Murray, 1957
- Stoeckl, Agnes de. *Mistress of Versailles: The Life of Madame Du Barry*. John Murray, 1966
- Sutherland, Douglas Johnson DMG. *France 1789-1815, Revolution and Counterrevolution*. Fontana, 1985
- Thomas, Chantal, translated by Moishe Black. *Farewell My Queen*. Phoenix, 2004
- Tour du Pin, Lucie de la, edited and translated by Walter Geer. *Memoirs*. London: Jonathan Cape, 1921
- Tourzel, Louise-Félicité de. *Memoires de Madame la Duchesse de Tourzel, Gouvernante des Enfants de France Pendant les Années 1789, 1790, 1791, 1792, 1793, 1794, 1795*. Paris: E. Plon, 1883
- Trollope, Anthony, edited with an introduction by W. J. McCormack, gazetteer prepared by Selina Guinness. *La Vendée*. Oxford University Press, 1994
- Turquan, Joseph, edited by Lady Theodora Davidson. *Madame Royale – the Last Dauphine Marie-Thérèse-Charlotte de France, Duchesse d'Angoulême*. London: T. Fisher Unwin, 1910
- Vansittart, Peter. *Voices of the Revolution*. Collins, 1989
- Viel-Castel, Baron Louis de. *Histoire de la Restauration*. Paris: Michel Lévy Frères, 1860-1878
- Villeneuve, Pons Louis François, Marquis de. *Charles X et Louis XIX en exil: Mémoires inédits du Marquis de Villeneuve, publiés par son arrière petit fils*. Paris: E. Plon, Norrit et Cie, 1889
- Webster, N. H. *French Revolution: A study in democracy*. London: Constable, 1920
- Whalley, Thomas Sedgewick, edited, with a memoir and illustrative notes, by the Rev. Hill Wickham, M.A. *Whalley DD: journals and correspondence of Thomas Sedgewick Whalley DD of Mendip Lodge, Somerset*. London: Richard Bentley, 1862
- Wheatcroft, Andrew. *The Habsburgs – Embodying Empire*. Penguin Books, 1996
- Williams, H. Noel. *A Princess of Adventure: Marie Caroline, Duchesse de Berry*. London: Methuen and Co. Ltd, 1911
- Williams-Wynn, Frances, edited with notes by A. Hayward,

Esq., Q.C. *Diaries of a lady of quality from 1797 to 1844.* London: Longman, Roberts & Green, 1864

- Wormeley, Katharine Prescott. *The Life and Letters of Madame Elisabeth de France followed by the Journal of the Temple by Cléry and the Narrative of Marie Thérèse de France Duchesse d'Angoulême.* London: William Heinemann, 1902
- Wylock, Paul. *The life and times of Guillaume Dupuytren*. Brussels University Press, 2010
- Yalom, Marilyn. *Blood Sisters: The French Revolution in Women's Memory*. Pandora, 1995
- Zamoyski, Adam. *1812 Napoleon's Fatal March on Moscow*. HarperCollins, 2004
- Zamoyski, Adam. *Rites of Peace: The Fall of Napoleon and the Congress of Vienna*. HarperCollins, 2007
- Ziegler, Philip. *The Duchess of Dino, Chatelaine of Europe*. Phoenix, 1962

Acknowledgements

With grateful thanks to you for your support, comments and encouragement to Cathy Sanderson, Sheena and the late and much missed Mike Watson, Janice Pearce, Anna and Paul Farrow, Sophie Mellis, Christine Knights, Jenny Baggott, George Bull.

Index

Abbé Edgeworth
Irish background 81
confessor at the execution of Louis XVI 82-3, 117
describes Louis XVI's death to Marie Thérèse 138
offered annuity in London 138
joins Louis XVIII as chaplain in Brunswick 122, 138
conducts marriage service of Marie Thérèse 139
negotiates with Napoleon 145
leaves Mittau 152
becomes confessor to Marie Thérèse 154
journals 77, 157
death in 1807 161-2
Abbé Marie 144, 154
Abrantès, Duchesse d' 208-9
Adélaïde d'Orléans 21, 214, 246, 250, 259-60, 268-9, 276, 284, 289, 332
Adelaide, Queen, wife of William IV 314-15
Adélaïde, Tante 30, 46, 53-5, 117, 119-20, 132, 145, 335
Agoult, Henriette d' 270, 299, 316, 319, 325, 333, 342
Agoult, Vicomte d' 168, 217
Alexander I of Russia 157-62, 180-3, 195-202, 239, 274-5
Algeria 281-2, 354
Amalia, Archduchess of Austria 124, 127, 129
American War of Independence 37, 42, 52
Amiens 192-3
Angoulême, Louis-Antoine, Duc d' *passim*
Angoulême, Marie Thérèse, Duchesse d' *passim*
Arblay, Madame d' 174, 186, 217-19, 258 *see also* Burney, Fanny
Artois, Comte d', *see* Charles X
Artois, Comtesse d' 16, 26, 118, 130-2, 161, 240
Artois, Mademoiselle Louise Marie d' 245-6, 273-4, 314, 332
Arundell, Lady 301, 303-4

Austria
Treaty of Versailles 4
Marie Antoinette's origins 4, 6-7, 17, 23-4, 27-8, 32, 155-6
rumours of intervention 41, 69, 107
France declares war 68, 106
exchange of Marie Thérèse 102, 107, 111
possible marriage for Marie Thérèse 108, 111, 114, 129
Marie Thérèse in exile 109-29
Napoleon defeats Austria 171
Napoleon's second marriage 171
alliance against Napoleon 178, 183-4, 204, 230
Congress of Vienna 203
Marie Thérèse's second exile 300, 314-17, 327, 333-6, 340-2, 362
final home at Frohsdorf 347-352
1848 revolutions 353
Avaray, Duc d' 65, 144, 147, 160-1, 173
Barras, Paul 94, 96-7, 105
Barry, Madame du 24
Bastille 40, 53, 68, 71, 203, 300
Béarn, Pauline de 28, 30, 33, 45, 53, 75-6, 102-3, 105-6, 191-2, 207, 256, 287
Beauharnais, Joséphine de, *see* Joséphine de Beauharnais
Bénézech, Pierre 107-9, 116
Bernadotte, Maréchal 128, 182, 194
Berry, Charles Ferdinand, Duc de
succession 15, 162, 221, 239
soldier 117-19, 133, 179-80, 264
suitors 161, 163-4, 239, 351
mistresses 168-9, 203-4, 223, 245, 350
marriage to Marie Caroline 240-7
assassination 249-52
Mass for his death 313
Berry, Duchesse de, *see* Marie Caroline
Blacas, Comte de 173, 175, 193, 197, 201, 303-4, 306, 313, 319-20, 329, 332-5, 338-9, 341, 346, 348, 360
Blaze de Bury, Baroness 348, 357
Boigne, Madame de, diarist
supporter of Orléans 196, 246, 268-9, 280
bias against Marie Thérèse 208, 234, 239-40, 243, 262, 279, 309
on Alexander I 182, 195-6, 274
o n Charles X 263, 265-7, 280
o n Comte d'Artois 190
on Court life 242, 270
on Duc d'Angoulême 248-9, 257, 264, 275
on Duc de Berry 179, 241, 243-5, 250-2
on Duc de Bordeaux 252-3, 273-4, 278
on Louis XVIII 254, 259, 261
on Mme de Guéméné 14
on Tuileries 232, 256
on Versailles 42, 46
Bonaparte, Joseph, King of Spain 180, 224, 255
Bonaparte, Napoleon
assumes power 105
at war 126, 133-4, 145, 158, 160, 163, 174, 177-80, 202-3, 274
dealings with Louis XVIII 144-6, 153, 158, 162, 168, 176, 198
crowned Emperor 156, 213

second marriage 171, 195
abdication and exile 182-3, 188, 197
loyalists to Napoleon 195, 199-200, 202-3, 206, 208, 220, 233-4, 249, 254
Hundred Days 220-5, 228, 257, 265, 279, 285, 310, 325
Second Restoration 231-2
death 254-5
Bonnay, Marquis de 123
Borbons of Spain 14, 51, 101, 118, 139, 224, 255
Bordeaux 179, 181-2, 219-28, 231, 234-5, 249, 255, 257, 264, 278-9
Bordeaux, Duc de, *see* Henri V
Bougon, Dr 249-51, 298, 306, 334-5, 342, 344, 358
Bouillé, Marquis de 55-6
Bourgogne, Duc de 127, 284, 293
Brown, Amy 168, 204, 239, 245, 250, 322, 350
Brunswick, Duke of 72, 79
Brunyer, Madame 59
Brunyer, Pierre-Edouard 59, 84
Buckingham, Marquis of 163-4, 186
Budweiss 118, 136, 140, 334
Burney, Fanny 165, 186, 193, 204, 217-19
Campan, Madame, biographer of Marie Antoinette 8, 10, 13, 18-19, 23, 27, 29, 32, 37, 40, 42, 47, 49, 53, 55, 58, 60, 64, 66, 68, 113, 120, 131, 189, 206, 208, 254
Carlsbad 321, 324-6, 334
Carlton House, London 174-5, 185, 187
Catherine II of Russia 51, 122, 274, 351
Cayla, Comtesse du 254, 259, 323
Châlons-sur-Marne 57, 61, 63, 79
Chambord, Comte de, *see* Henri V
Chambord, Comtesse de 351-2, 355, 359-60
Champ de Mars 53, 71, 203, 275, 277
Chanclos, Madame de 120, 127-8
Chanterenne, Madeleine de 100-3, 107, 109, 111, 118, 247, 341
Charles II of Bourbon-Parme 350
Charles III, married to Louise 350
Charles IV of Spain 14
Charles X of France, Comte d'Artois
succession 15, 28, 99, 135, 167, 177, 238, 268-9, 293, 327, 332, 336, 340
portraits 17, 347
in Paris 31, 34, 40, 74, 131
father to Duc d'Angoulême 37, 115, 127, 130, 144-5
in exile 41, 49, 51, 83, 114, 132-3
in England and Scotland 117-18, 133-5, 146, 159, 163-5, 176
other relationships 133, 146, 240
opposition to Napoleon 146, 158-9, 168, 179
during Restoration 184, 190, 197, 200, 204, 211
during Hundred Days 223-4, 228
Second Restoration 232, 234, 248
father to Duc de Berry 239-43, 252-3, 328-33
becomes King 260-7, 275
signing Ordinances 283-5
abdication 289-91, 294, 296
exile in Scotland 297-314
exile in Europe 316-21, 326-35
death from cholera 335-6, 361

Charlet, Baron 286-7, 301, 303, 312-14, 316-17, 327, 331, 334-5, 341, 349, 360
Charlotte, Queen 175, 185, 217
Charter of Louis XVIII 199, 223, 264, 278, 280, 284, 298
Chartres, Duc de 38, 276, 287, 304
Châteaubriand, Vicomte de 140, 181, 201, 255-6, 321, 324-6, 339, 356
Choiseul, Duc de 4, 58
Choisy, Mlle de 120, 144, 193, 217
cholera 313-15, 334-6
Clausel, General 225, 278
Cléry, Jean-Baptiste 75-7, 79, 107, 115, 117, 248
Clotilde, Madame 101, 117-18, 132, 158, 358
Coblenz 41, 49, 51, 58, 71
Coco 99, 110, 143, 152, 157, 171
Committee of Public Safety 92, 97, 100-1, 236
Compiègne 4, 193, 195-7, 200
Condé, Prince de 41, 83, 101, 111, 117, 122, 159, 163, 170, 173, 188, 271, 281, 339
Condé Army 41, 119, 122, 134, 136, 140, 142, 155, 174, 301
Constitution 49, 51, 54, 61, 66-7, 71, 132, 183, 199, 263-4
Courland, Duchy of 122, 139, 141, 160-1, 200
Coutts Bank 300, 304
Damas, Comte de 144, 154, 165, 175, 278, 289, 298, 304, 316-17, 330
Dawes, Sophie 271
Decazes, Duc 250-1, 254
Declaration of Hartwell 175-7, 184
Declaration of Regency 83
Declaration of Saint-Ouën 197
Dino, Duchesse de 310, 329, 333, 343, 362
Drouet, Jean-Baptiste 61, 102, 111
Duras, Duchesse de 191, 217
Edgeworth, Maria 162
Edinburgh 115, 118, 134-5, 165, 262, 305-12, 317, 329
Élisabeth, Madame, sister of Louis XVI
early education and religion 30, 33, 36, 95
at the Trianon 20, 23, 34
portrait 24, 172
Household and property 26, 29
in the Tuileries 42, 47-8, 51, 53
joins escape party 55-65
attacked by Paris mob 69-72
in the Temple 75-7, 85-6, 89, 92, 324
Marie Antoinette's final letter 88, 216, 236-7
on trial 86-7, 91-2
execution 92, 206
memorial Mass 209
Elysée Palace 243-4, 249-50, 267, 280
Enghien, Duc d' 83, 117, 159, 222
Estates General 39-40, 131, 283
Esterhazy, Comtesse d' 120, 316, 325, 352
Fallon, P.J. 306, 308-9, 312
Fare, Monseigneur de la 117, 119-21, 125-6, 140, 266
Ferdinand, Archduke 17
Ferdinand I, Emperor of Austria 333, 340, 350, 355
Ferdinand IV, King of Naples 240-1
Ferdinand V, Emperor of Austria 353
Ferdinand VII of Spain 255

Ferdinand d'Este 359
Fersen, Axel von 52, 55-7, 60-1, 124, 172
Flahaut, M. de 343, 350
Fontainebleau 44, 183, 222, 242, 287
Fouché, Joseph 202, 221, 228, 233
Francis I of the Two Sicilies 240, 279, 307
Francis II, Holy Roman Emperor, later Francis I of Austria 67, 85, 102, 112-14, 123, 128-9, 171, 178, 225, 315, 323, 333, 350
Francis II of France 45, 305
Francis IV Duke of Modena 351
Frederick William II of Prussia 122
Frederick William III of Prussia 122, 153, 233
Frohsdorf 336, 346-63
Garde Nationale, *see* National Guard
Genlis, Madame de 6, 131, 246
George III of England 34, 275
George IV of England 38, 267, 299
Georgiana, Duchess of Devonshire 17
Gomin, Jean-Baptiste 98-9, 106-7
Gontaut, Madame de 34, 41, 51, 58, 122, 134, 168, 184, 188, 203-4, 246, 251, 253, 262, 268-9, 272, 274, 276, 300-1, 304, 306, 319, 332-3, 338
Goritz 334-6, 340-1, 346-7, 352, 361-2
Gosfield Hall, Essex 163, 165
Gourbillon, Madame de 65, 136, 140, 147, 161
Gramont, Duc and Mme de 41, 319, 343
Greville, Charles, diarist, 166, 173, 205, 210, 254, 261, 287-8, 293, 299-301
Guéméné, Princesse de, governess, 13-14, 19, 25, 28-9, 44
guillotine 78, 80, 82, 88, 92, 94, 117, 125, 171, 206-7, 236, 250, 269
Gustav III of Sweden 14, 38, 51, 67
Gustav IV Adolph of Sweden 67, 159, 163, 173
Habsburgs 32-3, 102, 112, 121, 139, 171, 214, 225, 240, 242, 315, 318, 333-4, 351
Hartwell House, Bucks 166-85, 214
Hautpoul, General 331
Hébert, Jacques René 32, 86-7, 215, 237
Henri II 45
Henri III 45
Henri IV 201, 274, 328, 357
Henri V, Duc de Bordeaux, Comte de Chambord 252-3, 267-9, 273-4, 277, 289, 293, 298, 307, 312, 322, 328, 331-4, 339-42, 345-6, 350, 353-5, 361-2
Henri VII 214
Holyroodhouse 134, 304-8, 312
Hortense de Beauharnais, Queen of Holland, 180-1, 189-90, 195-8, 206, 221, 225, 232, 253-4
Hradschin Palace 317, 328, 331, 333, 340
Huë, Baron 75, 89, 101, 104, 110, 117, 129, 248
Huë, Madame Henriette 25, 100, 129, 143-4
Hundred Days 220-5, 228, 257, 265, 279, 285, 310, 325
Isle of Wight 299
Italy 45, 145, 279, 323
Italian language 33, 100, 152, 241, 243, 338
Jacobins 66-9, 71
Jesuits 255, 264, 275, 278, 330-2
Joinville, Prince de 266, 269, 281
Joseph II of Austria 6-8, 27, 51
Joséphine de Beauharnais, wife of Napoleon 144, 171, 181, 189-90, 196, 198-9, 202, 208, 216
Kirchberg 334, 336, 340, 343

Korff, Madame de 57, 124
Lafayette, Marquis de 42, 52-3, 56, 58, 60, 65, 286, 289
Lamballe, Madame de 7, 9, 11, 30, 39, 46-7, 71-2, 76, 78, 205, 354
Lambriquet, Marie Philippine, 'Ernestine', 32-4, 46, 48, 59, 65
Lamorlière, Rosalie 85, 193
Laurent, Christophe 97-100
Laurent, Madame 17
Laxenberg Palace 23, 34
Leopold I of Austria 112
Leopold II of Austria 51, 65, 67, 350
Leopold I of Belgium 345
Lévis, Duc de 228, 360
libelles 7, 32, 48, 63, 310
Lille, Comte de, *see* Louis XVIII
London
  Madame de Polignac 48
  Comte d'Artois, Charles X 133-4, 146, 165, 262, 275, 314
  Duc d'Angoulême 135, 174, 345
  Abbé Edgeworth 138
  Duc d'Orléans 159, 228
  Duc de Berry 168, 179
  Duchesse d'Angoulême 169, 174-5, 185-7, 227-9, 314
  Louis XVIII 174, 185-7
  Marie Caroline 305
  Henri V 345-6
  Louis Philippe I 356
London press 23, 34, 131, 224, 227; *see also The Times*
Louis Joseph, First Dauphin 27-8, 34, 37, 39
Louis XIII 21, 235, 376
Louis XIV 21, 32, 43, 45, 49, 74, 146, 184, 231, 306
Louis XV 5, 21, 24, 38, 49, 212
Louis XVI
  marriage to Marie Antoinette 4-5, 8, 20, 24, 52
  portraits 5, 14, 307, 325, 360
  reticent nature 6-7, 38, 54
  dealings with National Assembly 49, 54, 66, 72
  belief in royal supremacy 50-1, 54, 283
  trial and execution 79-83, 304
  reburial and Will 215-16, 236
  debts 124, 155-6
  grief of Marie Thérèse 138, 198, 207, 209
Louis XVII, Dauphin Louis Charles, Duc de Normandie
  birth 34
  becomes Dauphin 39-40
  portraits 45, 62
  upbringing 41-8, 53, 76, 85
  becomes King 83
  imprisoned 84-9, 93, 96-8
  death and burial 98-100, 209-10, 343
Louis XVIII, Comte de Provence
  succession 14-15, 19-20, 83, 99, 130, 135-6, 145, 167, 177, 209, 238, 244-6
  portrait 15, 177
  at Luxembourg Palace 46, 57, 59, 65
  and Marie Thérèse 56, 101, 103-5, 108-9, 112-16, 119, 127-8, 133, 137-9, 201, 206-7, 247, 325

becomes King 104, 263
in exile 106, 116-17, 122-3, 138, 142, 153-6, 160-2, 171, 176, 222, 238
and foreign powers 107, 113, 118, 127-9, 141, 147, 151, 155, 255
relations with wife 136, 171-2
health 144, 162, 177, 185-6, 196, 201, 221, 232, 260, 358
negotiations with Napoleon 145, 158, 175, 198
and Britain 155, 159, 163-5, 169, 173-6, 185-7, 258, 339
Restoration 180-3, 190-2, 195-200, 212-16
Napoleon's Hundred Days 221-8, 265, 279, 285
Second Restoration 228-34, 248, 312
and Madame du Cayla 254, 323
death 259-61
Louis XIX, *see* Duc d'Angoulême
Louis Philippe I, Duc d'Orléans
and Marie Thérèse 21, 38, 43, 170, 187, 269, 354
and government 39, 182
exile in England 159, 163, 170, 228, 247, 345, 355
marriage to Marie Amélie 213-14, 245
and Napoleon 222
Second Restoration 246-7
and Charles X 266-7, 270, 284, 288-9, 293, 336
and Palais-Royal 271, 279-80
made King 287-9, 293-4, 309-10
death of son 342-3
deposed by revolution 353
death 356
Louise, Queen of Prussia 153, 157
Louvel, Louis Pierre 249-50
Lulworth Castle 300-2, 304
Luxembourg Palace 46, 65, 73
Mackau, Baronne de 25, 29-30, 35-6, 59, 65, 105, 107
Madame Royale, *see* Angoulême, Duchesse de
Maria Carolina, Queen of Naples, *see* Naples, Queen Maria Carolina
Maria Theresa, Empress of Austria 4, 6, 14, 25-6, 32, 83, 129, 213, 240, 315, 317, 321
Marie Amélie of Naples 213-15, 245-7, 266, 268-9, 271, 276, 289, 303, 307, 312-13, 322, 342, 345, 356
Marie Anne, wife of Emperor Ferdinand 126, 350
Marie Antoinette, Queen of France
marriage to Louis XVI 4-5, 192, 260
portraits 6, 9, 14, 89
birth and upbringing of Marie Thérèse 6-11, 17-20, 25-7, 29-33, 50
in the Trianon 22-3, 31, 48
birth of three siblings 27-8, 34
poisoning of reputation 7, 32, 36, 42, 48, 68, 95
arranging marriage of Marie Thérèse 18, 37-8, 104, 113, 130-1, 135
in the Tuileries 44-9, 65, 203
seeking foreign support 51, 54-5, 79, 113
relations with Axel von Fursen 52, 124
escape to Varennes 56-64, 113
imprisonment in the Temple 74-7, 84, 94, 141, 206
execution of Louis XVI 80-3
sentencing and death of Marie Antoinette 85-9, 215-16, 236-8, 362-3
Marie Thérèse's grief 97, 198, 207, 209
financial affairs 124-5, 155, 316

Marie Caroline, Duchesse de Berry
birth as Maria Carolina 240-1
marriage to Duc de Berry 241-3
birth of children 245-6, 251-2
assassination of husband 249-50
titles 261-2, 305
widowhood 267-8, 270-3, 275, 280, 297-9, 303
championing her son 288-9, 293, 305-7, 312-13, 322
scandal of remarriage 323-30
Prague and Austria 328-31, 348, 350, 352, 357
Marie Élisabeth, Archduchess of Austria 127
Marie Joséphine, wife of Louis XVIII 14, 16, 26, 59, 65, 118, 132, 136-7, 159-61, 164, 167, 171-2, 259, 261
Marie Louise, daughter of Marie Caroline 323
Marie Louise, second wife of Napoleon 112, 120, 171, 178, 180-1, 183, 195, 200, 208, 222, 242, 255, 312, 315, 326, 350, 353-4
Marmont, Maréchal 182, 195, 224, 265, 275, 285, 287-8, 293, 298
Mary Queen of Scots 305, 307
Maximilian, Archduke 350, 355, 357
Méchin, M. 110
Metternich 340, 342, 350
Meudon, Château de 37, 46, 54
Mittau 122-5, 129-30, 136-47, 151-3, 160-5, 198, 234, 239, 269
Modena, Duke of 313, 336, 351
Moniteur 197, 224, 263, 278, 283-4
Montgolfier brothers 31, 197
Montmorency, Cardinal 139, 144
Montmorency, Mathieu de 210, 217-18
Naples 37, 55, 101, 152, 167-8, 241, 303, 313, 323
Naples, Maria Carolina, Queen of 37, 55, 112, 119, 213, 240-1, 280
Napoleon I, *see* Bonaparte
Napoleon III 252
National Assembly 40, 43, 48-9, 51-5, 63, 65, 69, 71-3, 86, 91, 132, 202
National Guard 42, 48, 53-6, 61-4, 69, 71-2, 82, 86, 188, 200, 222, 226, 251, 286, 292
Ney, Madame 195, 208-9, 233-4
Ney, Maréchal 183, 195, 199, 208-9, 221, 223-4, 233-4
Nicholas I of Russia 340, 351
Noailles, Madame de 30, 291
Oberkirch, Madame d' 23, 29, 35-6
Ordinances of 1828 278
Ordinances of 1830 282-5, 288
Orléans branch of the Royal Family 21-2, 34, 131, 196, 214, 253, 268-9, 326, 332
Orléans, Duc d', *see* Louis Philippe I
Orléans, Madame Adélaïde d', *see* Adélaïde d'Orléans
Orléans, Duchesse d', *see* Marie Amélie
Osmond, Comte and Comtesse d' 46, 206, 257, 261, 270
Palais-Royal 21, 214, 247, 271, 279-80, 284
Parma 101, 353-4
Paul I of Russia 122, 139, 141-2, 147, 151, 167, 274
Peace of Amiens 157
Philippe Égalité 21, 80, 118, 215, 246, 293
Pitt, William the Younger 134, 138, 155
Pius VII, Pope 156
Polignac, Duc de 198, 263, 280-1, 285, 288, 306-7, 320
Polignac, Duchesse de 7, 11, 29-30, 37, 41, 44, 48, 144, 251

Pompadour, Marquise de 4, 21-2, 24
Portugal 174, 178
Prague 122, 126-9, 255, 310, 317-21, 326-33, 337-8, 340, 355
Prince Regent, later George IV 38, 163, 173-5, 182, 184-8, 219, 228, 247, 275
Provence, Comte de, *see* Louis XVIII
Provence, Comtesse de, *see* Marie Joséphine
Prussia 77, 122, 152-3, 158, 160, 178, 182, 184, 200, 230
Puymaigre, M. de 281, 283
Radziwill, Princess 270
Rambouillet 287-8, 290-1, 300
Reichstadt, Duc de 315-16
Rheims 50, 173, 178, 265-7
Richelieu, Duc de 142, 252, 256-7
Richemont, Baron de 355
Robespierre, Maximilien 92-4, 208, 236
Rohan, Cardinal and family 14, 162, 326, 339
Roman Catholicism
for Marie Thérèse 33, 165, 236, 269, 344, 346, 362
and marriage restrictions 38, 164, 239, 340, 351
in relation to state 55, 156, 264
Abbé's conversion 81, 162
in England and Scotland 133, 167, 172, 192, 300, 305, 308, 312
and canonisation 138, 206
in Bourbon Court 142, 211, 253, 259, 266, 322, 357
Rome 55, 117, 119, 145, 156, 180, 183, 222, 252-3, 313, 323, 342
Rosny-sur-Seine 267, 271, 273, 280, 311
Royal Guards 42, 68, 138, 214, 285
Russia
armed forces 41, 168, 178-9, 204, 274
view of monarchy 51, 122, 151, 174, 183, 195-6, 340
sanctuary in Mittau 122, 129, 138, 141, 147, 151, 153-4, 160, 162
Marie Thérèse's wedding 139, 142
peace with Napoleon 162
Napoleon defeated 177-8
Alexander I enters Paris 180, 182, 184, 200, 230
prospective Royal marriages 239-40, 340, 350-1
death of Alexander I 274
Nicholas I 340
Russian Orthodox Church 139, 239, 340
Sainte-Preuve, Madame de 359-60
Salic Law 13, 100, 102
Sardinia 41, 118, 164, 172, 355
Savoy 24, 133
Scotland 117, 134-5, 305-8, 312-14; *see also* Edinburgh and Holyroodhouse
Sérent, Duc and Madame de 131, 135, 144, 154, 175, 186, 217, 257
Sèze, M. de 79, 304, 306, 308-9
Sicily 37, 213, 240-1, 243, 279, 307
Simon, Antoine 84, 210
Sixth Alliance 178, 184, 275
Sophie, Archduchess of Austria 315, 342, 350, 353, 358-9
Sophie Hélène Beatrix, baby sister of Marie Thérèse 34, 246
Sophie, Tante 30
Soucy, Madame de 25, 107, 110, 113-15
Spain 14, 51, 101, 145, 168, 174, 178, 180, 213, 224, 227, 235, 255-6, 267, 303, 322, 348
St Cloud 53, 55-6, 65, 131, 191, 203, 212, 232, 252, 256, 261, 263, 267, 280, 283, 285, 287, 300

St Petersburg 122, 141, 145, 202
Stowe 163-4
Swiss Guards 72, 191, 216, 226
Talleyrand, Charles 179-80, 182-3, 190-1, 197, 200, 202-3, 220, 231, 233, 240, 284, 332, 342
Temple
  painting 3
  imprisonment 73-110, 141, 147, 206, 209-10, 324
  and Napoleon 170
Tennis Court Oath 40, 69
Terror 78, 80, 92, 94, 100, 102, 116, 231, 233
Times, The 156-7, 182, 204, 223, 225, 227-8, 235, 375
Tippoo Sahib 36
Tour du Pin, Cécile de la 192
Tour du Pin, Lucie de la
  on Court life 6, 28-30, 36, 38, 54
  on Paris riots 40, 47
  on von Fersen 52, 61
  on Comte d'Artois 130-2
  on Marie Thérèse 192-4
Tour du Pin, M. de la 43, 192
Tourzel, Madame de
  as governess 30, 42, 44-5
  on Paris mob 43, 48, 68-73
  on Marie Thérèse 49-50, 65, 96, 101-5, 108
  in escape party 56-63
  on politics 65, 67-9
  at Temple 75-6, 78, 84-5, 94-6, 100-2, 105-6
  and Louis XVIII 104-8
Tourzel, Pauline de, *see* Béarn, Mme de
Treaty of Campo Formio 12
Treaty of Fontainebleau 183
Treaty of Paris 202
Treaty of Versailles, 1756 4, 7
Trébuquet, Abbé 331, 359
Tressan, Abbé de 136-8
Trianon Palace 7-8, 19, 21-3, 33-4, 48-9, 130, 141, 195, 213, 256
Trieste 145, 334
Trobriand family 156, 292, 297, 352
Tuileries Palace 44-9, 52-60, 62-73, 78, 101, 146, 191, 198, 202-7, 210, 215-17, 223-4, 230-2, 235, 244, 256, 260-1, 267-70, 279, 325
Ultra movement 231, 255, 275, 278-80
Valmy 79
Varennes 61, 71, 101, 111, 116, 132, 191, 281, 286, 292, 297, 316
Vendée 125-6, 135, 194, 228, 257, 322, 328
Venice 122, 145, 300, 352-3, 357-8
Vermond, Abbé de 9, 27, 35
Verona 104-5, 112, 117, 122, 300
Versailles
  marriage of Louis XVI 4
  Court life 6-38, 45, 90, 94, 97, 103, 120, 122, 125, 138, 141, 145, 161, 163, 167, 189, 195, 208, 249, 251, 295
  Estates General 39-40, 43, 131, 283
  Paris mob 41-3, 46-7, 56, 180, 190-1, 201, 300
  revisiting 212-13, 232, 256
  Louis Philippe's restoration 337

Victoire, Madame 30, 46, 53-5, 117, 119, 132, 145, 335
Victor Amadeus III, King of Sardinia 41, 118, 133
Victoria, Queen 252, 262, 345-7, 354-6
Vienna
childhood of Marie Antoinette 23, 27, 34, 51, 76, 120
marriage of Marie Antoinette 4, 7-8, 26
death of Emperor Leopold 67
protest at Marie Antoinette's imprisonment 89
possible marriage for Marie Thérèse 108, 111, 114, 129
exchange of Marie Thérèse 102, 107, 111
Marie Thérèse in exile 107-29, 135, 143-4, 155, 162, 171, 174, 188, 191, 194, 211, 217, 225, 312
Congress of Vienna 203, 274
Duc de Reichstadt 253
1832 visit 315-17
Henri V visits 342, 351
1845, 1851 visits 352-3, 358
Papal Nuncio and Chief Physician 359
Vigée Le Brun, Madame 9, 24-5, 34, 272
Villeneuve, Marquis de
and Marie Thérèse 79, 281, 318, 337, 339
in Prague 319-20, 328, 332-6
Légitimist stance 327-8, 330, 336, 339-40
and Duc de Bordeaux 338
Villeneuve-l'Étang 256, 304
Waddesdon Manor 4, 213
Wallace Collection 213
Walsch, Vicomte 327-8, 337
Warsaw 152-5, 157-60, 165, 167, 174, 185
Waterloo 225, 228, 230-3
Weld, Thomas 300, 302
Wellington, Duke of 174, 179-80, 204, 210, 225, 230, 232-3, 253, 255, 305, 312
William IV of England 299, 314
Worth Bank 303, 316

www.ingramcontent.com/pod-product-compliance
Ingram Content Group UK Ltd.
Pitfield, Milton Keynes, MK11 3LW, UK
UKHW062303290726
14090UKWH00017B/857

9 781916 267701